Course   Supply Chain Management Vol. 2
Humber College
Applied Technology

http://create.mcgraw-hill.com

ISBN-10: 0071059601   ISBN-13: 9780071059602

Contents

Credits

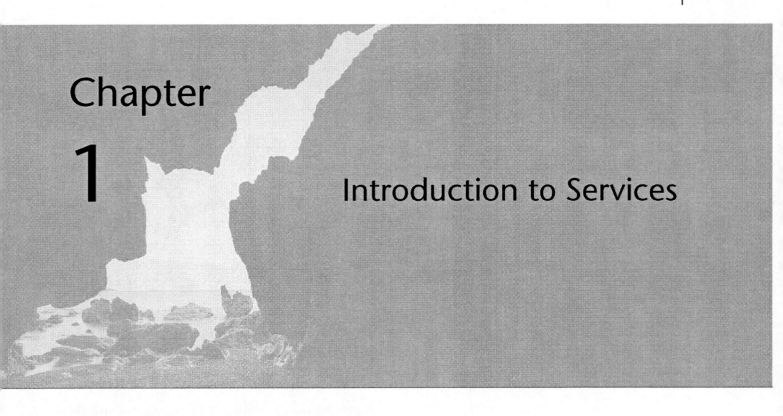

Chapter 1

Introduction to Services

THIS CHAPTER'S OBJECTIVES ARE TO

1. Explain what services are and identify important trends in services.

2. Explain the need for special services marketing concepts and practices and why the need has developed and is accelerating.

3. Explore the profound impact of technology on service.

4. Outline the basic differences between goods and services and the resulting challenges and opportunities for service businesses.

5. Introduce the expanded marketing mix for services and the philosophy of customer focus, as powerful frameworks and themes that are fundamental to the rest of the text.

NEW WAVE OF SERVICES: IBM TRANSFORMS INTO A SERVICES POWERHOUSE

IBM (www.ibm.ca) has transformed itself into a service provider. Like many businesses that were once viewed as manufacturing giants, IBM is shifting its focus. Back in 2001, Louis Gerstner, IBM's former CEO, predicted that soon "hardware and software will be sold inside a services wrapper." A headline in *eWeek* in early 2005 confirmed his prediction, proclaiming that IBM now sells services first, boxes second.

In a company brochure, IBM states that it is the largest *service* business in the world. Through its Global Services Canada division, IBM offers product support services, professional consulting services, and network computing services around the world. Many businesses have outsourced entire service functions to IBM. IBM Canada has won major multiyear service contracts with Scotiabank (worth about $900 million), TD Bank Financial Group ($720 million), and National Bank ($200 million). Although service are less lucrative than its other lines—operating margins are about 25 percent, as against 31 percent in hardware and a heady 87 percent in software—only services are capable of delivering the growth the company wants.

Going forward, IBM's strategy is to focus on total solutions and to be a truly valued, trusted, and indispensable partner for its key clients. This strategy means providing clients with total service solutions in such wide-ranging areas as human resources, marketing, product design, and customer relationship management.

No one in IBM would suggest that these positive results have been easily achieved. Switching from a manufacturing to a service and customer focus requires changes in management mindset, culture, and the way people work and are rewarded, and requires finding new ways of implementing customer solutions. At IBM this change has evolved over decades. It is suggested that Lou Gerstner's legacy at IBM may well be the definitive switch that the company has made from hardware to services and the strategic focus on customers.

Many of IBM's competitors have viewed the company's success and are attempting to make the same transformation. Underscoring its own commitment to the service sector, Hewlett-Packard recently signed a seven-year $2 billion outsourcing contract with CIBC. The agreement, at the time, was the largest in HP's history. Switching to services is not as easy as it looks, though. In moving into services, companies discover what service businesses such as hospitality, consulting, health care, financial services, and telecommunications have known for years: services marketing and management are different—not totally unique, but different. Selling and delivering a computer is not the same as selling and delivering a service that solves a customer's problem.[1]

Source: IBM. The IBM logo is a registered trademark of IBM in the United States and other countries and is used under license.

As the opening vignette suggests, services are not limited to service industries, services can be very profitable, and services are challenging to manage and market. Services represent a huge and growing percentage of the world economy; yet customer perceptions of service are not good.[2] Given the economic growth in services, their profit and competitive advantage potential, and the overall decline in customer satisfaction with services, it seems that the potential and opportunities for companies who can excel in services marketing, management, and delivery have never been greater.

This text will give you a lens with which to approach the marketing and management of services. What you learn can be applied in a company like IBM with a traditional manufacturing history or in pure service businesses. You will learn tools, strategies, and approaches for developing and delivering profitable services that can provide competitive advantage to firms. At the base of services marketing and management you will find a strong customer focus that extends across all functions of the firm—hence the subtitle of this book, "Integrating Customer Focus Across the Firm."

WHAT ARE SERVICES?

Put in the most simple terms, *services are deeds, processes, and performances.* Our opening vignette illustrates what is meant by this definition. The services offered by IBM are not tangible things that can be touched, seen, and felt, but rather are intangible deeds and performances. To be concrete, IBM offers repair and maintenance service for its equipment, consulting services for IT and e-commerce applications, training services, Web design and hosting, and other services. For the most part, the entire service is represented to the client through problem analysis activities, meetings with the client, follow-up calls, and reporting—a series of deeds, processes, and performances. Similarly, the core offerings of hospitals, hotels, banks, and utilities comprise primarily deeds and actions performed for customers.

Services include "all economic activities whose output is not a physical product or construction, is generally consumed at the time it is produced, and provides added value in forms (such as convenience, amusement, timeliness, comfort, or health) that are essentially intangible concerns of its first purchaser."[3] The breadth of industries making up the service sector of the Canadian economy is illustrated in Figure 1.1.

Service Industries, Services as Products, Customer Service, and Derived Service

As we begin our discussion of services marketing and management, it is important to draw distinctions between *service industries and companies, services as products, customer service,* and *derived service.* Sometimes when people think of service, they think only of customer service, but service can be divided into four distinct categories. The tools and strategies you will learn in this text can be applied to any of these categories.

Service industries and companies include those industries and companies typically classified within the service sector whose core product is a service. All of the following companies and organizations can be considered pure service companies: Marriott International (lodging), WestJet (transportation), Sun Life Financial (financial services), Athabasca University (education). The total services sector comprises a wide range of service industries, as suggested by Figure 1.1. Companies in these industries sell services as their core offering.

FIGURE 1.1   Contributions of Service Industries to Canadian Gross Domestic Product, 2004

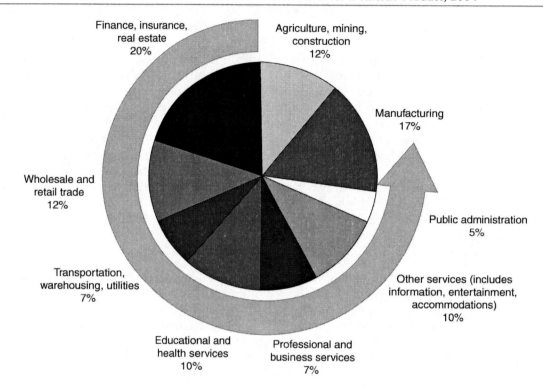

Source: Adapted from Statistics Canada website: www.statcan.ca. Accessed August 8, 2006.

Services as products represent a wide range of intangible product offerings that customers value and pay for in the marketplace. Service products are sold by service companies and by nonservice companies such as manufacturers and technology companies. For example, IBM and Hewlett-Packard offer information technology consulting services to the marketplace, competing with firms such as EDS and Accenture, which are traditional pure service firms. Other industry examples include department stores, like Chapters, that sell services such as gift wrapping and shipping, and pet stores, like Petcetera, that sell pet grooming and photography and training services.

Customer service is also a critical aspect of what we mean by "service." Customer service is the service provided in support of a company's core products. Companies typically do not charge for customer service. Customer service can occur onsite (as when a retail employee helps a customer find a desired item or answers a question), or it can occur over the phone or via the Internet. Many companies operate customer service call centres, often staffed around the clock. Quality customer service is essential to building customer relationships. It should not, however, be confused with the services provided for sale by the company.

Derived service is yet another way to look at what service means. In a recent article in the *Journal of Marketing*, Steve Vargo and Bob Lusch argue for a new dominant logic for marketing that suggests that all products and physical goods are valued for the services they provide.[4] Drawing on the work of respected economists, marketers, and philosophers, the two authors suggest that the value derived from physical goods is really the service provided by the good, not the good itself. For

6 Part 1 *Foundations for Services Marketing*

FIGURE 1.2 Tangibility Spectrum

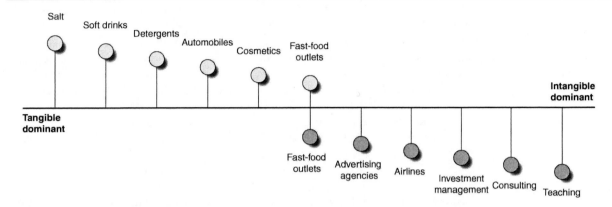

Source: G. Lynn Shostack, "Breaking Free from Product Marketing," *Journal of Marketing* 41 (April 1977), pp. 73–80. Reprinted with permission of the American Marketing Association.

example, they suggest that a pharmaceutical provides medical services, a razor provides barbering services, and computers provide information and data manipulation services. Although this view is somewhat abstract, it suggests that in the future we may think even more broadly about services than we currently do.

Tangibility Spectrum

The broad definition of services implies that intangibility is a key determinant of whether an offering is a service. Although this is true, it is also true that very few products are purely intangible or totally tangible. Instead, services tend to be *more intangible* than manufactured products, and manufactured products tend to be *more tangible* than services. For example, the fast-food industry, while classified as a service, also has many tangible components such as the food, the packaging, and so on. Automobiles, while classified within the manufacturing sector, also supply many intangibles, such as transportation. The tangibility spectrum shown in Figure 1.2 captures this idea. Throughout this text, when we refer to services we will be assuming the broad definition of services and acknowledging that there are very few "pure services" or "pure goods." The issues and approaches we discuss are directed toward those offerings that lie on the right side, the intangible side, of the spectrum shown in this figure.

WHY SERVICES MARKETING?

Why is it important to learn about services marketing, service quality, and service management? What are the differences in services versus manufactured-goods marketing that have led to the demand for books and courses on services? Many forces have led to the growth of services marketing, and many industries, companies, and individuals have defined the scope of the concepts, frameworks, and strategies that define the field. The field of services marketing and management has evolved as a result of these combined forces.

Service-Based Economies

First, services marketing concepts and strategies have developed in response to the growth of service industries and their increased importance to Canadian and other world economies. Although Canada has traditionally been viewed as a production-based economy that relies heavily on natural resources processing, our service sector is far more substantial than many may think, and it has recently been increasing in importance. Today, service industries in Canada account for almost 75 percent of our country's output and employment, having increased from a 50 percent share of each in the 1960s, and are attracting significantly more research and development dollars.[5]

Another indicator of the economic importance of services is that trade in services is growing worldwide and Canada's share of international share of service trade is increasing accordingly. The United States is the world's largest exporter of services and Canada's largest services trading partner as well. While, in contrast to the U.S., which generates a large trade surplus in services, Canada generates slight deficits, we are still the 12th-largest service exporter worldwide and our export rates have been increasing steadily since the 1980s.[6] And Canadian-based services available internationally may be more important still; many of our services are sold and delivered by affiliates based in foreign countries that are not accounted for in the trade balance calculation.

Finally, there is an increasing dominance of services in economies worldwide, as Table 1.1 indicates. The tremendous growth and economic contributions of the service sector have drawn increasing attention to the issues and challenges of service sector industries worldwide.

Service as a Business Imperative in Manufacturing and IT

Early in the development of the field of services marketing and management, most of the impetus came from service industries such as banking, transportation, and health care. As these traditional service industries evolve and become more competitive, the need for effective services management and marketing strategies continues. Now, however, manufacturing and technology industries such as automobiles, computers, and software are also recognizing the need to provide quality service and revenue-producing services in order to compete worldwide.

TABLE 1.1

Service Sector Contribution to Selected Economies Worldwide

Source: Central Intelligence Agency, *The World Factbook 2004*, available www.umsl.edu/services/govdocs/wofact2004/index.html, accessed September 14, 2006.

Country	Percent of GDP Attributed to Services
Bahamas	90
United States	79
Japan	74
United Kingdom	73
France	73
Canada	71
Sweden	69
Australia	68
Germany	68
Singapore	67
Brazil	51
India	48
China	33

8 Part 1 *Foundations for Services Marketing*

From IBM and HP to President's Choice Financial, and General Motors, companies are recognizing the opportunity to grow and profit through services.[7] Why? Because the quick pace of developing technologies and increasing competition make it difficult to gain strategic competitive advantage through physical products alone. Plus, customers are more demanding. Not only do they expect excellent, high-quality goods and technology, they also expect high levels of customer service and total service solutions along with them.

At GE the services strategy began in the mid-1990s under then-CEO Jack Welch when he launched what has been termed the "third revolution." A major thrust of the third revolution was to push GE's growth strategies even deeper into services such as aftermarket services, financial services, broadcasting, management consulting, and other services as far afield as health care and utilities. GE now generates more than 75 percent of its revenues from services.[8] At General Motors, the services strategy is absolutely critical. Since 2002, GM has *lost* US$5.2 billion manufacturing vehicles but *earned* US$9.8 billion selling loans, insurance, and (even) mortgages. As noted by the *Globe and Mail*, during that time the Bank of GM made more money than the Bank of Nova Scotia!

Besides differentiating themselves with financial services such as GMAC Automotive, Insurance, and Mortgages, full-featured online banking, and educational loans, GM offers their On-Star in-vehicle safety and security system.[9] (See Figure 1.3.) Visit GM's website for a tour of its varied services (www.gm.com/company/financial_svc).

As manufacturers such as GM and IT companies such as IBM (see the opening vignette) transition to become services organizations, the need for special concepts and approaches for managing and marketing services is increasingly apparent.[10]

Deregulated Industries and Professional Service Needs

Specific demand for services marketing concepts has come from deregulating industries and professional services as both these groups have gone through rapid changes in the ways they do business. Over the past several decades, many very large service industries have been deregulated. While this is more pronounced in the United States than in Canada, the impacts are international. At the time of the publication of this book, major uncertainty existed in Canada related to possible bank mergers, CRTC reviews of digital services, and a whole spectrum of possible regulatory changes regarding telecommunications. Deregulation typically means that marketing decisions once made by the government are now partially or totally controlled by the industry.

Providers of professional services (such as physicians, lawyers, accountants, engineers, and architects) have also demanded new concepts and approaches for their businesses as these industries have become increasingly competitive and as professional standards have been modified to allow advertising. Whereas traditionally the professions avoided even using the word *marketing*, they are now seeking better ways to understand and segment their customers, to ensure the delivery of quality services, and to strengthen their positions amid a growing number of competitors.

Services Marketing Is Different

As the forces described above coincided and evolved, businesspeople realized that marketing and managing services presented issues and challenges not faced in manufacturing and packaged goods companies. These differences and challenges were captured in a series of interviews by management consultant Gary Knisely in 1979.[11] For example, when a firm's core offering is a deed performed by an employee (such

FIGURE 1.3

Services such as OnStar are critical to GM's future success.

Source: Reprinted with permission of *OnStar* magazine.

as engineering consulting), how can the firm ensure consistent product quality to the marketplace? As service businesses began to turn to marketing and decided to hire marketing people, they naturally recruited from the best marketers in the world—Procter & Gamble, General Foods, Kodak. People who moved from marketing in packaged goods industries to marketing in health care, banking, and other service industries found that their skills and experiences were not directly transferable. They faced issues and dilemmas in marketing services that their experiences in packaged goods and manufacturing had not prepared them for. These people realized the need for new concepts and approaches for marketing and managing service businesses.

Service Equals Profits

A dedication to quality service has been the foundation for success for many firms, across industries. In his book *Discovering the Soul of Service*, Leonard Berry describes in detail 14 such companies.[12] The companies featured in his book had been in business an average of 31 years in 1999 when the book was written. These companies had been profitable in all but five of their combined 407 years of existence due to nine common service themes, among them values-driven leadership, commitment to investments in employee success, and trust-based relationships with customers and other partners at the foundation of the organization.

Researchers are building a convincing case that service strategies, implemented appropriately, can be very profitable. Work sponsored by the Marketing Science Institute suggests that corporate strategies focused on customer satisfaction, revenue generation, and service quality may actually be more profitable than strategies focused on cost cutting or strategies that attempt to do both simultaneously.[13] Research out of the Harvard Business School builds a case for the "service–profit chain," linking internal service and employee satisfaction to customer value and ultimately to profits.[14] And considerable research shows linkages from customer satisfaction (often driven by service outcomes) to profits.[15] From the University of Michigan American Customer Satisfaction Index (ACSI) even comes data suggesting that customer satisfaction is directly linked to shareholder value. Firms in the top 50 percent of the ACSI rankings show significantly higher shareholder value than firms in the bottom 50 percent.[16] Finally, research from Canada's National Quality Institute (NQI) found that from 1990 to 2005, CAE winners achieved a 143.1 increase in shareholder value. This is in contrast to an overall gain of 88.1 for the TSE 300 index.[17]

An important key to these successes is that the right strategies are chosen and that these strategies are implemented appropriately and well. Much of what you learn from this text will guide you in making such correct choices and in providing superior implementation. Throughout the text we will point out the profit implications and tradeoffs to be made with service strategies. In Chapter 18 we will come back to this issue by providing integrated coverage of the financial and profit impact of service.

But "Service Stinks"

Despite the importance of service and the bottom-line profit potential for service, consumers perceive that overall the quality of service is declining.[18] We see *BusinessWeek* magazine blatantly condemning service in its cover story "Why Service Stinks."[19] And although there are exceptions in every industry, American Customer Satisfaction Index (ACSI) scores for service industries are generally lower than the average for all industries. Particularly low are ACSI scores in the transportation, communications, and utilities sectors. For example, whereas the national ACSI average across all industries has risen to 74.4, cable and satellite television and the wireless telecommunication industries overall receive ratings in the low-to-mid-60s, and most airlines score in the mid-60s.[20]

Halifax-based author Laura Penny, in her book *Your Call Is Important to Us: The Truth About Bullshit*, expresses the mood well: "If my call is so important, why isn't anyone answering the damn phone?"[21]

This condemnation of service is troubling when, at some level, service has never been better. For example, think of just one industry—health care. The ability to prevent and treat diseases has never been greater, resulting in an ever-increasing life expectancy in most industrialized countries. So clearly, in some ways and in many industries, services are better than ever.

Despite these obvious improvements, there is hard evidence that consumers perceive a lower quality of service overall and are less satisfied. There are many theories as to why this decline in customer satisfaction with services has occurred. Plausible theories include:

- With more companies offering tiered service based on the calculated profitability of different market segments, many customers are in fact getting less service than they have in the past.

- Increasing use by companies of self-service and technology-based service is perceived as less service, because no human interaction or human personalization is provided.

- Technology-based services (automated voice systems, Internet-based services, technology kiosks) are hard to implement, with many failures and with poorly designed systems in place.

- Customer expectations are higher because of the excellent service they receive from some companies. Thus, they expect the same from all and are frequently disappointed.

- Organizations have cut costs to the extent that they are too lean and too under-staffed to provide quality service.

- The competitive job market results in less-skilled people working in front-line service jobs; talented workers soon get promoted or leave for better opportunities.

- Many companies give lip service to customer focus and service quality, but they fail to provide the training, compensation, and support needed to actually deliver quality service.

- Delivering consistent, high-quality service is not easy, yet many companies promise it.

For managers, students, and teachers of services marketing and management, the message is clear: services can be profitable, and yet overall quality perceptions and customer satisfaction are declining. In this text we will provide many examples of best practices—companies that understand how to get it right and are succeeding with service. We will also delineate many tools, concepts, and strategies that can help to reverse the "service stinks" mindset.

SERVICE AND TECHNOLOGY

The preceding sections examined the roots of services marketing and the reasons why the field exists. Another major trend—technology, specifically information technology—is currently shaping the field and profoundly influencing the practice of services marketing. In this section we explore trends in technology (positive *and* negative) to set the stage for topics that will be discussed throughout this text. In each chapter you will find a Technology Spotlight box that highlights the influence of technology on issues related to the particular chapter. We will also raise technology and service issues as appropriate throughout the general discussion in the text and have included several cases that explore the opportunities and challenges of services and technology. Together with globalization, the influence of technology is the most profound trend affecting services marketing today.

Potential for New Service Offerings

Looking to the recent past, it is apparent how technology has been the basic force behind service innovations now taken for granted. Automated voice mail, interactive voice response systems, fax machines, ATMs, and other common services were possible only because of new technologies. Just think how dramatically different your world would be without these basic technology services.

More recently, people have seen the explosion of the Internet, resulting in a host of new services. Internet-based companies like Amazon.ca and eBay offer services previously unheard of. And established companies find that the Internet provides a way to offer new services as well.[22] For example, the *Globe and Mail* offers an interactive version called *Insider Edition* that allows customers to organize the newspaper's content to suit their individual preferences.

Many new technology services are on the horizon. For example, some researchers project that the "connected car" will allow people to access all kinds of existing and new services while on the road. Already many cars are equipped with map and routing software that direct drivers to specific locations. In the future, in-car systems may provide recommendations for shopping by informing drivers when they are within a certain number of kilometres of their preferred retailer. On a road trip, the system may provide weather forecasts and warnings, and when it is time to stop for the night, the car's system might book a room at a nearby hotel, recommend a restaurant, and make dinner reservations.[23]

New Ways to Deliver Service

In addition to providing opportunities for new service offerings, technology is providing vehicles for delivering existing services in more accessible, convenient, productive ways. Technology facilitates basic customer service functions (bill paying, questions, chequing account records, tracking orders), transactions (both retail and business-to-business), and learning or information seeking. Our Technology Spotlight traces how, through history, evolving technologies have changed customer service forever. Companies have moved from face-to-face service to telephone-based service to widespread use of interactive voice response systems to Internet-based customer service and now wireless service. Interestingly, many companies are coming full circle and now offer human contact as the ultimate form of customer service.

Technology also facilitates transactions by offering a direct vehicle for making purchases. Technology giant Cisco Systems offers virtually all its customer service and ordering functions to its business customers via technology. Over 90 percent of its transactions with customers are completed online. On the consumer side, online shopping and transactions have already revolutionized the music and book businesses. Predictions suggest that online ordering will also rewrite the rules for purchasing jewellery, real estate, hotel rooms, and software.

Finally, technology, specifically the Internet, provides an easy way for customers to learn and research. Access to information has never been easier. For example, over 20,000 websites currently offer health-related information. Many provide answers to specific disease, drug, and treatment questions.[24]

Enabling Both Customers and Employees

Technology enables both customers and employees to be more effective in getting and providing service.[25] Through self-service technologies, customers can serve themselves more effectively. Via online banking, customers can access their accounts, check balances, apply for loans, shift money among accounts, and take care of just about any banking need they might have—all without the assistance of the bank's employees. All of Canada's financial institutions have moved increasing amounts of their business online. These services are just one example of the types of self-service technologies that are proliferating across industries.

For employees, technology can provide tremendous support in making them more effective and efficient in delivering service. Customer relationship management and sales support software are broad categories of technology that can aid front-line employees in providing better service. By having immediate access to information about their product and service offerings as well as about particular customers, employees

Technology Spotlight

The Changing Face of Customer Service

Excellent customer service—the daily, ongoing support of a company's offerings—is critical in creating brand identity and ultimate success. It includes answering questions, taking orders, dealing with billing issues, handling complaints, scheduling appointments, and similar activities. These essential functions can make or break an organization's relationships with its customers. The quality of customer care can significantly impact brand identity for service, manufacturing, and consumer products companies. Because of its importance in creating impressions and sustaining customer relationships, customer service has sometimes been called the "front door" of the organization or its "face."

So how has the "face" of customer service changed with the influx of technology? Long ago all customer service was provided face-to-face through direct personal interaction between employees and customers. The telephone changed this, allowing customers to call companies and speak directly with employees. Customer service became less personal, but without a doubt more efficient. With the evolution of computer technology, customer service representatives (CSRs) became even more efficient. Through computer information systems and customer data files, CSRs are able to call up customer records at their workstations to answer questions on the spot.

Over time, because communication and computer technologies allowed it, large organizations began to centralize their customer service functions, consolidating into a few large call centres that could be located anywhere in the world. For example, a large percentage of IBM's customer service calls in North America are handled out of its sales and service centre in Toronto, 24 hours a day. But still, in these types of call centres, customer service is for the most part an interpersonal event with customers talking directly, one-on-one with an employee.

The advent and rapid proliferation of the efficient, but much-maligned, automated voice response systems have changed personal customer service in many organizations into menu-driven, automated exchanges. In almost every industry, consumers encounter these types of systems, and many are quite frustrating—for example, when a system has a long, confusing set of menu options or when no menu option seems to fit the purpose of the call. Similarly, consumers become angry when they cannot get out of the system easily, or when there is no option to speak to a live person.

Some companies have overcome these obstacles, however, and have well-designed automated telephone systems that work well for customers. For instance, Rogers has recently redesigned their Customer Service Phone Line on the basis of customer feedback. The new system is available 24 hours a day, is easier to navigate, and allows callers to connect with a human when necessary. At Charles Schwab, the vice-president of retail voice technology occupies a senior management position, thereby communicating the importance of this function throughout the company. This may be partly why their customer satisfaction is rated among the highest in any industry.

Beyond automated telecom systems, the explosion of the Internet is also dramatically changing customer service for many companies. Service can now be provided on the Internet via email, website robots, FAQs, and online chats. In these cases there is no direct human interaction, and customers actually perform their own service. Ford Motor Company's dealership customers can set their own service appointments, send messages regarding their specific repair needs, and monitor the status of their vehicles, all online.

Why do companies continue to invest? One answer is that customers are demanding choice in how they get customer service. However, the cost to companies cannot be ignored. The typical service phone call involving human interaction is estimated to cost $7. Internet transactions involving human response cost $2.25. But a self-service phone call—no human interaction—costs less than $0.50. Although customers often enjoy technology-based service, and even demand it in many cases, it often doesn't work reliably,

continued

Technology Spotlight

The Changing Face of Customer Service—continued

doesn't seem to have any advantages over the interpersonal service alternatives, and lacks systems to recover from failures. Interestingly, when things don't work as they are supposed to on an Internet site or through an automated response system, customers are quick to look for more traditional interpersonal (in-person or via telephone) options, coming back to where they started!

Sources: J. A. Nickell, "To Voice Mail Hell and Back," *Business 2.0*, July 10, 2001, pp. 49–53; D. Ward, "The Web's Killer App: A Human Being," *Revolution*, March 2000, pp. 82–88; M. L. Meuter, A. L. Ostrom, R. I. Roundtree, and M. J. Bitner, "Self-Service Technologies: Understanding Customer Satisfaction with Technology-Based Service Encounters," *Journal of Marketing* 64 (July 2000), pp. 50–64; B. Horovitz, "Whatever Happened to Customer Service?" *USA Today*, September 25, 2003, available www.usatoday.com/money/economy/services/2003-09-25-services-frontcover_x.htm, accessed September 14, 2006.

are better able to serve them. This type of information allows employees to customize services to fit the customer's needs. They can also be much more efficient and timely than in the old days when most customer and product information was in paper files or in the heads of sales and customer service representatives.

Extending the Global Reach of Services

Technology infusion results in the potential for reaching out to customers around the globe in ways not possible before. The Internet itself knows no boundaries, and therefore information, customer service, and transactions can move across countries and across continents, reaching any customer who has access to the Web. Technology also allows employees of international companies to stay in touch easily—to share information, to ask questions, to serve on virtual teams together. All this technology facilitates the global reach as well as the effectiveness of service businesses. Our Global Feature focuses on the migration of service jobs and the ability to produce services almost anywhere.

The Internet *Is* a Service

An interesting way to look at the influence of technology is to realize that the Internet is just "one big service." All businesses and organizations that operate on the Internet are essentially providing services—whether they are giving information, performing basic customer service functions, or facilitating transactions. Thus all the tools, concepts, and strategies you learn in studying services marketing and management have direct application in an Internet or e-business world. Although technology and the Internet are profoundly changing how people do business and what offerings are possible, it is clear that customers still want basic service. They want what they have always wanted: dependable outcomes, easy access, responsive systems, flexibility, apologies, and compensation when things go wrong. But now they expect these same outcomes from technology-based businesses and from e-commerce solutions.[26] With hindsight it is obvious that many dot-com startups suffered and even failed because of lack of basic customer knowledge and failure of implementation, logistics, and service follow-up.[27]

Global Feature

The Migration of Service Jobs

With the ever-growing sophistication of information technology, the global reach of organizations is increasing at a spectacular rate. Activities that used to require close proximity and personal contact can now often be accomplished via the Internet, video, and telecommunication technologies. This advancement means that the jobs that produce and support these activities can be done almost anywhere in the world. The result has been referred to as a "migration of service jobs" out of countries such as Canada, the United States, and the United Kingdom to countries such as India, Pakistan, the Philippines, and Eastern European countries.

This globalization of services is in many ways inevitable, but it comes with considerable controversy. One clear concern is that some of the highest-paying service jobs are being "lost" to lower-wage countries, and this concern is very real for the individuals whose jobs are lost. However, the numbers are not as large as perhaps imagined. Critics of the global outsourcing of service jobs tend to be much more vocal in the United States than in Canada, though the Canadian media has not been silent on the issue. Some of the difference in concern noted between the two countries may be warranted. U.S.-based companies account for 70 percent of services outsourcing, and Forrester Research estimates that by the year 2015, 3.3 million high-tech and service jobs will move from the united States. Similarly, PricewaterhouseCoopers warns that 75,000 Canadian IT service jobs could be exported by 2010. However, in contrast with the United States, Canada is viewed as a "prime destination" for outsourced service jobs, and it currently ranks third worldwide as an outsourcing destination for information technology and business processes totalling $5.7 billion. Global outsourcing of service jobs can also be viewed as beneficial, because doing so can increase gross domestic product through increased innovation and job creation in other areas.

Although the specific outcomes of service job migration are not totally known, it is safe to say that the globalization of services will continue, resulting in further shrinking of the boundaries among people and countries.

Why is service job migration happening now? The root of the acceleration is the rapid development and accessibility of sophisticated information technologies. Services are information-intensive, and information can now be shared readily without direct personal contact. For example, researchers worldwide can work on a project simultaneously and share information instantaneously. Other services can easily be performed without regard for national boundaries. Canadian Imperial Bank of Commerce outsources its credit card processing to the United States; Indian financial analysts digest the latest disclosures of U.S. companies and file reports the next day; and other workers in India sort through mounds of consumer data provided by non-Indian company clients to determine behaviour patterns and develop ideas for marketing. In each of these cases, *where* the work is done is not important or meaningful to the client as long as it is done well and on time.

continued

Source: Indranil Mukerjee/Getty Images.

Global Feature

The Migration of Service Jobs—continued

A major reason that this movement of jobs is possible is that countries outside the developed world are now producing highly skilled, well-educated workforces, particularly in China and India. These workers typically work for far less compensation, allowing global companies to reduce labour costs on the one hand and increase overall productivity on the other. The quality of the work can be very high as well, with many companies citing quality and performance among their reasons for moving service jobs overseas.

Sources: U. Karmarkar, "Will You Survive the Services Revolution?" *Harvard Business Review,* June 2004, pp. 100–107; D. Goldfarb, "How Canada Wins from Global Services Outsourcing," *Commentary* (C. D. Howe Institute), November 2004, p. 1. M. Kripalani and P. Engardio, "The Rise of India," *BusinessWeek,* December 8, 2003; "Mapping Offshore Markets," white paper by neoIT, at www.neoIT.com; S. A. Teicher, "A Not So Simple Path," *Christian Science Monitor,* February 23, 2004; M. N. Baily and D. Farrell, "Exploding the Myths of Offshoring," *The McKinsey Quarterly,* online at www.mckinseyquarterly.com, July 2004.

The Paradoxes and Dark Side of Technology and Service

Although there is clearly great potential for technology to support and enhance services, there are potential negative outcomes as well. Mick and Fournier, well-regarded consumer researchers, have pointed out the many paradoxes of technology products and services for consumers, as shown in Table 1.2.[28] This section highlights some of the general concerns.

Customer concerns about privacy and confidentiality raise major issues for firms as they seek to learn about and interact directly with customers through the Internet. These types of concerns are what have stymied and precluded many efforts to advance technology applications in the health care industry, for example. Nor are all customers equally interested in using technology as a means of interacting with companies. Research exploring "customer technology readiness" suggests that some customers are simply not interested or ready to use technology.[29] Employees can also be reluctant to accept and integrate technology into their work lives—especially when they perceive, rightly or wrongly, that the technology will substitute for human labour and perhaps eliminate their jobs.

With technology infusion comes a loss of human contact, which many people believe is detrimental purely from a quality of life and human relationships perspective. Parents may lament that their children spend hours in front of computer screens, interacting with games, seeking information, and relating to their friends only through instant messaging without any face-to-face human contact. And workers in organizations become more and more reliant on communicating through technology—even communicating via email with the person in the next office!

Finally, the payback in technology investments is often uncertain. It may take a long time for an investment to result in productivity or customer satisfaction gains. Sometimes it never happens. For example, McKinsey & Company reports that a firm projected a $40 million savings from moving its billing and service calls to the Web. Instead it suffered a $16 billion loss as a result of lower usage by customers than projected, unanticipated follow-up calls and emails to the call centre from those who

TABLE 1.2 Eight Central Paradoxes of Technological Products

Paradox	Description
Control/chaos	Technology can facilitate regulation or order, and technology can lead to upheaval or disorder.
Freedom/enslavement	Technology can facilitate independence or fewer restrictions, and technology can lead to dependence or more restrictions.
New/obsolete	New technologies provide the user with the most recently developed benefits of scientific knowledge, and new technologies are already or soon to be outmoded as they reach the marketplace.
Competence/incompetence	Technology can facilitate feelings of intelligence or efficacy, and technology can lead to feelings of ignorance or ineptitude.
Efficiency/inefficiency	Technology can facilitate less effort or time spent in certain activities, and technology can lead to more effort or time in certain activities.
Fulfils/creates needs	Technology can facilitate the fulfilment of needs or desires, and technology can lead to the development or awareness of needs or desires previously unrealized.
Assimilation/isolation	Technology can facilitate human togetherness, and technology can lead to human separation.
Engaging/disengaging	Technology can facilitate involvement, flow, or activity, and technology can lead to disconnection, disruption, or passivity.

Source: D. G. Mick and S. Fournier, "Paradoxes of Technology: Consumer Cognizance, Emotions, and Coping Strategies," *Journal of Consumer Research* 25 (September 1998), pp. 123–47. © 1998 University of Chicago Press. Reprinted by permission.

had used the Web application initially, and loss of revenue from lack of cross-selling opportunities.[30]

CHARACTERISTICS OF SERVICES COMPARED TO GOODS

There is general agreement that there is a difference between goods and services and that the distinctive characteristics discussed in this section result in challenges (as well as advantages) for managers of services.[31] But it is also important to realize that each of these characteristics can be arranged on a continuum similar to the tangibility spectrum shown in Figure 1.1. That is, although services tend to be more heterogeneous, more intangible, more difficult to evaluate than goods, the differences between goods and services are not black and white by any means.[32]

Table 1.3 summarizes the differences between goods and services and the implications of these characteristics. Many of the strategies, tools, and frameworks in this text were developed to address these characteristics, which, until the 1980s, had been largely ignored by marketers. Recently it has been suggested that these distinctive characteristics should not be viewed as unique to services but that they are also relevant to goods, that "all products are services," and that "economic exchange is fundamentally about service provision."[33] Although this view is rather abstract, it does suggest that all types of organizations may be able to gain valuable insights from services marketing frameworks, tools, and strategies.

Intangibility

The most basic distinguishing characteristic of services is intangibility. Because services are performances or actions rather than objects, they cannot be seen, felt, tasted,

TABLE 1.3 Goods vs. Services

Goods	Services	Resulting Implications
Tangible	Intangible	Services cannot be inventoried. Services cannot be easily patented. Services cannot be readily displayed or communicated. Pricing is difficult.
Standardized	Heterogeneous	Service delivery and customer satisfaction depend on employee and customer actions. Service quality depends on many uncontrollable factors. There is no sure knowledge that the service delivered matches what was planned and promoted.
Production separate from consumption	Simultaneous production and consumption	Customers participate in and affect the transaction. Customers affect each other. Employees affect the service outcome. Decentralization may be essential. Mass production is difficult.
Nonperishable	Perishable	It is difficult to synchronize supply and demand with services. Services cannot be returned or resold.

Source: A. Parasuraman, V. A. Zeithaml, and L. L. Berry, "A Conceptual Model of Service Quality and Its Implications for Future Research," *Journal of Marketing* 49 (Fall 1985), pp. 41–50. Reprinted by permission of the American Marketing Association.

or touched in the same manner that you can sense tangible goods. For example, health care services are actions (such as surgery, diagnosis, examination, and treatment) performed by providers and directed toward patients and their families. These services cannot actually be seen or touched by the patient, although the patient may be able to see and touch certain tangible components of the service (like the equipment or hospital room). In fact, many services such as health care are difficult for the consumer to grasp even mentally. Even after a diagnosis or surgery has been completed the patient may not fully comprehend the service performed, although tangible evidence of the service (e.g., incision, bandaging, pain) may be quite apparent.

Resulting Marketing Implications Intangibility presents several marketing challenges. Services cannot be inventoried, and therefore fluctuations in demand are often difficult to manage. For example, there is tremendous demand by Canadians to visit Florida in the winter, and much less demand in July. Yet resort owners have the same number of rooms to sell year-round. Services cannot be easily patented, and new service concepts can therefore easily be copied by competitors. Services cannot be readily displayed or easily communicated to customers, so quality may be difficult for consumers to assess. Decisions about what to include in advertising and other promotional materials are challenging, as is pricing. The actual costs of a "unit of service" are hard to determine, and the price–quality relationship is complex.

Heterogeneity

Because services are performances, frequently produced by humans, no two services will be precisely alike. The employees delivering the service frequently are the service in the customer's eyes, and people may differ in their performance from day to day or even hour to hour. Heterogeneity also results because no two customers are precisely alike; each will have unique demands or experience the service in a unique way. Thus the heterogeneity connected with services is largely the result of human interaction (between and among employees and customers) and all of the vagaries that accompany it. For example, a tax accountant may provide a different service experience to two different customers on the same day depending on their individual needs and personalities and on whether the accountant is interviewing them when he or she is fresh in the morning or tired at the end of a long day of meetings.

Resulting Marketing Implications Because services are heterogeneous across time, organizations, and people, ensuring consistent service quality is challenging. Quality actually depends on many factors that cannot be fully controlled by the service supplier, such as the ability of the consumer to articulate his or her needs, the ability and willingness of personnel to satisfy those needs, the presence (or absence) of other customers, and the level of demand for the service. Because of these complicating factors, the service manager cannot always know for sure that the service is being delivered in a manner consistent with what was originally planned and promoted. Sometimes services may be provided by a third party, further increasing the potential heterogeneity of the offering.

Simultaneous Production and Consumption

Whereas most goods are produced first, then sold and consumed, most services are sold first and then produced and consumed simultaneously. For example, an automobile can be manufactured in Windsor, shipped to Vancouver, sold two months later, and consumed over a period of years. But restaurant services cannot be provided until they have been sold, and the dining experience is essentially produced and consumed at the same time. Frequently this situation also means that the customer is present while the service is being produced and thus views and may even take part in the production process. Simultaneity also means that customers will frequently interact with each other during the service production process and thus may affect each others' experiences. For example, strangers seated next to each other in an airplane may well affect the nature of the service experience for each other. That passengers understand this fact is clearly apparent in the way business travellers will often go to great lengths to be sure they are not seated next to families with small children. Another outcome of simultaneous production and consumption is that service producers find themselves playing a role as part of the product itself and as an essential ingredient in the service experience for the consumer.

Resulting Marketing Implications Because services often are produced and consumed at the same time, mass production is difficult. The quality of service and customer satisfaction will be highly dependent on what happens in "real time," including actions of employees and the interactions between employees and customers. Clearly the real-time nature of services also results in advantages in terms of opportunities to customize offerings for individual consumers. Simultaneous production and consumption also means that it is not usually possible to gain significant economies of scale through centralization. Often, operations need to be relatively decentralized so that the service can be delivered directly to the consumer in convenient locations, although the growth of technology-delivered services is changing this requirement for many services. Also, because of simultaneous production and consumption, the customer is involved in and observes the production process and thus may affect (positively or negatively) the outcome of the service transaction.

Perishability

Perishability refers to the fact that services cannot be saved, stored, resold, or returned. A seat on an airplane or in a restaurant, an hour of a lawyer's time, or telephone line capacity not used cannot be reclaimed and used or resold at a later time. Perishability is in contrast to goods that can be stored in inventory or resold another day, or even returned if the consumer is unhappy. Wouldn't it be nice if a bad haircut could be returned or resold to another consumer? Perishability makes this action an unlikely possibility for most services.

Resulting Marketing Implications   A primary issue that marketers face in relation to service perishability is the inability to inventory. Demand forecasting and creative planning for capacity utilization are therefore important and challenging decision areas. The fact that services cannot typically be returned or resold also implies a need for strong recovery strategies when things do go wrong. For example, although a bad haircut cannot be returned, the hairdresser can and should have strategies for recovering the customer's goodwill if and when such a problem occurs.

Challenges and Questions for Service Marketers

Because of the basic characteristics of services, marketers of services face some very real and distinctive challenges. Answers to questions such as the ones listed here still elude managers of services:

How can service quality be defined and improved when the product is intangible and nonstandardized?

How can new services be designed and tested effectively when the service is essentially an intangible process?

How can the firm be certain it is communicating a consistent and relevant image when so many elements of the marketing mix communicate to customers and some of these elements are the service providers themselves?

How does the firm accommodate fluctuating demand when capacity is fixed and the service itself is perishable?

How can the firm best motivate and select service employees who, because the service is delivered in real time, become a critical part of the product itself?

How should prices be set when it is difficult to determine actual costs of production and price may be inextricably intertwined with perceptions of quality?

How should the firm be organized so that good strategic and tactical decisions are made when a decision in any of the functional areas of marketing, operations, and human resources may have significant impact on the other two areas?

How can the balance between standardization and personalization be determined to maximize both the efficiency of the organization and the satisfaction of its customers?

How can the organization protect new service concepts from competitors when service processes cannot be readily patented?

How does the firm communicate quality and value to consumers when the offering is intangible and cannot be readily tried or displayed?

How can the organization ensure the delivery of consistent quality service when both the organization's employees and the customers themselves can affect the service outcome?

SERVICES MARKETING MIX

The preceding questions are some of the many raised by managers and marketers of services that will be addressed throughout the text through a variety of tools and strategies. Sometimes these tools are adaptations of traditional marketing tools, as with the services marketing mix presented here. Other times they are radically new, as in the case of service blueprinting presented in Chapter 9.

Traditional Marketing Mix

One of the most basic concepts in marketing is the marketing mix, defined as the elements an organization controls that can be used to satisfy or communicate with customers. The traditional marketing mix is composed of the four Ps: *product, price, place* (distribution), and *promotion*.[34] These elements appear as core decision variables in any marketing text or marketing plan. The notion of a mix implies that all the variables are interrelated and depend on each other to some extent. Further, the marketing mix philosophy implies an optimal mix of the four factors for a given market segment at a given point in time.

Key strategy decision areas for each of the four Ps are captured in the first four columns in Table 1.4. Careful management of product, place, promotion, and price will clearly also be essential to the successful marketing of services. However, the strategies for the four Ps require some modifications when applied to services. For example,

TABLE 1.4

Expanded Marketing Mix for Services

Product	Place	Promotion	Price
Physical good features	Channel type	Promotion blend	Flexibility
Quality level	Exposure	Salespeople	Price level
Accessories	Intermediaries	Selection	Terms
Packaging	Outlet locations	Training	Differentiation
Warranties	Transportation	Incentives	Discounts
Product lines	Storage	Advertising	Allowances
Branding	Managing channels	Media types	
		Types of ads	
		Sales promotion	
		Publicity	
		Internet/Web strategy	

People	Physical Evidence	Process	
Employees	Facility design	Flow of activities	
Recruiting	Equipment	Standardized	
Training	Signage	Customized	
Motivation	Employee dress	Number of steps	
Rewards	Other tangibles	Simple	
Teamwork	Reports	Complex	
Customers	Business cards	Customer	
Education	Statements	involvement	
Training	Guarantees		

traditionally promotion is thought of as involving decisions related to sales, advertising, sales promotions, and publicity. In services these factors are also important, but because services are produced and consumed simultaneously, service delivery people (such as clerks, ticket takers, nurses, and phone personnel) are involved in real-time promotion of the service even if their jobs are typically defined in terms of the operational function they perform.

Expanded Mix for Services

Because services are usually produced and consumed simultaneously, customers are often present in the firm's factory, interact directly with the firm's personnel, and are actually part of the service production process. Also, because services are intangible, customers will often be looking for any tangible cue to help them understand the nature of the service experience. For example, in the hotel industry the design and decor of the hotel as well as the appearance and attitudes of its employees will influence customer perceptions and experiences.

Acknowledgment of the importance of these additional variables has led services marketers to adopt the concept of an expanded marketing mix for services shown in the three remaining columns in Table 1.4.[35] In addition to the traditional four Ps, the services marketing mix includes *people, physical evidence,* and *process.*

> **People** All human actors who play a part in service delivery and thus influence the buyer's perceptions: namely, the firm's personnel, the customer, and other customers in the service environment.

All the human actors participating in the delivery of a service provide cues to the customer regarding the nature of the service itself. How these people are dressed, their personal appearance, and their attitudes and behaviours all influence the customer's perceptions of the service. The service provider or contact person can be very important. In fact, for some services, such as consulting, counselling, teaching, and other professional relationship-based services, the provider *is* the service. In other cases the contact person may play what appears to be a relatively small part in service delivery—for instance, a telephone installer, an airline baggage handler, or an equipment delivery dispatcher. Yet research suggests that even these providers may be the focal point of service encounters that can prove critical for the organization.

In many service situations, customers themselves can also influence service delivery, thus affecting service quality and their own satisfaction. For example, health care patients greatly affect the quality of service they receive when they either comply or don't comply with health regimens prescribed by the provider.

Customers not only influence their own service outcomes, but they can influence other customers as well. In a theater, at a ball game, or in a classroom, customers can influence the quality of service received by others—either enhancing or detracting from other customers' experiences.

> **Physical evidence** The environment in which the service is delivered and where the firm and customer interact, and any tangible components that facilitate performance or communication of the service.

The physical evidence of service includes all the tangible representations of the service such as brochures, signage, and equipment. In some cases it includes the physical facility where the service is offered—the "servicescape"—for example, the retail bank branch facility. In other cases, such as telecommunication services, the physical facility may be irrelevant. In this case other tangibles such as billing statements and appearance of the repair truck may be important indicators of quality. Physical evidence cues provide

⟼ EXHIBIT 1.1

WestJet: Aligning People, Processes, and Physical Evidence

WestJet, founded only 10 years ago, has quickly come to occupy a solid position in the minds of Canadian travellers. Modelled on the success of Southwest Airlines, WestJet positions itself on value, and all aspects of its services marketing mix must sing from the same page if it hopes to remain successful.

Since its inception as a regional carrier flying to five cities with three used planes, WestJet now flies to more than 30 cities across North America with five times as many planes—many of which are new 737-700s. Besides expansion itself, other tangible demonstrations of its successful service strategy include being named Canada's third-most-respected corporation in a 2004 survey conducted by Ipsos Reid (it placed second in the same survey a year earlier).

Success has come for a number of reasons. The cornerstone of the value proposition is, of course, low pricing, which is made possible by having the lowest cost structure coupled with an engaged, high-performing staff. The combination makes for great value. It is clear that all of WestJet's marketing mix is aligned around this value proposition. The three new marketing mix variables all reinforce the same message:

- *People.* WestJet has a unique employee culture—so unique that it placed first in the 2005 Canadian Corporate Culture study conducted by *Canadian Business* magazine and Waterstone Human Capital, Ltd. It was especially singled out for its "entrepreneurial spirit," "delivering what they promise," and "winning attitude." Employees are carefully selected, well trained, and empowered to get the job done. The company celebrates its success, provides the necessary tools and training, promotes from within, shares its profits, and encourages employees to become owners through a generous matching share-purchase program. All advertisements seem to be targeted as much at its own employees ("An Important Message from an Owner") as its customers. In 2004, WestJet was rated first in customer service.

- *Processes.* The service delivery process must also reinforce value. Like Southwest, WestJet reduces pilot training and maintenance costs by buying only one type of aircraft. They also focus on short average flight durations and quick airport turnaround times, permitting them to fly more people more cheaply. WestJet does not transfer

baggage to connecting flights, charges for all food, and encourages "guests" to buy their tickets online and use Web Check-In or Self-Serve Check-In Kiosks. Unlike Southwest, though, they do permit travellers to pre-select their seats. To date, WestJet's processes have been rated first in providing high-quality products and services, and on-time performance hovers in the low 90 percent range—good enough to be ranked number two in North America. Even its Investors Relations group is well regarded for its efficiency, being voted "Best Communication within the Retail Industry" by *IR Magazine*.

- *Physical evidence.* WestJet's tangible evidence reinforces its low-cost, fun atmosphere. Employees dress casually to reinforce the fun and to further emphasize the airline's commitment to its employee's comfort; advertisements stress the corporate culture and the key role of the employee; and the website plays up the fun image with amazing trivia—did you know for instance, that Canadians eat more KD (Kraft Dinner) per capita than any other nation on earth or that WestJet has 31 Karens, 39 Lisas, 61 Jens, 67 Davids, 46 Michelles, 86 Michaels, and 1 Yoga?

But as it continues to expand, WestJet's services marketing mix is gradually changing. Some observers are beginning to wonder if these changes are putting WestJet's strategy at risk. Consider the following decisions: purchasing new Boeing 737-700s; leather seats; seatback ExpressVu TVs; and Air Miles rewards and the launch of an expensive TV campaign rather than continuing to rely on print and radio. As well, with the addition of long-haul flights (including Honolulu, Maui, Miami, and Orlando), the company is moving away from its strategy of short-haul, point-to-point, rapid turnaround, no-layover flights. With Air Canada bringing down its services (removal of free meals and charging for pillows and blankets in economy class) and WestJet increasing its services, is WestJet at risk of losing its differentiation?

Sources: CCNMatthews, "WestJet Corporate Culture Most Admired in Canada Independent Study Reveals," news release, October 20, 2005, available www2.ccnmatthews.com/scripts/dnrp/release.asp?d=/cnrpxml/2005/10/20/292445_1_1020200583810AM.xml&t=WJA, accessed September 14, 2006; N. Ramage, "WestJet on the Fly," *Marketing* 110, no. 22 (June 20, 2005), p. 13; www.westjet.com.

Source: Courtesy of WestJet.

excellent opportunities for the firm to send consistent and strong messages regarding the organization's purpose, the intended market segments, and the nature of the service.

Process The actual procedures, mechanisms, and flow of activities by which the service is delivered—the service delivery and operating systems.

The actual delivery steps that the customer experiences, or the operational flow of the service, also give customers evidence on which to judge the service. Some services are very complex, requiring the customer to follow a complicated and extensive series of actions to complete the process. Another distinguishing characteristic of the process that can provide evidence to the customer is whether the service follows a production-line/standardized approach or whether the process is an empowered/customized one. For example, two successful airline companies, WestJet and Singapore Airlines, follow very different process models. WestJet is a no-frills, low-priced airline that offers mostly frequent, relatively short flights. All the evidence it provides is consistent with its vision and market position, as illustrated in Exhibit 1.1. Singapore Airlines, on the other hand, focuses on the business traveller and is concerned with meeting individual traveller needs. Thus, its process is highly customized to the individual, and employees are empowered to provide nonstandard service when needed. Both airlines have been very successful.

The three new marketing mix elements (people, physical evidence, and process) are included in the marketing mix as separate elements because any or all of them may influence the customer's level of satisfaction and repurchase decisions. The traditional elements as well as the new marketing mix elements will be explored in depth in future chapters.

STAYING FOCUSED ON THE CUSTOMER

A critical theme running throughout this text is *customer focus*. In fact, the subtitle of the book is "Integrating Customer Focus Across the Firm." From the firm's point of view, all strategies are developed with an eye to the customer, and all implementations are carried out with an understanding of their impact on the customer. From a practical perspective, decisions regarding new services and communication plans will integrate the customer's point of view; operations and human resource decisions will be considered in terms of their impact on customers. All the tools, strategies, and frameworks included in this text have customers at their foundation. The services marketing mix just described is clearly an important tool that addresses the uniqueness of services, keeping the customer at the centre.

In this text, we also view customers as assets to be valued, developed, and retained. The strategies and tools we offer thus focus on customer relationship building and loyalty as opposed to a more transactional focus in which customers are viewed as one-time revenue producers. This text looks at customer relationship management not as a software program but as an entire architecture or business philosophy. Every chapter in this text can be considered a component needed to build a complete customer relationship management approach.

SUMMARY

This chapter has set the stage for further learning about services marketing by presenting information on changes in the world economy and business practice that have driven the focus on service: the fact that services dominate the modern economies of the world; the focus on service as a competitive business imperative; specific needs of the deregulated and professional service industries; the role of new service concepts growing from technological advances; and the realization that the characteristics of services result in unique challenges and opportunities. The chapter presented a broad definition of services as deeds, processes, and performances, and it drew distinctions between pure services, value-added services, customer service, and derived service.

Building on this fundamental understanding of the service economy, the chapter went on to present the key characteristics of services that underlie the need for distinct strategies and concepts for managing service businesses. These basic characteristics are that services are intangible, heterogeneous, produced and consumed simultaneously, and perishable. Because of these characteristics, service managers face a number of challenges in marketing, including the complex problem of how to deliver quality services consistently.

The chapter ended by describing two themes that provide the foundation for future chapters: the expanded marketing mix for services; and customer focus as a unifying theme. The remainder of the text focuses on exploring the unique opportunities and challenges faced by organizations that sell and deliver services and on developing solutions that will help you become an effective services champion and manager.

⊢⟶ Discussion Questions

1. What distinguishes service offerings from customer service? Provide specific examples.
2. How is technology changing the nature of service?
3. What are the basic characteristics of services vs. goods? What are the implications of these characteristics for IBM Global Service or for WestJet?
4. One of the underlying frameworks for the text is the services marketing mix. Discuss why each of the three new mix elements (process, people, and physical evidence) is included. How might each of these communicate with or help to satisfy an organization's customers?
5. Think of a service job you have had or currently have. How effective, in your opinion, was or is the organization in managing the elements of the services marketing mix?
6. Again, think of a service job you have had or currently have. How did or does the organization handle relevant challenges listed in Table 1.3?
7. How can quality service be used in a manufacturing context for competitive advantage? Think of your answer to this question in the context of automobiles or computers or some other manufactured product you have actually purchased.

⊢⟶ Exercises

1. Roughly calculate your budget for an average month. What percentage of your budget goes for services vs. goods? Do the services you purchase have value? In what sense? If you had to cut back on your expenses, what would you cut out?
2. Visit two local retail service providers that you believe are positioned very differently (such as Dollarama and The Bay or Burger King and a fine restaurant). From your own observations, compare their strategies on the elements of the services marketing mix.

3. Try a service you have never tried before on the Internet. Analyze the benefits of this service. Was enough information provided to make the service easy to use? How would you compare this service to other methods of obtaining the same benefits?

Notes

1. D. Kirkpatrick, "Inside Sam's $100 Billion Growth Machine," *Fortune*, June 14, 2004, pp. 80–98; D. Kirkpatrick, "IBM, from Big Blue Dinosaur to E-Business Animal," *Fortune*, April 26, 1999, pp.116-26; W.M. Bulkeley, "These Days, Big Blue Is About Big Services Not Just Big Boxes," *The Wall Street Journal*, June 11, 2001, p. A1; David Kirkpatrick, "IBM Shares Its Secrets," *Fortune* 152, no. 5 (September 5, 2005), p. 128; Darryl K. Taft, "Research to the Rescue: IBM Research Unit Turns to Services to Help Propel High-Value Business Opportunities," *eWeek* 21, no. 26 (June 28, 2004), p. 20; Shane Schick, "IBM Inks TD Desktop Deal for $720M," *Computing Canada* 29, no. 21, p. 1.

2. D. Brady, "Why Service Stinks," *BusinessWeek,* October 23, 2000, pp. 118–28.

3. J. B. Quinn, J. J. Baruch, and P. C. Paquette, "Technology in Services," *Scientific American* 257, no. 6 (December 1987), pp. 50–58.

4. S. L. Vargo and R. F. Lusch, "Evolving to a New Dominant Logic for Marketing," *Journal of Marketing* 68 (January 2004), pp. 1–17.

5. International Trade Canada, "Canada and Trade in Services," March 29, 2006, available www.dfait-maeci.gc.ca/tna-nac/TS/canada-ts-en.asp, accessed September 14, 2006, and Anonymous, "Meeting the Challenges of a Services Economy," *Micro: The Micro-Economic Research Bulletin* 10, no. 1 (Winter/Spring 2005), p. 1.

6. International Trade Canada, "Canada and Trade in Services"; Industry Canada, "Services Industries," 2003, available www.strategis.gc.ca, accessed November 8, 2005.

7. M. Sawhney, S. Balasubramanian, and V. V. Krishnan, "Creating Growth with Services," *Sloan Management Review,* Winter 2004, pp. 34–43.

8. T. Smart, "Jack Welch's Encore," *BusinessWeek,* October 28, 1996, pp. 155–60; and GE company data, 2000.

9. D. Decloet, "Selling the Bank of GM Is Probably a Sign of Desperation," GlobeandMail.com, October 20, 2005.

10. J. A. Alexander and M. W. Hordes, *S-Business: Reinventing the Services Organization* (New York: SelectBooks, 2003); R. Oliva and R. Kallenberg, "Managing the Transition from Products to Services," *International Journal of Service Industry Management* 14, no. 2 (2003), pp. 160–72.

11. This discussion is based on interviews conducted by Gary Knisely that appeared in *Advertising Age* on January 15, 1979; February 19, 1979; March 19, 1979; and May 14, 1979.

12. L. Berry, *Discovering the Soul of Service* (New York: The Free Press, 1999).

13. R. T. Rust, C. Moorman, and P. R. Dickson, "Getting Return on Quality: Revenue Expansion, Cost Reduction, or Both?" *Journal of Marketing* 66 (October 2002), pp. 7–24.

14. J. L. Heskett, T. O. Jones, G. W. Loveman, W. E. Sasser Jr., and L. A. Schlesinger, "Putting the Service–Profit Chain to Work," *Harvard Business Review,* March/April 1994, pp. 164–74.

15. E. W. Anderson and V. Mittal, "Strengthening the Satisfaction–Profit Chain," *Journal of Service Research* 3, no. 2 (November 2000), pp. 107–20.

16. "Predictive Capabilities," www.theacsi.org, accessed October 13, 2004.

17. Adam J. Stoehr, "Impressive Stock Performance of CAE Winners from 1990–2005," November 1, 2005, available www.nqi.ca/articles/article_details.aspx?ID=547, accessed September 14, 2006.

18. C. Fishman, "But Wait, You Promised . . . ," *Fast Company,* April 2001, pp. 116–27.

19. D. Brady, "Why Service Stinks," *BusinessWeek,* October 23, 2000, pp. 116–28.

20. "Latest Increase in ACSI Bodes Well for the Economy," www.theacsi.org releases. Posted June 4, 2004, accessed October 13, 2004.

21. Laura Penny, *Your Call Is Important to Us: The Truth About Bullshit* (Toronto: McClelland & Stewart Ltd., 2005), back cover.

22. L. P. Willcocks and R. Plant, "Getting from Bricks to Clicks," *Sloan Management Review,* Spring 2001, pp. 50–59.

23. "Revolution Digital Tomorrow Report: Technologies That Will Change Marketing," *Revolution,* February 2001, pp. 51–65.

24. S. Fox and L. Rainie, "Vital Decisions," Washington, DC: The Pew Internet & American Life Project, available at www.pewinternet.org, 2002, accessed September 25, 2006.

25. M. J. Bitner, S. W. Brown, and M. L. Meuter, "Technology Infusion in Service Encounters," *Journal of the Academy of Marketing Science* 28 (Winter 2000), pp. 138–49.

26. M. J. Bitner, "Self-Service Technologies: What Do Customers Expect?" *Marketing Management,* Spring 2001, pp. 10–11.

27. R. Hallowell, "Service in E-Commerce: Findings from Exploratory Research," Harvard Business School, Module Note, N9-800-418, May 31, 2000.

28. D. G. Mick and S. Fournier, "Paradoxes of Technology: Consumer Cognizance, Emotions, and Coping Strategies," *Journal of Consumer Research* 25 (September 1998), pp. 123–47.

29. A. Parasuraman and C. L. Colby, *Techno-Ready Marketing: How and Why Your Customers Adopt Technology* (New York: The Free Press, 2001).

30. D. Khandelwal and S. Kell, "Customer Care in a New World," North American Contact Center Summit, January 23, 2002.

31. Discussion of these issues is found in many services marketing publications. The discussion here is based on V. A. Zeithaml, A. Parasuraman, and L. L. Berry, "Problems and Strategies in Services Marketing," *Journal of Marketing* 49 (Spring 1985), pp. 33–46.

32. For research supporting the idea of goods–services continua, see D. Iacobucci, "An Empirical Examination of Some Basic Tenets in Services: Goods–Services Continua," in *Advances in Services Marketing and Management,* ed. T. A. Swartz, D. E. Bowen, and S. W. Brown (Greenwich, CT: JAI Press, 1992), vol. 1, pp. 23–52.

33. S. L. Vargo and R. F. Lusch, "The Four Service Marketing Myths," *Journal of Service Research* 6 (May 2004), pp. 324–35.

34. E. J. McCarthy and W. D. Perrault Jr., *Basic Marketing: A Global Managerial Approach* (Burr Ridge, IL: Richard D. Irwin, 1993).

35. B. H. Booms and M. J. Bitner, "Marketing Strategies and Organizational Structures for Service Firms," in *Marketing of Services,* ed. J. H. Donnelly and W. R. George (Chicago: American Marketing Association, 1981), pp. 47–51.

Chapter

2

Conceptual Framework of This Book: The Gaps Model of Service Quality

THIS CHAPTER'S OBJECTIVES ARE TO

→ 1. Introduce a framework, called the gaps model of service quality, which is used to organize this textbook.

→ 2. Demonstrate that the gaps model is a useful framework for understanding service quality in an organization.

→ 3. Demonstrate that the most critical service quality gap to close is the customer gap, the difference between customer expectations and perceptions.

→ 4. Show that four gaps that occur in companies, which we call provider gaps, are responsible for the customer gap.

→ 5. Identify the factors responsible for each of the four provider gaps.

SERVICE QUALITY AT DELTA HOTELS

Source: Courtesy of Delta Hotels.

Delta Hotels (www.deltahotels.ca) is one of the largest and most successful hotel chains in Canada. Rising from humble beginnings as a single unit motor inn in British Columbia over 40 years ago, Delta boasts 40 properties, 11,300 rooms, and 7,000 employees nationwide. The chain has become a recognized service leader in North America—a rare distinction among hotel operators. It received two Canada Awards for Excellence—for quality (2000) and for a healthy workplace (2004)—from the National Quality Institute. It has also been voted one of "The 50 Best Employers in

Canada" by the *Globe and Mail*'s magazine Report on Business, in five of the past six years. The company prides itself on its innovative service offerings, including its famous "One-Minute Check-In" that guarantees free rooms to members of Delta Privilege, its guest recognition program, who wait longer than one minute for check-in service; its "Blue Ribbon" guarantee that promises rooms in perfect order at check-in; its pet policy that allows animals to stay onsite; and its chain-wide family program.

Take a moment to examine Delta's mission statement:

The mission of Delta Hotels is to be the full service, Canadian, hotel management company of choice with the dominant first-class brand. In carrying out this mission, Delta will be guided by our Quality Approach, and will be known:

To Owners as:
- The brand of choice for the hotel owner of first-class hotels
- An efficient operator who generates superior returns on their assets

To Guests as:
- A hotel company that offers great value
- A hotel company that has warm, friendly, sincere, customer-focused employees
- A hotel company that offers consistent delivery of products and services, is innovative, and [is] consistently improving service

To Employees as:
- A company where employees can contribute and grow
- A great place to work where a culture exists that recognizes "the way we deal with our employees will be reflected in the manner that they interact with our guests"
- A company that demonstrates and encourages an attitude that is supportive of the social needs of the community[1]

You may now be wondering why other North American hotels haven't been recognized with awards similar to Delta. This textbook is focused on highlighting strategies and tactics that companies can use to minimize any gaps that might occur between what customers expect in a service encounter and what they believe they have received in that encounter. Delta Hotels' mission statement, its more innovative service offerings briefly highlighted here, and its recent accolades indicate that the company values its customers and employees, invests a great deal of importance in service design and standards, and can deliver on its promises. As you will read in this chapter and throughout the text, each of these plays an important strategic part in matching customer perceptions with expectations.

Effective services marketing is a complex undertaking that involves many different strategies, skills, and tasks. Executives have long been confused about how to approach this complicated topic in an organized manner. This textbook is designed around one approach: viewing services in a structured, integrated way called the *gaps model of service quality*.[2] Sections of the book are tied to each of the gaps described in this chapter.

THE CUSTOMER GAP

The *customer gap* is the difference between customer expectations and perceptions (see Figure 2.1). Customer expectations are standards or reference points that customers bring into the service experience, whereas customer perceptions are subjective assessments of actual service experiences. Customer expectations often consist of what a customer believes should or will happen. For example, when you visit an expensive restaurant, you expect a high level of service, one that is considerably superior to the level you would expect in a fast-food restaurant. Closing the gap between what customers expect and what they perceive is critical to delivering quality service; it forms the basis for the gaps model.

Because customer satisfaction and customer focus are so critical to the competitiveness of firms, any company interested in delivering quality service must begin with a clear understanding of its customers. This understanding is relatively easy for an organization as small as the Island Hotel but very difficult for a large organization in which managers are not in direct contact with customers. For this reason, we will devote the first section of the textbook to describing the relevant customer concepts so that the focus of everything can relate back to these concepts. Considerable evidence exists that consumer evaluation processes differ for goods and services and that these differences affect the way service providers market their organizations. Unfortunately, much of what is known and written about consumer evaluation processes pertains specifically to goods. The assumption appears to be that services, if not identical to goods, are at least similar enough in the consumer's mind that they are chosen and evaluated in the same manner. We will detail what is known about customer behaviour in services in Chapter 3.

The sources of customer expectations are marketer-controlled factors (such as pricing, advertising, sales promises) as well as factors that the marketer has limited ability to

FIGURE 2.1

The Customer Gap

The Customer Gap

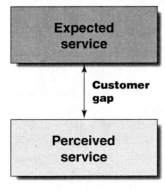

affect (innate personal needs, word-of-mouth communications, competitive offerings). In a perfect world, expectations and perceptions would be identical. In practice, there is often a gap between what customers expect and what they receive, and we will devote virtually the entire textbook to describing strategies and practices designed to close this customer gap. We will describe customer expectations in detail in Chapter 4 and customer perceptions in Chapter 5.

⟼ THE PROVIDER GAPS

To close the all-important customer gap, the gaps model suggests that four other gaps—the *provider gaps*—need to be closed. These gaps occur within the organization providing the service (hence the term *provider gaps*) and include

Gap 1: Not knowing what customers expect

Gap 2: Not selecting the right service designs and standards

Gap 3: Not delivering to service designs and standards

Gap 4: Not matching performance to promises

The rest of this chapter is devoted to a description of the full Gaps model.

Provider Gap 1: Not Knowing What Customers Expect

Provider Gap 1 is the difference between customer expectations of service and company understanding of those expectations. A primary cause for not meeting customers' expectations is that the firm lacks accurate understanding of exactly what those expectations are. Many reasons exist for managers not being aware of what customers expect: they may not interact directly with customers, they may be unwilling to ask about expectations, or they may be unprepared to address them. In this text, we broaden the responsibility for the first provider gap from managers alone to any employee with the authority to influence service policies. In today's organizations, the authority to make adjustments in service delivery is often delegated to empowered teams and front-line people.

Figure 2.2 shows the key factors responsible for Provider Gap 1. An inadequate marketing research orientation is one of the critical factors. When management or empowered employees do not acquire accurate information about customers' expectations, Provider Gap 1 is large. Formal and informal methods to capture information about customer expectations must be developed through marketing research. This chapter's Global Feature discusses techniques that IKEA and other companies have used to identify customer expectations.

Another key factor that is related to Provider Gap 1 is lack of upward communication. Front-line employees often know a great deal about customers; if management is not in contact with frontline employees and does not understand what they know, the gap widens.

Also related to Provider Gap 1 is a lack of company strategies to retain customers and strengthen relationships with them, an approach called relationship marketing. When organizations have strong relationships with existing customers, Provider Gap 1 is less likely to occur. Relationship marketing is distinct from transactional marketing, the term used to describe the more conventional emphasis on acquiring new customers rather than retaining them. When companies focus too much

32 Part 1   *Foundations for Services Marketing*

FIGURE 2.2

Key Factors Leading
to Provider Gap 1

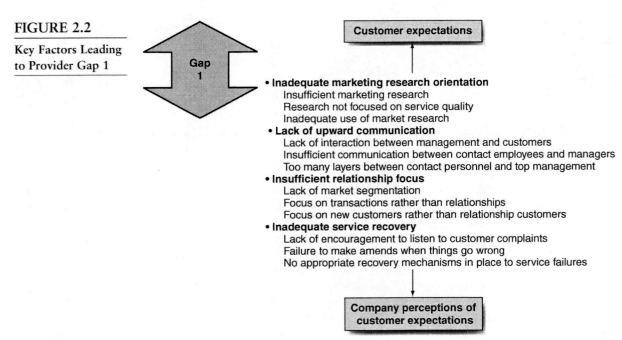

Customer expectations

- **Inadequate marketing research orientation**
   Insufficient marketing research
   Research not focused on service quality
   Inadequate use of market research
- **Lack of upward communication**
   Lack of interaction between management and customers
   Insufficient communication between contact employees and managers
   Too many layers between contact personnel and top management
- **Insufficient relationship focus**
   Lack of market segmentation
   Focus on transactions rather than relationships
   Focus on new customers rather than relationship customers
- **Inadequate service recovery**
   Lack of encouragement to listen to customer complaints
   Failure to make amends when things go wrong
   No appropriate recovery mechanisms in place to service failures

Company perceptions of customer expectations

on attracting new customers, they may fail to understand the changing needs and expectations of their current customers. Technology affords companies the ability to acquire and integrate vast quantities of data on customers that can be used to build relationships. Frequent-flyer travel programs conducted by airlines, car rental companies, and hotels are among the most familiar programs of this type.

The final key factor associated with Provider Gap 1 is lack of service recovery. Even the best companies, with the best of intentions and clear understanding of their customers' expectations, sometimes fail. It is critical for an organization to understand the importance of service recovery—why people complain, what they expect when they complain, and how to develop effective service recovery strategies for dealing with inevitable service failures. Such strategies might involve a well-defined complaint-handling procedure and an emphasis on empowering employees to react on the spot, in real time, to fix the failure; other times it involves a service guarantee or ways to compensate the customer for the unfulfilled promise.

To address the factors in Provider Gap 1, this text will cover topics that include how to understand customers through multiple research strategies (Chapter 6), how to build strong relationships and understand customer needs over time (Chapter 7), and how to implement recovery strategies when things go wrong (Chapter 8). Through these strategies, Provider Gap 1 can be minimized.

Provider Gap 2: Not Having the Right Service Designs and Standards

Accurate perceptions of customers' expectations are necessary, but not sufficient, for delivering superior quality service. Another prerequisite is the presence of service designs and performance standards that reflect those accurate perceptions. A recurring theme in service companies is the difficulty in translating customer expectations into service quality specifications that employees can understand and execute. These problems are reflected in Provider Gap 2, the difference between

Global Feature

An International Retailer Puts Customers in the Wish Mode to Begin Closing the Gaps

Finding out what customers expect is the first step in closing all the gaps in the organization to provide service excellence. In Chapter 6 we will talk about many ways that companies determine customer perceptions, including customer surveys and complaints, but understanding what customers expect can often be more challenging. Putting customers in the "wish mode" is an innovative approach to closing Gap 1 that proved successful for IKEA (www.ikea.ca), the world's largest furniture retailer, when it opened its Chicago retail outlet.

In this approach, nine groups of a dozen customers each were asked to dream up their ideal IKEA shopping experience. They were told to pretend that all IKEA stores had been destroyed and that new ones had to be designed from scratch. How would the store look? What would the shopping experience be like? Jason Magidson, who helped IKEA create the process, reported that customers responded with statements like the following:

> "I never feel disoriented because I always know exactly where I am in relation to every department."

> "If I am buying one item, all of the other items that go with it are nearby."

> "Shopping is a pleasant, relaxing experience."

Even though they were not technical experts, customers were asked to actually draw up a design for a store that would satisfy their needs.

What is significant about IKEA's approach is not just that the company asked customers what they expected but that they subsequently incorporated these expectations into the service design for the store. Designers created a multistorey octagonal building with an atrium in the centre that formed a home base for shoppers, addressing their concern about being able to find items easily. In keeping with another customer expectation, items were grouped together with related products. When shoppers were tired or hungry, they could go to the cafeteria-style restaurant on the upper floor that served Swedish food. IKEA's customers were so satisfied with the store (85% rated it as "excellent" or "very good") that they returned more and spent about an hour longer than they did in other IKEA stores. These actions close Gap 2, because service design was based on customer expectations.

IKEA has done an excellent job of closing all four provider gaps. The company's supplier network is carefully chosen and managed to ensure quality and consistency. Despite the fact that the company has stores in more than 34 countries, it keeps standards, designs, and approaches very consistent everywhere, thereby reducing Gap 2. Servicescapes—the indoor and outdoor physical environments—are unique and customer-focused, further closing Gap 2. IKEA is also well known for its strong employee culture and careful hiring and training, factors that help reduce Gap 3. In Chapter 13, we will tell you about another way the company closes Gap 3: its innovative service concept that involves customers in the delivery, assembly and creation of its products. To accomplish this service, the company educates its customers thoroughly with its scriptlike catalogues, thereby helping to close Gap 4.

Source: Michael Newman/Photo Edit.

Sources: Jason Magidson and Gregg Brandyberry, "Putting Customers in the 'Wish Mode,'" *Harvard Business Review*, September 2001, pp. 26–27; Barbara Solomon, "A Swedish Company Corners the Business: Worldwide," *Management Review*, April 1991, pp. 10–13; Richard Normann and Rafael Ramfrez, "From Value Chain to Value Constellation: Designing Interactive Strategy," *Harvard Business Review*, July/August 1993, pp. 65–77; www.ikea.ca.

company understanding of customer expectations and development of customer-driven service designs and standards. Customer-driven standards are different from the conventional performance standards that companies establish for service in that they are based on pivotal *customer* requirements that are *visible* to and *measured* by customers. They are operations standards set to correspond to customer expectations and priorities rather than to company concerns such as productivity or efficiency.

As shown in Figure 2.3, Provider Gap 2 exists in service organizations for a variety of reasons. Those people responsible for setting standards, typically management, sometimes believe that customer expectations are unreasonable or unrealistic. They may also believe that the degree of variability inherent in service defies standardization and therefore that setting standards will not achieve the desired goal. Although some of these assumptions are valid in some situations, they are often only rationalizations of management's reluctance to tackle the challenges of creating standards to deliver excellent service.

Because services are intangible, they are difficult to describe and communicate. This difficulty becomes especially evident when new services are being developed. It is critical that everyone (managers, front-line employees, and behind-the-scenes support staff) work with the same concepts of the new service. For a service that already exists, any attempt to improve it will also suffer unless everyone has the same vision of the service. One of the most important ways to avoid Provider Gap 2 is to clearly design services without oversimplification, incompleteness, subjectivity, and bias. To do so, tools are needed to ensure that new and existing services are carefully developed and improved. Chapter 9 describes the tools that are most effective in service development and design, including service blueprinting, a unique tool for services.

The quality of service delivered by customer contact personnel is critically influenced by how they are evaluated and compensated. Standards signal to contact personnel what the management priorities are and which types of performance really count. When service standards are absent or when standards do not reflect

FIGURE 2.3

Key Factors Leading
to Provider Gap 2

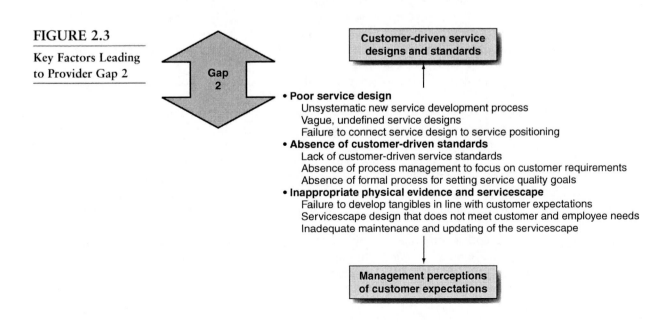

Gap 2

Customer-driven service designs and standards

• **Poor service design**
Unsystematic new service development process
Vague, undefined service designs
Failure to connect service design to service positioning

• **Absence of customer-driven standards**
Lack of customer-driven service standards
Absence of process management to focus on customer requirements
Absence of formal process for setting service quality goals

• **Inappropriate physical evidence and servicescape**
Failure to develop tangibles in line with customer expectations
Servicescape design that does not meet customer and employee needs
Inadequate maintenance and updating of the servicescape

Management perceptions of customer expectations

customers' expectations, quality of service is likely to suffer. When standards do reflect what customers expect, the quality of service they receive is likely to be enhanced. The Technology Spotlight in this chapter shows how Amazon.com uses customer-defined standards as the basis for its excellent service performance. Chapter 10 develops the topic of customer-defined service standards and shows that if they are developed appropriately they can have a powerful impact on closing both Provider Gap 2 and the customer gap.

In Chapter 11 we focus on the roles of physical evidence in service design and in meeting customer expectations. The *servicescape,* the physical setting where the service is delivered, is a particular focus of Chapter 11. Think of a restaurant, a hotel, a theme park, a health club, a hospital, or a school. The servicescape—the physical facility—is critical in these industries in terms of communicating about the service and making the entire experience pleasurable. In these cases the servicescape plays a variety of roles, from serving as a visual metaphor for what the company stands for to actually facilitating the activities of both consumers and employees.

Provider Gap 3: Not Delivering to Service Designs and Standards

Once service designs and standards are in place, it would seem that the firm is well on its way to delivering high-quality services. This assumption is true, but is still not enough to deliver excellent service. The firm must have systems, processes, and people in place to ensure that service delivery actually matches (or is even better than) the designs and standards.

Provider Gap 3 is the discrepancy between development of customer-driven service standards and actual service performance by company employees. Even when guidelines exist for performing services well and treating customers correctly, high-quality service performance is not a certainty. Standards must be backed by appropriate resources (people, systems, and technology), and employees must be measured and compensated on the basis of performance along those standards. Thus, even when standards accurately reflect customers' expectations, if the company fails to provide support for those standards—if it does not facilitate, encourage, and require their achievement—standards do no good. When the level of service delivery falls short of the standards, it falls short of what customers expect as well. Narrowing Gap 3—by ensuring that all the resources needed to achieve the standards are in place—reduces the customer gap.

Research has identified many of the critical inhibitors to closing Gap 3 (see Figure 2.4). These factors include employees who do not clearly understand the roles they are to play in the company, employees who experience conflict between customers and company management, poor employee selection, inadequate technology, inappropriate compensation and recognition, and lack of empowerment and teamwork. These factors all relate to the company's human resource function and involve internal practices such as recruitment, training, feedback, job design, motivation, and organizational structure. To deliver better service performance, these issues must be addressed across functions (such as with both marketing and human resources).

Another important variable in Provider Gap 3 is the customer. Even if contact employees and intermediaries are 100 percent consistent in their service delivery, the uncontrollable variables of the customer can introduce variability in service delivery. If customers do not perform their roles appropriately—if, for example, they fail to

36 Part 1 *Foundations for Services Marketing*

FIGURE 2.4

Key Factors Leading
to Provider Gap 3

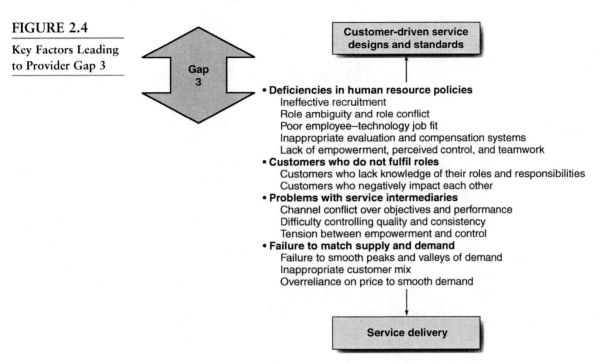

provide all the information necessary to the provider or neglect to read and follow instructions—service quality is jeopardized. Customers can also negatively influence the quality of service received by others if they are disruptive or take more than their share of a service provider's time. Understanding customer roles and how customers themselves can influence service delivery and outcomes are critical.

A third difficulty associated with Provider Gap 3 involves the challenge in delivering service through such intermediaries as retailers, franchisees, agents, and brokers. Because quality in service occurs in the human interaction between customers and service providers, control over the service encounter by the company is crucial, yet it rarely is fully possible. Most service (and many manufacturing) companies face an even more formidable task: attaining service excellence and consistency in the presence of intermediaries who represent them and interact with their customers yet are not under their direct control. Franchisers of services depend on their franchisees to execute service delivery as they have specified it. And it is in the execution by the franchisee that the customer evaluates the service quality of the company. With franchises and other types of intermediaries, someone other than the producer is responsible for the fulfilment of quality service. For this reason, a firm must develop ways to either control or motivate these intermediaries to meet company goals.

Another issue in Provider Gap 3 is the need in service firms to synchronize demand and capacity. Because services are perishable and cannot be inventoried, service companies frequently face situations of overdemand or underdemand. Lacking inventories to handle overdemand, companies lose sales when capacity is inadequate to handle customer needs. On the other hand, capacity is frequently underutilized in slow periods. Most companies rely on operations strategies such as cross-training or varying the size of the employee pool to synchronize supply and demand. Marketing strategies for managing demand—such as price changes, advertising, promotion, and alternative service offerings—can supplement approaches for managing supply.

Technology Spotlight

Amazon.ca Closes the Gaps

Can an online company be an excellent service provider, identifying customer expectations and meeting them by closing the four provider gaps? Amazon (www.amazon.ca) is a company that exemplifies the use of the strategies needed to provide consistent, accurate, and even personalized service.

Understanding customer expectations is a strategy that Amazon begins when a customer first starts shopping at its online store. From the very first time customers make choices, the company's computers begin profiles on them, offering selections based on a database of previous customers that read similar books or listened to similar music. In the beginning some offerings may not seem on target, but the longer customers shop at Amazon, the more accurately the company identifies their preferences and the more appropriate suggestions become. In time, the company even begins to send emails that are so specific ("We noticed that you purchased the last book by Jonathan Kellerman and we want you to know that he has just published a new book") that it almost seems like the local librarian is calling to let you know your new book is in. One of the company's unique features is "Your Store," a tab on the home page that sends customers to a selection of items that past purchases indicate would be of interest to them.

Customer-defined standards exist for virtually all activities at Amazon, from delivery to communication to service recovery. When you buy a product from Amazon, you select the mode of delivery and the company tells you the expected number of days it will take to receive your merchandise. Standard shipping is three to five days, but two- and one-day shipping are also available. The company has standards for how quickly you are informed when a product is unavailable (immediately), how fast you find out whether an out-of-print book can be located (three weeks), how long you can return items (30 days), and whether you pay return shipping costs (not if it is Amazon's error).

Service performance is where Amazon excels. Orders almost always arrive ahead of the promised date, are accurate, and are in excellent condition because of careful shipping practices. The company's copyrighted 1-Click Ordering allows regular customers to make purchases instantaneously without creating a shopping cart. Customers can track packages and review previous orders at any time. Amazon also makes sure that all its partners, who sell used and new books and other items direct to customers, perform to Amazon's standards. The company verifies performance of each purchase by asking the customer how well the merchant performed, then it posts scores where customers can see them easily.

Managing promises is handled by clear and careful communication on the website. Virtually every page is easy to understand and navigate. For example, the page dealing with returns eliminates customer misunderstanding by clearly spelling out what can be returned (almost everything) and what cannot (items that are gas powered or have flammable liquids, large televisions, opened CDs). The page describes how to repack items and when refunds are given. The page dealing with a customer's account shows all previous purchases and exactly where every ordered item is in the shipping process.

amazon.ca™

Source: Amazon, Amazon.com, the Amazon.com logo, and 1-Click are registered trademarks of Amazon.com, Inc. or its affiliates.

Now visit Chapters' Canadian-owned online store (www.chapters.indigo.ca) to see how it handles each of these provider gaps. Is Chapters as effective as Amazon in closing each gap?

Source: www.Amazon.ca.

We will discuss strategies to deal with the roles of employees in Chapter 12, customers in Chapter 13, intermediaries in Chapter 14, and demand and capacity in Chapter 15.

Provider Gap 4: Not Matching Performance to Promises

Provider Gap 4 illustrates the difference between service delivery and the service provider's external communications. Promises made by a service company through its media advertising, sales force, and other communications can raise customer expectations. The discrepancy between actual and promised service therefore has an adverse effect on the customer gap. Broken promises can occur for many reasons: overpromising in advertising or personal selling, inadequate coordination between operations and marketing, and differences in policies and procedures across service outlets. Figure 2.5 shows the key factors that lead to Provider Gap 4.

In addition to elevating expectations through exaggerated claims, there are other, less obvious ways in which external communications influence customers' assessments. Service companies frequently fail to educate customers appropriately. They also neglect to manage customer expectations of what will be delivered in service transactions and relationships.

One of the major difficulties associated with Provider Gap 4 is that communications to consumers involve issues that cross organizational boundaries. Because service advertising promises what people do, and because what *people* do cannot be controlled like machines, this type of communication involves more than the marketing department. This type of marketing is what we call *interactive marketing*—the marketing between contact people and customers—and it must be coordinated with the conventional types of *external marketing*. When employees do not understand the reality of service delivery, they are likely to make exaggerated promises or fail to communicate well. The result is poor service quality perceptions. Effectively coordinating actual

FIGURE 2.5

Key Factors Leading
to Provider Gap 4

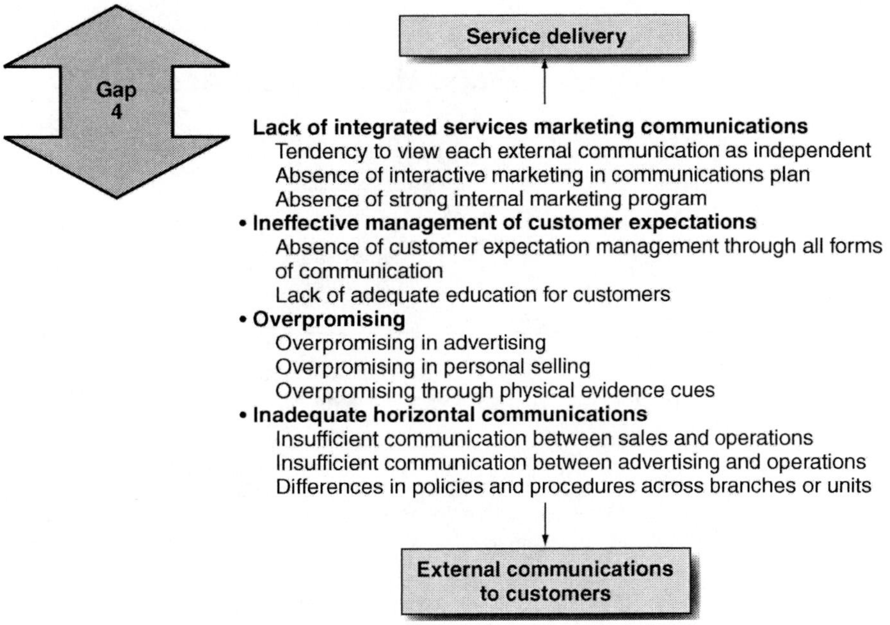

Gap 4

Service delivery

Lack of integrated services marketing communications
  Tendency to view each external communication as independent
  Absence of interactive marketing in communications plan
  Absence of strong internal marketing program
• **Ineffective management of customer expectations**
  Absence of customer expectation management through all forms
  of communication
  Lack of adequate education for customers
• **Overpromising**
  Overpromising in advertising
  Overpromising in personal selling
  Overpromising through physical evidence cues
• **Inadequate horizontal communications**
  Insufficient communication between sales and operations
  Insufficient communication between advertising and operations
  Differences in policies and procedures across branches or units

**External communications
to customers**

service delivery with external communications, therefore, narrows Provider Gap 4 and favourably affects the customer gap as well.

Another issue in Provider Gap 4 is associated with the pricing of services. With goods, customers possess enough price knowledge before purchase to be able to judge whether a price is fair. With services, customers often have no internal reference points for prices before purchase and consumption. Pricing strategies such as discounting, "everyday prices," and couponing obviously need to be different in services in which the customer has no initial sense of prices. Techniques for developing prices for services are more complicated than those for pricing tangible goods.

In summary, external communications—whether from marketing communications or pricing—can create a larger customer gap by raising expectations about service delivery. In addition to improving service delivery, companies must also manage all communications to customers so that inflated promises do not lead to higher expectations. Chapter 16 will discuss integrated services marketing communications, and Chapter 17 will cover pricing to accomplish these objectives.

PUTTING IT ALL TOGETHER: CLOSING THE GAPS

The full conceptual model shown in Figure 2.6 conveys a clear message to managers wishing to improve their quality of service: the key to closing the customer gap is to close Provider Gaps 1 through 4 and keep them closed. To the extent that one or more Provider Gaps exist, customers perceive service quality shortfalls. The gaps model of service quality therefore serves as a framework for organizations attempting to improve quality service and services marketing. Exhibit 2.1 provides a service quality gaps audit based on the model.

The model begins where the process of improving service quality begins: with an understanding of the nature and extent of the customer gap. Given the service organization's need to focus on the customer and to use knowledge about the customer to drive business strategy, we believe that this emphasis is warranted.

FIGURE 2.6

Gaps Model of
Service Quality

Gaps Model of Service Quality

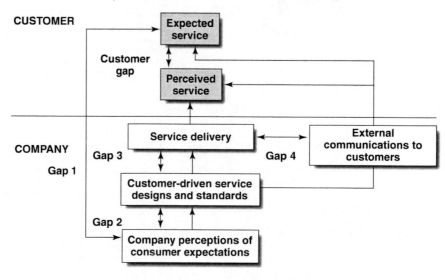

EXHIBIT 2.1

Using the Gaps Model to Assess an Organization's Service Strategy

The gaps model featured in this chapter and used as a framework for this textbook is a useful way to audit the service performance and capabilities of an organization. The model has been used by many companies as an assessment or service audit tool, because it is comprehensive and offers a way for companies to examine all the factors that influence service quality. To use the tool, a company documents what it knows about each gap and the factors that affect the size of the gap. Although you will learn much more about each of these gaps throughout the book, we provide here a basic gaps audit. In Exercise 1 at the end of this chapter, we propose that you use this audit with a company to determine its service quality gaps.

Service Quality Gaps Model Audit
For each of the following factors in the gaps, indicate the effectiveness of the organization on that factor. Use a 1 to 10 scale where I is "poor" and 10 is "excellent."

Customer Gap	*1 = poor* *10 = excellent*
1. How well does the company understand customer expectations of service quality? 2. How well does the company understand customer perceptions of service?	

Provider Gap I	*1 = poor* *10 = excellent*

1. **Market Research Orientation**
   Is the amount and type of market research adequate to understand customer expectations of service?
   Does the company use this information in decisions about service provision?
2. **Upward Communication**
   Do managers and customers interact enough for management to know what customers expect?
   Do contact people tell management what customers expect?
3. **Relationship Focus**
   To what extent does the company understand the expectations of different customer segments?
   To what extent does the company focus on relationships with customers rather than transactions?
4. **Service Recovery**
   How effective are the service recovery efforts of the organization?
   How well does the organization plan for service failures?
   Score for Provider Gap 1	

Provider Gap 2	*1 = poor* *10 = excellent*

5. **Systematic Service Design**
   How effective is the company's service development process?
   How well are new services defined for customers and employees?
6. **Presence of Customer-Defined Standards**
   How effective are the company's service standards?
   Are they defined to correspond to customer expectations?
   How effective is the process for setting and tracking service quality goals?	

> **EXHIBIT 2.1**
>
> *—continued*

7. **Appropriate Physical Evidence and Servicescape**

   How appropriate, attractive, and effective are the company's physical facilities, equipment, and other tangibles?

   Score for Provider Gap 2

Provider Gap 3	*1 = poor* *10 = excellent*

8. **Effective Human Resource Policies**

   How effectively does the company recruit, hire, train, compensate, and empower employees?

   Is service quality delivery consistent across employees, teams, units, and branches?

9. **Effective Role Fulfilment by Customers**

   Do customers understand their roles and responsibilities?

   Does the company manage customers to fulfil their roles, especially customers that are incompatible?

10. **Effective Alignment with Service Intermediaries**

    How well are service intermediaries aligned with the company?

    Is there conflict over objectives and performance, costs and rewards?

    Is service quality delivery consistent across the outlets?

11. **Alignment of Supply and Demand**

    How well is the company able to match supply with demand fluctuations?

    Score for Provider Gap 3

Provider Gap 4	*1 = poor* *10 = excellent*

12. **Integrated Services Marketing Communications**

    How well do all company communications—including the interactions between company employees and customers—express the same message and level of service quality?

13. **Effective Management of Customer Expectations**

    How well does the company communicate to customers about what will be provided to them?

14. **Accurate Promising in Advertising and Personal Selling**

    Does the company avoid overpromising and overselling?

15. **Adequate Horizontal Communications**

    How well do different parts of the organization communicate with each other so that service quality equals what is promised?

    Score for Provider Gap 4

The score for each gap should be compared to the maximum score possible. Are certain gaps weaker than others? Which areas in each gap need attention?

SUMMARY

This chapter presented the integrated gaps model of service quality (shown in Figure 2.6), a framework for understanding and improving service delivery. The entire text is organized around this model of service quality, which focuses on five pivotal gaps in delivering and marketing service:

The customer gap: Difference between customer expectations and perceptions

Provider Gap 1: Not knowing what customers expect

Provider Gap 2: Not selecting the right service designs and standards

Provider Gap 3: Not delivering to service designs and standards

Provider Gap 4: Not matching performance to promises

The gaps model positions the key concepts in services marketing in a manner that begins with the customer and builds the organization's tasks around what is needed to close the gap between customer expectations and perceptions. The final chapter in the book, Chapter 18, discusses the financial implications of service quality, reviewing the research and company data that indicates linkages between service quality and financial performance.

Discussion Questions

1. Think about a service you receive. Is there a gap between your expectations and perceptions of that service? What do you expect that you do not receive?
2. Consider the "wish mode" discussion about IKEA. Think about a service that you receive regularly and put yourself in the wish mode. How would you change the service and the way it is provided?
3. If you were the manager of a service organization and wanted to apply the gaps model to improve service, which gap would you start with? Why? In what order would you proceed to close the gaps?
4. Can Provider Gap 4 be closed prior to closing any of the other three provider gaps? How?
5. Which of the four provider gaps do you believe is hardest to close? Why?

Exercises

1. Choose an organization to interview, and use the integrated gaps model of service quality as a framework. An audit form is provided in Exhibit 2.1. Ask the manager whether the organization suffers from any of the factors listed in the figures in this chapter. Which factor in each of Figures 2.2 through 2.5 does the manager consider the most troublesome? What does the company do to try to address the problems?
2. Use the Internet to locate the website of Walt Disney, Marriott, Ritz-Carlton, or any other well-known, high-quality service organization. Which provider gaps has the company closed? How can you tell?

3. Interview a nonprofit or public sector organization in your area (it might be some part of your school). Find out if the integrated gaps model of service quality framework makes sense in the context of its organization.

⟶ Notes

1. "Our Mission," Delta Hotels site, www.deltahotels.ca/en/about/mission.html, accessed September 18, 2006.

2. The gaps model of service quality that provides the structure for this text was developed by and is fully presented in Valarie A. Zeithaml, A. Parasuraman, and Leonard L. Berry, *Delivering Quality Service: Balancing Customer Perceptions and Expectations* (New York: The Free Press, 1990).

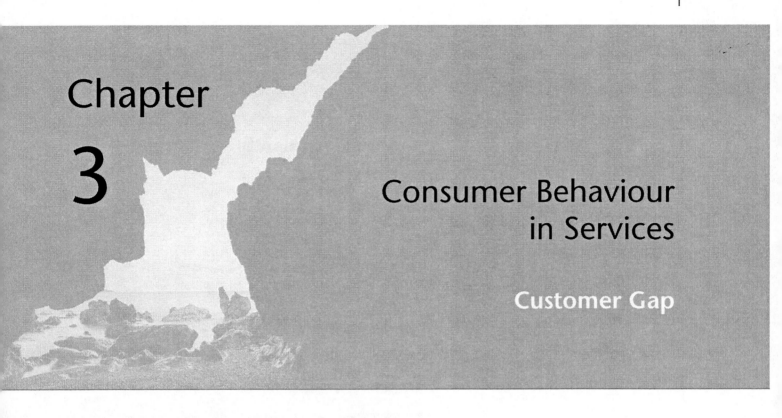

Chapter

3

Consumer Behaviour in Services

Customer Gap

THIS CHAPTER'S OBJECTIVES ARE TO

1. Enhance understanding of how consumers choose and evaluate services, through focusing on factors that are particularly relevant for services.

2. Describe how consumers judge goods versus services in terms of search, experience, and credence criteria.

3. Develop the elements of consumer behaviour that a services marketer must understand: choice behaviour, consumer experiences, and postexperience evaluation.

4. Explore how differences among consumers (cultural differences, group decision making) affect consumer behaviour and influence services marketing strategies.

CONSUMER PROBLEM: TIME DEFICIENCY

Today's dual-career couples, single-parent families, and two-job families are realizing a burning consumer need: more time. Individuals in these and other nontraditional family configurations are overstressed with their work and home obligations and find that dealing with many of life's everyday tasks is overwhelming. As depicted in the Time Crunch Meter, created from a recent Ipsos Reid survey, feeling that there is not enough time in the day to do what is needed to be done is a global phenomenon (see Figure 3.1). And, although Canada was not included in the survey, the situation is similar

44

FIGURE 3.1

Ipsos Reid Time Crunch Meter
Do you agree strongly, agree somewhat, disagree somewhat, or disagree strongly with the statement "There is never enough time in the day to get done what I want to get done."

*Urban-only samples.
**China's urban-only sample includes Hong Kong.

Source: Courtesy of Ipsos.

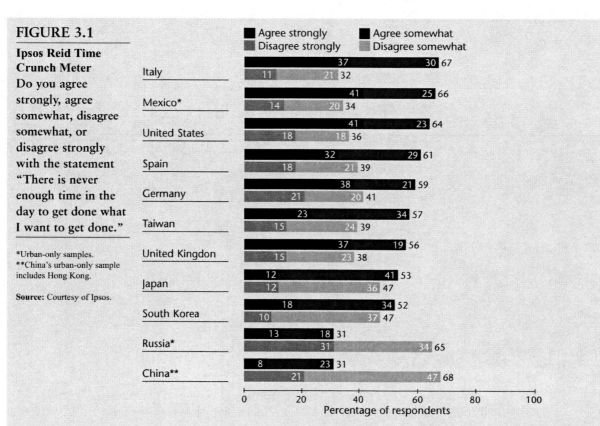

Legend: Agree strongly, Agree somewhat, Disagree strongly, Disagree somewhat

Country	Agree strongly	Agree somewhat	Total agree	Disagree strongly	Disagree somewhat	Total disagree
Italy	37	30	67	11	21	32
Mexico*	41	25	66	14	20	34
United States	41	23	64	18	18	36
Spain	32	29	61	18	21	39
Germany	38	21	59	21	20	41
Taiwan	23	34	57	15	24	39
United Kingdon	37	19	56	15	23	38
Japan	12	41	53	12	36	47
South Korea	18	34	52	10	37	47
Russia*	13	18	31	31	34	65
China**	8	23	31	21	47	68

Percentage of respondents

here. As John Torella from Toronto's J. C. Williams Group remarked about the time-poor customer, "They just don't have the time to do the kind of conventional shopping they've done in the past. It's particularly that young married segment—husband and wife working, a couple of kids."[1] For many customers, all types of shopping have become "drudgery or worse."[2] Faced with this dilemma, consumers have choices: They can continue to do all these tasks for themselves, or they can decide to employ the services of professionals or friends and relatives to help them out.[3]

The antidote to this time deficiency is found in many new services and service features that recover time for consumers. Innovative new services—plant watering, wedding advising, baby-proofing, executive organizing, and personal shopping—are emerging to deal with tasks that used to be performed by the household but now can be purchased by the time-buying consumer.[4] Conventional services such as retailing, banking, and restaurants[5] are also adding peripheral services to make shopping easier, increasing their hours to suit customer schedules, reducing transaction time, improving delivery, and providing merchandise or services at home or work. Increased use of the Internet is also saving time for customers. With the Web and home delivery, many shopping tasks can be carried out by customers without even leaving the house and at any time of the day or night.

And there is an increasingly popular parallel phenomenon in business today known as *outsourcing*, which means purchasing whole service functions (such as billing, payroll, secretarial support, maintenance, inventory, network operations, and marketing) from other firms rather than executing them in-house. The motivation for corporations is not so much saving time as it is saving money, better use of limited resources, and focusing on core competencies. Companies that use outsourcing effectively have discovered that in many cases purchasing services outright from another company can be far more economical than the payroll and capital costs of performing them inside. Another benefit, particularly for smaller businesses, is that outsourcing allows the company to focus on its core competencies without the distraction of less central tasks.

The primary objectives of services producers and marketers are identical to those of all marketers: to develop and provide offerings that satisfy consumer needs and expectations, thereby ensuring their own economic survival. To achieve these objectives, service providers need to understand how consumers choose, experience, and evaluate their service offerings.

This chapter shows that services' characteristics result in some differences in consumer evaluation processes compared to those used in assessing goods. Consumers have a more difficult time evaluating and choosing most services partly because services are intangible and nonstandardized and partly because consumption is so closely intertwined with production. These characteristics lead to differences in consumer evaluation processes for goods and services in all stages of the buying and consumption process.

FIGURE 3.2

Service tasks contribute to consumers' time deficiency.

Source: Ryan McVay/ Photodisc/Getty Images.

SEARCH, EXPERIENCE, AND CREDENCE PROPERTIES

One framework for isolating differences in evaluation processes between goods and services is a classification proposed by economists.[6] Economists first distinguished between two categories of properties of consumer products: **search qualities**, attributes that a consumer can determine before purchasing a product; and **experience qualities**, attributes that can be discerned only after purchase or during consumption. Search qualities include colour, style, price, fit, feel, hardness, and smell; experience qualities include taste and wearability. Products such as automobiles, clothing, furniture, and jewellery are high in search qualities because their attributes can be almost completely determined and evaluated before purchase. Products such as vacations and restaurant meals are high in experience qualities because their attributes cannot be fully known or assessed until they have been purchased and are being consumed. A third category, **credence qualities**, includes characteristics that the consumer may find impossible to evaluate even after purchase and consumption.[7] Examples of offerings high in credence qualities are treatments for some medical conditions and brake relinings on automobiles. Few consumers possess medical or mechanical skills sufficient to evaluate whether these services are necessary or are performed properly, even after they have been prescribed and produced by the seller. The ad shown in Figure 3.3 vividly shows that cholesterol treatment is strong in credence properties. People often don't know the extent of the condition until it is too late.

Figure 3.4 arrays products high in search, experience, or credence qualities along a continuum ranging from easy to evaluate to difficult to evaluate. Products high in search qualities are the easiest to evaluate (left end of the continuum). Products high in experience qualities are more difficult to evaluate, because they must be purchased and consumed before assessment is possible (centre of continuum). Products high in credence qualities are the most difficult to evaluate, because

FIGURE 3.3

Cholesterol treatment is high in credence properties.

Source: © 2006 Pfizer Canada Inc.

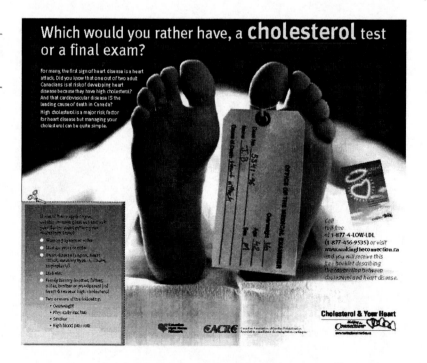

50 Part 2 *Focus on the Customer*

FIGURE 3.4

Continuum of Evaluation for Different Types of Products

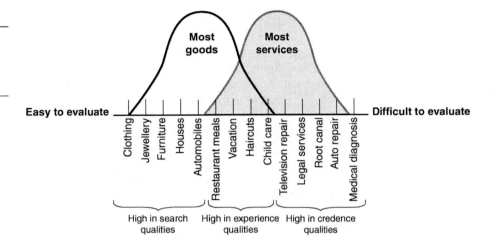

the consumer may be unaware of whether the offerings satisfy given wants or needs even after consumption (right end of the continuum). The major premise of this chapter is that most goods fall to the left of the continuum, whereas most services fall to the right because of the distinguishing characteristics described in Chapter 1. These characteristics make services more difficult to evaluate than goods, particularly in advance of purchase. Difficulty in evaluation, in turn, forces consumers to rely on different cues and processes when assessing services.

The next sections of this chapter build from these basic differences to explore the stages of consumer decision making and evaluation for services. This discussion is organized around three broad stages of consumer behaviour, as shown in Figure 3.5: consumer choice, consumer experience, and postexperience evaluation. Within each of these stages, you will see similarities and differences between goods and services.

CONSUMER CHOICE

The first important area of consumer behaviour is how customers choose and make decisions and the steps that lead to the purchase of a particular service. This process is similar to that used for goods in some ways and different in others. Customers follow a logical sequence, including need recognition, information search, evaluation of alternatives, and purchase. The following sections discuss this sequence, particularly focusing on the ways in which services decision making is different from goods decision making.

FIGURE 3.5   Stages in Consumer Decision Making and Evaluation of Services

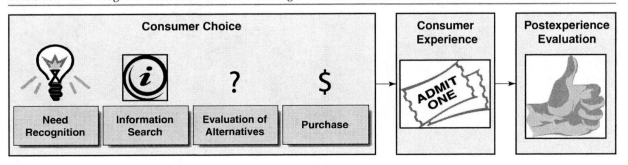

Need Recognition

The process of buying a service begins with the recognition that a need or want exists. Although there are many different ways to characterize needs, the most widely known is Maslow's hierarchy, which specifies five need categories arranged in a sequence from basic lower-level needs to higher-level needs. Services can fill all these needs, and they become increasingly important for higher-level social, ego, and self-actualization needs (see Figure 3.6).

The hierarchical nature of Maslow's need categorization has been disputed, and evidence exists that people with unfilled basic needs can be motivated to self-actualize. We are not concerned with the hierarchical nature in this section; we use it only as a way to discuss different drives that lead customers to the next stages of consumer behaviour in services.

Information Search

Once they recognize a need, consumers obtain information about goods and services that might satisfy this need. Seeking information may be an extensive, formalized process if the service is important to the consumer (e.g., a European vacation package). In other cases, the information search may be quick (e.g., a restaurant for a quick lunch). Consumers use both personal sources (e.g., friends or experts) and nonpersonal sources (e.g., mass media and websites) to gain information about goods and services. Seeking information is a way of reducing risk, helping consumers feel more confident about their choices.

Personal and Nonpersonal Sources

When purchasing goods, consumers make use of both personal and nonpersonal sources because both convey information about search qualities. When purchasing services, on the other hand, consumers seek and rely to a greater extent on *personal* sources for several reasons.

First, mass and selective media can convey information about search qualities but can communicate far less about experience qualities. By asking friends or experts about services, however, the consumer can obtain information vicariously about experience qualities.

FIGURE 3.6

Teeth whitening is a growing service that is driven by consumers' ego needs.

Source: Courtesy BriteSmile.

A second reason for greater use of personal sources of information for services is that many types of nonpersonal sources of information are not as readily available for services. Many service providers are local, independent merchants without the funds to advertise. Furthermore, cooperative advertising is used infrequently with services because most local providers are both producer and retailer of the service. And, because professional associations banned advertising for so long, both professionals and consumers tend to resist its use even though it is now permitted.

Finally, because consumers can assess few attributes *before* purchase of a service, they may feel greater risk in selecting a little-known alternative. Personal influence becomes pivotal as product complexity increases and when objective standards by which to evaluate a product decrease (i.e., when experience qualities are high).[8] Managers in service industries clearly recognize the strong influence of word-of-mouth communication (Figure 3.7).

Interestingly, consumers are now able through the Internet to seek more nonpersonal information about services in the form of visuals, photographs, and even virtual tours.[9] In addition to these tangible representations of the service experience, consumers can also seek the personal opinions of others via the Web through chat rooms, online ratings, and consumer complaint websites. Some consumer complaint websites even target a specific firm's current and prospective customers, offering unsolicited information.[10]

Perceived Risk

Although some degree of perceived risk may be inevitable, more risk appears to be involved in the purchase of services, because services are more intangible, variable, and perishable. Risk can come in the form of financial risk, time risk, performance risk, social risk, or psychological risk.

The intangible nature of services and their high level of experience qualities imply that services generally must be selected with less prepurchase information. There is clear evidence that greater intangibility increases perceptions of risk.[11] And because services are nonstandardized, the consumer will feel some uncertainty about the outcome and consequences each time a service is purchased. In addition, services purchases may involve more perceived risk than other purchases because, with some exceptions, services are not accompanied by warranties or guarantees. Dissatisfied

FIGURE 3.7

Consumers seek and rely on personal sources in purchasing experience goods and services.

Source: Mark Lewis/Getty Images.

customers can rarely "return" a service; they have already consumed it by the time they realize their dissatisfaction. Finally, many services are so technical or specialized that consumers often can't evaluate whether they are satisfied, even after they have consumed the service.

The increase in perceived risk in purchasing services suggests the use of strategies to reduce risk. Risk reduction can be accomplished through tactics that reduce risk directly (e.g., guarantees) or by addressing the factors that contribute to the perception of risk (e.g., making the service more tangible).[12] For example, Canada Post and FedEx provide tracking numbers for customers so they can follow their shipments online and know exactly where a package is. This system helps reduce the risk for consumers. Offering a free or reduced-cost trial period for a service would be another means to reduce risk. For example, child care centres often encourage a free trial day for prospective clients and their children to reduce the sense of risk in this important decision. To the extent possible, service providers should emphasize employee training and other procedures to standardize their offerings so that consumers learn to expect a given level of quality, again reducing perceived risk.

Evaluation of Service Alternatives

The evoked set of alternatives—that group of products that a consumer considers acceptable options—is likely to be smaller with services. One reason involves differences in retailing between goods and services. To purchase goods, consumers generally shop in retail stores that display competing products in close proximity, clearly demonstrating the possible alternatives. To purchase services, on the other hand, the consumer visits an establishment (such as a bank, a dry cleaner, or a hair salon) that almost always offers only a single "brand" for sale. A second reason for the smaller evoked set is that consumers are unlikely to find more than one or two businesses providing the same services in a given geographic area, whereas they may find numerous retail stores carrying the identical manufacturer's product. A third reason for a smaller evoked set is the difficulty of obtaining adequate prepurchase information about services.

Faced with the task of collecting and evaluating experience qualities, consumers may simply select the first acceptable alternative rather than searching many alternatives. The Internet has the potential to widen the set of alternatives and already has done so in some industries. This trend is most notable in airlines and hotels where comparable information is available through providers such as Travelocity, Orbitz, and Expedia.

For nonprofessional services, consumers' decisions often entail the choice between performing the services for themselves or hiring someone to perform them.[13] Working people may choose between cleaning their own homes or hiring housekeepers, or even between staying home to take care of their children or engaging a day care centre to provide child care. Consumers may consider themselves as sources of supply for many services, including lawn care, tax preparation, and preparing meals. Thus, the customer's evoked set frequently includes self-provision of the service. Self-service via technology is also a viable alternative for many services, as the Technology Spotlight demonstrates.

Service Purchase

Following consideration of alternatives, consumers decide to purchase a particular service or to do it themselves. One of the most interesting differences between goods and services is that most goods are fully produced (at the factory) prior to being purchased by consumers. Thus, consumers, prior to making their decision, can see and frequently

Technology Spotlight

Self-Service Technologies: How Much Do Customers Like Providing Their Own Services?

One major change in consumer behaviour is the growing tendency for consumers to interact with technology to create services instead of interacting with a live service firm employee. *Self-service technologies (SSTs)* are technological interfaces that allow customers to produce services independent of direct service employee involvement. Examples of SSTs that you are probably very familiar with are automated teller machines, pay-at-the-pump terminals at gas stations, automated hotel checkout and check-in, and any service over the Internet. Some Internet-based companies have begun selling divorce kits to speed up processing time, and some online divorce services will send all the legal paperwork after an individual completes a series of short questions over the Internet. Electronic self-ordering is being developed at fast-food chains, and self-scanning at grocery stores is available through companies such as Loblaws.

The table here shows a comprehensive set of categories and examples of SSTs in use today. The columns of the matrix represent the types of technologies that companies are using to interface with customers in self-service encounters, and the rows show purposes of the technologies from the customer perspective. As you can see, customers use the technologies to provide customer service, to conduct transactions, and to provide self-help.

A recent study asked customers across a wide range of industries and applications what they think of SSTs and found that customers have very strong feelings about them. They both love and hate SSTs, depending on a few key conditions. Customers love them when:

- *SSTs bail them out of difficult situations.* A single parent with a sleeping child in the car needs to get gas and money for work the following morning. Using a pay-at-the-pump gas station and drive-up ATM allows the parent to accomplish these tasks without leaving the sleeping child.

- *SSTs are better than the interpersonal alternative.* SSTs have the potential to save customers time, money, and psychological costs. The Internet allows customers to shop at any time and complete transactions

Source: Reproduced with the permission of Air Canada.

more quickly than they could in person. Internet loans and mortgages allow customers to avoid the anxiety of meeting a banker in person and feeling judged.

- *SSTs work.* When SSTs work as they are supposed to, customers are impressed. When these transactions work smoothly, as they usually do after the proper setup, the transactions are satisfying.

On the other hand, customers hate SSTs when the following problems occur:

- *SSTs fail.* The researchers found that 60 percent of the negative stories they heard stemmed from failures of SSTs. Broken machines, failed PINs, websites that were down, and items not shipped as promised all frustrate consumers.

- *SSTs are poorly designed.* Poorly designed technologies that are difficult to use or understand create hassles for customers, making them feel as though

continued

Technology Spotlight

Self-Service Technologies: How Much Do Customers Like Providing Their Own Services?—continued

the SST is not worth using. Websites that are difficult to manoeuvre are particularly troublesome. If customers cannot reach information they need within a few clicks (some researchers say that two clicks are all that customers will tolerate), customers shun the website.

- *The customer messes up.* Customers dislike using technologies that they feel they cannot perform adequately. Even though they feel partial responsibility, they will avoid using them in the future. A common frustration today is having various usernames and passwords for different websites.

- *There is no service recovery.* When the process or technology fails, SSTs rarely provide ways to recover on the spot. In these cases customers must then call or

visit the company, precisely what they were trying to avoid by using the self-service technology.

It is increasingly evident that these technological innovations will be a critical component of customer–firm interactions. If these SSTs are to succeed, the researchers contend, they must become more reliable, be better than the interpersonal alternatives, and have recovery systems in place when they fail.

Sources: M. L. Meuter, A. L. Ostom, R. I. Roundtree, and M. J. Bitner, "Self-Service Technologies: Understanding Customer Satisfaction with Technology-Based Service Encounters," *Journal of Marketing* 64 (July 2000), pp. 50–64; M. J. Bitner, "Self-Service Technologies: What Do Customers Expect?" *Marketing Management*, Spring 2001, pp. 10–11.

Interface / Purpose	**Categories and Examples of SSTs in Use**			
	Telephone/Interactive Voice Response	**Online/Internet**	**Interactive Kiosks**	**Video/CD**
Customer Service	• Telephone banking • Flight information • Order status	• Package tracking • Account information	• ATMs • Hotel checkout	
Transactions	• Telephone banking • Prescription refills	• Retail purchasing • Financial transactions	• Pay at the pump • Hotel checkout • Car rental	
Self-Help	• Information telephone lines	• Internet information search • Distance learning	• Blood pressure machines • Tourist information	• Tax preparation software • Television/CD-based training

try the exact object that they will buy. For services, much is still unknown at the point of purchase. In many cases, the service is purchased and produced almost simultaneously—as with a restaurant meal or live entertainment. In other cases, consumers pay all or part of the purchase price up-front for a service they will not fully experience until it is produced for them much later. This situation arises with services such as vacation tours or home remodelling, or ongoing services such as health club memberships or university educations. In business-to-business situations, long-term contracts for services (such as payroll, network integration, or landscaping) may be signed prior to anything being produced at all.

Because of the inherent risk in the purchase decision for services, some providers offer "free" (or "deeply discounted") initial trials or extensive tours of their facilities (e.g., prospective student and parent tours at universities) in order to reduce risk in the final purchase decision. In business-to-business situations, trust in the provider is paramount when customers sign long-term service contracts, and frequently the contracts themselves spell out in detail the service-level agreements and penalties for nonperformance.

CONSUMER EXPERIENCE

Because the choice process for services is inherently risky with many unknowns, the experience itself often dominates the evaluation process. As noted, services are high in experience and credence qualities relative to goods; thus, how consumers evaluate the actual experience of the service is very critical in their evaluation process and their decision to repurchase later. In fact, noted customer experience experts have stated that "the experience is the marketing."[14]

Much has been written recently about customer experiences and their important role in influencing consumer behaviour. Goods and services companies alike are being admonished to create "memorable experiences for their customers."[15]

In this section we describe elements of consumer behaviour that are relevant to understanding service experiences and how customers evaluate them. We do not limit our discussion to fun, exciting, or memorable experiences only. Instead, we use the term *customer experience* to encompass service processes that span the mundane to the spectacular. Customers purchasing building maintenance and dry cleaning services still have experiences, albeit less exciting ones than customers of entertainment or travel services. All services *are* experiences—some are long in duration and some are short; some are complex and others are simple; some are mundane, whereas others are exciting and unique. Creating and managing effective processes and experiences are always essential management tasks for service organizations. Many subsequent chapters in this book will provide you with tools and approaches for managing specific elements of the customer experience—the heart of services marketing and management.

Services as Processes

Because services are performances done for and with customers, they typically involve a sequence of steps. Consider medical services. Some of the steps in medical care involve patients interacting with their physician, other steps may be carried out by the customers themselves (e.g., "following the doctor's orders," taking medications), and other steps may involve third parties (e.g., going to a lab for blood work). The combination of these steps, and many others along the way, constitute a process, a service experience that is evaluated by the consumer. It is the combination of steps, or the "experience," that is evaluated by the customer. In many cases, the customer's experience comprises interactions with multiple, interconnected organizations, as in the case of medical services or home buying. Diverse sets of experiences across the network of firms (e.g., a doctor's office, medical laboratory, hospital, and physical therapy clinic) will likely influence consumers' overall impressions of their experience.[16] Whether or not the provider acknowledges it, it is inevitable that the customer will have an experience—good, bad, or indifferent.

Service Provision as Drama

The metaphor of a theatre is useful for analyzing service performances. Both the theatre and service organizations aim to create a desirable impression before an audience and recognize that the way to accomplish this is by carefully managing the actors and the physical setting.[17] The service marketer must play many drama-related roles—including director, choreographer, and writer—to be sure the performances of the actors are pleasing to the audience. The Walt Disney Company (Figure 3.8) explicitly considers its service provision a "performance," even using show business terms such as *cast member*, *onstage*, and *show* to describe the operations at Disneyland and Walt Disney World.[18]

The skill of the service **actors** in performing their routines, the way they appear, and their commitment to the "show" are all essential to service delivery. Although service actors are present in most service performances, their importance increases in three conditions. First, service actors are critical when the degree of direct personal contact is high. Consider the difference between a visit to Denny's and a trip to a Japanese restaurant like Benihana. In many cases customers go to Japanese steakhouses as much for the show as for the food, and they eagerly anticipate the performance of the real-time chef who twirls knives, jokes with the guests, and even flips shrimp into his hat or onto guests' plates. The second condition in which service actors' skills are critical is when the services involve repeat contact. Nurses in hospitals, favourite waiters, or captains on cruises are essential characters in service theatre, and their individual performances can make or break the success of the services. The third condition in which contact personnel are critical is when they have discretion in determining the nature of the service and how it is delivered. When you consider the quality of the education you are receiving in college, you are certain to focus much of your evaluation on your professors' delivery of classes. In education, as in other services such as medical and legal services, the professional is the key actor in the performance.[19]

Ray Fisk and Steve Grove, two experts in the area of service dramaturgy, point out that service actors' performances can be characterized as sincere or cynical.[20] A sincere performance occurs when an actor becomes one with the role that she is playing, whereas a cynical performance occurs when an actor views a performance only

FIGURE 3.8

At Disney World the delivery of service is conceived as drama.

Source: Freelance Consulting Services/Corbis.

as a means to an end, such as getting paid for doing the job. When a service employee takes the time to listen and help, the performance is sincere and often noteworthy. Unfortunately, too many examples of cynical performances exist in which front-line "actors" seem to care little about the "audience" of customers. As Grove and Fisk point out, a single employee can ruin the service experience by ridiculing other cast members' efforts, failing to perform his role correctly, or projecting the wrong image. To create the right impression, three characteristics are necessary: loyalty, discipline, and circumspection.[21]

The **physical setting** of the service can be likened to the staging of a theatrical production, including scenery, props, and other physical cues. Among a setting's features that may influence a service are the colours or brightness of the surroundings; the volume and pitch of sounds in the setting; the smells, movement, freshness, and temperature of the air; the use of space; the style and comfort of the furnishings; and the setting's design and cleanliness.[22] As an example, the service provided by a cruise ship features its layout (broad and open), decor and comfort (large, cushioned deck chairs), furnishings (lots of polished wood and brass), and cleanliness ("shipshape"). The setting increases in importance when the environment distinguishes the service. Consider how critical the setting is for a downtown law firm, which must appear professional, capable, even imposing.[23] In essence, the delivery of service can be conceived as drama, where service personnel are the actors, service customers are the audience, physical evidence of the service is the setting, and the process of service assembly is the performance.[24]

The drama metaphor offers a useful way to improve service performances. Selection of personnel can be viewed as auditioning the actors. An actor's personal appearance, manner, facial expression, gestures, personality, and demographic profile can be determined in large part in the interview or audition. Training of personnel can become rehearsing. Clearly defining the role can be seen as scripting the performance. Creation of the service environment involves setting the stage. Finally, deciding which aspects of the service should be performed in the presence of the customer (onstage) and which should be performed in the back room (backstage) helps define the performances the customer experiences.

Service Roles and Scripts

Roles are combinations of social cues that guide and direct behaviour in a given setting.[25] Just as there are roles in dramatic performances, there are roles in service delivery. For example, the role of a hostess in a restaurant is to acknowledge and greet customers, find out how many people are in their group, and then lead them to a table where they will eat. The success of any service performance depends in part on how well the role is performed by the service actor and how well the team of players—employees and customers—act out their roles.[26] Service employees need to perform their roles according to the expectations of the customer; if they do not, the customer may be frustrated and disappointed. If customers are informed and educated about their roles and if they cooperate with the provider in following the script, successful service provision is likely.

One factor that influences the effectiveness of role performance is the **script**—the logical sequence of events expected by the customer, involving her as either a participant or an observer.[27] Service scripts consist of sequences of actions associated with actors and objects that, through repeated involvement, define what the customer expects.[28] (See Figure 3.9 for a "service script" that was misread!)

Receiving a dental checkup is a service experience for which a well-defined script exists. For a checkup the consumer expects the following sequence: Enter the

FIGURE 3.9

These "service actors" must have two different scripts!

reception area, greet a receptionist, sit in a waiting room, follow the dental hygienist to a separate room, recline in a chair while his teeth are cleaned by the hygienist, be examined by the dentist, then pay for the services. When the service conforms to this script, the customer has a feeling of confirmed expectations and satisfaction. Deviations from the service script lead to confusion and dissatisfaction. Suppose, on moving to a new town, you went to a dentist who had no receptionist and no waiting area, only a doorbell in a cubicle. Suppose, on answering the doorbell, an employee in shorts took you to a large room where all patients were in dental chairs facing each other. These actions and objects are certainly not in the traditional service script for dentistry and might create considerable uncertainty and doubt in patients.

Some services are more scripted than others. Customers would expect very expensive, customized services such as spa vacations to be less scripted than mass-produced services such as fast food ("Have a nice day!") and airline travel.

The Compatibility of Service Customers

We have just discussed the roles of employees and customers receiving service. We now want to focus on the role of *other customers* receiving service at the same time. Consider how central the mere presence of other customers is in churches, restaurants, dances, bars, clubs, and spectator sports.[29] The way other customers behave with many services—such as airlines, education, clubs, and social organizations—exerts a major influence on a customer's experience.[30] In general, the presence, behaviour, and similarity of other customers receiving services has a strong impact on the satisfaction and dissatisfaction of any given customer.[31]

Customers can be incompatible for many reasons—differences in beliefs, values, experiences, abilities to pay, appearance, age, and health, to name just a few. The service marketer must anticipate, acknowledge, and deal with heterogeneous consumers who have the potential to be incompatible. The service marketer can also bring homogeneous customers together and solidify relationships between them, which increases the cost to the customer of switching service providers.[32] Customer compatibility is a factor that influences customer satisfaction, particularly in high-contact services. Recently, for instance, Westin Hotels decided to ban smoking in all their Canadian hotels—not just in certain rooms. For nonsmokers this is likely to be considered very good news. But smokers may not be so pleased.

Customer Coproduction

In addition to being audience members, as suggested by the drama metaphor, service customers also play a coproduction role that can have profound influence on the service experience.[33] For example, counselling, personal training, or educational services have little value without the full participation of the client, who will most likely have extensive work to do between sessions. In this sense, the client coproduces the service. In business-to-business contexts such as consulting and architecture, customers also coproduce the service.[34] It has been suggested that customers therefore need to understand their roles and be "trained" in ways that are similar to the training of service employees, so that they will have the motivation, ability, and role clarity to perform.[35] The customer coproduction role is particularly relevant in self-service situations, as noted in this chapter's Technology Spotlight.

The idea of customers as "partners" in the cocreation of products is gaining ground across all industries, not just services.[36] Postmodern consumer behaviour experts propose an even broader interpretation of this idea. They suggest that a fundamental characteristic of the postmodern era is consumers' assertiveness as active participants in creating their world—often evidenced in their demands to adjust, change, and use products in customized ways.[37]

Emotion and Mood

Emotion and mood are feeling states that influence people's (and therefore customers') perceptions and evaluations of their experiences. Moods are distinguished from emotions in that *moods* are transient feeling states that occur at specific times and in specific situations, whereas *emotions* are more intense, stable, and pervasive.[38]

Because services are experiences, moods and emotions are critical factors that shape the perceived effectiveness of service encounters. If a service customer is in a bad mood when she enters a service establishment, service provision will likely be interpreted more negatively than if she were in a buoyant, positive mood. Similarly, if a service provider is irritable or sullen, his interaction with customers will likely be colored by that mood. Furthermore, when other customers in a service establishment are cranky or frustrated, whether from problems with the service or from existing emotions unrelated to the service, their mood affects the provision of service for all customers who sense the negative mood.

In what specific ways can mood affect the behaviour of service customers? First, positive moods can make customers more obliging and willing to participate in behaviours that help service encounters succeed.[39]

A second way that moods and emotions influence service customers is to bias the way they judge service encounters and providers. Mood and emotions enhance and amplify experiences, making them either more positive or more negative than they might seem in the absence of the moods and emotions.[40] The positive mood of a customer at a dance will heighten the experience, leading to positive evaluations of the service establishment (Figure 3.10). The direction of the bias in evaluation is consistent with the polarity (positive or negative) of the mood or emotion.

Finally, moods and emotions affect the way information about service is absorbed and retrieved in memory. As memories about a service are encoded by a consumer, the feelings associated with the encounter become an inseparable part of the memory. If travellers fall in love during a vacation in the Bahamas, they may hold favourable assessments of the destination due more to their emotional state than to the destination itself.

FIGURE 3.10

Positive moods of customers in a dance club heighten their service experiences.

Source: Mark Richards/Photo Edit.

Because emotions and moods play such important roles in influencing customer experiences, "organizations must manage the emotional component of experiences with the same rigor they bring to the management of product and service functionality."[41] Organizations may observe customers' emotional responses and attempt to create places, processes, and interactions to enhance certain emotions. Some firms believe that consumers' emotional responses may be the best predictors of their ultimate loyalty. Thus, many companies are now beginning to measure emotional responses and connections as well—going beyond traditional measures of satisfaction and behavioural loyalty.

POSTEXPERIENCE EVALUATION

Following the service experience, customers form an evaluation that determines to a large degree whether they will return or continue to patronize the service organization (see Figure 3.5). Historically within the field of marketing, more attention has been paid to *prepurchase* evaluations and consumer choice. Yet *postpurchase* and postexperience evaluations are typically most important in predicting subsequent consumer behaviours and repurchase, particularly for services.

Postexperience evaluation is captured by companies in measures of satisfaction, service quality, loyalty, and sometimes emotional engagement. We devote an entire chapter (Chapter 5) to exploring the specifics of customer satisfaction and service quality. Another chapter (Chapter 7) will examine the topic of relationships and loyalty.

Word-of-Mouth Communication

Postexperience evaluations will significantly impact what consumers tell others about the service. Because service consumers are strongly influenced by the personal opinions of others, understanding and controlling word-of-mouth communication becomes even more important for service companies. When service is dissatisfactory, it is critical to have an effective service recovery strategy (see Chapter 8) to curb negative word of mouth.

Attribution of Dissatisfaction

When consumers are disappointed with purchases, they may attribute their dissatisfaction to the producers, the retailers, or themselves. Because consumers participate to a greater extent in services, they may feel more responsible for their dissatisfaction when they purchase services than when they purchase goods. As an example, consider a consumer purchasing a haircut; receiving the cut she desires depends in part on her clear specifications of her needs to the stylist. If disappointed, she may blame either the stylist (for lack of skill) or herself (for choosing the wrong stylist or for not communicating her own needs clearly).

The quality of many services depends on the information the customer brings to the service encounter: a doctor's accurate diagnosis requires a conscientious case history and a clear articulation of symptoms; and a dry cleaner's success in removing a spot depends on the consumer's knowledge of its cause. Dissatisfaction may not be blamed completely on the retailer or producer, because consumers must adequately perform their part in the production process also.

With products, on the other hand, a consumer's main form of participation is the act of purchase. The consumer may attribute failure to receive satisfaction to her own decision-making error, but she holds the producer responsible for product performance. Goods usually carry warranties or guarantees with purchase, emphasizing that the producer believes that if something goes wrong, it is not the fault of the consumer.

Positive or Negative Biases

Research suggests that people remember negative events more than positive ones and are more influenced by negative information than by positive information, and that it is easier for consumers to remember the negative service experiences they have than to think of the many routine, or even positive, experiences.

Research also that says that customers will weigh negative information about a product attribute more heavily than positive information in forming their overall brand attitudes. Yet some very interesting and recent research suggests "positivity bias" for services.[42] The research showed that consumers tend to infer positive qualities for the firm and its employees if they have a good experience with one service employee. When individual service providers are regarded positively, customers' positive perceptions of other service providers in the company are also raised. On the other hand, customers who have a negative experience with one employee are less likely to draw a negative inference about all employees or the firm. That is, customers are more likely to attribute that negative experience to the individual provider, not the entire firm. Although this is just one study, the results and implications are intriguing.

Brand Loyalty

The degree to which consumers are committed to particular brands of goods or services depends on a number of factors: the cost of changing brands (switching cost), the availability of substitutes, social ties to the company, the perceived risk associated with the purchase, and the satisfaction obtained in the past. Because it may be more costly to change brands of services, because awareness of substitutes is limited, and because higher risks may accompany services, consumers are more likely to be loyal to services than to goods.

The difficulty of obtaining information about services means that consumers may be unaware of alternatives or substitutes for their brands. Monetary fees may accompany brand switching in many services: physicians often require complete physicals on the initial visit; dentists sometimes demand new X-rays; and health clubs frequently charge "membership fees" at the outset to obtain long-term commitments from customers.

If consumers perceive greater risks with services, as is hypothesized here, they probably depend on brand names to a greater extent than when they purchase products. Brand loyalty, described as a means of economizing decision effort by substituting habit for repeated, deliberate decision, functions as a device for reducing the risks of consumer decisions.

A final reason that consumers may be more brand-loyal with services is the recognition of the need for repeated patronage in order to obtain optimum satisfaction from the seller. Becoming a "regular customer" allows the seller to gain knowledge of the customer's tastes and preferences, ensures better treatment, and encourages more interest in the consumer's satisfaction. Thus a consumer may exhibit brand loyalty to cultivate a satisfying relationship with the seller.

Brand loyalty has two sides. The fact that a service provider's own customers are brand-loyal is, of course, desirable. The fact that the competitors' customers are difficult to capture, however, creates challenges. Marketers can also facilitate switching from competitors' services by reducing switching costs, as was done by TD Canada Trust with its Easy Switch program.

→ UNDERSTANDING DIFFERENCES AMONG CONSUMERS

To this point in the chapter, we have discussed consumer decision making and evaluation processes that are applicable across a wide range of consumers and types of services. In these last sections of the chapter, we examine the role of national and ethnic cultures in shaping consumer behaviour.

Global Differences: The Role of Culture

Culture represents the common values, norms, and behaviours of a particular group and is often identified with nations or ethnicity. Culture is learned, shared, multidimensional, and transmitted from one generation to the next. Understanding cultural differences is important in services marketing because of its effects on the ways that customers evaluate and use services. Culture also influences how companies and their service employees interact with customers. Culture is important in international services marketing—taking services from one country and offering them in others—but it is also critical within countries. More and more, individual countries are becoming multicultural, and organizations need to understand how this factor affects evaluation, purchase, and use of services even within countries.

Research provides considerable evidence that there are differences in how consumers perceive services across cultures. For example, a study of service quality perceptions in Taiwan revealed that much greater emphasis is placed on the interpersonal dimensions of service than is generally true in studies of U.S. consumers.[43] Another study showed notable differences in how fast-food and grocery consumers in eight different countries (Australia, China, Germany, India, Morocco, the Netherlands, Sweden, and the United States) evaluate these services.[44] Research also recommends that firms carefully consider global differences in the ways they measure service quality in

64 Part 2 *Focus on the Customer*

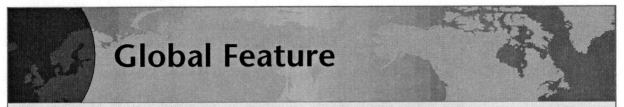

Global Feature

Differences in the Service Experience in the United States and Japan

As we emphasize in this chapter, the way service experiences differ across cultures influences how consumers evaluate service. Until recently, service differences across cultures were observed anecdotally rather than systematically, and researchers had few guidelines or criteria on which to evaluate these differences. One notable exception is a study that examined differences in the service experience across two cultures, in the United States and Japan, and provided both vivid examples and solid evidence of cultural subtleties that affect service encounters. The examples came from interviews with Japanese students studying at an American university and are categorized by dimensions of service behaviour. Following these examples, which come directly from the study, are a few of the interesting research findings.

- *Authenticity.* In Japan, "every clerk has the same type of smile ... the smile is not natural," and "everything is done according to the manual." In the United States, clerks "act independently," and "there is more variation in treatment."

- *Caring.* Caring or concern is the most important dimension in Japan, where "The customer is God." In the United States, sales clerks are always answering "I don't know"; another comment was that "they don't seem to care."

- *Control.* Control seems very important to Americans. In Japan, on the other hand, customers are "kind of timid or nervous. They tend to give the controlling interest to the clerk." Control is not important in Japan.

- *Courtesy.* In Japan, "if we find something bad about the service like, for example, they didn't apologize for spilling water, we never go back there again." Courtesy is very important in Japan.

- *Formality.* In Japan, formal treatment is a requirement for all service. Treatment in the United States is much more informal.

- *Friendliness.* "In the U.S. I feel like I'm supposed to treat serving people as equals. In Japan, that is not so." In Japan, friendliness can be disrespectful, and formality is usually preferred. In the United States, friendliness is expected.

- *Personalization.* "In Japan, you are treated the same." The waiters "are almost faceless, too businesslike and whoever comes, they treat them like the same person." In the United States, service is much more personalized and names are used more frequently.

- *Promptness.* "In the U.S., the sales clerk and the customer expect to have a nice little chat ... in Japan, many people would prefer a sales clerk who is quick but unfriendly."

After measuring and testing cultural dimensions across samples from the two countries, the study's author developed several compelling insights that are critical for understanding what service providers need to do to influence perceptions and evaluations of service encounters.

First, themes of friendliness, being personal, authenticity, and promptness dominate in the United States, whereas caring and concern are central in Japan. This difference can be explained by the cultural focus on individualism in the United States and the emphasis on empathy (being attentive, caring, and kind) in Japan. Civility, an important dimension in both countries, had different meanings: in the United States it meant paying attention and providing good service, whereas in Japan it due to being patient and fair. Authenticity is a relevant dimension in the United States but not in Japan, likely due to the Japanese focus on playing a role rather than expressing individual feelings.

It is evident from this study, and from others like it, that understanding culture is pivotal to being evaluated as an effective service provider. Providing the same service experience offered in the home country may not be successful when a service is extended to other cultural groups.

Source: Reprinted with permission of Elsevier Science Limited from K. F. Winsted, "The Service Experience in Two Cultures," *Journal of Retailing* 73, no. 3 (1997), pp. 337–60.

order to make valid comparisons across cultures.[45] Because of the importance of the global dimensions of business and cultural differences among consumers, we include a Global Feature in every chapter to illustrate how global differences affect services management as well as consumer behaviour. Our Global Feature in this chapter illustrates differences in how consumers experience and evaluate services in the United States compared to Japan.

Despite the clear differences in cultures, human nature dictates that people tend to view other cultures through the often cluttered lens of their own.[46] These prejudices are important, because they reflect a fundamental issue in services. As we discuss in Chapters 4 and 5, the intangibility of services makes their evaluation very much a matter of individual perception. And perceptions, at least when it comes to cultural differences, are what count, even if these perceptions are wrong.

In a recent study reported in *Science*, researchers looked at 30 personality traits among college students in 49 countries—everything from openness, agreeableness, conscientiousness, and warmth to straightforwardness, modesty, and competence. They then compared the stereotypes that subjects in each country would use to describe themselves using actual personality traits as measured using standardized tests. The result? We all have stereotypes of our own cultures, but our actual personalities are quite different.

Canadians, for instance, believe we are quite different from Americans. We describe ourselves as extremely agreeable. Americans describe themselves as very disagreeable. We believe we are calm and not irritable. Americans think they are more anxious and more hostile. According to the principal investigator, though, Canadians and Americans have almost identical personality traits. Time after time, the researchers found that people from all cultures hold strong stereotypes of themselves but that their own responses to the personality tests don't match the stereotype.[47]

So the truth of the matter is that, at the level of individual personality, we aren't very different from other people. But because we think we are, we have a tendency to evaluate things from our preexisting stereotypes. Another expert, Geert Hofstede, sums up the message of one of his books as follows:

> Everybody looks at the world from behind the windows of a cultural home, and everybody prefers to act as if people from other countries have something special about them (a national character) but home is normal. Unfortunately, there is no normal position in cultural matters."[48]

Differences in how services are evaluated across cultures can be traced to basic factors that distinguish cultures from each other. In the next sections, we highlight some of the major differences that can influence how people choose, use, and evaluate services, including values and attitudes, manners and customers, material culture, aesthetics, and educational and social institutions. Language, another obvious cultural difference particularly important for services, is discussed in Chapter 16.

Values and Attitudes Differ Across Cultures

Values and attitudes help determine what members of a culture think is right, important, and/or desirable. Because behaviours, including consumer behaviours, flow from values and attitudes, services marketers who want their services adopted across cultures must understand these differences.

Although North American brands often have an "exotic" appeal to other cultures, firms should not count on this appeal as a long-term strategy. In the late 1990s Wal-Mart found that the cachet of U.S. brands was falling in Mexico. The Mexican news media alerted consumers to shoddy foreign goods, and some Wal-Mart customers turned to a spirit of nationalism. The retailer responded with an "Hecho en Mexico" program similar to the "Made in the Canada" program that was successful here. In some situations it is more than a case of nationalism: brand attitudes are negatively influenced by specific prejudices toward "dominating" cultures. The Korean ban on Japanese movies and the French phobia about Euro Disney are good examples of the latter.

Manners and Customs

Manners and customs represent a culture's views of appropriate ways of behaving. It is important to monitor differences in manners and customs because they can have a direct effect on the service encounter. Central and Eastern Europeans are perplexed by Western expectations that unhappy workers "put on a happy face" when dealing with customers. As an example, McDonald's requires Polish employees to smile whenever they interact with customers. Such a requirement strikes many employees as artificial and insincere. The fast-food giant has learned to encourage managers in Poland to probe employee problems and to assign troubled workers to the kitchen rather to the food counter.[49]

Habits are similar to customs, and these tend to vary by culture. Japanese take very few vacations, and when they do they like to spend 7 to 10 days. Their vacations are unusually crammed with activities—Rome, Geneva, Paris, and London in 10 days is representative.[50]

Material Culture

Material culture consists of the tangible products of culture, or as comedian George Carlin puts it, "our stuff." Cars, houses, clothes, and furniture are examples of material culture.

The majority of Mexicans do not own cars, limiting retailers' geographic reach. Further, most Mexicans own small refrigerators and have limited incomes that restrict the amount of groceries they can purchase at one time. Instead of the once-per-week shopping trip typical in North America, Mexicans make frequent, smaller trips. Promotional programs in Mexico are also constrained by the availability of media. Limited ownership of televisions and radios affects the ability of services marketers to reach target audiences.

Terms of mortgages are another interesting area of cross-cultural differences in financial services. The typical mortgage in Canada is issued for five years with repeated financing every five years, whereas in the United States mortgages are issued for thirty years at the outset. In Mexico, most people pay cash for houses because mortgages are virtually unavailable. And in Japan, 100-year mortgages are quite common and often pass along with the house or flat to the next generation.

Aesthetics

Aesthetics refers to cultural ideas about beauty and good taste. These ideas are reflected in music, art, drama, and dance as well as the appreciation of colour and form (Figure 3.11).

Perhaps Alanis Morissette and MuchMusic sell well internationally, but even so, the adage "There's no accounting for taste" still rings quite true with most consumers around the world. A summer stroll through one of Madrid's important tourist attractions, Parque de Retiro, provides a simple but memorable lesson in how aesthetics vary across cultures. Trash cans are everywhere, but somehow the refuse doesn't make it into them. From the North American perspective, the litter detracts from the

FIGURE 3.11

Ideas about aesthetics differ across cultures.

Source: Ryan McVay/ Photodisc/Getty Images.

otherwise beautiful park. German tourists, used to the clean organization of their own fastidiously tidy forests, react negatively.

Educational and Social Institutions

Both educational and social institutions are affected by and transmit culture. Culture manifests itself most dramatically in the people-to-people contact of social institutions. Classroom interactions, for example, vary substantially around the world. Notice if the student from Japan sitting next to you in class verbally disagrees with your instructor. Japanese students are used to listening to lectures, taking notes, and asking questions only after class, if at all. In Japan the idea of grading class participation is nonsense. Alternatively, because Spaniards are used to huge undergraduate classes (hundreds rather than dozens), they tend to talk to their friends even when the instructor is talking.

Like education, health care delivery systems and doctor–patient interactions also reflect cultural differences. Canadians ask questions and get second opinions about medical care. Alternatively, the social hierarchy is heavily reflected in the Japanese health care system; instead of patients being most important, the doctors command deference. Thus the Japanese health care system, while delivering the best longevity statistics of any country, is relatively unresponsive to concerns of patients.

Group Decision Making

A group is defined as two or more individuals who have implicitly or explicitly defined relationships to one another such that their behaviour is interdependent.[51] When groups make decisions about services—a household purchasing a family vacation or an organization purchasing marketing research services—many of the same issues arise as for individuals: greater perceived risk; more reliance on word-of-mouth communication; greater difficulty in comparing alternatives; and often a higher level of customer participation. For example, although many large organizations have very clear evaluation processes for buying goods, their processes and decision rules for purchasing services are often not as well defined. The intangibility and variability of business services make them more risky and often difficult to compare. Thus, organizations often rely on established partnerships, long-term relationships, or referrals from others when it comes to major service purchases. Similar issues arise for households who rely heavily on personal referrals in making significant services purchases such as home repair, remodelling, landscaping, medical care, and vacation trips. Even smaller household decisions—where to eat dinner or choice of a dry cleaner—may be influenced by referrals and may involve a great deal of risk, depending on the occasion. Where to have Grandma's 40-year-old wedding dress drycleaned can be a decision that carries considerable risk.

Despite these similarities, aspects that are different for group buying are collective decision making, mixed motives or goals, roles in the purchasing process, and group culture. We will highlight some of these differences for two major groups: households and organizations.

Households

When a family makes a service purchase decision, it has a collective style of decision making that often differs from what any of the individuals would use if making an independent choice. When a family chooses a vacation destination, for example, its style may involve one of the following: (1) one parent makes a unilateral decision that the family will go on vacation to Disneyland; (2) the family discusses possible vacation destinations at the dinner table, taking each person's ideas and suggestions into account, and selects three locations that a parent will investigate further; (3) the parents provide a budget and a list of the destinations that can be visited within that budget, then allow the children to choose among them. Once a destination has been chosen, the mix of motives or goals of the group comes into play. The mother may want to sightsee, the father to rest, and the children to visit local theme parks. In this and other group purchasing decisions, the needs and goals of the various members must be balanced so that the service (in this case the vacation) delivers optimal satisfaction for as many members as possible. Group roles are also a key consideration. In a household, one individual often identifies a need and initiates the purchase, someone else may influence which service provider is selected, someone else may pay, and someone else may become the ultimate user of the service. For example, the father may decide that the family needs to visit the dentist, a teenager may recommend a dentist that her friend uses, the mother may pay the bills, and all the family members may go to the dentist to receive treatment. Finally, national and ethnic culture affects household purchase and consumption behaviours. For example, ethnic groups vary, with some being very patriarchal, others egalitarian, and still others autocratic.

Organizations

Organizational consumers are a special category of group consumers. These days, companies spend millions on information technology services, call centres, travel management, and payroll services, and outsourced services for human resource management. Making the right decision on services purchases can be absolutely critical for an organization's success. How do companies make these important decisions?

For routine and even complex purchases, organizations often rely on a small number of buyers within the company, many of whom specialize in purchasing. These buyers are typically organized either formally or informally into buying centres, which include all people involved in the decision process.[52] Each of these roles may be taken by a different person, or one person may assume all roles in some cases.

- The *initiator* identifies the organization's service needs.

- The *gatekeeper* collects and controls information about the purchase.

- The *decider* determines what service to purchase.

- The *buyer* or purchasing agent physically acquires the service.

- The *user* consumes the service and may or may not have any influence over the purchase decision.

Among the characteristics that distinguish organizational from individual decision making are economic forces such as current business climate and technology trends; organizational strategies and culture; whether purchasing is a centralized or decentralized function; and the group forces that influence purchasing decisions.[53] Organizational purchases also tend to differ by magnitude and include new task purchases (large purchases that require careful consideration of needs and evaluation of alternatives), straight rebuys (simple reorders of past service purchases), and modified rebuys (a mix of new and straight rebuy features).[54]

As companies outsource more services and particularly when these services are outsourced around the globe, purchase decisions become complex and difficult. Often companies must rely on outside expertise to help them with these multifaceted and financially risky decisions.

Organizational purchasers also rely on references and the experience of other organizations in making their service purchase decisions. Referrals and testimonials can be very helpful to other organizations considering similar business service purchases. In fact, many business service providers have customer stories, cases, and testimonials on their websites to help reduce the risk of these complex decisions.

SUMMARY

The intent of this chapter was to provide understanding for how consumers choose and evaluate services. Services possess high levels of experience and credence properties, which in turn make them challenging to evaluate, particularly prior to purchase. The chapter isolated and discussed three stages of consumer behaviour for services, and it looked at how experience and credence properties result in challenges and opportunities in all three stages. The three stages are consumer choice (including need recognition, information search, evaluation of alternatives, and service purchase); consumer experience; and postexperience evaluation. Consumer behaviour theories, current research, and insights for managers were highlighted in each of these sections.

Although the three stages are relevant for all types of consumer behaviour in services, important differences exist in behaviour across global cultures and for groups vs. individuals. Global differences in consumer behaviour were presented, particularly as they relate to service consumption. The chapter ended with a discussion of the differences in group versus individual consumer decision making related to households and organizations.

Discussion Questions

1. Based on the chapter, which aspects of consumer behaviour are similar and which are different for services versus goods?

2. Where does a college education fit on the continuum of evaluation for different types of products? Where does computer software fit? Consulting? Retailing? Fast food? What are the implications for consumer behaviour?

3. What are examples (other than those given in the chapter) of services that are high in credence properties? How do high credence properties affect consumer behaviour for these services?

4. For what types of services might consumers depend on mass communication (nonpersonal sources of information, including the Internet) in the purchase decision?

5. Which of the aspects discussed in the chapter describe your behaviour when it comes to purchasing services? Does your behaviour differ for different types of services?

6. Why are consumer experiences so important in the evaluation process for services?

7. Using the service drama metaphor, describe the services provided by a health club, a fine restaurant, or a vacation cruise line.

8. What are some differences in service choice, purchase, and consumption processes for organizations and households compared to individuals? What are some similarities?

Exercises

1. Choose a particular end-consumer services industry and one type of service provided in that industry (such as the financial services industry for mortgage loans, the legal services industry for wills, or the travel industry for a vacation package). Talk to five customers who have purchased that service and determine to what extent the information in this chapter described their behaviour in terms of consumer choice, consumer experience, and postexperience evaluation for that service.

2. Choose a particular business-to-business service industry and one type of service provided in that industry (such as the information services industry for computer maintenance services or the consulting industry for management consulting). Talk to five customers in that industry and determine to what extent the information in this chapter described their behaviour in terms of consumer choice, consumer experience, and postexperience evaluation for that service.

3. Visit a service provider of your choice. Experience the service firsthand if possible and observe other customers for a period of time. Describe the consumer (service) experience in detail in terms of what happened throughout the process and how customers, including yourself, felt about it. How could the service experience be improved?

4. Interview three people who come from countries other than your own. Ask them about their consumer behaviour patterns. Note the differences and similarities to your own consumer behaviour. What are possible causes of the differences?

⟼ Notes

1. S. Okalow, "Marketers Go Mobile," *Strategy Magazine*, March 22, 2004.
2. E. H. Fram, "Stressed-Out Consumers Need Timesaving Innovations," *Marketing News,* March 2, 1992, p. 10.
3. M. J. Dorsch, S. J. Grove, and W. R. Darden, "Consumer Intentions to Use a Service Category," *Journal of Services Marketing* 14, no. 2 (2000), pp. 92–117.
4. L. L. Berry, "The Time-Buying Customer," *Journal of Retailing* 55, no. 4 (Winter 1979), pp. 58–69.
5. A. Spector, "Menu Marketers Deliver Dinner, Incremental Sales," *Nation's Restaurant News,* May 19, 2003, p. 154.
6. P. Nelson, "Information and Consumer Behavior," *Journal of Political Economy* 78, no. 20 (1970), pp. 311–29.
7. M. R. Darby and E. Karni, "Free Competition and the Optimal Amount of Fraud," *Journal of Law and Economics* 16 (April 1973), pp. 67–86.
8. T. S. Robertson, *Innovative Behavior and Communication* (New York: Holt, Rinehart & Winston, 1971).
9. P. Berthon, L. Pitt, C. S. Katsikeas, and J. P. Berthon, "Virtual Services Go International: International Services in the Marketspace," *Journal of International Marketing* 7, no. 3 (1999), pp. 84–105.
10. J. C. Ward and A. L. Ostrom, "Online Complaining via Customer-Created Web Sites: A Protest Framing Perspective," working paper, W. P. Carey School of Business, Arizona State University, 2004.
11. M. Laroche, G. H. G. McDougall, J. Bergeron, and Z. Yang, "Exploring How Intangibility Affects Perceived Risk," *Journal of Service Research* 6, no. 4 (May 2004), pp. 373–89; K. B. Murray and J. L. Schlacter, "The Impact of Services versus Goods on Consumers' Assessment of Perceived Risk and Variability," *Journal of the Academy of Marketing Science* 18 (Winter 1990), pp. 51–65; M. Laroche, J. Bergeron, and C. Goutaland, "How Intangibility Affects Perceived Risk: The Moderating Role of Knowledge and Involvement," *Journal of Services Marketing* 17, no. 2 (2003), pp. 122–40.
12. M. Laroche et al., "Exploring How Intangibility Affects Perceived Risk."
13. R. F. Lusch, S. W. Brown, and G. J. Brunswick, "A General Framework for Explaining Internal vs. External Exchange," *Journal of the Academy of Marketing Science* 10 (Spring 1992), pp. 119–34; Dorsch, Grove, and Darden, "Consumer Intentions to Use a Service Category."
14. J. H. Gilmore and B. J. Pine II, "The Experience Is the Marketing," report from Strategic Horizons LLP, 2002.
15. See, for example, B. J. Pine II and J. H. Gilmore, *The Experience Economy* (Boston: Harvard Business School Press, 1999); B. H. Schmitt, *Experiential Marketing* (New York: The Free Press, 1999); B. H. Schmitt, *Customer Experience Management* (Hoboken, NJ: John Wiley & Sons, 2003).
16. S. S. Tax and F. N. Morgan, "Toward a Theory of Service Delivery Networks," working paper, W. P. Carey School of Business, Arizona State University, 2004.
17. S. J. Grove and R. P. Fisk, "Service Theater: An Analytical Framework for Services Marketing," in *Services Marketing,* 4th ed., ed. Christopher Lovelock (Englewood Cliffs, NJ: Prentice Hall, 2001), pp. 83–92.

18. S. J. Grove, R. P. Fisk, and M. J. Bitner, "Dramatizing the Service Experience: A Managerial Approach," in *Advances in Services Marketing and Management,* vol. 1, ed. T. A. Swartz, D. E. Bowen, and S. W. Brown (Greenwich, CT: JAI Press, 1992), pp. 91–121.

19. Grove, Fisk, and Bitner, "Dramatizing the Service Experience."

20. Grove and Fisk, "Service Theater."

21. Ibid.

22. Grove, Fisk, and Bitner, "Dramatizing the Service Experience."

23. Ibid.

24. Ibid.

25. M. R. Solomon, C. Surprenant, J. A. Czepiel, and E. G. Gutman, "A Role Theory Perspective on Dyadic Interactions: The Service Encounter," *Journal of Marketing* 49 (Winter 1985), pp. 99–111.

26. Ibid.

27. R. F. Abelson, "Script Processing in Attitude Formation and Decision Making," in *Cognition and Social Behavior,* ed. J. S. Carroll and J. S. Payne (Hillsdale, NJ: Erlbaum, 1976).

28. R. A. Smith and M. J. Houston, "Script-Based Evaluations of Satisfaction with Services," in *Emerging Perspectives on Services Marketing,* ed. L. Berry, G. L. Shostack, and G. Upah (Chicago: American Marketing Association, 1982), pp. 59–62.

29. J. E. G. Bateson and M. K. M. Hui, "Crowding in the Service Environment," in *Creativity in Services Marketing: What's New, What Works, What's Developing,* ed. M. Venkatesan, D. M. Schmalensee, and C. Marshall (Chicago: American Marketing Association, 1986), pp. 85–88.

30. J. Baker, "The Role of the Environment in Marketing Services: The Consumer Perspective," in *The Services Challenge: Integrating for Competitive Advantage,* ed. J. A. Czepiel, C. A. Congram, and J. Shanahan (Chicago: American Marketing Association, 1987), pp. 79–84.

31. C. L. Martin and C. A. Pranter, "Compatibility Management: Customer-to-Customer Relationships in Service Environments," *Journal of Services Marketing* 3 (Summer 1989).

32. Ibid.

33. N. Bendapudi and R. P. Leone, "Psychological Implications of Customer Participation in Co-Production," *Journal of Marketing* 67 (January 2003), pp. 14–28.

34. L. A. Bettencourt, A. L. Ostrom, S. W. Brown, and R. I. Roundtree, "Client Co-production in Knowledge-Intensive Business Services," *California Management Review* 44, no. 4 (Summer 2002), pp. 100–128.

35. S. Dellande, M. C. Gilly, and J. L. Graham, "Gaining Compliance and Losing Weight: The Role of the Service Provider in Health Care Services," *Journal of Marketing* 68 (July 2004), pp. 78–91; M. L. Meuter, M. J. Bitner, A. L. Ostrom, and S. W. Brown, "Choosing Among Alternative Service Delivery Modes: An Investigation of Customer Trial of Self-Service Technologies," *Journal of Marketing* 69, no. 2, p. 61.

36. C. K. Prahalad and V. Ramaswamy, "The New Frontier of Experience Innovation," *Sloan Management Review*, Summer 2003, pp. 12–18.

37. A. F. Firat and A. Venkatesh, "Liberatory Postmodernism and the Reenchantment of Consumption," *Journal of Consumer Research* 22, no. 3 (December 1995), pp. 239–67.

38. M. P. Gardner, "Mood States and Consumer Behavior: A Critical Review," *Journal of Consumer Research* 12 (December 1985), pp. 281–300.

39. Ibid., p. 288.

40. S. S. Tomkins, "Affect as Amplification: Some Modifications in Theory," in *Emotion: Theory, Research, and Experience,* ed. R. Plutchik and H. Kellerman (New York: Academic Press, 1980), pp. 141–64.

41. L. L. Berry, L. P. Carbone, and S. H. Haeckel, "Managing the Total Customer Experience," *Sloan Management Review*, Spring 2002, pp. 85–89.

42. V. S. Folkes and V. M. Patrick, "The Positivity Effect in Perceptions of Services: Seen One, Seen Them All?" *Journal of Consumer Research* 30 (June 2003), pp. 125–37.

43. B. Imrie, J. W. Cadogan, and R. McNaughton, "The Service Quality Construct on a Global Stage," *Managing Service Quality* 12, no. 1 (2002), p. 10–18.

44. B. D. Keillor, G. T. M. Hult, D. Kandemir, "A Study of the Service Encounter in Eight Countries," *Journal of International Marketing* 12, no. 1 (2004), pp. 9–35.

45. A. M. Smith and N. L. Reynolds, "Measuring Cross-Cultural Service Quality: A Framework for Assessment," *International Marketing Review* 19, no. 5 (2001), pp. 450–81.

46. R. B. Money, M. C. Gilly, and J. L. Graham, "Explorations of National Culture and Word-of-Mouth Referral Behavior in the Purchase of Industrial Services in the United States and Japan," *Journal of Marketing* 62 (October 1998), pp. 76–87.

47. A. Terracciano et al., "National Character Does Not Reflect Mean Personality Trait Levels in 49 Cultures," *Science* 310, no. 5745 (October 7, 2005), pp. 96–100.

48. G. Hofstede, *Culture and Organizations: Software of the Mind* (New York: McGraw-Hill, 1991), p. 235.

49. D. E. Murphy, "New East Europe Retailers Told to Put on a Happy Face," *Los Angeles Times,* November 26, 1994, pp. A1, A18.

50. "Japanese Put Tourism on a Higher Plane," *International Herald Tribune*, February 3, 1992, p. 8.

51. E. Arnould, L. Price, and G. Zinkhan, *Consumers*, 2nd ed. (New York: McGraw-Hill, 2004).

52. For excellent coverage of buyer behaviour in organizations, see M. D. Hutt and T. W. Speh, *Business Marketing Management,* 8th ed. (Mason, OH: South-Western, 2004), ch. 3.

53. Ibid., pp. 68–69.

54. Ibid., pp. 62–67.

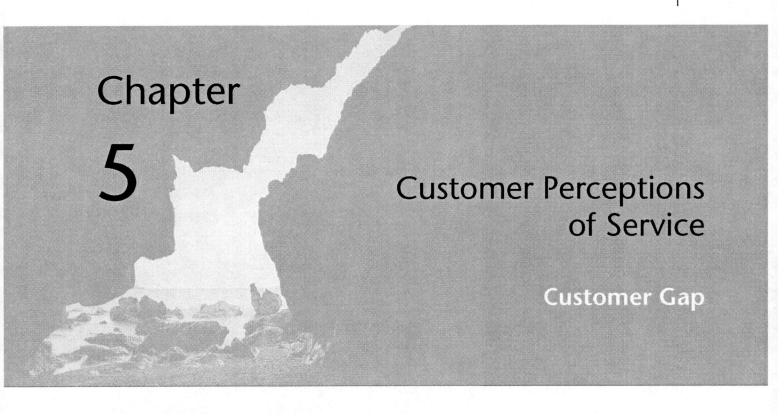

Chapter

5

Customer Perceptions of Service

Customer Gap

THIS CHAPTER'S OBJECTIVES ARE TO

↦ 1. Show what influences customer perceptions of service and the relationships among customer satisfaction, service quality, and individual service encounters.

↦ 2. Demonstrate the importance of customer satisfaction—what it is, the factors that influence it, and the significant outcomes resulting from it.

↦ 3. Develop critical knowledge of service quality and its five key dimensions: reliability, responsiveness, empathy, assurance, and tangibles.

↦ 4. Show that service encounters or the "moments of truth" are the essential building blocks from which customers form their perceptions.

EXCEEDING CUSTOMER EXPECTATIONS

Try to think of an example of great customer service you have received. What made the service you received so special?

Now, what if someone told you the service they received at Wal-Mart (www. walmart.ca) was great? Would you be surprised? Maybe—it all depends on your expectations of the service and your perception of how well the service provider has met or exceeded those expectations. Consider these examples provided by Wal-Mart customers.[1]

Sheila risked her own safety when she jumped in front of a car to prevent a little boy from being struck, Phyllis administered CPR to a customer who had suffered a heart attack in her store, Joyce threw a plate on the floor to assure a young mother that a set of dishes truly was unbreakable, and Annette gave up the Power Ranger she had on layaway for her own son so a customer's son could have his birthday wish.

Each of these examples demonstrates times when employees were able to exceed the expectations of those customers, and illustrates the kind of service Sam Walton expected his employees to provide. He summarized his service philosophy as follows:

> Exceed your customers' expectations. If you do, they'll come back over and over. Give them what they want—and a little more. Let them know you appreciate them. Make good on all your mistakes, and don't make excuses ... apologize. Stand behind everything you do. The two most important words I ever wrote were on that first Wal-Mart sign, "Satisfaction Guaranteed." They're still up there, and they have made all the difference.

Great prices, good merchandise quality and selection, friendly service, and unexpected over-the-top gestures by employees all add up to the satisfaction of shoppers at Wal-Mart. The same is true for other landmark service companies such as Lands' End, Delta Hotels, and IBM Global Services. In all of these companies the quality of the core product and exemplary customer service result in high customer service ratings.

So what is it that brings about customer satisfaction? How do customers evaluate service quality? How do they form their perceptions of service? Answers to these questions are the subjects of this chapter.

Source: Courtesy Wal-Mart Canada Corp.

CUSTOMER PERCEPTIONS

How customers perceive services, how they assess whether they have experienced quality service, and whether they are satisfied are the subjects of this chapter. We will be focusing on the *perceived service* box in the Gaps model. As we move through this chapter, keep in mind that perceptions are always considered relative to expectations. Because expectations are dynamic, evaluations may also shift over time—from person to person and from culture to culture. The things that satisfy customers today may be different tomorrow. Also keep in mind that the entire discussion of quality and satisfaction is based on *customers' perceptions of the service*—not some predetermined objective criteria of what service is or should be.

Satisfaction vs. Service Quality

Practitioners and writers in the popular press tend to use the terms *satisfaction* and *quality* interchangeably, but researchers have attempted to be more precise about the meanings and measurement of the two concepts, resulting in considerable debate.[2] Consensus is that the two concepts are fundamentally different in terms of their underlying causes and outcomes.[3] Although they have certain things in common, **satisfaction** is generally viewed as a broader concept, whereas **service quality** focuses specifically on dimensions of service. Based on this view, **perceived service quality** is a component of customer satisfaction. Figure 5.1 graphically illustrates the relationships between the two concepts.

As shown in the figure, service quality is a focused evaluation that reflects the customer's perception of: reliability, assurance, responsiveness, empathy, and tangibles.[4] Satisfaction, on the other hand, is more inclusive: it is influenced by perceptions of service quality, product quality, and price as well as situational factors and personal factors. For example, *service quality* of a health club is judged on attributes such as whether equipment is available and in working order when needed, how responsive the staff are to customer needs, how skilled the trainers are, and whether the facility is well maintained. *Customer satisfaction* with the health club is a broader concept that will certainly be influenced by perceptions of service quality but that will also include perceptions of product quality (such as quality of products sold in the pro shop), price of membership,[5] personal factors such as the consumer's emotional state, and even uncontrollable situational factors such as weather conditions and experiences driving to and from the health club.[6]

Transaction vs. Cumulative Perceptions

In considering perceptions, it is also important to recognize that customers will have perceptions of single, transaction-specific encounters as well as overall perceptions of a company based on all their experiences.[7] For example, a bank customer will

FIGURE 5.1

Customer
Perceptions
of Quality
and Customer
Satisfaction

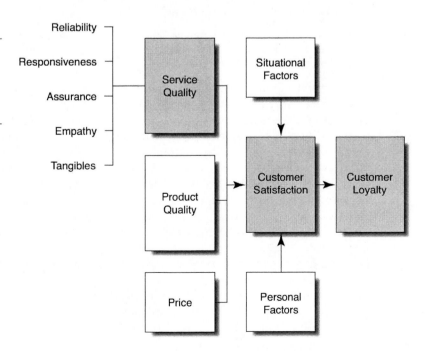

have a perception of how he or she was treated in a particular encounter with a bank employee at a branch. That perception is at a very micro, transaction-specific level. That same bank customer will also have overall perceptions of the bank based on all his encounters over a period of time. These experiences might include online banking experiences and experiences using the bank's ATMs. At an even more general level, the customer may have perceptions of the whole banking industry as a result of all his or her experiences with banks.

Research suggests that it is important to understand all these types of perceptions for different reasons and that the viewpoints are complementary rather than competing.[8] Understanding perceptions at the transaction-specific level is critical for diagnosing service issues and making immediate changes. These isolated encounters are also the building blocks for overall, cumulative experience evaluations, as you will learn later in this chapter. On the other hand, cumulative experience evaluations are likely to be better predictors of overall loyalty to a company. That is, customer loyalty most often results from the customer's assessment of all experiences, not just a single encounter.

In this chapter, we will begin with an overview of the broadest of these perceptions—satisfaction—and then turn our attention to the more specific concept of service quality. Finally, we will discuss the most specific concept—service encounters. These encounters, or "moments of truth," are the building blocks for the more general assessments of quality and satisfaction.

⟶ CUSTOMER SATISFACTION

What Is Customer Satisfaction?

"Everyone knows what satisfaction is, until asked to give a definition. Then, it seems, nobody knows."[9] This quote from Richard L. Oliver expresses the challenge of defining this most basic of customer concepts. Building from previous definitions, Oliver offers his own formal definition (p. 13):

> Satisfaction is the consumer's fulfillment response. It is a judgment that a product or service feature, or the product or service itself, provides a pleasurable level of consumption-related fulfillment.

We interpret this to mean simply that *satisfaction* is the customer's evaluation of whether a service has met his or her needs and expectations. Failure to meet needs and expectations is assumed to result in *dissatisfaction* with the product or service.

In addition to a sense of *fulfilment* in the knowledge that one's needs have been met, satisfaction can also be related to other types of feelings, depending on the particular context or type of service.[10] For example, satisfaction can be viewed as *contentment*—more of a passive response. It may also be associated with feelings of *pleasure*. For those services that really surprise the consumer in a positive way, satisfaction may mean *delight*. In some situations, involving removal of a negative, the consumer may associate a sense of *relief* with satisfaction. Finally, satisfaction may be associated with feelings of *ambivalence* when there is a mix of positive and negative experiences associated with the product or service.

Although consumer satisfaction tends to be measured at a particular point in time as if it were static, satisfaction is a dynamic, moving target that may evolve over time, influenced by a variety of factors.[11] Particularly when the service experience takes place over time, satisfaction may be highly variable depending on which experience cycle one is focusing on. Similarly, in the case of a service not previously experienced, customer expectations may be barely forming at the point of initial purchase; these expectations will solidify as the process unfolds and the consumer begins to form his or her perceptions. Through the service cycle the consumer may have a variety of different experiences—some good, some not good—and each will ultimately impact satisfaction.

What Determines Customer Satisfaction?

As shown in Figure 5.1, customer satisfaction is influenced by specific product or service features, perceptions of product and service quality, and price. In addition, personal factors such as the customer's mood or emotional state and situational factors such as family member opinions will also influence satisfaction.

Product and Service Features

Customer satisfaction is influenced significantly by the customer's evaluation of service features.[12] For a service such as a resort hotel, important features might include the pool area, access to golf facilities, restaurants, room comfort and privacy, helpfulness and courtesy of staff, room price, and so forth. In conducting satisfaction studies, most firms will determine what the important features and attributes are for their service and then measure perceptions of those features as well as overall service satisfaction. Research has shown that customers make tradeoffs among different service features (e.g., price level vs. quality vs. friendliness of personnel), depending on the type of service being evaluated and the criticality of the service.[13]

Consumer Emotions

Customers' emotions can also affect their perceptions of satisfaction.[14] These emotions can be stable, preexisting ones—for example, mood state or life satisfaction. Think of times when you are very happy (such as when you are on vacation), and your happy mood and positive frame of mind have influenced how you feel about the services you experience. Alternatively, when you are in a bad mood, your negative feelings may carry over into how you respond to services, causing you to respond negatively to any little problem.

Specific emotions may also be induced by the consumption experience itself, influencing a consumer's satisfaction with the service. Research done in a river-rafting context showed that the river guides had a strong effect on their customers' emotional responses to the trip and that those feelings (both positive and negative) were linked to overall trip satisfaction.[15] Positive emotions such as happiness, pleasure, elation, and a sense of warmheartedness enhanced customers' satisfaction with the rafting trip. In turn, negative emotions such as sadness, sorrow, regret, and anger led to diminished customer satisfaction. Overall, in the rafting context, positive emotions had a stronger effect than negative ones (as is apparent in Figure 5.2.) Similar effects of emotions on satisfaction were found in a Finnish study that looked at consumers' satisfaction with a government labour bureau service.[16] In that study, negative emotions including anger, depression, guilt, and humiliation had a strong effect on customers' dissatisfaction ratings.

Attributions for Service Success or Failure

Attributions—the perceived causes of events—influence perceptions of satisfaction as well.[17] When they have been surprised by an outcome (the service is either much better or much worse than expected), consumers tend to look for the

100 Part 2 *Focus on the Customer*

FIGURE 5.2

River rafters experience many positive emotions, increasing their satisfaction with the service.

Source: River Odysseys West, www.rowinc.com.

reasons, and their assessments of the reasons can influence their satisfaction. For example, if a customer of a weight-loss organization fails to lose weight as hoped for, she will likely search for the causes—was it something she did, was the diet plan ineffective, or did circumstances simply not allow her to follow the diet regimen—before determining her level of satisfaction or dissatisfaction with the weight-loss company.[18] For many services, customers take at least partial responsibility for how things turn out.

Even when customers do not take responsibility for the outcome, customer satisfaction may be influenced by other kinds of attributions. For example, research done in a travel agency context found that customers were less dissatisfied with a pricing error made by the agent if they felt that the reason was outside the agent's control or if they felt that it was a rare mistake, unlikely to occur again.[19]

Perceptions of Equity or Fairness

Customer satisfaction is also influenced by perceptions of equity and fairness.[20] Customers ask themselves: Have I been treated fairly compared with other customers? Did other customers get better treatment, better prices, or better quality service? Did I pay a fair price for the service? Was I treated well in exchange for what I paid and the effort I expended? Notions of fairness are central to customers' perceptions of satisfaction with products and services, particularly in service recovery situations. As you will learn in Chapter 8, satisfaction with a service provider following a service failure is largely determined by perceptions of fair treatment.

Other Consumers, Family Members, and Coworkers

In addition to product and service features and one's own individual feelings and beliefs, consumer satisfaction is often influenced by other people.[21] For example, satisfaction with a family vacation trip is a dynamic phenomenon, influenced by the reactions and expressions of individual family members over the duration of the vacation. Later, what family members express in terms of satisfaction or dissatisfaction with the trip will be influenced by stories that are retold among the family and selective memories of the events. Similarly, the satisfaction of the rafters in Figure 5.2 is certainly influenced by individual perceptions, but it is also influenced greatly by the experiences, behaviour, and views of the other rafters.

National Customer Satisfaction Indexes

Because of the importance of customer satisfaction to firms, many countries have a national index that measures customer satisfaction at a macro level.[22] Many public policymakers believe that these measures could and should be used as tools for evaluating the health of the nation's economy, along with traditional measures of productivity and price. Customer satisfaction indexes begin to get at the *quality* of economic output, whereas more traditional economic indicators tend to focus only on *quantity*. The first such measure was the Swedish Customer Satisfaction Barometer introduced in 1989.[23] Throughout the 1990s similar indexes were introduced in Germany (Deutsche Kundenbarometer, or DK, in 1992), the United States (American Customer Satisfaction Index, ACSI, in 1994), and Switzerland (Swiss Index of Customer Satisfaction, SWICS, in 1998).[24] Canada has not yet developed a national satisfaction index. Although the National Quality Institute devotes its resources to assisting its members improve the overall quality of its products and services, it does not have a national scoring system. NQI does have a scoring system for healthy workplaces, however, which we will return to in a later chapter.

In the United States, data compiled by the ACSI shows that consumers tend to be most satisfied with non-durables (like soft drinks and personal care products), somewhat less satisfied with durables (like automobiles and appliances), and least satisfied with services. This trend has been consistently observed over the entire history of the ACSI index.

We can only conjecture about the reasons for lower satisfaction with services in general. Perhaps it is because downsizing and right-sizing in service businesses has resulted in stressed and overworked front-line service providers who are unable to provide the level of service demanded. Perhaps it is due to the inherent heterogeneity of services discussed in Chapter 1; in other words, because services are difficult to standardize, and each customer has his or her own unique expectations, the result may be greater variability and potentially lower overall satisfaction. Perhaps it is due to difficulty finding qualified front-line service providers for consumer-service businesses. Perhaps it is due to rising customer expectations rather than any real or absolute decline in actual service. Whatever the reason, there is much room for improvement in customer satisfaction ratings across service industries.

Outcomes of Customer Satisfaction

Why all this attention to customer satisfaction? Satisfaction is an important indicator of quality of life. Further, customer satisfaction is correlated with other measures of economic health such as corporate earnings and stock value.

Individual firms have discovered that increasing levels of customer satisfaction can be linked to customer loyalty and profits.[25] As shown in Figure 5.3, there is an important relationship between customer satisfaction and customer loyalty. This relationship is particularly strong when customers are very satisfied. Xerox Corporation was one of the first companies to pinpoint this relationship. In the 1980s Xerox discovered through its extensive customer research that customers giving Xerox a 5 (very satisfied) on a satisfaction scale were six times more likely to repurchase Xerox equipment than were those giving the company a 4 (somewhat satisfied).[26] As another example, Enterprise Rent-A-Car learned through its research that customers who gave

102 Part 2 *Focus on the Customer*

FIGURE 5.3

Relationship
Between Customer
Satisfaction
and Loyalty in
Competitive
Industries

Source: J. L. Heskett, W.
E. Sasser Jr., and L. A.
Schlesinger, *The Service
Profit Chain: How Leading
Companies Link Profit and
Growth to Loyalty, Satisfaction,
and Value* (New York: The Free
Press, 1997), p. 83. © 1997
by J. L. Heskett, W. E. Sasser,
Jr., and L. A. Schlesinger.
Reprinted with the permission
of The Free Press, a Division of
Simon & Schuster, Inc.

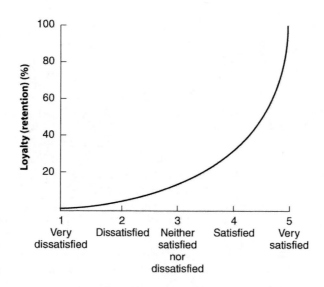

the highest rating to their rental experience were three times more likely to rent again than those who gave the company the second-highest rating.[27] Many other companies have drawn similar conclusions.

At the opposite end of the satisfaction spectrum, researchers have also found that there is a strong link between dissatisfaction and disloyalty—or defection. Customer loyalty can fall off precipitously when customers reach a particular level of dissatisfaction or when they are dissatisfied with critically important service attributes.[28] We discuss these relationships and the implications for relationship and loyalty marketing in Chapter 7. Thus, many companies are spending more time and money understanding the underpinnings of customer satisfaction and ways that they can improve.

SERVICE QUALITY

We now turn to *service quality,* a critical element of customer perceptions. In the case of pure services (e.g., health care, financial services, education), service quality will be the dominant element in customers' evaluations. In cases in which customer service or services are offered in combination with a physical product (e.g., IT services, auto services), service quality may also be very critical in determining customer satisfaction. Figure 5.1, which is our model of the relationship between quality and satisfaction, highlighted these relationships. We will focus here on the left side of that figure, examining the underlying factors that form perceptions of service quality. First we discuss *what* customers evaluate; then we look specifically at the five dimensions of service that customers rely on in forming their judgments.

Outcome, Interaction, and Physical Environment Quality

What is it that consumers evaluate when judging service quality? Researchers have suggested that consumers judge the quality of services according to the technical outcome provided, the process by which that outcome was delivered, and the quality of the physical surroundings where the service is delivered.[29] For example, a restaurant customer will judge the service on her perceptions of the meal (technical outcome quality) and on how the meal was served and how the employees interacted with her (interaction quality). The decor and surroundings (physical environment quality) will also impact perceptions of overall service quality.

This depiction of service quality as outcome quality, interaction quality, and physical environment quality is most recently captured by Michael Brady and Joseph Cronin in their empirical research published in the *Journal of Marketing*.[30] Other researchers have defined similar aspects of service in their examinations of service quality.[31]

Service Quality Dimensions

Research suggests that customers do not perceive quality in a unidimensional way but rather judge quality based on multiple factors. The dimensions of service quality have been identified through the pioneering research of Parsu Parasuraman, Valarie Zeithaml, and Leonard Berry. Their research identified five specific dimensions of service quality that apply across a variety of service contexts.[32] The five dimensions defined here are shown in Figure 5.1 as drivers of service quality. These five dimensions appear again in Chapter 6, along with the scale developed to measure them, SERVQUAL.

- *Reliability.* Ability to perform the promised service dependably and accurately

- *Responsiveness.* Willingness to help customers and provide prompt service

- *Assurance.* Employees' knowledge and courtesy and their ability to inspire trust and confidence

- *Empathy.* Caring, individualized attention given to customers

- *Tangibles.* Appearance of physical facilities, equipment, personnel, and written materials

These dimensions represent how consumers organize information about service quality in their minds. On the basis of exploratory and quantitative research, these five dimensions were found relevant for banking, insurance, appliance repair and maintenance, securities brokerage, long-distance telephone service, automobile repair service, and others. Sometimes customers will use all the dimensions to determine service quality perceptions, at other times not. For example, for an ATM, empathy is not likely to be a relevant dimension. And in a phone encounter to schedule a repair, tangibles will not be relevant. Research suggests that cultural differences will also affect the relative importance placed on the five dimensions, as discussed in our Global Feature. In the following pages we expand on each of the dimensions and provide illustrations of how customers judge them.

Reliability: Delivering on Promises

Of the five dimensions, reliability has been consistently shown to be the most important determinant of perceptions of service quality.[33] **Reliability** is defined as the ability to perform the promised service dependably and accurately. In its broadest sense, reliability means that the company delivers on its promises—promises about delivery, service provision, problem resolution, and pricing. Customers want to do business with companies that keep their promises, particularly their promises about the service outcomes and core service attributes.

One company that effectively communicates and delivers on the reliability dimension is FedEx. The reliability message of FedEx—"When it absolutely, positively has to get there overnight"—reflects the company's service positioning. See also Home

FIGURE 5.4

This ad demonstrates the "reliability" dimension of service quality.

Source: Reprinted by permission of Home Depot, Canada.

Depot's use of TV celebrity Mike Holmes to position its installation services on quality and reliability dimensions, illustrated in Figure 5.4.

Responsiveness: Being Willing to Help

Responsiveness is the willingness to help customers and to provide prompt service. This dimension emphasizes attentiveness and promptness in dealing with customer requests, questions, complaints, and problems. Responsiveness is communicated to customers by the length of time they have to wait for assistance, answers to questions, or attention to problems. Responsiveness also captures the notion of flexibility and ability to customize the service to customer needs. In Figure 5.5 on the next page, we see how one of Canada's biggest law firms, Borden Ladner Gervais, humorously positions itself on responsiveness.

To excel on the dimension of responsiveness, a company must view the process of service delivery and the handling of requests from the customer's point of view rather than from the company's point of view. Standards for speed and promptness that reflect the company's view of internal process requirements may be very different from the customer's requirements for speed and promptness. To truly distinguish themselves on responsiveness, companies need well-staffed customer service departments as well as responsive front-line people in all contact positions. Responsiveness perceptions diminish when customers wait to get through to a company by telephone, are put on hold, are put through to a complex voice mail system, or have trouble accessing the firm's website.

Assurance: Inspiring Trust and Confidence

Assurance is defined as employees' knowledge and courtesy and the ability of the firm and its employees to inspire trust and confidence. This dimension is likely to be particularly important for services that customers perceive as high risk or for services of which they feel uncertain about their ability to evaluate outcomes—for example, banking, insurance, brokerage, medical, and legal services.

FIGURE 5.5

This ad stresses the "responsiveness" dimension of service quality.

Source: Cartoon Bank, a division of the New Yorker/ Danny Shanahan, Cartoonist/ Mary Secord, Copy Writer, FCB Canada/Annie Lee, Art Director, FCB Canada.

Trust and confidence may be embodied in the person who links the customer to the company, such as securities brokers, insurance agents, lawyers, or counsellors. In such service contexts the company seeks to build trust and loyalty between key contact people and individual customers. The "personal banker" concept captures this idea: customers are assigned to a banker who will get to know them individually and who will coordinate all their banking services.

In other situations, trust and confidence are embodied in the organization itself. Insurance companies such as Allstate ("You're in good hands with Allstate") and Prudential ("Own a piece of the rock") illustrate efforts to create trusting relationships between customers and the company as a whole. A recent ad campaign by FedEx uses the tag line "Relax, it's FedEx," going beyond its traditional reliability message to focus on assurance and trust.

Empathy: Treating Customers as Individuals

Empathy is defined as the caring, individualized attention that the firm provides its customers. The essence of empathy is conveying, through personalized or customized service, that customers are unique and special and that their needs are understood. Customers want to feel understood by and important to firms that provide service to them. Personnel at small service firms often know customers by name and build relationships that reflect their personal knowledge of customer requirements and preferences. When such a small firm competes with larger firms, the ability to be empathetic may give the small firm a clear advantage.

Tangibles: Representing the Service Physically

Tangibles are defined as the appearance of physical facilities, equipment, personnel, and communication materials. Service industries that emphasize tangibles in their strategies include hospitality services in which the customer visits the establishment

Global Feature

Importance of Service Quality Dimensions Across Cultures

The development of the service quality dimensions of reliability, responsiveness, assurance, empathy, and tangibles was based on research conducted across multiple contexts within the United States. As a general rule, reliability comes through as the most important dimension of service quality in the United States, with responsiveness also being relatively important when compared to the remaining three dimensions. But what happens when we look across cultures? Are the service quality dimensions still important? Which ones are most important? Answers to these questions can be extremely valuable for companies delivering services across cultures or in multicultural environments.

Researchers have used Hofstede's well-established cultural dimensions to assess whether service quality importance would vary across different cultural orientations. For example, *power distance* refers to the extent to which status differences are expected and accepted within a culture. Research has suggested that most Asian countries are characterized by high power distance, whereas many Western countries score lower on power distance measures. Broadly speaking, *individualism* reflects a self-orientation that is characteristic of Western culture whereas its opposite, *collectivism,* is more typical of the East. Similar comparisons across cultures have been made for the other dimensions: *masculinity, uncertainty avoidance,* and *long-term orientation.* The question is whether these types of cultural differences may affect the importance consumers place on the service quality dimensions.

The figure shown here from research published by Furrer, Liu, and Sudharshan suggests strong differences in the importance of service quality dimensions across clusters of customers defined by different

continued

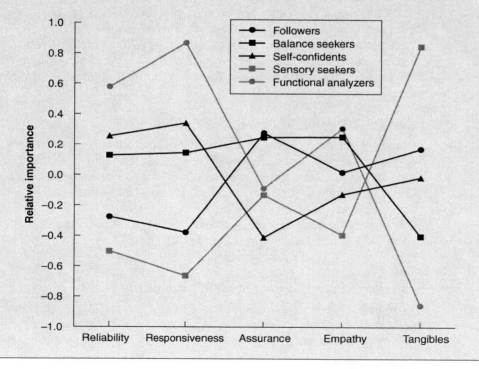

Global Feature

Importance of Service Quality Dimensions Across Cultures—continued

cultural dimensions. The cultural profile of the clusters is described here:

Followers: Large power distance, high collectivism, high masculinity, neutral uncertainty avoidance, and short-term orientation.

Balance seekers: Small power distance, high collectivism, neutral masculinity, high uncertainty avoidance, and medium-term orientation.

Self-confidents: Small power distance, high individualism, medium femininity, low uncertainty avoidance, and long-term orientation.

Sensory seekers: Large power distance, medium individualism, high masculinity, low uncertainty avoidance, and short-term orientation.

Functional analyzers: Small power distance, medium individualism, high femininity, high uncertainty avoidance, and long-term orientation.

From this figure it is clear that the service quality dimensions are important across cultures, but their relative importance varies depending on cultural value orientation. For example, small power distance cultures with high to medium individualism and long-term orientation (self-confidents and functional analyzers) rate reliability and responsiveness as most important. On the other hand, cultures with large power distance and high masculinity (followers and sensory seekers) rate these same dimensions as less important. The tangibles dimension shows the widest variation, with sensory seekers rating it most important and functional analyzers rating it least important.

The researchers in this study suggest a number of implications for companies serving multiple cultures. For example, if the target market has a follower cultural profile, service providers may want to emphasize training their employees to have professional knowledge and be trustworthy to gain the trust of these customers, combined with tangibles and empathy to convey service quality. On the other hand, to serve self-confidents, providers should emphasize equipping and empowering the employees so they are capable of providing reliable, responsive service.

Sources: G. Hofstede, *Cultures and Organizations: Software of the Mind* (New York, McGraw-Hill, 1991); O. Furrer, B. Shaw-Ching Liu, and D. Sudharshan, "The Relationships Between Culture and Service Quality Perceptions," *Journal of Service Research* 2, no. 4 (May 2000), pp. 355–71.

to receive the service, such as restaurants and hotels, retail stores, and entertainment companies.

Although tangibles are often used by service companies to enhance their image, provide continuity, and signal quality to customers, most companies combine tangibles with another dimension to create a service quality strategy for the firm. For example, Mr. Lube emphasizes both responsiveness and tangibles—providing fast, efficient service and a comfortable, clean waiting area.

Table 5.1 provides examples of how customers judge each of the five dimensions of service quality across a variety of service contexts.

TABLE 5.1 Examples of How Customers Judge the Five Dimensions of Service Quality

	Reliability	Responsiveness	Assurance	Empathy	Tangibles
Car repair (consumer)	Problem fixed the first time and ready when promised	Accessible; no waiting; responds to requests	Knowledgeable mechanics	Acknowledges customer by name; remembers previous problems and preferences	Repair facility; waiting area; uniforms; equipment
Airline (consumer)	Flights to promised destinations depart and arrive on schedule	Prompt and speedy system for ticketing, in-flight baggage handling	Trusted name; good safety record; competent employees	Understands special individual needs; anticipates customer needs	Aircraft; ticketing counters; baggage area; uniforms
Medical care (consumer)	Appointments are kept on schedule; diagnoses prove accurate	Accessible; no waiting; willingness to listen	Knowledge; skills; credentials; reputation	Acknowledges patient as a person; remembers previous problems; listens well; has patience	Waiting room; exam room; equipment; written materials
Architecture (business)	Delivers plans when promised and within budget	Returns phone calls; adapts to changes	Credentials; reputation; name in the community; knowledge and skills	Understands client's industry; acknowledges and adapts to specific client needs; gets to know the client	Office area; reports; plans themselves; billing statements; dress of employees
Information processing (internal)	Provides needed information when requested	Prompt response to requests; not "bureaucratic"; deals with problems promptly	Knowledgeable staff; well trained; credentials	Knows internal customers as individuals; understands individual and departmental needs	Internal reports; office area; dress of employees
Internet brokerage (consumer and business)	Provides correct information and executes customer requests accurately	Quick website with easy access and no down time	Credible information sources on the site; brand recognition; credentials apparent on site	Responds with human interaction as needed	Appearance of the website and collateral

e-Service Quality

The growth of e-tailing and e-services has led many companies to wonder how consumers evaluate service quality on the Web and whether the criteria are different from those used to judge the quality of non-Internet services.[34] A study sponsored by the Marketing Science Institute has been conducted to understand how consumers judge e-service quality.[35] In that study, e-SQ is defined as the extent to which a website facilitates efficient and effective shopping, purchasing, and delivery. Through exploratory focus groups and two phases of empirical data collection and analysis, this research identified seven dimensions that are critical for core service evaluation (four dimensions) and service recovery evaluation (three dimensions).

The four core dimensions that customers use to judge websites at which they experience no questions or problems are listed below. Do you agree with them?

- *Efficiency.* The ability of customers to get to the website, find their desired product and information associated with it, and check out with minimal effort

- *Fulfilment.* The accuracy of service promises, having products in stock, and delivering the products in the promised time

- *Reliability.* The technical functioning of the site, particularly the extent to which it is available and functioning properly

- *Privacy.* The assurance that shopping behaviour data are not shared and that credit information is secure

The study also revealed three dimensions that customers use to judge recovery service when they have problems or questions:

- *Responsiveness.* The ability of e-tailers to provide appropriate information to customers when a problem occurs, to have mechanisms for handling returns, and to provide online guarantees

- *Compensation.* The degree to which customers are to receive money back and are reimbursed for shipping and handling costs

- *Contact.* The availability of live customer service agents online or through the phone

SERVICE ENCOUNTERS: THE BUILDING BLOCKS FOR CUSTOMER PERCEPTIONS

We have just finished a discussion of customer perceptions, specifically customer satisfaction and service quality. Here we turn to the building blocks for customer perceptions—service encounters, or "moments of truth." Service encounters are where promises are kept or broken and where the proverbial rubber meets the road—sometimes called "real-time marketing." It is from these service encounters that customers build their perceptions.

Service Encounters or Moments of Truth

From the customer's point of view, the service encounters in a hotel include checking in, being taken to a room by a bellperson, eating a restaurant meal, requesting a wakeup call, and checking out. You might think of the linking of these moments of truth as a service encounter cascade (see Figure 5.6). It is in these encounters that

FIGURE 5.6

A Service Encounter Cascade for a Hotel Visit

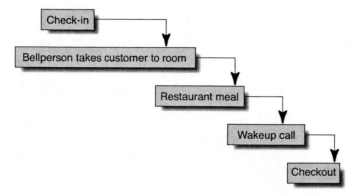

customers receive a snapshot of the organization's service quality, and each encounter contributes to the customer's overall satisfaction and willingness to do business with the organization again. From the organization's point of view, each encounter thus presents an opportunity to prove its potential as a quality service provider and to increase customer loyalty, as suggested by the ad for Doubletree Hotels shown in Figure 5.7 on the next page.

Some services have few service encounters, and others have many. The Disney Corporation estimates that each of its amusement park customers experiences about 74 service encounters and that a negative experience in any one of them can lead to a negative overall evaluation. Mistakes or problems that occur in the early levels of the service cascade may be particularly critical. Marriott Hotels learned this through their extensive customer research to determine what service elements contribute most to customer loyalty. They found that four of the top five factors came into play in the first 10 minutes of the guest's stay.[36]

The Importance of Encounters

Although early events in the encounter cascade are likely to be especially important, *any* encounter can potentially be critical in determining customer satisfaction and loyalty. If a customer is interacting with a firm for the first time, that initial encounter will create a first impression of the organization. In these first-encounter situations, the customer frequently has no other basis for judging the organization, and the initial phone contact or face-to-face experience can take on excessive importance in the customer's perceptions of quality. Even if the technical quality of the firm's repair service is superior, the firm may not get the chance to demonstrate it if the initial telephone encounter drives the customer away.

Logic suggests that not all encounters are equally important in building relationships. For every organization, certain encounters are probably key to customer satisfaction. For Marriott Hotels, as noted, the early encounters are most important. In a hospital context, a study of patients revealed that encounters with nursing staff were more important than encounters with meal service or patient discharge personnel.[37] And research at GTE Laboratories documented that small business customers' relationships with GTE depended on specific installation, repair, and sales encounters.[38]

In addition to these key encounters, there are some momentous encounters that, like the proverbial "one bad apple," simply ruin the rest and drive the customer away no matter how many or what type of encounters have occurred in the past. These momentous encounters can occur in connection with very important events (such

FIGURE 5.7

Every service
encounter is an
opportunity to build
satisfaction and
quality.

Source: Reprinted
with permission, Hilton
Hospitality, Inc./Doubletree
® Hotels, Suites, Resorts,
Clubs. Photographer: Chris
Schrameck.

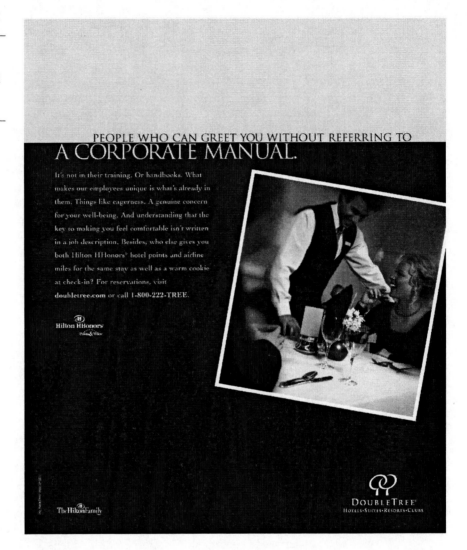

as the failure to deliver an essential piece of equipment before a critical deadline),
or they may seem inconsequential, as in the story of the bank customer described in
Exhibit 5.1. Similarly, momentous positive encounters can sometimes bind a customer
to an organization for life.

Sources of Pleasure and Displeasure in Service Encounters

Because of the importance of service encounters in building perceptions, researchers have extensively analyzed service encounters in many contexts to determine the
sources of customers' favourable and unfavourable impressions. The research uses
the critical incident technique to get customers and employees to provide verbatim
stories about satisfying and dissatisfying service encounters they have experienced.[39]
With this technique, customers (either internal or external) are asked the following
questions:

> Think of a time when, as a customer, you had a particularly *satisfying* (or
> *dissatisfying*) interaction with _____.

EXHIBIT 5.1

One Critical Encounter Destroys 30-Year Relationship

"If you have $1 in a bank or $1 million, I think they owe you the courtesy of stamping your parking ticket," said John Barrier. One day in 1989 Mr. Barrier paid a visit to his bank in Spokane, Washington. He was wearing his usual shabby clothes and pulled up in his pickup truck, parking in the lot next to the bank. After cashing a cheque, he went outside to drive away and was stopped by a parking attendant who told him there was a 60 cent fee, but that he could get his parking slip validated in the bank and park for free. No problem, Barrier thought, and he went back into the bank (where, by the way, he had been banking for 30 years). The teller looked him up and down and refused to stamp his slip, telling him that the bank validated parking only for people who have transactions with the bank and that cashing a cheque wasn't a transaction. Mr. Barrier then asked to see the bank manager, who also looked him up and down, stood back, and "gave me one of those kinds of looks," also refusing to validate the parking bill. Mr. Barrier then said, "Fine. You don't need me, and I don't need you." He withdrew all his money and took it down the street to a competing bank, where the first cheque he deposited was for $1,000,000.

Source: "Shabby Millionaire Closes Account, Gives Bank Lesson About Snobbery." Reprinted with permission of United Press International from *The Arizona Republic* issue of February 21, 1989, p. A3.

When did the incident happen?

What specific circumstances led up to this situation?

Exactly what did the employee (or firm member) say or do?

What resulted that made you feel the interaction was *satisfying* (or *dissatisfying*)?

What could or should have been done differently?

Sometimes contact employees are asked to put themselves in the shoes of a customer and answer the same questions: "Put yourself in the shoes of *customers* of your firm. In other words, try to see your firm through your customers' eyes. Now think of a recent time when a customer of your firm had a particularly *satisfying/unsatisfying* interaction with you or a fellow employee." The stories are then analyzed to determine common themes of satisfaction/dissatisfaction underlying the events. On the basis of thousands of service encounter stories, four common themes—recovery (after failure), adaptability, spontaneity, and coping—have been identified as the sources of customer satisfaction/dissatisfaction in memorable service encounters.[40] Each of the themes is discussed here, and sample stories of both satisfying and dissatisfying incidents for each theme are given in Exhibit 5.2. The themes encompass service behaviours in encounters spanning a wide variety of industries.

Recovery—Employee Response to Service Delivery System Failures

The first theme includes all incidents in which there has been a failure and an employee is required to respond to consumer complaints. The failure may be, for example, a hotel room that is not available, an airplane flight that is delayed six hours, or a critical error on an internal document. The content or form of the employee's response is what causes the customer to remember the event favourably or unfavourably.

Adaptability—Employee Response to Customer Needs and Requests

A second theme underlying satisfaction/dissatisfaction is the adaptability of the service delivery system when the customer has special needs that make demands

━━▶ EXHIBIT 5.2
Service Encounter Themes

THEME 1: RECOVERY

Satisfactory

They lost my room reservation but the manager gave me the VIP suite for the same price.

Even though I did not make any complaint about the hour-and-a-half wait, the waitress kept apologizing and said the bill was on the house.

Dissatisfactory

We had made advance reservations at the hotel. When we arrived we found we had no room—no explanation, no apologies, and no assistance in finding another hotel.

One of my suitcases was all dented up and looked like it had been dropped from 30,000 feet. When I tried to make a claim for my damaged luggage, the employee insinuated that I was lying and trying to cheat them.

THEME 2: ADAPTABILITY

Satisfactory

I did not have an appointment to see a doctor; however, my allergy nurse spoke to a practitioner's assistant and worked me into the schedule. I received treatment after a 10-minute wait. I was very satisfied with the special treatment I received, the short wait, and the quality of the service.

It was snowing outside—my car broke down. I checked 10 hotels and there were no rooms. Finally, one understood my situation and offered to rent me a bed and set it up in a small banquet room.

Dissatisfactory

My young son, flying alone, was to be assisted by the flight attendant from start to finish. At Toronto she left him alone in the airport with no one to escort him to his connecting flight.

Despite our repeated requests, the hotel staff would not deal with the noisy people partying in the hall at 3 a.m.

THEME 3: SPONTANEITY

Satisfactory

We always travel with our teddy bears. When we got back to our room at the hotel we saw that the cleaning person had arranged our bears very comfortably in a chair. The bears were holding hands.

The anaesthesiologist took extra time to explain exactly what I would be aware of and promised to take special care in making sure I did not wake up during surgery. It impressed me that the anaesthesiologist came to settle my nerves and explain the medicine I was getting because of my cold.

Dissatisfactory

The lady at the front desk acted as if we were bothering her. She was watching TV and paying more attention to that than to the hotel guests.

I needed a few more minutes to decide on a dinner. The waitress said, "If you would read the menu and not the road map, you would know what you want to order."

THEME 4: COPING

Satisfactory

A person who became intoxicated on a flight started speaking loudly, annoying the other passengers. The flight attendant asked the passenger if he would be driving when the plane landed and offered him coffee. He accepted the coffee and became quieter and friendlier.

Dissatisfactory

An intoxicated man began pinching the female flight attendants. One attendant told him to stop, but he continued and then hit another passenger. The copilot was called and asked the man to sit down and leave the others alone, but the passenger refused. The copilot then "decked" the man, knocking him into his seat.

on the process. In these cases, customers judge service encounter quality in terms of the flexibility of the employees and the system. Incidents categorized within this theme contain an implicit or explicit request for customization of the service to meet a need. Much of what customers see as special needs or requests may actually be rather routine from the employee's point of view; what is important is that the customers perceive that something special is being done for them according to their individual needs. External customers and internal customers alike are pleased when the service provider puts forth the effort to accommodate and adjust the system. On the flip side, they are angered and frustrated by an unwillingness to try to accommodate and by promises that are never followed through. Contact employees also see their abilities to adapt the system as being a prominent source of customer satisfaction, and often they are equally frustrated by constraints that keep them from being flexible.

Spontaneity—Unprompted and Unsolicited Employee Actions

Even when there is no system failure and no special request or need, customers can still remember service encounters as being very satisfying or very dissatisfying. Employee spontaneity in delivering memorably good or poor service is the third theme. Satisfying incidents in this group represent very pleasant surprises for the customer (special attention, being treated like royalty, receiving something nice but not requested), whereas dissatisfying incidents in this group represent negative and unacceptable employee behaviours (rudeness, stealing, discrimination, ignoring the customer).

Coping—Employee Response to Problem Customers

The incidents categorized in this group came to light when employees were asked to describe service encounter incidents in which customers were either very satisfied or dissatisfied. In addition to describing incidents of the types outlined under the first three themes, employees described many incidents in which customers were the cause of their own dissatisfaction. Such customers were basically uncooperative—that is, unwilling to cooperate with the service provider, other customers, industry regulations, and/or laws. In these cases nothing the employee could do would result in the customer feeling pleased about the encounter. The term *coping* is used to describe these incidents, because coping is the behaviour generally required of employees to handle problem customer encounters. Rarely are such encounters satisfying from the customers' point of view.[41]

Table 5.2 on page 116 summarizes the specific employee behaviours that cause satisfaction and dissatisfaction in service encounters according to the four themes just presented: recovery, adaptability, spontaneity, and coping. The left side of the table suggests what employees do that results in positive encounters, whereas the right side summarizes negative behaviours within each theme.

Technology-Based Service Encounters

All the research described thus far is based on interpersonal services. Recently researchers have also begun to look at the sources of pleasure and displeasure in technology-based service encounters.[42] These types of encounters involve customers interacting with Internet-based services, automated phone services, kiosk services, and services delivered via CD or video technology. Often these systems are referred to as *self-service technologies* (SSTs), because the customer essentially provides his or her own service.

Technology Spotlight

Customers Love Amazon.com

Although its stock price suffered in 2000–2001, along with that of just about every other Internet-based company, and although the company had never reported a profit until-early in 2002, just prior to entering Canada, customers have always loved Amazon.com. In 2003 the company completed its first full year of profitable quarters and the stock price was back up. The 2004 American Customer Satisfaction Index reflected a rating of 88 for Amazon—one of the highest ratings of any company in any industry, and certainly much higher than the 80 average rating for e-commerce endeavours and the 60–75 ratings for many other service businesses. And, although Amazon's ACSI rating fell to 84 in 2005, it is still one of the highest scores recorded.

Jeff Bezos, CEO of Amazon, whose name has become a household word worldwide, believes that his customers come first. With a continued focus on customers, relationships, value, and the brand itself, Bezos and others believe that sales will continue to grow (almost $7 billion in 2004) and profits will continue. According to Bezos, "Customers come first. If you focus on what customers want and build a relationship, they will allow you to make money."

Few would deny that Amazon is a master of technology and technology-based services for consumers. In fact, other companies, such as Toys "R" Us and Office Depot have sought a technology partnership with Amazon in order to benefit from the company's experience and success with customers. Amazon now provides Internet retail services for both these companies.

Amazon has taken a historically interpersonally dominated transaction and successfully transformed it to a Web-based service experience. Let's take a closer look at what the company is doing and why customers love it so much. Since its inception in July 1995, Amazon has grown to the point where it offers more book titles than any bricks-and-mortar bookstore could ever hope to stock. So selection and availability of titles are one key to its popularity with customers. But that is just the beginning.

In addition to a wide selection, Amazon has invested significant effort to simulate the feel of a neighbourhood bookstore, where a patron can mingle with other customers, discuss books, and get recommendations from bookstore employees. Amazon allows customers to find related books on virtually any topic by simply typing keywords and initiating a search of its massive database. Its one-to-one marketing system allows the company to track what individual consumers buy and let them know of additional titles that might interest them. This marketing is done while the customer is shopping as well as through periodic direct email that identifies books specifically related to the customer's past purchase patterns and interests.

Currently, customers can buy much more than books from Amazon. In fact, Bezos hopes that they can buy just about anything they want through the Amazon website. His goal from the beginning was "to create the world's most customer-centric company, the place where you can find and buy anything you want online." Bezos continues to take risks that are combined with a long-term view of success, and to reflect all new ideas against a customer-focused filter. It is hard to predict where these basic strategies may lead in the future, but even doubters are beginning to believe that Amazon will continue to succeed and be around for a long time. As noted in our Technology Spotlight in Chapter 2, Amazon is a great example of a technology company that addresses all the gaps in the service quality gaps model.

amazon.com®

Sources: S. Alsop, "I'm Betting on Amazon.com," *Fortune*, April 30, 2001, p. 48; ACSI results at www.theacsi.org; Robert D. Hof, "How Amazon Cleared That Hurdle," *BusinessWeek*, February 4, 2002, pp. 60–61; A. Deutschman, "Inside the Mind of Jeff Bezos," *Fast Company*, August 2004, pp. 52–58.

TABLE 5.2 General Service Behaviours Based on Service Encounter Themes—Dos and Don'ts

Theme	Do	Don't
Recovery	Acknowledge problem	Ignore customer
	Explain causes	Blame customer
	Apologize	Leave customer to fend for himself or herself
	Compensate/upgrade	Downgrade
	Lay out options	Act as if nothing is wrong
	Take responsibility	"Pass the buck"
Adaptability	Recognize the seriousness of the need	Ignore
	Acknowledge	Promise, but fail to follow through
	Anticipate	Show unwillingness to try
	Attempt to accommodate	Embarrass the customer
	Adjust the system	Laugh at the customer
	Explain rules/policies	Avoid responsibility
	Take responsibility	"Pass the buck"
Spontaneity	Take time	Exhibit impatience
	Be attentive	Ignore
	Anticipate needs	Yell/laugh/swear
	Listen	Steal from customers
	Provide information	Discriminate
	Show empathy	
Coping	Listen	Take customer's dissatisfaction personally
	Try to accommodate	Let customer's dissatisfaction affect others
	Explain	
	Let go of the customer	

The research on SSTs reveals some different themes in terms of what drives customer satisfaction and dissatisfaction. The following themes were identified from analysis of hundreds of critical incident stories across a wide range of contexts, including Internet retailing, Internet-based services, ATMs, automated phone systems, and others.

For Satisfying SSTs

- *Solved an intensified need.* Customers in this category were thrilled that the technology could bail them out of a difficult situation—for example, a cash machine that came to the rescue, allowing the customer to get cash to pay a cab driver and get to work on time when a car had broken down.

- *Better than the alternative.* Many SST stories related to how the technology-based service was in some way better than the alternative—easy to use, saved time, available when and where the customer needed it, saved money.

- *Did its job.* Because there are so many failures of technology, many customers are simply thrilled when the SST works as it should!

For Dissatisfying SSTs

- *Technology failure.* Many dissatisfying SST stories relate to the technology simply not working as promised—it is not available when needed, PINs do not work, or systems are offline.

- *Process failure.* Often the technology seems to work, but later the customer discovers that a back-office or follow-up process, which the customer assumed was connected, does not work. For example, a product order seems to be placed successfully, but it never arrives or the wrong product is delivered.

- *Poor design.* Many stories relate to the customer's dissatisfaction with how the technology is designed, in terms of either the technical process (technology is confusing, menu options are unclear) or the actual service design (delivery takes too long, service is inflexible).

- *Customer-driven failure.* In some cases the customers told stories of their own inabilities or failures to use the technology properly. These types of stories are (of course) much less common than stories blaming the technology or the company.

For all of the dissatisfying SST stories, there is clearly an element of service failure. Interestingly, the research revealed little attempt in these technology-based encounters to recover from the failure—unlike the interpersonal service encounters described earlier, in which excellent service recovery can be a foundation for retaining and even producing very satisfied customers. As companies progress further with SSTs and become better at delivering service this way, we expect that growing numbers will be able to deliver superior service via technology. Many are doing it already, as our Technology Spotlight on Amazon.com illustrates. In the future we believe that many firms will be able to deliver highly reliable, responsive, customized services via technology and will offer easy and effective means for service recovery when failure does occur.[43]

The Evidence of Service

Because services are intangible, customers are searching for evidence of service in every interaction they have with an organization.[44] Figure 5.8 depicts the three major categories of evidence as experienced by the customer: people, process, and physical evidence. These categories together represent the service and provide the evidence that makes the offering tangible. Note the parallels between the elements of evidence of service and the new marketing mix elements presented in Chapter 1. The new mix elements essentially *are* the evidence of service in each moment of truth.

FIGURE 5.8

The Evidence of Service (from the Customer's Point of View)

Source: M. J. Bitner, "Managing the Evidence of Service," *The Service Quality Handbook*, ed. E. E. Scheuing and W. F. Christopher. Reprinted by permission of the American Marketing Association.

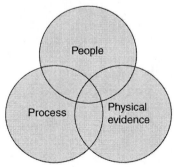

- Contact employees
- Customer him/herself
- Other customers

People

- Operational flow of activities
- Steps in process
- Flexibility vs. standard
- Technology vs. human

Process

Physical evidence

- Tangible communication
- Servicescape
- Guarantees
- Technology
- Website

SUMMARY

This chapter described customer perceptions of service by first introducing you to two critical concepts: customer satisfaction and service quality. These critical customer perceptions were defined and discussed in terms of the factors that influence each of them. You learned that customer satisfaction is a broad perception influenced by features and attributes of the product as well as by customers' emotional responses, their attributions, and their perceptions of fairness. Service quality, the customer's perception of the service component of a product, is also a critical determinant of customer satisfaction. Sometimes, as in the case of a pure service, service quality may be the *most* critical determinant of satisfaction. You learned that perceptions of service quality are based on five dimensions: reliability, assurance, empathy, responsiveness, and tangibles.

Another major purpose of the chapter was to introduce the idea of service encounters, or "moments of truth," as the building blocks for both satisfaction and quality. You learned that every service encounter (whether remote, over the phone, or in person) is an opportunity to build perceptions of quality and satisfaction. The underlying themes of pleasure and displeasure in service encounters were also described. The importance of managing the evidence of service in each and every encounter was discussed.

Chapters 3, 4, and 5 have provided you with a grounding in customer issues relevant to services. The three chapters together are intended to give you a solid understanding of customer behaviour issues and of service expectations and perceptions. Through the rest of the book, we illustrate strategies that firms can use to close the gap between customer expectations and perceptions.

⟼ Discussion Questions

1. What is customer satisfaction, and why is it so important? Discuss how customer satisfaction can be influenced by each of the following: product attributes and features, customer emotions, attributions for success or failure, perceptions of fairness, and family members or other customers.

2. Why do service companies generally receive lower satisfaction ratings than non-durable and durable product companies?

3. Discuss the differences between perceptions of service quality and customer satisfaction.

4. List and define the five dimensions of service quality. Describe the services provided by a firm you do business with (your bank, your doctor, your favourite restaurant) on each of the dimensions. In your mind, has this organization distinguished itself from its competitors on any particular service quality dimension?

5. Describe a remote encounter, a phone encounter, and a face-to-face encounter that you have had recently. How did you evaluate the encounter, and what were the most important factors determining your satisfaction/dissatisfaction in each case?

6. Describe an "encounter cascade" for an airplane flight. In your opinion, what are the most important encounters in this cascade for determining your overall impression of the quality of the airline?

7. Why did the gentleman described in Exhibit 5.1 leave his bank after 30 years? What were the underlying causes of his dissatisfaction in that instance, and why would that cause him to leave the bank?

8. Assume that you are a manager of a health club. Discuss general strategies you might use to maximize customers' positive perceptions of your club. How would you know if you were successful?

Exercises

1. Keep a journal of your service encounters with different organizations (at least five) during the week. For each journal entry, ask yourself the following questions: What circumstances led up to this encounter? What did the employee say or do? How did you evaluate this encounter? What exactly made you evaluate the encounter that way? What should the organization have done differently (if anything)? Categorize your encounters according to the four themes of service encounter satisfaction/dissatisfaction (recovery, adaptability, spontaneity, coping).

2. Interview someone with a different cultural background from you. Ask the person about service quality, whether the five dimensions of quality are relevant, and which are most important in determining quality of banking services (or some other type of service) in the person's country.

3. Think of an important service experience you have had in the last several weeks. Analyze the encounter according to the evidence of service provided (see Figure 5.8). Which of the three evidence components was (or were) most important for you in evaluating the experience, and why?

4. Interview an employee of a local service business. Ask the person to discuss each of the five dimensions of quality with you as it relates to the person's company. Which dimensions are most important? Are any dimensions *not* relevant in this context? Which dimensions does the company do best? Why? Which dimensions could benefit from improvement? Why?

5. Interview a manager, owner, or president of a business. Discuss with this person the strategies he or she uses to ensure customer satisfaction. How does service quality enter into the strategies, or does it? Find out how this person measures customer satisfaction and/or service quality.

6. Visit Amazon.com's website. Visit a traditional bookstore. How would you compare the two experiences? Compare and contrast the factors that most influenced your satisfaction and perceptions of service quality in the two different situations. When would you choose to use one rather than the other?

Notes

1. "Exceeding Customer Expectations," Wal-Mart Stores site, www.walmartstores. com, accessed September 25, 2006.

2. For more discussion of the debate on the distinctions between quality and satisfaction, see A. Parasuraman, V. A. Zeithaml, and L. L. Berry, "Reassessment of Expectations as a Comparison Standard in Measuring Service Quality: Implications for Future Research," *Journal of Marketing* 58 (January 1994), pp. 111–24;

R. L. Oliver, "A Conceptual Model of Service Quality and Service Satisfaction: Compatible Goals, Different Concepts," in *Advances in Services Marketing and Management,* vol. 2, ed. T. A. Swartz, D. E. Bowen, and S. W. Brown (Greenwich, CT: JAI Press, 1994), pp. 65–85; M. J. Bitner and A. R. Hubbert, "Encounter Satisfaction vs. Overall Satisfaction vs. Quality: The Customer's Voice," in *Service Quality: New Directions in Theory and Practice,* ed. R. T. Rust and R. L. Oliver (Newbury Park, CA: Sage, 1993), pp. 71–93; and D. Iacobucci et al., "The Calculus of Service Quality and Customer Satisfaction: Theory and Empirical Differentiation and Integration," in *Advances in Services Marketing and Management,* vol. 3, ed. T. A. Swartz, D. E. Bowen, and S. W. Brown (Greenwich, CT: JAI Press, 1994), pp. 1–67; P. A. Dabholkar, C. D. Shepherd, and D. I. Thorpe, "A Comprehensive Framework for Service Quality: An Investigation of Critical Conceptual and Measurement Issues through a Longitudinal Study," *Journal of Retailing* 7, no. 2 (Summer 2000), pp. 139–73; J. J. Cronin, Jr., M. K. Brady, and G. T. M. Hult, "Assessing the Effects of Quality, Value, and Customer Satisfaction on Consumer Behavioral Intentions in Service Environments," *Journal of Retailing* 7 (Summer 2000), pp. 193–218.

3. See in particular Parasuraman, Zeithaml, and Berry, "Reassessment of Expectations"; Oliver, "A Conceptual Model of Service Quality"; and M. K. Brady and J. J. Cronin Jr., "Some New Thoughts on Conceptualizing Perceived Service Quality: A Hierarchical Approach," *Journal of Marketing* 65 (July 2001), pp. 34–49.

4. A. Parasuraman, V. A. Zeithaml, and L. L. Berry, "SERVQUAL: A Multiple-Item Scale for Measuring Consumer Perceptions of Service Quality," *Journal of Retailing* 64 (Spring 1988), pp. 12–40.

5. Parasuraman, Zeithaml, and Berry, "Reassessment of Expectations."

6. Oliver, "A Conceptual Model of Service Quality."

7. See V. Mittal, P. Kumar, and M. Tsiros, "Attribute-Level Performance, Satisfaction, and Behavioral Intentions over Time," *Journal of Marketing* 63 (April 1999), pp. 88–101; L. L. Olsen and M. D. Johnson, "Service Equity, Satisfaction, and Loyalty: From Transaction-Specific to Cumulative Evaluations," *Journal of Service Research* 5 (February 2003), pp. 184-95.

8. Olsen and Johnson, "Service Equity, Satisfaction, and Loyalty."

9. R. L. Oliver, *Satisfaction: A Behavioral Perspective on the Consumer* (New York: McGraw-Hill, 1997).

10. For a more detailed discussion of the different types of satisfaction, see E. Arnould, L. Price, and G. Zinkhan, *Consumers,* 2nd ed., ch. 18, "Consumer Satisfaction" (New York: McGraw-Hill, 2004), pp. 754–96.

11. S. Fournier and D. G. Mick, "Rediscovering Satisfaction," *Journal of Marketing* 63 (October 1999), pp. 5–23.

12. Oliver, *Satisfaction,* ch. 2.

13. A. Ostrom and D. Iacobucci, "Consumer Trade-offs and the Evaluation of Services," *Journal of Marketing* 59 (January 1995), pp. 17–28.

14. For more on emotions and satisfaction, see Oliver, *Satisfaction,* ch. 11; and L. L. Price, E. J. Arnould, and S. L. Deibler, "Consumers' Emotional Responses to Service Encounters," *International Journal of Service Industry Management* 6, no. 3 (1995), pp. 34–63.

15. L. L. Price, E. J. Arnould, and P. Tierney, "Going to Extremes: Managing Service Encounters and Assessing Provider Performance," *Journal of Marketing* 59 (April 1995), pp. 83–97.

16. V. Liljander and T. Strandvik, "Emotions in Service Satisfaction," *International Journal of Service Industry Management* 8, no. 2 (1997), pp. 148–69.

17. For more on attributions and satisfaction, see V. S. Folkes, "Recent Attribution Research in Consumer Behavior: A Review and New Directions," *Journal of Consumer Research* 14 (March 1988), pp. 548–65; and Oliver, *Satisfaction,* ch. 10.

18. A. R. Hubbert, "Customer Co-creation of Service Outcomes: Effects of Locus of Causality Attributions," doctoral dissertation, Arizona State University, Tempe, Arizona, 1995.

19. M. J. Bitner, "Evaluating Service Encounters: The Effects of Physical Surrounding and Employee Responses," *Journal of Marketing* 54 (April 1990), pp. 69–82.

20. For more on fairness and satisfaction, see E. C. Clemmer and B. Schneider, "Fair Service," in *Advances in Services Marketing and Management,* vol. 5, ed. T. A. Swartz, D. E. Bowen, and S. W. Brown (Greenwich, CT: JAI Press, 1996), pp. 109–26; Oliver, *Satisfaction,* ch. 7; and Olsen and Johnson, "Service Equity, Satisfaction, and Loyalty."

21. Fournier and Mick, "Rediscovering Satisfaction."

22. C. Fornell, M. D. Johnson, E. W. Anderson, J. Cha, and B. E. Bryant, "The American Customer Satisfaction Index: Nature, Purpose, and Findings," *Journal of Marketing* 60 (October 1996), pp. 7–18.

23. E. W. Anderson, C. Fornell, and D. R. Lehmann, "Customer Satisfaction, Market Share, and Profitability: Findings from Sweden," *Journal of Marketing* 58 (July 1994), pp. 53–66.

24. M. Bruhn and M. A. Grund, "Theory, Development and Implementation of National Customer Satisfaction Indices: The Swiss Index of Customer Satisfaction (SWICS)," *Total Quality Management* 11, no. 7 (2000), pp. S1017–S1028; A. Meyer and F. Dornach, "The German Customer Barometer," www. servicebarometer.de.or.

25. J. L. Heskett, W. E. Sasser Jr., and L. A. Schlesinger, *The Service Profit Chain* (New York: Free Press, 1997).

26. M. A. J. Menezes and J. Serbin, *Xerox Corporation: The Customer Satisfaction Program,* case no. 591-055 (Boston: Harvard Business School, 1991).

27. F. F. Reichheld, "The One Number You Need to Grow," *Harvard Business Review,* December 2003, pp. 47–54.

28. E. W. Anderson and V. Mittal, "Strengthening the Satisfaction–Profit Chain," *Journal of Service Research* 3 (November 2000), pp. 107–20.

29. Brady and Cronin, "Some New Thoughts on Conceptualizing Perceived Service Quality."

30. Ibid.

31. See C. Gronroos, "A Service Quality Model and Its Marketing Implications," *European Journal of Marketing* 18, no. 4 (1984), pp. 36–44; R. T. Rust and R. L. Oliver, "Service Quality Insights and Managerial Implications from the Frontier," in *Service Quality: New Directions in Theory and Practice,* ed. R. T. Rust and R. L. Oliver (Thousand Oaks, CA: Sage, 1994), pp. 1–19; M. J. Bitner, "Managing the Evidence of Service," in *The Service Quality Handbook,* ed. E. E. Scheuing and W. F. Christopher (New York: AMACOM, 1993), pp. 358–70.

32. Parasuraman, Zeithaml, and Berry, "SERVQUAL: A Multiple-Item Scale." Details on the SERVQUAL scale and the actual items used to assess the dimensions are provided in Chapter 6.

33. Ibid.

34. For a review of what is known about service quality delivery via the Web, see V. A. Zeithaml, A. Parasuraman, and A. Malhotra, "Service Quality Delivery Through Web Sites: A Critical Review of Extant Knowledge," *Journal of the Academy of Marketing Science* 30, no. 4 (2002), pp. 362–75.

35. V. Zeithaml, A. Parasuraman, and A. Malhotra, "A Conceptual Framework for Understanding e-Service Quality: Implications for Future Research and Managerial Practice," Marketing Science Institute working paper, Report No. 00-115, 2001.

36. "How Marriott Makes a Great First Impression," *The Service Edge* 6, no. 5 (May 1993), p. 5.

37. A. G. Woodside, L. L. Frey, and R. T. Daly, "Linking Service Quality, Customer Satisfaction, and Behavioral Intention," *Journal of Health Care Marketing* 9 (December 1989), pp. 5–17.

38. R. N. Bolton and J. H. Drew, "Mitigating the Effect of Service Encounters," *Marketing Letters* 3, no. 1 (1992), pp. 57–70.

39. For detailed discussions of the Critical Incident Technique, see J. C. Flanagan, "The Critical Incident Technique," *Psychological Bulletin* 51 (July 1954), pp. 327–58; M. J. Bitner, J. D. Nyquist, and B. H. Booms, "The Critical Incident as a Technique for Analyzing the Service Encounter," in *Services Marketing in a Changing Environment,* ed. T. M. Bloch, G. D. Upah, and V. A. Zeithaml (Chicago: American Marketing Association, 1985), pp. 48–51; S. Wilson-Pessano, "Defining Professional Competence: The Critical Incident Technique 40 Years Later," presentation to the Annual Meeting of the American Educational Research Association, New Orleans, 1988; I. Roos, "Methods of Investigating Critical Incidents," *Journal of Service Research* 4 (February 2002), pp. 193–204; D. D. Gremler, "The Critical Incident Technique in Service Research," *Journal of Service Research* 7 (August 2004), pp. 65–89.

40. For a complete discussion of the research on which this section is based, see M. J. Bitner, B. H. Booms, and M. S. Tetreault, "The Service Encounter: Diagnosing Favorable and Unfavorable Incidents," *Journal of Marketing* 54 (January 1990), pp. 71–84; M. J. Bitner, B. H. Booms, and L. A. Mohr, "Critical Service Encounters: The Employee's View," *Journal of Marketing* 58, no. 4 (1994), pp. 95–106; D. Gremler and M. J. Bitner, "Classifying Service Encounter Satisfaction across Industries," in *Marketing Theory and Applications,* ed. C. T. Allen et al. (Chicago: American Marketing Association, 1992), pp. 111–18; and D. Gremler, M. J. Bitner, and K. R. Evans, "The Internal Service Encounter," *International Journal of Service Industry Management* 5, no. 2 (1994), pp. 34–56.

41. Bitner, Booms, and Mohr, "Critical Service Encounters."

42. This discussion is based on research and results presented in M. L. Meuter, A. L. Ostrom, R. I. Roundtree, and M. J. Bitner, "Self-Service Technologies: Understanding Customer Satisfaction with Technology-Based Service Encounters," *Journal of Marketing* 64 (July 2000), pp. 50–64.

43. M. J. Bitner, S. W. Brown, and M. L. Meuter, "Technology Infusion in Service Encounters," *Journal of the Academy of Marketing Science* 28, no. 1, pp. 138–49.

44. Bitner, "Managing the Evidence of Service."

Chapter

6

Listening to Customers Through Research

Provider Gap 1

↦ 1. Present the types of and guidelines for marketing research in services.

↦ 2. Show how marketing research information can and should be used for services.

↦ 3. Describe the strategies by which companies can facilitate interaction and communication between management and customers.

↦ 4. Present ways that companies can and do facilitate interaction between contact people and management.

TD BANK FINANCIAL GROUP EXCELS AT RESEARCH IN SERVICES

Toronto-Dominion Bank Financial Group (TDBFG, www.td.com), headquartered in Toronto, has the best customer service among the five major banks in the country. TDBFG, ranking number one overall on a 2005 customer service index kept by independent market research company Synovate (www.synovate.com), outperformed competitors in eight of eleven categories, including "overall quality of customer service" and "staff service at my branch." And the accolades do not stop there. The 150-year-old company has won numerous awards for having the best customer Internet bank in the nation, and has been honoured with SQM's Contact Centre Industry Service Quality Award for Excellence.

The SQM award constitutes recognition that the company's focus is on the customer. As TDBFG's 2004 Corporate Responsibility Report indicates,

"Our customers are why we exist so paying attention to what counts to them is the overarching focus that propels our business." However, with 52,000 employees and 14 million customers worldwide, knowing just what the customer expects can be a challenge. TDBFG uses a variety of research sources to listen to their customers.

Among the company's most detailed customer research initiatives is the Voice of the Customer study, which entails administering hundreds of thousands of customer surveys annually within a few days of a banking experience. The results are used to tabulate a Customer Satisfaction Index (CSI), providing an internal measure of how the company is performing in the eyes of the customer. As with the external validation the company has received on their customer-focused initiatives, customers are increasingly satisfied with their Toronto-Dominion experience. The CSI has increased every year from 81.9 in 2002 to 86.8 in 2005.

Other customer-focused research initiatives at TDBFG are focus groups conducted with front-line employees and a formal Customer Problem Resolution process. Additionally, the company maintains a comprehensive data warehouse and employs a team of analysts to sift through the reams of data for further insight.

TD Bank Financial Group has been successful in satisfying customers because their research lets them know what customers expect so that strategies can be implemented to provide customers with the service they desire, resolve problems as they arise, and, in turn, maintain a loyal customer base.[1]

 Bank Financial Group

Source: Courtesy of TD Bank Financial Group.

Despite a genuine interest in meeting customer expectations, many companies miss the mark by thinking inside out—they believe they know what customers *should* want, rather than finding out what they *do* want. (See Figure 6.1 for a humorous take on "listening to customers.") When this happens, companies provide services that do not match customer expectations. Because services have few clearly defined and tangible cues, this difficulty may be considerably larger than it is in manufacturing firms. A better approach involves thinking outside in—determining customer expectations and then delivering to them. Thinking outside in uses research to understand customers and their requirements fully. Research, the subject of this chapter, involves far more than conventional surveys. It consists of a portfolio of listening strategies that allow companies to deliver service to customer expectations.

USING RESEARCH TO UNDERSTAND CUSTOMER EXPECTATIONS

In this section we discuss the elements of services research programs that help companies identify customer expectations and perceptions. In the sections that follow, we

FIGURE 6.1

An example of how *not* to listen to your customers.

Source: © Graham Harrop.

will discuss ways in which the tactics of general research may need to be adjusted to maximize its effectiveness in services.

Research Objectives for Services

The first step in designing services research is the most critical: defining the problem and research objectives. This is where the services marketer poses the questions to be answered with research. In spite of the importance of this first stage, many research studies are initiated without adequate attention to objectives.

Research objectives in services are similar in many ways to the research conducted for physical products. However, they incorporate additional elements that require specific attention.

First, services research must continually track service performance, because performance is subject to human variability and heterogeneity. Conducting performance research at a single point in time, as might be done for a physical product, would be insufficient in services. Another focus of services research involves documenting the process by which service is performed. Even when service employees are performing well, a service provider must continue to track performance, because the potential for variation in service delivery always exists.

A second distinction in services research is the need to consider and monitor the gap between expectations and perceptions. This gap is dynamic because both perceptions and expectations fluctuate. Does the gap exist because performance is declining, because performance varies with demand and supply level, or because expectations are escalating?

Exhibit 6.1 lists a number of services research objectives. Once objectives such as these have been identified, they will point the way to decisions about the most appropriate type of research, methods of data collection, and ways to use the information. The additional columns in this table are described in sections of this chapter.

→ EXHIBIT 6.1

Elements in an Effective Marketing Research Program for Services

Type of Research	Primary Research Objectives	Qualitative/Quantitative	Costs of Information		Frequency
			Monetary	Time	
Complaint solicitation	To identify/attend to dissatisfied customers To identify common service failure points	Qualitative	Low	Low	Continuous
Critical incident studies	To identify "best practices" at transaction level To identify customer requirements as input for quantitative studies To identify common service failure points To identify systemic strengths and weaknesses in customer-contact services	Qualitative	Low	Moderate	Periodic
Requirements research	To identify customer requirements as input for quantitative research	Qualitative	Moderate	Moderate	Periodic
Relationship surveys and SERVQUAL surveys	To monitor and track service performance To assess overall company performance compared with that of competition To determine links between satisfaction and behavioural intentions To assess gaps between customer expectations and perceptions	Quantitative	Moderate	Moderate	Annual
Trailer calls	To obtain immediate feedback on performance of service transactions To measure effectiveness of changes in service delivery To assess service performance of individuals and teams To use as input for process improvements To identify common service failure points	Quantitative	Low	Low	Continuous

Research	Purpose	Type			Frequency
Service expectation meetings and reviews	To create dialogue with important customers To identify what individual large customers expect and then to ensure that it is delivered To close the loop with important customers	Qualitative	Moderate	Moderate	Annual
Process checkpoint evaluations	To determine customer perceptions of long-term professional services during service provision To identify service problems and solve them early in the service relationship	Quantitative	Moderate	Moderate	Periodic
Market-oriented ethnography	To research customers in natural settings To study customers from cultures other than North America in an unbiased way	Qualitative	Moderate	High	Periodic
Mystery shopping	To measure individual employee performance for evaluation, recognition, and rewards To identify systemic strengths and weaknesses in customer-contact services	Quantitative	Low	Low	Quarterly
Customer panels	To monitor changing customer expectations To provide a forum for customers to suggest and evaluate new service ideas	Qualitative	Moderate	Moderate	Continuous
Lost customer research	To identify reasons for customer defection To assess gaps between customer expectations and perceptions	Qualitative	Low	Low	Continuous
Future expectations research	To forecast future expectations of customers To develop and test new service ideas	Qualitative	High	High	Periodic
Database marketing research	To identify the individual requirements of customers using information technology and database information	Quantitative	High	High	Continuous

FIGURE 6.2

Criteria for an
Effective Services
Research Program

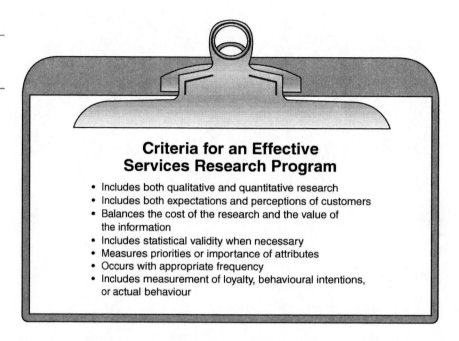

**Criteria for an Effective
Services Research Program**

- Includes both qualitative and quantitative research
- Includes both expectations and perceptions of customers
- Balances the cost of the research and the value of the information
- Includes statistical validity when necessary
- Measures priorities or importance of attributes
- Occurs with appropriate frequency
- Includes measurement of loyalty, behavioural intentions, or actual behaviour

Criteria for an Effective Services Research Program

A **services research program** can be defined as the composite of all research needed to address the objectives and execute an overall measurement strategy. Understanding the criteria for an effective services research program (see Figure 6.2) will help a company evaluate different types of research and choose the ones most appropriate for its research objectives. In this section we discuss these criteria.

Includes Qualitative and Quantitative Research

Research is not limited to surveys and statistics. Some forms of research, called *qualitative research*, are exploratory and preliminary, and are conducted to clarify problem definition, to prepare for more formal research, or to gain insight when more formal research is not necessary. Insights gained through one-on-one conversations, customer focus groups, critical incidents research, and direct observation of service transactions show the marketer the right questions to ask of consumers. Because the results of qualitative research play a major role in designing quantitative research, it is often the first type of research done. Qualitative research can also be conducted after quantitative research to make the numbers in computer printouts meaningful by giving managers the perspective required for interpreting data and initiating improvement efforts.[2]

Quantitative research in marketing is designed to describe the nature, attitudes, or behaviours of customers empirically and to test specific hypotheses that a services marketer wants to examine. These studies are key for quantifying the customers' satisfaction, the importance of service attributes, the extent of service quality gaps, and perceptions of value. Such studies also provide managers with benchmarks for evaluating competitors. Finally, results from quantitative studies can highlight specific service deficiencies that can be more deeply probed through follow-up qualitative research.

Includes Both Perceptions and Expectations of Customers

As we discussed in Chapter 4, expectations serve as standards or reference points for customers. In evaluating service quality, customers compare what they perceive they get in a service encounter with their expectations of that encounter. For this reason, a measurement program that captures only perceptions of service is missing a critical part of the service quality equation. Companies need also to incorporate measures of customer expectations.

Measurement of expectations can be included in multiple ways. First, research that relates to customers' requirements—that identifies the service features that matter to customers—can be considered expectation research. In this form, the *content* of customer expectations is captured, initially in some form of qualitative research such as focus group interviews. Research on the *levels* of customer expectations also is needed. This type of research assesses the levels of customer expectations and compares these with perception levels, usually by calculating the gap between expectations and perceptions.

Balances the Cost of the Research and the Value of the Information

An assessment of the cost of research compared with its benefits is another key criterion. One cost is monetary, including costs to marketing research companies, payments to respondents, and internal costs incurred by employees collecting the information. Time costs are also important, including the time needed by employees to administer the research and the interval between data collection and availability for use by the firm. These costs must be weighed against the gains to the company in improved decision making, retained customers, and successful new service launches. As in many other marketing decisions, costs are easier to estimate than the value of the information. For this reason, we include only costs, not value, in Exhibit 6.1. In later chapters we describe approaches to estimating the value of customers to a company, approaches that are useful as input to the tradeoff analysis needed to address this criterion.

Includes Statistical Validity When Necessary

We have already shown that research has multiple objectives. These objectives determine the research methodology. To illustrate, some research is used by companies to build relationships with customers—to allow contact employees to find out what customers desire, to diagnose the strengths and weaknesses of the firm, to prepare a plan to meet requirements, and to confirm that the company has executed the plan. The underlying objective of this type of research is to allow contact people to identify specific action items that will gain the maximum return in customer satisfaction. This type of research does not need sophisticated quantitative analysis, anonymity of customers, careful control of sampling, or strong statistical validity.

On the other hand, research used to track overall service quality that will be used for bonuses and salary increases must be carefully controlled for sampling bias and statistical validity. Not all forms of research have statistical validity, and not all forms need it. Most forms of qualitative research, for example, do not possess statistical validity.

Measures Priorities or Importance

Customers have many service requirements, but not all are equally important. One of the most common mistakes managers make in trying to improve service is spending resources on the wrong initiatives, only to become discouraged because the firm's

Technology Spotlight

Conducting Marketing Research on the Web

One of the most intriguing applications of the Internet is online research, replacing comment cards and intrusive telephone calls with cyber-surveys that are challenging and fun for consumers. The application is growing rapidly, for obvious reasons: Internet research has been touted to have many benefits to marketers besides more willing respondents, including the following:

- *Speed.* Rather than months required to collect data through mail questionnaires, or weeks needed to train interviewers and obtain data from telephone questionnaires, online surveys can be prepared and executed quickly. A sample of 300 to 400, large enough for many studies, can be completed in a weekend and available for viewing by clients on a secure website.

- *Ability to target hard-to-reach populations.* One of the traditional difficulties in research, particularly segmentation research, is to identify and access hard-to-reach consumers. One firm overcoming this difficulty is Toronto's In-Sync (www.insyncresearch. com), which conducts Virtual Roundtables (online focus groups). About 12 participants stay together (virtually) for a week, and visit a designated website where they respond to questions and perform exercises. Another Canadian firm doing interesting work is Tangency (www.tangency.ca), whose findings suggest that young males are more comfortable in virtual focus groups than they would be in traditional ones. The resulting richer conversations lead to increased understanding of both group and individual expectations and perceptions.

- *Ability to target customers with money.* Online research allows service companies to reach customers who have higher incomes, higher education levels, and greater willingness to spend. Consumers with computers who use online services regularly tend to be in these demographic target groups, and they can be effectively surveyed with online research. Compared with the sample that

would be obtained from traditional research using all telephone subscribers, the sample of online users is far better in terms of marketing potential.

- *Opportunity to use multimedia to present video and audio.* Telephone surveys are limited to voice alone, whereas mail surveys are constrained to two-dimensional visuals. In the past, to present the full range of audio and video needed to give respondents the true sense of a service being researched, surveys had to be conducted in person and were therefore very expensive ($30 to $150 per person depending on the topic and sample). Online research offers broader stimuli potential through all multimedia possibilities at a fraction of the cost.

- *No interviewers.* And therefore no interviewer errors or interviewer bias. Bias occurs when the interviewer is in a bad mood, tired, impatient, or not objective. These problems occur with human interviews but not cyber-interviews. Interviewer error is another age-old research problem, described well by a research professional:

  > The first survey I ever designed was on the subject of home heating systems. When I went to observe the first day of field, I was surprised and horrified to realize that most of my interviewers could not pronounce many of the technical terms that I had used in the survey, and virtually none of them knew what those terms meant. It wasn't exactly the best way to collect data.

- *Control over data quality.* This can eliminate contradictory or nonsensical answers. With traditional surveys, researchers need a step called "data cleaning and editing" in which all data are checked for such problems; electronic checks can be built into online surveys that take care of this problem as it occurs.

- *Inexpensive research.* Data collection costs can be the most expensive part of a study, and the

continued

Technology Spotlight

Conducting Marketing Research on the Web—*continued*

most expensive part of data collection can be paying subjects to participate. Online marketing research, astonishingly, is 10 to 80 percent less expensive than other approaches. The Internet also eliminates postage, phone, labour, and printing costs that are typical with other survey approaches. Respondents also seem to complete Web-based surveys in half the time it would take an interviewer to conduct the survey, perhaps contributing to the lack of need for incentives.

One additional but to date undersubstantiated benefit is higher response rate—reportedly as high as 70 percent—possibly stemming from the fact that the interactive nature of cyber-research can make answering surveys fun for respondents. While it is getting more difficult to get consumers to answer traditional surveys, the entertainment value of cyber-surveys makes it easy to recruit participants. One study shows that consumers are five times more likely to complete an electronic survey as they are to do the same survey with written materials and that researchers obtain the following three additional benefits: (1) consumers "play" an e-survey longer, answering more questions than in a traditional survey; (2) people tend to concentrate more fully on their answers; and (3) the entertainment value of an e-survey actually lowers the respondent's perceived time to complete the survey.

The advantages of online research likely far outnumber the disadvantages. However, marketers need to be aware of certain drawbacks. Perhaps the major problem is the composition of the sample. Unlike the process used with most telephone and mail surveys, the population of responders is not usually selected but is a matter of convenience, consisting of whoever responds to the survey. This is a particular problem when respondents are recruited from other websites and click through to the survey. In these cases marketers may not even know who the responders are and whether they in fact fit the profile for answering the survey. To address this problem, companies are prequalifying respondents by telephone or email, then asking for enough demographic information to ensure that the respondents meet the desired requirements.

Sources: A. Hogg, "Online Research Overview," MarketingPower.com, updated 2004; D. McCullough, "Web-Based Market Research Ushers in New Age," *Marketing News*, September 14, 1998, p. 28; R. Weible and J. Wallace, "Cyber Research: The Impact of the Internet on Data Collection," *Marketing Research*, Fall 1998, pp. 19–24; R. Nadilo, "On-Line Research Taps Consumers Who Spend," *Marketing News*, June 8, 1998, p. 12; and S. Yaffe, "Going Deep: Getting to Know Customers Better Than They Know Themselves Means Asking Different Questions Differently," *Strategy Magazine*, February 2005, p. 55.

service does not improve! Measuring the relative importance of service dimensions and attributes helps managers to channel resources effectively; therefore, research must document the priorities of the customer. Prioritization can be accomplished in multiple ways. *Direct importance measures* ask customers to prioritize dimensions of service. One effective approach involves asking respondents to allocate a total of 100 points across the various service dimensions. *Indirect importance measures* are estimated using the statistical procedures of correlation and regression analysis, which show the relative contribution of questionnaire items or requirements to overall service quality. Both indirect and direct importance measures provide evidence of customer priorities.

Occurs with Appropriate Frequency

Because customer expectations and perceptions are dynamic, companies need to institute a research *process*, not just do isolated studies. A single study provides only a snapshot of one moment in time. For full understanding, marketing research must be ongoing.

Just what does "ongoing research" mean in terms of frequency? As we discuss the different types in the following section, you will see the frequency with which each type of research could be conducted.

Includes Measures of Loyalty, Behavioural Intentions, or Behaviour

An important trend in services research involves measuring the positive and negative consequences of service quality along with overall satisfaction or service quality scores. Among the most important generic behavioural intentions are willingness to recommend the service to others and repurchase intent. Positive behavioural intentions include saying positive things about the company, recommending the company to others, remaining loyal, spending more with the company, and paying a price premium. Negative behavioural intentions include saying negative things to others, doing less business with the company, switching to another company, and complaining to outside organizations such as the Better Business Bureau.

Summary

The research criteria discussed here should be incorporated into a services marketing research program. As we discuss the elements in such a program, we will indicate how these approaches satisfy the criteria. In addition to the types and techniques of research shown in Exhibit 6.1, the boxes in this chapter also show how electronic and other technologies add to the information that managers can collect.

ELEMENTS IN AN EFFECTIVE SERVICES RESEARCH PROGRAM

A good services research program includes multiple types of research studies. If a company were to engage in virtually all types of service research, the portfolio would look like Exhibit 6.1, but few companies do all types of research. The particular portfolio for any company will match company resources and address the key areas needed to understand its customers. So that it will be easier for you to identify the appropriate type of research for different research objectives, we list the objectives in column 2 of Exhibit 6.1. In the following sections we describe each major type of research and show the way each type addresses the criteria associated with it. The Technology Spotlight discusses research conducted online.

Complaint Solicitation

Many of you have complained to employees of service organizations, only to find that nothing happens with your complaint. No one rushes to solve it, and the next time you experience the service the same problem is present. How frustrating! Good service organizations take complaints seriously. Not only do they listen to complaints—they also seek complaints as communications about what can be done to improve their service and their service employees.

Firms that use complaints as research use the information to identify dissatisfied customers, correct individual problems where possible, and identify common service

FIGURE 6.3

Participants in a focus group discuss services using the critical incidents technique.

Source: Getty Images.

failure points. Although this research is used for both goods and services, it has a critical real-time purpose in services—to improve failure points and to improve or correct the performance of contact personnel. Research on complaints is one of the easiest types of research for firms to conduct, leading many companies to depend solely on complaints to stay in touch with customers. Unfortunately, research provides evidence that customer complaints alone are a woefully inadequate source of information: only a small percentage of customers with problems actually complain. The rest will stay dissatisfied, telling other people about their dissatisfaction.

To be effective, complaint solicitation requires rigorous recording of numbers and types of complaints through many channels, and then working to eliminate the most frequent problems. Complaint channels include employees at the front line, intermediary organizations like retailers who deliver service, managers, and complaints to third parties such as customer advocate groups. Companies must both solve individual customer problems and seek overall patterns to eliminate failure points.

Critical Incidents Studies

In Chapter 5, we discussed the critical incident technique (CIT), a qualitative interview procedure in which customers are asked to provide verbatim stories about satisfying and dissatisfying service encounters they have experienced (Figure 6.3). According to a recent summary of the use of the technique in services, CIT has been reported in hotels, restaurants, airlines, amusement parks, automotive repair, retailing, banking, cable television, public transportation, and education.[3] The studies have explored a wide range of service topics: consumer evaluation of services, service failure and recovery, employees, customer participation in service delivery, and service experience.

CIT has many benefits. First, data are collected from the respondent's perspective and are usually vivid because they are expressed in consumers' own words and reflect the way they think. Second, the method provides concrete information about the way the company and its employees behave and react, thereby making the research easy to translate into action. Third, like most qualitative methods, the research is particularly useful when the topic or service is new and very little other information exists. Finally, the method is well suited for assessing perceptions of customers from different cultures because it allows respondents to share their perceptions rather than answer researcher-defined questions.[4]

Requirements Research

Requirements research involves identifying what customers expect in a service. Because these studies are so foundational, qualitative techniques are appropriate to begin them. Quantitative techniques may follow, usually during a pretest stage of survey development. Unfortunately, many companies do inadequate requirements research, often developing surveys on the basis of intuition or company direction rather than thorough customer probing.

An example of requirements research is *structured brainstorming*, a technique developed by researchers in IBM's Advanced Business Systems unit.[5] In this technique a sample of customers and potential customers is assembled. A facilitator leads the group through a series of exercises on creativity and then has the customers describe the ideal provider of the service—what they would want if they could have their ideal service. The facilitator asks "what" customers want (to elicit fundamental requirements), "why" they want it (to elicit the underlying need or benefit sought), and "how" they will know when they receive it (to elicit specific service features). IBM's Global Banking Industry used a similar format, with 100 audience members looking on. Ontario's The Glasgow Group assisted with the subsequent breakout sessions in which discussions with the audience members reflected on the roundtable topics.

Some researchers, though, suggest there are limits to what can be achieved with this approach. Jake McCaul, founder of Toronto-based Second Sight Innovation, says, "You can't ask customers what they want anymore; technology is moving too fast and there are too many [variables] at play."[6] Instead, many researchers, including Second Sight and Toronto-based InSync, believe the best way to understand the targets is to empower them to research themselves. "We charge them with exercises that direct them to become reflective of their needs and their relationships to a brand."[7]

Burger King tried taking their customers to lunch. Customers visited both Burger King and competitors' locations. In each case they went through the entire process from ordering to paying to eating (and leaving). Then they attended a full-day session devoted to understanding customer expectations and how the company might respond.

Relationship and SERVQUAL Surveys

Relationship surveys pose questions about all elements in the customer's relationship with the company (including service, product, and price). This comprehensive approach can help a company diagnose its relationship strengths and weaknesses. These surveys typically track service performance annually with an initial survey providing a baseline. Relationship surveys are also effective in comparing company performance with that of competitors, often focusing on the best competitor's performance as a benchmark. When used for this purpose, the sponsor of the survey is not identified and questions are asked about both the focal company and one or more competitors.

A good example of a relevant satisfaction survey is the *Globe and Mail*'s University Report Card, which, unlike the university rankings used by *Maclean's*, surveys students nationwide asking them how satisfied they are with their university experience.

(To see the respective studies, go to www.theglobeandmail.com/generated/realtime/specialReportCard2005.html and www.macleans.ca/universities.)

A sound measure of service quality is necessary for identifying needed performance improvement and evaluating the impact of improvement efforts. Unlike goods quality, which can be measured objectively by such indicators as durability and number of defects, service quality is abstract and is best captured by surveys that measure customer evaluations of service. One of the first measures to be developed specifically to measure service quality was the SERVQUAL survey.

The SERVQUAL scale involves a survey containing 21 service attributes, grouped into the five service quality dimensions (discussed in Chapter 5) of reliability, responsiveness, assurance, empathy, and tangibles. The survey sometimes asks customers to provide two different ratings on each attribute—one reflecting the level of service they would expect from excellent companies in a sector and the other reflecting their perception of the service delivered by a specific company within that sector. The difference between the expectation and perception ratings constitutes a quantified measure of service quality. Exhibit 6.2 shows the items on the basic SERVQUAL scale as well as the phrasing of the expectations and perceptions portions of the scale.[8]

Data gathered through a SERVQUAL survey can be used for a variety of purposes:

- To determine the average gap score (between customers' perceptions and expectations) for each service attribute

- To assess a company's service quality along each of the five SERVQUAL dimensions

- To track customers' expectations and perceptions (on individual service attributes and/or on the SERVQUAL dimensions) over time

- To compare a company's SERVQUAL scores against those of competitors

- To identify and examine customer segments that differ significantly in their assessments of a company's service performance

- To assess internal service quality (i.e., the quality of service rendered by one department or division of a company to others within the same company)

SERVQUAL is used all over the world in service industries. Published studies have used it, and adaptations of it, in a variety of contexts: real estate brokers, physicians in private practice, public recreation programs, dental schools, business school placement centres, and higher education. Many of the findings are unpublished and/or proprietary. However, from our knowledge of some of these applications, one example will be briefly described here.

The Ceramic Products Division of Corning, Inc., developed a systematic process for monitoring and improving its service quality as perceived by its customers, and the SERVQUAL approach was an integral component of this process. Corning's Ceramic Products Division began its service improvement process by focusing on its largest client, a multinational company. This division modified the SERVQUAL instrument for assessing its service quality as perceived by multiple levels within this company. The SERVQUAL survey was re-administered a year later to assess the impact of the corrective actions. Results indicated significant improvements in most of the targeted attributes and also identified additional areas for further corrective action. The success of SERVQUAL in this pilot application prompted Corning to make this process an ongoing activity in the Ceramics Product Division and to expand its implementation to other divisions and customer groups.

EXHIBIT 6.2

SERVQUAL: A Multidimensional Scale to Capture Customer Perceptions and Expectations of Service Quality

The SERVQUAL scale was first published in 1988 and has undergone numerous improvements and revisions since then. The scale currently contains 21 perception items that are distributed throughout the five service quality dimensions. The scale also contains expectation items. Although many different formats of the SERVQUAL scale are now in use, we show here the basic 21 perception items as well as a sampling of ways the expectation items have been posed.

PERCEPTIONS

	Strongly disagree						Strongly agree

Perceptions Statements in the Reliability Dimension

1. When XYZ Company promises to do something by a certain time, it does so.   1 2 3 4 5 6 7
2. When you have a problem, XYZ Company shows a sincere interest in solving it.   1 2 3 4 5 6 7
3. XYZ Company performs the service right the first time.   1 2 3 4 5 6 7
4. XYZ Company provides its services at the time it promises to do so.   1 2 3 4 5 6 7
5. XYZ Company insists on error-free records.   1 2 3 4 5 6 7

Statements in the Responsiveness Dimension

1. XYZ Company keeps customers informed about when services will be performed.   1 2 3 4 5 6 7
2. Employees in XYZ Company give you prompt service.   1 2 3 4 5 6 7
3. Employees in XYZ Company are always willing to help you.   1 2 3 4 5 6 7
4. Employees in XYZ Company are never too busy to respond to your request.   1 2 3 4 5 6 7

Statements in the Assurance Dimension

1. The behaviour of employees in XYZ Company instils confidence in you.   1 2 3 4 5 6 7
2. You feel safe in your transactions with XYZ Company.   1 2 3 4 5 6 7

3. Employees in XYZ Company are consistently courteous with you.   1 2 3 4 5 6 7
4. Employees in XYZ Company have the knowledge to answer your questions.   1 2 3 4 5 6 7

Statements in the Empathy Dimension

1. XYZ Company gives you individual attention.   1 2 3 4 5 6 7
2. XYZ Company has employees who give you personal attention.   1 2 3 4 5 6 7
3. XYZ Company has your best interests at heart.   1 2 3 4 5 6 7
4. Employees of XYZ Company understand your specific needs.   1 2 3 4 5 6 7
5. XYZ Company has operating hours that are convenient to all its customers   1 2 3 4 5 6 7

Statements in the Tangibles Dimension

1. XYZ Company has modern-looking equipment.   1 2 3 4 5 6 7
2. XYZ Company's physical facilities are visually appealing.   1 2 3 4 5 6 7
3. XYZ Company's employees appear neat.   1 2 3 4 5 6 7
4. Materials associated with the service (such as pamphlets or statements) are visually appealing at XYZ Company.   1 2 3 4 5 6 7

⟼ EXHIBIT 6.2
— continued

EXPECTATIONS: Several Formats for Measuring Customer Expectations Using Versions of SERVQUAL

Matching Expectations Statements (Paired with the Previous Perception Statements)

	Strongly disagree					Strongly agree
When customers have a problem, excellent firms will show a sincere interest in solving it.	1 2 3 4 5 6 7					

Referent Expectations Formats

1. Considering a "world class" company to be a "7," how would you rate XYZ Company's performance on the following service features?

	Low					High
Sincere, interested employees	1 2 3 4 5 6 7					
Service delivered right the first time	1 2 3 4 5 6 7					

2. Compared with the level of service you expect from an excellent company, how would you rate XYZ Company's performance on the following?

	Low					High
Sincere, interested employees	1 2 3 4 5 6 7					
Service delivered right the first time	1 2 3 4 5 6 7					

Combined Expectations/Perceptions Statements

For each of the following statements, circle the number that indicates how XYZ Company's service compares with the level you expect:

	Lower than my desired service level			The same as my desired service level			Higher than my desired service level		
1. Prompt service	1	2	3	4	5	6	7	8	9
2. Courteous employees	1	2	3	4	5	6	7	8	9

Expectations Distinguishing Between Desired Service and Adequate Service

For each of the following statements, circle the number that indicates how XYZ Company's performance compares with your *minimum service level* and with your *desired service level.*

	Compared with my *minimum* service level XYZ's service performance is:			Compared with my *desired* service level XYZ's service performance is:		
When it comes to . . .	Lower	Same	Higher	Lower	Same	Higher
1. Prompt service	1 2 3 4 5 6 7 8 9			1 2 3 4 5 6 7 8 9		
2. Employees who are consistently courteous	1 2 3 4 5 6 7 8 9			1 2 3 4 5 6 7 8 9		

Source: A. Parasuraman, V. A. Zeithaml, and L. L. Berry, "SERVQUAL: A Multiple-Item Scale for Measuring Consumer Perceptions of Service Quality," *Journal of Retailing* 64, no. 1 (Spring 1988). Reprinted by permission of C. Samuel Craig.

Corning's use of SERVQUAL touches on virtually all the potential applications of the instrument listed earlier. It also illustrates the fact that SERVQUAL can be adapted for use in a variety of contexts, including industrial product and internal service contexts.

Trailer Calls or Posttransaction Surveys

Whereas the purpose of SERVQUAL surveys is usually to gauge the overall relationship with the customer, the purpose of transaction surveys is to capture information about the key service *encounters* with the customer. In this method, customers are asked a short list of questions immediately after a particular transaction (hence the name *trailer calls*) about their satisfaction. Because the surveys are administered continuously to a broad spectrum of customers, they are more effective than complaint solicitation (in which the information comes only from dissatisfied customers).

At checkout, immediately after staying at Fairfield Inns, customers are asked to use a computer terminal to answer four or five questions about their stay in the hotel. This novel approach has obvious benefits over the ubiquitous comment cards left in rooms—the response rate is far higher, because the process engages customers and takes only a few minutes. In other companies, transaction surveys are administered by telephone several days after a transaction. Because they occur close to service transactions, these surveys are useful in identifying sources of dissatisfaction and satisfaction. For example, Enterprise Rent-A-Car often calls customers a day after a car has been rented (and is still in the customer's possession) to ensure that customers are satisfied.

A strong benefit of this type of research is that it often appears to customers that the call is following up to ensure that they are satisfied; consequently the call does double duty as a market research tool and as customer service. This type of research is simple and fresh and provides management with continuous information about interactions with customers. Further, the research allows management to associate service quality performance with individual contact personnel so that high performance can be rewarded and low performance corrected. It also serves as an incentive for employees to provide better service because they understand how and when they are being evaluated.

Service Expectation Meetings and Reviews

In business-to-business situations, research that is highly effective involves eliciting the expectations of the client at a specified time of the year and then following up later (usually after a year) to discuss whether the expectations were fulfilled. Unlike other forms of research, these meetings are not conducted by unbiased researchers but are instead facilitated by senior members of the account team so that they can listen carefully to the client's expectations. You may be surprised to find that such interaction does not come naturally to sales teams who are used to talking to clients rather than listening carefully to their needs. Consequently, teams have to be carefully trained not to defend or explain but instead to comprehend. One company found that the only way it could teach its salespeople not to talk on these interviews was to take a marketing researcher along to gently kick the salesperson under the table whenever he or she strayed from the format!

The format, when appropriate, consists of (1) asking clients what they expect in terms of 8 to 10 basic requirements determined from focus group research, (2) inquiring what particular aspects of these requirements the account team performed well in the past as well as what aspects need improvement, and (3) requesting that the client rank the relative importance of the requirements. After getting the input, senior account members go back to their teams and plan their goals for the year around client requirements. The next step is verifying with the client that the account plan will satisfy requirements or, when it will not, managing expectations to let the client know what cannot be accomplished. After executing the plan for the year, the senior account personnel then return to the client, determine whether the plan has been successfully executed and expectations met, then establish a new set of expectations for the coming year.

Process Checkpoint Evaluations

With professional services such as consulting, construction, and architecture, services are provided over a long period, and there are not obvious ways or times to collect customer information. Waiting until the entire project is complete—which could last years—is undesirable because unresolvable problems could have occurred by then. But discrete service encounters to calibrate customer perceptions are also not usually available. In these situations, the smart service provider defines a process for delivering the services and then structures the feedback around the process, checking in at frequent points to ensure that the client's expectations are being met. For example, a management consulting firm might establish the following process for delivering its services to clients: (1) collect information, (2) diagnose problems, (3) recommend alternative solutions, (4) select alternatives, and (5) implement solutions. Next, it could agree with the client up front that it will communicate at major process checkpoints—after diagnosing the problem, before selecting the alternative, and so on—to make certain that the job is progressing as planned.

Market-Oriented Ethnography

Many of the types of research we discuss in this section are particularly relevant for Canada and cultures similar to it. Structured questionnaires, for example, make key assumptions about what people are conscious of or can recall about

In professional services, evaluations are made at important checkpoints in the process.

Source: Digital Vision/Getty Images.

their behaviour and what they are willing to explain to researchers about their opinions. These assumptions are based on our own culture. Even focus group interviews are inherently culture-based, because they depend on norms of participation, or what people are willing to say in front of others and to researchers. To fully understand how customers of other cultures assess and use services, it is necessary and effective to use other approaches, such as market-oriented ethnography. This set of approaches allows researchers to observe consumption behaviour in natural settings. The goal is to enter the consumer's world as much as possible—observing how and when a service is used in an actual home environment.

LeoShe—a research division made up of female employees of Toronto-based Leo Burnett—has conducted year-long studies in which women participants are invited to ask six to eight female friends to have regular dinner dates in which they talk about specified topics. These "friendship groups" show that deeper insights are possible when people are in natural settings.

Observation can also involve entering the experience as a participant observer and watching what occurs rather than asking questions about it. One-on-one interviews, particularly with key informants in the culture rather than consumers themselves, can provide compelling insights about culture-based behaviour. Studying existing documents and cultural artifacts can also provide valuable insights, especially about lifestyles and usage patterns.[9]

Best Western International used this technique to better understand its senior market. Rather than bringing participants into focus group facilities and asking them questions, the company paid 25 over-55 couples to videotape themselves on cross-country journeys. The firm was able to listen to how couples actually made decisions rather than the way they reported them. The insights they gained from this research were decidedly different from what they would have learned otherwise. Most noteworthy was the finding that seniors who talked hotel clerks into better deals on rooms did not need the lower price to afford staying at the hotel—they were simply after the thrill of the deal, as illustrated in this description:

> The 60-ish woman caught on the grainy videotape is sitting on her hotel bed, addressing her husband after a long day spent on the road. "Good job!" she exults. "We beat the s—t out of the front desk and got a terrific room."[10]

These customers then spent their discount money on better dinners elsewhere, contributing nothing to Best Western. "The degree of discount clearly isn't what it used to be in importance—and we got that right out of the research," claimed the manager of programs for Best Western.[11] This finding would be highly unlikely using traditional research and asking customers directly, for few customers would admit to being willing to pay a higher price for a service!

Mystery Shopping

In this form of research, which is unique to services (including retailing),[12] companies hire outside research organizations to send people into service establishments and experience the service as if they were customers. These "mystery shoppers" are trained in the criteria important to customers of the establishment. They deliver objective assessments about service performance by completing questionnaires about service standards. Questionnaires contain items that represent important quality or service issues to customers. Central, a regional chain of home improvement retail stores located in Nova Scotia, and Canadian Tire Automotive are just two examples of firms that use this technique. The mystery shoppers ask questions of service personnel and/or purchase products, then fill out a form detailing the level of service they received. The service experience might be evaluated on any number of predetermined criteria, such as employee helpfulness, employee knowledge, promptness of service, and store cleanliness.

Mystery shopping keeps workers on their toes, because they know they may be evaluated at any time. They know they are being judged on the company's service standards and therefore carry out the standards more consistently than if they were not going to be judged.

Customer Panels

Customer panels are ongoing groups of customers assembled to provide attitudes and perceptions about a service over time. They offer a company regular and timely customer information—virtually a pulse on the market. Firms can use customer panels to represent large segments of end customers.

Customer panels are used in the entertainment industry to screen movies before they are released. After a rough cut of a film has been created, the movie is viewed by a panel of consumers that matches the demographic target. In the most basic of these panels, consumers report on their responses to the movie. On the basis of these panels, movies are revised and edited to ensure that they will succeed in the marketplace. In extreme situations, entire endings of movies have been changed to be more consistent with customer attitudes. In some of the most sophisticated consumer panel research on movies (also used for television shows and commercials) consumers have digital devices in their seats through which they indicate their responses as they watch films. This instantaneous response allows the producers, directors, and editors to make changes at the appropriate places in the film to ensure that the story line, characters, and scenery are "tracking."

Lost Customer Research

This type of research involves deliberately seeking customers who have dropped the company's service to inquire about their reasons for leaving. Some lost customer research is similar to exit interviews with employees in that it asks open-ended, in-depth questions to expose the reasons for defection and the particular events that led to dissatisfaction. For example, Sobeys, a leading national grocer, had store managers telephone customers who had suddenly stopped shopping in their stores. It is also possible to use more standard surveys on lost customers.

One benefit of this type of research is that it identifies failure points and common problems in the service and can help establish an early-warning system for future defectors. Another benefit is that the research can be used to calculate the cost of lost customers.

Future Expectations Research

Customer expectations are dynamic and can change very rapidly. As competition increases, as tastes change, and as consumers become more knowledgeable, companies must continue to update their information and strategies. One such "industry" is interactive video, representing the merger of computer, telecommunications, and cable television. The technologies available in this industry are revolutionary. In dynamic market situations, companies want to understand not just current customer expectations but also future expectations—the service features desired in the future. Future expectations research is new and includes different types. First, *features research* involves environmental scanning and querying of customers about desirable features of possible services. *Lead user research* brings in customers who are opinion leaders/innovators and asks them what requirements are not currently being met by existing products or services. Another form of this research is the *synectics approach*, which defines lead users more broadly than in standard lead user research.

The question of customer involvement in expectation studies is often debated. Designers and developers claim that consumers do not know what they might want, especially in industries or services that are new and rapidly changing. Consumers and marketing researchers, on the other hand, counter that services developed independent of customer input are likely to be targeted at needs that do not exist. To study this question, researchers assessed the contributions made by users compared with professional developers for end-user telecom services. Three groups were studied: users alone, developers alone, and users with a design expert present to provide information on feasibility. Findings showed that users created more original but less producible ideas. However, inviting users to test and explore possibilities once a prototype has been created can produce positive results.[13]

ANALYZING AND INTERPRETING RESEARCH FINDINGS

One of the biggest challenges facing a researcher is converting a complex set of data to a form that can be read and understood quickly by employees who will make decisions. Many of the people who use marketing research findings have not been trained in statistics and have neither the time nor the expertise to analyze computer printouts and other technical research information. The goal in this stage of the research process is to communicate information clearly to the right people in a timely fashion. Among considerations are the following: Who gets this information? Why do they need it? How will they use it? Does it mean the same thing across cultures? (See the Global Feature box.) When users feel confident that they understand the data, they are far more likely to apply it appropriately. When managers do not understand how to interpret the data, or when they lack confidence in the research, the investment of time, skill, and effort will be lost.

Depicting research findings graphically is a powerful way to communicate research information. Here are a sample of graphic representations of the types of research data we have discussed throughout this chapter.

Tracking of Performance, Gap Scores, and Competition

A simple way of tracking performance is shown in Figure 6.4. Both expectations and perceptions are plotted, and the gap between them shows the service quality shortfall. Although any attribute or dimension of service can be tracked, Figure 6.4 shows only the scores for service reliability. Competitor service performance is another frequently tracked service quality measurement. It allows managers to have a better grasp of service improvement priorities for their firm by comparing the firm's service strengths and weaknesses against those of key competitors.[14]

Zones of Tolerance Charts

When companies collect data on the dual expectation levels described in Chapter 4 —desired service and adequate service—along with performance data, they can

FIGURE 6.4

Tracking of
Customer
Expectations and
Perceptions of
Service Reliability

Source: E. Sivadas, "Europeans
Have a Different Take on
CS [Customer Satisfaction]
Programs," *Marketing News*,
October 26, 1998, p. 39.
Reprinted by permission
of the American Marketing
Association.

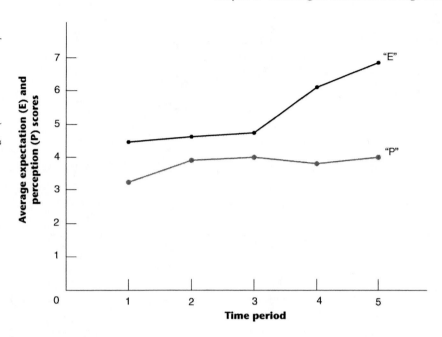

convey the information concisely on zones of tolerance charts. Figure 6.5 plots
customer quality perceptions relative to customers' zones of tolerance. Perceptions
of company performance are indicated by the circles, and the zones of tolerance
boxes are bounded on the top by the desired service score and on the bottom by the
adequate service score. When the perception scores are within the boxes, as in the
figure, the company is delivering service that is above customers' minimum level
of expectations. When the perception scores are below the boxes, the company's
service performance is lower than the minimum level, and customers are dissatisfied
with the company's service.[15]

FIGURE 6.5

Service Quality
Perceptions
Relative to Zones
of Tolerance by
Dimensions

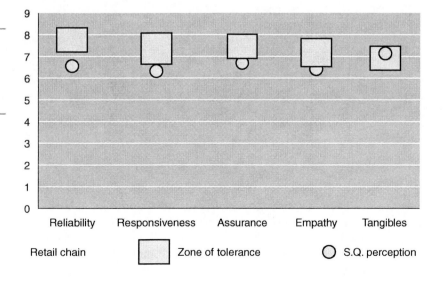

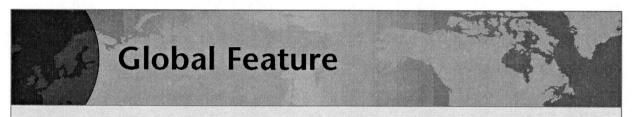

Global Feature

Culture Influences Marketing Research

Marketing research practices that are developed in North America are not always directly transferable to other cultures. Customer satisfaction measurement and CRM (customer relationship management), both created in the United States, are easily used in Canada with little modification. They do, however, have relevance in other countries and geographies but must be adapted to key differences that require a deep understanding of culture. In this box, we discuss how customer research, and specifically CRM, must be adapted in Asia.

CUSTOMER RELATIONSHIP MANAGEMENT IN ASIA

Don Peppers and Martha Rogers, consultants in CRM and related areas, have noted the Western orientation of CRM and have emphasized that inherent values in the CRM literature do not fit with Asian values. Whereas CRM literature in the United States assumes that customers will "unerringly respond [on] the basis of self-interest and self-gratification," Asian values—such as delayed gratification, loyalty to family and clan, and *Guanxi* (networks of obligations and connections)—must be taken into account if CRM is to succeed in Asia. As the consultants point out, customer relationships are different in Asia in these ways:

• Language preferences are more complex in China than in the United States. Chinese/Malaysian customers may speak one Chinese dialect

formally, transact business in Bahasa Malay, and complete legal documents in English. Knowing these differences customizes a relationship, but very few CRM systems can accommodate this level of customization.

• Customer names are very different in societies that are racially diverse. Some names are very long and do not have surnames. Chinese names start with the last (family) names and then are followed by the first and second given names. As you probably know from your Chinese classmates, Chinese people also sometimes give themselves Western names. Recognizing all these differences is very difficult for a CRM system.

• Some Asian customers have more than one marriage, family, and address. Sending information, such as for life insurance or financial services, to the wrong address violates privacy and can create very difficult situations!

• Asians will rarely tell anyone their net worth, because of a cultural bias against flaunting wealth. Therefore, it is difficult to find out which customers are most valuable on the basis of their income.

For these and other reasons, CRM has been adopted much more slowly in Asia than in Canada and the U.S.

Source: A. Berhad and T. Tyler, "Customer Relationship Management in Asia: A Cross Cultural Case Study Based on Aetna Universal Insurance" (Norwalk, CT: Peppers & Rogers Group, 2001).

Importance/Performance Matrices

One of the most useful forms of analysis in marketing research is the importance/performance matrix. Such a chart combines information about customer perceptions and importance ratings. An example is shown in Figure 6.6. Attribute importance is represented on the vertical axis from high (top) to low (bottom). Performance is shown on the horizontal axis from low (left) to high (right). There are many variations of these matrices; some companies define the horizontal axis as the gap between expectations

FIGURE 6.6

Importance/
Performance Matrix

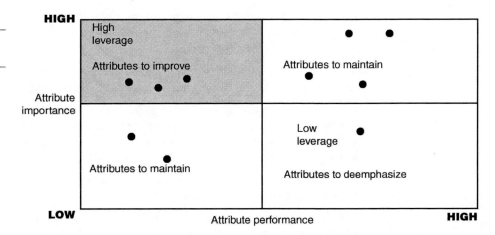

and perceptions, or as performance relative to competition. The shading on the chart indicates the area of highest leverage for service quality improvements—where importance is high and performance is low. In this quadrant are the attributes that most need to be improved. In the adjacent upper quadrant are attributes to be maintained, ones that a company performs well and that are very important to customers. The lower two quadrants contain attributes that are less important, some of which are performed well and others poorly. Neither of these quadrants merit as much attention in terms of service improvements as the upper quadrants because customers are not as concerned about the attributes that are plotted in them as they are the attributes in the upper quadrants.

MODEL SERVICES RESEARCH PROGRAMS

We have chosen three companies to illustrate comprehensive and effective programs that have sustained close customer–company relationships.

Disney

Most visitors to Walt Disney theme parks see magic, but the magic is based on solid research discipline. Disney conducts over 200 different external surveys a year, tracking satisfaction along with demographic profiles of its customers. The company also conducts price-sensitivity analysis to determine the tolerance of guests for various levels of pricing. One recent outcome of this analysis was the FastPass, a premium-priced ticket to the park that allows its purchasers to avoid lines and expedite their access to rides and other attractions. The company also has guests evaluate its different attractions, noting the aspects that are pleasing or troublesome and changing aspects to ensure that the attractions run as smoothly as possible. In addition, the company monitors tens of thousands of letters and comment cards it receives and practises "management by walking around." By doing so, Disney gathers critical information and enables the design of a service experience that delights its guests.[16]

FedEx

FedEx, the first major service company to win the U.S. Malcolm Baldridge National Quality Award, has a strong and comprehensive program of marketing and customer satisfaction research.[17] Its program includes:

- Customer requirements and expectations, gleaned from multiple qualitative and quantitative research studies, feedback from sales professionals, and feedback from customer service professionals.

- Toll-free numbers for complaints, which are systematically captured and dispatched to responsible parties. Trends are also tracked and analyzed.

- Customer satisfaction studies, with objectives of assessing satisfaction, identifying reasons for dissatisfaction, and monitoring satisfaction over time. This involves 2,400 telephone interviews per quarter measuring 17 domestic service attributes, 22 export service attributes, eight drop-box attributes, and eight service centre attributes.

- Ten targeted satisfaction studies on specialized business functions. These are direct-mail, self-administered surveys.

- Satisfaction monitoring at every point of interaction with the customer, some through transaction-based studies and others using operational measures driven by customer requirements.

- A comment card program, monitoring satisfaction with counter service.

- Customer satisfaction studies in world markets, focusing on understanding how service delivery must be adapted to global markets.

MuchMusic

MuchMusic, recently dubbed *Strategy Magazine*'s "Overall Brand of the Year," has taken listening to its customers to a whole new level, and that can't be easy when its target customers are changing as quickly as Canadian teenagers.

Listening closely to its audience is a core brand value at MuchMusic (Figure 6.7). The policy is based not only on traditional marketing research, but also—and even more so—on interacting with the audience and letting the audience set the agenda. MuchMusic has perfected listening with its MuchOnDemand program. Razer is a brand extension that lets customers program, select, and even host shows. PunchMuch lets customers request videos and join onscreen chats and polling—naturally, the polls drive the program.

FIGURE 6.7

MuchMusic is an industry leader in listening to its customers.

Source: Courtesy of MuchMusic.

Now MuchMusic has formalized its listening with an online research panel of 2,000 viewers aged 12 to 34. "It's an opportunity to have access to our viewers. ... [Moreover] it provides us with a framework on a balanced research level."[18]

Conducting research about customer expectations is only the first part of understanding the customer, even if the research is appropriately designed, executed, and presented. A service firm must also use the research findings in a meaningful way—to drive improvement in the way service is delivered. The misuse (or even nonuse) of research data can lead to a large gap in understanding customer expectations. Understanding how to make the best use of research—to apply what has been learned to the business—is a key way to close Provider Gap 1, the gap between customer expectations and management perceptions of customer expectations.

⟶ UPWARD COMMUNICATION

In some service firms, especially small ones, owners or managers may be in constant contact with customers. But in large service organizations, managers do not always get the opportunity to experience firsthand what their customers want.

The larger a company is, the more difficult it will be for managers to interact directly with the customer and the less firsthand information they will have about customer expectations. To truly understand customer needs, management benefits from hands-on knowledge of what really happens in stores, on customer service telephone lines, in service queues, and in face-to-face service encounters. If Gap 1 is to be closed, managers in large firms need some form of customer contact.

Objectives for Upward Communication

Exhibit 6.3 shows the major research objectives for improving upward communication. These objectives can be met by two types of interactive activities in the organization: one designed to improve the type and effectiveness of communications from customers to management, and the other designed to improve communications between employees and management.

Research for Upward Communication

Executive Visits to Customers

This approach is frequently used in business-to-business services marketing. In some visits, executives of the company make sales or service calls with customer contact personnel (salespeople). In other situations, executives of the selling company arrange meetings with executives at a similar level in client companies. When Lou Gerstner became CEO of IBM, one of his first actions was to arrange a meeting with 175 of the company's biggest customers for a discussion of how IBM can better meet their needs.

Executive or Management Listening to Customers

The marketing director at Milliken, a textile and chemicals firm, called his experience working the swing shift "naive listening," and he described its benefits as follows:

> Getting close to the customer is a winner! ... I worked the second shift (3:00 p.m. to midnight) and actually cleaned carpeting as well as hard-surface floors. I operated all the machinery they used daily, plus handled the same housekeeping problems .... Now I can put together my trade advertising as well as my entire merchandising program based directly upon the needs of my customers as I observed them. ... I'm learning—from new-product introduction to maintenance of existing products—exactly what our health care customers require.[19]

→ EXHIBIT 6.3

Elements in an Effective Program of Upward Communication

Type of Interaction or Research	Research Objective	Qualitative/ Quantitative	Cost of Information		
			Money	**Time**	**Frequency**
Executive visits to customers	To gain firsthand knowledge about customers	Qualitative	Moderate	Moderate	Continuous
Executive listenings	To gain firsthand knowledge about customers	Qualitative	Low	Low	Continuous
Research on intermediate customers	To gain in-depth information on end customers	Quantitative	Moderate	Moderate	Annual
Employee internal satisfaction surveys	To improve internal service quality	Quantitative	Moderate	Moderate	Annual
Employee visits or listenings	To gain firsthand knowledge about employees	Qualitative	Moderate	Moderate	Continuous
Employee suggestions	To obtain ideas for service improvements	Qualitative	Low	Low	Continuous

As this example illustrates, direct interaction with customers adds clarity and depth to managers' understanding of customer expectations and needs.

Managers can also spend time on the line, interacting with customers and experiencing service delivery. A formal program for encouraging informal interaction is often the best way to ensure that the contact takes place. At Loyalty Marketing Group Canada Inc., which operates Canada's most widely recognized loyalty program, the AIR MILES® Reward Program (Figure 6.8), the entire marketing department "double-jacks" on the phones in the customer care centre. AIR MILES president Bryan Pearson also meets with call centre specialists during regular lunchtime meetings.[20]

Research on Intermediate Customers

Intermediate customers (such as contact employees, dealers, distributors, agents, and brokers) are people the company serves who serve the end customer. Researching the needs and expectations of these customers *in serving the end customer* can be a useful and efficient way to both improve service to and obtain information about end users. It can also help the company learn about and satisfy the service expectations of intermediate customers, a process critical in their providing quality service to end customers.

FIGURE 6.8

Air Miles® marketing staff "double-jack" on the call centre phones to ensure they know what their customers expect.

Source: Reprinted by permission of The Loyalty Group.

Research on Internal Customers (Employees)

Employees who perform services are themselves customers of internal services on which they depend heavily to do their jobs well. There is a strong and direct link between the quality of internal service that employees receive and the quality of service they provide. For this reason it is important to conduct employee research that focuses on the service that internal customers give and receive. In many companies this focus requires adapting existing employee opinion research to focus on service satisfaction. Employee research complements customer research when service quality is the issue being investigated. Customer research provides insight into what is occurring, whereas employee research provides insight into why. The two types of research play unique and equally important roles in improving service quality. Companies that focus service quality research exclusively on external customers are missing a rich and vital source of information.[21]

Executive or Management Listening Approaches to Employees

Employees who actually perform the service have the best possible vantage point for observing the service and identifying impediments to its quality. Customer contact personnel are in regular contact with customers and thereby come to understand a great deal about customer expectations and perceptions.[22] If the information they know can be passed on to top management, top managers' understanding of the customer may improve. In fact, it could be said that in many companies, top management's understanding of the customer depends largely on the extent and types of communication received from customer contact personnel and from noncompany contact personnel (like independent insurance agents and retailers) who represent the company and its services. When these channels of communication are closed, management may not get feedback about problems encountered in service delivery and about how customer expectations are changing.

Sam Walton, the late founder of Wal-Mart, once remarked, "Our best ideas come from delivery and stock boys."[23] To stay in touch with the source of new ideas, Walton spent endless hours in stores working the floor, helping clerks, or approving personal cheques, even showing up at the loading dock with a bag of doughnuts for a surprised crew of workers.[24] He was well known for having his plane drop him next to a wheat field where he would meet a Wal-Mart truck driver. Giving his pilot instructions to meet him at another landing strip more than 320 kilometres down the road, he would make the trip with the Wal-Mart driver, listening to what he had to say about the company.

Managers who stay close to their contact people benefit not only by keeping their employees happy but also by learning more about their customers.[25] These companies encourage, appreciate, and reward upward communication from contact people. VIA Rail is instituting face-to-face meetings of cross-functional teams and meetings between customer relations and marketing staff to get deeper insights into the customers' experience. Through these important channels, management learns about customer expectations from employees in regular contact with customers and can thereby reduce the size of Gap 1.

Employee Suggestions

Most companies have some form of employee suggestion program whereby contact personnel can communicate to management their ideas for improving work. Suggestion systems have come a long way from the traditional suggestion box. Effective suggestion systems are ones in which employees are empowered to see their suggestions through, where supervisors can implement proposals immediately, where employees participate for continuous improvement in their jobs, where supervisors respond quickly to ideas, and where coaching is provided in ways to handle suggestions. (Recall the chapter opening vignette featuring Toronto-Dominion Bank Financial Group, which illustrated the value placed on employee insight for that firm.) In today's companies, suggestions from employees are facilitated by self-directed work teams that encourage employees to identify problems and then work to develop solutions to those problems.

SUMMARY

This chapter discussed the role of marketing research in understanding customer perceptions and expectations. After first describing criteria for effective services research, the chapter defined key forms of services research including critical incidents studies, mystery shopping, service expectation meetings and reviews, process checkpoint evaluations, and database research. Important topics in researching services—including developing research objectives and presenting data—were also described. Finally, upward communication, ways in which management obtains and uses information from customers and customer contact personnel, was discussed. These topics combine to close Provider Gap 1 between customer expectations and company understanding of customer expectations, the first of four Provider Gaps in the Gaps model of service quality.

⟶ Discussion Questions

1. Give five reasons why research objectives must be established before marketing research is conducted.

2. Why are both qualitative and quantitative research methods needed in a services marketing research program?

3. Why does the frequency of research differ across the research methods shown in Exhibit 6.1?

4. Compare and contrast the types of research that help a company identify common failure points (see column 2 in Exhibit 6.1). Which of the types do you think produces better information? Why?

5. In what situations does a service company need requirements research?

6. What reasons can you give for companies' lack of use of research information? How might you motivate managers to use the information to a greater extent? How might you motivate front-line workers to use the information?

7. Given a specific marketing research budget, what would be your recommendations for the percentage to be spent on customer research versus upward communication? Why?

8. What kinds of information might be gleaned from research on intermediate customers? What would intermediate customers know that service providers might not?

9. For what types of products and services would research on the Internet be preferable to traditional research?

⟶ Exercises

1. Choose a local services organization to interview about marketing research. Find out what the firm's objectives are and the types of marketing research it currently uses. Using the information in this chapter, think about the effectiveness of its marketing research. What are the strengths? Weaknesses?

2. Choose one of the services you consume. If you were in charge of creating a survey for that service, what questions would you ask on the survey? Give several examples. What type of survey (relationship vs. transaction-based) would be most appropriate for the service? What recommendations would you give to management of the company about making such a survey actionable?

3. If you were the marketing director of your college or university, what types of research (see Exhibit 6.1) would be essential for understanding both external and internal customers? If you could choose only three types of research, which ones would you select? Why?

4. Using the SERVQUAL scale in this chapter, create a questionnaire for a service firm that you use. Give the questionnaire to 10 people, and describe what you learn.

5. To get an idea of the power of the critical incidents technique, try it yourself with reference to restaurant service. Think of a time when, as a customer, you had a particularly satisfying interaction with a restaurant. Follow the instructions here,

which are identical to the instructions in an actual study, and observe the insights you obtain about your requirements in restaurant service:

a. When did the incident happen?

b. What specific circumstances led up to this situation?

c. Exactly what did the employee (or firm) say or do?

d. What resulted that made you feel the interaction was satisfying?

e. What could or should have been done differently?

Notes

1. TD Bank annual report, 2005, available at www.td.com.

2. A. Parasuraman, L. L. Berry, and V. A. Zeithaml, "Guidelines for Conducting Service Quality Research," *Marketing Research: A Magazine of Management and Applications*, December 1990, pp. 34–44.

3. This section is based on a comprehensive assessment of the critical incident technique in D. D. Gremler, "The Critical Incident Technique in Service Research," *Journal of Service Research* 7 (August 2004), pp. 65–89.

4. Ibid.

5. E. E. Lueke and T. W. Suther III, "Market-Driven Quality: A Market Research and Product Requirements Methodology," *IBM Technical Report*, June 1991.

6. Jake McCaul, quoted in S. Yaffe, "Going Deep: Getting to Know Customers Better Than They Know Themselves Means Asking Different Questions Differently," *Strategy Magazine*, February 2005, p. 9.

7. Susan Bardwell, quoted in S. Yaffe, p. 9.

8. See V. A. Zeithaml and A. Parasuraman, *Service Quality*, MSI Relevant Knowledge Series (Cambridge, MA: Marketing Science Institute, 2004) for a complete review of this research, including the many publications by the original authors of SERVQUAL and the extensions by other authors.

9. E. Day, "Researchers Must Enter Consumer's World," *Marketing News*, August 17, 1998, p. 17.

10. G. Khermouch, "Consumers in the Mist," *BusinessWeek*, February 26, 2001, pp. 92–93.

11. Ibid., p. 92.

12. For examples, see S. J. Grove and R. P. Fiske, "Observational Data Collection Methods for Services Marketing: An Overview," *Journal of the Academy of Marketing Science* 20 (Summer 1992), pp. 117–214.

13. P. R. Magnusson, J. Mathing, and P. Kristensson, "Managing User Involvement in Service Innovation: Experiments with Innovating End Users," *Journal of Service Research* 6 (November 2003), pp. 111–24.

14. V. A. Zeithaml, A. Parasuraman, and L. L. Berry, Delivering Quality Service: *Balancing Customer Perceptions and Expectations* (New York: Free Press, 1990), p. 28.

15. A. Parasuraman, V. A. Zeithaml, and L. L. Berry, "Moving Forward in Service Quality Research," *Marketing Science Institute Report No. 94-114*, September 1994.

16. R. Johnson, "A Strategy for Service—Disney Style," *Journal of Business Strategy*, September/October 1991, pp. 38–43.

17. "Multiple Measures Give FedEx Its 'Good' Data," *The Service Edge*, June 1991, p. 6.
18. Natalia Williams, "Much Accomplishment," *Strategy Magazine*, November 2005, p. 37.
19. T. J. Peters and N. Austin, *A Passion for Excellence* (New York: Random House, 1985), p. 16.
20. L. D'Innocenzo, *Strategy Magazine*, November 2005, p. 14.
21. "Baldridge Winner Co-convenes Quality Summit," *Executive Report on Customer Satisfaction*, October 30, 1992.
22. M. J. Bitner, B. Booms, and L. Mohr, "Critical Service Encounters: The Employee's Viewpoint," *Journal of Marketing* 58 (October 1994), pp. 95–106.
23. S. Koepp, "Make That Sale, Mr. Sam," *Time*, May 18, 1987.
24. Ibid.
25. Zeithaml, Parasuraman, and Berry, *Delivering Quality Service*, p. 64.

Chapter 7

Building Customer Relationships

Provider Gap 1

THIS CHAPTER'S OBJECTIVES ARE TO

THIS CHAPTER'S OBJECTIVES ARE TO

1. Explain relationship marketing, its goals, and the benefits of long-term relationships for firms and customers.

2. Explain why and how to estimate customer relationship value.

3. Introduce the concept of customer profitability segments as a strategy for focusing relationship marketing efforts.

4. Present relationship development strategies—including quality core service, switching barriers, and relationship bonds.

5. Identify challenges in relationship development, including the somewhat controversial idea that "the customer is not always right."

REALITY TELEVISION HAS BEGUN BUILDING RELATIONSHIPS WITH VIEWERS

Gone are the days when individuals had only a handful of television channels from which to choose to satisfy their at-home entertainment needs. Today, with a variety of different media options, including several hundred television channels readily accessible, it is becoming increasingly difficult for show creators and networks to create and retain loyal viewers. That is, it was—until reality television made its debut in North America just a few years ago.

These shows have been able to quickly acquire millions of viewers. Discussion of their content has replaced news topics and other traditional programming in many "water cooler conversations" across the continent. These shows seem to offer something for everyone in a variety of genres. There are game shows such as *Survivor, Fear Factor*, and *The Amazing Race*; makeover programs such as *Extreme Makeover* and *The Biggest Loser*; and talent competitions such as *American Idol* (www.americanidol. com), *Canadian Idol* (www.idol.ctv.ca), *Nashville Star* (www.usanetwork. com/series/nashvillestar), and *Rock Star Supernova* (www.rockstar.msn. com). As will be discussed in Chapter 7, simply acquiring customers (or viewers) does not a relationship make; but it is a necessary first step.

Among reality shows, the talent genre as a whole seems to have taken its relationship-building efforts with viewers to the next level. On the *American Idol* model, the *Canadian Idol* franchise and shows like it have begun allowing greater levels of interactivity with their audiences in several ways. First, the shows allow viewers to voice their opinion in a very tangible way—they can vote for contestants and influence the show's outcome. Also, most programming of this kind engages in cross-promotion with wireless companies, and all have created online communities with many interesting relationship programs to make the TV experience more personal. Some sites provide access to chat rooms; one *Nashville Star* judge sought and answered viewer questions on the show's site; *Rock Star* contestants regularly post entries in online journals; and *Canadian Idols* blog regularly, and have even designed their own T-shirts sold through the site.

By maintaining greater contact with viewers and monitoring audience feedback, show producers can begin to close Provider Gap 1—Not Knowing What Customers Expect—and increase their focus on viewer retention.

Source: Canadian Idol is a trademark of 19 TV Limited and FremantleMedia North America Inc. (www. fremantlemedia.com). Logo used with permisssion from FremantleMedia North America, Inc.

As noted at the beginning of Chapter 6, closing Provider Gap 1—Not Knowing What Customers Expect—is easier for companies who focus on keeping their customers and building long-term relationships with them. However, many companies fail to understand customers accurately, because they fail to focus on customer relationships. They tend to fixate on acquiring new customers rather than viewing customers as assets that they need to nurture and retain. By concentrating on new customers, firms can fall into the traps of short-term promotions, price discounts, or catchy ads that bring customers in but are not enough to bring them back. By adopting a relationship philosophy, on the other hand, companies begin to understand customers over time and in great depth, and are better able to meet their changing needs and expectations. In so doing, they can help to ensure Provider Gap 1 is kept as small as possible.

⟼ RELATIONSHIP MARKETING

> There has been a shift from a transactions to a relationship focus in marketing. Customers become partners and the firm must make long-term commitments to maintaining those relationships with quality, service, and innovation.[1]

Relationship marketing essentially represents a paradigm shift within marketing—away from an acquisitions/transaction focus toward a retention/relationship focus.[2] Relationship marketing is a philosophy of doing business that focuses on *keeping and improving* relationships with current customers rather than on acquiring new customers. This philosophy assumes that many customers prefer to have an ongoing relationship with one organization than to switch continually among providers in their search for value. Building on this assumption and the fact that it is usually much cheaper to keep a current customer than to attract a new one, successful marketers are working on effective strategies for retaining customers.

It has been suggested that firms frequently focus on attracting customers (the "first act") but then pay little attention to what they should do to keep them (the "second act").[3] Ideas expressed in an interview with James L. Schorr, then executive vice-president of marketing at Holiday Inns, illustrate this point.[4] In the interview he stated that he was famous at Holiday Inns for what is called the "bucket theory of marketing." By this he meant that marketing can be thought of as a big bucket: it is what the sales, advertising, and promotion programs do that pours business into the top of the bucket. As long as these programs are effective, the bucket stays full. However, "There's only one problem," he said, "there's a hole in the bucket." When the business is running well and the hotel is delivering on its promises, the hole is small and few customers are leaving. When the operation is weak and customers are not satisfied with what they get, however, people start falling out of the bucket through the holes faster than they can be poured in through the top.

The bucket theory illustrates why a relationship strategy that focuses on plugging the holes in the bucket makes so much sense. Historically, marketers have been more concerned with acquisition of customers, so a shift to a relationship strategy often represents changes in mindset, organizational culture, and employee reward systems. For example, the sales incentive systems in many organizations are set up to reward bringing in new customers. There are often fewer (or no) rewards for retaining current accounts. Thus, even when people see the logic of customer retention, the existing organizational systems may not support its implementation.

The Evolution of Customer Relationships

Firms' relationships with their customers, like other social relationships, tend to evolve over time. Scholars have suggested that marketing exchange relationships between providers and customers often have the potential to evolve from strangers to acquaintances to friends to partners. Exhibit 7.1 illustrates different issues at each successive level of the relationship.[5]

Customers as Strangers

Strangers are those customers who are not aware of or, perhaps, those who have not yet had any transactions (interactions) with a firm. Consequently, the firm's primary goal with these potential customers ("strangers") is to initiate communication with them in order to *attract* them and *acquire* their business.

━━▶ EXHIBIT 7.1

A Typology of Exchange Relationships

Customers As ...	Strangers	Acquaintances	Friends	Partners
Product offering	Attractive relative to competative offerings or alternative purchases.	Parity product as a form of industry standard.	Differentiated product adapted to specific market segments.	Customized product and dedicated resources adapted to an individual customer or organization.
Source of competitive advantage	Attractiveness	Satisfaction	Satisfaction + trust	Satisfaction + trust + commitment
Buying activity	Interest, exploration, and trial.	Satisfaction facilitates and reinforces buying activity and reduces need to search for market information.	Trust in firm is needed to continue the buying activity without perfect information.	Commitment in the form of information sharing and idiosyncratic investments is needed to achieve customized product and to adjust product continuously to changing needs and situations.
Focus of selling	Awareness of firm's offerings (encouraging trial) facilitates initial selling.	Familiarity and general knowledge of customer (identification) facilitates selling.	Specific knowledge of customer's connection to segment need and situation facilitates selling.	Specific knowledge of customer's need and situation and idiosyncratic investments facilitates selling.
Relationship time horizon	None: Buyer may have had no previous interactions with or knowledge of the firm.	Short: Generally short because the buyer can often switch firms without much effort or cost.	Medium: Generally longer than aquaintance relationships because trust in a differentiated position takes a longer time to build and imitate.	Long: Generally long because it takes time to build and replace interconnected activities and to develop a detailed knowledge of a customer's needs and the unique resources of a supplier to commit resources to the relationship.

continued

EXHIBIT 7.1
—continued

Customers As ...	Strangers	Acquaintances	Friends	Partners
Sustainability of competitive advantage	Low: Generally low, as firm must continually find ways to be attractive, in terms of the value offered, in order to induce trial.	Low: Generally low, but competitors can vary in how they build unique value into selling and serving even if the product is a form of industry standard.	Medium: Generally medium but depends on competitors' ability to understand heterogeneity of customer needs and situations and the ability to transform this knowledge into meaningful, differentiated products.	High: Generally high but depends on how unique and effective the interconnected activities between customer and supplier are organized.
Primary relationship marketing goal	*Acquire* customer's business.	*Satisfy* customer's needs and wants.	*Retain* customer's business.	*Enhance* relationship with customer.

Source: Adapted from M. D. Johnson and F. Seines, "Customer Portfolio Management: Toward a Dynamic Theory of Exchange Relationships," *Journal of Marketing* 68 (April 2004), p. 5. Reprinted by permission of the American Marketing Association.

Customers as Acquaintances

Once customer awareness and trial are achieved, familiarity is established and the customer and the firm become acquaintances, creating the basis for an exchange relationship. A primary goal for the firm at this stage of the relationship is *satisfying* the customer. In the acquaintance stage, firms are generally concerned about providing a value proposition to customers that is comparable with that of competitors. An acquaintanceship is effective as long as the customer is relatively satisfied with what is being received. With repetitive interactions, the customer gains experience and becomes more familiar with the firm. These encounters can help reduce uncertainty about the benefits expected in the exchange and, therefore, increase the attractiveness of the company relative to the competition. Repetitive interactions improve the firm's knowledge of the customer, helping to facilitate marketing, sales, and service efforts. Thus, an acquaintance relationship facilitates transactions primarily through the reduction of the customer's perceived risk and the provider's costs.

Customers as Friends

As a customer continues to make purchases from a firm, the firm begins to acquire specific knowledge of the customer's needs, allowing it to create an offering that directly addresses the customer's situation. The provision of a unique offering, and thus differential value, transforms the exchange relationship from acquaintance to friendship. This transition from acquaintanceship to friendship, particularly in service exchange relationships, requires the development of trust.[6] As discussed in an earlier chapter, customers may not be able to assess a service outcome prior to purchase and consumption, and for those services high in credence qualities, customers may not be able to discern service performance even after experiencing it. Therefore, customers must trust the provider to do what is promised. As customers become friends they not only become familiar with the company but also come to trust that it provides superior value.

A primary goal for firms at the friendship stage of the relationship is customer *retention*. Given their likelihood of past satisfying experiences and repeated purchases, these customers ("friends") are more likely to appreciate the firm's product offerings and are more open to other related services. A firm's potential to develop sustainable competitive advantage through friends should be higher than for acquaintances, because the offering is more unique (and more difficult for competition to imitate) and the customer comes to trust that uniqueness.[7]

Customers as Partners

As a customer continues to interact with a firm, the level of trust often deepens and the customer may receive more customized product offerings and interactions. The trust developed in the friendship stage is a necessary but not sufficient condition for a customer–firm partnership to develop.[8] That is, the creation of trust leads to (ideally) the creation of commitment—and that is the condition necessary for customers to extend the time perspective of a relationship.[9] The deepening of trust and the establishment of commitment reduce the customer's need to solve problems in the traditional sense of "finding a better alternative." Thus, in order to move the relationship into a partner relationship, a firm must use customer knowledge and information systems to deliver highly personalized and customized offerings.

At the partnership stage, the firm is concerned with *enhancing* the relationship. Customers are more likely to stay in the relationship if they feel that the company understands their changing needs and is willing to invest in the relationship by constantly improving and evolving its product and service mix. By enhancing these relationships, the firm expects such customers to be less likely to be lured away by competitors and more likely to buy additional products and services from the company over time. These loyal customers not only provide a solid base for the organization, they may represent growth potential. A bank chequing account customer becomes a better customer when she sets up a savings account, takes out a loan, and/or uses the financial advising services of the bank. And a corporate account becomes a better customer when it chooses to do 75 percent of its business with a particular supplier rather than splitting the business equally among three suppliers. In recent years, in fact, many companies have aspired to be the "exclusive supplier" of a particular product or service for their customers. Over time these enhanced relationships can increase market share and profits for the organization. Our Technology Spotlight features Ritz-Carlton, which is successfully using information technology to enhance relationships with its customers.

The Goal of Relationship Marketing

The discussion of the evolution of customer relationships demonstrates how a firm's relationship with its customers might be enhanced as customers move further along this relationship continuum. As the relationship value of a customer increases, the provider is more likely to pursue a closer relationship. Thus, the primary goal of relationship marketing is *to build and maintain a base of committed customers who are profitable for the organization.* Figure 7.1 graphically illustrates the goals of relationship marketing. The overriding goal is to move customers up the ladder (i.e., along the relationship continuum) from the point at which they are strangers that need to be attracted through to the point at which they are highly valued, long-term customers whose relationship with the firm has been enhanced. From a customer's problem-solving perspective, the formation of satisfaction, trust, and commitment corresponds to being an acquaintance, friend, and partner, respectively. From a firm's resource-allocation perspective, the delivery of differential value corresponds to the extent of its desire to create an acquaintance, friend, or partner relationship with the customer. The AIC print ad shown in Figure 7.2 shows how one firm tries to communicate the need for a long-term relationship.

Benefits for Customers and Firms

Both parties in the customer–firm relationship can benefit from customer retention. That is, it is not only in the best interest of the organization to build and maintain a loyal customer base, but customers themselves also benefit from long-term associations.

Benefits for Customers

Assuming they have a choice, customers will remain loyal to a firm when they receive greater value relative to what they expect from competing firms. *Value* represents a tradeoff for the consumer between the "give" and the "get" components. Consumers are more likely to stay in a relationship when the gets (quality, satisfaction, specific

FIGURE 7.1

Customer goals of relationship marketing: acquiring customers, satisfying customers, retaining customers, and enhancing customers.

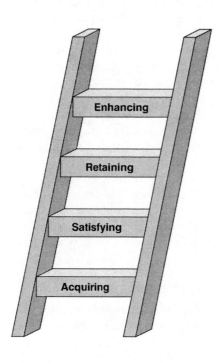

Enhancing

Retaining

Satisfying

Acquiring

FIGURE 7.2

AIC's way of showing that a long-term relationship is best.

Source: Reprinted with permission of AIC Limited.

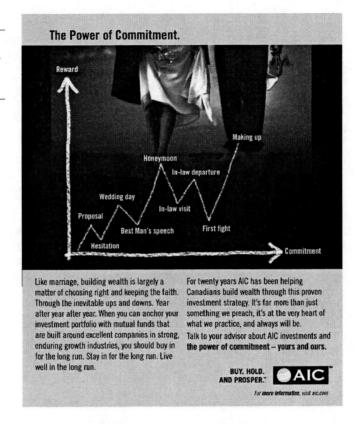

benefits) exceed the gives (monetary and nonmonetary costs). When firms can consistently deliver value from the customer's point of view, clearly the customer benefits and has an incentive to stay in the relationship. As noted in our Technology Spotlight, customers can't afford to forget about renewing important medical prescriptions. Being reminded can be a real help.

Beyond the specific inherent benefits of receiving service value, customers also benefit in other ways from long-term associations with firms. Sometimes these relationship benefits keep customers loyal to a firm more than the attributes of the core service. Research has uncovered specific types of relational benefits that customers experience in long-term service relationships including confidence benefits, social benefits, and special treatment benefits.[10]

Confidence Benefits Confidence benefits comprise feelings of trust or confidence in the provider along with a sense of reduced anxiety in knowing what to expect. Across all the services studied in the research just cited, confidence benefits were the most important to customers.

Human nature is such that most consumers would prefer not to change service providers, particularly when there is a considerable investment in the relationship. The costs of switching are frequently high in terms of dollar costs and associated psychological and time-related costs. Most customers have many competing demands on their time and money and are continually searching for ways to balance and simplify decision making to improve the quality of their lives. When they can maintain a relationship with a service provider, they free up time for other concerns and priorities.

Technology Spotlight

Customer Information Systems Help Enhance the Customer Relationship

The potential of today's customer information systems far exceeds any traditional marketing information system that has gone before. These new systems differ from the old in their scale (thousands of bits of information on tens of millions of customers), the depth of information that can be captured on each individual or household, and the ways in which the information can be used. In many cases, access to this type of information about individual customers allows the organization to customize to the individual level what previously would have been undifferentiated services.

For example, The Ritz-Carlton Hotel Company L.L.C. (www.ritzcarlton.com) targets its services to industry executives, meeting and corporate travel planners, and affluent travellers. Although there are many dimensions to the company's success, one of the keys is the quality of its customer database. By training each employee to note the likes and dislikes of regular guests and to enter this information immediately into the customer's file, employees at any Ritz-Carlton Hotel are able to personalize services to the Ritz-Carlton's 240,000 repeat customers. The employees can know in advance the guest's preferences and be prepared to provide individualized service even before the guest's arrival. For example, if a guest prefers a feather pillow, wants extra brown sugar with her oatmeal, or always orders a glass of sherry before retiring, this information can be entered into the database and these needs anticipated—often much to the guest's surprise.

Other examples abound. Dentist offices send reminders or make phone calls to patients when it is time to make an appointment for regular cleanings. The technology required is very simple, but the firm must still have made the commitment to deploy it.

In the Canadian retail sector, a growing concern among health care workers is the ongoing tendency for people to quit taking their medication. For conditions such as blood pressure, anxiety, cholesterol, or asthma, symptoms can eventually disappear. However, that often means the condition is merely under control, not cured. When patients stop taking their prescriptions, sometimes a visit to the emergency room is the result. A technologically simple, yet effective, way to reduce their risk of non-adherence is for pharmacies to set up a database and automatically fill soon-to-expire prescriptions. They then call the patient to advise them that their prescription is ready. This way, everyone benefits.

Welcome

TO

THE RITZ-CARLTON

How may we be of Assistance?

The Ritz-Carlton provides the finest personal service and facilities throughout the world. The atmosphere is warm and relaxed and the ambience embraces the uniqueness of the local culture. The variety of services offered will enable you to create your own experience.

Social Benefits   Over time, customers develop a sense of familiarity and even a social relationship with their service providers. These ties make it less likely that they will switch, even if they learn about a competitor that might have better quality or a lower price. This customer's description of her hair stylist illustrates the concept of social benefits: "I like him. . . . He's really funny and always has lots of good jokes. He's kind of like a friend now. . . . It's more fun to deal with somebody that you're used to. You enjoy doing business with them."

In some long-term customer–firm relationships, a service provider may actually become part of the consumer's social support system.[11] Hairdressers, as in the example just cited, often serve as personal confidants.

These types of personal relationships can develop for business-to-business customers as well as for end consumers of services. The social support benefits resulting from these relationships are important to the consumer's quality of life above and beyond the technical benefits of the service provided. Many times the close personal and professional relationships that develop between service providers and clients are the basis for the customer's loyalty. The flip side of this customer benefit is the risk to the firm of losing customers when a valued employee leaves the firm and takes customers with him or her.[12] We're probably all familiar with advertisements for hair stylists or automobile salespeople inviting former friends and clients to visit them at their new locations following a change in employers.

Special Treatment Benefits   Special treatment includes getting the benefit of the doubt, being given a special deal or price, or getting preferential treatment as exemplified by the following quote from the research:

> I think you get special treatment [when you have established a relationship]. My pediatrician allowed me to use the back door to the office so my daughter could avoid contact with other sick children. Other times I have been in a hurry and they take me right back.

Interestingly, special treatment benefits are less important than the other types of benefits received in service relationships.

Benefits for Firms

The benefits to organizations of developing a loyal customer are numerous. In addition to the economic benefits, a variety of customer behaviour benefits and human resource management benefits are also often received.

Economic Benefits   Research based on information contained in the Compustat and Compact Disclosure databases reveals that over the long run, relationship-oriented service firms achieve higher overall returns than do transaction-oriented firms.[13] These bottom-line benefits come from a variety of sources, including increased revenues over time from the customer, reduced marketing and administrative costs, and the ability to maintain margins without reducing prices.

One of the most commonly cited economic benefits of customer retention is increased purchases over time, as illustrated in Figure 7.3. The figure summarizes studies showing that customers generally spent more each year with a particular relationship partner than they did in the preceding period.[14] As customers get to know a firm, they give more of their business to the firm.

Another economic benefit is lower costs. Some estimates suggest that repeat purchases by established customers require as much as 90 percent less marketing expenditure.[15] Many startup costs are associated with attracting new customers, including advertising and other promotion costs, the operating costs of setting up new accounts, and time costs of getting to know the customers. Sometimes these initial costs can outweigh the revenue expected from the new customers in the short term, so it is to the firm's advantage to cultivate long-term relationships. In Chapter 18 we will provide more specifics on the financial impact of customer retention.

Customer Behaviour Benefits   The contribution that loyal customers make to a service business can go well beyond their direct financial impact on the firm.[16] The first benefit that a firm receives from long-term customers is free word-of-mouth advertising. When a product is difficult to evaluate and when risk is involved in the decision to buy it—as is the case with many services—consumers often look to

FIGURE 7.3

Profit Generated by a Customer over Time

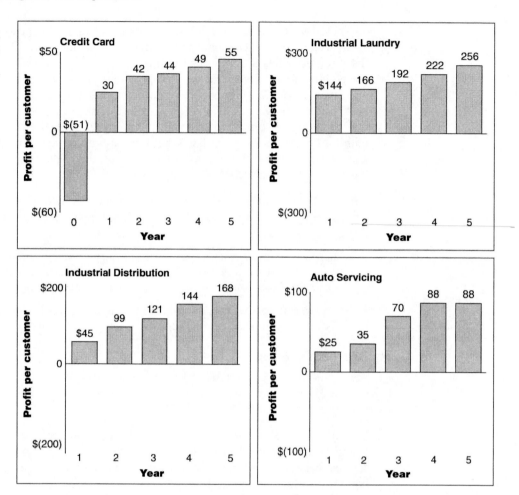

others for advice on which providers to consider. Satisfied, loyal customers are likely to provide a firm with strong word-of-mouth endorsements. This form of advertising can be more effective than any paid advertising that the firm might use, and it has the added benefit of reducing the costs of attracting new customers. Imagine, for instance, that you and your friends are planning an outdoor adventure vacation to British Columbia. Wouldn't you feel better about your decision of which tour operator to use if a close friend gave a glowing recommendation for a particular firm? Now, if you were that firm, wouldn't it be worth a little extra effort to ensure your former customers always gave glowing recommendations?

In addition to word-of-mouth communication, there is a second consumer behaviour benefit sometimes labelled customer voluntary performance;[17] in a restaurant, such behaviour might include reporting messy restrooms to an employee or picking up trash in the parking lot. Such behaviours support the firm's ability to deliver quality services. Third, for some services loyal customers may provide social benefits to other customers in the form of friendships or encouragement. At a physical therapy clinic, for example, a patient recovering from knee surgery is likely to think more highly of the clinic when fellow patients provide encouragement and emotional support during the rehabilitation process. That is precisely what happens at Shouldice, a famous Canadian hospital specializing in hernia operations (discussed in Chapter 11). Finally, loyal customers may serve as mentors and, because of their experience with the provider, help other customers understand the explicitly or implicitly stated rules of conduct.[18]

Human Resource Management Benefits Loyal customers may also provide a firm with human resource management benefits. First, loyal customers may be able to contribute to the co-production of the service by assisting in service delivery; often the more experienced customers can make the service employees' job easier. For example, a regular patient of a medical service provider is likely to know how the system works; she would know to bring her medication with her on a visit, to plan on paying by cheque (having previously learned that the office cannot process credit cards), and to schedule an annual mammogram without waiting for her doctor to prompt her. A second benefit relates to one of the benefits for customers that we have already discussed. We noted that loyal customers receive social benefits as a result of being in a relationship with a firm; employees who regularly interact with the same customers may also receive similar social benefits.[19] A third benefit of customer retention is employee retention. It is easier for a firm to retain employees when it has a stable base of satisfied customers. People like to work for companies whose customers are happy and loyal. Their jobs are more satisfying, and they are able to spend more of their time fostering relationships than scrambling for new customers. In turn, customers are more satisfied and become even better customers—a positive upward spiral. Because employees stay with the firm longer, service quality improves and costs of turnover are reduced, adding further to profits.

RELATIONSHIP VALUE OF CUSTOMERS

Relationship value of a customer is a concept or calculation that looks at customers from the point of view of their lifetime revenue and/or profitability contributions to a company. This type of calculation is obviously needed when companies start thinking of building long-term relationships with their customers. Just what is the potential financial value of those long-term relationships? And what are the financial implications of *losing* a customer? Here we will only summarize the factors that influence a customer's relationship value. In Chapter 18 we provide more detail on lifetime value financial calculations.

Factors That Influence Relationship Value

The lifetime or relationship value of a customer is influenced by the length of an average "lifetime," the average revenues generated per relevant time period over the lifetime, sales of additional products and services over time, referrals generated by the customer over time, and costs associated with serving the customer. *Lifetime value* sometimes refers to lifetime revenue stream only; but most often when costs are considered, lifetime value truly means "lifetime profitability."

Estimating Customer Lifetime Value

If companies knew how much it really costs to lose a customer, they would be able to accurately evaluate investments designed to retain customers. One way of documenting the dollar value of loyal customers is to estimate the increased value or profits that accrue for each additional customer who remains loyal to the company rather than defecting to the competition. This is what Bain & Co. has done for a number of industries, as shown in Figure 7.4.[20] The figure shows the percentage of increase in

FIGURE 7.4

Profit Impact of
5 Percent Increase in
Retention Rate

Source: Reprinted with
permission of the American
Marketing Association. From
F. F. Reichheld, "Loyalty and
the Renaissance of Marketing,"
Marketing Management 2, no.
4 (1994), p. 15.

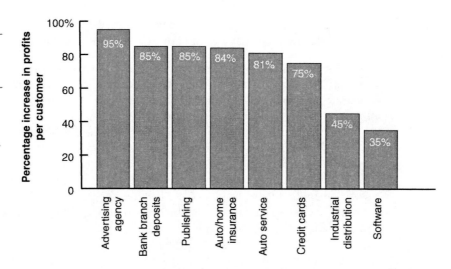

total firm profits when the retention or loyalty rate rises by 5 percentage points. The increases are dramatic, ranging from 35 to 95 percent. These increases were calculated by comparing the net present values of the profit streams for the average customer life at current retention rates with the net present values of the profit streams for the average customer life at 5 percent higher retention rates.[21]

Linking Customer Relationship Value to Firm Value

The emphasis on estimating the relationship value of customers has increased substantially in the past decade. Part of this emphasis has resulted from an increased appreciation of the economic benefits that firms accrue with the retention of loyal customers. Interestingly, recent research suggests that customer retention has a large impact on firm value and that relationship value calculations can also provide a useful proxy for assessing the value of a firm.[22] That is, a firm's market value can be roughly determined by carefully calculating customer lifetime value. The approach is straightforward: estimate the relationship value of a customer, forecast the future growth of the number of customers, and use these figures to determine the value of a company's current and future base. To the extent that the customer base forms a large part of a company's overall value, such a calculation can provide an estimate of a firm's value—a particularly useful figure for young, high-growth firms for which traditional financial methods (e.g., discounted cash flow) do not work well.

CUSTOMER PROFITABILITY SEGMENTS

Companies may want to treat all customers with excellent service, but they generally find that customers differ in their relationship value and that it may be neither practical nor profitable to meet (and certainly not to exceed) *all* customers' expectations.[23] FedEx Corporation, for example, has categorized its customers internally as the good, the bad, and the ugly—based on their profitability. Rather than treating all its customers the same, the company pays particular attention to enhancing their relationships with the good, tries to move the bad to the good, and discourages the ugly.[24] Other companies also try to identify segments—or, more appropriately, tiers of customers—that differ in current and/or future profitability to a firm. This approach goes beyond usage or volume segmentation, because it tracks costs and revenues for segments of customers, thereby capturing their financial worth to companies. After identifying profitability bands, the firm offers services and service levels in line with the identified segments. Building a high-loyalty customer base of the right customers increases profits. At MBNA Canada, a leading financial services firm, a 5 percent jump in retention increased the company profits 60 percent by the fifth year.[25]

Profitability Tiers—The Customer Pyramid

Although some people may view the FedEx grouping of customers into "the good, the bad, and the ugly" as negative, descriptive labels of the tiers can be very useful internally. Labels are especially valuable if they help the company keep track of which customers are profitable.

Virtually all firms are aware that their customers differ in profitability, in particular, that a minority of their customers accounts for the highest proportion of sales or profit. This finding has often been called the "80/20 rule"—20 percent of customers produce 80 percent of sales or profit.

In this version of tiering, 20 percent of the customers constitute the top tier, those who can be identified as the most profitable in the company. The rest are indistinguishable from each other but differ from the top tier in profitability. Most companies realize that there are differences among customers within this tier but do not possess the data or capabilities to analyze the distinctions. The 80/20 two-tier scheme assumes that consumers within the two tiers are similar, just as conventional market segmentation schemes typically assume that consumers within segments are similar.

However, more than two tiers are likely and can be used if the company has sufficient data to analyze customer tiers more precisely. Different systems and labels can be helpful. One useful four-tier system, shown in Figure 7.5, includes the following:

1. The *platinum tier* describes the company's most profitable customers, typically those who are heavy users of the product, are not overly price-sensitive, are willing to invest in and try new offerings, and are committed customers of the firm. Closing Provider Gap 1 is most critical for this group. Unfortunately, many firms don't know who those customers are and therefore can't focus attention on them.

2. The *gold tier* differs from the platinum tier in that profitability levels are not as high, perhaps because the customers want price discounts that limit margins or are not as loyal. They may be heavy users who minimize risk by working with multiple vendors rather than just the focal company.

3. The *iron tier* contains essential customers who provide the volume needed to utilize the firm's capacity, but their spending levels, loyalty, and profitability are not substantial enough for special treatment.

4. The *lead tier* consists of customers who are costing the company money. They demand more attention than they are due given their spending and profitability and are sometimes problem customers—complaining about the firm to others and tying up the firm's resources.

Examples of effective use of the customer pyramid approach exist in a number of business contexts. Financial services firms are leading the way, perhaps because of the vast amounts of data already housed in those firms. Bank of Montreal has managed to classify approximately one-third of its more than 5 million customers as profitable and

FIGURE 7.5

The Customer Pyramid

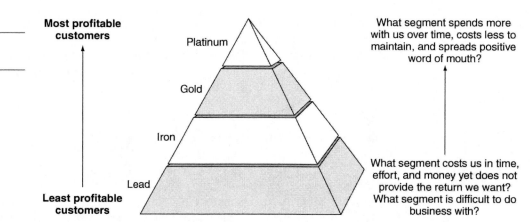

Most profitable customers

Least profitable customers

Platinum

Gold

Iron

Lead

What segment spends more with us over time, costs less to maintain, and spreads positive word of mouth?

What segment costs us in time, effort, and money yet does not provide the return we want? What segment is difficult to do business with?

plans to continue focus on these clients. Similarly, Royal Bank, using CRM technology, has segmented a group of customers it refers to as the Growth Market. Its commitment to better serve such core customers required revamping whole departments.[26]

Once a system has been established for categorizing customers, the multiple levels can be identified, motivated, served, and expected to deliver differential levels of profit. Companies improve their opportunities for profit when they increase shares of purchases by customers who either have the greatest need for the services or show the greatest loyalty to a single provider. By strengthening relationships with the loyal customers, increasing sales with existing customers, and increasing the profitability on each sale opportunity, companies thereby increase the potential of each customer.

The Customer's View of Profitability Tiers

Whereas profitability tiers make sense from the company's point of view, customers don't appreciate being categorized into a less desirable segment.[27] For example, at some companies the top clients have their own individual account representative whom they can contact personally. The next tier of clients may be handled by representatives who each have 100 clients. Meanwhile, the majority of clients are served by an 800 number, an automated voice response system, or referral to a website. Customers are aware of this unequal treatment, and many resist and resent it.

Therefore, it is increasingly important that firms communicate with customers so they understand the level of service they can expect and what they would need to do to get better service. The most significant issues result when customers do not understand, believe they have been singled out for poor service, or feel that the system is unfair.

The ability to segment customers narrowly based on profitability implications also raises questions of privacy for customers. In order to know who is profitable and who is not, companies must collect large amounts of individualized data on consumers. Many consumers today resent what they perceive as an intrusion into their lives, especially when it results in differential treatment that they perceive is unfair.

Making Business Decisions Using Profitability Tiers

Prudent business managers are well aware that past customer purchase behaviour, although useful in making predictions, can be misleading.[28] What a customer spends today, or has spent in the past, may not necessarily be reflective of what he or she will do (or be worth) in the future. Banks serving university and college students know this well—a typical such student generally has minimal financial services needs (i.e., a chequing account) and tends to not have a high level of deposits. However, within a few years that student may embark on a professional career, start a family, and/or purchase a house, and thus require several financial services and become a very profitable bank customer. Generally speaking, a firm would like to keep its consistent big spenders and lose the erratic small spenders. But all too often a firm also has two other groups they must consider: erratic big spenders and consistent small spenders. So, in some situations in which consistent cash flow is a concern, it may be helpful to a firm to have a portfolio of customers that includes steady customers, even if they have a history of being less profitable. Some service providers have actually been quite successful in targeting customers who were previously considered to be unworthy of another firm's marketing efforts.[29] For example, brokerage firms such as The Cash Store provide small short-term loans for clients, many of whom may not qualify for financing through a more traditional lending institution. Firms, therefore, need to be cautious in blindly applying customer value calculations without thinking carefully about the implications.

RELATIONSHIP DEVELOPMENT STRATEGIES

To this point in the chapter, we have focused on the rationale for relationship marketing and the benefits (to both firms and customers) of the development of strong exchange relationships. In this section we examine factors that influence the development of strong customer relationships, including the customer's overall evaluation of a firm's offering, bonds created with customers by the firm, and barriers that the customer faces in leaving a relationship. These factors, illustrated in Figure 7.6, provide the rationale for specific strategies that firms use to keep their current customers.

FIGURE 7.6

Relationship Development Model

Source: Adapted from D. D. Gremler and S. W. Brown, "Service Loyalty: Antecedents, Components, and Outcomes," in *1998 AMA Winter Educators' Conference: Marketing Theory and Applications*, Vol. 9, D. Grewal and C. Pechmann, eds. (Chicago: American Marketing Association,) pp. 165–166.

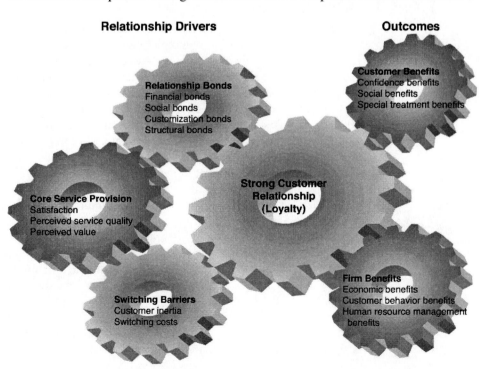

Core Service Provision

Retention strategies will have little long-term success unless the firm has a solid base of customer satisfaction on which to build. The firm does not necessarily have to be the very best among its competitors. It must be competitive, however, and frequently better than that. All the retention strategies that we describe in this section are built on the assumption of competitive quality and value being offered. Clearly, a firm needs to begin the relationship development process by providing good core service that, at minimum, meets customer expectations; it does no good to design relationship strategies for inferior services.

Switching Barriers

When considering a switch in service providers, a customer may face a number of barriers that make it difficult to leave one service provider and begin a relationship with another. Literature suggests that switching barriers influence consumers' decisions to exit from relationships with firms and, therefore, help to facilitate customer retention.[30] This might be called the "negative reinforcement" model.

Customer Inertia

One reason that customers commit to developing relationships with firms is that a certain amount of effort may be required to change firms. Sometimes consumers simplistically state that "it's just not worth it" to switch providers. Inertia may even explain why some dissatisfied customers stay with a provider. In discussing why people remain in relationships (in general) that they no longer find satisfying, scholars suggest that people may stay because breaking the relationship would require them to restructure their life—to develop new habits of living, to refashion old friendships, and to find new ones.[31] In other words, people do not like to change their behaviour.

Switching Costs

In many instances, customers develop loyalty to an organization in part because of costs involved in changing to and purchasing from a different firm. These costs, both real and perceived, monetary and nonmonetary, are termed *switching costs*. Switching costs include investments of time, money, or effort—such as setup costs, search costs, learning costs, and contractual costs—that make it challenging for the customer to move to another provider.[32] To illustrate, a patient may incur *setup costs* such as paying for a complete physical when changing doctors or for new X-rays when switching dentists. Because services often have characteristics that make them difficult to evaluate—including intangibility, nonstandardization, and inseparability of production and consumption as well as high experience and credence qualities—high *search costs* may be required to obtain suitable information about alternative services. *Learning costs* are those costs associated with learning the idiosyncrasies of how to use a product or service; in many situations, a customer who wishes to switch firms may need to accumulate new user skills or customer know-how. *Contractual costs* arise when the customer is required to pay a penalty to switch providers (e.g., prepayment charges for customer-initiated switching of mortgage companies or mobile telephone services), making it financially difficult, if not impossible, for the customer to initiate an early termination of the relationship.

In order to retain customers, some firms even increase switching costs. Therefore, to attract new customers, a service provider should consider implementing strategies designed to *lower* the switching costs of customers not currently using the provider.

FIGURE 7.7

What if banks really listened to their customers?

Source: © Graham Harrop

For example, providers might complete the customer's required paperwork themselves.

Banks, for example, might offer both automatic deposits and automatic payments. IBM, which provides banking services to large Canadian firms, learned that account opening is both intensive and repetitive. They are now actively trying to help banks simplify the process. This will make it easier for people to switch to IBM's customers. (Figure 7.7 provides a humorous look at what might happen if banks really listened to their customers.)

Relationship Bonds

Relationship bonds attempt to give customers reasons to *want to be loyal*—as opposed to feeling they *might as well* or *have to be loyal*.[33] We call this the positive reinforcement model of customer retention.

Recall that Provider Gap 1—Not Knowing What Customers Expect—is magnified when service providers focus on generating transactions and acquiring new customers instead of fostering relationships with existing customers. Hence, assuming a company has a clearly defined position in the market and has chosen its customer segments carefully, that company can use different relationship strategies to reduce Gap 1. As is depicted in Figure 7.8, these relationship strategies can be grouped into four categories according to the type of relationship bonds the company is pursuing—financial bonds, social bonds, customization bonds, and structural bonds.

Level 1—Financial Bonds

Financial bonds, the first and weakest level of relationship bond, provide some type of economic incentive for a customer to continue a relationship with a company, such as the guarantee of stable prices or discounts or reward miles associated with frequent

174   Part 3   *Understanding Customer Requirements*

FIGURE 7.8

Levels of
Relationship
Strategies

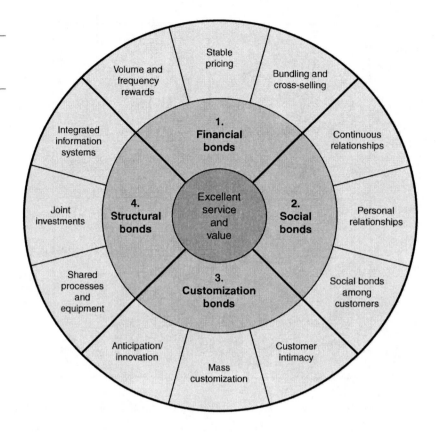

shopper or loyalty cards. They are the weakest level because they are easily imitated by competitors.[34]

Level 2—Social Bonds

Social bonds, the level-two strategies, provide additional attraction for customers. Retention marketers enhance relationships previously based on financial bonds with social and interpersonal relationships. Many service providers use strategies to create social bonds with clients. Lawyers, teachers, and hairdressers, when referring to their clients by name and who bring personal details into conversations, are using these level-two strategies.

Sometimes relationships are formed with the organization because of the social bonds that develop *among customers* rather than between customers and the provider of the service. Such bonds are often formed in health clubs, country clubs, educational settings, and other service environments where customers interact with each other. Over time the social relationships they have with other customers are important factors that keep them from switching to another organization. One company that has built a significant strategy around customer-to-customer bonds is Harley Davidson, with its local Harley Owners Groups, or HOGs. HOGs are involved in local rallies, tours, and parties as well as in national HOG events organized by the company. Through the HOGs, Harley customers come to know each other and develop a sense of community around their common interest—motorcycle riding—as illustrated in Figure 7.9.

Social bonds alone may not tie the customer permanently to the firm, but they are much more difficult for competitors to imitate than price incentives. In the absence of

FIGURE 7.9

Harley Davidson riders develop customer-to-customer bonds through Harley Owners Group (HOG) activities.

Source: EyeWire Collection/ Getty Images.

strong reasons to shift to another provider, interpersonal bonds can encourage customers to stay in a relationship.[35] In combination with financial incentives, social bonding strategies may be very effective.

Level 3—Customization Bonds

Customization bonds, or level-three strategies, may have commonalities with level-one and level-two strategies, but they are stronger still. These types of relationships are often established by companies that have intimate knowledge of customers and personalized services to meet their needs. Even large companies with many clients can develop one-to-one relationships with sophisticated technology solutions as indicated in our Global Feature.

Level 4—Structural Bonds

Structural bonds are the strongest, because they are the most difficult to imitate. This type of bond is often realized in business-to-business relationships where companies become structurally tied to each other (frequently with technology) but also exhibit customization, social, and financial bonds. Structural bonds are created by providing services to the client that are frequently designed right into the service delivery, and are characterized by some type of integration between the organizations.

An example of structural bonds can be seen in the long competitive battle between UPS and Federal Express (now known as FedEx).[36] In the mid-1990s, both firms attempted to tie their clients closer to them by providing them with free computers—Federal Express's PowerShips and UPS's MaxiShips—that stored addresses and shipping data, printed mailing labels, and helped track packages. By tying into one of the systems, a company saved time overall and could better track daily shipping records. As technology has continued to advance, the two companies have tied their customers to them through the Web and now through wireless technology, as shown in the UPS ad in Figure 7.10.

But there is also a potential downside to this arrangement from the customer's perspective. Customers may fear that tying themselves too closely to one provider may not allow them to take advantage of potential price savings from other providers in the future.

FIGURE 7.10

UPS uses technology to build ties to customers.

Source: Courtesy of UPS; Photo by William Howard © The Martin Agency.

RELATIONSHIP CHALLENGES

Given the many benefits of long-term customer relationships, it would seem that a company would not want to refuse or terminate a relationship with any customer. Yet situations arise in which either the firm, the customer, or both want to end (or have to end) their relationship. The final section of this chapter discusses situations in which the firm might actually consider ending the relationship and how that might occur. In the next chapter we discuss situations in which the customer decides to terminate the relationship and switch providers.

The Customer Is *Not* Always Right

The assumption that all customers are good customers is very compatible with the belief that "The customer is always right," an almost sacrosanct tenet of business. However, the preceding section on profitability tiers reminded us that *not* all customers are good customers. To close Gap 1, it is as important to know what unprofitable customers want and expect as it is to know what profitable customers want and expect. If these expectations can't be met profitably—and the reason is not simply that the firm lacks the will to raise the level of its game—the firm must find ways to reallocate its scarce resources.

Why are many customers unprofitable? Some of the time, in our opinion, it is because the firm hasn't given these customers sufficient reason to be loyal. The service simply isn't good enough. But sometimes the reasons lie elsewhere. It may be, for

Global Feature

Developing Loyal Customers at Boots The Chemists

Boots The Chemists is one of the best-known and trusted brands in the United Kingdom and is the United Kingdom's leading health and beauty retailer. The company was founded in 1887, spanning three centuries of successful operations. Currently offering its products through 1,400 retail stores in the United Kingdom, numerous satellite stores within other retail outlets in the United States, Europe, Asia, and New Zealand, and an online store at www.boots.com, the company is deservedly called the "Chemist to the Nation." On its website, the Boots Company states that it intends to become the global leader in well-being products and services and is expanding globally through Boots Retail International.

A foundation for Boots's success in recent years is its increased focus on the customer and a desire to develop customer loyalty through a number of retention and relationship strategies. At the heart of the company's loyalty strategy is its Advantage Card, started in 1997. The Advantage Card is right now the world's largest smart card loyalty scheme, with close to 14 million members. Over 50 percent of Boots's current sales are now linked to the card. The card offers a number of benefits to customers and has helped the company increase sales, but more than that, it has been the foundation for building greater loyalty among Boots's best customers.

Using the card for purchases, Boots's customers receive 4 points for every pound spent. These points can be redeemed for selected products, aimed to treat customers to something special rather than simply to offer discounts off purchases. In fact the card is *not* about discounts; rather, it is about treating oneself. Customers can use their points to treat themselves to a simple lunch or to a full day of pampering at a spa. From a financial perspective, the company has seen increasing average transaction values among higher-spending customers. Boots managers say that they have increased loyalty and

spending from people who were already good and profitable customers—a clear win for the company.

A number of initiatives are tied to the Advantage Card, taking it beyond a pure points reward program from the customer's perspective. For example, Boots now mails a first-class health and beauty magazine to the top spending 3 million Advantage Card holders. The magazine is Britain's biggest health and beauty magazine; it is not viewed as a "Boots" magazine but rather as a health and beauty magazine sent by Boots. Cardholders also have access to additional benefits and discounts using interactive kiosks in over 380 stores. The card can be used for purchases at the online store through the www.boots.com site that was launched jointly with Granada Media in 2001. Many products are offered on the site that are not available in Boots stores. In addition, the site provides access to an online magazine, answers to questions, a chat room, and other features and services. A credit card version of the Advantage Card was launched in 2001. And Boots joined with the Department of Health to enable Advantage Card holders to register with the National Health Service Organ Donor program and to carry an Advantage Card featuring the program's logo.

continued

Source: Newscast.

Global Feature

Developing Loyal Customers at Boots The Chemists—continued

From the company's perspective as well, the card is much more than a reward program. Data generated through the card is used to understand customers and to anticipate and identify individual needs in health and beauty care products. In fact, the goals with the Advantage Card program back in 1997 were to gain customer insight; build a database that would allow the company to tailor offerings to individual customers' needs; develop incremental sales by building customer loyalty; and use the customer knowledge to develop and introduce new products and services. A great deal of planning and testing went into developing the program, and this planning paid off in customer loyalty. Buy-in from the company's 60,000 staff members also aided in

the rapid success of the program. All associates were signed up as members six months before the launch of the card. After experiencing the benefits of the card firsthand, they became enthusiastic advocates, encouraging customers to sign up.

Through the program, Boots has learned that the more broadly customers buy, in more categories over time, the more they increase visits to Boots stores. The result has been customization of product and service offerings and more sales and greater loyalty from its best customers.

Sources: Frederick Newell, *Loyalty.com,* New York: McGraw-Hill, 2000, Chapter 24, pp. 239–45; www.boots-plc.com, 2002; www.wellbeing.com, 2002.

example, that the customers simply represent the wrong segment, are unprofitable in the long run, or are too difficult to deal with.

The Wrong Segment

A company cannot target its services to all customers; some segments will be more appropriate than others. It would not be beneficial to either the company or the customer for a company to establish a relationship with a customer whose needs the company cannot meet. For example, a school offering only a lockstep, daytime MBA program in downtown Montreal would not encourage full-time working people to apply for its program, nor would a law firm based in Ottawa that specializes in government issues establish a relationship with individuals seeking advice on divorce. These examples seem obvious. Yet firms frequently do give in to the temptation to make a sale by agreeing to serve a customer who would be better served by someone else.

Similarly, it would not be wise to forge relationships simultaneously with incompatible market segments. In many service businesses (such as restaurants, hotels, tour package operators, entertainment, and education), customers experience the service together and can influence each other's perceptions about value received. Thus, to maximize service to core segments, an organization may choose to turn away marginally profitable segments that would be incompatible. For example, a conference hotel may find that mixing executives in town for a serious educational program with students in town for a regional track meet may not be wise. If the executive group is a key long-term customer, the hotel may choose to pass up the sports group in the interest of retaining the executives.

Not Profitable in the Long Term

In the absence of ethical or legal mandates, organizations will prefer *not* to have long-term relationships with unprofitable customers. Some segments of customers will not be profitable for the company even if their needs can be met by the services offered. Some examples of this situation are when there are not enough customers in the segment to make it profitable to develop a marketing approach, when the segment cannot afford to pay the cost of the service, or when the projected revenue flows from the segment would not cover the costs incurred to originate and maintain the business. For example, in the banking industry it has been estimated that 40 to 70 percent of customers served in a typical bank are not profitable in the sense that the costs of serving these customers exceed the revenues generated.[37]

At the individual customer level, it may not be profitable for a firm to engage in a relationship with a particular customer who has bad credit or who is a poor risk for some other reason. Retailers, banks, mortgage companies, and credit card companies routinely refuse to do business with individuals whose credit histories are unreliable. Although the short-term sale may be beneficial, the long-term risk of nonpayment makes the relationship unwise from the company's point of view. Similarly, some car rental companies check into the driving records of customers and reject bad-risk drivers.[38] This practice, while controversial, is logical from the car rental companies' point of view because they can cut back on insurance costs and accident claims (thus reducing rental costs for good drivers) by not doing business with accident-prone drivers.

Beyond the monetary costs associated with serving the wrong customers, there can be substantial time investments in some customers that, if actually computed, would make them unprofitable for the organization. Everyone has had the experience of waiting in a bank, a retail store, or even an education setting while a particularly demanding customer seems to use more than his share of the service provider's time. The dollar value of the time spent with a specific customer is typically not computed or calculated into the price of the service.

In a business-to-business relationship, the variability in time commitment to customers is even more apparent. Some customers may use considerable resources of the supplier organization through inordinate numbers of phone calls, excessive requests for information, and other time-consuming activities. In the legal profession, clients are billed for every hour of the firm's time that they use in this way because time is essentially the only resource the firm has. Yet in other service businesses, all clients essentially pay the same regardless of the time demands they place on the organization.

Difficult Customers

Managers have repeated the dictum "The customer is always right" so often that you would expect it to be accepted by every employee in every service organization. So why isn't it? Perhaps because it simply is not true. The customer is not always right. No matter how frequently it is said, repeating that mantra does not make it become reality, and service employees know it.

In many situations, firms have service encounters that fail because of *dysfunctional customers.* Dysfunctional customer behaviour refers to actions by customers who intentionally, or perhaps unintentionally, act in a manner that in some way disrupts otherwise functional service encounters.[39] Such customers have been described as "customers from hell," "problem customers," or "jay customers." One of us was awakened during a recent hotel stay at 4 a.m. by drunk customers who were arguing with each other in a room above; management eventually called the police and asked them to escort the customers off the property. An Enterprise Rent-A-Car customer demanded that she not be charged for any of the two weeks that she had a car because, near the end of the rental period, she found a small stain in the back seat.[40] These customers often have the objective of gaining faster, superior, or perhaps free service, but their behaviour is considered dysfunctional from the perspective of the service provider and perhaps fellow customers.

Dysfunctional customer behaviour can affect employees, other customers, and the organization. Research suggests that exposure to dysfunctional customer behaviour can have psychological, emotional, behavioural, and physical effects on employees.[41] For example, customer-contact employees who are exposed to rude, threatening, obstructive, aggressive, or disruptive behaviour by customers often have their mood or temper negatively affected as well as their motivation and morale. Such customers are difficult to work with and often create stress for employees. (See Figure 7.11 for one example.) Dysfunctional customers can also have an impact on other customers. Such behaviour can spoil the service experience for other customers, or become contagious, particularly if it includes vociferous or illegitimate complaining. Finally, dysfunctional customer behaviour can create both direct costs and indirect costs for the organization. Direct costs of such behaviour can include the expense of restoring damaged property, increased insurance premiums, property loss by theft, costs incurred in compensating customers affected by the dysfunctional behaviour of others, and the costs incurred through illegitimate claims by dysfunctional customers. Additionally, indirect costs might include increased workloads for staff required to deal with dysfunctional behaviour as well as increased costs for attracting and retaining appropriate personnel and, perhaps, for absenteeism payments.

Although often these difficult customers will be accommodated and employees can be trained to recognize and deal with them appropriately, at times the best choice may be to not maintain the relationship at all—especially at the business-to-business level, where long-term costs to the firm can be substantial. Take, for example, the view of some of Bay Street's major ad agencies. "Some ad agencies say some accounts are so difficult to work with that they simply cannot—or will not—service them."[42] Difficult clients paralyze an ad agency for a variety of reasons. Some ask that a particular ad campaign work for all their diverse constituencies at the same time, which in some cases may be next to impossible. Others require so much up-front work and ad testing

FIGURE 7.11

Some customers may be difficult, if not impossible, to serve.

Source: Masterfile.

before selecting an agency that the work is essentially done for free by those agencies not selected. Other clients are stingy, require dozens of storyboards before settling on a concept, or require a lot of direct, frequently disruptive, involvement in the production process. As a result, agencies have become more wary of chasing every client that comes along. "As in a marriage, all agencies and all clients don't work well together."[43]

Ending Business Relationships

Managers should not only know how to establish a relationship but also how to end one. A company may *not* want to continue in a relationship with every customer. However, gracefully exiting a relationship may not be easy. Customers may end up feeling disappointed, confused, or hurt if a firm attempts to terminate the relationship.

Relationship Endings

Relationships end in different ways—depending on the type of relationship in place.[44] In some situations, a relationship is established for a certain purpose and dissolves when it has served its purpose. For example, a house painting service may be engaged while painting the house exterior, but both parties understand that the end of the relationship is predetermined—the end occurs when the house has been painted. Sometimes a relationship has a natural ending. Piano lessons for children often cease as the child gets older and develops interests in other musical areas. Or an ending may occur because the customer is not fulfilling his or her obligations. For example, a bank may choose to end the relationship with a customer who regularly has insufficient funds in the chequing account. Whatever the reason for ending the relationship, firms should clearly communicate their reasons for wanting (or needing) to terminate it so that customers understand what is occurring and why.

Should Firms Fire Their Customers?

A logical conclusion to be drawn from the discussion of the challenges firms face in customer relationships is that perhaps firms should seek to get rid of those customers who are not right for the company. More and more companies are making these types of decisions in the belief that troublesome customers are usually less profitable and less loyal and that it may be counterproductive to attempt to retain their business.[45] Another reason for "firing" a customer is the negative effect that these customers can have on employee quality of life and morale.

One company came to this conclusion when a client, the CEO of an Internet startup company, paged one of its employees at her home on the West Coast at 4 a.m. and asked her to order a limousine for him in New York City.[46] This incident was enough to push the employee over the edge and cause her boss to agree that the company should fire this client. It did so by directly telling him that the relationship was not working out and to take his business elsewhere.

Although it may sound like a good idea, firing customers is not that simple and needs to be done in a way that avoids negative publicity or negative word of mouth. Sometimes raising prices or charging for services that previously had been given away for free can move unprofitable customers out of the company. Helping a client find a new supplier who can better meet its needs is another way to gracefully exit a nonproductive relationship. If the customer has become too demanding, the relationship may be salvaged by negotiating expectations or finding more efficient ways to serve the client. If not, both parties may find an agreeable way to end the relationship.

One of the key benefits to paying attention to Provider Gap 1 is that firms will develop a better appreciation for what their customers expect. When this is tied to recognition that not all customers are profitable, it is possible to assess what expectations *un*profitable customers have. If these expectations can't be met without excessive cost, firms must transition their business to a greater focus on those customers whose expectations they *can* satisfy. Going forward, firms must also attempt to identify what aspects of their strategy may have inadvertently attracted the wrong segments.

SUMMARY

In this chapter we focused on the rationale for, benefits of, and strategies for developing long-term relationships with customers. It should be obvious by now that organizations that focus only on acquiring new customers may well fail to understand their current customers; thus, while a company may be bringing customers in through the front door, equal or greater numbers may be exiting. Estimates of lifetime relationship value accentuate the importance of retaining current customers.

The particular strategy that an organization uses to retain its current customers can and should be customized to fit the industry, the culture, and the customer needs of the organization. However, in general, customer relationships are driven by a variety of factors that influence the development of strong customer relationships, including (1) the customer's overall evaluation of the quality of a firm's core service offering, (2) the switching barriers that the customer faces in leaving a relationship, and (3) the relationship bonds developed with that customer by the firm. By developing strong relationships with customers and by focusing on factors that influence customer relationships, the organization will accurately understand customer expectations over time and consequently will narrow Provider Gap1.

The chapter concluded with a discussion of the challenges that firms face in developing relationships with customers. Although long-term customer relationships are critical and can be very profitable, firms should not attempt to build relationships with just any customer. In other words, the customer is *not* always right. Indeed, in some situations it may be best for firms to discontinue relationships with some customers—for the sake of the customer, the firm, or both.

⟼ Discussion Questions

1. Discuss how relationship marketing or retention marketing is different from the traditional emphasis in marketing.

2. Describe how a firm's relationships with customers may evolve over time. For each level of relationship discussed in the chapter, identify a firm with which you have that level of relationship and discuss how its marketing efforts differ from other firms.

3. Think about a service organization that retains you as a loyal customer. Why are you loyal to this provider? What are the benefits to you of staying loyal and not switching to another provider? What would it take for you to switch?

4. With regard to the same service organization, what are the benefits to the organization of keeping you as a customer? Calculate your "lifetime value" to the organization.

5. Describe the logic behind "customer profitability segmentation" from the company's point of view. Also discuss what customers may think of the practice.

6. Describe the various switching barriers discussed in the text. What switching barriers might you face in switching banks? Mobile telephone service providers? Universities?

7. Describe the four levels of retention strategies, and give examples of each type. Again, think of a service organization to which you are loyal. Can you describe the reason(s) you are loyal in terms of the different levels? In other words, what ties you to the organization?

8. Have you ever worked as a front-line service employee? Can you remember having to deal with difficult or "problem" customers? Discuss how you handled such situations. As a manager of front-line employees, how would you help your employees deal with difficult customers?

↦ Exercises

1. Interview the manager of a local service organization. Discuss with the manager the target market(s) for the service. Estimate the lifetime value of a customer in one or more of the target segments. To do this estimate, you will need to get as much information from the manager as you can. If the manager cannot answer your questions, make some assumptions.

2. In small groups in class, debate the question "Is the customer always right?" In other words, are there times when the customer may be the wrong customer for the organization?

3. Design a customer appreciation program for the organization with whom you currently work. Why would you have such a program, and to whom would it be directed toward?

4. Choose a specific company context (your class project company, the company you work for, or a company in an industry you are familiar with). Calculate the lifetime value of a customer for this company. You will need to make assumptions to do this calculation, so make your assumptions clear. Using ideas and concepts from this chapter, describe a relationship marketing strategy to increase the number of lifetime customers for this firm.

↦ Notes

1. F. E. Webster Jr., "The Changing Role of Marketing in the Corporation," *Journal of Marketing,* October 1992, pp. 1–17.

2. For discussions of relationship marketing and its influence on the marketing of services, consumer goods, strategic alliances, distribution channels, and buyer–seller interactions, see *Journal of the Academy of Marketing Science* 23, Special Issue on Relationship Marketing (Fall 1995). Some of the early roots of this paradigm shift can be found in C. Gronroos, *Service Management and Marketing* (New York: Lexington Books, 1990) and E. Gummesson, "The New Marketing—Developing Long-Term Interactive Relationships," *Long Range Planning* 20 (1987), pp. 10–20. For current thinking and excellent reviews of relationship

marketing across a spectrum of topics, see J. N. Sheth, *Handbook of Relationship Marketing* (Thousand Oaks, CA: Sage Publications, 2000).

3. L. L. Berry and A. Parasuraman, *Marketing Services* (New York: Free Press, 1991), chap. 8.

4. G. Knisely, "Comparing Marketing Management in Package Goods and Service Organizations," a series of interviews appearing in *Advertising Age,* January 15, February 19, March 19, and May 14, 1979.

5. This discussion is based on M. D. Johnson and F. Selnes, "Customer Portfolio Management: Toward a Dynamic Theory of Exchange Relationships," *Journal of Marketing* 68 (April 2004), pp. 1–17.

6. R. M. Morgan and S. D. Hunt, "The Commitment-Trust Theory of Relationship Marketing," *Journal of Marketing* 58 (July 1994), pp. 20–38; N. Bendapudi and L. L. Berry, "Customers' Motivations for Maintaining Relationships with Service Providers," *Journal of Retailing* 73 (Spring 1997), pp. 15–37.

7. Johnson and Selnes, "Customer Portfolio Management."

8. Ibid.

9. See also D. Siredeshmukh, J. Singh, and B. Sabol, "Customer Trust, Value, and Loyalty in Relational Exchanges," *Journal of Marketing* 66 (January 2002), pp. 15–37.

10. The three types of relational benefits discussed in this section are drawn from K. P. Gwinner, D. D. Gremler, and M. J. Bitner, "Relational Benefits in Service Industries: The Customer's Perspective," *Journal of the Academy of Marketing Science* 26 (Spring 1998), pp. 101–14.

11. See M. B. Adelman, A. Ahuvia, and C. Goodwin, "Beyond Smiling: Social Support and Service Quality," in *Service Quality: New Directions in Theory and Practice,* ed. R. T. Rust and R. L. Oliver (Thousand Oaks, CA: Sage Publications, 1994), pp. 139–72; and C. Goodwin, "Private Roles in Public Encounters: Communal Relationships in Service Exchanges," unpublished manuscript, University of Manitoba, 1993.

12. N. Bendapudi and R. P. Leone, "How to Lose Your Star Performer Without Losing Customers, Too," *Harvard Business Review,* November 2001, pp. 104–15.

13. P. Kumar, "The Impact of Long-Term Client Relationships on the Performance of Business Service Firms," *Journal of Service Research* 2 (August 1999), pp. 4–18.

14. F. F. Reichheld and W. E. Sasser Jr., "Zero Defections: Quality Comes to Services," *Harvard Business Review,* September/October 1990, pp. 105–11; and F. F. Reichheld, *The Loyalty Effect* (Boston: Harvard Business School Press, 1996).

15. R. Dhar and R. Glazer, "Hedging Customers," *Harvard Business Review* 81 (May 2003), pp. 86–92.

16. D. D. Gremler and S. W. Brown, "The Loyalty Ripple Effect: Appreciating the Full Value of Customers," *International Journal of Service Industry Management* 10, no. 3 (1999), pp. 271–91.

17. L. A. Bettencourt, "Customer Voluntary Performance: Customers as Partners in Service Delivery," *Journal of Retailing* 73 (Fall 1997), pp. 383–406.

18. S. J. Grove and R. P. Fisk, "The Impact of Other Customers on Service Experiences: A Critical Incident Examination of 'Getting Along,'" *Journal of Retailing* 73 (Spring 1997), pp. 63–85.

19. L. L. Price, E. J. Arnould, and A. Hausman, "Commercial Friendships: Service Provider–Client Relationship Dynamics," in *Frontiers in Services,* ed. R. T. Rust and R. L. Oliver (Nashville: Vanderbilt University, 1996).

20. Reichheld and Sasser, "Zero Defections."

21. Additional frameworks for calculating lifetime customer value that include a variety of other variables can be found in W. J. Reinartz and V. Kumar, "The Impact of Customer Relationship Characteristics on Profitable Lifetime Duration," *Journal of Marketing* 67 (January 2003), pp. 77–99; Dhar and Glazer, "Hedging Customers"; H. K. Stahl, K. Matzler, and H. H. Hinterhuber, "Linking Customer Lifetime Value with Shareholder Value," *Industrial Marketing Management* 32, no. 4 (2003), pp. 267–79.

22. S. Gupta, D. R. Helmann, and J. A. Stuart, "Valuing Customers," *Journal of Marketing Research* 41 (February 2004), pp. 7–18.

23. For more on customer profitability segments and related strategies, see V. A. Zeithaml, R. T. Rust, and K. N. Lemon, "The Customer Pyramid: Creating and Serving Profitable Customers," *California Management Review* 43 (Summer 2001), pp. 118–42.

24. R. Brooks, "Alienating Customers Isn't Always a Bad Idea, Many Firms Discover," *The Wall Street Journal*, January 7, 1999, p. A1.

25. F. Reichheld, "Loyalty-Based Management," *Harvard Business Review,* March/April 1993, pp. 64–74.

26. L. Young, "Cutting Through All the Hype About CRM: A Handful of Pioneers Such as the Bank of Montreal Are Turning CRM into More Than Just a Buzzword," *Marketing Magazine*, February 12, 2001, p. 15.

27. D. Brady, "Why Service Stinks," *BusinessWeek,* October 23, 2000, pp. 118–28.

28. Dhar and Glazer, "Hedging Customers."

29. D. Rosenblum, D. Tomlinson, and L. Scott, "Bottom-Feeding for Blockbuster Businesses," *Harvard Business Review* 81 (March 2003), pp. 52–59.

30. See T. A. Burnham, J. K. Frels, and V. Mahajan, "Consumer Switching Costs: A Typology, Antecedents, and Consequences," *Journal of the Academy of Marketing Science* 32 (Spring 2003), pp. 109–26; F. Selnes, "An Examination of the Effect of Product Performance on Brand Reputation, Satisfaction, and Loyalty," *European Journal of Marketing* 27, no. 9 (2003), 19–35; P. Klemperer, "The Competitiveness of Markets with Switching Costs," *Rand Journal of Economics* 18 (Spring 1987), pp. 138–50.

31. T. L. Huston and R. L. Burgess, "Social Exchange in Developing Relationships: An Overview," in *Social Exchange in Developing Relationships*, ed. R. L. Burgess and T. L. Huston (New York: Academic Press, 1979), pp. 3–28; L. White and V. Yanamandram, "Why Customers Stay: Reasons and Consequences of Inertia in Financial Services," *Managing Service Quality* 14, nos. 2/3 (2004), pp. 183–94.

32. See J. P. Guiltinan, "A Classification of Switching Costs with Implications for Relationship Marketing," in *Marketing Theory and Practice*, ed. Terry L. Childers et al. (Chicago: American Marketing Association, 1989), pp. 216–20; Klemperer, "The Competitiveness of Markets with Switching Costs"; C. Fornell, "A National Customer Satisfaction Barometer: The Swedish Experience," *Journal of Marketing* 56 (January 1992), pp. 6–21; P. G. Patterson and T. Smith, "A

Cross-Cultural Study of Switching Barriers and Propensity to Stay with Service Providers," *Journal of Retailing* 79 (Summer 2003), pp. 107–20.

33. See Bendapudi and Berry, "Customers' Motivations for Maintaining Relationships with Service Providers"; H. S. Bansal, P. G. Irving, and S. F. Taylor, "A Three-Component Model of Customer Commitment to Service Providers," *Journal of the Academy of Marketing Science* 32 (Summer 2004), pp. 234–50.

34. For more information on cautions to be considered in implementing rewards strategies, see L. O'Brien and C. Jones, "Do Rewards Really Create Loyalty?" *Harvard Business Review,* May/June 1995, pp. 75–82; and G. R. Dowling and M. Uncles, "Do Customer Loyalty Programs Really Work?" *Sloan Management Review,* Summer 1997, pp. 71–82.

35. D. D. Gremler and S. W. Brown, "Service Loyalty: Its Nature, Importance, and Implications," in *Advancing Service Quality: A Global Perspective*, ed. Bo Edvardsson et al. (Jamaica, NY: International Service Quality Association, 1996), pp. 171–80; H. Hansen, K. Sandvik, and F. Selnes, "Direct and Indirect Effects of Commitment to a Service Employee on the Intention to Stay," *Journal of Service Research* 5 (May 2003), pp. 356–68.

36. L. M. Grossman, "Federal Express, UPS Face Off on Computers," *The Wall Street Journal,* September 17, 1993, p. B1.

37. R. Brooks, "Alienating Customers Isn't Always a Bad Idea." P. Carroll and S. Rose, "Revisiting Customer Retention," *Journal of Retail Banking* 15, no. 1 (1993), pp. 5–13.

38. J. Dahl, "Rental Counters Reject Drivers Without Good Records," *The Wall Street Journal,* October 23, 1992, p. B1.

39. See L. C. Harris and K. L. Reynolds, "The Consequences of Dysfunctional Customer Behavior," *Journal of Service Research* 6 (November 2003), p. 145 for cites; also, see A. A. Grandey, D. N. Dickter, and H. P. Sin, "The Customer Is *Not* Always Right: Customer Aggression and Emotion Regulation of Service Employees," *Journal of Organizational Behavior* 25 (2004), pp. 397–418.

40. K. Ohnezeit, recruiting supervisor for Enterprise Rent-A-Car, personal communication, February 12, 2004.

41. See Harris and Reynolds, "The Consequences of Dysfunctional Customer Behavior."

42. L. Bird, "The Clients That Exasperate Madison Avenue," *The Wall Street Journal,* November 2, 1993, p. B1.

43. Ibid.

44. For a detailed discussion on relationship ending, see A. Halinen and J. Tähtinen, "A Process Theory of Relationship Ending," *International Journal of Service Industry Management* 13, no. 2 (2002), 163–80.

45. M. Schrage, "Fire Your Customers," *The Wall Street Journal,* March 16, 1992, p. A8.

46. S. Shellenbarger, "More Firms, Siding with Employees, Bid Bad Clients Farewell," *The Wall Street Journal,* February 16, 2000, p. B1.

Chapter

8

Service Recovery

Provider Gap 1

1. Illustrate the importance of recovering from service failures.

2. Discuss consumer complaints and why people do and do not complain.

3. Discuss what customers expect and the kind of responses they want when they do complain.

4. Present strategies for effective service recovery, together with examples of what does and does not work.

5. Discuss service guarantees—what they are, the benefits of guarantees, and when to use them—as a particular type of service recovery strategy.

TORONTO MAPLE LEAFS SPORTS AND ENTERTAINMENT—EMPLOYEE EMPOWERMENT PREVENTS OUTRAGED FANS

Toronto Maple Leafs Sports and Entertainment manage the fan experience at the Air Canada Centre (www.theaircanadacentre.com) for Leafs hockey games, Raptors basketball games, and also any of the many concerts that take place in the venue. And, with Toronto Maple Leafs ticket holders being 97 percent season-pass customers, retaining the loyalty of such valued patrons requires not only being able to meet clients' basic expectations for clean facilities and friendly service, but also being able to prevent fan outrage by quickly recovering when service does falter. Director of Client Services

Chris Gibbs therefore instils in his employees the importance of three rules for service recovery: "Recover quickly, recover effectively, and improve the situation."

In order to quickly and effectively recover and improve a poor situation at the Air Canada Centre, employees must be empowered to act. Ushers are therefore responsible for their own areas. When a fan spills a drink, for instance, the usher quickly replaces the item and has the area cleaned. For larger concerns, like a patron requiring relocation, the customer service department may need to be contacted to find an available location. Finally, senior staff sometimes need to take action to remedy larger situations, as was the case at a Julio Iglesias concert. When many attendees experienced poor sound quality and complained, the entire section was given complimentary tickets to the next Julio concert.

Gibbs has also managed to defuse other potentially damaging situations by using a problem to create an opportunity to delight the customer and build goodwill. Consider, for example, the situation when three visiting Israeli patrons missed a Raptors game due to miscalculating the time change from their home. It would have been easy to politely explain to these fans that there was nothing that could (or would) be done because the Centre was not at fault. Instead, Gibbs and his employees functioned as travel agents for the group, rescheduling their flights, finding a cheap

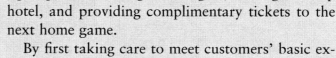

hotel, and providing complimentary tickets to the next home game.

By first taking care to meet customers' basic expectations, empowering employees to act quickly and responsibly to diffuse negative experiences, and leading by example in service recovery efforts, Toronto Maple Leafs Sports and Entertainment are well positioned to build and maintain stronger relationships with their clientele.[1]

Source: www.theaircanadacentre.com.

The preceding two chapters have given you grounding in understanding customers through research as well as through knowing them as individuals and developing strong relationships with them. These strategies are designed to help minimize Provider Gap 1—Not Knowing What Customers Expect. But, in all service contexts—whether customer service, consumer services, or business-to-business services—service failure is inevitable. This is true even for the best of firms with the best of intentions, even for those with world-class service systems. To continue closing Provider Gap 1, firms must also know what their customers expect when service failures occur, and must implement effective strategies for service recovery.

THE IMPACT OF SERVICE FAILURE AND RECOVERY

Service recovery refers to the actions taken by an organization in response to a service failure. Failures occur for all kinds of reasons—the service may be unavailable when promised, it may be delivered late or too slowly, the outcome may be incorrect or poorly executed, or employees may be rude or uncaring.[2] All these types of failures bring about negative feelings and responses from customers. Left unfixed, they can result in customers leaving, telling other customers about their negative experiences, and even challenging the organization through consumer rights organizations or legal channels.

Service Recovery Effects

Research has shown that resolving customer problems effectively has a strong impact on customer satisfaction, loyalty, word of mouth communication, and bottom-line performance.[3] That is, customers who experience service failures but who are ultimately satisfied based on recovery efforts by the firm, will be more loyal than those whose problems are not resolved. That loyalty translates into profitability, as you learned in Chapter 7. Data from the Technical Assistance Research Program (TARP) verifies this relationship, as shown in Figure 8.1.[4] Customers who complain and have their problems resolved quickly are much more likely to repurchase than those whose complaints are not resolved. Those who never complain are *least* likely to repurchase.

Hampton Inn Hotels directly realized the benefits of effective service recovery through their service guarantee. They achieved $11 million in additional annual revenue and the highest customer retention rate in their industry after implementing the 100 percent customer satisfaction guarantee shown in Figure 8.2.[5] The guarantee reimburses customers who experience service failures in their hotels—and is part of an overall service recovery and customer retention strategy.

An effective service recovery strategy has multiple potential impacts. It can increase customer satisfaction and loyalty and generate positive word of mouth communication. A well-designed, well-documented service recovery strategy also provides information that can be used to improve service as part of a continuous improvement effort. By making adjustments to service processes, systems, and

FIGURE 8.1

Unhappy Customers' Repurchase Intentions

Source: Adapted from data reported by the Technical Assistance Research Program.

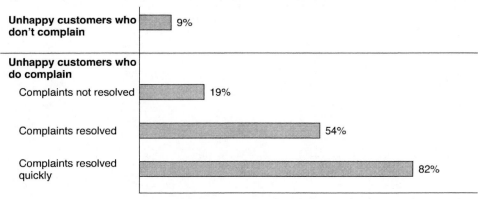

Percentage of customers who will buy again after a major complaint (over $100 losses)

FIGURE 8.2

The 100 Percent
Hampton Inn Hotels
Guarantee

Source: Courtesy of Hampton
Inn® Hotels.

Friendly service, clean rooms, comfortable surroundings, every time.
If you're not satisfied, we don't expect you to pay.
That's our commitment & your guarantee. That's 100% Hampton.

outcomes based on previous service recovery experiences, companies increase the likelihood of "doing it right the first time." In turn, this reduces costs of failures and increases initial customer satisfaction.

An interesting example of a very visible service recovery is provided by Canadian Imperial Bank of Commerce (CIBC). See Figure 8.3. The bank went to a lot of trouble to recover from a service failure that might have gone completely unnoticed. The cost of producing, mailing, and processing the cheques was certainly much more than would have been incurred had they simply credited the affected accounts. But it communicated that the CIBC took the error seriously and could be trusted to do the right thing.

Unfortunately, many firms do not employ effective recovery strategies. A recent study suggests that 50 percent of customers who experienced a serious problem received no response from the firm.[6] There are tremendous downsides to having weak service recovery strategies. Poor recovery following a bad service experience can lead to customers who are so dissatisfied that they become "terrorists," actively pursuing

FIGURE 8.3

CIBC's High-Profile
Service Recovery

Source: Reprinted by
permission of CIBC.

Re: Personal overdraft protection service reimbursement

We recently discovered an error in the amount we charged to some customers on their overdraft protection service. The amounts involved are quite small; we estimate the average amount per account to be $3.46. We have corrected this error and are working diligently to reimburse customers as promptly as possible.

Our records indicate that your account was not affected by this error in the period after May 1998. However, as an expression of good faith, we are also reimbursing you a proportional share of the total estimated amount our customers were overcharged for the pre-1998 period. We are doing this as part of our effort to make things right and to ensure that CIBC does not retain any of the money it received in error.

Accordingly, please find enclosed a cheque payable to you in the amount of $3.46. This amount includes interest calculated at the rate of 10% per year.

Please accept my apologies for this error. Should you have any questions, you can call us at 1-877-757-1535.

We appreciate your business and look forward to serving you in the future.

Yours truly

Robert Cummings
Senior Vice President
CIBC Mortgages & Lending

CIBC   Canadian Imperial Bank of Commerce
Main Branch-Commerce Court
Toronto ON M5L 1G9

Date   JUNE 10, 2004   Cheque Number   Account Number

PAY THE SUM OF   THREE 46/100************   VOID   Amount $3.46
                                                        Cdn. Dollars $
To

Payable through Canadian Imperial Bank of Commerce

Authorized Signature

→ EXHIBIT 8.1
Complainers Spread the Word

Doubletree Inns

When Web consultants Tom F. and Shane A. experienced poor service at a Doubletree Inn while on a business trip (not at one of the Canadian locations), they decided to create a PowerPoint presentation to vent their frustrations and chronicle their "shabby treatment." The men sent the presentation, not only to two managers at the hotel, but also to two clients and Shane's mother-in-law, encouraging these three latter people to "share it with a few of your friends." Within a month the presentation, titled "Yours is a Very Bad Hotel," had been circulated around the globe. As a result, the two men got more than 9,000 email messages from six continents, and there were stories about their experience in publications such as the *Wall Street Journal* and *Forbes*.

Just what had prompted the pair to react in this way? Well, upon arriving at their hotel with a confirmation and credit card guarantee for late arrival, they had discovered the hotel was overbooked and that their rooms had already been given away. Tom, a frequent business traveller and a Hilton Honors Gold VIP, understood the situation to be fairly common, but he and his companion did expect at least an apology and prompt resolution. Instead

they received "insolence and insults," and were given two smoking rooms in a "dump" of a hotel several kilometres away and farther from the downtown area where they needed to be.

Finally, after all the publicity generated by the circulation of their presentation, Hilton offered a free two-night stay at any Hilton hotel and informed Tom and Shane of actions taken to improve employee training and overbooking policies. The men declined the free hotel and requested instead that a $1,000 charitable donation be made to a local organization.

Citizens Bank

Another example of a disgruntled customer generating quite a bit of media attention in Canada is Don Rogers. The retired Kingston-area gentleman, after discovering that his bank was outsourcing some of its credit card processing to the United States, decided to pay his $230 Visa bill in 985 instalments, sometimes only pennies at a time. Upset that U.S. authorities could technically access his personal information under the *Patriot Act*, Rogers asked Vancouver-based Citizens Bank to abandon the practice. His request being refused, Rogers thought it necessary to find a way to get the company's attention and perhaps eventually achieve the results he desired. To date, his "creative solution" has generated stories in the *Globe and Mail* and on *CTV News*, has garnered him a one-on-one conversation with the Citizens Bank CEO and privacy officer, has jammed the bank's system, has forced employees to process some payments manually, and has created a 35-page Visa statement—but the bank still has not changed its Visa processing company and there is no indication that they intend to do so.

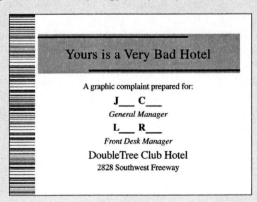

Sources: L. Bly, "Online Complaint About Bad Hotel Service Scores Bull's-Eye," *USA Today*, January 4, 2002, p. D6; S. Stewart, "Irate Client Pays Visa Pennies," *Globe and Mail*, November 23, 2005, p. A11.

opportunities to openly criticize the company.[7] When customers experience a service failure, they talk about it to others no matter what the outcome. That recent study also found that customers who were satisfied with a firm's recovery efforts talked to an average of seven people, whereas those customers who were dissatisfied with the response talked to an average of 25 people.[8] With the ability to share such stories on the Internet, the potential reach of such dissatisfied customers is even greater. (See Exhibit 8.1 about the two dissatisfied Doubletree Inn customers.) Further, repeated service failures can aggravate employees. The costs in employee morale and even lost employees is an often overlooked cost of not having effective service recovery.

The Recovery Paradox

Some businesses have customers who are initially dissatisfied with a service and then experience excellent service recovery, seemingly leading them to be more satisfied after they experience a service failure than they otherwise would have been![9] To illustrate, consider a hotel customer who arrives to check in and finds that no room is available. In an effort to recover, the front desk person immediately upgrades this guest to a better room at the original price. The customer, thrilled with this compensation, reports that she is even more impressed with the hotel than before, and vows to be loyal into the future. Although such extreme instances are relatively rare, this idea—that an initially disappointed customer who has experienced good service recovery might be even more satisfied and loyal as a result—has been labelled the *recovery paradox.*

So, should a firm "screw up" so that it can "fix the problem" superbly? If doing so would actually lead to more satisfied customers, is this strategy worth pursuing? First, as we indicated earlier in this chapter, a vast majority of customers do not complain when they experience a problem. The possibility of a recovery exists only in situations in which the firm is aware of a problem and is able to recover well; if customers do not make the firm aware of the failure—and most do not—dissatisfaction is most likely to be the result. Second, it is expensive to fix mistakes; re-creating a service may be quite costly. Third, it is ludicrous to encourage service failures—after all, reliability ("doing it right the first time") is the most critical determinant of service quality. Finally, although the recovery paradox suggests that a customer *may* end up more satisfied after experiencing excellent recovery, there is certainly *no* guarantee that the customer actually *will* end up more satisfied. The recovery paradox is highly dependent on the context and situation; although one customer may find it easy to forgive a restaurant who provides him with a gift certificate for a later date for having lost his dinner reservation, another customer who had planned to propose marriage to his date over dinner may not be so happy with the same recovery scenario.

The intrigue stimulated by the recovery paradox has led to empirical research specifically on this issue. Although anecdotal evidence provides limited support for the recovery paradox, research seems to indicate that this phenomenon is not pervasive. In one study, researchers found that only the very highest levels of customers' service recovery ratings resulted in increased satisfaction and loyalty.[10] This research suggests that customers weigh their most recent experiences heavily in their determination of whether to buy again. If the most recent experience is negative, feelings about the company decrease and repurchase intentions diminish significantly. A second study found that overall satisfaction was consistently lower for those customers who experienced a service failure than for those who experienced no failure, no matter what the recovery effort.[11] An explanation for why no recovery paradox occurred is suggested by the magnitude of the service failure in this study—a three-hour airplane flight delay. Perhaps this type of failure may be too much to be overcome by any recovery effort. However, in this study, strong service recovery was able to mitigate, if not reverse, the effects of the failure by reducing overall dissatisfaction. Finally, a rather recent study suggests that the recovery paradox phenomenon *may* only exist after *one* service failure; however, if a customer experiences a *second* service failure, the likelihood of the customer's evaluation of the service being greater after the second failure is minimal.[12]

Given the mixed opinions on the extent to which the recovery paradox exists, "doing it right the first time" is still the best and safest strategy in the long run. However, when a failure does occur, every effort should be made to mitigate its negative effects. If the failure can be fully overcome, if the failure is less critical, or if the recovery effort is clearly superlative, it may be possible to observe the recovery paradox.

HOW CUSTOMERS RESPOND TO SERVICE FAILURES

Customers who experience service failures can respond in a variety of ways, as illustrated in Figure 8.4.[13] Research suggests that a variety of negative emotions follow service failure, including anger, discontent, disappointment, self-pity, and anxiety.[14] These initial negative responses affect how customers evaluate the service recovery and their ultimate decision to return or not.[15]

Many customers are passive about their dissatisfaction, simply saying or doing nothing. As we have pointed out, customers who do not complain are least likely to return. For companies, customer passivity in the face of dissatisfaction is a threat to future success. If dissatisfied customers don't complain, the company won't learn about their failure and will be less likely to correct it. For that reason, complaints have sometimes been referred to as "gifts." And although there are times when the firm receiving such a "gift" might prefer it otherwise (as in Exhibit 8.1), companies that are sincerely committed to meeting customer expectations are better off knowing what it is they are doing wrong and thus minimizing Gap 1.

Why People Do (and Do Not) Complain

Some customers are more likely to complain than others for a variety of reasons. These consumers believe that positive consequences may occur, that there are social benefits to complaining, and that their personal norms support complaining behaviour. They believe they should and will be provided compensation for the service failure. They also believe that in cases of service failure, someone should make good. In some

FIGURE 8.4   **Customer Complaint Actions Following Service Failure**

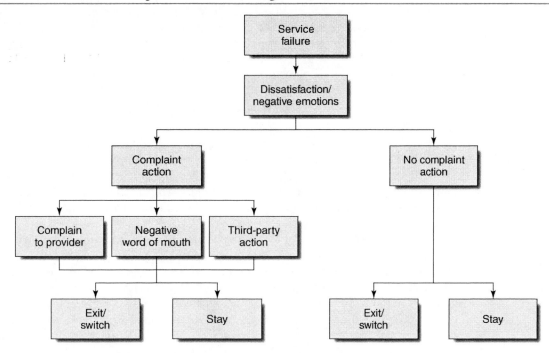

FIGURE 8.5

Sometimes customers don't complain because it doesn't seem "worth it."

Source: © Graham Harrop.

cases they feel a social obligation to complain—to help others avoid similar situations or to punish the service provider. A very small number of consumers even have "complaining personalities"—they just like to complain or cause trouble!

Consumers who are unlikely to take any action believe the opposite. They see complaining as a waste of time. (See Figure 8.5 for another angle on this!) Sometimes they do not know how to complain—they do not understand that avenues are open to them to voice their complaints. In some cases noncomplainers may engage in "emotion-focused coping" to deal with their negative experiences. This type of coping involves self-blame, denial, and possibly seeking social support.[16] They may feel that the failure was somehow their fault and that they do not deserve redress.

Personal relevance of the failure can also influence whether people complain.[17] The situation at Doubletree Inn, which is described in Exhibit 8.1, illustrates a failure that had been considered especially important to two customers. Consumers are also more likely to complain about services that are expensive, high-risk, and ego-involving (like vacation packages, airline travel, and medical services) than they are about less expensive, frequently purchased services (fast-food drive-through service, a cab ride, a call to a customer service help line). These latter services are simply not important enough to warrant the time to complain. Unfortunately, even though the experience may not be important to the consumer at the moment, a dissatisfying encounter can still drive him or her to a competitor next time the service is needed.

Types of Customer Complaint Actions

If customers initiate actions following service failure, the action can be of various types. A dissatisfied customer can choose to complain on the spot to the service provider, giving the company the opportunity to respond immediately. This reaction is often the best-case scenario for the company because it has a second chance right at that moment to satisfy the customer. Customers who do not complain immediately may choose to complain later to the provider by phone, in writing, or via the Internet. Again, the company has a chance to recover.

Some customers choose not to complain directly to the provider but rather spread negative word of mouth to friends and coworkers. This negative word of mouth can be extremely detrimental, because it can reinforce the customer's feelings of negativism and spread that negative impression to others as well. Further, the company has no chance to recover. In recent years, customers have taken to complaining via the Internet. A variety of websites[18] have been created to facilitate customer complaints and have provided customers with the possibility of spreading negative word-of-mouth

FIGURE 8.6

The Government of Canada has instituted a process for people to complain.

Source: Reproduced with the permission of the Minister of Public Works and Government Services, 2006.

communication to a much broader audience. Some customers become so dissatisfied with a product or service failure that they construct websites targeting the firm's current and prospective customers. On these sites,[19] angry customers convey their grievances against the firm in ways designed to convince other consumers of the firm's incompetence and evil.[20]

Finally, customers may choose to complain to third parties such as the Better Business Bureau, to consumer affairs arms of the government, to a licensing authority, to a professional association, or potentially to a private attorney. The Government of Canada has even instituted a process for people to complain (see Figure 8.6).

Types of Complainers

Research suggests that people can be grouped into categories according to how they respond to failures. Four categories of response types were identified in a study that focused on grocery stores, automotive repair services, medical care, and banking and financial services[21]: *passives, voicers, irates,* and *activists.*

Passives

This group of customers is least likely to take any action. They are unlikely to say anything to the provider, less likely than others to spread negative word of mouth, and unlikely to complain to a third party. They often doubt the effectiveness of complaining. Sometimes their personal values or norms argue against complaining. These customers tend to feel less alienated from the marketplace than irates and activists.

Voicers

These customers actively complain to the service provider, but they are less likely to spread negative word of mouth, to switch patronage, or to go to third parties with their complaints. *These customers should be viewed as the service provider's best friends!* They actively complain and thus give the company a second chance. As with the passives, these customers are less alienated from the marketplace than those in the next two groups. They tend to believe complaining has social benefits. They believe that the consequences of complaining can be very positive, and they believe less in other types of complaining such as spreading word of mouth or talking to third parties. Their personal norms are consistent with complaining. Don Rogers, the Kingston, Ontario man who wanted Citizens Bank to change its policies as described in Exhibit 8.1, is clearly a "voicer."

Irates

These consumers are more likely than others to engage in negative word-of-mouth communication and to switch providers. They are about average in their propensity to complain to the provider. They are unlikely to complain to third parties. They tend to feel somewhat alienated from the marketplace. As their label suggests, they are more angry with the provider, although they do believe that complaining to the provider can have social benefits. They are less likely to give the service provider a second chance and instead will switch to a competitor, spreading the word to friends and relatives along the way.

Activists

These consumers are most likely to complain: they will complain to the provider, they will tell others, and they are more likely to complain to third parties. Complaining fits with their personal norms. As with the irates, these consumers are more alienated from the marketplace than the other groups. They have a very optimistic sense of the potential positive consequences of all types of complaining. In extreme cases these consumers can become "terrorists," as in the Starbucks Coffee case described at the end of this text.

⟼ CUSTOMERS' RECOVERY EXPECTATIONS

When they take the time and effort to complain, customers generally have high expectations. Our "Story of a Service Hero," Exhibit 8.2, epitomizes this kind of service recovery.

Understanding and Accountability

In many service failure situations, customers are not looking for extreme actions from the firm; however, they want to understand what happened and for firms to be accountable.[22] One study identified the seven most common "remedies" that customers seek when they experience a serious problem[23]; three remedies were to have the service fixed, to be reimbursed all their money, or to be reimbursed part of their money. Interestingly, however, the other four remedies—including an apology, an explanation, assurance that the problem would not be repeated, and an opportunity for the customer to vent—cost the firm very little.

These four nonmonetary remedies consist primarily of providing employees the opportunity to communicate with customers. Customers expect an apology when things go wrong; they also want to know what the company is going to do to ensure that the problem does not recur.[24]

Demonstrating an understanding of customer concerns requires cultural sensitivity, too. One of us recently took two flights to Paris, the first with Air Canada and the second with Air France. Both airlines lost our luggage, but the respective recovery efforts were a bit different. Air Canada provided the usual toothpaste, comb, shaving gel, etc.; Air France provided all this plus one additional item—a condom.

Fair Treatment

Customers also want justice and fairness in handling their complaints. Service recovery experts Steve Brown and Steve Tax have documented three specific types of justice that customers are looking for following their complaints: *outcome fairness,*

→ EXHIBIT 8.2
Story of a Service Hero

A good recovery can turn angry, frustrated customers into loyal ones. It can, in fact, create more goodwill than if things had gone smoothly in the first place. Consider how Club Med–Cancun, part of the Paris-based Club Mediter-ranèe, recovered from a service nightmare and won the loyalty of one group of vacationers.

The vacationers had nothing but trouble getting from New York to their Mexican destination. The flight took off 6 hours late, made two unexpected stops, and circled 30 minutes before it could land. Because of all the delays and mishaps, the plane was en route for 10 hours more than planned and ran out of food and drinks. It finally arrived at two o'clock in the morning, with a landing so rough that oxygen masks and luggage dropped from overhead. By the time the plane pulled up to the gate, the soured passengers were faint with hunger and convinced that their vacation was ruined before it had even started. One lawyer on board was already collecting names and addresses for a class-action lawsuit.

Silvio de Bortoli, the general manager of the Cancun resort and a legend throughout the organization for his ability to satisfy customers, got word of the horrendous flight and immediately created an antidote. He took half the staff to the airport, where they laid out a table of snacks and drinks and set up a stereo system to play lively music. As the guests filed through the gate, they received personal greetings, help with their bags, a sympathetic ear, and a chauffeured ride to the resort. Waiting for them at Club Med was a lavish banquet, complete with mariachi band and champagne. Moreover, the staff had rallied other guests to wake up and greet the newcomers, and the partying continued until sunrise. Many guests said it was the most fun they'd had since college.

In the end, the vacationers had a better experience than if their flight from New York had gone like clockwork. Although the company probably couldn't measure it, Club Mediterranèe won market share that night. After all, the battle for market share is won not by analyzing demographic trends, ratings points, and other global measures, but rather by pleasing customers one at a time.

Source: Reprinted by permission of *Harvard Business Review.* An excerpt from C. W. L. Hart, J. L. Heskett, and W. E. Sasser, Jr., "The Profitable Art of Service Recovery," *Harvard Business Review,* July/August 1990, pp. 148, 149. © 1990 by the Harvard Business School Publishing Corporation. All rights reserved.

---

procedural fairness, and *interactional fairness.*[25] Outcome fairness concerns the results that customers receive from their complaints; procedural fairness refers to the policies, rules, and timeliness of the complaint process; and interactional fairness focuses on the interpersonal treatment received during the complaint process.[26] Exhibit 8.3 shows examples of each type of fairness taken from Brown and Tax's study of consumers who reported on their experiences with complaint resolution.

Outcome Fairness

Customers expect outcomes, or compensation, that match the level of their dissatisfaction. This compensation can take the form of actual monetary compensation, an apology, future free services, reduced charges, repairs, and/or replacements. Customers expect equity in the exchange—that is, they want to feel that the company has "paid" for its mistakes in a manner at least equal to what the customer has suffered. The company's "punishment should fit the crime." Outcome fairness is especially important in settings in which customers have particularly negative emotional responses to the service failure; in such situations recovery efforts should focus on improving the outcome from the customer's point of view.[27]

In the Club Med example in Exhibit 8.2, customers were compensated in a variety of ways. These guests had suffered a lot and the compensation definitely was adequate. Note that in this case the service failure was not even Club Med's fault.

On the other hand, customers can be uncomfortable if they are overly compensated. Early in its experience with service guarantees, Domino's Pizza offered not to charge

EXHIBIT 8.3
Fairness Themes in Service Recovery

	Fair	Unfair
Outcome fairness: The results that customers receive from complaints	*"The waitress agreed that there was a problem. She took the sandwiches back to the kitchen and had them replaced. We were also given a free drink."* *"They were very thorough with my complaint. One week later I received a coupon for a free oil change and an apology from the shop owner."*	*"Their refusal to refund our money or make up for the inconvenience and cold food was inexcusable."* *"If I wanted a refund, I had to go back to the store the next day. It's a 20-minute drive; the refund was barely worth the trouble."* *"All I wanted was for the ticket agent to apologize for doubting my story. I never got the apology."*
Procedural fairness: The policies, rules, and timeliness of the complaint process	*"The hotel manager said that it didn't matter to her who was at fault, she would take responsibility for the problem immediately."* *"The sales manager called me back one week after my complaint to check if the problem was taken care of to my satisfaction."*	*"They should have assisted me with the problem instead of giving me a phone number to call. No one returned my calls, and I never had a chance to speak to a real person."* *"I had to tell my problem to too many people. I had to become irate in order to talk with the manager, who was apparently the only one who could provide a solution."*
Interactional fairness: The interpersonal treatment received during the complaint process	*"The loan officer was very courteous, knowledgeable, and considerate—he kept me informed about the progress of the complaint."* *"The teller explained that they had a power outage that morning so things were delayed. He went through a lot of files [effort] so that I would not have to come back the next day."*	*"The person who handled my complaint about the faulty air conditioner repair wasn't going to do anything about it and didn't seem to care."* *"The receptionist was very rude; she made it seem like the doctor's time was important but mine was not."*

for the pizza if the driver arrived after the 30-minute guaranteed delivery time. Many customers were not comfortable asking for this level of compensation, especially if the driver was only a few minutes late. In this case "the punishment was greater than the crime."

Procedural Fairness

In addition to fair compensation, customers expect fairness in terms of policies, rules, and timeliness of the complaint process. They want easy access to the complaint process, and they want things handled quickly, preferably by the first person they contact. They appreciate companies that can be adaptable in their procedures so that the recovery effort can match their individual circumstances. In some cases, particularly in business-to-business services, companies actually ask the customer, "What can we do to compensate you for our failure?" Many times what the customer asks for is actually less than the company might have expected.

Fair procedures are characterized by clarity, speed, and absence of hassles. Unfair procedures are those that customers perceive as slow, prolonged, and inconvenient. Customers also feel it is unfair if they have to prove their case—when the assumption seems to be they are wrong or lying until they can prove otherwise.

In the Club Med case in Exhibit 8.2, the recovery happened as quickly as possible when the passengers landed in Mexico. And the vacationers had no more hassles once they were on the ground.

Interactional Fairness

Above and beyond their expectations of fair compensation and hassle-free, quick procedures, customers expect to be treated politely, with care and honesty. This form of fairness can dominate the others if customers feel the company and its employees have uncaring attitudes and have done little to try to resolve the problem. This type of behaviour on the part of employees may seem strange—why would they treat customers rudely or in an uncaring manner under these circumstances? Often it is due to lack of training and empowerment—a frustrated front-line employee who has no authority to compensate the customer may easily respond in an aloof or uncaring manner, especially if the customer is angry and/or rude.

In the Club Med case in Exhibit 8.2, Silvio de Bortoli and his staff were gracious, caring, and upbeat when they greeted the long-delayed passengers. They personally met them at the airport even though it was late at night. They even involved other guests already staying at the resort to greet the new arrivals.

⟼ SWITCHING VS. STAYING FOLLOWING SERVICE RECOVERY

Whether customers switch to a new provider following service failure will depend on a number of factors. The more serious the failure, the more likely the customer is to switch no matter what the recovery effort.[28]

The nature of the customer's relationship with the firm may also influence whether the customer stays or switches providers. Research suggests that customers who have "true relationships" with their service providers are more forgiving and less likely to switch than those who have a "first-time encounter" relationship.[29]

Other research reveals that the individual customer's attitude toward switching will strongly influence whether he or she ultimately stays with the provider and that this attitude toward switching will be even more influential than basic satisfaction with the service.[30] This research suggests that certain customers will have a greater propensity to switch service providers no matter how their service failure situations are handled. Research in an online service context showed that the profile of an "online service switcher" is a person who was influenced to subscribe to the service through positive word of mouth; who used the service less; who was less satisfied and less involved with the service; who had a lower income and education level; and who also had a lower propensity for taking risks.[31]

Finally, the decision to switch may not occur immediately following poor service recovery. That is, service switching can be viewed as a process resulting from a series of critical service encounters over time rather than one specific moment in time.[32] This

FIGURE 8.7

Causes Behind Service Switching

Source: Reprinted with permission of the American Marketing Association. From S. Keaveney, "Customer Switching Behavior in Service Industries: An Exploratory Study," *Journal of Marketing* 59 (April 1995), pp. 71–82.

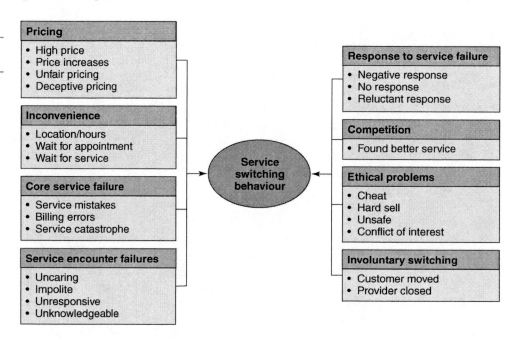

process orientation suggests that companies could potentially track customer interactions and predict the likelihood of defection based on a series of events, intervening earlier in the process to head off the customer's decision to switch.

Another study identified eight broad themes underlying the decision to defect.[33] These themes (pricing, inconvenience, core service failure, service encounter failure, response to service failure, competition, ethical problems, and involuntary switching) are shown in Figure 8.7. As these findings suggest, service failure can cause customers to switch companies. To minimize the impact of service failure, excellent service recovery is needed. In the next section we discuss several service recovery strategies that attempt to keep dissatisfied customers from defecting.

SERVICE RECOVERY STRATEGIES

Many companies have learned the importance of providing excellent recovery for disappointed customers. In this section we examine their strategies and share examples of benchmark companies and what they are doing. It will become clear that excellent service recovery is really a combination of a variety of strategies that need to work together, as illustrated in Figure 8.8. We discuss each of the strategies shown in the figure, starting with the basic "Do it right the first time."

Make the Service Fail-Safe—Do It Right the First Time!

The first rule of service quality is to do it right the first time. In this way recovery is unnecessary, customers get what they expect, and the costs of redoing the service and compensating for errors can be avoided.[34]

Dick Chase, noted service operations expert, suggests that services adopt the notion of *poka yokes* to improve service reliability.[35] Poka yokes are automatic warnings or controls in place to ensure that mistakes are not made; essentially they are quality control mechanisms, typically used on assembly lines. Chase suggests that poka yokes can be devised in service settings to "mistakeproof" the service. In a

FIGURE 8.8

Service Recovery
Strategies

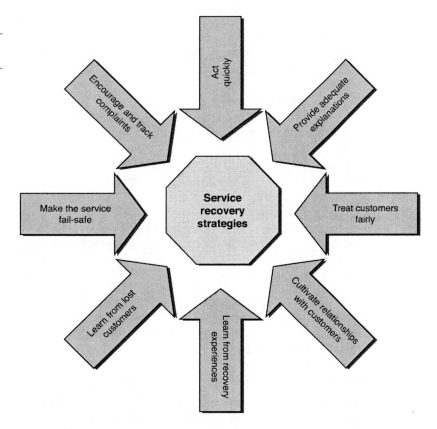

hospital setting, poka yokes ensure that procedures are followed to avoid potentially life-threatening mistakes. For example, trays for surgical instruments have indentations for specific instruments, and each instrument is nested in its appropriate spot. In this way surgeons and their staff know that all instruments are in their places prior to closing the patient's incision.[36]

Similarly, poka yokes can be devised to ensure that the tangibles associated with the service are clean and well maintained and that documents are accurate and up to date. Poka yokes can also be implemented for employee behaviours (checklists, role-playing and practice, reminder signs) and even for ensuring that customers perform effectively. Many of the strategies we discuss in Parts 4 and 5 of the text ("Aligning Service Design and Standards" and "Delivering and Performing Service") are aimed at ensuring service reliability and can be viewed as applications of the basic fail-safe notion of poka yokes.

Even more fundamentally, it is important for a firm to create a culture of zero defections to ensure doing it right the first time.[37] Within a zero-defections culture, everyone understands the importance of reliability. Employees and managers aim to satisfy every customer and look for ways to improve service. Employees in a zero-defections culture fully understand and appreciate the "relationship value of a customer" concept presented in Chapter 7. Thus they are motivated to provide quality service *every time* and to *every customer.*

Encourage and Track Complaints

Even in a zero-defections organization, failures occur. A critical component of a service recovery strategy is thus to encourage and track complaints.

Firms can utilize a number of ways to encourage and track complaints. Customer research can be designed for this purpose through satisfaction surveys, critical incidents studies, and lost customer research, as discussed in Chapter 6. Toll-free call centres, email, and pagers are now used to facilitate, encourage, and track complaints. Software applications in a number of companies also allow complaints to be analyzed, sorted, responded to, and tracked automatically.[38] Our Technology Spotlight shows how a world-class airline, British Airways, encourages, facilitates, and employs technology to track customer complaints as a critical component of its service recovery process.

In some cases technology can anticipate problems and complaints, allowing service employees to diagnose problems before the customer recognizes they exist. At companies such as IBM and Caterpillar, information systems are being implemented to anticipate equipment failures and to send out an electronic alert to the local field technician with the nature of the problem as well as which parts and tools will be needed to make the repair—a repair the customer does not yet know is needed.[39]

Act Quickly

Complaining customers want quick responses.[40] Thus, if the company welcomes, even encourages, complaints, it must be prepared to act on them quickly. Immediate response requires not only systems and procedures that allow quick action but also empowered employees.

Take Care of Problems on the Front Line

Customers want the persons who hear their complaints to solve their problems whether a complaint is registered in person, over the phone, or via the Internet. The Ritz-Carlton, for example, insists that the first person to hear a complaint from a customer "owns" that complaint until the employee is sure it is resolved. If a maintenance employee hears a complaint from a customer while the employee is in the middle of fixing a light in the hotel corridor, he owns that complaint and must be sure that it is handled appropriately before returning to his work.

Finally, if your company knows of a service failure and wants to be proactive, you can always take out an ad in the local paper. That's exactly what the Halifax *Chronicle Herald* did when they were having service delays. (It certainly makes it easier when you don't have to pay for the ad!) "Thank you for your understanding" said the ad, addressed "To Our Valued Readers," explaining that the delays were due to modernization at one of their printing plants.

Empower Employees

Employees must be trained and empowered to solve problems as they occur. A problem not solved can quickly escalate. Take, for example, the true story of a corporate vice-president who sent an email to his bank to register a complaint while he was attempting a transaction through its Internet banking service. The email was never answered. The customer then sent an email directly to the president of the bank. That one was never answered either. Ultimately the customer withdrew his approximately $70,000 account because his complaint was not handled in a timely manner. In this case the technology was not effectively linked to other systems, nor ultimately to employees. The Internet access encouraged the complaint, but the response never occurred.

Global Feature

September 11, 2001: Rebuilding a Firm—Service Recovery in the Wake of Disaster

"As I watched TV on September 11, 2001, I was struck with horror along with the rest of the world at the sight of the World Trade Center towers in New York City collapsing. My immediate thoughts that morning were, as for many, of friends and loved ones who worked in those towers, wondering where they were and if they were all right. In my case, it was a friend of over 30 years who worked in the North Tower of the World Trade Center, on the 55th floor, in a law firm where he is a partner. Other friends and I immediately started to think of ways to reach him, and eventually one of us did, that afternoon. He was safe."

M.J.B.

The story of how Sidley Austin Brown & Wood was able to rebuild itself and serve its clients and employees was reported in *The New York Times* the following Sunday, September 16. The remarkable story is the ultimate example of service recovery in its most monumental proportions. All but one of the firm's 600 employees who worked in the WTC survived the disaster, and they were back in business, able to serve their clients, within six days.

Sidley Austin Brown & Wood is the fourth-largest law firm in the United States, employing 1,325 attorneys and serving large corporate, financial, and government clients. The firm is the result of a merger in 2001 of two firms with long histories—Sidley & Austin was founded in 1866 in Chicago, Brown & Wood in 1914 in New York. The firm has primary offices in New York and Chicago and additional offices in San Francisco, Los Angeles, Washington (DC), Seattle, Dallas, Shanghai, Tokyo, Hong Kong, Beijing, Singapore, and London.

How did the firm achieve its remarkable recovery following September 11? Some of it had to do with careful planning as a result of surviving the WTC bombing in 1993. A lot of it had to do with courageous, focused employees as well as cooperative,

helpful suppliers and understanding clients. We can capture here only a tiny bit of what happened.

The first and highest priority of the firm was, of course, its employees and their safety. All 13 offices of the firm around the world were shut down the day following the collapse of the Towers, and three centres of activity were established to deal with the aftermath. Once it was learned that most employees were accounted for and out of the building, the firm's administrators and managing partners focused on reestablishing the New York office and began assessing what it needed to do to serve its employees and its corporate and government clients.

Within three hours of the disaster, a partner in the firm had secured leases on four additional floors of a building in midtown New York where the firm already had some space. The cost of the space was not discussed, and a firm that was due to move into the space agreed to delay its move to give the space to Sidley, at least temporarily. By the end of the day, others had arranged for the delivery of 800 desks, 300 computers, and hundreds of cell phones. Contractors were hired that day to string cable and reestablish the firm's computer network. Normal rules of business were bypassed as suppliers and even competitors offered to help. Nightly backups of the firm's entire electronic network enabled everything up to the night before the attacks to be restored. The backup tapes were stored in New Jersey by two independent firms and needed to be shipped immediately to Chicago so they could be restored and readied for use. Because no planes were flying for several days, these companies offered to have their own employees drive the tapes to Chicago from New Jersey.

On September 12 a letter to "our colleagues, clients, and friends" appeared on the firm's website to assure clients of the progress being made to serve

continued

Global Feature

September 11, 2001: Rebuilding a Firm—Service Recovery in the Wake of Disaster—continued

them without interruption, ending with the following statement: "We will not let down our predecessors, or our current colleagues, clients, and friends. From this tragedy, we have the opportunity to build something stronger and more energized than ever before, and we intend to do so. Thank you for your thoughts and prayers. We will keep you informed." The firm was back in business, serving its clients, in its new midtown offices on September 17.

During and following all the hectic efforts to reopen the firm for business, people remained a primary concern. Once the safety of employees, friends, and loved ones was assured, the firm turned to providing counselling, to ensuring that employees' pay was not interrupted, to bringing people together to see each other and share their feelings, and to

ensuring the security of the workplace. Heroic stories of employee actions and sad accounts of the things they felt and saw in those days in September have become part of the fabric and culture of the firm. Six hundred of its employees worked in the WTC and were displaced on that day in September. All but one of those employees survived the disaster.

Sources: J. Schwartz, "Up from the Ashes, One Firm Rebuilds," *The New York Times*, September 16, 2001, sec. 3, p. 1. For a follow-up story see John Schwartz, "Rebuilding a Day at a Time: Law Firm Pushes Two Steps Forward for Every Step Back," *The New York Times*, December 14, 2001, p. C1. See also: "Our Test," a personal account of the events surrounding September 11, 2001, by Thomas Cole, chairperson of the executive committee of Sidley Austin Brown & Wood, at www.sidley.com, news and events; accessed November 15, 2004; Sidley Austin Brown & Wood website; www.sidley.com.

Sometimes employees can even anticipate problems before they arise and surprise customers with a solution. For example, flight attendants on a flight severely delayed because of weather anticipated everyone's hunger, particularly the young children's. Once in flight, they announced to the harried travellers, "Thank you for your extreme patience in waiting with us. Now that we're on our way, we'd like to offer you complimentary beverages and dinner. Because we have a number of very hungry children on board, we'd like to serve them first, if that's OK with all of you." The passengers nodded and applauded their efforts, knowing that hungry, crying children could make the situation even worse. The flight attendants had anticipated a problem and solved it before it escalated.

Service employees have a specific and real need for recovery training. Because customers demand that service recovery take place on the spot and quickly, front-line employees need the skills, authority, and incentives to engage in effective recovery. Effective recovery skills include hearing the customer's problems, taking initiative, identifying solutions, improvising, and perhaps bending the rules from time to time.

Not only do employees need the authority to act (usually within certain defined limits), but they also should not be punished for taking action. In fact, incentives should exist that encourage employees to exercise their recovery authority. At the Ritz-Carlton, employees are authorized to spend $2,000 on behalf of the customer to solve a problem. This amount of money is rarely needed, but knowing that they have it encourages employees to be responsive without fear of retribution.

Allow Customers to Solve Their Own Problems

Another way problems or complaints can be handled quickly is by building systems that allow customers to actually solve their own service needs and fix their own problems. Typically this is acheived through technology that the customers directly interface with, and that provides them with instant answers. FedEx uses this in its package tracking services, for example.

Provide Adequate Explanations

In many service failures, customers try to understand why the failure occurred. Research suggests that when the firm's ability to provide an adequate *outcome* is not successful, further dissatisfaction can be reduced if an adequate *explanation* is provided to the customer.[41] In order for an explanation to be perceived as adequate, it must possess two primary characteristics. First, the explanation must be appropriate; relevant facts and pertinent information are important in helping the customer understand what occurred. Second, how the explanation is delivered can also reduce customer dissatisfaction. This includes the personal characteristics of the explanation givers, including their credibility and sincerity. Part of the frustration of the Doubletree Inn customers mentioned in Exhibit 8.1 was the result of not receiving an adequate explanation from the hotel.

Treat Customers Fairly

In responding quickly, it is also critical to treat each customer fairly. In the section "Customers' Recovery Expectations," we discussed results of research that focused on fairness in service recovery. Here we remind you that fair treatment is an essential component of an effective service recovery strategy.

Cultivate Relationships with Customers

A benefit of relationship marketing is that if the firm fails in service delivery, customers who have a strong relationship with the firm are more forgiving and more open to service recovery efforts. Research suggests that strong customer–firm relationships can help shield the firm from the negative effects of failures on customer satisfaction.[42] To illustrate, one study demonstrated that the presence of rapport between customers and employees provided several service recovery benefits, including increased post-failure satisfaction, increased loyalty intentions, and decreased negative word-of-mouth communication.[43] Another study found that customers who expect the relationship to continue also tend to have lower service recovery expectations and may demand less immediate compensation for a failure, because they consider the balance of equity across a longer time horizon.[44] Thus, cultivation of strong customer relationships can provide an important buffer to service firms when failures occur.

Learn from Recovery Experiences

"Problem-resolution situations are more than just opportunities to fix flawed services and strengthen ties with customers. They are also a valuable—but frequently ignored or underutilized—source of diagnostic, prescriptive information for improving customer service."[45] By conducting root-cause analysis, firms can identify the sources of problems and modify processes, sometimes eliminating almost completely the need for recovery.

Technology Spotlight

British Airways—Complaint Handling Model Pays Off

Ads for British Airways (BA) reinforce the company's branding strategy as the "World's Favourite Airline." Indeed, British Airways is a favourite among world travellers—but it was not always so. The success in turning BA around from a bureaucratic institution that regarded itself as doing the public a favour by allowing them to fly on its planes to a customer-responsive, world-class service provider can be attributed to its CEO at the time, Sir Colin Marshall. Marshall (currently chair of the board) was brought in to head up a major change for BA in the 1980s—and he did. His legacy has sustained and further propelled the airline to its current level of success.

A big part of this success was achieved in new ways of listening to customers and new approaches to dealing with customer complaints. One of the first things Marshall did was to install video booths at Heathrow airport so that upset customers could immediately go to the video booth while still at the airport and complain directly to him. In addition to this type of innovative action, Marshall instituted a series of systems and training changes to encourage and be responsive to customer complaints. To quote him directly, "I ardently believe that customer complaints are precious opportunities to hold on to customers who otherwise might take their business elsewhere and to learn about problems that need to be fixed."

Initially BA did research to understand the effect that dissatisfied or defecting customers had on the business. It learned that 50 percent of the dissatisfied customers who did *not* tell BA about their problems left the airline for a competitor. However, of those who *did* tell the company of their problems, 87 percent remained loyal to BA. It quickly became obvious that complaints should be encouraged! Considering that an average business class passenger has a lifetime value of $150,000, encouraging complaints and retaining their business was obviously critical.

Source: Newscast.

BA responded by building a model for "Making Customers into Champions." Goals of the new system were to (1) use customer feedback more effectively to improve quality; (2) strive to prevent future service problems through teamwork; (3) compensate customers on their terms, not the company's; and (4) practise customer retention, not adjudication. The bottom-line objective: to prevent customer defections.

To accomplish this objective, BA set up a four-step process to guide development of its technical and human delivery systems. This process was based on knowledge of how customers would like their complaints handled. The first step in the process was to *apologize and own the customer's problem*—not to search for someone to blame but rather to become the customer's advocate. The second essential was to *respond quickly*—taking absolutely no longer than 72 hours, and preferably providing an immediate solution. The third step was to *assure the customer that the problem is being fixed.* Finally, as much as possible, *handle complaints by phone.* BA found that customers with problems were delighted to speak personally to a customer service representative who could solve their problems.

To facilitate the process just described required major investments in systems and people. First, BA

continued

Technology Spotlight

British Airways—Complaint Handling Model Pays Off—continued

invested in a computer system called Caress that eliminated all paper by scanning or manually entering all customer information relevant to a complaint into a customer complaint database. A particular customer's information was thus easily accessed, and the data could be analyzed for patterns as well. The process for dealing with a complaint was also shortened by eliminating a number of unnecessary and redundant steps: the number of steps required to deal with a complaint was reduced from 13 to 3. Further, customer service representatives were given the tools and authority—they were empowered—to use whatever resources were needed to retain the customer's business. New training on listening skills, how to handle anger, and how to negotiate win-win solutions were put in place for customer service representatives. Finally, customers were encouraged to complain. Prior to the new initiatives, BA knew that only about 10 percent of its customers ever communicated with the airline directly—whether for good or bad reasons. The airline thus worked hard to get customers to complain and provide input by establishing 12 different "listening posts" or ways of communicating, including postage-paid cards, customer forums, surveys, and a "Fly with Me" program, in which customer service representatives flew with customers to experience and hear their responses firsthand.

Not only did BA use the information and systems it developed to directly retain dissatisfied customers, it also built systems to use the data and information to improve systems for the future. It used the information to design out common failure patterns and to design early-warning mechanisms to alert the company to potential future failures.

BA found that all its efforts toward complaint management paid off. For every £1 spent in customer retention efforts, BA found it had a £2 return. BA continues to take great pride in delivering the highest levels of customer service. In January 2000 the company unveiled £600,000,000 worth of new customer service initiatives to be rolled out over the following two years.

Sources: J. Barlow and C. Moller, *A Complaint Is a Gift* (San Francisco: Berrett-Koehler Publishers, 1996), pp. 16–18; C. R. Weiser, "Championing the Customer," *Harvard Business Review*, November/December 1995, pp. 113–15; S. E. Prokesch, "Competing on Service: An Interview with British Airways' Sir Colin Marshall," *Harvard Business Review*, November/December 1995, pp. 101–16; and www.britishairways.com, 2002.

At Ritz-Carlton Hotels, all employees carry service recovery forms called "instant action forms" with them at all times so that they can immediately record service failures and suggest actions to address them. In turn, the employees report to management these sources of service failure and the remedies. This information is then entered into the customer database and analyzed for patterns and systemic service issues that need to be fixed. If common themes are observed across a number of failure situations, changes are made to service processes or attributes. In addition, the information is entered into the customer's personal data file so when that customer stays at the Ritz-Carlton again (no matter what hotel), employees can be aware of the previous experience, ensuring that it does not happen again for that particular customer.

Learn from Lost Customers

Another key component of an effective service recovery strategy is to learn from the customers who decide to leave. Formal market research to discover the reasons customers have left can assist in preventing failures in the future. This type of research is difficult, even painful for companies. No one really likes to examine their failures. Yet such examination is essential for preventing the same mistakes.[46]

As presented in Chapter 6, lost customer research is most effectively obtained by depth interviews, administered by interviewers who truly understand the business. It may be best to have this type of research done by senior people in the company, particularly in business-to-business contexts in which customers are large and the impact of even one lost customer is great. The type of depth analysis often requires a series of "why" questions or "tell me more about that" questions to get at the actual, core reason for the customer's defection.[47]

In conducting this kind of research, a firm must focus on important or profitable customers who have left—not just everyone who has left the company. An insurance company in Australia once began this type of research to learn about their lost customers, only to find that the customers they were losing tended to be their least profitable customers anyway. They quickly determined that research on how to keep these *un*profitable customers would not be a good investment!

SERVICE GUARANTEES

A guarantee is a particular type of recovery tool. Guarantees have only recently been used for services. Traditionally, people believed that services could not be guaranteed given their intangible and variable nature. With a product, the customer is guaranteed that it will perform as promised and if not, that it can be returned. With services, it is generally not possible to take returns or to "undo" what has been performed. The skepticism about service guarantees is being dispelled, however, as more and more companies find they can guarantee their services and that there are tremendous benefits to doing so.

FIGURE 8.9   Corus Radio offers Canadians a performance guarantee.

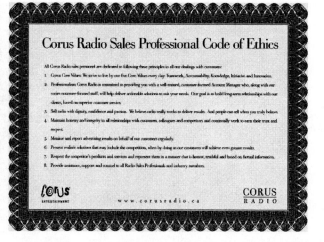

Source: Corus Entertainment Inc., 2005.

Companies are finding that effective service guarantees can complement the company's service recovery strategy—serving as one tool to help accomplish the service recovery strategies depicted in Figure 8.8. The Hampton Inn Hotels guarantee shown in Figure 8.3 is an example of such an effective guarantee. The Corus Radio guarantee depicted in Figure 8.9 is another.

Benefits of Service Guarantees

"Service organizations, in particular, are beginning to recognize that guarantees can serve not only as a marketing tool but as a means for defining, cultivating, and maintaining quality throughout an organization."[48] The benefits to the company of an effective service guarantee are numerous:[49]

- *A good guarantee forces the company to focus on its customers.* To develop a meaningful guarantee, the company must know what is important to its customers—what they expect and value. In many cases "satisfaction" is guaranteed, but in order for the guarantee to work effectively, the company must clearly understand what satisfaction means for its customers (what they value and expect).

- *An effective guarantee sets clear standards for the organization.* It prompts the company to clearly define what it expects of its employees and to communicate that expectation to them. The guarantee gives employees service-oriented goals that can quickly align employee behaviors around customer strategies. For example, Pizza Hut's guarantee that "If you're not satisfied with your pizza, let our restaurant know. We'll make it right or give you your money back" lets employees know exactly what they should do if a customer complains. It is also clear to employees that making it right for the customer is an important company goal.

- *A good guarantee generates immediate and relevant feedback from customers.* It provides an incentive for customers to complain and thereby provides more representative feedback to the company than simply relying on the relatively few customers who typically voice their concerns. The guarantee communicates to customers that they have the right to complain.

- *When the guarantee is invoked there is an instant opportunity to recover,* thus satisfying the customer and helping retain loyalty.

- *Information generated through the guarantee can be tracked and integrated into continuous improvement efforts.* A feedback link between customers and service operations decisions can be strengthened through the guarantee.

- *Studies of the impact of service guarantees suggest that employee morale and loyalty can be enhanced as a result.* A guarantee generates pride among employees. Through feedback from the guarantee, improvements can be made in the service that benefit customers and, indirectly, employees.

- *For customers, the guarantee reduces their sense of risk* and builds confidence in the organization. Because services are intangible and often highly personal or ego-involving, customers seek information and cues that will help reduce their sense of uncertainty. Guarantees have been shown to reduce risk and increase positive evaluation of the service prior to purchase.[50]

The bottom line for the company is that an effective guarantee can affect profitability through building customer awareness and loyalty, through positive word of mouth, and through reduction in costs as service improvements are made and service recovery expenses are reduced. Indirectly, the guarantee can reduce costs of employee turnover through creating a more positive service culture.

Types of Service Guarantees

Satisfaction vs. Service Attribute Guarantees

Service guarantees can be *unconditional satisfaction guarantees* or *service attribute guarantees*. Hampton Inn Hotels' guarantee is an unconditional satisfaction guarantee. In another context, Bain & Company, a management consulting firm, has offered some clients an unconditional guarantee for its services.[51] If clients are unhappy, they do not pay for the services. Lands' End, a catalogue retailer, has abbreviated its guarantee to "Guaranteed. Period."

In other cases, firms offer guarantees of particular aspects of the service that are important to customers. FedEx guarantees package delivery by a certain time. In introducing a new seat design in first class, British Airways advertised "Comfort guaranteed or you get 25,000 miles." McDonald's advertised a guarantee that stated "Hot Food; Fast, Friendly Delivery; Double-Check Drive-Thru Accuracy...We'll make it right, or your next meal is on us." In all these cases, the companies have guaranteed elements of the service that they know are important to customers.

Another type of service guarantee, a *combined guarantee,* combines the wide scope of the total satisfaction guarantee with specific attribute performance standards. Research suggests that this type of guarantee can be more effective than either of the other two types.[52]

External vs. Internal Guarantees

Interestingly, guarantees do not have to be only for external customers. Some companies are finding that internal service guarantees—one part of the organization guaranteeing its services to others—are effective ways of aligning internal service operations. At one direct-mail firm, the sales force guarantees to give the production department all the specifications needed to provide service to the external customer, or the offending salesperson will take the production department to lunch, sing a song at their next department meeting, or personally input all the specs into the computer.[53]

Characteristics of Effective Guarantees

No matter what the type of guarantee, certain characteristics make some guarantees more effective than others. Characteristics of effective guarantees are shown in Exhibit 8.4. But companies shouldn't expect the development of a guarantee to happen overnight. Travelocity.com recently launched its "Travelocity Service Guarantee." According to one of the company's VPs who worked on it, "It's taken a year of planning and a [huge] investment to be able to get the infrastructure in place to stand behind our guarantee. To do it correctly, you can't do it overnight."[54]

When to Use (or Not Use) a Guarantee

Service guarantees are not appropriate for every company and certainly not in every service situation. Before putting a guarantee strategy in place, a firm needs to address a number of important questions (see Exhibit 8.5). A guarantee is probably *not* the right strategy when:

---> EXHIBIT 8.4

Characteristics of an Effective Service Guarantee

UNCONDITIONAL

- The guarantee should make its promise unconditionally—no strings attached.

MEANINGFUL

- The firm should guarantee elements of the service that are important to the customer.
- The payout should cover fully the customer's dissatisfaction.

EASY TO UNDERSTAND AND COMMUNICATE

- Customers need to understand what to expect.
- Employees need to understand what to do.

EASY TO INVOKE AND COLLECT

- The firm should eliminate hoops or red tape in the way of accessing or collecting on the guarantee.

Source: C. W. L. Hart, "The Power of Unconditional Guarantees," *Harvard Business Review*, July/August 1988, pp. 54–62.

- *Existing service quality in the company is poor.* Before instituting a guarantee, the company should fix any significant quality problems. Otherwise the costs of implementing the guarantee might easily outweigh any benefits.

- *A guarantee does not fit the company's image.* Research suggests that the benefits of offering a guarantee for a high-end hotel like the Four Seasons may be significantly less than the benefits that a hotel of lesser quality would enjoy.[55]

- *Service quality is truly uncontrollable.* Uncontrollable service quality is often merely an excuse for not employing a guarantee. However, there are situations in which service quality is truly uncontrollable. For example, it would not be a good practice for a training organization to guarantee that all participants would pass a certification exam on completion of the training course if passing depends too much on the participants' own effort. The company might, however, guarantee satisfaction with the training or certain aspects of the training process.

- *Potential exists for customer abuse of the guarantee.* Fear of opportunistic customer behaviour, including customer cheating or fraudulent invocation of service guarantees, is a common reason that firms hesitate to offer guarantees.[56] In general, however, customer abuse of service guarantees is fairly minimal and not at all widespread.[57]

- *Costs of the guarantee outweigh the benefits.* As with any quality investment, the company will want to carefully calculate expected costs (payouts for failures and costs of making improvements) against anticipated benefits (customer loyalty, quality improvements, attraction of new customers, word-of-mouth advertising).

- *Customers perceive no risk in the service.* If there is no risk, a guarantee will likely produce little benefit for the company other than perhaps some promotional value.[58]

- *Customers perceive little variability in service quality between competitors.* Unless industries exhibit extreme variability in quality between competitors, a guarantee will yield little benefit.[59]

EXHIBIT 8.5

Questions to Consider in Implementing a Service Guarantee

DECIDING WHO DECIDES

- Is there a guarantee champion in the company?
- Is senior management committed to a guarantee?
- Is the guarantee design a team effort?
- Are customers providing input?

WHEN DOES A GUARANTEE MAKE SENSE?

- How high are quality standards?
- Can we afford a guarantee?
- How high is customer risk?
- Are competitors offering a guarantee?
- Is the company's culture compatible with a guarantee?

WHAT TYPE OF GUARANTEE SHOULD WE OFFER?

- Should we offer an unconditional guarantee or a specific-outcome one?

- Is our service measurable?
- What should our specific guarantee be about?
- What are the uncontrollables?
- Is the company particularly susceptible to unreasonable triggerings?
- What should the payout be?
- Will a refund send the wrong message?
- Could a full refund make customers feel guilty?
- Is the guarantee easy to invoke?

Source: A. L. Ostrom and C. W. L. Hart, "Service Guarantees: Research and Practice," in *Handbook of Services Marketing and Management*, ed. D. Iacobucci and T. Swartz (Thousand Oaks, CA: Sage Publications, 2000). © 2000 by Sage Publications. Reprinted by permission of Sage Publications.

SUMMARY

Part 3 of this text (Chapters 6, 7, and 8) focused on the critical importance of understanding customer expectations as well as many of the strategies firms use to accomplish this goal. Part of understanding customer expectations is being prepared for and knowing what to do when things go wrong or when the service fails. In this chapter we focused on service recovery, the actions taken by an organization in response to a service failure.

You learned in this chapter the importance of an effective service recovery strategy for retaining customers and increasing positive word of mouth communication. Another major benefit of an effective service recovery strategy is that the information it provides can be useful for service improvement. The potential downsides of poor service recovery are tremendous—negative word of mouth, lost customers, and declining business when quality issues are not addressed.

In this chapter you learned how customers respond to service failures and why some complain while others do not. You learned that customers expect to be treated fairly when they complain—not just in terms of the actual outcome or compensation they receive, but also in terms of the procedures that are used and how they are treated interpersonally. We pointed out in this chapter that there is tremendous room for improvement in service recovery effectiveness across firms and industries.

The second half of the chapter focused on specific strategies that firms are using for service recovery: (1) making the service fail-safe, or doing it right the first time, (2) encouraging and tracking complaints, (3) acting quickly, (4) providing adequate explanations, (5) treating customers fairly, (6) cultivating relationships with customers, (7) learning from recovery experiences, and (8) learning from lost customers. The chapter ended with a discussion of service guarantees as a tool used by many firms to build a foundation for service recovery. You learned the benefits of service guarantees, the elements of a good guarantee, and the pros and cons of using guarantees under various circumstances.

⟼ Discussion Questions

1. Why is it important for a service firm to have a strong recovery strategy? Think of a time when you received less-than-desirable service from a particular service organization. Was any effort made to recover? What should/could have been done differently? Do you still buy services from the organization? Why or why not? Did you tell others about your experience?

2. Discuss the benefits to a company of having an effective service recovery strategy. Describe an instance in which you experienced (or delivered as an employee) an effective service recovery. In what ways did the company benefit in this particular situation?

3. Explain the recovery paradox, and discuss its implications for a service firm manager.

4. Discuss the types of actions that customers can take in response to a service failure. What type of complainer are you? Why? As a manager, would you want to encourage your customers to be voicers? If so, how?

5. Review Exhibits 8.1 and 8.2. What would you have done if you were on the management team at Doubletree Inn, Ctizens Bank, or Club Med?

6. Explain the logic behind these two quotes: "A complaint is a gift" and "The customer who complains is your friend."

7. Choose a firm you are familiar with. Describe how you would design an ideal service recovery strategy for that organization.

8. What are the benefits to the company of an effective service guarantee? Should every service organization have one?

9. Describe three service guarantees that are currently offered by companies or organizations in addition to the ones already described in the chapter. (Examples are readily available on the Internet.) Are your examples good guarantees or poor guarantees based on the criteria presented in this chapter?

⟼ Exercises

1. Write a letter of complaint (or voice your complaint in person) to a service organization from which you have experienced less-than-desirable service. What do you expect the organization to do to recover? (Later, report to the class the results of your complaint, whether you were satisfied with the recovery, what could/should have been done differently, and whether you will continue using the service.)

2. Interview five people about their service recovery experiences. What happened, and what did they expect the firm to do? Were they treated fairly according to the definition of recovery fairness presented in the chapter? Will they return to the company in the future?

3. Interview a manager about service recovery strategies used in his or her firm. Use the strategies shown in Figure 8.8 to frame your questions.

4. Visit Cisco Systems' website (www.cisco.com). Consider what the company is currently doing to help its customers solve their own problems. Compare what Cisco is doing with the self-service efforts of another service provider of your choice.

5. Choose a service you are familiar with. Explain the service offered and develop a good service guarantee for it. Discuss why your guarantee is a good one, and list the benefits to the company of implementing it.

Notes

1. As quoted in F. Van Bennekom, "A Sporting Service Recovery," Great Brook site, 2005, www.greatbrook.com/complaint_handling.htm, accessed September 30, 2006.

2. For research that shows different types of service failures, see M. J. Bitner, B. H. Booms, and M. S. Tetreault, "The Service Encounter: Diagnosing Favorable and Unfavorable Incidents," *Journal of Marketing* 54 (January 1990), pp. 71–84; and S. M. Keaveney, "Customer Switching Behavior in Service Industries: An Exploratory Study," *Journal of Marketing* 59 (April 1995), pp. 71–82.

3. For research on important outcomes associated with service recovery, see S. S. Tax, S. W. Brown, and M. Chandrashekaran, "Customer Evaluations of Service Complaint Experiences: Implications for Relationship Marketing," *Journal of Marketing* 62 (April 1998), pp. 60–76; S. S. Tax and S. W. Brown, "Recovering and Learning from Service Failure," *Sloan Management Review,* Fall 1998, pp. 75–88; A. K. Smith and R. N. Bolton, "An Experimental Investigation of Customer Reactions to Service Failure and Recovery Encounters," *Journal of Service Research* 1 (August 1998), pp. 65–81; S. W. Kelley, K. D. Hoffman, and M. A. Davis, "A Typology of Retail Failures and Recoveries," *Journal of Retailing* 69 (Winter 1993), pp. 429–52; R. N. Bolton, "A Dynamic Model of the Customer's Relationship with a Continuous Service Provider: The Role of Satisfaction," *Marketing Science* 17, no. 1 (1998), pp. 45–65; A. K. Smith and R. N. Bolton, "The Effect of Customers' Emotional Responses to Service Failures on Their Recovery Effort Evaluations and Satisfaction Judgments," *Journal of the Academy of Marketing Science,* 30 (Winter 2002), pp. 5–23.

4. Technical Assistance Research Program, "Consumer Complaint Handling in America: An Update Study" (Washington, DC: Department of Consumer Affairs, 1986).

5. B. Ettorre, "Phenomenal Promises That Mean Business," *Management Review,* March 1994, pp. 18–23.

6. M. Granier, J. Kemp, and A. Lawes, "Customer Complaint Handling—The Multimillion Pound Sinkhole: A Case of Customer Rage Unassuaged," study conducted by the Customer Care Alliance, 2004.

7. Tax and Brown, "Recovering and Learning from Service Failure."

8. Granier, Kemp, and Lawes, "Customer Complaint Handling—The Multimillion Pound Sinkhole."

9. See C. W. Hart, J. L. Heskett, and W. E. Sasser Jr., "The Profitable Art of Service

Recovery," *Harvard Business Review* 68 (July/August 1990), pp. 148–56; M. A. McCollough and S. G. Bharadwaj, "The Recovery Paradox: An Examination of Consumer Satisfaction in Relation to Disconfirmation, Service Quality, and Attribution Based Theories," in *Marketing Theory and Applications,* ed. C. T. Allen et al. (Chicago: American Marketing Association, 1992), p. 119.

10. Smith and Bolton, "An Experimental Investigation of Customer Reactions to Service Failure and Recovery Encounters."

11. M. A. McCullough, L. L. Berry, and M. S. Yadav, "An Empirical Investigation of Customer Satisfaction After Service Failure and Recovery," *Journal of Service Research,* 3 (November 2000), pp. 121–37.

12. J. G. Maxham III and R. G. Netemeyer, "A Longitudinal Study of Complaining Customers' Evaluations of Multiple Service Failures and Recovery Efforts," *Journal of Marketing* 66 (October 2002), pp. 57–71.

13. For research foundations on typologies of customer responses to failures, see R. L. Day and E. L. Landon Jr., "Towards a Theory of Consumer Complaining Behavior," in *Consumer and Industrial Buying Behavior,* ed. A. Woodside, J. Sheth, and P. Bennett (Amsterdam: North-Holland Publishing Company, 1977); J. Singh, "Consumer Complaint Intentions and Behavior: Definitional and Taxonomical Issues," *Journal of Marketing* 52 (January 1988), pp. 93–107; and J. Singh, "Voice, Exit, and Negative Word of mouth Behaviors: An Investigation Across Three Service Categories," *Journal of the Academy of Marketing Science* 18 (Winter 1990), pp. 1–15.

14. Smith and Bolton, "The Effect of Customers' Emotional Responses to Service Failures."

15. Ibid.

16. N. Stephens and K. P. Gwinner, "Why Don't Some People Complain? A Cognitive–Emotive Process Model of Consumer Complaining Behavior," *Journal of the Academy of Marketing Science* 26 (Spring 1998), pp. 172–89.

17. Ibid.

18. T. Hennig-Thurau, K. P. Gwinner, G. Walsh, and D. D. Gremler, "Electronic Word of mouth via Consumer-Opinion Platforms: What Motivates Consumers to Articulate Themselves on the Internet?" *Journal of Interactive Marketing* 18 (Winter 2004), pp. 38–52.

19. Many such websites exist; examples include www.untied.com (for United Airlines experiences), www.starbucked.com (for Starbucks), and www.walmart sucks.org (for Wal-Mart).

20. J. C. Ward and A. L. Ostrom, "Online Complaining via Customer-Created Web Sites: A Protest Framing Perspective," working paper, W. P. Carey School of Business, Arizona State University, 2004.

21. J. Singh, " A Typology of Consumer Dissatisfaction Response Styles," *Journal of Retailing* 66 (Spring 1990), pp. 57–99.

22. J. R. McColl-Kennedy and B. A. Sparks, "Application of Fairness Theory to Service Failures and Service Recovery," *Journal of Service Research* 5 (February 2003), pp. 251–66; M. Davidow, "Organizational Responses to Customer Complaints: What Works and What Doesn't," *Journal of Service Research* 5 (February 2003), pp. 225–50.

23. Granier, Kemp, and Lawes, "Customer Complaint Handling—The Multimillion Pound Sinkhole."

24. Davidow, "Organizational Responses to Customer Complaints."

25. See Tax, Brown, and Chandrashekaran, "Customer Evaluations of Service Complaint Experiences"; Tax and Brown, "Recovering and Learning from Service Failure."

26. Tax and Brown, "Recovering and Learning from Service Failure."

27. Smith and Bolton, "The Effect of Customers' Emotional Responses to Service Failures."

28. McCullough, Berry, and Yadav, "An Empirical Investigation of Customer Satisfaction After Service Failure and Recovery."

29. A. S. Mattila, "The Impact of Relationship Type on Customer Loyalty in a Context of Service Failures," *Journal of Service Research* 4 (November 2001), pp. 91–101; see also R. L. Hess Jr., S. Ganesan, and N. M. Klein, "Service Failure and Recovery: The Impact of Relationship Factors on Customer Satisfaction," *Journal of the Academy of Marketing Science* 31 (Spring 2003), pp. 127–45; R. Priluck, "Relationship Marketing Can Mitigate Product and Service Failures," *Journal of Services Marketing* 17, no. 1 (2003), pp. 37–52.

30. H. S. Bansal and S. F. Taylor, "The Service Provider Switching Model (SPSM)," *Journal of Service Research* 2 (November 1999), pp. 200–218.

31. S. M. Keaveney and M. Parthasarathy, "Customer Switching Behavior in Online Services: An Exploratory Study of the Role of Selected Attitudinal, Behavioral, and Demographic Factors," *Journal of the Academy of Marketing Science* 29, no. 4 (2001), pp. 374–90.

32. I. Roos, "Switching Processes in Customer Relationships," *Journal of Service Research* 2 (August 1999), pp. 68–85.

33. Keaveney, "Customer Switching Behavior in Service Industries."

34. A. Parasuraman, V. A. Zeithaml, and L. L. Berry, "SERVQUAL: A Multiple-Item Scale for Measuring Consumer Perceptions of Service Quality," *Journal of Retailing* 64 (Spring 1988), pp. 64–79.

35. R. B. Chase and D. M. Stewart, "Make Your Service Fail-Safe," *Sloan Management Review,* Spring 1994, pp. 35–44.

36. Ibid.

37. F. R. Reichheld and W. E. Sasser Jr., "Zero Defections: Quality Comes to Services," *Harvard Business Review,* September/October 1990, pp. 105–7.

38. L. M. Fisher, "Here Comes Front-Office Automation," *Strategy and Business* 13 (Fourth Quarter, 1999), pp. 53–65; and R. A. Shaffer, "Handling Customer Service on the Web," *Fortune,* March 1, 1999, pp. 204, 208.

39. S. W. Brown, "Service Recovery Through IT," *Marketing Management,* Fall 1997, pp. 25–27.

40. Davidow, "Organizational Responses to Customer Complaints."

41. J. Dunning, A. Pecotich, and A. O'Cass, "What Happens When Things Go Wrong? Retail Sales Explanations and Their Effects," *Psychology and Marketing* 21, no. 7 (2004), pp. 553–72; McColl-Kennedy and Sparks, "Application of Fairness Theory to Service Failures and Service Recovery"; Davidow, "Organizational Responses to Customer Complaints."

42. Hess, Ganesan, and Klein, "Service Failure and Recovery"; Priluck, "Relationship Marketing Can Mitigate Product and Service Failures."

43. T. DeWitt and M. K. Brady, "Rethinking Service Recovery Strategies: The Effect of Rapport on Consumer Responses to Service Failure," *Journal of Service Research* 6 (November 2003), pp. 193–207.

44. Hess, Ganesan, and Klein, "Service Failure and Recovery."

45. L. L. Berry and A. Parasuraman, *Marketing Services* (New York: Free Press, 1991), p. 52.
46. F. F. Reichheld, "Learning from Customer Defections," *Harvard Business Review,* March/April 1996, pp. 56–69.
47. Ibid.
48. A. L. Ostrom and C. W. L. Hart, "Service Guarantees: Research and Practice," in *Handbook of Services Marketing and Management,* ed. D. Iacobucci and T. Swartz (Thousand Oaks, CA: Sage Publications, 2000), pp. 299–316.
49. See ibid.; C. W. L. Hart, "The Power of Unconditional Guarantees," *Harvard Business Review,* July/August 1988, pp. 54–62; and C. W. L. Hart, *Extraordinary Guarantees* (New York: AMACOM, 1993).
50. A. L. Ostrom and D. Iacobucci, "The Effect of Guarantees on Consumers' Evaluation of Services," *Journal of Services Marketing* 12, no. 5 (1998), pp. 362–78; S. B. Lidén and P. Skålén, "The Effect of Service Guarantees on Service Recovery," *International Journal of Service Industry Management* 14, no. 1 (2003), pp.-36–58.
51. Ostrom and Hart, "Service Guarantees."
52. J. Wirtz and D. Kum, "Designing Service Guarantees: Is Full Satisfaction the Best You Can Guarantee?" *Journal of Services Marketing* 15, no. 4 (2001), pp. 282–99.
53. Example cited in Ostrom and Hart, "Service Guarantees."
54. As quoted in *Strategy Magazine*, November 2005, p. 15.
55. J. Wirtz, D. Kum, and K. S. Lee, "Should a Firm with a Reputation for Outstanding Service Quality Offer a Service Guarantee?" *Journal of Services Marketing* 14, no. 6 (2000), pp. 502–12.
56. J. Wirtz, "Development of a Service Guarantee Model," *Asia Pacific Journal of Management* 15 (April 1998), pp. 51–75; Wirtz and Kim, "Consumer Cheating on Service Guarantees," *Journal of the Academy of Marketing Science* 32 (Spring 2004), pp. 159–75.
57. Wirtz, "Development of a Service Guarantee Model."
58. Ostrom and Iacobucci, "The Effect of Guarantees."
59. Wirtz, "Development of a Service Guarantee Model."

Chapter 10

Customer-Defined Service Standards

Provider Gap 2

FEDEX SETS STANDARDS THROUGH SQI

Marketing research data are not the only numbers that FedEx (www.fedex.com) tracks to run its business. The company, which began delivery to Canada more than 25 years ago, drives its operations with the aid of the most comprehensive, customer-defined index of service standards and measures in the world. FedEx's service quality indicator (SQI) was designed as "unforgiving internal performance measurement" to ensure that the company delivered to its goal of "100 percent customer satisfaction after every interaction and transaction and 100 percent service performance on every package handled."[1] The development and implementation of SQI led to a U.S.-based Malcolm Baldrige National Quality Award.

What makes this service index different from those of other companies is its foundation in customer feedback. Since the 1980s, FedEx has documented customer complaints and used the information to improve internal processes. Its composite listing of the 12 most common customer complaints, called the "Hierarchy of Horrors," included wrong-day delivery, right-day late delivery, pickup not made, lost package, customer misinformed by FedEx, billing and paperwork mistakes, employee performance failures, and damaged packages. Although this list was useful, it fell short of giving management the ability to anticipate and eliminate customer complaints before they occurred.

The company developed the 12-item statistical SQI to be a more "comprehensive, pro-active, customer-oriented measure of customer satisfaction and service quality."[2] The SQI consists of the following components and weighting (based on relative importance of each component to customers):

Indicator	Weight
Right-day late deliveries	1
Wrong-day late deliveries	5
Traces not answered	1
Complaints reopened	5
Missing proofs of delivery	1
Invoice adjustments	1
Missed pickups	10
Damaged packages	10
Lost packages	10
Aircraft delay minutes	5
Overgoods	5
Abandoned calls	1

Another distinguishing feature of the SQI is its reporting in terms of *numbers* of errors rather than percentages. Management of the company strongly believes that percentages distance the company from the consumer: to report 1 percent of packages late diminished the reality of 20,000 unhappy customers (1% of the approximately 2 million packages shipped a day). The service quality indicator report is disseminated weekly to everyone in the company. On receipt of the report, root causes of service failures are investigated. With a senior officer assigned to each component, and with bonuses for everyone in the company tied to performance on the SQI, the company drives continuously closer to its goal of 100 percent satisfaction with every transaction.[3]

As we saw in Chapters 6, 7, and 8, understanding customer requirements is the first step in delivering high service quality. Once managers accurately understand what customers expect, they face a second critical challenge: using this knowledge to set service quality standards for the organization. Service companies experience difficulty in setting standards partly because doing so requires that the marketing and operations departments within a company work together. In most service companies, integrating the work of the marketing function and the operations function (appropriately called *functional integration*) is not a typical approach; more frequently these two functions operate separately. The reason that operations and marketing must work hard to achieve better integration has its roots in how firms have evolved. Until recently, marketing wasn't even a function in many service firms. Consider Canada Post. Its operations staff were responsible for "getting the job done." That job might be delivering the mail, shipping parcels, providing forwarding addresses, and so forth. Metrics for these activities were based on efficiency, speed, accuracy, and cost. When Canada Post realized that they must do more to compete with firms like FedEx, they added marketing staff, trained their clerks, and tried to become customer-responsive. These first steps were, however, relatively superficial, because the firm still had not changed the way it did business and measured itself.

To this day, many formerly operationally driven companies continue to find it hard to change the way they run their businesses. It is only gradually, and with significant difficulty, that many service firms are actually integrating concern for their customers into their business.

But although closing Gap 2 is taking a while, progress is being made. Customer standards are replacing or being added to company standards—marketing is slowly integrating with operations.

⟶ FACTORS NECESSARY FOR APPROPRIATE SERVICE STANDARDS

Standardization of Service Behaviours and Actions

The translation of customer expectations into specific service standards depends on the degree to which tasks can be standardized (Figure 10.1). Some managers believe that services cannot be standardized—that customization is essential. Managers also may feel that standardizing tasks is inconsistent with employee empowerment—that employees will feel controlled by the company if tasks are standardized. Further, they feel that services are too intangible to be measured. This view leads to vague and loose standard setting with little or no measurement or feedback.

In reality, many service tasks are routine (such as those needed for opening chequing accounts or spraying lawns for pests), and for these, specific rules and standards can be fairly easily established. Employees may welcome knowing how to perform actions most efficiently: it frees them to use their ingenuity in the more personal aspects of their jobs.

According to one observer, standardization of service can take three forms: (1) substitution of technology for personal contact (2) improvement in work methods, and (3) combinations of these two methods.[4] Examples of technology substitution include automatic teller machines and automatic car washes. Improvements in work methods are illustrated by restaurant salad bars.

Standardization, whether accomplished by technology or by improvements in work processes, reduces Gap 2. Standardization does not mean that service is performed in a rigid, mechanical way. Customer-defined standardization ensures that the most critical

FIGURE 10.1

Federal Express has standardized service behaviours and actions, resulting in superior employee performance.

elements of a service are performed as expected by customers, not that every action in a service is executed in a uniform manner. Using customer-defined standardization can, in fact, allow for and be compatible with employee empowerment. For instance, companies such as Amex Bank of Canada, in using customer priorities rather than company priorities, have no set standard for the amount of time an employee spends on the telephone with a customer. Instead, they have standards that focus on making the customer satisfied and comfortable, allowing telephone representatives to use their own judgment about the time limits.

Formal Service Targets and Goals

Successful companies are noted for establishing formal standards to guide employees. These companies have an accurate sense of how well they are performing—how long it takes to conduct transactions, how frequently service fails, how quickly they settle customer complaints—and strive to improve by defining goals that lead them to meet or exceed customer expectations.

One type of formal goal setting that is relevant in service businesses involves specific targets for individual behaviours. As an example, consider the behaviour "calls the customer back quickly," an action that signals responsiveness in contact employees. If the service goal for employee behaviour is stated in such a general term as "call the customer back quickly," the standard provides little direction. Different employees will interpret this vague objective in their own way: some may call the customer back in 10 minutes whereas others may wait two to four days. And the firm itself will not be able to determine when or if individual employees meet the goal because its expression is not measurable—one could justify virtually any amount of time as "quickly." On the other hand, if the individual employee's service goal is to call each customer back within four hours, employees have a specific, unambiguous guideline about how quickly they should execute the action (four hours). If you have ever done a performance review at your workplace, you will immediately recognize the importance of having specific metrics. Vague standards lead to many misunderstandings.

Another type of formal goal setting involves the overall department or company. For example, a department might set as its overall goal "to call the customer back within four hours 97 percent of the time" and collect data over a month's or year's time to evaluate the extent to which it meets the target.

Customer- Not Company-Defined Standards

Virtually all companies possess service standards that are *company-defined*—they are established to reach internal company goals for productivity, efficiency, cost, or technical quality. A current company-defined standard that does not meet customer expectations is the common practice of voice-activated telephone support systems that do not allow consumers to speak to humans. Because these systems save companies money many organizations have switched to them. To close Gap 2, standards set by companies must be based on customer requirements and expectations rather than just on internal company goals. In this chapter we make the case that *company-defined* standards are not typically successful in driving behaviours that close Provider Gap 2. Instead, a company must set *customer-defined standards:* operational standards based on pivotal customer requirements that are visible to and measured by customers. These standards are deliberately chosen to match customer expectations and to be calibrated the way the customer views and expresses them. Because these goals are essential to the provision of excellent service, the rest of this chapter focuses on customer-defined standards.

Knowing customer requirements, priorities, and expectation levels can be both effective and efficient. Anchoring service standards on customers can save money by identifying what the customer values, thus eliminating activities and features that the customer either does not notice or will not pay for.

On the other hand, many firms create standards and policies to suit their own needs that are so counter to the wishes of customers that the companies endanger their customer relationships. When the hotel industry was booming, many hotels initiated policies penalizing late arrivals and early departures as well as imposing minimum-stay requirements. Some began to charge guests $50 when they stayed fewer days than agreed to at check-in. B&Bs often kept guests' one-night deposits unless they cancelled at least three days prior to arrival. And then, of course, there is the famous *Seinfeld* episode in which George is charged for missing his appointment with Elaine's friend, the masseuse! Businesses defend these policies on the basis of self-protection, but they are clearly not customer-oriented.

Although customer-defined standards need not conflict with productivity and efficiency, they are not developed for these reasons. Rather, they are anchored in and steered by customer perceptual measures of service quality or satisfaction. The service standards that evolve from a customer perspective are likely to be different from company-defined service standards.

Virtually all organizations have lists of actions that they measure regularly, most of which fall into the category of company-defined standards. As noted earlier, often these standards deal with activities or actions that reflect the history of the business rather than the reality of the needs of current customers.

⟶ TYPES OF CUSTOMER-DEFINED SERVICE STANDARDS

The type of standards that close Provider Gap 2 are *customer-defined standards*: operational measures based on customer requirements that are visible to customers rather than on company concerns such as productivity or efficiency. Two major types of customer-defined service standards can be distinguished: "hard" and "soft." These standards will be discussed in the following two sections.

Hard Customer-Defined Standards

All the FedEx standards that comprise the SQI fall into the category of hard standards and measures: *things that can be counted, timed, or observed through audits.* A series of 35 studies across numerous industries from the Arthur D. Little management consulting firm found that the most frequently cited customer complaint was late product and service delivery (44%), followed by product and service quality mistakes (31%).[5]

Reliability is the single most important concern of service customers. One of the best examples of customer-defined hard standards in the Internet context is the set of summary metrics that Dell Computer uses for fulfilment.[6] They include:

- *Ship to target (SSTT)*—the percentage of orders delivered on time with complete accuracy

- *Initial field incident rate (IFIR)*—the frequency of customer problems

- *On-time first-time fix (OTFTF)*—the percentage of problems fixed on the first visit by a service representative arriving at the time promised

Dell tracks its performance to these standards and rewards employees on the basis of their "met promises" or reliability, which is often higher than 98 percent.

When it comes to providing service across cultures and continents, service providers need to recognize that customer-defined service standards often need to be adapted. In Canada we expect waiters to bring the cheque promptly. In fact, if we do not receive it shortly after the last course, and without our asking for it, we evaluate the service as slow and nonresponsive. In Spain, however, customers consider it rude for the waiter to bring the bill to the table without being asked to do so. They feel rushed, a state they dislike during meals.

Hard service standards for responsiveness are set to ensure the speed or promptness with which companies deliver products (within two working days), handle complaints (by sundown each day), answer questions (within two hours), answer the telephone (see the Technology Spotlight), and arrive for repair calls (within 30 minutes of the estimated time). In addition to standard setting that specifies levels of response, companies must have well-staffed customer service departments.

FIGURE 10.2

Reliability—"getting it done right"—is the most important dimension of service quality.

Source: By permission of Dave Coverly and Creators Syndicate, Inc.

Responsiveness perceptions diminish when customers wait to get through to the company by telephone, are put on hold, or are dumped into a phone mail system.

The Global Feature in this chapter provides some real examples of these hard customer-defined standards, along with some soft customer-defined standards, which will be discussed next.

Soft Customer-Defined Standards

Not all customer priorities can be counted, timed, or observed through audits. As Albert Einstein once said, "Not everything that counts can be counted, and not everything that can be counted, counts." In contrast to hard measures, soft measures are those that must be documented using perceptual data. We call these standards *soft standards and measures,* because they are opinion-based and cannot be directly observed. They must be collected by talking to customers, employees, or others. Soft standards provide direction, guidance, and feedback to employees in ways to achieve customer satisfaction and can be quantified by measuring customer perceptions and beliefs.

Mini Maid Services, a firm that franchises home and office janitorial services, successfully built a business by developing a repertoire of 22 customer-defined soft standards for daily cleaning chores. The company sends out crews of four who perform these 22 tasks in an average time of 55 minutes for a fee ranging from approximately $45 to $55. These standards are considered soft because they are measured by follow-up trailer calls that survey customer perceptions.

One-Time Fixes

When customer research is undertaken to find out what aspects of service need to be changed, requirements can sometimes be met using one-time fixes. One-time fixes are *technology, policy, or procedure changes that, when instituted, address customer requirements.* We include one-time fixes in our discussion of standards because organizations with multiple outlets often must clearly define these standards to ensure consistency. As an example, Hampton Inns' new "Make It Hampton" program requires that all inns institute 60 new product and service standards, many of which are one-time fixes. These include providing lap desks in rooms, outdoor planter gardens to hide trash containers, red-carpet welcome mats, and new lobby artwork and music that celebrates travel.[7] Performance standards do not typically need to be developed for these dissatisfiers, because the one-time change in technology, policy, or procedures accomplishes the desired change.

Examples of successful one-time fixes include Hertz and other rental car companies' express check-in and GM Saturn's one-price policy for automobiles. In each of these examples, customers expressed a desire to be served in ways different from the past. Hertz's customers had clearly indicated their frustration at waiting in long lines. Saturn customers disliked haggling over car prices in dealer showrooms.

Whereas most companies in these industries decided for various reasons not to address these customer requirements, Hertz and Saturn each responded with one-time fixes that virtually revolutionized the service quality delivered by their companies. Hertz used technology to create Express Checkout, a one-time fix that also resulted in productivity improvements and cost reductions. The company also pioneered a similar one-time fix for hotel Express Check-In, again in response to customers' expressed desires. Saturn countered industry tradition and offered customers a one-price policy that eliminated the haggling characteristics of automobile dealerships.

Technology Spotlight

The Power of a Good Telephone Responsiveness Standard

Customer-defined service standards resulted for all United States public service agencies after a 1993 National Performance Review, when all government agencies that dealt directly with the public were required to survey customers and establish service standards on the basis of the feedback. By 1998 more than 4,000 customer service standards had been created by 570 agencies. One of the most successful came from the Social Security Administration (SSA) and illustrates a customer-defined hard standard relating to a technology issue that all customers face in dealing with public and private companies alike: telephone responsiveness.

The SSA knew that access—getting through to the agency on its 800 number—was the single biggest driver of customer satisfaction and public perception of the agency's competency. Unfortunately, customers more often than not repeatedly encountered busy signals on the 60 million calls they placed to the SSA's high-volume 800 number. The National Performance Review suggested to the agency that its service standard ought to be that everyone who called its 800 number would get through on the first try: 100 percent access! The SSA balked, recognizing that its telephone technology, limited employee resources, and wide fluctuations in demand would prevent the standard from being met.

The agency ultimately settled on a more reasonable standard: 95 percent of all callers would be served within five minutes. This standard became a very clear and focused goal that "everybody knew and everybody was shooting for," according to an SSA manager. Early measurements indicated less-than-stellar performance; in 1995 only 73.5 percent of callers got through in five minutes.

What followed was an impressive effort of technology, people, and measurement. According to an expert, "SSA endured tremendous expense, dislocation, pain—and even failure—to meet its standard." First, SSA officials developed a new phone system with AT&T (www.att.sbc.com) that involved a sophisticated call-routing approach. Second, the organization trained virtually all technical people who held jobs other than in teleservices in those skills so that they could be shifted during peak hours to help with the volume. Third, the agency restricted leave for teleservice representatives at peak time, increased the use of overtime, and worked with employees to change processes and rules to improve performance.

The low point in performance to the standard was during the transition to the new system. In November 1995 only 57.2 percent of callers got through within five minutes. Even worse was that on the first day back to work in January 1996, the AT&T 800-number system crashed, leading to even more busy signals. By February, after AT&T fixed the system and the organization got used to its changes, performance improved significantly. The five-minute access rate was 92.1 percent in February, 95.9 percent in November, and above 95 percent ever since.

The SSA standard was successful because it was specific, measurable, and meaningful to customers. Because its results were documented and publicized both within and outside the agency, both employees and management were accountable for performance. Unlike many of the vague, meaningless standards that resulted from the National Performance Review's work with government agencies, this one was a winner.

Source: D. Osborne, "Higher Standards," *Government Executive,* July 2000, pp. 63–71.

Source: Royalty-Free/CORBIS.

Global Feature

Distinguishing Hard and Soft Customer-Defined Standards

Even though Canadians do not have access to Cingular Wireless, you have likely seen some of their television commercials. The spring 2006 advertising campaign that had the company promoting itself as the wireless network with "the fewest dropped calls" serves as a good illustration of a hard customer-defined standard.

In an industry that had been competing on price, wireless carriers are now moving to a more service-oriented differentiation strategy. Thinking that consumers care more about calls getting through than their cost, Cingular Wireless appears to have adopted a hard customer-defined standard to differentiate itself from the competition. Its assertion that it has the fewest dropped calls is specific, measurable, and seemingly meaningful to customers.

Not to be left out, competitors Sprint and Verizon were touting similar claims: that they were each the most reliable wireless carrier. However, these competitors' advertising did not point to hard standards. The difference was that Sprint's ads declared it was "America's most reliable wireless" without pointing to specific, measurable attributes, and Verizon's only implied the reliability of their network by asking, "Can you hear me now?"

Table 10.1 presents some more North American examples of some hard and soft customer-defined standards.

Sources: B. Mohl, "The Fewest Dropped Calls," *The Boston Globe*, April 23, 2006, available www.boston.com/business/articles/2006/04/23/the_fewest_dropped_calls, accessed October 1, 2006; "The Ritz-Carlton Basics," flyer distributed by The Ritz-Carlton Hotel Company L.L.C. to all employees.

One-time fixes are often accomplished by technology. Technology can simplify and improve customer service, particularly when it frees company personnel by handling routine, repetitive tasks and transactions. Effective use of information databases is illustrated in this example from Pizza Hut:

> Pizza Hut centralized and computerized its home delivery operations. Rather than having the separate tasks of order taking, baking, and delivery all in the same location, the company developed a system that works more effectively for both the company and the customer. Operators in a customer service center (not a bakery) take requests for pizza. Working from a database that shows past orders, trained operators take an average of 17 seconds to verify directions to a caller's home and enter his or her request. Operators then route the orders to the closest bake shops, which are strategically located throughout cities to ensure fast deliveries. Cooks in the satellite bake shops prepare pizzas on instructions sent to bake shop printers from order-takers' computers. Drivers aim to complete their deliveries within a half hour of a customer's call, and usually succeed.[8]

One-time fixes also deal with the aspects of service that go beyond human performance: rules and policies, operating hours, product quality, and price. "Poka yokes," discussed in Chapter Eight, are also excellent illustrations of one-time fixes. Recall that poka yokes include, for instance, trays for surgical instruments that include indentations for each specific instrument to ensure that surgeons know all instruments are back in their proper place prior to closing a patient's incision.

TABLE 10.1   Examples of Hard and Soft Customer-Defined Standards

Hard Customer-Defined Standards		
Company	**Customer Priorities**	**Customer-Defined Standards**
FedEx	On-time delivery	Number of packages right day late Number of packages wrong day late Number of missed pickups
Dell Computer	On-time delivery Computer works properly	Ship to target Initial field incident rate Missing wrong and damaged rate Service delivery on time first-time fix
LensCrafters	Quick turnaround on eyeglasses	Glasses ready in one hour
Honeywell Home and Building Division	Fast delivery On-time delivery Order accuracy	Orders entered first day received Orders delivered when promised Order 100% accurate
Texas Instruments Defense Systems	Compliance with commitments More personal contact	On-time delivery Product compliance to requirements Increased number of personal visits
Soft Customer-Defined Standards		
General Electric	Interpersonal skills of operators: • Tone of voice • Problem solving • Summarizing actions • Closing	Taking ownership of the call; following through with promises made; being courteous and knowledgeable; understanding the customer's question or request
The Ritz-Carlton Hotel Company L.L.C.	Being treated with respect	"Gold Standards" • Uniforms are to be immaculate. • Wear proper and safe footwear. • Wear name tag. • Adhere to grooming standards. • Notify supervisor immediately of hazards. • Use proper telephone etiquette. • Ask the caller, "May I place you on hold?" • Do not screen calls. • Eliminate call transfers when possible.
L. L. Bean	Calming human voice; minimal customer anxiety	Tone of voice; other tasks (e.g., arranging gift boxes) not done while on the telephone with customers
American Express	Resolution of problems Treatment Courtesy of representative	Resolve problem at first contact (no transfers, other calls, or multiple contacts); communicate and give adequate instructions; take all the time necessary. Listen; do everything possible to help; be appropriately reassuring (open and honest). Put card member at ease; be patient in explaining billing process; display sincere interest in helping card member; listen attentively; address card member by name; thank card member at end of call.

DEVELOPMENT OF CUSTOMER-DEFINED SERVICE STANDARDS

Basing Standards on the Service Encounter Sequence

Performance requirements are rarely the same across all parts of a company; instead, they are associated with particular service processes and encounters.

A customer's overall service quality evaluation is the accumulation of evaluations of multiple service experiences. Service encounters are the component pieces needed to establish service standards in a company. Therefore, one of the first steps in establishing customer-defined standards is to delineate the service encounter sequence. Identifying the sequence can be done by listing the sequential steps and activities that the customer experiences in receiving the service. Alternatively, service blueprints (see Chapter 9) can be used to identify the sequence by noting all the customers' activities across the top of the blueprint. Vertical lines from customer activities into the lower levels of the blueprint signal the points at which service encounters take place. Standards that meet customer expectations can then be established.

Because many services have multiple encounters, companies and researchers have examined whether some encounters (e.g., the first or the last) are more important than others. The Marriott Corporation identified the encounters that occur in the first 10 minutes of a hotel stay as the most critical, leading the hospitality company to focus on hotel front desk experiences (such as Express Check-In) when making improvements. Although service practice and management literature have emphasized strong starts, recent research indicates that strong finishes in the final event of the encounter have a greater impact on overall satisfaction. Further, the research shows that consistent performance throughout the encounter—widely believed to produce the most favourable evaluations—is not as effective as a pattern of improving performance that culminates in a strong finish.[9] An implication of this research for hotels is that managers should focus on the "back end" of the hotel experience—checkout, parking, bellperson services—to leave a strong final impression.

Expressing Customer Requirements as Specific Behaviours and Actions

Effective service standards are defined in very specific ways that enable employees to understand what they are being asked to deliver. At best, these standards are set and measured in terms of specific responses of human behaviours and actions.

Figure 10.3 shows different levels of abstraction/concreteness for standards in a service firm, arrayed from top (most abstract) to bottom (most concrete and specific). At the very abstract level are customer requirements that are too general to be useful to employees: customers want satisfaction, value, and relationships. One level under these very general requirements are abstract dimensions of service quality already discussed in this text, such as reliability, responsiveness, empathy, assurance, and tangibles. One level further are attributes more specific in describing requirements. If we dig still deeper beneath the attribute level, we get to specific behaviours and actions that are at the right level of specificity for setting standards.

A real-world example of the difference in requirements across these levels will illustrate their practical significance. In a traditional measurement system for a major company's training division, only one aspect of the instructor was included in its class evaluation: ability of instructor. During qualitative research relating to the attributes that satisfy students, three somewhat more specific requirements were elicited: (1) instructor's style, (2) instructor's expertise, and (3) instructor's management of class.

FIGURE 10.3   What Customers Expect: Getting to Actionable Steps

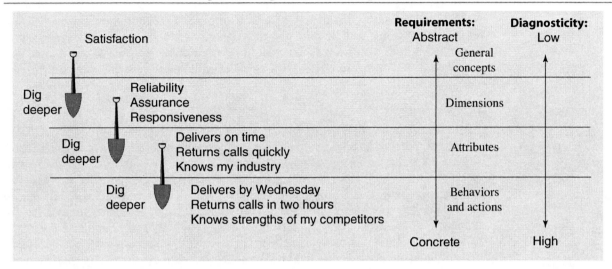

Although the articulation of the three attributes was more helpful to instructors than the broad "ability of instructor," management found that the attributes were still too broad to help instructors wanting to improve their course delivery. When the company invested in a customer-defined standards project, the resulting measurement system was far more useful in diagnosing student requirements, because the research focused on *specific behaviours and actions* of instructors that met student requirements. Instead of a single broad requirement or three general attributes, the requirements of students were articulated in 14 specific behaviours and actions that related to the instructor and 11 specific behaviours and actions that related to the course content. These behaviours and actions were clearly more diagnostic for communicating what was good and bad in the courses. An additional benefit of this approach was that feedback on behaviours and actions was less personal than feedback on traits or personal characteristics. It was also easier for employees of the company to make changes that related to behaviours rather than to personality traits.

Measuring Behaviours and Actions

Hard Measurements

Hard measurements consist of counts that provide feedback about the performance of a service standard. To demonstrate, here are some of the actual hard measurements for components of the FedEx SQI:

- *Missing proofs of delivery*—the number of invoices that do not include proof-of-delivery paperwork

- *Overgoods*—lost and found packages that lack, or have lost, identifying labels for the sender and the addressee and are sent to the Overgoods Department

- *Wrong-day late deliveries*—number of packages delivered after the commitment date

- *Traces*—the number of "proof of performance" requests from customers that cannot be answered through data contained in the computer system[10]

In these and other hard measurements, the actual gauge involves a count of the number and type of actions or behaviours that are correct or incorrect. Somewhere in the operation system these actions and behaviours are tabulated, frequently through information technology.

The appropriate hard measure to deliver to customer requirements is not always intuitive or obvious, and the potential for counting or tracking an irrelevant aspect of operations is high. For this reason it is desirable to link the measure of operational performance with soft measures (surveys or trailer calls) to be sure that they are strongly correlated.

Soft Measurements

Two types of perceptual measurement that were described in Chapter 6 can document customers' opinions about whether performance met the standards established: trailer calls and relationship surveys. Relationship and SERVQUAL surveys cover all aspects of the customer's relationship with the company, are typically expressed in attributes, and are usually completed once per year. Trailer calls are associated with specific service encounters, are short (approximately six or seven questions), and are administered as close in time to a specific service encounter as possible. Trailer calls are administered continuously, whenever a customer experiences a service encounter of the type being considered, and they provide data on a continuous basis. The company must decide on a survey strategy combining relationship surveys and trailer calls to provide soft measurement feedback.

Adapting Standards Globally or Locally

How do companies adjust for cultural or local differences in service standards if they recognize that these geographic differences are related to varying customer expectations? Companies with worldwide brands have much to lose if their service standards vary too much across countries, and therefore they must find ways to achieve universally high quality while still allowing for local differences.

As one of the world's leading operators of luxury hotels and resorts, the Four Seasons Hotel manages 63 properties in 29 countries, and successfully accomplishes this goal by balancing universal services standards with standards that vary by country.[11] The company, world-famous for its service, owes at least some of its success to its seven "service culture standards" expected of *all* staff *all* over the world at *all* times. The seven standards, which form the acrostic SERVICE, are:

1. **Smile:** Employees will actively greet guests, smile, and speak clearly in a friendly manner.

2. **Eye:** Employees will make eye contact, even in passing, with an acknowledgment.

3. **Recognition:** All staff will create a sense of recognition by using the guest's name, when known, in a natural and discreet manner.

4. **Voice:** Staff will speak to guests in an attentive, natural, and courteous manner, avoiding pretension and in a clear voice.

5. **Informed:** All guest contact staff will be well informed about their hotel, their product, will take ownership of simple requests, and will not refer guests elsewhere.

6. **Clean:** Staff will always appear clean, crisp, well-groomed, and well-fitted.

7. **Everyone:** Everyone, everywhere, all the time, show their care for our guests.

In addition to these culture standards that are expected of all staff all over the world, the hotel has 270 core standards that apply to different aspects of service provision

FIGURE 10.4

The Four Seasons in Toronto standardizes a long list of in-room service activities to ensure consistency.

Source: Tibor Kolley/The Globe and Mail.

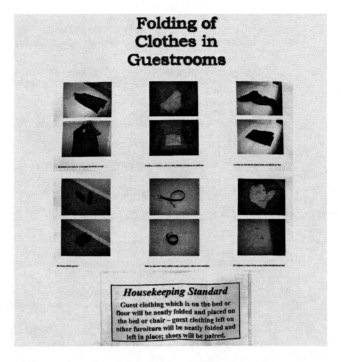

(examples include "the staff will be aware of arriving vehicles and will move toward them, opening doors within 30 seconds" and "unanswered guest room phones will be picked up within 5 rings, or 20 seconds"). Exceptions to these 270 standards are allowed if they make local or cultural sense. For example, in North America, coffee pots are left on tables at breakfast; in many parts of Europe, including France, customers perceive this practice as a lack of service and servers personally refill coffee cups as needed. Standards for uniforms and decor differ across cultures, but minimum expectations must be met everywhere.

Developing Customer-Defined Standards

Figure 10.5 shows the general process for setting customer-defined service standards.

Step 1: Identify Existing or Desired Service Encounter Sequence

The first step involves delineating the service encounter sequence. A service blueprint may be used to identify the service encounter sequence. Ideally, the company would be open to discovering customers' desired service encounter sequences, exploring the ways customers want to do business with the firm.

Step 2: Translate Customer Expectations into Behaviours and Actions for Each Service Encounter

The input to step 2 is existing research on customer expectations. In this step, abstract customer requirements and expectations must be translated into concrete, specific behaviours and actions associated with each service encounter. Abstract requirements (like reliability) can call for a different behaviour or action in each service encounter, and these differences must be probed. Eliciting these behaviours and actions is likely to require additional qualitative research because in most service companies, marketing information has not been collected for this purpose.

262   Part 4   *Aligning Service Design and Standards*

FIGURE 10.5

Process for Setting
Customer-Defined
Standards

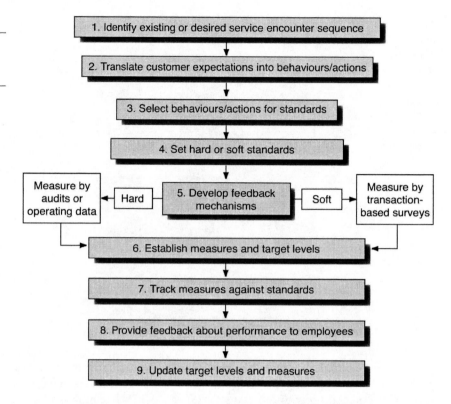

Information on behaviours and actions must be gathered and interpreted by an objective source such as a research firm or an inside department with no stake in the ultimate decisions. If the information is filtered through company managers or front-line people with an internal bias, the outcome would be company-defined rather than customer-defined standards. When this happens, Gap 2 usually gets wider.

Research techniques discussed in Chapter 6 that are relevant for eliciting behaviours and actions include in-depth interviewing of customers, focus group interviews, and other forms of research such as partnering.

Step 3: Select Behaviours and Actions for Standards

This stage involves prioritizing the behaviours and actions, of which there will be many, into those for which customer-defined standards will be established. The following are the most important criteria for creation of the standards:

1. *The standards are based on behaviours and actions that are very important to customers.* Customers have many requirements for the products and services that companies provide. Customer-defined standards need to focus on what is *very important* to customers.

2. *The standards cover performance that needs to be improved or maintained.* The company gets the highest leverage or biggest impact from focusing on behaviours and actions that need to be improved. Figure 10.6 shows an importance/performance matrix for a computer manufacturer. It combines the importance and performance criteria and indicates them by the shading in the cell in the matrix where behaviours and actions should be selected to meet those criteria.

3. *The standards cover behaviours and actions employees can improve.* Employees perform according to standards consistently only if they understand, accept, and

FIGURE 10.6

Importance/
Performance Matrix:
Delivery, Installing,
Performing

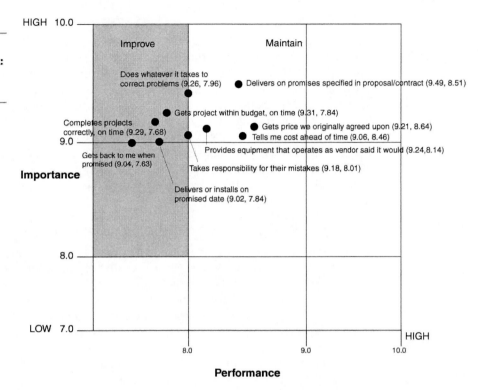

have control over the behaviours and actions specified in the standards. Holding contact people to standards that they cannot control (such as product quality or time lag in introduction of new products) does not result in improvement. For this reason, service standards should cover controllable aspects of employees' jobs.

4. *The standards are accepted by employees.* Employees will perform to standards consistently only if they understand and accept the standards. Imposing standards on unwilling employees often leads to resistance, resentment, absenteeism, even turnover. Many companies establish standards for the amount of time it should take (rather than for the time it does take) for each service job and gradually cut back on the time to reduce labour costs. This practice inevitably leads to increasing tensions among employees. In these situations, managers, financial personnel, and union employees can work together to determine new standards for the tasks.

5. *The standards are predictive rather than reactive.* Customer-defined standards should not be established on the basis of complaints or other forms of reactive feedback. Reactive feedback deals with past concerns of customers rather than with current and future customer expectations. Rather than waiting for dissatisfied customers to complain, the company should actively seek both positive and negative perceptions of customers in advance of complaints.

6. *The standards are challenging but realistic.* A large number of studies on goal setting show that highest performance levels are obtained when standards are challenging but realistic. If standards are not challenging, employees get little reinforcement for mastering them. On the other hand, unrealistically high standards leave an employee feeling dissatisfied with performance and frustrated by not being able to attain the goal.

Step 4: Decide Whether Hard or Soft Standards Are Appropriate

The next step involves deciding whether hard or soft standards should be used to capture the behaviour and action. One of the biggest mistakes companies make in this step is to choose a hard standard hastily. Companies are accustomed to operational measures and have a bias toward them. However, unless the hard standard adequately captures the expected behaviour and action, it is not customer-defined. The best way to decide whether a hard standard is appropriate is to first establish a soft standard by means of trailer calls and then determine over time which operational aspect most correlates to this soft measure. Figure 10.7 shows the linkage between speed of complaint handling (a hard measure) and satisfaction (a soft measure); the figure illustrates that satisfaction strongly depends on the number of hours it takes to resolve a complaint.

Step 5: Develop Feedback Mechanisms for Measurement to Standards

Once companies have determined whether hard or soft standards are appropriate and which specific standards best capture customer requirements, they must develop feedback mechanisms that adequately capture the standards. Hard standards typically involve mechanical counts or technology-enabled measurement of time or errors. Soft standards require perceptual measurements through the use of trailer surveys or employee monitoring. Employee monitoring is illustrated by the practice of supervisors listening in on employee calls. You may have experienced this when you called customer service numbers for many organizations and noticed that the voice prompts tell you that calls may be monitored for quality purposes. The purpose of this monitoring is to provide feedback on employee performance to the standards set by the organization to meet customer needs. One critical aspect of developing feedback mechanisms is ensuring that performance captures the process from the customer's view rather than the company's perspective. A supervisor monitoring an employee's handling of a customer service call, for example, should focus not so much on how quickly the employee gets the customer off the phone as on how adequately he or she handles the customer's request.

FIGURE 10.7

Linkage Between
Soft and Hard
Measures for Speed
of Complaint
Handling

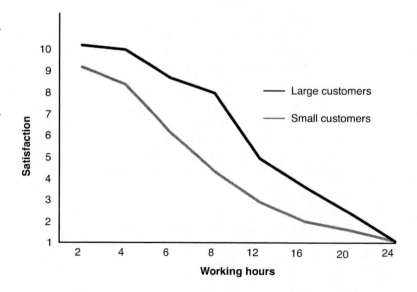

Step 6: Establish Measures and Target Levels

The next step requires that companies establish target levels for the standards. Without this step the company lacks a way to quantify whether the standards have been met. When the service consists of repetitive processes, companies can relate levels of customer satisfaction with actual performance of a behaviour or task. Consider, for example, a study to determine the standard for customers' wait time in a line. The information needed includes customer perceptions of their wait in line (soft perceptual measure) and the amount of time they actually stand in line (hard operations measure). The joint collection of these data over many transactions provides evidence of the sensitivity of customers to different wait times.

An airline conducted precisely this study by having a flight attendant intercept customers as they approached the ticket counter. As each customer entered the line, the attendant stamped the entry time on a ticket (using a machine like those in parking lots) and handed the customer the stamped ticket. As the customer exited the line at the end of the transaction, the flight attendant restamped the ticket with the exit time and asked the customer three or four questions about perceptions of the wait in line and satisfaction with the transaction. Aggregating the individual customer data provided a graph that allowed the company to evaluate the impact on perceptions of various levels of line waits.

Step 7: Track Measures Against Standards

Roger Milliken, former head of Milliken Industries, is reported to have said, "In God we trust, all others bring data." Successful service businesses, such as FedEx and Walt Disney, have careful and comprehensive fact-based systems about their operations. One company that has recently made a very significant commitment to fact-based decision making is the TD Bank Financial Group. Following the merger between TD and Canada Trust, they had their hands full combining products and services, systems, branches, and of course management and staff. Naturally, such a process can lead to customer service problems. To address these, TD Canada Trust implemented a Customer Problem Resolution Process. Employees were invited to identify obstacles to customer service and customers were regularly surveyed to track progress.[12]

Since the quality movement of the 1980s, many techniques have been developed to track measures against standards. W. Edwards Deming, one of the most influential leaders of the quality movement, developed an approach called the P-D-C-A cycle (Plan-Do-Check-Act) that is applied to processes to measure and continuously improve their performance. Joseph Juran, another founder of the quality movement, was one of the first to apply statistical methods to improvement, leading to the widespread use of statistical process control as a way to measure performance to standards.

Step 8: Provide Feedback About Performance to Employees

FedEx communicates the performance on its service quality indicator daily so that everyone in the company knows how the company is performing. When problems occur, they can be identified and corrected. The SQI measurement gives everyone in the company immediate feedback on activity that is strongly related to customer perceptions. In a general sense, data and facts need to be analyzed and distributed to support evaluation and decision making at multiple levels within the company. The data also must be deployed quickly enough that the people who need it to make decisions about service or processes can do so. Responsibility for meeting service requirements must also be communicated throughout the organization. All parts of the organization must be measuring their services to internal customers and, ultimately, measuring how that performance relates to external customer requirements.[13]

Step 9: Periodically Update Target Levels and Measures

The final step involves revising the target levels, measures, and even customer requirements regularly enough to keep up with customer expectations.

Developing Service Performance Indexes

One outcome from following the process for developing customer-defined standards is a service performance index. *Service performance indexes* are comprehensive composites of the most critical performance standards. Development of an index begins by identifying the set of customer-defined standards that the company will use to drive behaviour. Not all service performance indexes contain customer-defined standards, but the best ones, like FedEx's SQI, are based on them. Most companies build these indexes by (1) understanding the most important requirements of the customer, (2) linking these requirements to tangible and measurable aspects of service provision, and (3) using the feedback from these indexes to identify and improve service problems. The most progressive companies also use the feedback for reward and recognition systems within the company. Here are a few examples of service performance indexes in some companies.

TD Bank Financial Group

As part of its ongoing desire to improve service, TD Canada Trust has created its Customer Service Index (CSI). In 2005, TD surveyed approximately 400,000 customers. Categories tracked included treating customers in a respectful manner, processing transactions quickly and accurately, handling customer requests, giving customers individual attention, and greeting customers pleasantly. In the same year, TD Canada Trust was rewarded for its efforts with the Contact Centre Industry Service Quality of Excellence Award. It also placed first among Canada's major banks in the national Synovate Survey on eight of eleven categories including "overall quality of service." According to their Corporate Social Responsibility Report, "Our customers are why we exist so paying attention to what counts to them is the overarching focus that propels our business" (p. 36).[14]

The Ritz-Carlton Hotel Company L.L.C.

The Ritz-Carlton has created a Service Quality Indicator that is patterned on FedEx's SQI (discussed in this chapter's opening). The Ritz's SQI spells out the 12 most serious defects that can occur in the operation of a hotel and weights them by their seriousness. The defects and points associated with them include:

1. Missing guest preferences (10 points)
2. Unresolved difficulties (50 points)
3. Inadequate guestroom housekeeping (1 point)
4. Abandoned reservation calls (5 points)
5. Guestroom changes (5 points)
6. Inoperable guestroom equipment (5 points)
7. Unready guestroom (10 points)
8. Inappropriate hotel appearance (5 points)

9. Meeting event difficulties (5 points)

10. Inadequate food/beverage (1 point)

11. Missing/damaged guest property/accidents (50 points)

12. Invoice adjustment (3 points)

The hotel calculates the SQI by multiplying the total number of occurrences by their points, totals the points, and divides by the number of working days to get an average daily point value. This value is communicated daily to employees.[15]

Among the issues that companies must tackle when developing service performance indexes are (1) the number of components to be contained, (2) what overall or summary measures will be included, (3) whether the index should be weighted or unweighted (to put greater emphasis on the performance of the attributes considered most important to customers), and (4) whether all parts of the business (departments, sectors, or business units) will be held to the same performance measures. One of the most important goals of an index is to simply and clearly communicate business performance in operational and perceptual terms. Companies must develop the rigour in these measurement areas that they have in financial performance.

Recently, subscribers to Aliant (Atlantic Canada's major telecommunications firm) received an insert in their monthly statements. This insert reported on a CRTC-mandated set of customer-driven measures that all Canadian telecommunications firms had to track to avoid a monetary penalty. Go to the CRTC website at www.crtc. gc.ca/ENG/publications/reports/8660/8660.htm to find out how companies in your part of the country performed.

SUMMARY

This chapter discussed the discrepancy between company perceptions of customer expectations and the standards they set to deliver to these expectations. Among the major causes for Provider Gap 2 are inadequate standardization of service behaviours and actions, absence of formal processes for setting service quality goals, and lack of customer-defined standards. These problems were discussed and detailed, along with strategies to close the gap.

Customer-defined standards are at the heart of delivery of service that customers expect: they are the link between customers' expressed expectations and company actions to deliver to those expectations. Creating these service standards is not a common practice in many firms. Doing so requires that companies' marketing and operations departments work together by using marketing research as input for operations. Unless the operations standards are defined by customer priorities, they are not likely to have an impact on customer perceptions of service.

⟼ Discussion Questions

1. How does the service measurement that we describe in this chapter differ from the service measurement in Chapter 6? Which of the two types do you think is most important? Why?

2. In what types of service industries are standards most difficult to develop? Why? Recommend three standards that might be developed in one of the firms from the industries you specify. How would employees react to these standards? How could you gain buy-in for them?

3. Given the need for customer-defined service standards, do firms need company-defined standards at all? Could all standards in a company be customer-defined? Why or why not? What functional departments in a firm would object to having all standards customer-defined?

4. What is the difference between hard and soft standards? Which do you think would be more readily accepted by employees? By management? Why?

5. Consider the university or school you currently attend. What are examples of hard standards, soft standards, and one-time fixes that would address student requirements? Does the school currently use these standards for delivery of service to students? Why or why not? Do you think your reasons would apply to private-sector companies as well? To public or nonprofit companies?

6. Think of a service that you currently use, then map out the service encounter sequence for that service. What is your most important requirement in each interaction? Document these requirements, and make certain that they are expressed at the concrete level of behaviours and actions.

7. Which of the service performance indexes described at the end of this chapter is the most effective? Why? What distinguishes the one you selected from the others? How would you improve each of the others?

Exercises

1. Select a local service firm. Visit the firm and ascertain the service measurements that the company tracks. What hard measures does it monitor? Soft measures? On the basis of what you find, develop a service performance index.

2. Choose one of the peripheral services (such as computer, library, placement) provided by your school. What hard standards would it be useful to track to meet student expectations? What soft standards? What one-time fixes would improve service?

3. Think of a service company you have worked for or know about. Using Figure 10.3, write in customer requirements at each of the levels. How far down in the chart can you describe requirements? Is that far enough?

4. Look at three websites from which you can order products (such as Amazon.ca or LLBean.com). What are the companies' delivery promises? What types of standards might they set for these promises? Are these customer- or company-defined standards?

Notes

1. "Taking the Measure of Quality," *Service Savvy*, March 1992, p. 3.
2. Ibid.
3. Speech by Federal Express Manager in Baltimore, Maryland, June 1993.
4. T. Levitt, "Industrialization of Service," *Harvard Business Review*, September/October 1976, pp. 63–74.
5. "Fast, Reliable Delivery Processes Are Cheered by Time-Sensitive Customers," *The Service Edge* 4, no. 3 (1993): 1.

6. F. Reichhold, "e-Loyalty," *Harvard Business Review*, July/August 2000, pp. 105–13.

7. J. Weinstein, "Redesigning the Box," *Hotels* 38, no. 3 (2004), p. 7.

8. "Fast, Reliable Delivery Processes," p. 21.

9. D. E. Hansen and P. J. Danaher, "Inconsistent Performance During the Service Encounter: What's a Good Start Worth?" *Journal of Service Research* 1 (February 1999), pp. 227–35.

10. "Taking the Measure of Quality," p. 3.

11. This discussion about the Four Seasons is based on R. Hallowell, D. Bowen, and C. Knoop, "Four Seasons Goes to Paris," *Academy of Management Executive* 16, no. 4 (2002), pp. 7–24.

12. *TDBFG Corporate Social Responsibility Report*, 2003, pp. 28, 29.

13. "Taking the Measure of Quality," p. 3.

14. *TDBFG Corporate Social Responsibility Report*, 2004, p. 36; *TDBFG Annual Report*, 2005.

15. 1999 Application Summary for The Ritz-Carlton Hotel Company L.L.C., Malcolm Baldrige National Quality Award, 2000.

Chapter

15

Managing Demand and Capacity

Closing Provider Gap 3

THIS CHAPTER'S OBJECTIVES ARE TO

1. Explain the underlying issue for capacity-constrained services: lack of inventory capability.

2. Present the implications of time, labour, equipment, and facilities constraints combined with variations in demand patterns.

3. Lay out strategies for matching supply and demand through (a) shifting demand to match capacity or (b) adjusting capacity to meet demand.

4. Demonstrate the benefits and risks of yield management strategies in forging a balance among capacity utilization, pricing, market segmentation, and financial return.

5. Provide strategies for managing waiting lines for times when capacity and demand cannot be aligned.

How to Fill 1,590 Rooms 365 Days of the Year

The Delta Chelsea Hotel (www.deltahotels.com), located in the heart of downtown Toronto, is Canada's largest hotel. It has 1,590 rooms, three restaurants, three lounges, two pools, a health club, and spacious meeting and conference facilities.[1] These restaurants and meeting facilities are available to guests 365 days and nights of the year. Yet natural demand for them can vary widely. Since the hotel is located in Canada's top tourist destination,[2] demand for rooms is understandably high during the peak tourist season, between June and October. But though Toronto has one of the milder climates in Canada, the winter months are still cold, with temperatures getting as low as –10 degrees Celsius. Consequently, tourism declines in the winter. Because the hotel caters to business travellers and business meetings, demand has a weekly cycle in addition to the seasonal fluctuations. Business travellers do not stay over weekends. Thus, demand for rooms from the hotel's primary market segment drops on Friday and Saturday nights.

To balance demand and capacity throughout the year, the Delta Chelsea targets more than just business travellers. Group business (primarily business conferences) is pursued throughout the year to fill the lower demand periods. A variety of special events, sports, weddings, and getaway packages are offered year-round to increase weekend demand for rooms. And promotions that encourage more local clientele or are run in conjunction with local attractions or events like "Shop 'N Stay" can help round out demand during the traditionally slower times of the year. The Shop 'N Stay package features exclusive discounts to some of Toronto's best shopping and entertainment venues, all just steps away from the comfort of a hotel room. This package includes accommodation as well as special offers from well-known retailers such as the Eaton Centre, The Shoe Company, Sam the Record Man, and The Bay, Queen Street. Area attractions such as the Royal Ontario Museum, the Art Gallery of Ontario, Olympic Spirit, and CanStage are also offering reduced rates on admission and ticket prices. Of note now as well is their Gas Up and Go promotion: with gasoline prices continuing to rise, people generally travel less, so the Gas Up and Go initiative includes gasoline rebates.

Source: Courtesy of Delta Chelsea Hotel.

Most downtown hotels in urban areas face the same weekly demand fluctuations that the Delta Chelsea deals with, and many have found a partial solution by catering to families and children on the weekends.[3] For many dual-career couples, weekend getaways are a primary form of relaxation and vacation. The downtown hotels cater to these couples and families by offering discounted room rates, child-oriented activities and amenities, and an environment in which families feel comfortable. The Delta Chelsea has recently been dubbed "The Entertainment Hotel" for its ability to combine a variety of entertainment options with a hotel stay, including many activities for children. The hotel boasts being home to Toronto's only indoor water slide, which happens to be four storeys tall. Families also like the fact that the hotel has Camp Chelsea available on weekends, whereby children can partake in a variety of activities supervised by hotel staff while parents are free to enjoy other aspects of Toronto life.

For the Delta Chelsea in Toronto, managing demand and utilizing the hotel's fixed capacity of rooms, restaurants, and meeting facilities can be a seasonal, weekly, and even daily challenge. Although the hotel industry epitomizes the challenges of demand and capacity management, many service providers face similar problems. For some businesses, demand is predictable, as for a tax accountant. For others, such as management or technology consultants, demand may be less predictable, fluctuating according to customer needs and business cycles. Sometimes firms experience too much demand for the existing capacity and sometimes capacity sits idle.

Overuse or underuse of a service can directly contribute to Gap 3—failure to deliver what was designed and specified. For example, when demand for services exceeds maximum capacity, the quality of service may drop because staff and facilities are overtaxed. And some customers may be turned away, not receiving the service at all. During periods of slow demand it may be necessary to reduce prices or cut service amenities, changing the makeup of the clientele and the nature of the service and thus running the risk of not delivering what customers expect.[4]

In this chapter we focus on the challenges of matching supply and demand in capacity-constrained services. Gap 3 can occur when organizations fail to smooth the peaks and valleys of demand, overuse their capacities, attract an inappropriate customer mix in their efforts to build demand, or rely too much on price in smoothing demand. The chapter gives you an understanding of these issues and strategies for addressing them. The effective use of capacity is frequently a key success factor for service organizations.

→ THE UNDERLYING ISSUE: LACK OF INVENTORY CAPABILITY

The fundamental issue underlying supply and demand management in services is the lack of inventory capability. Unlike manufacturing firms, service firms cannot build up inventories during periods of slow demand to use later when demand increases. This lack of inventory capability is due to the perishability of services and their simultaneous production and consumption. An airline seat that is not sold on a given flight cannot be resold the following day. The productive capacity of that seat has perished. Similarly, an hour of a lawyer's billable time cannot be saved from one day to the next. Services also cannot be transported from one place to another or transferred from person to person. Thus the Delta's services cannot be moved to an alternative location in the winter months.

The lack of inventory capability combined with fluctuating demand leads to a variety of potential outcomes, as illustrated in Figure 15.1.[5] The horizontal lines in the figure indicate service capacity, and the curved line indicates customer demand for the service. In many services, capacity is fixed; thus capacity can be designated by a flat horizontal line over a certain time period. Demand for service frequently fluctuates, however, as indicated by the curved line. The topmost horizontal line in the figure represents maximum capacity. For example, in our opening vignette, the horizontal line would represent the Delta's maximum number of rooms, or it could represent the approximately 10,000 seats in the Halifax Metro Centre. The rooms and the seats remain constant, but demand for them fluctuates. The band between the second and third horizontal lines represents optimum capacity—the best use of the capacity from the perspective of both customers and the company (the difference between optimal and maximum capacity utilization is discussed later in the chapter).

390 Part 5 *Delivering and Performing Service*

FIGURE 15.1 Variations in Demand Relative to Capacity

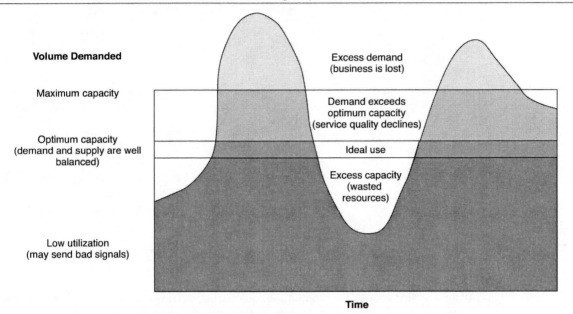

Source: Reprinted from C. Lovelock, "Getting the Most out of Your Productive Capacity," *Product Plus* (Boston: McGraw Hill, 1994), ch. 16, p. 241. © 1994 by The McGraw-Hill Companies, Inc. Reprinted by permission of The McGraw-Hill Companies.

The areas in the middle of the figure are labelled to represent four basic scenarios that can result from different combinations of capacity and demand:

1. *Excess demand.* The level of demand exceeds maximum capacity. In this situation some customers will be turned away, resulting in lost business opportunities. For the customers who do receive the service, its quality may not match what was promised because of crowding or overtaxing of staff and facilities.

2. *Demand exceeds optimum capacity.* No one is being turned away, but the quality of service may still suffer because of overuse, crowding, or staff being pushed beyond their abilities to deliver consistent quality.

3. *Demand and supply are balanced at the level of optimum capacity.* Staff and facilities are occupied at an ideal level. No one is overworked, facilities can be maintained, and customers are receiving quality service without undesirable delays.

4. *Excess capacity.* Demand is below optimum capacity. Productive resources in the form of labour, equipment, and facilities are underutilized, resulting in lost productivity and lower profits. Customers may receive excellent quality on an individual level because they have the full use of the facilities, no waiting, and complete attention from the staff. If, however, service quality depends on the presence of other customers, customers may be disappointed or may worry that they have chosen an inferior service provider.

Not all firms will be challenged equally in terms of managing supply and demand. The seriousness of the problem will depend on the *extent of demand fluctuations over time,* and the *extent to which supply is constrained* (Table 15.1).[6] Some types of organizations will experience wide fluctuations in demand (telecommunications,

TABLE 15.1

Demand versus
Supply

Extent to Which Supply Is Constrained	Extent of Demand Fluctuations over Time	
	Wide 1	**Narrow** 2
Peak demand can usually be met without a major delay	Electricity Natural gas Hospital maternity unit Police and fire emergencies	Insurance Legal services Banking Laundry and dry cleaning
	4	3
Peak demand regularly exceeds capacity.	Accounting and tax preparation Passenger transportation Hotels Restaurants Hospital emergency rooms	Services similar to those in 2 that have insufficient capacity for their base level of business

Source: C. H. Lovelock, "Classifying Services to Gain Strategic Marketing Insights," *Journal of Marketing* 47 (Summer 1983), p. 17. Reprinted by permission from the American Marketing Association.

hospitals, transportation, restaurants), whereas others will have narrower fluctuations (insurance, laundry, banking). For some, peak demand can usually be met even when demand fluctuates (electricity, natural gas), but for others peak demand may frequently exceed capacity (hospital emergency rooms, restaurants, hotels). Those firms with wide variations in demand (cells 1 and 4 in the table), and particularly those with wide fluctuations in demand that regularly exceed capacity (cell 4), will find the issues and strategies in this chapter particularly important to their success. Those firms that find themselves in cell 3 need a "one-time-fix" to expand their capacity to match regular patterns of excessive demand. The example industries in the table are provided to illustrate where *most* firms in those industries would likely be classified. In reality, an individual firm from any industry could find itself in any of the four cells, depending on its immediate circumstances.

To identify effective strategies for managing supply and demand fluctuations, an organization needs a clear understanding of the constraints on its capacity and the underlying demand patterns.

CAPACITY CONSTRAINTS

Later in the chapter, we present some creative ways to expand and contract capacity in the short and long term, but for our discussion now, you can assume that service capacity is fixed. Depending on the type of service, critical fixed-capacity factors can be time, labour, equipment, facilities, or (in many cases) a combination of these.

Time, Labour, Equipment, Facilities

For some service businesses, the primary constraint on service production is *time*. For example, a lawyer, a consultant, a hairdresser, a plumber, and a psychological counselor all primarily sell their time. If their time is not used productively, profits are lost. If there is excess demand, time cannot be created to satisfy it. From the point of view of the individual service provider, time is the constraint.

From the point of view of a firm that employs a large number of service providers, *labour* or staffing levels can be the primary capacity constraint. A law firm, a university department, a consulting firm, a tax accounting firm, and a repair and maintenance contractor may all face the reality that at certain times demand for their organizations' services cannot be met because the staff is already operating at peak capacity. However, it does not always make sense (nor may it be possible in a competitive labour market) to hire additional service providers if low demand is a reality at other times.

In other cases, *equipment* may be the critical constraint. For trucking or air-freight delivery services, the trucks or airplanes needed to service demand may be the capacity limitation. During the Christmas holidays, Purolator, Canada Post, and other delivery service providers face this issue. Health clubs also deal with this limitation, particularly at certain times of the day (before work, during lunch hours, after work) and in certain months of the year. For network service providers, bandwidth, servers, and switches represent their perishable capacity.

Finally, many firms face restrictions brought about by their limited *facilities*. Hotels have only a certain number of rooms to sell, airlines are limited by the number of seats on the aircraft, educational institutions are constrained by the number of rooms and the number of seats in each classroom, and restaurant capacity is restricted to the number of tables and seats available.

Understanding the primary capacity constraint, or the combination of factors that restricts capacity, is a first step in designing strategies to deal with supply and demand issues (Table 15.2).

TABLE 15.2

Constraints on Capacity

Nature of the Constraint	Type of Service*
Time	Legal
	Consulting
	Accounting
	Medical
Labour	Law firm
	Accounting firm
	Consulting firm
	Health clinic
Equipment	Delivery services
	Telecommunications
	Network services
	Utilities
	Health club
Facilities	Hotels
	Restaurants
	Hospitals
	Airlines
	Schools
	Theatres
	Churches

*The examples illustrate the most common capacity constraint for each type of service. In reality, any of the service organizations listed can be operating under multiple constraints. For example, a law firm may be operating under constrained labour capacity (too few attorneys) and facilities constraints (not enough office space) at the same time.

Optimal vs. Maximum Use of Capacity

To fully understand capacity issues, it is important to know the difference between optimal and maximum use of capacity. As suggested in Figure 15.1, optimum and maximum capacity may not be the same. Using capacity at an optimum level means that resources are fully employed but not overused and that customers are receiving quality service in a timely manner. Maximum capacity, on the other hand, represents the absolute limit of service availability. In the case of a football game, optimum and maximum capacity may be the same. The entertainment value of the game is enhanced for customers when every single seat is filled, and obviously the profitability for the team is greatest under these circumstances (Figure 15.2). On the other hand, in a university classroom it is usually not desirable for students or faculty to have every seat filled. In this case, optimal use of capacity is less than the maximum. In some cases, maximum use of capacity may result in excessive waiting by customers, as in a popular restaurant. From the perspective of customer satisfaction, optimum use of the capacity will be less than maximum use.

In the case of equipment or facilities constraints, the maximum capacity at any given time is obvious. There are only a certain number of weight machines in the health club, a certain number of seats in the airplane, and a limited amount of space in a cargo carrier. In the case of a bottling plant, when maximum capacity on the assembly line is exceeded, bottles begin to break and the system shuts down. Thus it is relatively easy to observe the effects of exceeding maximum equipment capacity.

When the limitation is people's time or labour, maximum capacity is harder to specify because people are in a sense more flexible than facilities and equipment. When an individual service provider's maximum capacity has been exceeded, the result is likely to cause decreased service quality, customer dissatisfaction, and employee burnout and turnover, but these outcomes may not be immediately observable even

FIGURE 15.2

For sports and other entertainment venues, maximal and optimal capacity use are close to the same.

Source: CP/Larry MacDougal.

to the employee herself. It is often easy for a consulting firm to take on one more assignment, taxing its employees beyond their maximum capacity, or for a clinic to schedule a few more appointments in a day, stretching its staff and physicians beyond their maximum capacity. Given the potential costs in terms of reduced quality and customer and employee dissatisfaction, it is critical for the firm to understand optimum and maximum human capacity limits.

DEMAND PATTERNS

To manage fluctuating demand in a service business, it is necessary to have a clear understanding of demand patterns, why they vary, and the market segments that comprise demand at different points in time.[7] A number of questions need to be answered regarding the predictability and underlying causes of demand.

The Charting of Demand Patterns

First, the organization needs to chart the level of demand over relevant time periods. Organizations that have good computerized customer information systems can chart this information very accurately. Others may need to chart demand patterns more informally. Daily, weekly, and monthly demand levels should be followed, and if seasonality is a suspected problem, graphing should be done for data from at least the past year. In some services, such as restaurants or health care, hourly fluctuations within a day may also be relevant. Sometimes demand patterns are intuitively obvious; in other cases patterns may not reveal themselves until the data are charted.

Predictable Cycles

In looking at the graphic representation of demand levels, is there a predictable cycle daily (variations occur by hours), weekly (variations occur by day), monthly (variations occur by day or week), and/or yearly (variations occur according to months or seasons)? In some cases, predictable patterns may occur at all periods. For example, in the restaurant industry, especially in seasonal tourist locations, demand can vary predictably by month, by week, by day, and by hour.

If a predictable cycle is detected, what are its underlying causes? The Delta in Toronto knows that demand cycles are based on seasonal weather patterns and that weekly variations are based on the workweek (business travellers do not stay at the hotel over the weekend). Tax accountants can predict demand on the basis of when taxes are due. Services catering to children respond to variations in school hours and vacations. Retail services have peak periods at certain holidays and times of the week and day. When predictable patterns exist, generally one or more causes can be identified. A surprising pattern even exists for hospital maternity wards. You might expect that births would always be randomly spread over the course of a week, but it turns out that a full moon occasions a predictable spike in births.

Random Demand Fluctuations

Sometimes the patterns of demand appear to be random—there is no apparent predictable cycle. Yet even in this case, causes can often be identified. For example, day-to-day changes in the weather may affect use of recreational, shopping, or entertainment facilities. Although the weather cannot be predicted far in advance, it may be possible to anticipate demand a day or two ahead. Health-related events also cannot be predicted. Accidents and heart attacks increase demand for hospital services, but the level of demand cannot generally be determined in advance. Natural disasters such as floods, fires, and hurricanes can dramatically increase the need for such services as insurance, telecommunications, and health care. Canada has had its share of floods and hurricanes. Whether we look at flooding in western Canada, the ice storm in Quebec, or Hurricane Juan in Nova Scotia, natural disasters cause unpredicted demand fluctuations.

Our Global Feature illustrates how one company with seemingly random and chaotic demand for its services was able to change its business to serve customers. The feature is also a good example of organizational learning across cultures.

Demand Patterns by Market Segment

An organization that has detailed records on customer transactions may be able to disaggregate demand by market segment, revealing patterns within patterns. Or the analysis may reveal that demand from one segment is predictable whereas demand from another segment is relatively random. For example, for a bank, the visits from its commercial accounts may occur daily at a predictable time, whereas personal account holders may visit the bank at seemingly random intervals. Health clinics often notice that walk-in or "care needed today" patients tend to concentrate their arrivals on Monday, with fewer needing immediate attention on other days of the week. Knowing that this pattern exists, some clinics schedule more future appointments (which they can control) for later days of the week, leaving more of Monday available for same-day appointments and walk-ins.

STRATEGIES FOR MATCHING CAPACITY AND DEMAND

When an organization has a clear grasp of its capacity constraints and an understanding of demand patterns, it is in a good position to develop strategies for matching supply and demand. There are two general approaches for accomplishing this match. The first is to smooth the demand fluctuations themselves by shifting demand to match existing supply. This approach implies that the peaks and valleys of the demand curve (Figure 15.1) will be flattened to match as closely as possible the horizontal optimum capacity line. The second general strategy is to adjust capacity to match fluctuations in demand. This implies moving the horizontal capacity lines shown in Figure 15.1 to match the ups and downs of the demand curve. Each of these two basic strategies is described next with specific examples.

Shifting Demand to Match Capacity

With this strategy an organization seeks to shift customers away from periods in which demand exceeds capacity, perhaps by convincing them to use the service during periods of slow demand. This change may be possible for some customers but not for others. For example, many business travellers are not able to shift their needs for airline, car rental, and hotel services; pleasure travellers, on the other hand, can often shift the timing of their trips. Customers who cannot shift and cannot be accommodated will represent lost business for the firm.

During periods of slow demand, the organization seeks to attract more and/or different customers to utilize its productive capacity. A variety of approaches, detailed

Global Feature

Cemex Creatively Manages Chaotic Demand for Its Services

Imagine a business in which customers' orders are unpredictable, where more than half of all customer orders are changed, often repeatedly and at the last minute, and where the product being delivered is never more than 90 minutes from spoiling. Welcome to the concrete delivery business. Cemex (www. cemex.com), based in Monterrey, Mexico, and founded in 1906, is a highly successful global player in this industry. Having grown substantially through acquisitions, the company now operates in more than 50 countries with more than 50,000 employees and annual sales in excess of $15 billion.

Yet, when two internal consultants examined the business several years ago, they were amazed at the chaos that ruled the industry. Wild weather, unpredictable traffic, spontaneous labour disruptions, and sporadic government inspections of construction sites all combined with ever-changing customer orders to create a sense of chaos and uncontrollability in the business. Combine this chaos with 8,000 grades of concrete available through a half-dozen regional mixing plants, and you have an extremely complex system to manage.

Historically, Cemex had attempted to run the business through controlling its customers to stick with their orders and by imposing fines for changed orders. Efficiency ruled, not customers—in order to conquer the natural randomness of demand and the customers' needs to change orders at the last minute.

The company began searching for new ways to do business. It turned to FedEx and to the 911 emergency dispatch centre in Houston, Texas, for ideas. What it found were organizations that, instead of trying to control demand for their services, had developed people and technology to be flexible in meeting customers' seemingly random demand patterns. Instead of penalizing customers for changing their orders, FedEx does not restrict its customers and, in fact, guarantees delivery at a certain time to any and all locations. This ability to serve customers is made possible by sophisticated information systems that track demand and schedule pickups and deliveries, customer-focused front-line employees, and a customer-centric corporate culture that supports it all. From the 911 centre in Houston, Cemex learned that even seemingly random occurrences such as emergency health needs and accidents occur in sufficient number to allow patterns of demand to be discerned and planned for. In terms of Figure 15.1, what FedEx and the 911 emergency centre did was adjust their capacity to meet the peaks and valleys of customer demand rather than insist that the customers adjust their demand to fit the company's constrained capacity.

The experiences at FedEx and in Houston at the 911 centre were a revelation to Cemex's team. The company went back to Mexico determined to embrace the complexity of its marketplace and to do business on the customers' terms. The company launched a project called Sincronizacion Dinamica de Operaciones: the dynamic synchronization of operations. It unleashed trucks from previous zone assignments, allowing them to roam the city. It outfitted the trucks with transmitters and receivers connected to a GPS system so that locations, direction, and speed of every vehicle could be tracked. It enrolled its drivers in secondary education classes over a period of two years so they would be more service-oriented and able to deal with customers.

Impressed with FedEx's guaranteed service, Cemex worked toward being able to offer "same-day service, with free, unlimited order changes." Now, if a load fails to arrive within 20 minutes of its scheduled delivery time, the buyer gets back 20 pesos per cubic metre—"guarantia 20 × 20"—amounting to roughly 5 percent of the total cost.

Cemex embraced the chaos of its industry instead of trying to adjust and change it. By using technology, people, and systems, it was able to match its capacity

continued

Global Feature

Cemex Creatively Manages Chaotic Demand for Its Service—*continued*

constraints with its customers' wildly fluctuating demands. And the company came out a winner. Cemex can afford to offer its 20 × 20 guarantee now that its reliability exceeds 98 percent!

Today, the company's focus on the customer is clearly stated in the slogan across the top of its website: "By connecting with customer needs, we deliver value worldwide."

Sources: T. Petzinger Jr., "This Promise Is Set in Concrete," *Fast Company,* April 1999, pp. 216–18. See also T. Petzinger Jr., *The New Pioneers* (New York: Simon & Schuster, Inc., 1999), pp. 91–93. M. Dickerson, "Foundation Rock Solid for Mexico's Cement Giant," *Chicago Tribune,* online edition, May 30, 2006, www.chicagotribune.com, accessed June 1, 2006. Reprinted with the permission of Simon & Schuster, Inc. © 1999 by Thomas Petzinger Jr.; updated with company information from the Cemex website, www.cemex.com, 2004.

in the following sections, can be used to shift or increase demand to match capacity. Frequently a firm uses a combination of approaches. Ideas for how to shift demand during both slow and peak periods are shown in Figure 15.3. Note that providing incentives to customers for usage during non-peak times is a very common practice of WestJet's (Figure 15.4).

Vary the Service Offering

One approach is to change the nature of the service offering, depending on the season of the year, day of the week, or time of day. For example, Whistler Mountain, a ski resort near Vancouver, offers its facilities for executive development and training programs during the summer when skiing is not possible. Accounting firms focus on tax preparation late in the year and until April 30, when taxes are due. During other times of the year they can focus on audits and general tax consulting activities. Airlines even

FIGURE 15.3 Strategies for Shifting Demand to Match Capacity

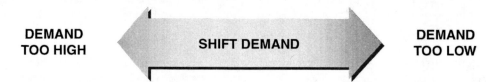

| DEMAND TOO HIGH | SHIFT DEMAND | DEMAND TOO LOW |

- Use signage to communicate busy days and times.
- Offer incentives to customers for usage during nonpeak times.
- Take care of loyal or "regular" customers first.
- Advertise peak usage times and benefits of nonpeak use.
- Charge full price for the service—no discounts.

- Use sales and advertising to increase business from current market segments.
- Modify the service offering to appeal to new market segments.
- Offer discounts or price reductions.
- Modify hours of operation.
- Bring the service to the customer.

398 Part 5 *Delivering and Performing Service*

FIGURE 15.4

WestJet uses price incentives to encourage travel during non-peak times. As WestJet increases its penetration of the business traveller segment, midweek demand should gradually increase.

Source: Courtesy of WestJet.

AN IMPORTANT MESSAGE FROM AN OWNER

"To fit your busy business schedule, we've expanded ours."

Ramel Gutierrez, Specialty Sales Super Agent

Save **40%** when you travel on Tuesdays, Wednesdays and Thursdays.

change the configuration of their plane seating to match the demand from different market segments. Some planes may have no first-class section at all. On routes with a large demand for first-class seating, a significant proportion of seats may be placed in first class. Our opening vignette featured ways in which downtown hotels have changed their offerings to appeal to the family market segment on weekends. In all these examples, the service offering and associated benefits are changed to smooth customer demand for the organization's resources.

Care should be exercised in implementing strategies to change the service offering, because such changes may easily imply and require alterations in other marketing mix variables—such as promotion, pricing, and staffing—to match the new offering. Unless these additional mix variables are altered effectively to support the offering, the strategy may not work. Even when done well, the downside of such changes can be a confusion in the organization's image from the customers' perspective, or a loss of strategic focus for the organization and its employees.

Communicate with Customers

Another approach for shifting demand is to communicate with customers, letting them know the times of peak demand so they can choose to use the service at alternative times and avoid crowding or delays. For example, signs in banks and post offices that let customers know their busiest hours and busiest days of the week can serve as a warning, allowing customers to shift their demand to another time if possible. Research in a bank context found that customers who were forewarned about the bank's busiest hours were more satisfied even when they had to wait than were customers who were not forewarned.[8]

In addition to signage that communicates peak demand times to customers, advertising and other forms of promotion can emphasize different service benefits during peak and slow periods. Advertising and sales messages can also remind customers about peak demand times.

Modify Timing and Location of Service Delivery

Some firms adjust their hours and days of service delivery to more directly reflect customer demand. Historically, banks were open only during "bankers' hours" from 10 a.m. to 3 p.m. every weekday. Obviously these hours did not match the times when most people preferred to do their personal banking. Now many banks open early, stay open until 6 p.m., and are often open on Saturdays, better reflecting customer demand patterns. TD Canada Trust in particular has chosen to expand its hours of operation by staying open late—a strategy they have extensively promoted. Online banking has also shifted demand from branches to "anytime, anywhere" websites. Theatres accommodate customer schedules by offering matinees on weekends and holidays when people are free during the day for entertainment. Movie theatres are sometimes rented during weekdays by business groups—an example of varying the service offering during a period of low demand.

Differentiate on Price

A common response during slow demand is to discount the price of the service. This strategy relies on basic economics of supply and demand. To be effective, however, a price differentiation strategy depends on solid understanding of customer price-sensitivity and demand curves. For example, business travellers are far less price-sensitive than families travelling for pleasure. For the Delta Hotel (the subject of our opening vignette), lowering prices during the slow summer months is not likely to increase bookings from business travellers dramatically. However, the lower summer prices attract considerable numbers of families and local guests who want an opportunity to experience a luxury hotel but are not able to afford the rooms during peak season.

The maximum capacity of any hotel, airline, restaurant, or other service establishment could be reached if the price were low enough. But the goal is always to ensure the highest level of capacity utilization without sacrificing profits. We explore this complex relationship among price, market segments, capacity utilization, and profitability later in the chapter in the section on yield management.

Heavy use of price differentiation to smooth demand can be a risky strategy. Over-reliance on price can result in price wars in an industry in which eventually all competitors suffer. Price wars are well known in the airline industry, and total industry profits often suffer as a result of airlines simultaneously trying to attract customers through price discounting. Another risk of relying on price is that customers grow accustomed to the lower price and expect to get the same deal the next time they use the service. If communications with customers are unclear, customers may not understand the reasons for the discounts and will expect to pay the same during peak demand periods. Overuse or exclusive use of price as a strategy for smoothing demand is also risky because of the potential impact on the organization's image, the potential for attracting undesired market segments, and the possibility that higher-paying customers will feel they have been treated unfairly. Recently, residents and business owners in Whistler have begun planning how to discourage an undesirable influx of high school students from Vancouver who show up in droves on the May long weekend. During this time, partying students clash with traditional and full-time residents.

Adjusting Capacity to Meet Demand

A second strategic approach to matching supply and demand focuses on adjusting capacity. The fundamental idea here is to adjust, stretch, and align capacity to match customer demand (rather than working on shifting demand to match capacity, as just

FIGURE 15.5 Strategies for Adjusting Capacity to Match Demand

DEMAND TOO HIGH   **ADJUST CAPACITY**   **DEMAND TOO LOW**

- Stretch time, labour, facilities, and equipment.
- Cross-train employees.
- Hire part-time employees.
- Request overtime work from employees.
- Rent or share facilities.
- Rent or share equipment.

- Subcontract or outsource activities.
- Perform maintenance, renovations.
- Schedule vacations.
- Schedule employee training.
- Lay off employees.

described). During periods of peak demand the organization seeks to stretch or expand its capacity as much as possible. During periods of slow demand it tries to shrink capacity so as not to waste resources. General strategies for adjusting the four primary service resources (time, people, equipment, and facilities) are discussed throughout the rest of this section. In Figure 15.5, we summarize specific ideas for adjusting capacity during periods of peak and slow demand. Often, a number of different strategies are used simultaneously.

Stretch Existing Capacity

The existing capacity of service resources can often be expanded temporarily to match demand. In such cases no new resources are added; rather the people, facilities, and equipment are asked to work harder and longer to meet demand.

Stretch Time It may be possible to extend the hours of service temporarily to accommodate demand. A health clinic might stay open longer during flu season, retailers are open longer hours during the holiday shopping season, and accountants have extended appointment hours (evenings and Saturdays) before tax deadlines.

Stretch Labour In many service organizations, employees are asked to work longer and harder during periods of peak demand. For example, consulting organizations face extensive peaks and valleys with respect to demand for their services. During peak demand, associates are asked to take on additional projects and work longer hours. And front-line service personnel in banks, tourist attractions, restaurants, and telecommunications companies are asked to serve more customers per hour during busy times than during hours or days when demand is low.

Stretch Facilities Theatres, restaurants, meeting facilities, and classrooms can sometimes be expanded temporarily by the addition of tables, chairs, or other equipment needed by customers. Or, as in the case of a commuter train, a car that holds a fixed number of people seated comfortably can "expand" by accommodating standing passengers.

Stretch Equipment Computers, power lines, and maintenance equipment can often be stretched beyond what would be considered the maximum capacity for short periods to accommodate peak demand.

In using these types of "stretch" strategies, the organization needs to recognize the wear and tear on resources and the potential for inferior quality of service that may go with the use. These strategies should thus be used for relatively short periods in order to allow for later maintenance of the facilities and equipment and refreshment of the people who are asked to exceed their usual capacity.

Align Capacity with Demand Fluctuations

This basic strategy is sometimes known as a "chase demand" strategy. By adjusting service resources creatively, organizations can in effect chase the demand curves to match capacity with customer demand patterns. Time, labour, facilities, and equipment are again the focus, this time with an eye toward adjusting the basic mix and use of these resources. Specific actions might include the following.[9]

Use Part-Time Employees   In this situation the organization's labour resource is being aligned with demand. Retailers hire part-time employees during the holiday rush. Restaurants often ask employees to work split shifts (work the lunch shift, leave for a few hours, and come back for the dinner rush) during peak mealtime hours.

Outsourcing   Firms that find they have a temporary peak in demand for a service that they cannot perform themselves may choose to outsource the entire service.

Rent or Share Facilities or Equipment   For some organizations it is best to rent additional equipment or facilities during periods of peak demand. For example, express mail delivery services rent or lease trucks during the peak holiday delivery season. It would not make sense to buy trucks that would sit idle during the rest of the year. Sometimes organizations with complementary demand patterns can share facilities. An example is a church that shares its facilities during the week with a preschool. The school needs the facilities Monday through Friday during the day; the church needs the facilities evenings and on the weekend.

Schedule Downtime During Periods of Low Demand   If people, equipment, and facilities are being used at maximum capacity during peak periods, then it is imperative to schedule repair, maintenance, and renovations during off-peak periods. This schedule ensures that the resources are in top condition when they are most needed. Vacations and training are also scheduled during slow demand periods.

Cross-Train Employees   If employees are cross-trained, they can shift among tasks, filling in where they are most needed. Cross-training increases the efficiency of the whole system and avoids underutilizing employees in some areas while others are being overtaxed. Many airlines cross-train their employees to move from ticketing to working the gate counters to assisting with baggage if needed. Grocery stores also use this strategy, most employees being able to move as needed from cashiering to stocking shelves to bagging groceries.

Modify or Move Facilities and Equipment   Sometimes it is possible to adjust, move, or creatively modify existing capacity to meet demand fluctuations. Hotels utilize this strategy by reconfiguring rooms—two rooms with a locked door between can be rented to two different parties in high demand times or turned into a suite during slow demand. The airline industry offers dramatic examples of this strategy. Using an approach known as "demand-driven dispatch," airlines have begun to experiment with methods that assign airplanes to flight schedules on the basis of fluctuating market needs.[10] The method depends on accurate knowledge of demand and the ability to quickly move airplanes with different seating capacities to flight assignments that match their capacity. The Boeing 777 aircraft is so flexible that it can be reconfigured within hours to vary the number of seats allocated to one, two, or three classes.[11] The plane can thus be quickly modified to match demand from different market segments, essentially molding capacity to fit demand.

Combining Demand and Capacity Strategies

Many firms use multiple strategies, combining marketing-driven demand management approaches with operations-driven capacity management strategies. Figuring out which is the best set of strategies for maximizing capacity utilization, customer satisfaction, and profitability can be challenging, particularly when the service offering is a constellation of offerings within one service setting, for example, theme parks with rides, restaurants, shopping; hotel vacation villages with hotels, shopping, spas, pools, restaurants; or ski resorts with ski slopes, spas, restaurants, and entertainment. Firms face complex problems in trying to balance demand across all the different offerings with an eye to quality and profitability.

⟶ YIELD MANAGEMENT: BALANCING CAPACITY UTILIZATION, PRICING, MARKET SEGMENTATION, AND FINANCIAL RETURN

Yield management is a term that has become attached to a variety of methods, some very sophisticated, matching demand and supply in capacity-constrained services. Using yield management models, organizations find the best balance at a particular point in time among the prices charged, the segments sold to, and the capacity used. The goal of yield management is to produce the best possible financial return from a limited available capacity. Specifically, yield management (also referred to as revenue management) has been defined as "the process of allocating the right type of capacity to the right kind of customer at the right price so as to maximize revenue or yield."[12]

Although the implementation of yield management can involve complex mathematical models and computer programs, the underlying effectiveness measure is the ratio of actual revenue to potential revenue for a particular measurement period:

$$\text{Yield} = \frac{\text{Actual revenue}}{\text{Potential revenue}}$$

where

$$\text{Actual revenue} = \text{Actual capacity used} \times \text{Average actual price}$$

$$\text{Potential evenue} = \text{Total capacity} \times \text{Maximum price}$$

The equations indicate that yield is a function of price and capacity used. Recall that capacity constraints can be in the form of time, labour, equipment, or facilities. Yield is essentially a measure of the extent to which an organization's resources (or capacities) are achieving their full revenue-generating potential. Assuming that total capacity and maximum price cannot be changed, yield approaches 1 as actual capacity utilization increases or when a higher actual price can be charged for a given capacity used. For example, in an airline context, a manager could focus on increasing yield by finding ways to bring in more passengers to fill the capacity, or by finding higher-paying passengers to fill a more limited capacity. In reality, expert yield managers work on capacity and pricing issues simultaneously to maximize revenue across different customer segments. Exhibit 15.1 shows simple yield calculations and the inherent tradeoffs for two types of services: hotel and legal.

> ## EXHIBIT 15.1
> ## Simple Yield Calculations: Examples from Hotel and Legal Services

You can do basic yield calculations for any capacity constrained service assuming you know the actual capacity, average price charged for different market segments, and maximum price that could be charged. Ideally, yield will approach the number 1, or 100 percent, where:

Yield = Actual revenue/Potential revenue

In this box we describe yield calculations for two simple examples—a 200-room hotel and a lawyer with a 40-hour work week—under different assumed pricing and usage situations. Although companies use much more complex mathematical models to determine yield, the underlying ideas are the same. The goal is to maximize the revenue-generating capability of the organization's capacity.

200-ROOM HOTEL WITH MAXIMUM ROOM RATE OF $100 PER ROOM PER NIGHT

Potential revenue = $100 × 200 rooms = $20,000 per night

1. Assume: the hotel rents all its rooms at a discounted rate of $50 per night.

   Yield = $50 × 200 rooms/$20,000 = 50%

   At this rate, the hotel is maximizing capacity utilization, but not getting a very good price.

2. Assume: the hotel charges its full rate, but can only rent 40 percent of its rooms at that price, due to price sensitivity.

   Yield = $100 × 80 rooms/$20,000 = 40%

   In this situation the hotel has maximized the per-room price, but the yield is even lower than in the first situation because so few rooms were rented at that relatively high rate.

3. Assume: the hotel charges its full rate of $100 for 40 percent of its rooms and then gives a discount of $50 for the remaining 120 rooms.

Yield = [($100 × 80) + ($50 × 120)]/$20,000 = $14,000/$20,000 = 70%

Clearly, the final alternative, which takes into account price-sensitivity and charges different prices for different rooms or market segments, will result in the highest yield.

40 HOURS OF A LAWYER'S TIME ACROSS A TYPICAL WORK WEEK AT $200 PER HOUR MAXIMUM (PRIVATE CLIENT RATE)

Potential revenue = 40 hours × $200 per hour = $8,000 per week

1. Assume: the lawyer is able to bill out 30 percent of her billable time at $200 per hour.

   Yield = $200 × 12 hours/$8,000 = 30%

   In this case the lawyer has maximized her hourly rate, but has only enough work to occupy 12 billable hours.

2. Assume: the lawyer decides to charge $100 for non-profit or government clients and is able to bill out all 40 hours at this rate for these types of clients.

   Yield = $100 × 40 hours/$8,000 = 50%

   In this case, although she has worked a full week, yield is still not very good given the relatively low rate per hour.

3. Assume: the lawyer uses a combined strategy in which she works 12 hours for private clients and fills the rest of her time with nonprofit clients at $100 per hour.

   Yield = [($200 × 12) + ($100 × 28)]/$8,000 = $5,200/$8,000 5 65%

   Again, catering to two different market segments with different price-sensitivities, is the best overall strategy in terms of maximizing revenue-generating capacity of the lawyer's time.

Implementing a Yield Management System

Our Technology Spotlight illustrates several examples of how information technology supports effective yield management applications. To implement a yield management system, an organization needs detailed data on past demand patterns by market segment as well as methods of projecting current market demand. The data can be combined through mathematical programming models, threshold analysis, or use of expert systems to project the best allocation of limited capacity at a particular point in time.[13]

404   Part 5   *Delivering and Performing Service*

Technology Spotlight

Information and Technology Drive Yield Management Systems

Yield management is not a new concept. In fact, the basic idea behind yield management—achieving maximum profits through the most effective use of capacity—has been around forever. It is easy to find examples of capacity-constrained businesses using price to shift demand: theatres that charge different prices for matinees vs. evening performances, inter-city trains with different prices on weekdays than on weekends, ski resorts with cheaper prices for night skiing, and restaurants with "twilight" dinner specials. All these strategies illustrate attempts to smooth the peaks and valleys of demand using price as the primary motivator.

The difference in these basic pricing strategies and more sophisticated yield management approaches currently in use by airlines, car rental companies, hotels, shippers, and others is the reliance of these latter strategies on massive databases, sophisticated mathematical algorithms, and complex analyses. These forms of yield management consider not only price but also market segments, price-sensitivity among segments, timing of demand, and potential profitability of customer segments—all simultaneously. What makes new forms of yield management possible are the technology and systems underlying them. Here we provide a few examples of what some companies and industries have done.

AUSTRIAN AIRLINES

Austrian Airlines (www.uau.com) has been one of the most consistently profitable airlines in Europe. Prior to deregulation of airlines in Europe, Austrian foresaw the need to develop a competitive advantage that would carry it into the deregulated future. The airline invested in a revenue management computer system to build a two-year historical database of booking data that would monitor flights up to 250 days into the future. Using the system, Austrian saw significant improvements in both number of passengers carried and revenue. By being more selective in its discounting practices than were its competitors, Austrian achieved excellent results.

Source: Courtesy of Marriott International Inc.

MARRIOTT HOTELS

The hotel industry has also embraced the concepts of yield management, and Marriott Hotels (www.marriott.com) has been a leader. The systems at Marriott, for example, maximize profits for a hotel across full weeks rather than by day. In their hotels that target business travellers, Marriott has peak days during the middle of the week. Rather than simply sell the hotel out on those nights on a first-come, first-served basis with no discounts, the revenue management system (which is reviewed and revised daily) now projects guest demand both by price and length of stay, providing discounts in some cases to guests who will stay longer, even on a peak demand night. One early test of the system was at the Munich Marriott during Oktoberfest. Typically no discounts would be offered during this peak period. However, the yield management system recommended that the hotel offer some rooms at a discount, but only for those guests who stayed an extended period before or after the peak days. Although the average daily rate was down 11.7 percent for the period, occupancy was up over 20 percent, and overall revenues were up 12.3 percent. Using yield management practices, Marriott Hotels estimates an additional $400 million per year in revenue.

YELLOW TRANSPORTATION

Pricing in the freight industry still seems to be stuck in a regulated mindset in which cost issues dominate, and discounts from class rates are determined by complex formulas. However, companies such as Yellow Transportation (www.myyellow.com, a subsidiary of YRC Worldwide Inc.) are moving toward market-driven models that price services consistently with the value

continued

Technology Spotlight

Information and Technology Drive Yield Management Systems—continued

as perceived by the customer. New pricing structures recognize the customers' and freight providers' desires for simplification, while combining this with sophisticated use of yield management models that take into account the most profitable use of resources. Yield management systems encourage more-rational scheduling of trucks and drivers by considering such subtle factors as equipment type and the skills of a particular driver.

The systems can match hundreds of drivers with loads in fractions of seconds to make the best dispatch and driver decisions. By analyzing its services, prices, and demand patterns in this way, Yellow has been able to project the success of its Exact Express service, which targets customers who recognize the value of guaranteed, time-definite delivery.

Sources: R. G. Cross, *Revenue Management* (New York: Broadway Books, 1997); N. Templin, "Your Room Costs $250 . . . No! $200 . . . No," *The Wall Street Journal*, May 5, 1999, p. B1; H. Richardson, "Simplify! Simplify! Simplify!," *Transportation and Distribution* 39 (October 1998), pp. 111–17; and C. Salter "On the Road Again," *Fast Company*, January 2002, pp. 50–58.

Source: Courtesy of YRC Worldwide.

Allocations of capacity for specific market segments can then be communicated to reservations staff as targets for selling rooms, seats, time, or other limited resources. Sometimes the allocations, once determined, remain fixed. At other times allocations change weekly, or even daily or hourly, in response to new information.

Recent research indicates that traditional yield management approaches are most profitable when (1) a service provider faces different market segments or customers, who arrive or make their reservations at different times and (2) customers who arrive or reserve early are more price-sensitive than those who arrive or reserve late.[14] These criteria exactly fit the situation for airlines and many hotels—industries that have effectively and extensively used yield management techniques to allocate capacity. In other services (entertainment, sports, fashion), those customers willing to pay the higher prices are the ones who buy early rather than late. People who really want to see a particular performance reserve their seats at the earliest possible moment. Discounting for early purchases would reduce profits. In these situations, the price generally starts out high and is reduced later to fill capacity if needed.

Interestingly, some airlines now use both these strategies effectively. They start with discounted seats for customers who are willing to buy early, usually leisure and discretionary travellers. They charge a higher fare for those who want a seat at the last minute, typically the less price-sensitive business travellers whose destinations and schedules are inflexible. However, in some cases a bargain fare can be found at the last minute as well, commonly via Internet sales, to fill seats that would otherwise go unoccupied. Online auctions and services offered by companies like Internet-based Priceline.com serve a purpose in filling capacity at the last minute, often charging much lower fares. (See the Technology Spotlight in Chapter 17 for examples of dynamic pricing via the Internet.)

Challenges and Risks in Using Yield Management

Yield management programs can significantly improve revenues. However, although yield management may appear to be an ideal solution to the problem of matching supply and demand, it is not without risks. By becoming focused on maximizing financial returns through differential capacity allocation and pricing, an organization may encounter these problems:[15]

- *Loss of competitive focus.* Yield management may cause a firm to overfocus on profit maximization and inadvertently neglect aspects of the service that provide long-term competitive success.

- *Customer alienation.* If customers learn that they are paying a higher price for service than someone else, they may perceive the pricing as unfair, particularly if they do not understand the reasons. However, a study done in the restaurant industry found that when customers were informed of different prices being charged by time of day, week, or table location, they generally felt the practice was fair, particularly if the price difference was framed as a discount for less desirable times rather than a premium for peak times or table locations.[16] Customer education is thus essential in an effective yield management program. Customers can be further alienated if they fall victim (and are not compensated adequately) to overbooking practices that are often necessary to make yield management systems work effectively.

- *Employee morale problems.* Yield management systems take much guesswork and judgment in setting prices away from sales and reservations people. Although some employees may appreciate the guidance, others may resent the rules and restrictions on their own discretion.

- *Incompatible incentive and reward systems.* Employees may resent yield management systems that do not match incentive structures. For example, many managers are rewarded on the basis of capacity utilization *or* average rate charged, whereas yield management balances the two factors.

- *Lack of employee training.* Extensive training is required to make a yield management system work. Employees need to understand its purpose, how it works, how they should make decisions, and how the system will affect their jobs.

- *Inappropriate organization of the yield management function.* To be most effective with yield management, an organization must have centralized reservations. Although airlines and some large hotel chains and shipping companies do have such centralization, smaller organizations may have decentralized reservations systems and thus find it difficult to operate a yield management system effectively.

WAITING LINE STRATEGIES: WHEN DEMAND AND CAPACITY CANNOT BE MATCHED

Sometimes it is not possible to manage capacity to match demand, or vice versa. It may be too costly—for example, most health clinics would not find it economically feasible to add additional facilities or physicians to handle peaks in demand during the winter flu season; patients usually simply have to wait to be seen. Sometimes

FIGURE 15.6

Waiting is common in many service industries.

Source: Photodisc Green/Getty Images.

waits may occur when demand backs up because of the variability in length of time for service. For example, even though patients are scheduled by appointments in a physician's office, frequently there is a wait because some patients take longer to serve than the time allotted to them. According to many sources, the misalignment in capacity and demand has reached crisis proportions in the emergency health care context, as is described in Exhibit 15.2.

For most service organizations, waiting customers are a fact of life at some point (see Figure 15.6). Waiting can occur on the telephone (customers put on hold when they call in to ask for information, order something, or make a complaint) and in person (customers waiting in line at the bank, post office, Disneyland, or a physician's office).

In today's fast-paced society, waiting is not something most people tolerate well. As people work longer hours, as individuals have less leisure, and as families have fewer hours together, the pressure on people's time is greater than ever. In this environment, customers are looking for efficient, quick service with no wait. Organizations that make customers wait take the chance that they will lose business or at the very least that customers will be dissatisfied.[17] To deal effectively with the inevitability of waits, organizations can utilize a variety of strategies, described next.

Employ Operational Logic

If customer waits are common, a first step is to analyze the operational processes to remove any inefficiencies. It may be possible to redesign the system to move customers along more quickly.

In introducing its express check-in, Marriott Hotels used an operations-based modification to eliminate much of the waiting previously experienced by its guests. Guests who use a credit card and preregister can avoid waiting in line at the hotel front desk altogether. The guest can make it from the curb outside the hotel to his or her room in as little as three minutes when escorted by a "guest service associate" who checks the

EXHIBIT 15.2

Overflow in the ER: How to Manage Capacity Constraints and Excess Demand in Hospital Emergency Departments

Nowhere is there a more vivid example of demand and capacity issues than in hospital emergency departments (EDs). (*Emergency department* is the preferred term within the medical community for what has traditionally been called the ER.) In a typical ED, rooms are filled, the corridors may be clogged with waiting patients, wait time may be anywhere from 15 minutes to 8 or 10 hours, and ambulances are routinely turned away to seek other hospitals on what is called "reroute" or "diversion." Many experts have referred to these issues as a national crisis in health care. The emergency department is the front door of hospitals and is also the treatment of last resort for many. Why has this overcrowding issue reached national proportions? Many factors come into play, including increased demand and severe capacity constraints.

INCREASED DEMAND FOR SERVICES

Emergency departments are to some extent victims of their own success. Decades of public health campaigns urging people to call 911 in case of medical emergency have been successful in educating people to do just that—and they end up in the ED. Many do indeed have life-threatening emergencies that belong in the ED. Others waiting in the ED are without a family doctor; the ED is their only option, and legally the ED must care for them. Also crowding EDs are patients who cannot get appointments with their doctors in a timely manner, or who learn that it may be their fastest entry into a hospital bed. Patients and their doctors are becoming aware that they can get sophisticated care in the ED relatively quickly. Thus the demand for ED services has increased.

CAPACITY CONSTRAINTS

It is not just an increase in demand that is causing the overcrowding. It is also a shrinkage or unavailability of critical capacity at the same time. Doctors are overbooked in private practices, so patients who don't want to wait turn to the ED. Also, a shortage of specialists who are willing to take patients on call from the ED results in increased waiting times because these patients waiting for specialized care occupy beds in the ED longer than necessary. Another very critical capacity constraint is the number of beds in hospitals. Over the years many hospitals across the country have, for financial reasons, reduced the number of beds available. So ED patients often cannot get beds right away even if they need one, again increasing waiting time for themselves and others. There is a shortage of nurses as well and staffing shortages in housekeeping play a role. A bed may be empty, but until it is cleaned and remade, it

is not available for a waiting patient. In some communities, patients may find that emergency room facilities are simply not available. Some hospitals have actually closed their emergency departments after determining that it is unprofitable to run them at current reimbursement rates. In other areas, population growth is outpacing hospital and ED construction.

To address this complex set of issues, a few changes are being made or considered.

Technology and Systems Improvements

A partial solution is to turn to technology to smooth the process of admitting patients into the ED and to track the availability of hospital beds. Some Web-based systems are used to reroute ambulances to hospitals that have capacity. Other systems help EDs track the availability of rooms in their own hospitals in terms of knowing exactly when a bed is vacant and when it has been cleaned and is available—similar to what hotels have done for decades. Wireless systems for registering patients at bedside and "radar screens" that track everything going on in the ED are other partial solutions. These screens can track patients, staff, carts, and equipment, making the service delivery process more efficient and quicker.

Other hospitals have segmented their patients and have developed parallel "fast track" processes for dealing with minor emergency patients that can account for 30 to 50 percent of total visits. This process can be separated from the major-emergency situations that may require more time and special equipment. Quicker admitting processes, sometimes done on wireless devices, are also being implemented. Instead of having a patient fill out long forms with detailed questions, the quicker process asks just three to four questions initially, saving the longer admitting forms for after treatment.

Yet another innovation is to have staff administer routine tests while the patient is waiting so that the doctor who finally sees the patient has information at hand. This solution also satisfies the patient's need for "something to happen" during the waiting time. Giving patients pagers so they can do something else while waiting is another way that EDs are helping patients cope with the long waits.

Increasing Capacity

Another set of partial solutions relates directly to hospital and staff capacity issues. Some hospitals have already begun adding rooms and other facilities. More urgent care centres are being built to take some of the pressure off EDs. For patients who need to be admitted to the

continued

➡ EXHIBIT 15.2
—*continued*

hospital, however, increasing capacity is not a total solution. The nursing and doctor shortage, one of the most critical problems, is very difficult to solve.

It is obvious that this classic dilemma of matching supply and demand in a service context has multiple, deeply rooted causes when examined in the context of emergency care. The solutions to the issues are also multifaceted—some can be undertaken by individual hospitals, whereas others need to be addressed by the entire health care industry. Some,

however, are societal issues with only long-term solutions. Yet all these issues play out daily in the very immediate environment of hospital emergency departments.

Sources: L. Landro, "ERs Now Turn to Technology to Help Deal with Overcapacity," *The Wall Street Journal,* July 13, 2001, p. B1; J.-Snyder, "Curing the ER," *The Arizona Republic,* December 9, 2001, p. D1+; N. Shute and M. B. Marcus, "Crisis in the ER," *US News & World Report,* September 10, 2001.

guest into the hotel, picks up keys and paperwork from a rack in the lobby, and then escorts the guest directly to the room.[18]

When queues are inevitable, the organization faces the operational decision of what kind of queuing system to use, or how to configure the queue. Queue configuration refers to the number of queues, their locations, their spatial requirement, and their effect on customer behaviour.[19] Several possibilities exist, as shown in Figure 15.7. In the multiple-queue alternative, the customer arrives at the service facility and must decide which queue to join and whether to switch later if the wait appears to be shorter in another line. In the single-queue alternative, fairness of waiting time is ensured in that the first-come, first-served rule applies to everyone; the system can also reduce the average time customers spend waiting overall. However, customers may leave if they perceive that the line is too long or if they have no opportunity to select a particular service provider. The last option shown in Figure 15.7 is the take-a-number option in which arriving customers take a number to indicate line position. Advantages are similar to the single-queue alternative with the additional benefit that customers are able to mill about, browse, and talk to each other. The disadvantage is that customers must be on the alert to hear their numbers when they are called. Recent research suggests that length of the

FIGURE 15.7

Waiting-Line Configurations

Source: J. A. Fitzsimmons and M. J. Fitzsimmons, *Service Management,* 4th ed. (New York: Irwin/McGraw-Hill, 2004), ch. 11, p. 296. © 2004 by The McGraw-Hill Companies, Inc. Reprinted by permission of The McGraw-Hill Companies.

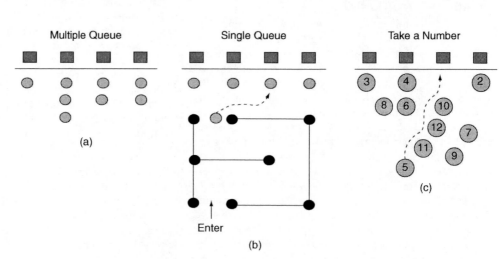

queue and perceived cost of waiting are not the only influences on customers' likelihood of staying in line. In a series of experiments and field tests, researchers showed that the larger the number of customers waiting in line *behind* a consumer, the more likely that consumer is to stay in line and wait for the service.[20]

Many service businesses have become experts at handling queues effectively in terms of minimizing customer dissatisfaction. Some of the benchmarks include Disney, Marriott, and FedEx.

Establish a Reservation Process

When waiting cannot be avoided, a reservation system can help to spread demand. Restaurants, transportation companies, theatres, physicians, and many other service providers use reservation systems to alleviate long waits. The idea behind a reservation system is to guarantee that the service will be available when the customer arrives. Beyond simply reducing waiting time, a reservation system has the added benefit of potentially shifting demand to less desirable time periods. A challenge inherent in reservation systems, however, is what to do about "no-shows." Inevitably there will be customers who reserve a time but do not show up. Some organizations deal with this problem by overbooking their service capacity on the basis of past records of no-show percentages. If the predictions are accurate, overbooking is a good solution. When predictions are inaccurate, however, customers may still have to wait and sometimes may not be served at all, as when airlines overbook the number of seats available on a flight. Victims of overbooking may be compensated for their inconvenience in such cases. To minimize the no-show problem, some organizations (such as hotels, airlines, conferences/training programs, and theatres) charge customers who fail to show up or cancel their reservations within a certain time frame. While overbooking is an intentional strategy for many airlines, WestJet is taking a different approach (see Figure 15.8). By *not* overbooking, they hope to increase average load levels by attracting passengers who don't want to be unpleasantly surprised.

Differentiate Waiting Customers

Not all customers necessarily need to wait the same length of time for service. On the basis of need or customer priority, some organizations differentiate among customers, allowing some to experience shorter waits for service than others. Known as "queue discipline," such differentiation reflects management policies regarding whom to select next for service.[21] The most popular discipline is first-come, first-served.

FIGURE 15.8   WestJet promises not to overbook its flights.

However, other rules may apply. Differentiation can be based on factors such as the following:[22]

- *Importance of the customer.* Frequent customers or customers who spend large amounts with the organization can be given priority in service by providing them with a special waiting area or segregated lines.

- *Urgency of the job.* Those customers with the most urgent need may be served first. This strategy is used in emergency health care. It is also used by maintenance services such as air-conditioning repair that give priority to customers whose air conditioning is not functioning over those who call for routine maintenance.

- *Duration of the service transaction.* In many situations, shorter-service jobs get priority through "express lanes." At other times, when a service provider sees that a transaction is going to require extra time, the customer is referred to a designated provider who deals only with these special-needs customers.

- *Payment of a premium price.* Customers who pay extra (e.g., first class on an airline) are often given priority via separate check-in lines or express systems.

Make Waiting Fun, or at Least Tolerable

Even when they have to wait, customers can be more or less satisfied depending on how the wait is handled by the organization. Of course the actual length of the wait will affect how customers feel about their service experience. But it is not just the actual time spent waiting that has an impact on customer satisfaction—it is how customers feel about the wait and their perceptions during it. The type of wait (e.g., a standard queue versus a wait due to a delay of service) can also influence how customers will react.[23] In a classic article entitled "The Psychology of Waiting Lines," David Maister proposes several principles about waiting, each of which has implications for how organizations can make waiting more pleasurable or at least tolerable.[24]

Unoccupied Time Feels Longer Than Occupied Time

When customers are unoccupied they will likely be bored and will notice the passage of time more than when they have something to do. Providing something for waiting customers to do, particularly if the activity offers a benefit in and of itself or is related in some way to the service, can improve the customer's experience and may benefit the organization as well.[25] Examples include giving customers menus to look at while waiting in a restaurant, providing interesting information to read in a dentist's office, or playing entertaining programs over the phone while customers are on hold. At Macy's in New York, children waiting to see Santa Claus wind their way through displays of dancing teddy bears, elves, and electric trains that become part of the total service adventure.[26]

Preprocess Waits Feel Longer Than In-Process Waits

If wait time is occupied with activities that relate to the upcoming service, customers may perceive that the service has started and they are no longer actually waiting. This in-process activity will make the length of the wait seem shorter and will also benefit the service provider by making the customer better prepared when the service actually does begin. Filling out medical information while waiting to see the physician, reading a menu while waiting to be seated in a restaurant, and watching a videotape of the upcoming service event are all activities that can both educate the customer and reduce perceptions of waiting.

Research in a restaurant context found that customers reacted less negatively to in-process waits than to either preprocess or postprocess waits.[27] Other researchers have found the same for waits due to routine slowness of the process. However, if the wait is due to a service failure, then the in-process wait is viewed more negatively than the preprocess wait.[28] Thus, how customers perceive preprocess, in-process, and postprocess waits may depend to some extent on the cause of the wait.

Anxiety Makes Waits Seem Longer

When customers fear that they have been forgotten or do not know how long they will have to wait, they become anxious, and this anxiety can increase the negative impact of waiting. Anxiety also results when customers are forced to choose in a multiple-line situation and they discover they have chosen the "wrong line." To combat waiting-line anxiety, organizations can provide information on the length of the wait. At its theme parks, Disney uses signs at intervals along the line that let customers know how long the wait will be from that point on. Using a single line also alleviates customer anxiety over having chosen the wrong line. Explanations and reassurances that no one has forgotten them alleviate customer anxiety by taking away their cause for worry.

Uncertain Waits Are Longer Than Known, Finite Waits

Anxiety is intensified when customers do not know how long they will have to wait. Health care providers combat this problem by letting customers know when they check in how far behind the physician is that day. Some patients resolve this uncertainty themselves by calling ahead to ask. Maister provides an interesting example of the role of uncertainty, which he terms the "appointment syndrome." Customers who arrive early for an appointment will wait patiently until the scheduled time, even if they arrive very early. However, once the expected appointment time has passed, customers grow increasingly anxious. Before the appointment time the wait time is known; after that, the length of the wait is not known.

Research in an airline context has suggested that as uncertainty about the wait increases, customers become more angry, and their anger in turn results in greater dissatisfaction.[29] Research also shows that giving customers information on the length of the anticipated wait and/or their relative position in the queue can result in more positive feelings and acceptance of the wait and ultimately more positive evaluation of the service.[30]

Unexplained Waits Are Longer Than Explained Waits

When people understand the causes for waiting, they frequently have greater patience and are less anxious, particularly when the wait is justifiable. An explanation can reduce customer uncertainty and may help customers estimate how long they will be delayed. Customers who do not know the reason for a wait begin to feel powerless and irritated.

Unfair Waits Are Longer Than Equitable Waits

When customers perceive that they are waiting while others who arrived after them have already been served, the apparent inequity will make the wait seem even longer. This situation can easily occur when there is no apparent order in the waiting area and many customers are trying to be served. Queuing systems that work on a first-come, first-served rule are best at combating perceived unfairness. However, other approaches may be required to determine who will be served next. For example, in an emergency medical care situation, the most seriously ill or injured patients would be seen first. When customers understand the priorities and the rules are clearly communicated and enforced, fairness of waiting time should not be an issue.

The More Valuable the Service, the Longer the Customer Will Wait

Customers who have substantial purchases or who are waiting for a high-value service will be more tolerant of long wait times and may even expect to wait longer. For example, in a supermarket, customers who have a full cart of groceries will generally wait longer than customers who have only a few items and expect to be checked through quickly. And diners expect to wait longer for service in an expensive restaurant than they do when eating at a "greasy spoon."

Solo Waits Feel Longer Than Group Waits

People will wait longer when they are in a group than when they are alone because of the distractions provided by other members of the group. People also feel comfort in waiting with a group rather than alone.[31] In some group waiting situations, such as at Disneyland or when patrons are waiting in long lines to purchase concert tickets, customers who are strangers begin to talk to each other and the waiting experience can actually become fun and a part of the total service experience.

SUMMARY

Because service organizations lack the ability to inventory their products, the effective use of capacity can be critical to success. Idle capacity in the form of unused time, labour, facilities, or equipment represents a direct drain on bottom-line profitability. When the capacity represents a major investment (e.g., airplanes, expensive medical imaging equipment, or lawyers and physicians paid on a salary), the losses associated with underuse of capacity are even more accentuated. Overused capacity is also a problem. People, facilities, and equipment can become worn out over time when used beyond optimum capacity constraints. People can quit, facilities become run down, and equipment can break. From the customer's perspective, service quality also deteriorates. Organizations focused on delivering quality service, therefore, have a natural drive to balance capacity utilization and demand at an optimum level in order to meet customer expectations.

This chapter has provided you with an understanding of the underlying issues of managing supply and demand in capacity-constrained services by exploring the lack of inventory capability, the nature of service constraints (time, labour, equipment, facilities), the differences in optimal versus maximum use of capacity, and the causes of fluctuating demand.

Based on grounding in the fundamental issues, the chapter presented a variety of strategies for matching supply and demand. The basic strategies fall under two headings: *demand strategies* (shifting demand to match capacity) and *supply strategies* (adjusting capacity to meet demand). Demand strategies seek to flatten the peaks and valleys of demand to match the flat capacity constraint, whereas supply strategies seek to align, flex, or stretch capacity to match the peaks and valleys of demand. Organizations frequently employ several strategies simultaneously to solve the complex problem of balancing supply and demand.

Yield management was presented as a sophisticated form of supply and demand management that balances capacity utilization, pricing, market segmentation, and financial return. This strategy, long practised by the passenger airline industry, is growing in use by hotel, shipping, car rental, and other capacity-constrained industries in which bookings are made in advance. Essentially, yield management allows organizations to

414 Part 5 *Delivering and Performing Service*

decide on a monthly, weekly, daily, or even hourly basis to whom they want to sell their service capacity at what price.

All strategies for aligning capacity and demand need to be approached with caution. Any one of them is likely to imply changes in multiple marketing mix elements to support the strategy. Such changes, even if done well, carry a risk that the firm will lose focus or inadvertently alter its image in pursuit of increased revenues. Although a different focus or image is not necessarily bad, the potential strategic impact on the total organization should be considered.

In the last section of the chapter, we discussed situations in which it is not possible to align supply and demand. In these unresolved capacity utilization situations, the inevitable result is customer waiting. We described strategies for effectively managing waiting lines, such as employing operational logic, establishing a reservation process, differentiating waiting customers, and making waiting fun or at least tolerable.

⟼ Discussion Questions

1. Why do service organizations lack the capability to inventory their services? Compare a car repair and maintenance service with an automobile manufacturer/dealer in terms of inventory capability.

2. Discuss the four scenarios illustrated in Figure 15.1 and presented in the text (excess demand, demand exceeds optimum capacity, demand and supply are balanced, excess capacity) in the context of a professional basketball team selling seats for its games. What are the challenges for management under each scenario?

3. Discuss the four common types of constraints (time, labour, equipment, facilities) facing service businesses and give an example of each (real or hypothetical).

4. How does optimal capacity utilization differ from maximum capacity utilization? Give an example of a situation in which the two might be the same and one in which they are different.

5. Choose a local restaurant or some other type of service with fluctuating demand. What is the likely underlying pattern of demand? What causes the pattern? Is it predictable or random?

6. Describe the two basic strategies for matching supply and demand, and give at least two specific examples of each.

7. What is yield management? Discuss the risks in adopting a yield management strategy.

8. How might yield management apply in the management of the following: a Broadway theatre? A consulting firm? A commuter train?

9. Describe the four basic waiting-line strategies, and give an example of each, preferably based on your own experiences as a consumer.

⟼ Exercises

1. Choose a local service organization that is challenged by fixed capacity and fluctuating demand. Interview the marketing manager (or other knowledgeable person) to learn (*a*) in what ways capacity is constrained, (*b*) the basic patterns of

demand, and (*c*) strategies the organization has used to align supply and demand. Write up the answers to these questions, and make your own recommendations regarding other strategies the organization might use.

2. Assume you manage a winter ski resort in Banff or Colorado. *(a)* Explain the underlying pattern of demand fluctuation that is likely to occur at your resort and the challenges it would present to you as a manager. Is the pattern of demand predictable or random? (*b*) Explain and give examples of how you might use both demand-oriented and supply-oriented strategies to smooth the peaks and valleys of demand during peak and slow periods.

3. Choose a local organization in which people have to wait in line for service. Design a waiting-line strategy for the organization.

4. Visit the website of Wells Fargo Bank (www.wellsfargo.com), a leader in online banking. What online services does the bank currently offer? How do these online services help Wells Fargo manage the peaks and valleys of customer demand? How do its strategies to use more ATMs, in-store bank branches, and other, alternative delivery strategies complement the online strategies?

Notes

1. www.deltahotels.com, accessed October 2, 2006.
2. "Toronto's Key Industry Clusters: Tourism," Toronto.ca, www.toronto.ca/economic_profile/tourism.htm, accessed October 2, 2006.
3. J. S. Hirsch, "Vacationing Families Head Downtown to Welcoming Arms of Business Hotels," *The Wall Street Journal,* June 13, 1994, p. B1.
4. Ibid.
5. C. Lovelock, "Getting the Most out of Your Productive Capacity," *Product Plus* (Boston: McGraw-Hill, 1994), ch. 16.
6. C. H. Lovelock, "Classifying Services to Gain Strategic Marketing Insights," *Journal of Marketing* 47 (Summer 1983), pp. 9–20.
7. Portions of this section are based on C. H. Lovelock, "Strategies for Managing Capacity-Constrained Service Organizations," in *Managing Services: Marketing, Operations, and Human Resources,* 2nd ed. (Englewood Cliffs, NJ: Prentice Hall, 1992), pp. 154–68.
8. E. C. Clemmer and B. Schneider, "Toward Understanding and Controlling Customer Dissatisfaction with Waiting During Peak Demand Times," in *Designing a Winning Service Strategy,* ed. M. J. Bitner and L. A. Crosby (Chicago: American Marketing Association, 1989), pp. 87–91.
9. Lovelock, "Getting the Most out of Your Productive Capacity."
10. M. E. Berge and C. A. Hopperstad, "Demand Driven Dispatch: A Method for Dynamic Aircraft Capacity Assignment, Models, and Algorithms," *Operations Research* 41 (January/February 1993), pp. 153–68.
11. Lovelock, "Getting the Most out of Your Productive Capacity."
12. See S. E. Kimes, "Yield Management: A Tool for Capacity-Constrained Service Firms," *Journal of Operations Management* 8 (October 1989), pp. 348–63; S. E. Kimes and R. B. Chase, "The Strategic Levers of Yield Management," *Journal of Service Research* 1 (November 1998), pp. 156–66; S. E. Kimes, "Revenue Management: A Retrospective," *Cornell Hotel and Restaurant Administration Quarterly* 44, no. 5/6 (2003), pp. 131–38.

13. Kimes, "Yield Management."

14. R. Desiraji and S. M. Shugan, "Strategic Service Pricing and Yield Management," *Journal of Marketing* 63 (January 1999), pp. 44–56.

15. Kimes, "Yield Management."

16. S. E. Kimes and J. Wirtz, "Has Revenue Management Become Acceptable? Findings from an International Study on the Perceived Fairness of Rate Fences," *Journal of Service Research* 6 (November 2003), pp. 125–35.

17. For research supporting the relationship between longer waits and decreased satisfaction, quality evaluations, and patronage intentions see Clemmer and Schneider, "Toward Understanding and Controlling Customer Dissatisfaction"; A. Th. H. Pruyn and A. Smidts, "Customer Evaluation of Queues: Three Exploratory Studies," *European Advances in Consumer Research* 1 (1993), pp. 371–82; S. Taylor, "Waiting for Service: The Relationship Between Delays and Evaluations of Service," *Journal of Marketing* 58 (April 1994), pp. 56–69; K. L. Katz, B. M. Larson, and R. C. Larson, "Prescription for the Waiting-in-Line Blues: Entertain, Enlighten, and Engage," *Sloan Management Review,* Winter 1991, pp. 44–53; S. Taylor and J. D. Claxton, "Delays and the Dynamics of Service Evaluations," *Journal of the Academy of Marketing Science* 22 (Summer 1994), pp. 254–64; D. Grewal, J. Baker, M. Levy, and G. B. Voss, "The Effects of Wait Expectations and Store Atmosphere on Patronage Intentions in Service-Intensive Retail Stores," *Journal of Retailing* 79 (Winter 2003), pp. 259–68.

18 R. Henkoff, "Finding, Training, and Keeping the Best Service Workers," *Fortune,* October 3, 1994, pp. 110–22.

19. J. A. Fitzsimmons and M. J. Fitzsimmons, *Service Management*, 3rd ed. (New York: Irwin/McGraw-Hill, 2000), ch. 11.

20. R. Zhou and D. Soman, "Looking Back: Exploring the Psychology of Queuing and the Effect of the Number of People Behind," *Journal of Consumer Research* 29 (March 2003), pp. 517–30.

21. Fitzsimmons and Fitzsimmons, *Service Management,* ch. 11.

22. Lovelock, "Getting the Most out of Your Productive Capacity."

23. For an excellent review of the literature on customer perceptions of and reactions to various aspects of waiting time, see S. Taylor and G. Fullerton, "Waiting for Services: Perceptions Management of the Wait Experience," in *Handbook of Services Marketing and Management,* ed. T. A. Swartz and D. Iacobucci (Thousand Oaks, CA: Sage Publications, 2000), pp. 171–89.

24. D. A. Maister, "The Psychology of Waiting Lines," in *The Service Encounter,* ed. J. A. Czepiel, M. R. Solomon, and C. F. Surprenant (Lexington, MA: Lexington Books, 1985), pp. 113–23.

25. S. Taylor, "The Effects of Filled Waiting Time and Service Provider Control over the Delay on Evaluations of Service," *Journal of the Academy of Marketing Science* 23 (Summer 1995), pp. 38–48.

26. A. Bennett, "Their Business Is on the Line," *The Wall Street Journal,* December 7, 1990, p. B1.

27. L. Dube-Rioux, B. H. Schmitt, and F. Leclerc, "Consumers' Reactions to Waiting: When Delays Affect the Perception of Service Quality," in *Advances in Consumer Research,* vol. 16, ed. T. Srull (Provo, UT: Association for Consumer Research, 1988), pp. 59–63.

28. M. K. Hui, M. V. Thakor, and R. Gill, "The Effect of Delay Type and Service Stage on Consumers' Reactions to Waiting," *Journal of Consumer Research* 24 (March 1998), pp. 469–79.
29. Taylor and Fullerton, "Waiting for Services."
30. M. K. Hui and D. K. Tse, "What to Tell Consumers in Waits of Different Lengths: An Integrative Model of Service Evaluation," *Journal of Marketing* 60 (April 1996), pp. 81–90.
31. J. Baker and M. Cameron, "The Effects of the Service Environment on Affect and Consumer Perception of Waiting Time: An Integrative Review and Research Propositions," *Journal of the Academy of Marketing Science* 24 (Fall 1996), pp. 338–49.

Chapter 17

Pricing of Services

Closing Provider Gap 4

THIS CHAPTER'S OBJECTIVES ARE TO

1. Discuss three major ways that service prices are perceived differently from goods prices by customers.

2. Articulate the key ways that pricing of services differs from pricing of goods from a company's perspective.

3. Demonstrate what value means to customers and the role that price plays in value.

4. Describe strategies that companies use to price services.

5. Give examples of pricing strategy in action.

WHAT DO CONSUMERS PAY FOR MUSIC ONLINE?

> Welcome to the post-Napster era of rent-a-tune when music is leased instead of bought, and when every recording, from electric guitars to chamber ensembles, comes with strings attached.[1]

In their heyday, free online music exchange services such as Napster, Fast-Track, and the Dutch firm KaZaA allowed more than 60 million Internet fans to download music free with virtually unrestricted availability of artists and selections. Pirated music, which included the use of these services, was estimated to have drained more than $23 million from the legitimate Canadian music market.[2] These companies were stopped from doing business by the major record companies and their artists, and "pay-for-play"

Source: Courtesy of Puretracks Inc.

services have taken over. Napster initially defined customer expectations for online music services—any time, anywhere, for free. Today many online music services, such as Canadian-owned Puretracks (www.puretracks.com) and Apple Computer's iTunes (www.apple.com/ca/itunes), charge a flat rate per track for downloads. Other services have pricing strategies that are more difficult to compare.

Legitimate digital download music sales account for only 1 percent of the Canadian market, but the competition between service providers is intensifying, particularly since the launch of Apple's iTunes in Canada in November 2004.[3] iTunes, built as an extension of Apple's overwhelmingly successful iPod music player, became immediately successful in the United States when it began offering $0.99 digital music downloads in April 2003, and thus set a standard for industry pricing. Perhaps in anticipation of iTunes' entry into Canada, Canadian-based Puretracks' pricing model mirrored that of the American giant. Today competitors tend to use pricing as part of their strategy to gain customers. Napster, for example, charges a monthly fee of $9.95, after which each download is only $1.19. Puretracks has begun varying prices as well, charging $0.79 for some older indie tracks and for certain promotions while maintaining a premium price of $1.19 for more current, popular songs such as KT Tunstall's "Black Horse & the Cherry Tree." The table here shows several top competitors in the Canadian market along with the prices and benefits they offer.[4]

Which service offers the best deal? As the table shows, service prices are neither straightforward nor consistent. Archambaultzik.ca has some tracks priced more expensively than all competitors and has the smallest catalogue, but the service offers francophone material. On services such as Napster, users obtain an unlimited number of streaming audios and downloads for $9.95 per month but must pay $1.19 for every song they burn to a CD. Users who discontinue their subscription wipe out their downloaded library, so the service is more similar to renting or leasing than owning. And services differ in whether CDs can be burned to play only on home, car, or portable stereos or on portable MP3 players. Only iTunes songs can be downloaded to iPods. Some services, such as Puretracks, offer higher-sound-quality downloads. Companies have added value to their offerings by making it easy to organize tunes into playlists, offering high-resolution album art, giving biographical notes on artists, creating music communities, and providing access to lyrics.

These differences in offerings illustrate an important issue about pricing that will be made clear in this chapter. Price is not only about monetary cost; it also involves time, convenience, and psychic payments. In each of these offerings from online music companies, consumers are constrained in what they receive. How valuable is music if you must sit in front of your computer to hear it? How much is it worth to be able to burn a CD or transfer online music to an MP3 player? Is it enough to rent or license music, or will users want to own it as they have in the past?

INTERNET MUSIC SERVICES:
What You Get, How Much It Costs

Service	Cost	Competitive Advantages	Competitive Disadvantages	Content
Archambaultzik.ca	Songs from $0.99 to $1.39 each	Bilingual site; best francophone selection; visitors can shop for physical product from Archambault's online store simultaneously	Limited catalogue; not iPod-compatible; downloads licensed for Canada only	300,000 tracks
iTunes	$0.99 per song; albums starting at $9.99	iPod-compatible; exclusive tracks; offers music videos; music can be shared with up to 5 Macs and PCs	None	Over one million tracks; 100,000 new tracks from independent artists; 5,000 audio books, 20,000 podcasts, and more than 1,000 music videos
Napster	$9.95 per month; $1.19 per song	Month-by-month subscription; music discovery and sharing through Napster community; Napster custom compilations	Downloads expire if subscription lapses	Over 700,000 tracks
Puretracks	Songs starting at $0.79; albums starting at $9.90	Highest-quality music files available in North America; independent artist mandate; substantial Canadian content; accepts payment via PayStone	Not iPod-compatible	More than one million tracks
Yahoo! Music	$8.99 per month or $83.88 per annum; songs starting at $0.89	Allows sharing of full files among subscription holders using Yahoo! Messenger	Not iPod-compatible; limited to Windows XP users	More than one million tracks

According to one of the leading experts on pricing, most service organizations use a "naive and unsophisticated approach to pricing without regard to underlying shifts in demand, the rate that supply can be expanded, prices of available substitutes, consideration of the price–volume relationship, or the availability of future substitutes."[5] What makes the pricing of services more difficult than pricing of goods? What approaches work well in the context of services?

This chapter builds on three key differences between customer evaluation of pricing for services and goods: (1) customers often have inaccurate or limited reference prices for services, (2) price is a key signal of quality in services, and (3) monetary price is not the only price relevant to service customers. As we demonstrate, these three differences can have a profound impact on the strategies companies use to set and administer prices for services.

The chapter also discusses common pricing structures including (1) cost-based, (2) competition-based, and (3) demand-based pricing. One of the most important aspects of demand-based pricing is perceived value, which must be understood by service providers so that they price in line with offerings and customer expectations. For that reason we also describe how customers define value and discuss pricing strategies in the context of value. You will notice many advertisements by Canadian companies that illustrate the various pricing approaches we describe. In particular, we have featured a number of ads by Air Canada, who have recently introduced a number of important price-based innovations.

But before we begin, it is worth briefly reiterating how pricing relates to our Gaps model. As you know from Chapter 2 and the introduction to Part 6, price sends a signal to an organization's clients. It is what customers give the firm in order to get something in return. Pricing is therefore a key determinant of customer expectations. Having too high (or too low) a price can be caused by Gap 1—Not Knowing What Customers Expect. This may be because the firm has inadequate marketing research, poor upward communication, insufficient relationship focus, or a service recovery process that isn't passing along key information about price perceptions to those in the company who set the prices. If the firm does not know what customers expect to pay or think the service is worth, pricing mistakes will occur.

Price is therefore one of the strongest forms of external communication a firm has under its control. If it is not handled properly, there will be a gap between what a firm does—including its pricing—and what it says. This will lead to an increase in Gap 4—Not Matching Performance to Promises.

In addition, price is the only element of the services marketing mix that generates revenue. All the other elements are cost drivers. Because of this, firms must be careful not only to match their performance to their promises, but also to do so at a profit. It would be a simple matter to offer great service at low prices, for instance. But while this would not lead to an increase in Gap 4, it wouldn't generate a profit, either. Service firms must be able to keep all four gaps closed while maintaining adequate cost control if they are to continue in business. Clearly, pricing plays a big role in a service company's strategy.

THREE KEY WAYS THAT SERVICE PRICES ARE DIFFERENT FOR CONSUMERS

What role does price play in consumer decisions about services? How important is price to potential buyers compared with other factors and service features? Service companies must understand how pricing works, but first they must understand how customers perceive prices and price changes. The three sections that follow describe what we know about the ways that customers perceive services, and each is central to effective pricing.

Customer Knowledge of Service Prices

To what extent do customers use price as a criterion in selecting services? How much do consumers know about the costs of services? Before you answer these questions, take the services pricing quiz in Exhibit 17.1. Were you able to fill in a price for each of the services listed? If you were able to answer the questions from memory, you have internal *reference prices* for the services. A reference price is *a price point in memory for a good or a service,* and can consist of the price last paid, the price most frequently paid, or the average of all prices customers have paid for similar offerings.[6]

To see how accurate your reference prices for services are, you can compare them with the actual price of these services from the providers in your hometown. If you are like many consumers, you feel quite uncertain about your knowledge of the prices of services, and the reference prices you hold in memory for services are not generally as accurate as those you hold for goods. There are many reasons for this difference.

• *Service variability limits knowledge.* Because services are not created on a factory assembly line, service firms have great flexibility in the configurations of services they offer. Firms can conceivably offer an infinite variety of combinations and permutations, leading to complex and complicated pricing structures. As an example, consider how difficult it is to get comparable price quotes when buying life insurance. With the multitude of types (such as whole-life vs. term), features (different deductibles), variations associated with customers (age, health risk, smoking or nonsmoking), few insurance companies offer exactly the same features and the same prices. Only an expert customer, one who knows enough about insurance to completely specify the options across providers, is likely to find prices that are directly comparable.

• *Providers are unwilling to estimate prices.* Another reason customers lack accurate reference prices for services is that many providers are unable or unwilling to estimate price in advance. For example, legal service providers are rarely able to estimate a price in advance. The fundamental reason is that they do not know themselves what the services will involve until they have fully examined the client's situation or until the process of service delivery (such as a trial) unfolds.

• *Individual customer needs vary.* Another factor that results in the inaccuracy of reference prices is that individual customer needs vary. Some hairstylists' service prices vary across customers on the basis of length of hair, type of haircut, and whether a conditioning treatment and style are included. Therefore, if you were to ask a friend what a cut costs from a particular stylist, chances are that your cut from the same stylist may be a different price. Now consider a service purchase as idiosyncratic as braces from a dentist or help from a lawyer. In these and many other services, customer differences in need will play a strong role in the price of the service.

• *Collection of price information is overwhelming in services.* Still another reason customers lack accurate reference prices for services is that customers feel overwhelmed with the information they need to gather. With most goods, retail stores display the products by category to allow customers to compare and contrast the prices of different brands and sizes. Rarely is there a similar display of services in a single outlet. If customers want to compare prices (such as for dry cleaning), they must drive to or call individual outlets. Have a look at Exhibit 17.1 and test your knowledge of service prices with question 1.

Here's one final test about reference prices. Suppose you were having a birthday party and wanted a celebrity—say, INXS, Sheryl Crow, or Shania Twain—to perform. Do you know what celebrities charge for a performance? Steve Einzig, who runs a celebrity-booking firm, reports these going rates for private performances. (www. bookingentertainment.com):[7]

Bette Midler	$750,000 to $1,000,000
Rod Stewart	$500,000
Harry Connick Jr.	$350,000
Chris Rock	$200,000
Lionel Richie	$200,000
Bill Cosby	$150,000

The fact that consumers often possess inaccurate reference prices for services has several important managerial implications. First, promotional pricing may not be as meaningful to consumers who often don't know what price they should *expect* to pay in the first place. Second, promotional pricing may create problems if the promotion—such as $50 for highlights at the salon—is the only price a customer sees; it might become the customer's new reference price, making the regular price of $75 look high. A third implication caused by the absence of accurate reference prices suggests that advertising prices may reduce uncertainty. By featuring its price, the company might overcome the fear of high cost by giving its target audience a reference price.

• *Prices are not visible.* One requirement for the existence of customer reference prices is *price visibility*—the price cannot be hidden or implicit. In many services, particularly financial services, most customers know about only the rate of return and not the costs they pay in the form of fund and insurance fees. American Express Financial Services, the parent company of Amex Bank of Canada, discovered through research that customers knew even less than expected: not only did they not understand *what* they were paying for many of their services, very few consumers understood *how* they pay for financial services in general. Only for financial products in which price was visible—such as with securities and term life insurance—were customers aware of fees. When price was invisible, such as in certificates, whole-life insurance, and annuities, customers did not know how they were charged and what they paid. The company also found that shopping behaviour in the category of financial services was extremely limited. Between 50 and 60 percent of customers bought financial products from the very first person they talked to.[8]

For all the reasons just listed, many customers do not see the price at all until *after* they receive certain services. Of course in situations of urgency, such as in accident or illness, customers must make the decision to purchase without respect to cost. And if cost is not known to the customer before purchase, it cannot be used as a key criterion for purchase, as it often is for goods. Price is likely to be an important criterion in *repurchase,* however. Furthermore, monetary price in repurchase may be an even more important criterion than in initial purchase.

EXHIBIT 17.1

What Do You Know About the Prices of Services?

1. What do the following services cost in your hometown?

   Dental checkup _____

   One-month fitness club membership _____

   Legal help with an impaired driving charge _____

   Dental braces _____

   Rental of a video or DVD for one night _____

   One hour of housecleaning _____

   Room at the Delta _____

   Haircut _____

   Oil change and lube _____

2. Which of the following would you select if you needed a filling replaced in a tooth?

   a. Dentist A—cost is $50, located 25 kilometres from your home, wait is three weeks for an appointment and 1.5 hours in waiting room

   b. Dentist B—cost is $75, located 25 kilometres from your home, wait is one week for appointment and 0.5 hour in waiting room

   c. Dentist C—cost is $125, located 5 kilometres from your job, wait is one week for appointment and no time in waiting room

   d. Dentist D—cost is $175, located 5 kilometres from your job, wait is one week for appointment and no time in waiting room; nitrous oxide used so no pain is involved

The Role of Nonmonetary Costs

Economists have long recognized that monetary price is not the only sacrifice consumers make to obtain products and services. Demand, therefore, is not just a function of monetary price but is influenced by other costs as well. Nonmonetary costs represent other sources of sacrifice perceived by consumers when buying and using a service. Time costs, search costs, and psychological costs often enter into the evaluation of whether to buy or rebuy a service and may at times be more important concerns than monetary price. Customers will trade money for these other costs.

- *Time costs.* Most services require direct participation of the consumer and thus consume real time: time waiting as well as time when the customer interacts with the service provider. Time becomes a sacrifice made to receive service in multiple ways. First, because service providers cannot completely control the number of customers or the length of time it will take for each customer to be served, customers are likely to expend time waiting to receive the service. As Jerry Seinfeld remarked, we are so conditioned to waiting for service that we aren't even surprised that doctors have "waiting" rooms. And when we've waited in the main waiting room long enough, we get to go into the inner rooms where we get to wait some more. Second, customers often wait for an available appointment from a service provider (in the price quiz, dentist A required a three-week wait whereas dentist D required only one week). Virtually everyone has waited to receive services.

- *Search costs.* Search costs—the effort invested to identify and select among services you desire—are often higher for services than for physical goods. Prices for services are rarely displayed on shelves of service establishments for customers to examine as they shop, so these prices are often known only when a customer has decided to experience the service. As an example, how well did you estimate the costs of an hour of housecleaning in the price quiz? As a student, it is unlikely that you regularly purchase housecleaning, and you probably have not seen the price of an hour of cleaning displayed in any retail store. Another factor that increases search costs is that every service establishment typically offers only one "brand" of a service (with the exception of brokers in insurance or financial services), so a customer must initiate contact with several different companies to get information across sellers. Price comparisons for some services (travel and hotels, for example) has been facilitated through the Internet.

- *Convenience costs.* There are also convenience (or, perhaps more accurately, inconvenience) costs of services. If customers have to travel to a service, they incur a cost, and the cost becomes greater when travel is difficult, as it is for elderly persons. Further, if service hours do not coincide with customers' available time, they must arrange their schedules to correspond to the company's schedule. And if consumers have to expend effort and time to prepare to receive a service (such as removing all food from kitchen cabinets in preparation for an exterminator's spraying), they make additional sacrifices.

- *Psychological costs.* Often the most painful nonmonetary costs are the psychological costs incurred in receiving some services. Fear of not understanding (insurance), fear of rejection (bank loans), fear of outcomes (medical treatment or surgery)—all these fears constitute psychological costs that customers experience as sacrifices when purchasing and using services. New services, even those that create positive change, bring about psychological costs that consumers factor into the purchase of services. Direct deposit, a clear improvement in banking service for the elderly with limited mobility, was viewed with suspicion until the level of comfort improved. And most customers rejected voice mail when it was first developed.

Nonmonetary Cost Priorities

You can assess your own priorities on these nonmonetary cost components—time, effort, search, psychological—by thinking about your answer to question 2 in the price quiz in Exhibit 17.1. If you chose dentist A, you are probably most concerned about monetary costs—you are willing to wait for an appointment and in the waiting room of the dentist's office. If you chose dentist B over dentist A, your time and convenience costs are slightly more important than your monetary costs, because you are willing to pay $25 more to reduce the waiting time. If you chose dentist C, you are much more sensitive to time and convenience costs, including travel time, than to monetary costs—you are willing to pay $125 more than what you would pay for dentist A to avoid the other nonmonetary costs. And if you chose dentist D, you want to minimize psychological costs as well, in this case fear and pain.

Reducing Nonmonetary Costs

The managerial implications of these other sources of sacrifice are compelling. First, a firm may be able to increase monetary price by reducing time and other costs. For example, a services marketer can reduce the perceptions of time and convenience costs when use of the service is embedded in other activities (such as when a convenience store cashes cheques, sells stamps, and serves coffee along with selling products). Second, customers may be willing to pay to avoid the other costs. Many customers willingly pay extra to have items delivered to their home—including restaurant meals—rather than transporting the services and products themselves. Some customers also pay a premium for fast check-in and checkout (as in joining the Hertz #1 club), and to avoid doing the work themselves (such as paying one-and-one-half times the price per litre to avoid having to put gas in a rental car before returning it). If time or other costs are pivotal for a given service, the company's advertising can emphasize these savings rather than monetary savings. The Greater Toronto Airport Authority's (GTAA) Valet Care advertisement (Figure 17.1) makes the case for recognizing the cost of inconvenience, and the monetary value travellers might put on being able to reduce this cost.

Many other services save time, thus actually allowing the customer to "buy" time. Household cleaning services, lawn care, babysitting, interactive cable shopping, personal shopper service, home banking, home delivery of groceries, painting, and carpet cleaning—all these services represent net gains in the discretionary time of consumers and can be marketed that way. Services that allow the customer to buy time are likely to have monetary value for busy consumers.

Price as an Indicator of Service Quality

One of the intriguing aspects of pricing is that buyers are likely to use price as an indicator of both service costs and service quality—price is at once an attraction variable and a repellent.[9] Customers' use of price as an indicator of quality depends on several factors, one of which is the other information available to them. When service cues to quality are readily accessible, when brand names provide evidence of a company's reputation, or when the level of advertising communicates the company's belief in the brand, customers may prefer to use those cues instead of price. In other situations, however, such as when quality is hard to detect or when quality or price varies a great deal within a class of services, consumers may believe that price is the best indicator of quality. Many of these conditions typify situations that face consumers when purchasing services.[10] Another factor that increases the dependence on price as a quality indicator is the risk associated with the service purchase. In high-risk situations, many of which involve credence services such as medical treatment or management consulting, the customer will look to price as a surrogate for quality.

Because customers depend on price as a cue to quality and because price sets expectations of quality, service prices must be determined carefully. In addition to being chosen to cover costs or match competitors, prices must be selected to convey the

FIGURE 17.1

Pearson Airport's Valet Care will reduce travellers' nonmonetary costs in exchange for a fee.

Source: Courtesy of Greater Toronto Airport Authority.

appropriate quality signal. Pricing too low can lead to inaccurate inferences about the quality of the service. Pricing too high can set expectations that may be difficult to match in service delivery.

→ APPROACHES TO PRICING SERVICES

Rather than repeat what you learned about pricing in your marketing principles class, we want to emphasize in this chapter the way that services prices and pricing differ from both the customer's and the company's perspective. We discuss these differences in the context of the three pricing structures typically used to set prices: (1) cost-based, (2) competition-based, and (3) demand-based pricing. These categories, as shown in Figure 17.2, are the same bases on which goods prices are set, but adaptations must be made in services. The figure shows the three structures interrelating, because companies need to consider each of the three to some extent in setting prices. In the following sections we describe in general each basis for pricing and discuss challenges that occur when the approach is used in services pricing. The figure summarizes those challenges.

Cost-Based Pricing

In cost-based pricing, a company determines expenses from raw materials and labour, adds amounts or percentages for overhead and profit, and thereby arrives at the price. This method is widely used by industries such as utilities, contracting, wholesaling, and advertising. The basic formula for cost-based pricing is

$$\text{Price} = \text{Direct costs} + \text{Overhead costs} + \text{Profit margin}$$

Direct costs involve materials and labour that are associated with delivering the service, overhead costs are a share of fixed costs, and the profit margin is a percentage of full costs (direct + overhead).

FIGURE 17.2

Three Basic Marketing Price Structures and Challenges Associated with Their Use for Services

Challenges
1. Small firms may charge too little to be viable.
2. Heterogeneity of services limits comparability.
3. Prices may not reflect customer value.

Challenges
1. Costs are difficult to trace.
2. Labour is more difficult to price than materials.
3. Costs may not equal the value that customers perceive the services are worth.

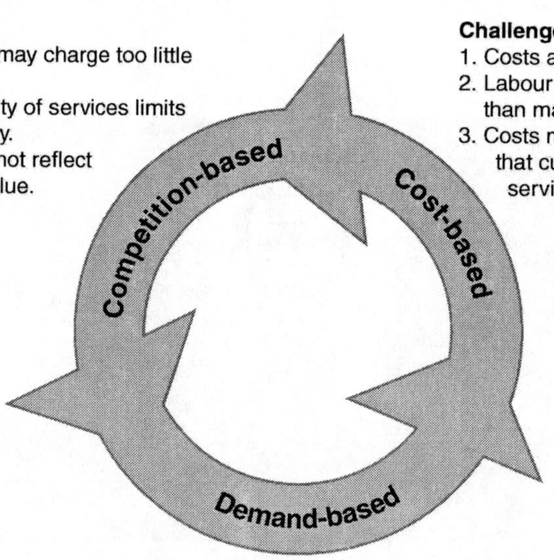

Competition-based · Cost-based · Demand-based

Challenges
1. Monetary price must be adjusted to reflect the value of nonmonetary costs.
2. Information on service costs is less available to customers; hence, price may not be a central factor.

Special Challenges in Cost-Based Pricing for Services

One of the major difficulties in cost-based pricing involves defining the units in which a service is purchased. Thus the price per unit—a well-understood concept in pricing of manufactured goods—is a vague entity. For this reason many services are sold in terms of input units rather than units of measured output. For example, most professional services (such as consulting, engineering, architecture, psychotherapy, and tutoring) are sold by the hour.

What is unique about services when using cost-based approaches to pricing? First, costs are difficult to trace or calculate in services businesses, particularly where multiple services are provided by the firm.[11] Consider how difficult it must be for a bank to allocate teller time accurately across its chequing, savings, and money market accounts in order to decide what to charge for the services. Or consider how hard it is for an auto insurer to track its customers' mileage and therefore exposure to the risk of having an accident. In this case, though, IBM is using GPS technology to assist insurance companies in delivering an entirely new service, "pay by the kilometre" insurance (see Figure 17.3). Second, a major component of cost is employee time rather than materials, and the value of people's time, particularly nonprofessional time, is not easy to calculate or estimate.

An added difficulty is that actual service costs may underrepresent the value of the service to the customer. A local tailor charges $10 for taking in a seam on a $350 ladies' suit jacket and an equal $10 for taking in a seam on a pair of $14 sweat shorts. The tailor's rationale is that both jobs require the same amount of time. What she neglects to see is that the customer would pay a higher price—and might even be happier about the alterations—for the expensive suit jacket, and that $10 is too high a price for the sweat shorts.

Examples of Cost-Based Pricing Strategies Used in Services

Cost-plus pricing is a commonly used approach in which component costs are calculated and a markup added. In product pricing, this approach is quite simple; in service industries, however, it is complicated because the tracking and identification of costs

FIGURE 17.3

IBM's innovative technology is helping insurers manage risk, and therefore costs, more precisely.

Source: Photographer: Christian Stoll.

are difficult. The approach is typically used in industries in which cost must be estimated in advance, such as construction, engineering, and advertising. In construction, bids are solicited by clients on the basis of the description of the service desired. Using their knowledge of the service (including the raw materials), labour, and margin, the company estimates a price for the finished service. A contingency amount—to cover the possibility that costs may be higher than estimated—is also stated because in large projects specifications can change as the service is provided.

Fee for service is the pricing strategy used by professionals; it represents the cost of the time involved in providing the service. Consultants, psychologists, accountants, and lawyers charge for their services on an hourly basis.

Lawyers and accountants must keep track of the time they spend for a given client, often down to 10-minute increments. For this reason the method has been criticized because it does not promote efficiency and sometimes ignores the expertise of the lawyers. Clients also fear padding of their legal bills, and may audit them. Despite these concerns, the hourly bill dominates the industry, the majority of revenues being billed this way.[12]

Competition-Based Pricing

The competition-based pricing approach focuses on the prices charged by other firms in the same industry or market. Competition-based pricing does not always imply charging the identical rate others charge but rather using others' prices as an anchor for the firm's price. This approach is used predominantly in two situations: (1) when services are standard across providers, such as in the dry cleaning industry, and (2) in oligopolies with a few large service providers, such as in the airline or rental car industry.

Special Challenges in Competition-Based Pricing for Services

Small firms may charge too little and not make margins high enough to remain in business. Many mom-and-pop service establishments—dry cleaning, retail, and tax accounting, among others—cannot deliver services at the low prices charged by chain operations.

Further, the heterogeneity of services across and within providers makes this approach complicated. Bank services illustrate the wide disparity in service prices. Customers buying chequing accounts, money orders, or foreign currency, to name a few services, find that prices are rarely similar across providers. The wide disparity in prices probably reflects the bank's difficulty in determining prices as well as their belief that financial customers do not shop around nor discern the differences (if any) among offerings from different providers. Only in very standardized services where there are few switching barriers (such as dry cleaning) are prices likely to be remembered *and* compared.

Examples of Competition-Based Pricing in Services Industries

Price signalling occurs in markets with a high concentration of sellers. In this type of market, any price offered by one company will be matched by competitors to avoid giving a low-cost seller a distinct advantage. The airline industry exemplifies price signalling in services. When any competitor drops the price of routes, others match the lowered price almost immediately.

Going-rate pricing involves charging the most prevalent price in the market. Rental car pricing is an illustration of this technique (and also an illustration of price signalling, because the rental car market is dominated by a small number of large companies). For years, the prices set by one company (Hertz) have been followed by the other companies. When Hertz instituted a new pricing plan that involved "no mileage charges, ever," other rental car companies imitated the policy. They then had to raise other factors such as base rates, size and type of car, daily or weekly rates, and dropoff charges to continue to make profits. Prices in different geographic markets, even cities, depend on the going rate in that location, and customers often pay different rates in contiguous cities. National toll-free reservation lines may offer better rates than are obtained by calling local rental car companies, because those rates are less influenced by the going rates in a particular area.[13]

The Global Feature in this chapter illustrates some of the practices in pricing that differ across countries.

Demand-Based Pricing

The two approaches to pricing just described are based on the company and its competitors rather than on customers. Neither approach takes into consideration that customers may lack reference prices, may be sensitive to nonmonetary prices, and may judge quality on the basis of price. All these factors can be accounted for in a company's pricing decisions. The third major approach to pricing, *demand-based pricing,* involves setting prices consistent with customer perceptions of value: prices are based on what customers will pay for the services provided.

Special Challenges in Demand-Based Pricing for Services

One of the major ways that pricing of services differs from pricing of goods in demand-based pricing is that nonmonetary costs and benefits must be factored into the calculation of perceived value to the customer. When services require time, inconvenience, and psychological and search costs, the monetary price must be adjusted to compensate. And when services save time, inconvenience, and psychological and search costs, the customer is willing to pay a higher monetary price. The challenge is to determine the value to customers of each of the nonmonetary aspects involved.

Another way services and goods differ with respect to this form of pricing is that information on service costs may be less available to customers, making monetary price not as salient a factor in initial service selection as it is in goods purchasing.

Four Meanings of Perceived Value

One of the most appropriate ways that companies price their services is basing the price on the perceived value of the service to customers. Among the questions a services marketer needs to ask are the following: What do consumers mean by *value?* How can we quantify perceived value in dollars so that we can set appropriate prices for our services? Is the meaning of value similar across consumers and services? How can value perceptions be influenced? To understand demand-based pricing approaches, we must fully understand what value means to customers.

This is not a simple task. When consumers discuss value, they use the term in many different ways and talk about myriad attributes or components. What constitutes value, even in a single service category, appears to be highly personal and idiosyncratic. Customers define value in four ways: (1) Value is low price. (2) Value is whatever I want in a product or service. (3) Value is the quality I get for the price I pay. (4) Value is what I get for what I give (Figure 17.4).[14] Let us take a look at each of these definitions more carefully.

Global Feature

Unique Pricing Around the World

TIPPING

A Cornell University study revealed an interesting fact about tipping: The custom of tipping is more prevalent in countries where citizens value status and prestige than in countries where they do not. Michael Lynn found that the number of service professionals tipped is relatively small in countries where citizens value recognition and esteem less. "Tipping is really a form of conspicuous consumption. We tip more people ... because we value status."

One measure of the differences in tipping is the number of service professionals who are given tips in different countries. The United States leads the list with about 35 different professions. Canada also ranks high on the list with 25 different professions. Other countries that place a high value on recognition and esteem also tip a large number of professionals. These include Spain (29), India (25), and Italy (24). In contrast, in Denmark and Sweden, the number of tipped professionals is under 10, reflecting the lower value placed on recognition and esteem in these countries.

SERVICE FEES

In Europe, Asia, and Latin America, fixed services charges rather than tips are added to customers' bills in restaurants. Except for large parties, this service charge had been an unusual practice in North American restaurants, perhaps for the reason cited in the previous paragraph. However, some U.S. establishments are exchanging tips for service charges in spite of the preference of guests to choose what to tip. The reason is that the IRS has been leaning on restaurants to have their waiters and waitresses report tips. If reported tip income is less than 8 percent of gross receipts, the IRS has now made restaurant owners liable for back taxes on unreported income unless they participate in a program to track their employee's tips. Service personnel do not like the change, partly because they make less money (the restaurant shares the service fee with kitchen personnel) and partly because they do not receive the instant gratification that tips provide. Guests are typically unfavourable as well: "We surveyed our guests and they seem to feel that they have a constitutional right to reward and punish waiters." Canadian guests have maintained such power. Although the Canada Revenue Agency expects earners to report tip income, the agency has not instituted any requirements for restaurants to force compliance on the part of their employees.

PRICELESS

A London restaurant called Just Around the Corner has an extraordinary demand-oriented pricing policy: It lets customers pay whatever they think the meal is worth. The policy has been extremely successful since it was started, with most customers paying more for their meals than the restaurant would charge if it

Source: Doug Menuez/Getty Images.

continued

Global Feature

Unique Pricing Around the World—continued

set the prices. Customers average 25 pounds ($51) for a three-course dinner, but some are especially careful to pay enough. "One night, four American government officials handed over nearly $1,000 for a meal worth less than $200. They asked if they had left enough." The owner, Michael Vasos, claims, "I make more money from this restaurant than from any of my other [four] establishments." He thinks his customers' generosity accounts for the success of the restaurant and its pricing policies, although others state that the fear of embarrassment common to the English prevents patrons from paying too little.

PAY BY THE MINUTE IN TOKYO

Some restaurants in Japan are charging for dinner according to how quickly customers eat. At Dai-ichi Hotel Tokyo Seafort, diners punch a time clock when they start their meals, then pay 25 cents per minute until they clock out. Fast diners—like two young girls who gulped down platefuls of cake in 10 minutes and

paid only $3—can get bargain meals. Perhaps that is why the restaurant is popular among college students! Other franchise restaurants throughout Japan put time limits on their all-you-can-eat buffets. Prices range from $10 an hour to $100 for 90 minutes. During that time, diners can consume unlimited quantities of top-quality sushi or shabu shabu, a Japanese specialty consisting of thin slices of beef cooked in boiling broth. At one restaurant, Mo Mo Paradise in Tokyo, for example, diners can pay $13.50 to eat for 90 minutes or $30 to eat as much as they want for as long as they want.

Sources: Andrea Sachs, "Eat All You Want; Pay by the Minute," *Washington Post,* September 26, 1999, p. H3; © 1999, *The Washington Post,* reprinted with permission. "Study Examines Tipping," *Hotel and Motel Management,* March 17, 1997, p. 14; B. Ortega, "No Tips, Please—Just Pay the Service Fee," *The Wall Street Journal,* September 4, 1998, p.-B1; "Priceless," *People,* February 15, 1999, p. 114; and I. Wall, "It May Be a Dog-Eat-Dog World, But This Restaurant Won't Prove It," *The Wall Street Journal,* December 11, 1998, p. B1.

Value Is Low Price   Some consumers equate value with low price, indicating that what they have to give up in terms of money is most salient in their perceptions of value.[15]

Value Is Whatever I Want in a Product or Service   Rather than focusing on the money given up, some consumers emphasize the benefits they receive from a service or product as the most important component of value. In the telecommunications industry, for example, business customers strongly value the reliability of the systems and are willing to pay for the safety and confidentiality of the connections.

Value Is the Quality I Get for the Price I Pay   Other consumers see value as a tradeoff between the money they give up and the quality they receive.

Value Is What I Get for What I Give   Finally, some consumers consider all the benefits they receive as well as all sacrifice components (money, time, effort) when describing value.

FIGURE 17.4

Four Customer Definitions of Value

Source: N. C. Mohn, "Pricing Research for Decision Making," *Marketing Research: A Magazine of Management and Applications* 7, no. 1 (Winter 1995), pp. 10–19. Reprinted by permission of the American Marketing Association.

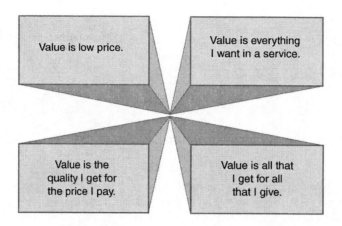

The four consumer expressions of value can be captured in one overall definition consistent with the concept of utility in economics: *Perceived value is the consumer's overall assessment of the utility of a service based on perceptions of what is received and what is given.* Although what is received varies across consumers (some may want volume, others high quality, still others convenience), as does what is given (some are concerned only with money expended, others with time and effort), value represents a tradeoff of the give and get components. Customers will make a purchase decision on the basis of perceived value, not solely to minimize the price paid. These definitions are the first step in identifying the elements that must be quantified in setting prices for services.

Incorporating Perceived Value into Service Pricing

The buyer's perception of total value prompts the willingness to pay a particular price for a service. To translate the customer's value perceptions into an appropriate price for a specific service offering, the marketer must answer a number of questions. What benefits does the service provide? How important is each of these benefits? How much is it worth to the customer to receive a particular benefit from a service? At what price will the service be economically acceptable to potential buyers? In what context is the customer purchasing the service?

The most important thing a company must do—and often a difficult thing—is to estimate the value to customers of the company's services. Value may be perceived differently by consumers because of idiosyncratic tastes, knowledge about the service, buying power, and ability to pay. In this type of pricing, what the consumers value—not what they pay—forms the basis for pricing. *Therefore its effectiveness rests solely on accurately determining what the market perceives the service to be worth.*

When the services are for the end consumer, most often service providers will decide that they cannot afford to give each individual exactly the bundle of attributes he or she values. They will, however, attempt to find one or more bundles that address segments of the market. On the other hand, when services are sold to businesses (or to end customers in the case of high-end services), the company can understand and deliver different bundles to each customer. Exhibit 17.2 presents an illustration of this approach to pricing.

An interesting manifestation of demand-oriented pricing is shown in the Technology Spotlight.

One of the most complex and difficult tasks of services marketers is setting prices internationally. If services marketers price on the basis of perceived value and if

Technology Spotlight

Dynamic Pricing on the Internet Allows Price Adjustments Based on Supply and Demand

When shopping for an airline ticket on the Internet, have you ever found a low-priced ticket that you did not purchase immediately, then returned four hours later to find the same ticket had increased $100 in price? This experience is dynamic pricing in action—the buying and selling of goods in markets in which prices move quickly in response to supply and demand fluctuations. In the case of your airline ticket, chances are that other travellers had purchased tickets at the original low price, reducing the airlines' inventory and allowing the airline to gamble on getting customers to buy the remaining seats at higher prices.

Dynamic pricing is estimated to account for 40 percent of $1.4 trillion in total online transactions in 2004. The approach—often incorporating auctions and other forms of online bidding—is typically used at the end of the supply chain to eliminate surplus inventory or perishable service capacity, as with airline seats. Dynamic pricing has allowed companies to generate significant revenue from excess supply or discontinued products, which they used to turn over to intermediaries. In the past, liquidators would receive unsold services, getting five cents on the dollar in liquidation fees in addition to whatever they could get from reselling the products. Not only did the firm not receive revenue from the sale of the services, but it would also have to pay for liquidation services.

AUCTIONS: EBAY AND 1,500 RIVALS

Online auctions represent dynamic pricing because customers pay what they are willing and they compete with each other on the goods they desire. In 1995, eBay pioneered the Internet auction, but more than 1,500 websites now offer person-to-person online trading. Market leader eBay now offers thousands of new items for auction every day, and reported revenue grew to more than $4.5 billion in 2005, a 39 percent increase over the previous year. Whereas eBay focuses on consumer-to-consumer transactions, uBid.com acts as a consignment house for manufacturers selling directly to customers. uBid, founded in 1997, offers leading manufacturers' merchandise to consumers and businesses at

prices lower than wholesale. Most uBid auctions begin at $1 and allow market dynamics to set the price. Interestingly, although uBid.com is an American-based auction and does not directly ship to Canada, the company encourages all international prospective customers to sign up for a U.S. mailing address using Access USA and then continue shopping their auctions.

DUTCH AUCTIONS: KLIK-KLOK.COM, WRHAMBRECHT.COM

Dutch auctions, which originated in Netherlands for selling services such as insurance or perishable items such as tulips, reverse the typical auction in that the prices go down as the auction progresses. Also unlike in typical auctions, in which one of a particular type of product is sold at a given time, in Dutch auctions multiple—albeit limited—quantities of the same services are sold at the same time. The duration of the auction is very short, and the price drops rapidly over this time. At any given time (or price point), a bidder can stop the clock by bidding at the instantaneous price. The bid with time, price, and quantity is then recorded. This bidding continues until all bids have been received. At that point all winning bidders pay the same price, which is the lowest "successful" bid. The catch here is that there is a limited supply of each product. As the clock progresses and the remaining available inventory decreases, the nonbidders (those waiting for the lowest selling price) risk not getting their desired quantities.

REVERSE AUCTIONS: PRICELINE.COM

Reverse auctions are used on the buy side, allowing buyers to see the lowest bid, but not identify the buyer or the seller. The brand or identity of the seller is revealed only if the seller decides to accept the bid offered by the buyer. An advantage for buyers is that they do not need to guess at the price and can receive the same products and services offered elsewhere with static prices at significant discounts. A disadvantage is that although buyers see a rating of the seller, they cannot be sure who the seller is and what the service outcome will be.

Technology Spotlight

Dynamic Pricing on the Internet Allows Price Adjustments Based on Supply and Demand—continued

The brand is eliminated as a communicator of quality. Furthermore, the buyer has to sacrifice control over some aspects of the service that is being consumed. For instance, on Priceline.com, the buyer does not have full control over time of the flights.

GROUP BUYING: ONLINECHOICE.COM, HAPPYMANY.COM

Group buying sites such as HappyMany.com aggregate demand for sellers. This site offers group rates on long distance, Internet, and cell phone services, and has recently introduced group rates on gasoline. The concept behind this form of dynamic pricing is that the greater the number of people who want to buy products, the lower the price will be for everyone. Sellers generally bucket the prices of the product being sold based on the number of buyers. For example, for 0 to 10 buyers, the price for each buyer is $100; for 10 to 20 buyers, the price for each buyer is $95, and so on. Word of mouth is critical, because interested buyers are encouraged to enlist their friends and relatives to get a cheaper price for the whole group. Sellers motivate this action by placing an "Invite Your Friend" icon right next to the service or price information. Advantages of this form of dynamic pricing are that the price decreases as a greater number of people bid and the exact service and its specifications are known to buyers when bidding.

FINDING THE LOWEST PRICE ACROSS INTERNET SITES: BUY.COM CANADA

Buy.com's slogan is "lowest prices on Earth." The Internet allows consumers to do quick price comparisons, and Buy.com wants to make sure its services and products end up being the lowest prices in everyone's search. To deliver on its promises, Buy.com uses software to monitor price changes for products on competing sites. When these price changes occur, the software then recommends price adjustments to Buy.com. The process is automated, but the decision to change prices is made by a manager, usually once a day rather than moment to moment. Buy.com relies on this strategy in highly competitive online categories such as computer software. The

software makes recommendations throughout the day, and decisions are made the next morning. Prices tend to fall more often than they go up.

DINING WITH DYNAMIC PRICING

Flexible, or dynamic, pricing in the restaurant industry involves changing menu prices by hour or time of day to attract diners in nonpeak hours, such as afternoons between 2 p.m. and 6 p.m. or late evenings. Restaurants may use discounts, such as 15 to 30 percent off the total check, to build traffic during off-hours. Typically the restaurants use a "dining aggregator," a site that collects and coordinates information about all restaurants in an area that want to offer dynamic pricing. For example, DinnerBroker.com is a novel dynamic-pricing website representing restaurants in some metropolitan areas of the United States and a few in Canada. The restaurants using DinnerBroker's service use off-peak discount programs to gain incremental business and new customers. DinnerBroker.com has an easy-to-use graphic matrix that allows users to see on one page all participating restaurants and the discounts they offer. The site also enables customers to make online reservations and offers access to prime-time tables. To participate in these services, DinnerBroker.com requires restaurants to pay a subscription of $49 a month and $1 for every off-hour reservation booked and fulfilled by the service.

Sources: Michael Bazeley, "eBay Has Strong Earnings in Quarter," *Knight Ridder Tribune Business News,* October 21, 2004, p. 1; Georgia Perakis, "Third Informs Revenue Management and Pricing Conference," *Journal of Revenue and Pricing Management,* January 2004, p. 388; Vaidyanathan Jayaraman and Tim Baker, "The Internet as an Enabler for Dynamic Pricing of Goods," *IEEE Transactions on Engineering Management,* November 2003, p. 470; Alan J. Liddle, "Using Web for Discounting Clicks with Digital Diners," *Nation's Restaurant News,* May 19, 2003, p. 172; Christopher T. Heun, "Dynamic Pricing Boosts Bottom Line," *Informationweek,* October 29, 2001; Michael Vizard, "With So Very Few Internet Players, Is Dynamic Pricing Good for Our Economy?" *InfoWorld,* March 26, 2001; Michael Vizard, Ed Scannel, and Dan Neel, "Suppliers Toy with Dynamic Pricing," *InfoWorld,* May 14, 2001.

perceived value and willingness to pay differ across countries (which they often do), then service firms may provide essentially the same service but charge different prices in different countries. Here, as in pricing domestically, the challenge is to determine the perceived value not just to different customers but to customers in different parts of the world. Pricing in Europe provides one of the most compelling examples of the pricing challenges that marketers face internationally.

Historically, Europe was considered to be a loosely aligned group of more than 12 separate countries, and a services marketer could have as many different pricing approaches as it had countries in which it offered the services. Although pricing was complex to administer, the marketer had full flexibility in pricing and could seek the profit-maximizing price in each country. The European Community created a single internal market, holding the potential to simplify marketing in the area but also creating grave concerns about pricing. The largest concern is that marketers will be required to offer all services at a single European price—the lowest price offered in any European country—which could dramatically reduce revenues and profits.

PRICING STRATEGIES THAT LINK TO THE FOUR VALUE DEFINITIONS

In this section we describe the approaches to services pricing that are particularly suited to each of the four value definitions.

Pricing Strategies When the Customer Means "Value Is Low Price"

When monetary price is the most important determinant of value to a customer, the company focuses mainly on price. This focus does not mean that the quality level and intrinsic attributes are always irrelevant, just that monetary price dominates in importance. To establish a service price in this definition of value, the marketer must understand to what extent customers know the objective prices of services in this category, how they interpret various prices, and how much is too much of a perceived sacrifice. These factors are best understood when the service provider also knows the relative dollar size of the purchase, the frequency of past price changes, and the range of acceptable prices for the service. Some of the specific pricing approaches appropriate when customers define value as low price include discounting, odd pricing, synchro-pricing, and penetration pricing (Figure 17.5).

Discounting

Service providers offer discounts or price cuts to communicate to price-sensitive buyers that they are receiving value. In Chapter 14, we noted that Air Canada had risked

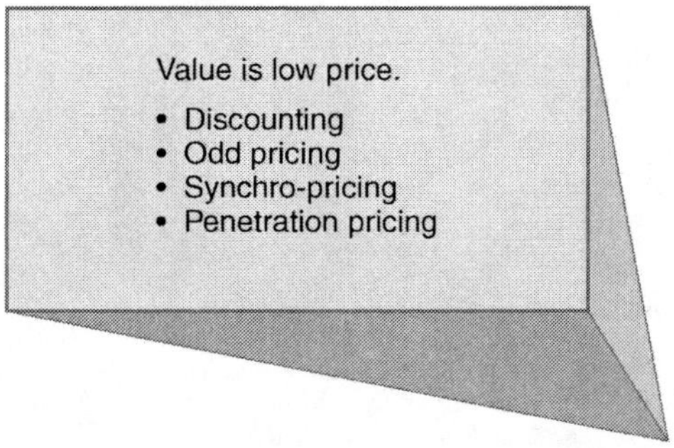

FIGURE 17.5

Pricing Strategies When the Customer Defines Value as Low Price

Value is low price.

- Discounting
- Odd pricing
- Synchro-pricing
- Penetration pricing

➡ EXHIBIT 17.2

Pricing for Customer-Perceived Value with Modular Service Pricing and Service Tiering

As described in this chapter, pricing a service in line with what customers perceive it is worth is often difficult. Two approaches that have gained favour in recent years are modular service pricing and service tiering.

MODULAR SERVICE PRICING

One of the reasons that pricing of services is more difficult than pricing of goods is that service units are more variable and difficult to identify than units of goods. Units of goods—automobiles, jeans, litres of milk, and microwaves—are easy to define. Units of service are more difficult in part because they are sold by a variety of units. Information services, for example, are sold by the minute, the web page, the file (as in buying online music), or the search (as in finding and purchasing magazine articles). The services of your doctor are sold by the length and type of the visit, the test performed, the shot given, and the X-rays taken. One approach to dealing with the complexity of pricing services is to develop modular service bundles.

Modular service pricing involves first identifying the basic and value-added services of a provider as components or building blocks for pricing. To create modules, the company first defines the full range of services both that could meet customer needs and for which customers will pay. In the airlines, for example, the base price is set for a seat, but customers will also pay for excess baggage, special ticketing, class of seats, animals, alcoholic beverages, and food. Customers of rental car companies pay by the day but also buy additional services such as liability insurance, collision insurance, dropoff services, and refuelling services.

To create modular pricing, firms need

1. A viable price for each different service

2. The ability to combine prices and services using easy rules

3. Minimum overlap among the service elements so that customers do not pay twice or more for the same service

SERVICE TIERING

Sometimes even good modular pricing can become too complex, and simpler ways to present the company's prices are needed. Service tiering, usually called versioning when applied to the pricing of goods, involves creating a set of prices that corresponds to the price points and value bundles of different customer segments.

In general, service tiers allow customers to quickly and simply match their desires and the price they are willing to pay with an offering from the company. The customer perceives a benefit in choosing one of the tiers because each tier provides a discount over individual services. The company enjoys a benefit because customers typically buy more services when they are sold in tiers than when they are offered individually.

Modular pricing and service tiering allow the company to maximize sales from all parts of a service that the customer desires without having to create unique service bundles for every customer.

Air Canada provides a good illustration of the use of service tiers. Note in the chart shown here how they have grouped their fares into five tiers. Interestingly, they have also added a modular component, so that even if a passenger booked a Tango fare, he or she can, for an additional fee, still change the reservation or get advance seat selection. To further assist passengers in deciding on what fare class to book, Air Canada's website (www.aircanada.com/en/news/oneway/index.html) provides short narratives of options accompanied by photos of the types of people who might choose each. If you read the suggested descriptions for passengers who would choose Tango over Executive Class, for instance, you will see very good illustrations of the "Value Is Low Price" and "Value Is Everything I Want in a Service" points of view, respectively.

Source: Courtesy of Air Canada.

Sources: R. Docters, M. Reopel, J. Sun, and S. Tanny, "Capturing the Unique Value of Services: Why Pricing of Services Is Different," *The Journal of Business Strategy* 25, no. 2 (2004), pp. 23–28.

the ire of its travel agents, the airline's key distribution channel, by removing its lowest fares from the agents' systems. Air Canada has branded these fares GO Discount, and this new fare option provides even lower fares than are available with standard Tango fares. Figure 17.6 shows a recent advertisement Air Canada used to help launch GO Discount, listing the conditions passengers must comply with to qualify for it.

Odd Pricing

Odd pricing is the practice of pricing services just below the exact dollar amount to make buyers perceive that they are getting a lower price. Dry cleaners charge $2.98 for a shirt rather than $3, health clubs have dues priced at $33.90 per month rather than $34, and haircuts are $9.50 rather than $10. Odd prices suggest discounting and bargains and are appealing to customers for whom value means low price.

Synchro-Pricing

Synchro-pricing is the use of price to manage demand for a service by capitalizing on customer sensitivity to prices. Certain services, such as tax preparation, passenger transportation, long-distance telephone, hotels, and theatres, have demand that fluctuates over time as well as constrained supply at peak times. For companies in these and other industries, setting a price that provides a profit over time can be difficult. Pricing can, however, play a role in smoothing demand and synchronizing demand and supply. Time, place, quantity, and incentive differentials have all been used effectively by service firms, as discussed in Chapter 15.

Place differentials are used for services in which customers have a sensitivity to location. The front row at concerts, the 50-yard line in football, centre court in tennis or basketball, oceanside rooms in resort hotels—all these represent place differentials that are meaningful to customers and that therefore command higher prices.

FIGURE 17.6

Air Canada has introduced a new discounted fare option called GO Discount.

Source: Courtesy of Air Canada.

Time differentials involve price variations that depend on when the service is consumed. Examples are cell phone service in the evening and on weekends, and airline tickets that include a Saturday night stay. By offering lower prices for underused time periods, a service company can smooth demand and also gain incremental revenue.

Quantity differentials are usually price decreases given for volume purchasing. This pricing structure allows a service company to predict future demand for its services. Customers who buy a booklet of coupons for a tanning salon or facial, a quantity of tokens for public bridges, or packages of advertising spots on radio or television are all responding to price incentives achieved by committing to future services. Air Canada has recently introduced Canada's first quantity differential for air travel (see Figure 17.7). This innovative pricing approach will likely appeal to tourists and business travellers. For $6,998 (plus GST), consumers can take unlimited flights to more than 100 destinations across North America.[16]

Differentials as incentives are lower prices for new or existing clients in the hope of encouraging them to be regular users or more frequent users. Some professionals—lawyers, dentists, electrologists, and even some physicians—offer free consultations at the front end, usually to overcome fear and uncertainty about high service prices. Other companies stimulate use by offering regular customers discounts or premiums during slow periods.

Penetration Pricing

Penetration pricing is a strategy in which new services are introduced at low prices to stimulate trial and widespread use. The strategy is appropriate when (1) sales volume of the service is very sensitive to price, even in the early stages of introduction; (2) it is possible to achieve economies in unit costs by operating at large volumes; (3) a service faces threats of strong potential competition very soon after introduction; and (4) there is no class of buyers willing to pay a higher price to obtain the service.[17] Penetration pricing can lead to problems when companies

FIGURE 17.7

Air Canada introduced Canada's first-ever subscription to unlimited flights.

Source: Courtesy of Air Canada.

then select a "regular" increased price. Care must be taken not to penetrate with so low a price that customers feel the regular price is outside the range of acceptable prices.

Pricing Strategies When the Customer Means "Value Is Everything I Want in a Service"

When the customer is concerned principally with the "get" components of a service, monetary price is not of primary concern. The more desirable intrinsic attributes a given service possesses, the more highly valued the service is likely to be and the higher the price the marketer can set. Figure 17.8 shows appropriate pricing strategies.

Prestige Pricing

Prestige pricing is a special form of demand-based pricing by service marketers who offer high-quality or status services. For certain services—restaurants, health clubs, airlines, and hotels—a higher price is charged for the luxury end of the business. Some customers of service companies who use this approach may actually value the high price because it represents prestige or a quality image. Others prefer purchasing at the high end because they are given preference in seating or accommodations and are entitled to other special benefits. In prestige pricing, demand may actually increase as price increases because the costlier service has more value in reflecting quality or prestige.

Care must be taken, though. Whistler Ski Resort (see Figure 17.9) has become known as "a snowy playground for the rich and famous," and this reputation has caused regular travellers to stay away (unless lured by deep discounts in the off-season, which, as we saw in Chapter 15, poses additional problems with segment incompatibility). This reputation as a super-rich resort is due, in part, to $2,000-a-night hotel rooms during the late 90s and illustrates the risks of prestige pricing. In this case, the resort benefited from the strategy during the boom times, but since 9/11 and the increase in value of the Canadian dollar, prestige pricing is no longer working.

Skimming Pricing

Skimming, a strategy in which new services are introduced at high prices with large promotional expenditures, is an effective approach when services are major improvements over past services. In this situation customers are more concerned about obtaining the service than about the cost of the service, allowing service providers to skim the customers most willing to pay the highest prices.

FIGURE 17.8

Pricing Strategies When the Customer Defines Value as Everything Wanted in a Service

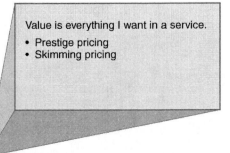

Value is everything I want in a service.
- Prestige pricing
- Skimming pricing

FIGURE 17.9

Whistler no longer wants to be seen as practising prestige pricing and would like to get rid of its image as a resort only for the super-rich.

Source: Lyle Stafford/Photo.

Pricing Strategies When the Customer Means "Value Is the Quality I Get for the Price I Pay"

Some customers primarily consider both quality and monetary price. The task of the marketer is to understand what *quality* means to the customer (or segments of customers) and then to match quality level with price level. Specific strategies are shown in Figure 17.10.

Value Pricing

The widely used term *value pricing* has come to mean "giving more for less." In current usage it involves assembling a bundle of services that are desirable to a wide group of customers and then pricing them lower than they would cost alone. Taco Bell pioneered value pricing with a $0.59 Value Menu. After sales at the chain rose 50 percent in two years to $2.4 billion, McDonald's and Burger King adopted the value pricing practice. WestJet also offers value pricing: a low cost for a bundle of desirable service attributes such as no overbooking, live seat-back TV, and free blankets (in competition with Air Canada who began to charge for their blankets in 2005). See Figure 17.11 for one of WestJet's value pricing advertisements.

FIGURE 17.10

Pricing Strategies When the Customer Defines Value as Quality for the Price Paid

Value is the quality I get for the price I pay.

- Value pricing
- Market segmentation pricing

470   Part 6   *Managing Service Promises*

FIGURE 17.11

WestJet exemplifies
a value pricing
approach with a
"more for less"
message.

Source: Courtesy of WestJet.

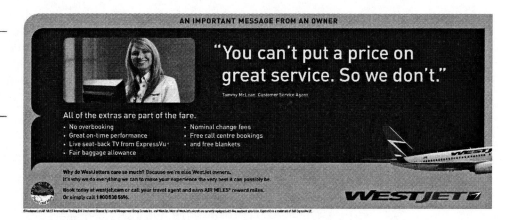

Market Segmentation Pricing

Market segmentation pricing, a service marketer charges different prices to groups
of customers, even though there may not be corresponding differences in the costs
of providing the service to each of these groups. This form of pricing is based on the
premise that segments show different price elasticities of demand and desire different
quality levels.

Services marketers often price by *client category.* This may be based on the recognition that some groups find it difficult to pay a recommended price. Health clubs
located in university and college communities will typically offer student memberships, recognizing that this segment of customers has limited ability to pay full price.
In addition to the lower price, student memberships may also carry with them reduced
hours of use, particularly in peak times. The same line of reasoning leads to memberships for "seniors," who are less able to pay full price but are willing to patronize the
clubs during daytime hours when most full-price members are working. Sometimes
clients may be *able* to pay but not very *willing.* In that case, marketers may also
offer price concessions to encourage business. One spa resort whose primary target
is women recognizes that men are less likely to stay. It therefore chooses the unique
strategy of "Men Stay Free." In so doing, St. Anne's (see Figure 17.12) hopes to get
more women during the midweek low demand period by making it possible for a
couple to stay for the same price the woman alone would have paid.

FIGURE 17.12

Ste. Anne's targets
women by letting
their partners stay
for free.

Source: Courtesy of Sainte
Anne's.

Companies also use market segmentation by *service version,* recognizing that not all segments want the basic level of service at the lowest price. When they can identify a bundle of attributes that are desirable enough for another segment of customers, they can charge a higher price for that bundle. Companies can configure service bundles that reflect price and service points appealing to different groups in the market. Hotels, for example, offer standard rooms at a basic rate but then combine amenities and tangibles related to the room to attract customers willing to pay more for the concierge level, jacuzzis, additional beds, and sitting areas.

Pricing Strategies When the Customer Means "Value Is All That I Get for All That I Give"

Some customers define value as including not just the benefits they receive but also the time, money, and effort they put into a service. Figure 17.13 illustrates the pricing strategies described in this definition of value.

Price Framing

Because many customers do not possess accurate reference prices for services, services marketers are more likely than product marketers to organize price information for customers so they know how to view it. Customers naturally look for price anchors as well as familiar services against which to judge focal services. If they accept the anchors, they view the price and service package favourably.

Price Bundling

Some services are consumed more effectively in conjunction with other services; other services accompany the products they support (such as extended service warranties, training, and expedited delivery). When customers find value in a package of services that are interrelated, price bundling is an appropriate strategy. Bundling, which means pricing and selling services as a group rather than individually, has benefits to both customers and service companies. Customers find that bundling simplifies their purchase and payment, and companies find that the approach stimulates demand for the firm's service line, thereby achieving cost economies for the operations as a whole while increasing net contributions.[18] Bundling also allows the customer to pay less than when purchasing each of the services individually, which contributes to perceptions of value.

The effectiveness of price bundling depends on how well the service firm understands the bundles of value that customers or segments perceive, and on the complementarity of demand for these services. Effectiveness also depends on the right choice of services from the firm's point of view. Because the firm's objective is to increase overall sales, the services selected for bundling should be those with a relatively small

FIGURE 17.13

Pricing Strategies When the Customer Defines Value as All That Is Received for All That Is Given

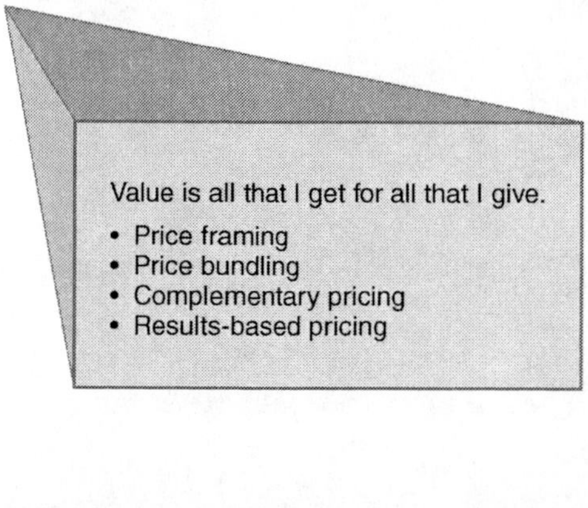

Value is all that I get for all that I give.

- Price framing
- Price bundling
- Complementary pricing
- Results-based pricing

sales volume without the bundling to minimize revenue loss from discounting a service that already has a high sales volume.

Approaches to bundling include mixed bundling and mixed-leader bundling.[19] In *mixed bundling,* the customer can purchase the services individually or as a package, but a price incentive is offered for purchasing the package. As an example, a health club customer may be able to contract for aerobics classes at $10 per month, weight machines at $15, and pool privileges at $15—or the group of three services for $27 (a price incentive of $13 per month).[20] In *mixed-leader bundling,* the price of one service is discounted if the first service is purchased at full price. For example, if cable TV customers buy one premium channel at full price, they can acquire a second premium channel at a reduced monthly rate. The objective is to reduce the price of the higher-volume service to generate an increase in its volume that "pulls" an increase in demand for a lower-volume but higher-contribution margin service.

Complementary Pricing

Services that are highly interrelated can be leveraged by using complementary pricing. This pricing includes three related strategies—captive pricing, two-part pricing, and loss leadership.[21] In *captive pricing* the firm offers a base service or product and then provides the supplies or peripheral services needed to continue using the service. In this situation the company could offload some part of the price for the basic service to the peripherals. For example, cable services often drop the price for installation to a very low level, then compensate by charging enough for the peripheral services to make up for the loss in revenue. With service firms, this strategy is often called *two-part pricing,* because the service price is broken into a fixed fee plus variable usage fees (also found in telephone services, health clubs, and commercial services such as rentals). *Loss leadership* is the term typically used in retail stores when providers place a familiar service on special largely to draw the customer to the store and then reveal other levels of service available at higher prices.

Results-Based Pricing

In service industries in which outcome is very important but uncertainty is high, the most relevant aspect of value is the *result* of the service. In personal injury lawsuits, for example, clients value the settlement they receive at the conclusion of the service. From tax accountants, clients value cost savings. From trade schools, students most value getting a job upon graduation. From Hollywood stars, production companies value high grosses. In these and other situations, an appropriate value-based pricing strategy is to price on the basis of results or outcome of the service.

The most commonly known form of results-based pricing is a practice called *contingency pricing* used by lawyers. Contingency pricing is the major way that personal injury and certain consumer cases are billed; in one study, contingency pricing accounted for 12 percent of commercial law billings.[22] In this approach, lawyers do not receive fees or payment until the case is settled, when they are paid a percentage of the money that the client receives. Therefore, only an outcome in the client's favour is compensated. From the client's point of view, the pricing makes sense in part because most clients in these cases are unfamiliar with and possibly intimidated by law firms. Their biggest fears are high fees for a case that may take years to settle. By using contingency pricing, clients are ensured that they pay no fees until they receive a settlement.

Sealed Bid Contingency Pricing Companies wishing to gain the most value from their services purchases are increasingly turning to a form of results-based pricing that involves sealed bids guaranteeing results. Consider the challenge of a school district with energy bills so high that money was diverted from its primary mission of educating students. The school board wanted a long-term solution to the problem. The EMS Company, an engineering firm providing services to control and reduce energy use in large buildings, proposed a computer-controlled system that monitored energy use and operated on/off valves for all energy-using systems. The proposal specified a five-year contract with a fixed price of $254,500 per year, with the additional guarantee that the school district would save at least that amount of money every year or EMS would refund the difference.[23]

Although two other firms submitted lower multiyear bids of $190,000 and $215,000 annually, neither bid provided any guarantee for energy savings. EMS was awarded the bid. During the first year, actual calculated savings exceeded $300,000. The use of contingency pricing by EMS removed the risk from the school board's decision and added profits at EMS.[24]

Money-Back Guarantees   Many colleges offer one major promise: to get students jobs upon graduation. So many schools commit to this promise—often blatantly in television advertising—that prospective students have come to distrust all promises from these colleges. To give substance to its promise, Brown-MacKenzie College, a for-profit institution, offered a tuition-back guarantee to any graduate who, after due effort, failed to obtain a suitable position within 90 days of program completion. A future-income-dependent payment plan has also been considered by many schools. Under such a plan, a student would receive a full scholarship and, after graduation, pay a fixed percentage of salary for a set period—for example, 5 percent of salary for 20 years.[25]

Commission   Many services providers—including real estate agents and advertising agencies—earn their fees through commissions based on a percentage of the selling price. In these and other industries, commission is paid by the supplier rather than the buyer. Advertising agencies are paid 15 percent commission by the print and broadcast

FIGURE 17.14

Summary of Service Pricing Strategies for Four Customer Definitions of Value

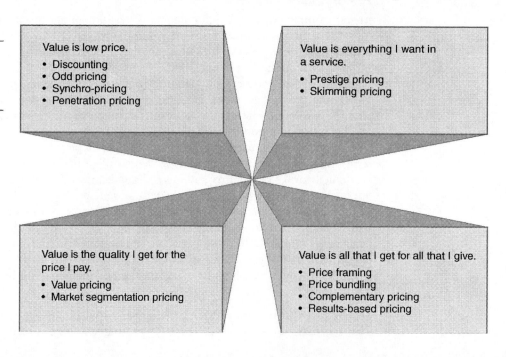

Value is low price.
- Discounting
- Odd pricing
- Synchro-pricing
- Penetration pricing

Value is everything I want in a service.
- Prestige pricing
- Skimming pricing

Value is the quality I get for the price I pay.
- Value pricing
- Market segmentation pricing

Value is all that I get for all that I give.
- Price framing
- Price bundling
- Complementary pricing
- Results-based pricing

media (newspaper, radio, TV, magazines) for the amount of advertising that they place with the media, but agencies are not paid by their clients. Real estate agents are usually paid 6 percent of the selling price of a house.

The commission approach to services pricing is compelling in that agents are compensated most when they find the highest rates and fares. It would seem that agents have an underlying motivation to avoid the lowest fares and rates for their clients.

SUMMARY

This chapter began with three key differences between customer evaluation of pricing for services and goods: (1) customers often have inaccurate or limited reference prices for services, (2) price is a key signal to quality in services, and (3) monetary price is not the only relevant price to service customers. These three differences can have profound impact on the strategies that companies use to set and administer prices for services. The chapter next discussed common pricing structures, including (1) cost-based, (2) competition-based, and (3) demand-based pricing. Central to the discussion were the specific challenges in each of these structures and the services pricing techniques that have emerged in practice.

Finally, the chapter defined customer perceptions of value and suggested appropriate pricing strategies that match each customer definition. Figure 17.14 summarizes these definitions and strategies. The four value definitions include (1) value is low price, (2) value is whatever I want in a product or service, (3) value is the quality I get for the price I pay, and (4) value is all that I get for all that I give.

Discussion Questions

1. Which approach to pricing (cost-based, competition-based, or demand-based) is the most fair to customers? Why?
2. Is it possible to use all three approaches simultaneously when pricing services? If you answer yes, describe a service that is priced this way.
3. For what consumer services do you have reference prices? What makes these services different from others for which you lack reference prices?
4. Name three services you purchase in which price is a signal to quality. Do you believe that there are true differences across services that are priced high and those that are priced low? Why or why not?
5. Describe the nonmonetary costs involved in the following services: getting an automobile loan, belonging to a health club, having allergies diagnosed and treated, attending an executive education class, and getting braces.
6. Consider the specific pricing strategies for each of the four customer value definitions. Which of these strategies could be adapted and used with another value definition?

Exercises

1. List five services for which you have no reference price. Now put yourself in the role of the service providers for two of those services and develop pricing strategies. Be sure to include in your description which of the value definitions you

believe customers will possess and what types of strategies would be appropriate given those definitions.

2. In the next week, find three price lists for services (such as from a restaurant, dry cleaner, or hairstylist). Identify the pricing base and the strategy used in each of them. How effective is each?

3. Consider that you are the owner of a new private college and can prepare a value/price package that is appealing to students. Describe your approach. How does it differ from existing offerings?

4. Go to Priceline.com and get familiar with how the site works.

⟼ Notes

1. Peter Lewis, "Pay to Play," *Fortune*, January 7, 2002, pp. 115–17.
2. Canadian Recording Industry Association, "Threat of Piracy to the Legitimate Industry," www.cria.ca/antipiracy.php, accessed October 3, 2006.
3. Larry LeBlanc, "Bell Dialing for Downloads," *Billboard*, March 18, 2006, p. 20.
4. Table compiled from information from company websites and "Archambault Group Launches Archambaultzik.ca, the First French-Language Music Download Site in Canada," January 16, 2004, www.quebecor.com, accessed October 3, 2006; Rob McIntyre, "Canada's Legal Music Download Services," www.music bymailcanada.com/CADOWN.html, accessed October 3, 2006; Fred Goodman, "Will Fans Pay for Music Online?" *Rolling Stone*, January 31, 2002, pp. 17–18; "Bell Canada Acquires Majority Interest in Puretracks, Nation's Premiere Online Digital Music Service," *The Spill*, March 1, 2006, available http://spillmagazine.com/news.htm, accessed October 3, 2006; Larry LeBlanc, "Music Industry Sees Bright Digital Future," *Billboard*, April 2, 2005, p. 44.
5. K. Monroe, "The Pricing of Services," *Handbook of Services Marketing,* ed. C. A. Congram and M. L. Friedman (New York: AMACOM, 1989), pp. 20–31.
6. Ibid.
7. "Rent a Star for the Holidays," *People,* December 15, 2003.
8. M. A. Ernst, "Price Visibility and Its Implications for Financial Services," presentation at the Effective Pricing Strategies for Service Providers Conference, Institute for International Research, Boston, October 1994.
9. Monroe, "The Pricing of Services."
10. V. A. Zeithaml, "The Acquisition, Meaning, and Use of Price Information by Consumers of Professional Services," in *Marketing Theory: Philosophy of Science Perspectives,* ed. R. Bush and S. Hunt (Chicago: American Marketing Association, 1982), pp. 237–41.
11. C. H. Lovelock, "Understanding Costs and Developing Pricing Strategies," *Services Marketing* (New York: Prentice Hall, 1991), pp. 236–46.
12. A. Stevens, "Firms Try More Lucrative Ways of Charging for Legal Services," *The Wall Street Journal,* November 25, 1994, pp. B1ff.
13. C. L. Grossman, "The Driving Forces Behind Rental Car Costs," *USA Today,* October 25, 1994, p. 50.
14. V. A. Zeithaml, "Consumer Perceptions of Price, Quality, and Value: A Means–End Model and Synthesis of Evidence," *Journal of Marketing* 52 (July 1988), pp. 2–22.

15. All comments from these four sections are based on those from Zeithaml, "Consumer Perceptions," pp. 13–14.

16. Sean Monke, *Canada NewsWire*, September 13, 2005, p. 1, quoted in *The Globe and Mail*.

17. Monroe, "The Pricing of Services."

18. Ibid.

19. Ibid.

20. J. P. Guiltinan, "The Price Bundling of Services: A Normative Framework," *Journal of Marketing* 51 (April 1987): 74–85.

21. G. J. Tellis, "Beyond the Many Faces of Price: An Integration of Pricing Strategies," *Journal of Marketing* 50 (October 1986): 146–60.

22. A. Stevens, "Clients Second-Guess Legal Fees," *The Wall Street Journal,* January 6, 1995, pp. B1, B6.

23. Ibid.

24. Ibid.

25. K. Fox, *Service Marketing Newsletter* (Chicago: American Marketing Association, 1984), pp. 1–2.

Chapter

18

The Financial and Economic Impact of Service

THIS CHAPTER'S OBJECTIVES ARE TO

1. Examine the direct effects of service on profits.

2. Consider the effect of service on getting new customers.

3. Evaluate the role of service in keeping customers.

4. Discuss what is known about the key service drivers of overall service quality, customer retention, and profitability.

5. Discuss the balanced performance scorecard that allows for strategic focus on measurements other than financials.

6. Describe the role of strategy maps in implementing the balanced performance scorecard.

"WHAT RETURN CAN I EXPECT ON SERVICE QUALITY IMPROVEMENTS?"

—A TYPICAL CEO

Consultants who work with companies to improve service quality find that the two most frequently asked questions are:

"How do I know that service quality improvements will be a good investment?"

"Where in the company do I invest money to achieve the highest return?"

For example, a restaurant chain, after conducting consumer research, found that service quality perceptions averaged 85 percent across the chain. The specific items receiving the lowest scores on the survey were appearance of the restaurant's exterior (70 percent), wait time for service

(78 percent), and limited menu (76 percent). The company's CEO wanted to know, first of all, whether making improvements in overall service quality or to any of the specific areas would result in revenues that exceeded their costs. Moreover, he wanted guidance as to which of the service aspects to tackle. He could determine how much each of the initiatives would cost to change, but that was as far as his financial estimates would take him. Clearly, the restaurant's exterior was most in need of change because it was rated lowest; but would it not also be by far the most expensive to change? What could he expect in return for improvements in each service area? Would adjustments in the other two factors be better investments? Which of the three service initiatives would generate noticeable improvements to raise the overall customer perceptions of the restaurant?

Ten years ago, these questions had to be answered on the basis of executive intuition. Today, more rigorous approaches exist to help managers make these decisions about service quality investments. The best-known and most widely respected approach is called return on service quality (ROSQ) and was developed by Roland Rust, Anthony Zahorik, and Tim Keiningham, a team of researchers and consultants.[1] The ROSQ approach is based on the following assumptions:

1. Quality is an investment.

2. Quality efforts must be financially accountable.

3. It is possible to spend too much on quality.

4. Not all quality expenditures are equally valid.

Their approach looks at investments in services as a chain of effects of the following form:

1. A service improvement effort will produce an increased level of customer satisfaction at the process or attribute level. For example, expending money to refurbish the exterior of the restaurants will likely increase customers' satisfaction level from the current low rating of 70 percent.

2. Increased customer satisfaction at the process or attribute level will lead to increased overall customer satisfaction. If satisfaction with the restaurant's exterior goes from 70 to 80 percent, overall service quality ratings may increase from 85 to 90 percent. (Both these percentage changes could be accurately measured the next time surveys are conducted and could even be projected in advance using the ROSQ model.)

3. Higher overall service quality or customer satisfaction will lead to increased behavioural intentions, such as greater repurchase intention and intention to increase usage. Customers who have not yet eaten at the restaurant will be drawn to do so, and many

who currently eat there once a month will consider increasing their patronage.

4. Increased behavioural intentions will lead to behavioural impact, including repurchase or customer retention, positive word of mouth, and increased usage. Intentions about patronizing the restaurant will become reality, resulting in higher revenues and more positive word-of-mouth communications.

5. Behavioural effects will then lead to improved profitability and other financial outcomes. Higher revenues will lead to higher profits for the restaurant, assuming that the original investment in refurbishing the exterior is covered.

The ROSQ methodology can help distinguish among all the company strategies, processes, approaches, and tactics that can be altered. The ROSQ approach is informative because it can be applied in companies to direct their individual strategies. Software has been developed to accompany the approach, and consulting firms work with companies to apply it. No longer do firms like the restaurant discussed here have to depend on intuition alone to guide them in their service quality investments.

In the current era of accountability, companies hunger for tools to monitor the payoff of new investments in service. Many managers still see service quality as costs rather than as contributors to profits, partly because of the difficulty involved in tracing the link between service and financial returns. Determining the financial impact of service parallels the age-old search for the connection between advertising and sales. Service quality's results—like advertising's results—are cumulative, and therefore, evidence of the link may not come immediately or even quickly after investments. And, like advertising, service quality is one of many variables—among them pricing, advertising, efficiency, and image—that simultaneously influence profits. Furthermore, spending on service per se does not guarantee results because strategy and execution must both also be considered.

In recent years, however, researchers and company executives have sought to understand the relationship between service and profits and have found strong evidence to support the relationship. For example, a recent study examined the comparative benefits of revenue expansion and cost reduction on return on quality. The research addressed a common strategic dilemma faced by executives: whether to reduce costs through the use of quality programs such as Six Sigma that focus on efficiencies and cost cutting, or to build revenues through improvements to customer service, customer satisfaction, and customer retention.[2] Using managers' reports as well as secondary data on firm profitability and stock returns, the study investigated whether the highest return on quality was generated from cost cutting, revenue expansion, or a combination of the two approaches. The results suggest that firms that adopt primarily a revenue expansion emphasis perform better and have higher return on quality than firms that emphasize either cost reduction or both revenue expansion and cost reduction together.[3]

Executives are also realizing that the link between service and profits is not simple. Service quality affects many economic factors in a company, some of them leading to profits through variables not traditionally in the domain of marketing. For example, the traditional total quality management approach expresses the financial impact of service quality in lowered costs or increased productivity. These relationships involve operational issues more than marketing issues.

More recently, other evidence has become available examining the relationship between service and profitability. The overall goal of this chapter is to synthesize that recent evidence and to identify relationships between service and profits. This chapter is divided into six sections, parallelling the chapter's objectives. In each section we assess the evidence and identify what is currently known about the topics. The chapter is organized using a conceptual framework linking all the variables in the topics.

SERVICE AND PROFITABILITY: THE DIRECT RELATIONSHIP

Figure 18.1 shows the underlying question at the heart of this chapter. Managers were first interested in this question in the 1980s when service quality emerged as a pivotal competitive strategy. Since that time, a significant amount of research has been conducted into the relationship between service and profit.[4] One study showed the favourable financial impact of complaint recovery systems.[5] Another found a significant and positive relationship between patient satisfaction and hospital profitability. In this study, specific dimensions of hospital service quality, such as billing and discharge processes, explained 17 to 27 percent of hospital earnings, net revenues, and return on assets.[6] Extending the definition of financial performance to include stock returns, another study found a significant positive link between changes in customer quality perceptions and stock return while holding constant the effects of advertising expenditures and return on investment.[7]

Research conducted by Canada's National Quality Institute (NQI) found the following results for Canada Awards for Excellence (CAE) winners:

- 91 percent improvement in employee turnover

- 215 percent increase in cost savings

- 90 percent increase in customer satisfaction

- 59 percent in price savings to client

- 57 percent decrease in injuries

From 1990 to 2005, CAE winners achieved a 143 percent increase in shareholder value. This compares to an overall gain of 88 percent for the TSE 300, a 78 percent gain among companies in the Dow Jones Industrial Average, and a 66 percent gain for the S&P 200.[8]

FIGURE 18.1

The Direct Relationship Between Service and Profits

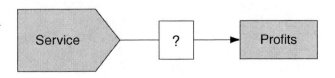

EXHIBIT 18.1
Linking Service to Profits

One way to view the relationship between service and profit has been developed by a group of Harvard professors and is called the "service-profit chain." The professors who created it argue many of the samepoints made in this chapter—that the longer customers stay with companies, the lower the costs to serve them, the higher the volume of purchases they make, the higher the price premium they tolerate, and the greater the positive word-of-mouth communication they engage in. These professors have provided evidence from in-depth studies in multiple companies.

At Sears, for instance, management spent a great deal of time developing a set of total performance indicators (TPI) that showed how well the company was doing:

> We use the TPI at every level of the company, in every store and facility; and nearly every manager has some portion of his or her compensation at risk on the basis of nonfinancial measures . . . . [I]n the course of the last 12 months, employee satisfaction on the Sears TPI has risen by almost 4% and customer satisfaction by 4% ... if our model is correct—and its predictive record is extremely good—that 4% improvement in customer satisfaction translates into more than $200 million in additional revenues in the past 12 months.

At BFI, the international waste management company, research showed that a 1 percent decline in customer defection led to an increase in pre-tax profit of $41 million. BFI worked backward from their customer satisfaction scores in order to further specify its causes—eventually

learning that the biggest cause was the dependability of trash pickups. This is consistent with the model we have used in this text, which stresses that the most important dimension of service quality is usually reliability. Once BFI had identified the significance of dependable pickups, they were able to specify what other actions were needed to deliver on their promises.

During the mid-90s, CIBC management faced issues similar to those Sears and BFI faced. Defection rates were high, and there was concern they would go even higher. According to CIBC's analysis, profits were driven by customer behaviour, which was found to be influenced by employee commitment. Employee commitment, in turn, was driven by management style and leadership. When their analysis was complete, the bank's business model showed that a 1 percent increase in any one of their loyalty measures led to an increased profit of $0.60 per customer per month. In addition, they found that a 5 percent increase in employee commitment resulted in a 2 percent increase in customer loyalty.

Sources: J. L. Heskett, W. E. Sasser Jr., and L. A. Schlesinger, *The Service Profit Chain* (New York: The Free Press, 1997); Marc C. Epstein and Robert A. Westbrook, "Linking Actions to Profits in Strategic Decision Making," *MIT Sloan Management Review* 42, no. 3 (Spring 2004), pp. 39–49; an exhibit from A. J. Rucci, S. P. Kirn, and R. T. Quinn, "The Employee-Customer-Profit Chain at Sears," *Harvard Business Review*, January/February 1998, pp. 83–97. © 1998 by the President and Fellows of Harvard College. All rights reserved. Reprinted by permission of *Harvard Business Review*.

Exhibit 18.1 shows how some of these relationships have been examined at Sears, BFI, and CIBC. Although some companies continued to approach the relationship between service and profit at a broad level, others began to focus more specifically on particular elements of the relationship. For example, executives and researchers soon recognized that service quality played a different role in getting new customers than it did in retaining existing customers.

OFFENSIVE MARKETING EFFECTS OF SERVICE: ATTRACTING MORE AND BETTER CUSTOMERS

Service quality can help companies attract more and better customers to the business through *offensive marketing*.[9] Offensive effects (shown in Figure 18.2) involve market share, reputation, and price premiums. When service is good, a company gains a positive reputation and through that reputation a higher market share and the ability to charge more than its competitors for services. These benefits were documented in a multiyear, multicompany study called PIMS (profit impact of marketing strategy).

FIGURE 18.2

Offensive Marketing
Effects of Service on
Profits

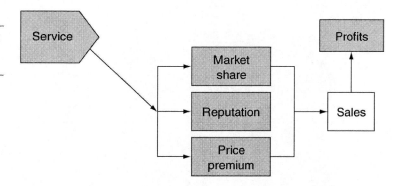

The PIMS research shows that companies offering superior service achieve higher-than-normal market share growth and that service quality influences profits through increased market share and premium prices as well as lowered costs and less rework.[10] The study found that businesses rated in the top fifth of competitors on relative service quality average an 8 percent price premium over their competitors.[11]

To document the impact of service on market share, a group of researchers described their version of the path between quality and market share, claiming that satisfied customers spread positive word of mouth, which leads to the attraction of new customers and then to higher market share. They claim that advertising service excellence without sufficient quality to back up the communications will not increase market share. Further, they confirm that there are time lags in market share effects, making the relationship between quality and market share difficult to discern in the short term.[12]

DEFENSIVE MARKETING EFFECTS OF SERVICE: CUSTOMER RETENTION

When it comes to keeping the customers a firm already has—an approach called *defensive marketing*[13]—researchers and consulting firms have in the last 15 years documented and quantified the financial impact of existing customers. In Chapter 7 we explained that customer defection, or "customer churn," is widespread in service businesses. Customer defection is costly to companies, because new customers must replace lost customers and replacement comes at a high cost. Getting new customers is expensive; it involves advertising, promotion, and sales costs as well as start-up operating expenses. New customers are often unprofitable for a period of time after acquisition. In the insurance industry, for example, the insurer does not typically recover selling costs until the third or fourth year of the relationship. Capturing customers from other companies is also an expensive proposition: A greater degree of service improvement is necessary to make a customer switch from a competitor than to retain a current customer. Selling costs for existing customers are much lower (on average 20 percent lower) than selling to new ones.[14]

In general, the longer a customer remains with the company, the more profitable the relationship is for the organization:

> Served correctly, customers generate increasingly more profits each year they stay with a company. Across a wide range of businesses, the pattern is the same: the longer a company keeps a customer, the more money it stands to make.[15]

484   Part 7   *Service and the Bottom Line*

FIGURE 18.3

TD Canada Trust offers an attractive incentive to new customers to get them to switch service providers.

Source: Photographer: Paul Weeks/Westside Studio.

The money a company makes from retention comes from four sources (shown in Figure 18.3): costs, volume of purchases, price premium, and word-of-mouth communication. This section provides research evidence for many of the sources.

Lower Costs

Attracting a new customer can be five times more costly than retaining an existing one. A recent example of the kind of costs needed to acquire new customers in what is typically a "sticky" industry with relatively low levels of churn is provided by TD Canada Trust. Note in Figure 18.4 their strategy of giving free iPods to new customers who transfer their main chequing accounts. Consultants who have focused on these relationships assert that customer defections have a stronger effect on a company's profits than market share, scale, unit costs, and many other factors usually associated with competitive advantage.[16] They also claim that, depending on the industry, companies can increase profits from 25 to 85 percent by retaining just 5 percent more of their customers. A U.S. study conducted on winners of the Malcolm Baldrige National Quality Award found that quality reduced costs: order processing time decreased on average by 12 percent per year, errors and defects fell by 10 percent per year, and cost of quality declined by 9 percent per year.

Consider the following facts about the role of service quality in lowering costs:

- "Our highest quality day was our lowest cost of operations day" (Fred Smith, FedEx).

- "Our costs of not doing things right the first time were from 25 to 30 percent of our-revenue" (David F. Colicchio, regional quality manager, Hewlett-Packard Company).[17]

FIGURE 18.4

Defensive Marketing
Effects of Service on
Profits

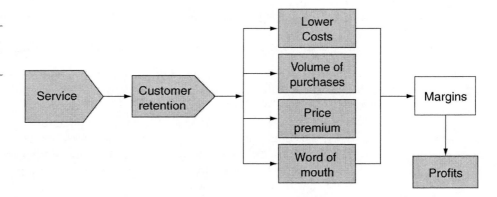

- Profit on services purchased by a 10-year customer is on average three times greater than for a 5-year customer.[18]

- Bain and Company, a consulting organization specializing in retention research, estimates that in the life insurance business, a 5 percent annual increase in customer retention lowers a company's costs per policy by 18 percent.

Volume of Purchases

Customers who are satisfied with a company's services are likely to increase the amount of money they spend with that company or the types of services offered. A customer satisfied with a broker's services, for example, will likely invest more money when it becomes available. Similarly, a customer satisfied with a bank's chequing services is likely to open a savings account with the same bank and to use the bank's loan services as well.

Price Premium

Evidence suggests that a customer who notices and values the services provided by a company will pay a price premium for those services. Graniterock, a winner of the Baldrige Award, has been able to command prices up to 30 percent higher than competitors for its rock (a product that many would claim is a commodity!) because it offers off-hour delivery and 24-hour self-service. In fact, most of the service quality leaders in industry command higher prices than their competitors: Purolator collects more for overnight delivery than Canada Post, Hertz rental cars cost more than Avis cars, and staying at the Ritz-Carlton is more expensive than staying at the Four Seasons.

Word-of-Mouth Communication

In Chapter 3, we described the valuable role of word-of-mouth communications in purchasing service. Because word of mouth is considered more credible than other sources of information, the best type of promotion for a service may well come from other customers who advocate the services provided by the company. Word of mouth brings new customers to the firm, and the financial value of this form of advocacy can be calibrated by the company in terms of the promotional costs it saves as well as the streams of revenues from new customers.

⟶ CUSTOMER PERCEPTIONS OF SERVICE AND PURCHASE INTENTIONS

In Chapter 5 we highlighted the links among customer satisfaction, service quality, and increased purchases. Here we provide more research and empirical evidence supporting these relationships. For example, researchers at Xerox offered a compelling insight about the relationship between satisfaction and purchase intentions. Initially, the company focused on satisfied customers, which they identified as those checking either a "4" or a "5" on a five-point satisfaction scale. Careful analysis of the data showed that customers giving Xerox 5s were six times more likely to indicate that they would repurchase Xerox equipment than those giving 4s. This relationship encouraged the company to focus on increasing the 5s rather than the 4s and 5s because of the strong sales and profitability implications.[19] Figure 18.5 shows this relationship.

Evidence also shows that customer satisfaction and service quality perceptions affect consumer intentions to behave in other positive ways—praising the firm, preferring the company over others, increasing volume of purchases, or agreeably paying a price premium. Most of the early evidence looked only at overall benefits in terms of purchase intention rather than examining specific types of behavioural intentions. One study, for example, found a significant association between overall patient satisfaction and intent to choose a hospital again.[20] Another, using information from a Swedish customer satisfaction barometer, found that stated repurchase intention is strongly related to stated satisfaction across virtually all product categories.[21]

More recently, studies have found relationships between service quality and more specific behavioural intentions. One study involving university students found strong links between service quality and other behavioural intentions of strategic importance to a university, including behaviour such as saying positive things about the school, planning to contribute money to the class pledge on graduation, and planning to recommend the school to employers as a place from which to recruit.[22] Another comprehensive study examined a battery of 13 specific behavioural intentions likely to result from perceived service quality. The overall measure was significantly correlated with customer perceptions of service quality.[23]

Individual companies have also monitored the impact of service quality on selected behavioural intentions. Toyota found that intent to repurchase a Toyota automobile increased from a base of 37 to 45 percent with a positive sales experience, from

FIGURE 18.5

The Effects of
Service

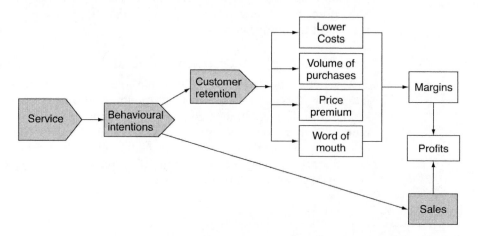

37 to 79 percent with a positive service experience, and from 37 to 91 percent with both positive sales and service experiences.[24] A similar study quantitatively assessed the relationship between level of service quality and willingness to purchase at AT&T. Of AT&T's customers who rated the company's overall quality as excellent, more than 90 percent expressed willingness to purchase from AT&T again. For customers rating the service as good, fair, or poor, the percentages decreased to 60, 17, and 0 percent, respectively. According to these data, willingness to repurchase increased at a steeper rate (by 43 percent) as the service quality rating improved from fair to good than when it went from poor to fair (17 percent) or from good to excellent (30 percent).[25]

Exhibit 18.2 shows a list of the questions that businesses still need to know more about on this topic and the others in this chapter.

THE KEY DRIVERS OF SERVICE QUALITY, CUSTOMER RETENTION, AND PROFITS

Understanding the relationship between overall service quality and profitability is important, but it is perhaps more useful to managers to identify specific drivers of service quality that most relate to profitability (shown in Figure 18.6). Doing so will help firms understand what aspects of service quality to change to influence the relationship, and therefore where to invest resources.

Most evidence for this issue has come from examining the aspects of service (such as empathy, responsiveness, and tangibles) on overall service quality, customer satisfaction, and purchase intentions rather than on financial outcomes such as retention or profitability. As you have discovered in this text, service is multifaceted, consisting of a wide variety of customer-perceived dimensions including reliability, responsiveness, and empathy and resulting from innumerable company strategies such as technology and process improvement. In research exploring the relative importance of service dimensions on overall service quality or customer satisfaction, the bulk of the support confirms that reliability is most critical; but other research has demonstrated the importance of customization and other factors. Because the dimensions and attributes are delivered in many cases with totally different internal strategies, resources must be allocated where they are most needed, and study in this topic could provide direction.

Some companies and researchers have viewed the effect of specific service encounters on overall service quality or customer satisfaction and the effect of specific behaviours within service encounters. As we discussed more fully in Chapters 5 and 8,

FIGURE 18.6

The Key Drivers of Service Quality, Customer Retention, and Profits

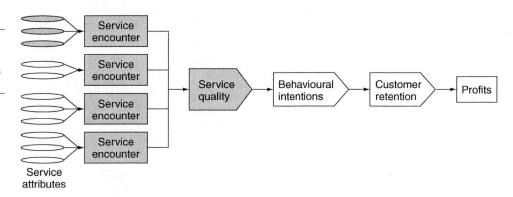

→ EXHIBIT 18.2

Service Quality and the Economic Worth of Customers: Businesses Still Need to Know More

Topic	Key Research Questions
Service quality and profitability: the direct relationship	1. What methodologies need to be developed to allow companies to capture the effect of service quality on profit? 2. What measures are necessary to examine the relationship in a consistent, valid, and reliable manner? 3. Does the relationship between service quality and profitability vary by industry, country, category of business (e.g., in services companies vs. goods companies, in industrial vs. packaged goods companies), or other variables? 4. What are the moderating factors of the relationship between service quality and profitability? 5. What is the optimal spending level on service in order to affect profitability?
Offensive effects of service quality	1. What is the optimal amount of spending on service quality to obtain offensive effects on reputation? 2. To obtain offensive effect, are expenditures on advertising or service quality itself more effective? 3. In what ways can companies signal high service quality to customers to obtain offensive effects?
Defensive effects of service quality	1. What is a loyal customer? 2. What is the role of service in defensive marketing? 3. How does service compare in effectiveness to other retention strategies such as price? 4. What levels of service provision are needed to retain customers? 5. How can the effects of word-of-mouth communication from retained customers be quantified? 6. What aspects of service are most important for customer retention? 7. How can defection-prone customers be identified?
Perceptions of service quality, behavioural intentions, and profits	1. What is the relationship between customer purchase intentions and initial purchase behaviour in services? 2. What is the relationship between behavioural intentions and repurchase in services? 3. Does the degree of association between service quality and behaviour change at different quality levels?
Identifying the key drivers of service quality, customer retention, and profits	1. What service encounters are most responsible for perceptions of service quality? 2. What are the key drivers in each service encounter? 3. Where should investments be made to affect service quality, purchase, retention, and profits? 4. Are key drivers of service quality the same as key drivers of behavioural intentions, customer retention, and profits?

Marriott Hotels conducted extensive customer research to determine what service elements contribute most to customer loyalty. They found that four of the top five factors came into play in the first 10 minutes of the guest's stay—those that involved the early encounters of arriving, checking in, and entering the hotel rooms. Other companies have found that mistakes or problems that occur in early service encounters are particularly critical, because a failure at early points results in greater risk for dissatisfaction in each ensuing encounter.

▶ COMPANY PERFORMANCE MEASUREMENT: THE BALANCED PERFORMANCE SCORECARD

Traditionally, organizations have measured their performance almost completely on the basis of financial indicators such as profit, sales, and return on investment. This short-term approach leads companies to emphasize financials to the exclusion of other performance indicators. Today's corporate strategists recognize the limitations of evaluating corporate performance on financials alone, contending that these income-based financial figures measure yesterday's decisions rather than indicate future performance. This recognition came when many companies' strong financial records deteriorated because of unnoticed declines in operational processes, quality, or customer satisfaction.[26] In the words of one observer of corporate strategy:

> Financial measures emphasize profitability of inert assets over any other mission of the company. They do not recognize the emerging leverage of the soft stuff—skilled people and employment of information—as the new keys to high performance and near-perfect customer satisfaction. ... If the only mission a measurement system conveys is financial discipline, an organization is directionless.[27]

For this reason, companies began to recognize that *balanced performance scorecards*—strategic measurement systems that captured other areas of performance—were needed. The developers of balanced performance scorecards defined them as follows:

> ... a set of measures that gives top managers a fast but comprehensive view of the business .... [that] complements the financial measures with operational measures of customer satisfaction, internal processes, and the organization's innovation and improvement activities—operational measures that are the drivers of future financial performance.[28]

Having a firm handle on what had been viewed as "soft" measures became the way to help organizations identify customer problems, improve processes, and achieve company objectives.

Balanced performance scorecards have become extremely popular. One recent report indicates that 70 percent of the *Fortune* 1,000 companies have or are experimenting with balanced performance scorecards and more than one-half of the largest companies worldwide use them. Furthermore, according to a report called "Measures That Matter" from Ernst and Young's Center for Business Innovation, investors give nonfinancial measures an average of one-third the weight when making a decision to buy or sell any given stock,[29] strongly demonstrating to companies that investors recognize the value of the new forms of measurement.

As shown in Figure 18.7, the balanced performance scorecard captures three perspectives in addition to the financial perspective: customer, operational, and learning. The balanced scorecard brings together, in a single management report, many of the previously separated elements of a company and forces senior managers to consider all the important measures together. The scorecard has been facilitated by recent developments in enterprise-wide software (discussed in the Technology Spotlight) that allow companies to create, automate, and integrate measurements from all parts of the company.

Methods for measuring financial performance are the most developed and established in corporations, having been created more than 400 years ago. In contrast, efforts to measure market share, quality, innovation, human resources, and customer satisfaction have only recently been created. Companies can improve their performance by developing this discipline in their measurement of all four categories. As noted

FIGURE 18.7 Sample Measurements for the Balanced Scorecard

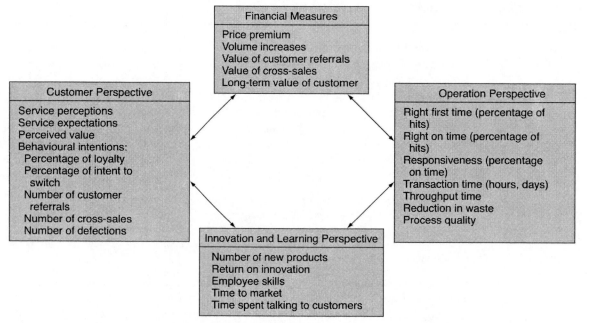

by researchers Marc Epstein and Robert Westbrook, "Much of what has been written about profitability modeling does not take a cross functional approach." A welcome exception to this is represented by Epstein's "Customer Profitability Analysis," recently published by the Society of Management Accountants of Canada (CMAs).[30]

Changes to Financial Measurement

One way that service leaders are changing financial measurement is to calibrate the defensive effect of retaining and losing customers. The monetary value of retaining customers can be projected through the use of average revenues over the lifetimes of customers. The number of customer defections can then be translated into lost revenue to the firm and become a critical company performance standard:

> Ultimately, defections should be a key performance measure for senior management and a fundamental component of incentive systems. Managers should know the company's defection rate, what happens to profits when the rate moves up or down and why defections occur.[31]

Companies can also measure actual increases or decreases in revenue from retention or defection of customers by capturing the value of a loyal customer, including expected cash flows over a customer's lifetime or lifetime customer value (as described in Chapter 7). Other possible financial measures (as shown in Figure 18.7) include the value of price premiums, volume increases, customer referrals, and cross sales.

Customer Perceptual Measures

Customer perceptual measures are leading indicators of financial performance. As we discussed in this chapter, customers who are not happy with the company will defect and will tell others about their dissatisfaction. As we also discussed, perceptual measures

Technology Spotlight

Automating the Balanced Scorecard

A study of the usage of balanced scorecards by North American organizations, sponsored by six organizations that are involved in their preparation and use (AICPA, CAM-I, CMA Canada, IQPC, Targus Corporation, and Hyperion Solutions), examined the factors that make the use of scorecards successful. One of the most important factors was software automation of the scorecards, and the study found that 70 percent of organizations who use balanced scorecards currently use some form of off-the-shelf or in-house software. The use of software allows companies to collect and report information quickly and continuously, removing the time-consuming task of updating data and freeing employees and management to focus on the strategic aspects of the scorecard.

Thirty-six percent of organizations that use software, and virtually all that have been using scorecards for more than five years, use Microsoft Excel spreadsheets, largely because they are easy to use, widely available, inexpensive, and flexible. Spreadsheets are flexible because a template can be created into which multiple parts of the organization can enter their data. Organizations also tend to add, eliminate, or change measures, and spreadsheets offer the flexibility of adapting. However, users have found that spreadsheets make benchmarking scorecards across performance units difficult because departments can interpret measures differently and can engage in gamesmanship. Spreadsheets are also difficult to maintain because the data are not collected electronically and must be updated by area.

The second-most-popular software is Hyperion's Performance Scorecard, one of the off-the-shelf packages that has been developed by software companies. Hyperion Solutions reports that 88 of the Fortune 100 companies, 66 of the Nikkei top 100, 53 of the Financial Times Europe Top 100, 10 of the top 10 banks and 5 of the top 5 industrial equipment companies use the company's Balanced Performance Scorecard software. These packages have the following advantages over spreadsheet software: better data security, a more focused tool, and more consistent information across the firm. These off-the-shelf programs can extract data from multiple transactional systems and integrate it into one version of the company's financial and operational performance. Therefore, all managers have the same facts and metrics, giving them a common understanding of the factors affecting overall performance.

Organizations use five different ways to communicate scorecard results: paper, email, the Web, LANs, and WANs. The method used by a company tends to be related to organizational size and the use of software. The smallest organizations (fewer than 100 employees)

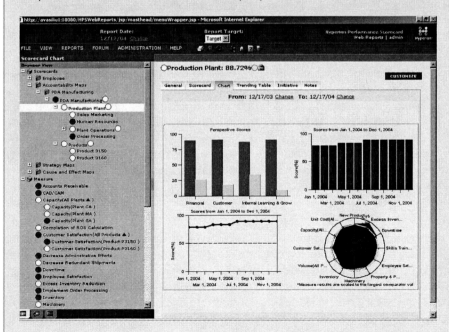

continued

Technology Spotlight

Automating the Balanced Scorecard—*continued*

typically use paper-based reporting. Medium-sized companies use email and the Web to report the results of spreadsheet software, and companies that use the Web are the most likely to report success. The largest organizations use technologically sophisticated techniques like the Web and LANs, which are easy to use in combination with off-the-shelf software.

The survey showed that the most important feature related to success in using software for balanced scorecards is the ability to provide Web-based reporting. This feature was followed by the ability to drill down to root data, the ability to customize reports, and the ability to link scorecards and roll them up. The system also needs to be able to access data from multiple legacy systems and other data sources and must be flexible enough to easily accommodate future changes to the scorecarding system.

Sources: R. Lawson, W. Stratton, and T. Hatch, "Automating the Balanced Scorecard," *CMA Management* 77, no. 9 (2004), pp. 39–44; www.hyperion.com.

reflect customer beliefs and feelings about the company and its products and services and can predict how the customer will behave in the future. Overall forms of the measurements we discussed in Chapters 5 and 6 (shown in the customer perspective box of Figure 18.7) are measures that can be included in this category. Among the measures that are valuable to track are overall service perceptions and expectations, customer satisfaction, perceptual measures of value, and behavioural intention measures such as loyalty and intent to switch. A company that notices a decline in these numbers should be concerned that the decline will translate into lost dollars for the company.

Operational Measures

Operational measures involve the translation of customer perceptual measures into the standards or actions that must be set internally to meet customers' expectations. Although virtually all companies count or calculate operational measures in some form, the balanced scorecard requires that these measures stem from the business processes that have the greatest effect on customer satisfaction. In other words, these measures are not independent of customer perceptual measures but instead are intricately linked with them. In Chapter 10 we called these customer-linked operational measures *customer-defined standards*—operational standards determined through customer expectations and calibrated the way the customer views and expresses them.

Innovation and Learning

The final area of measurement involves a company's ability to innovate, improve, and learn—by launching new products, creating more value for customers, and improving operating efficiencies. This measurement area is most difficult to capture quantitatively but can be accomplished using performance-to-goal percentages. For example, a company can set a goal of launching 10 new products a year, then measure what percentage of that goal it achieves in a year. If four new products are launched, its percentage for the year is 40 percent, which can then be compared with subsequent years.

The Global Feature shows that implementation of the balanced performance score-card can vary by culture.

The Balanced Scorecard in Practice

The balanced scorecard has been implemented not only in corporations but also in government and nonprofit organizations. In 2001 the University of Virginia Library (UVL), a system of 11 different libraries with holdings of four million volumes, be-came the first library in North America to begin using a balanced scorecard to improve its performance.[32]

Lynda White, associate director of management information services at UVL, says that the scorecard is currently used as a management tool to assess the health of the organization, to indicate areas in which it is doing well and other areas that need at-tention, and to assemble information in a meaningful way. The organization began development of the scorecard by prioritizing the many numbers in the statistics and data that it had collected over the years.

The library's scorecard uses four categories of measures: the user perspective, the internal processes perspective, the financial perspective, and the learning and growth perspective. Each of the four perspectives has four to six measures that tell the organi-zation how well the library is doing in each area. The first two categories, focusing on users and internal processes, were easy for the library to understand and measure. The metrics for user perspective helped the library improve customer service, as White describes:

> We measure how well we do in customer service, what faculty and students think of services and collections, what students think of user instruction, how much special collections is used, how much patrons use new books and electronic resources, how quickly we turn around requests (for searches, recalls, library electronic ordering [LEO] document delivery, interlibrary loan, scanning for e-reserves, new books), how fast and accurately we re-shelve, Web-site usability, renovation of public-service areas, increasing access to digital materials. And of course, measuring the unit cost of various services affects them as taxpayers or donors. It addresses whether we are using their money wisely and efficiently.[33]

According to Jim Self, director of management information services at the library, the other two categories were more difficult. Because UVL, like most libraries, is nonprofit, the financial perspective was the most challenging. In determining what to measure, the scorecard gave the library an opportunity to look at the financial aspects of its operation that had not been emphasized before, such as processing costs incurred in cataloging and acquisitions and transaction costs in reference, circulation, and interlibrary loan.

The organization realized the value of the scorecard when it compared its actual performance to its assumed performance. It found out, for example, that turnaround times for ordering books requested by users were much slower than its promises. It had been promising users that it could get new books for them in one week, but it found that only 17 percent of new books it ordered on request were ready in seven days. Through this comparison and others, the balanced scorecard helped the library look at its priorities, goals, and vision statements, align them with each other, and simplify its priority list. The library's special website (www.lib.virginia.edu/bsc) describes the history, measures, and implementation of the scorecard.

Global Feature

Challenges to Implementation of the Balanced Performance Scorecard in China

As China continues to develop into a world economic power, its organizations are recognizing the value of strategic management concepts to help them formulate and execute effective and competitive strategies. Chinese organizations are now joining the organizations in the world that have adopted the balanced performance scorecard.

Companies in China face many of the same external and internal challenges as Western companies face, including rapidly changing business conditions, increasing competition, and increasing customer expectations. However, many Chinese organizations are unfamiliar with the building blocks needed for strategy development—such as analysis of the business life cycle, SWOT (strengths, weaknesses, opportunities, and threats) analysis, and development of value propositions for target markets. Chinese companies had been successful largely based on entrepreneurship, intuition, or prior market dominance, approaches that have been unsuccessful as competition has intensified.

Consultants and companies that have implemented balanced scorecards in China recognize special challenges:

1. Goal-setting processes are not flexible enough to allow companies to adapt quickly, largely because companies lack the ability to track, analyze, and change goals.

2. Measurement data is either not readily available or is scattered across the organization, with no single system for recording or displaying the information. Enterprise software systems usually have data in the financial and operational areas but lack data in the customer and learning/growth perspectives.

3. Performance appraisal systems in China are particularly susceptible to the problems created by organizational silos, and managers are compensated based on functional performance.

4. Companies are less likely to have information technology systems to record data for employee evaluations. Therefore, human resource professionals or managers must manually calculate performance scores and bonuses.

Irv Beiman and Yong-Ling Sun of e-Gate Consulting Shanghai, consultants who have applied the balanced performance scorecard to workplaces in China, identify six critical success factors in implementing the scorecard methodology in workplaces: (1) committing and involving top management; (2) overcoming implementation hurdles; (3) overcoming functional silos; (4) establishing linkages to competency development and variable pay; (5) developing infrastructure to communicate the strategy, track performance, and make adjustments based on results; and (6) elevating human resources to the status of a strategic partner to line management. All these criteria are important for a firm in any country to have a successful balanced scorecard, but the challenges in China are harder to overcome, particularly in the area of human resources.

One of the biggest human resource issues is the way that executives, directors, and managers are paid. Variable pay, which creates incentives to aim for common goals, is infrequently used, and compensation is almost always based on individual departments' sales and revenue goals. For example, Chinese sales personnel are almost always paid exclusively for sales volume or revenue. Because of the way they are paid, they do not cooperate with other departments, which results in conflict and tension, particularly with production departments. Consider the experience of a private entrepreneurial company in China. Each department in the firm had developed its own way of approaching work, without coordinating with

continued

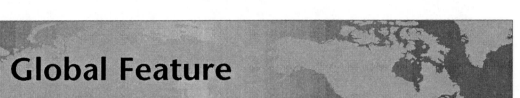

Global Feature

Challenges to Implementation of the Balanced Performance Scorecard in China
—continued

other departments. Compensation was based on each department's performance rather than common performance. When faced with increasing pressure from nternational competition in their domestic markets, the firm recognized that it needed to revise its strategy and focus on external customer needs. The company adopted the balanced scorecard methodology and initially found that managers constantly complained about employees in other departments, placing the blame on them. After implementation of the scorecard, managers began working more cooperatively with each other by sharing objectives across departments, improving cross-functional business processes, and fostering teamwork. Measurable improvements in company performance resulted.

Another human resource issue involves performance appraisal, performance management, and job

descriptions, which do not always exist in Chinese firms. When they do exist, they are created in each individual department, meaning that each department knows only a piece of the work done by the organization. As a result, training across departments is not connected with a focus on the customer or the firm's overall strategy. In situations in which the balanced performance scorecard approach has been used effectively, the human resource function assumes the responsibility for job descriptions, performance appraisals, variable compensation, and other policies that support strategy execution.

Sources: I. Beiman and Y. L. Sun, "Using the Balanced Scorecard for Strategy Execution in China," *China Staff* 9, no. 8 (2003), pp. 10–14; I. Beiman and Y. Sun, "Implementing a Balanced Scorecard in China: Steps for Success," *China Staff* 9, no. 9 (2003), pp. 11–15. Used with permission.

Strategy Maps to Enhance Balanced Scorecards

The strategy map is a concept that was recently developed to help companies deploy the balanced scorecard more effectively. A strategy map provides a single-page visual representation of a firm's strategy (see Figure 18.8) that links the four perspectives of the balanced scorecard and thereby shows the cause-and-effect relationships among them.[34] Instead of merely showing the four clusters of metrics as separate categories linked by arrows, as shown in the figure, the strategy map shows how the typical 20 to 30 measures in a balanced scorecard are integrated in the creation of a single unified strategy and clearly demonstrates which variables lead, lag, and feed back into other variables. The map also identifies the capabilities of the organization's intangible assets—human capital, information capital, and organization capital—that are required for superior performance.

The essence of the map is that financial outcomes are possible only if targeted customers are satisfied, a complicated process achieved with a set of interrelated capabilities. The mapping process forces managers to identify cause and effect and to clarify the logic of how the company will create value and for whom.[35] As part of the process, companies must identify the customer value proposition and then describe how it will generate sales and loyalty from targeted customers. The company then must link the critical internal processes that are most important to deliver the

496   Part 7   *Service and the Bottom Line*

FIGURE 18.8   A Strategy Map Helps Companies Align Strategy with Performance

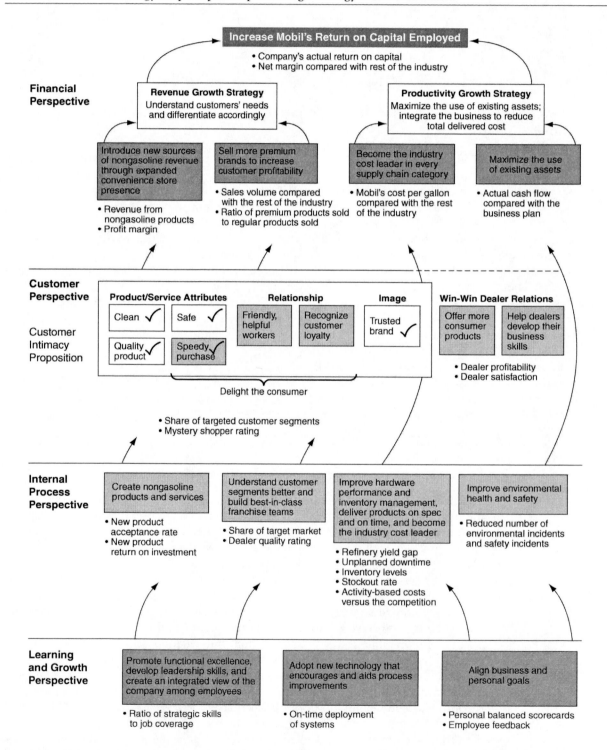

value proposition. Mapping helps identify any of the four categories in which management has not thought through metrics and strategies. Strategies are typically executed through a structure of strategic themes developed during the mapping.

Effective Nonfinancial Performance Measurements

According to field research conducted in 60 companies and survey responses from 297 senior executives, many companies do not identify and act on the correct nonfinancial measures.[36] One example involves a bank that surveyed satisfaction only from customers who physically entered the branches, a policy that caused some branch managers to offer free food and drinks in order to increase their scores. According to the authors of the study, companies make four major mistakes:

1. *Not linking measures to strategy.* Companies can easily identify hundreds of nonfinancial measures to track, but they also need to use analysis that identifies the most important drivers of their strategy. Successful organizations use value driver maps, tools that lay out the cause-and-effect relationships between drivers and strategic success. Figure 18.9 shows the causal model developed by a successful fast-food chain to understand the key drivers of shareholder value. The factors on

FIGURE 18.9

The measures that matter most: A causal model for a fast-food company shows the critical drivers of performance and the concepts that lead to shareholder value.

Source: Christopher D. Ittner and David F. Larcker, "Coming Up Short on Nonfinancial Performance Measurement," *Harvard Business Review,* November 2003, pp. 88–95.

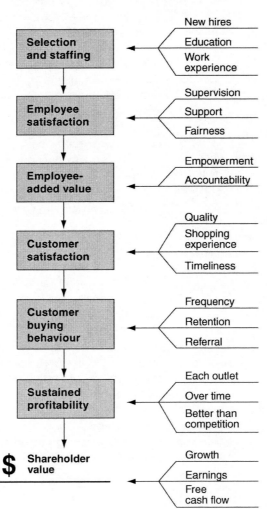

Customer Equity and Return on Marketing: Metrics to Match a Strategic Customer-Centred View of the Firm

Although the marketing concept has articulated a customer-centred viewpoint since the 1960s, marketing theory and practice have become incrementally customer-centred over the past 40 years. For example, marketing has only recently decreased its emphasis on short-term transactions and increased its focus on long-term customer relationships. Much of this refocus stems from the changing nature of the world's leading economies, which have undergone a century-long shift from the goods sector to the service sector.

Because service often tends to be more relationship based, this structural shift in the economy has resulted in more attention to relationships and therefore more attention to customers. This customer-centred viewpoint is starting to be reflected in the concepts and metrics that drive marketing management, including such metrics as customer value and voice of the customer. For example, the concept of brand equity, a fundamentally product-centred concept, is now being challenged by the customer-centred concept of *customer equity.*

> *Customer equity* is the total of the discounted lifetime values summed over all the firm's customers.

In other words, customer equity is obtained by summing up the customer lifetime values of the firm's customers. In fast-moving and dynamic industries that involve customer relationships, products come and go but customers remain. Customers and customer equity may be more central to many firms than brands and brand equity, although current management practices and metrics do not yet fully reflect this shift. The shift from product-centred thinking to customer-centred thinking implies the need for an accompanying shift from product-based metrics to customer-based metrics.

USING CUSTOMER EQUITY IN A STRATEGIC FRAMEWORK

Consider the issues facing a typical marketing manager or marketing-oriented CEO: How do I manage my brand? How will my customers react to changes in service and service quality? Should I raise price? What is the best way to enhance the relationships with my current customers? Where should I focus my efforts? Determining customer lifetime value, or customer equity, is the first step, but the more important step is to evaluate and test ideas and strategies using lifetime value as the measuring stick. At a very basic level, strategies for building customer relationships can affect five basic factors: retention rate, referrals, increased sales, reduced direct costs, and reduced marketing costs.

Rust, Zeithaml, and Lemon have developed an approach based on customer equity that can help business executives answer their questions. The model that represents this approach is shown in the accompanying figure. In this context, customer equity is a new approach to marketing and corporate strategy that finally puts the customer—and, more importantly, strategies that grow the value of the customer—at the heart of the organization. The researchers identify the drivers of customer equity—value equity, brand equity, and relationship equity—and explain how these drivers work, independently and together, to grow customer equity. Service strategies are prominent in both value equity and relationship equity. Within each of these drivers are specific, incisive actions ("levers") that the firm can take to enhance the firm's overall customer equity.

WHY IS CUSTOMER EQUITY IMPORTANT?

For most firms, customer equity—the total of the discounted lifetime values of all the firm's customers—is certain to be the most important determinant of the long-term value of the firm. Although customer equity will not be responsible for the entire value of the firm (consider, for example, physical assets, intellectual property, research and development competencies, etc.), the firm's current customers provide the most reliable source of future revenues and profits—and provide a focal point for marketing strategy.

Although it may seem obvious that customer equity is key to long-term success, understanding how to grow and manage customer equity is much more complex. Growing customer equity is of utmost importance, and doing it well can lead to significant competitive advantage.

continued

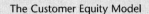

→ EXHIBIT 18.3
—continued

The Customer Equity Model

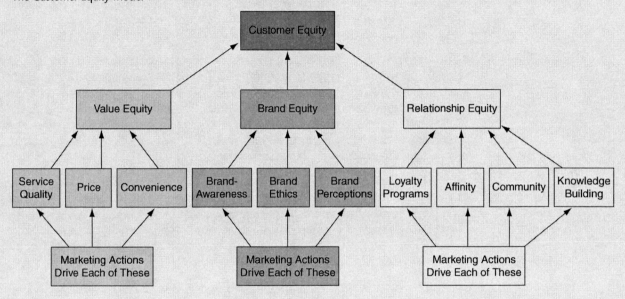

CALCULATING RETURN ON MARKETING USING CUSTOMER EQUITY

At the beginning of this chapter, we told you about an approach called return on quality that was developed to help companies understand where they could get the biggest impact from quality investments. A more general form of that approach is called return on marketing, which enables companies to look at all competing marketing strategy options and trade them off on the basis of projected financial return. This approach allows companies to not just examine the impact of service on financial return but also compare the impact of service with the impact of branding, price changes, and all other marketing strategies. Using the customer equity model, firms can analyze the drivers that have

the greatest impact, compare the drivers' performance with that of competitors' drivers, and project return on investment from improvements in the drivers. The framework enables what-if evaluation of marketing return on investment, which can include such criteria as return on quality, return on advertising, return on loyalty programs, and even return on corporate citizenship, given a particular shift in customer perceptions. This approach enables firms to focus marketing efforts on strategic initiatives that generate the greatest return.

Sources: R. T. Rust, K. N. Lemon, and V. A. Zeithaml, "Return on Marketing: Using Customer Equity to Focus Marketing Strategy," *Journal of Marketing* 68, no. 1 (January 2004), pp. 109; R. Rust, V. Zeithaml, and K. Lemon, *Driving Customer Equity* (New York: The Free Press, 2000).

the right were identified as most important in leading to the concepts on the left, and the sequence of concepts from top to bottom show the relationships among company strategies (such as selection and staffing) and intermediate results (such as employee and customer satisfaction) that result in financial results (such as sustained profitability and shareholder value). The study found that fewer than 30 percent of the firms surveyed used this causal modelling approach.

500   Part 7   *Service and the Bottom Line*

2. *Not validating the links.* Only 21 percent of companies in the study verify that the nonfinancial measures lead to financial performance. Instead, many firms decide what they are going to measure in each category and never link the categories. Many managers believed that the relationships were self-evident instead of conducting analysis to validate the linkages. Exhibit 18.3 shows one way companies can create this type of linkage. In general, it is critical that companies pull together all their data and examine the relationships among the categories.

3. *Not setting the right performance targets.* Companies sometimes aim too high in setting improvement targets. Targeting 100 percent customer satisfaction might seem to be a desirable goal, but many companies expend far too many resources to gain too little improvement in satisfaction. The study's authors found that a telecommunications company aiming for 100 percent customer satisfaction was wasting resources because customers who were 100 percent satisfied spent no more money than those who were 80 percent satisfied.[37]

4. *Measuring incorrectly.* Companies need to use metrics with statistical validity and reliability. Organizations cannot measure complex phenomenon with one or two simple measures, nor can they use inconsistent methodologies to measure the same concept, such as customer satisfaction. Another problem that companies may encounter is trying to use quantitative metrics to capture qualitative results for important factors such as leadership and innovation.

Creating a balanced scorecard in and of itself does not improve performance. Companies will not reap the benefits of techniques such as the balanced scorecard unless they address these four issues.

SUMMARY

This chapter is divided into six sections, five of which assess the evidence and identify what is currently known about the relationship between service and profitability. The chapter used a conceptual framework to link all the variables in these topics: (1) the direct relationship between service and profits; (2) offensive effects of service quality; (3) defensive effects of service quality; (4) the relationship between service quality and purchase intentions; (5) key drivers of service quality, customer retention, and profits. Considerable progress has been made in the last 10 years in the investigation of service quality, profitability, and the economic worth of customers, but managers are still lacking many of the answers that would help them make informed decisions about service quality investments. The chapter concluded with a discussion of the balanced performance scorecard approach to measuring corporate performance, which offers a strategic approach for measuring all aspects of a company's performance.

Discussion Questions

1. Why has it been difficult for executives to understand the relationship between service improvements and profitability in their companies?

2. What is the ROSQ model, and what is its significance to corporate America?

3. To this day, many companies believe that service is a cost rather than a revenue producer. Why might they hold this view? How would you argue the opposite view?

4. What is the difference between offensive and defensive marketing? How does service affect each of these?

5. What are the main sources of profit in defensive marketing?

6. What are the main sources of profit in offensive marketing?

7. How will the balanced performance scorecard help us understand and document the information presented in this chapter? Which of the five sections that discuss different aspects of the relationship between service quality and profits can it illuminate?

Exercises

1. On the Internet, use a search engine to locate three companies that make balanced scorecard software. What are the software companies' current offerings? How can the software firms help individual companies understand the concepts and relationships discussed in this chapter? Which of the three companies would you select based on the information you locate?

2. Interview a local firm and see what it knows about its key drivers of financial performance. What are the key service drivers of the firm? Does the company know whether these service drivers relate to profit?

3. Select a service industry (such as fast food) or a company (such as McDonald's) that you are familiar with, either as a customer or employee, and create a balanced scorecard. Describe the operational, customer, financial, and learning measures that could be used to capture performance.

Notes

1. R. T. Rust, A. J. Zahorik, and T. L. Keiningham, *Return on Quality* (Chicago: Probus, 1994).

2. R. T. Rust, C. Moorman, and P. R. Dickson, "Getting Return on Quality: Revenue Expansion, Cost Reduction, or Both?" *Journal of Marketing* 66 (October 2002), pp. 7–24.

3. Ibid.

4. J. Matthews and P. Katel, "The Cost of Quality: Faced with Hard Times, Business Sours on Total Quality Management," *Newsweek,* September 7, 1992, pp. 48–49; "The Cracks in Quality," *The Economist* 18 (April 1992), pp. 67–68; *Management Practice, U.S. Companies Improve Performance Through Quality Efforts,* Report No. GAO/NSIAD-91-190 (Washington, DC: U.S. General Accounting Office, 1992).

5. R. Rust, B. Subramanian, and M. Wells, "Making Complaints a Management Tool," *Marketing Management* 3 (1993), pp. 40–45.

6. E. Nelson, R. T. Rust, A. Zahorik, R. L. Rose, P. Batalden, and B. Siemanski, "Do Patient Perceptions of Quality Relate to Hospital Financial Performance?" *Journal of Healthcare Marketing,* December 1992, pp. 1–13.

7. D. A. Aaker and R. Jacobson, "The Financial Information Content of Perceived Quality," *Journal of Marketing* 58 (May 1994), pp. 191–201.

8. National Quality Institute, "Investing in Excellence: A Wise Choice. Celebrating Organizational Excellence in Canada," 2006, available www.nqi.ca/nqistore/product_details.aspx?ID=145, accessed October 3, 2006.

9. C. Fornell and B. Wernerfelt, "Defensive Marketing Strategy by Customer Complaint Management: A Theoretical Analysis," *Journal of Marketing Research* 24 (November 1987), pp. 337–46; see also C. Fornell and B. Wernerfelt, "A Model for Customer Complaint Management," *Marketing Science* 7 (Summer 1988), pp. 271–86.

10. B. Gale, "Monitoring Customer Satisfaction and Market-Perceived Quality," *American Marketing Association Worth Repeating Series,* no. 922CS01 (Chicago: American Marketing Association, 1992).

11. Ibid.

12. R. E. Kordupleski, R. T. Rust, and A. J. Zahorik, "Why Improving Quality Doesn't Improve Quality (or Whatever Happened to Marketing?)," *California Management Review* 35 (1993), pp. 82–95.

13. Fornell and Wernerfelt, "Defensive Marketing Strategy by Customer Complaint Management" and "A Model for Customer Complaint Management."

14. T. J. Peters, *Thriving on Chaos* (New York: Alfred A. Knopf, 1988).

15. F. Reichheld and E. Sasser, "Zero Defections: Quality Comes to Services," *Harvard Business Review,* September/October 1990, p. 106.

16. Ibid., p. 105.

17. D. F. Colicchio, regional quality manager, Hewlett-Packard Company, personal communication.

18. S. Rose, "The Coming Revolution in Credit Cards," *Journal of Retail Banking,* Summer 1990, pp. 17–19.

19. J. L. Heskett, W. E. Sasser, Jr. and L. A. Schlesinger, *The Service Profit Chain* (New York: The Free Press, 1997).

20. A. Woodside, L. Frey, and R. Daly, "Linking Service Quality, Customer Satisfaction and Behavioral Intentions," *Journal of Health Care Marketing* 9 (December 1989), pp. 5–17.

21. E. W. Anderson and M. Sullivan, "The Antecedents and Consequences of Customer Satisfaction for Firms," *Marketing Science* 12 (Spring 1992), pp. 125–43.

22. W. Boulding, R. Staelin, A. Kalra, and V. A. Zeithaml, "Conceptualizing and Testing a Dynamic Process Model of Service Quality," report no. 92-121, Marketing Science Institute, 1992.

23. V. A. Zeithaml, L. L. Berry, and A. Parasuraman, "The Behavioral Consequences of Service Quality," *Journal of Marketing* 60 (April 1996), pp. 31–46.

24. J. P. McLaughlin, "Ensuring Customer Satisfaction Is a Strategic Issue, Not Just an Operational One," presentation at the AIC Customer Satisfaction Measurement Conference, Chicago, December 6–7, 1993.

25. Gale, "Monitoring Customer Satisfaction."

26. R. S. Kaplan and D. P. Norton, "The Balanced Scorecard—Measures That Drive Performance," *Harvard Business Review,* January/February 1992, pp. 71–79.
27. Kaplan and Norton, "The Balanced Scorecard."
28. S. Silk, "Automating the Balance Scorecard," *Management Accounting,* May 1998, pp. 38–42.
29. D. A. Light, "Performance Measurement: Investors' Balance Scorecards," *Harvard Business Review,* November/December 1998, pp. 17–20.
30. Marc C. Epstein and Robert A. Westbrook, "Linking Actions to Profits in Strategic Decision Making," *MIT Sloan Management Review* 42, no. 3 (Spring 2004), pp. 39–49.
31. Reichheld and Sasser, "Zero Defections," p. 111.
32. A. Willis, "Using the Balanced Scorecard at the University of Virginia Library: An Interview with Jim Self and Lynda White," *Library Administration and Management* 18 (2004), pp. 64–67.
33. Ibid., p. 66.
34. R. Kaplan and D. Norton, "Plotting Success with 'Strategy Maps,'" *Optimize,* 2004, pp. 61–65.
35. R. S. Kaplan and D. P. Norton, "How Strategy Maps Frame an Organization's Objectives," *Financial Executive* 20 (2004), pp. 40–45.
36. The material in this section comes from C. D. Ittner and D. F. Larcker, "Coming Up Short on Nonfinancial Performance Measurement," *Harvard Business Review,* November 2003, pp. 88–95.
37. Ibid., p. 92.

Index

Chapter **6**

Master Production Scheduling

In this chapter, we discuss constructing and managing a master production schedule (MPS), a central module in the manufacturing planning and control system. An effective master production schedule provides the basis for making good use of manufacturing resources, making customer delivery promises, resolving trade-offs between sales and manufacturing, and attaining the firm's strategic objectives as reflected in the sales and operations plan. The prerequisites to master production scheduling are to define the MPS unit (and associated bill of materials) and to provide the master production scheduler with the supporting concepts and techniques described in this chapter.

This chapter is organized around the following eight topics:

- *The master production scheduling (MPS) activity:* What is the role of master production scheduling in manufacturing planning and control?
- *Master production scheduling techniques:* What are the basic MPS tasks and what techniques are available to aid this process?
- *Bill of materials structuring for the MPS:* How can nonengineering uses of the bill of materials assist the master production scheduling function?
- *The final assembly schedule:* How is the MPS converted into a final build schedule?
- *The master production scheduler:* What does a master production scheduler do and what are the key organizational relationships for this position?
- *Company examples:* How do actual MPS systems work in practice?
- *Master production schedule stability:* How can a stable MPS be developed and maintained?
- *Managing the MPS:* How can MPS performance be monitored and controlled?

This chapter is closely related to Chapter 2 on sales and operations planning and Chapter 3 on demand management. Both of these chapters describe modules that provide important inputs to the MPS function. Chapter 7 describes the material requirements planning activities and Chapter 10 describes the management of capacity. Both of these functions depend on the master production schedule to develop their plans. Chapter 13 describes the importance of aligning the production activities of the firm (largely operationalized through the MPS) with the firm's approach to the market and competition.

The Master Production Scheduling (MPS) Activity

We begin with a brief overview of the role of master production scheduling (MPS) in the manufacturing planning and control (MPC) system. We look at the fundamental role of the MPS in converting the disaggregated sales and operations plan into a specific manufacturing schedule. Next we consider how the environment in which the MPS activity takes place shapes the MPS task. Finally, we discuss the linkages between the MPS, other MPC modules, and other company activities.

At the conceptual level, the master production schedule translates the sales and operations plan of the company into a plan for producing specific products in the future. Where the sales and operations plan provides an aggregate statement of the manufacturing output required to reach company objectives, the MPS is a statement of the specific products that make up that output. The MPS is the translation of the sales and operations plan into producible products with their quantities and timing determined. Paraphrasing Tom Wallace, a noted MPC expert, the role of the sales and operations plan is to balance supply and demand volume, while the MPS specifies the mix and volume of the output.

On a day-to-day basis, the MPS provides the information by which sales and manufacturing are coordinated. The MPS shows when products will be available in the future, thereby providing the basis for sales to promise delivery to customers. These promises will be valid as long as manufacturing executes the MPS according to plan. When conditions arise that create customer promise dates that are unacceptable from a marketing or manufacturing perspective, the MPS provides the basis for making the required trade-offs.

At the operational level, the most basic concern is with the construction of the MPS record and updating it over time. The MPS record is developed to be compatible with the material requirements planning (MRP) system and to provide the information for coordinating with sales. Over time, as production is completed and products are used to meet customer requirements, the MPS record must be kept up to date. Doing this means implementing a periodic review and update cycle that we term "rolling through time." Updating the record involves processing MPS transactions, maintaining the MPS record, responding to exception conditions, and measuring MPS effectiveness on a routine basis. Performing these tasks effectively will keep manufacturing resources and output aligned with the sales and operations plan.

The MPS Is a Statement of Future Output

The master production schedule is a statement of planned future output. It specifies the products (or product options) that will be completed, the time of completion and the quantities to be completed. It is the anticipated build schedule for the company. As such, it is a statement of production, not a statement of demand. The MPS specifies how product will be supplied to meet future demand. We stress the fact that the MPS is *not* a forecast, since manufacturing is held responsible for meeting the MPS requirements.

The forecast is an important input into the planning process that determines the master production schedule, but the MPS differs from the forecast in significant ways. The MPS takes into account capacity limitations, the costs of production, other resource considerations, and the sales and operations plan. As a consequence, the MPS may specify large batches of product when the demand is for single units. Or production may take place in advance of market demand in order to better utilize production capacity. It is even possible that product for which there is forecast demand may not even be made.

As the statement of output, the master production schedule forms the basic communication link between the market and manufacturing. The MPS is stated in product specifications—in part numbers for which there are **bills of materials (BOM),** the language of product manufacturing. Since the MPS is a build schedule, it must be stated in terms used to determine component-part needs and other requirements. It can't, therefore, be stated in overall dollars or some other global unit of measure. It must be in terms that relate to a producible product.

The MPS can be stated in specific end-item product designations, but this is not always the case. The MPS units might be options or modules from which a variety of end products could be assembled. Alternatively, the MPS might be stated in a number of units of an "average" final product—for example, an average Dell Latitude D series laptop. Doing this requires a special **planning bill of materials** designed to produce the parts and components necessary to build a number of laptops whose "average" configuration would correspond to the average Latitude D laptop. Converting the options, parts, and components into specific end products would be controlled by a separate **final assembly schedule (FAS),** which isn't ascertained until the last possible moment. The choice of MPS unit is largely dictated by the environment in which the MPS is implemented, a topic to which we now turn our attention.

The Business Environment for the MPS

The business environment, as it relates to master production scheduling, encompasses the production approach used, the variety of products produced, and the markets served by the company. Three basic production environments have been identified: make-to-stock, make-to-order, and assemble-to-order. Each of these environments affects the design of the MPS system, primarily through the choice of the unit used for stating the MPS—that is whether the MPS is stated in end-item terms, some average end item, product modules or options, or specific customer orders.

The **make-to-stock** company produces in batches, carrying finished goods inventories for most, if not all, of its end items. The MPS is the production statement of how much of and when each end item is to be produced. Firms that make to stock are often producing consumer products as opposed to industrial goods, but many industrial goods, such as supply items, are also made to stock.

The choice of MPS unit for the make-to-stock company is fairly straightforward. All use end-item catalogue numbers, but many tend to group these end items into model groupings until the latest possible time in the final assembly schedule. Thus, the Ethan Allen Furniture Company uses a **consolidated item number** for items identical except for the finish color, running a separate system to allocate a lot size in the MPS to specific finishes at the last possible moment. Similarly, the Black & Decker tool manufacturing firm groups models in a series, such as sanders, which are similar, except for horsepower, attachments, and private-brand labels. All products so grouped are run together in batches to achieve economical runs for component parts and to exploit the learning curve in the final assembly areas.

The **make-to-order** (or **engineer-to-order**) company, in general, carries no finished-goods inventory and builds each customer order as needed. This form of production is often used when there's a very large number of possible production configurations, and, thus, a small probability of anticipating a customer's exact needs. In this business environment, customers expect to wait for a large portion of the entire design and manufacturing lead time. Examples include a tugboat manufacturer or refinery builder.

In the make-to-order company, the MPS unit is typically defined as the particular end item or set of items composing a customer order. The definition is difficult since part of the job is to define the product; that is, design takes place as construction takes place. Production often starts before a complete product definition and bill of materials have been determined.

The **assemble-to-order** firm is typified by an almost limitless number of possible end item configurations, all made from combinations of basic components and subassemblies. Customer delivery time requirements are often shorter than total manufacturing lead times, so production must be started in anticipation of customer orders. The large number of end-item possibilities makes forecasting exact end-item configurations extremely difficult, and stocking end items very risky. As a result, the assemble-to-order firm tries to maintain flexibility, starting basic components and subassemblies into production, but, in general, not starting final assembly until a customer order is received.

Examples of assemble-to-order firms include Dell and IBM with their endless variety of computer end-item combinations; the Hyster Company, which makes forklift trucks with such options as engine type, lift height, cab design, speed, type of lift mechanism, and safety equipment; and Mack Trucks, which produces trucks with many driver/owner-specified options. None of these firms know until the last minute the specific choices their customers will make.

The assemble-to-order firm typically doesn't develop a master production schedule for end items. The MPS unit is stated in planning bills of materials, such as an average Hyster forklift truck of some model series or an average Mack highway truck. The MPS unit has as its components a set of common part and options. The option usages are based on percentage estimates, and their planning in the MPS incorporates **buffering** or **hedging** techniques to maximize response flexibility to actual customer orders.

We've said here that the primary difference between make-to-stock, make-to-order, and assemble-to-order firms is in the definition of the MPS unit. However, most master production scheduling techniques are useful for any kind of MPS unit definition. Moreover, the choice of the MPS unit is somewhat open to definition by the firm. Thus some firms may produce end items that are held in inventory, yet still use assemble-to-order approaches. Also, some firms use more than one of these approaches at the same time, so common systems across all approaches are important.

Linkages to Other Company Activities

Figure 6.1 presents a partial schematic for the overall manufacturing planning and control system showing the linkages to master production scheduling. The detailed schedule produced by the MPS drives all the engine and, subsequently, the back-end systems, as well as the rough-cut capacity planning activities. All the feedback linkages aren't shown in the figure, however. For example, as execution problems are discovered, there are many mechanisms for their resolution, with feedback to the MPS and to the other MPC modules.

The linkages to the enterprise resource planning (ERP) system of the firm are shown as indirect, but they are important. All of the major ERP vendors have a master production

FIGURE 6.1
Master Production Scheduling in the MPC System

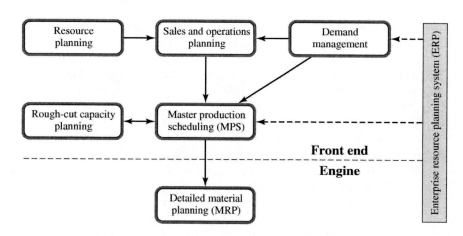

scheduling module. The role of the MPS in an ERP system is the same as we have described here: disaggregating the sales and operations plan, creating a statement of the output from the factory, and providing the information for coordinating sales and manufacturing. The records for a particular ERP system may look different from the version that we use here, but all of the functions will be included.

The demand management block in Figure 6.1 represents a company's forecasting, order entry, order promising, and physical distribution activities. Demand management collects data on all sources of demand for manufacturing capacity: customer orders, forecasts of future customer orders, warehouse replenishments, interplant transfers, spare parts requirements, and so forth. These forecasts are summarized and provided to sales and operations planning. Moreover, demand management books customer orders (enters the order, determines a delivery date with the customer and provides product details to manufacturing). These booked orders are also provided to master production scheduling to coordinate product availability with customer requirements.

In sales and operations planning, the forecasts from demand management will be consolidated and incorporated into the sales and operations plan. This is sometimes referred to as the *company game plan*. The operations plan is a statement of the aggregate output that will meet the objectives of the firm, both quantitatively and qualitatively. In some firms this plan is stated in terms of the sales dollars generated for the company as a whole or for individual plants or regions. In other firms it is stated as the number of units of output to be produced in the next year. The aggregate operations plan constrains the MPS, since the sum of the detailed MPS quantities must always equal the whole as defined by the operations plan.

Rough-cut capacity planning involves an analysis of the master production schedule to discover the existence of any manufacturing resources that represent potential bottlenecks in the production flow. This is the linkage that provides a rough evaluation of potential capacity problems with a particular MPS. If any problems are disclosed, they must be resolved before attempting to execute the MPS.

The disaggregation of the operations plan into production plans for specific products defines the product mix that will be produced. These plans also provide the basic demand "forecast" for each MPS production unit. It is on the basis of these forecast data that the master production schedule is developed. The MPS, in turn, provides the input (gross requirement) data to the material requirements planning system. The MPS, then, is the driver of all the detailed manufacturing activities needed to meet the output objectives of the firm.

The MPS also is the basis for key interfunctional trade-offs. The most profound of these is between production and sales. The specification of exact production output, in terms of products, dates, and quantities, provides the basis for promising delivery to customers. Moreover, when there is a request to increase the output for any one item, the MPS helps determine which item should be reduced in output in order to stay within the capacity constraints. If the production for no item can be reduced, by definition, the operations plan and resultant budget for manufacturing and the firm must be changed.

Since the MPS is an important input to the manufacturing budget, it follows that financial budgets should be integrated with master production scheduling activities. When the MPS is extended over a time horizon sufficient to make capital equipment purchases, a better basis is provided for capital budgets. On a day-to-day basis, both cash flow and profits can be better forecast by basing the estimates on the planned production output specified in the MPS.

Master Production Scheduling Techniques

This section presents some useful basic techniques for master production scheduling. We start out with the time-phased record to show relationships between production output, the "forecast" (derived from the sales and operations plan), and expected inventory balance. This record provides an integration of information that, up until the advent of ERP systems, was often scattered throughout the firm (and far too frequently still is). We then show how plans are revised as you roll through time during a review cycle. This is when actual conditions are taken into account and the record is updated. Finally, we present the process for promising delivery to customers. This process illustrates how the actual customer orders "consume" the forecast.

The Time-Phased Record

Using time-phased records as a basis for MPS preparation and maintenance means that they can be produced easily by computer, and they're consistent with MRP record formats. Figure 6.2 shows a highly simplified example of a master production schedule involving an item with a beginning inventory of 20 units, sales forecast of 10 units per week, and MPS of 10 units per week as well. The MPS row states the timing for *completion* of units available to meet demand. Data in this record show the expected conditions as of the current

FIGURE 6.2
MPS Example

| | Week Number | | | | | | | | | | | |
	1	2	3	4	5	6	7	8	9	10	11	12
Forecast	10	10	10	10	10	10	10	10	10	10	10	10
Available	20	20	20	20	20	20	20	20	20	20	20	20
MPS	10	10	10	10	10	10	10	10	10	10	10	10
On hand	20											

week (the first week in the master production schedule). The record covers a 12-week period (planning horizon) for which total sales forecast is 120 units. The total MPS is also 120 units.

The projected available inventory balance (available) is shown in the second row of the record in Figure 6.2. The "Available" row represents the expected inventory position at the end of each week in the 12-week schedule. It results from adding to the starting inventory of 20 units the MPS of 10 units per week, and subtracting the sales forecast of 10 units per week. Any negative values in the projected available inventory row represent expected back orders.

There are several reasons for maintaining a positive projected inventory balance. Forecasts involve some degree of error, and the MPS is a plan for production that may not be exactly achieved. The projected inventory balance provides a tolerance for errors that buffers production from sales variations. For example, in Figure 6.2, if actual sales in week 1 were 20 units and the MPS was achieved, there would be no back order. Furthermore, if the marketing department still expected total sales for the overall 12 weeks to be 120 units (implying some weeks' sales would be less than the forecast of 10), production can continue at the rate of 10 units per week and still end up with the same planned inventory at the end of week 12.

The MPS row indicates the quantity and time of completion of production. Details for starting production of the various components and assembly of the product are taken care of by the MRP system. In this sense, the MPS drives the MRP system, as shown in Figure 6.1. We'll discuss several of the many alternative MPS plans. All start from the basic logic used to project the expected available inventory balance.

Figure 6.3 presents a different sales forecast from that in Figure 6.2. In Figure 6.3, the marketing department expects sales of 5 units per week for the first 6 weeks and 15 units per week for the next 6 weeks. The overall result is the same: total sales of 120 units during the 12-week period, but sales are seasonal. Figures 6.3 and 6.4 show two different master production schedules to meet this sales forecast. The MPS in Figure 6.3 represents a level 10-unit-per-week production rate over the 12-week planning horizon. The MPS in

FIGURE 6.3
A Level Production MPS Approach to Seasonal Sales

	Week Number											
	1	2	3	4	5	6	7	8	9	10	11	12
Forecast	5	5	5	5	5	5	15	15	15	15	15	15
Available	25	30	35	40	45	50	45	40	35	30	25	20
MPS	10	10	10	10	10	10	10	10	10	10	10	10
On hand	20											

FIGURE 6.4
A Chase Sales MPS Approach to Seasonal Sales

	Week Number											
	1	2	3	4	5	6	7	8	9	10	11	12
Forecast	5	5	5	5	5	5	15	15	15	15	15	15
Available	20	20	20	20	20	20	20	20	20	20	20	20
MPS	5	5	5	5	5	5	15	15	15	15	15	15
On hand	20											

FIGURE 6.5
Lot Sizing in
the MPS

	Week Number											
	1	**2**	**3**	**4**	**5**	**6**	**7**	**8**	**9**	**10**	**11**	**12**
Forecast	5	5	5	5	5	5	15	15	15	15	15	15
Available	15	10	5	30	25	20	5	20	5	20	5	20
MPS				30				30		30		30
On hand	20											

Figure 6.4, however, adjusts for the difference in sales forecasts, calling for 5 units of production per week for the first 6 weeks, and 15 units per week for the next 6 weeks.

Comparing the projected available rows in Figures 6.3 and 6.4 indicates the difference in inventory between the two MPS plans during the 12-week period. They start and end with the same inventory; but the MPS in Figure 6.3 builds up inventory during the first six weeks, which is gradually depleted during the last six weeks, while the MPS in Figure 6.4 maintains a constant inventory. These two master production schedules represent two extreme strategies. The MPS in Figure 6.3 is a **"leveling" strategy;** the MPS in Figure 6.4 is a **"chase" strategy.** The level MPS calls for no production, workforce, or other capacity adjustments. The chase MPS, on the other hand, requires production adjustments to chase the demands of the marketplace. There are, obviously, many alternative MPS plans between these two extremes. The goal is to find that plan that best balances the cost and benefits.

Figure 6.5 presents the same sales forecast as Figure 6.3, but it incorporates a lot size of 30 units. In Figure 6.5, a lot of 30 units is scheduled for completion in any week when projected available balance would fall below 5 units. This trigger quantity of 5 units reflects a managerial trade-off between carrying inventory and incurring possible back orders.

The projected available balance starts at the beginning inventory position of 20 units and would drop below the 5-unit trigger in the fourth week, so a 30-unit order is scheduled for the fourth week. This order lasts until the eighth week, when the 5-unit level again would be broken. Figure 6.5 shows a total of 4 batches of 30 units being produced over the 12-week planning horizon. The first batch lasts for 6 weeks, while subsequent batches last only for 2 weeks.

Manufacturing in batches of 30 units produces inventories that last between production runs. This inventory, called **cycle stock,** is part of the projected available inventory row in Figure 6.5. The cycle stock could be cut by reducing the lot size for the whole schedule or even just during the first 6 weeks. Similarly, if the company felt overall inventory investment was too high for this MPS, the 5-unit trigger could be reduced. This would provide less **safety stock** protection against forecast errors or manufacturing problems.

Rolling through Time

Now let's turn to Murphy's law: If anything can go wrong, it will. Rolling through time requires updating the record to define how the MPS reflects actual conditions. It's necessary not only to construct the MPS but also to process actual transactions and modify the MPS.

Figure 6.6 shows the situation at the start of the second week (now for weeks 2 through 13), using the original MPS for the 12-week period as given in Figure 6.5. No material was received during the first week, since none was planned by the MPS. But actual sales were 10 units instead of 5 units, and actual inventory at the end of the first week (also the start of week 2) is 10 units (instead of 15).

176   Chapter 6   *Master Production Scheduling*

FIGURE 6.6
Using the Revised Forecast after One Week

	Week Number											
	2	3	4	5	6	7	8	9	10	11	12	13
Forecast	10	10	10	10	10	15	15	15	15	15	15	15
Available	0	−10	10	0	−10	−25	−10	−25	−10	−25	−10	−25
MPS			30				30		30		30	
On hand	10											

FIGURE 6.7
MPS Revisions to Accommodate Revised Forecast after One Week

	Week Number											
	2	3	4	5	6	7	8	9	10	11	12	13
Forecast	10	10	10	10	10	15	15	15	15	15	15	15
Available	30	20	10	30	20	5	20	5	20	5	20	5
MPS	30			30			30		30		30	
On hand	10											

In light of the higher-than-expected sales during the first week, it's reasonable to ask whether the sales forecast is still valid; that is, does the marketing department still believe that total sales for weeks 1 through 12 will be 120 units? What's the forecast for week 13? Let's say the marketing department has decided that the original forecast was incorrect. A new forecast at the end of the first week is for 10 units per week for the next 5 weeks (2 through 6) and 15 units per week for the following 7 weeks (7 through 13). This would total 155 units for the new 12-week planning horizon. Since the new 12-week forecast incorporates 35 more units than the original 12-week forecast, it's greater than the planned production indicated by the MPS of Figure 6.5. Figure 6.6 shows the implications of the new forecast without a revised MPS. Clearly, some adjustment to the MPS is required if anticipated customer needs are to be met. The first potential problem is seen in week 3 of the MPS, where projected available inventory goes negative. The original master production schedule called for the first batch of 30 units in week 4 and the next batch in week 8. That's not sufficient to meet the revised forecast made at the end of week 1.

The revised MPS in Figure 6.7 uses the same 5-unit trigger inventory logic used to establish the lot-sized master schedule in Figure 6.5. Figure 6.7 calls for five batches of 30 units to be produced during the MPS plan, instead of the four batches in Figures 6.5 and 6.6. This revision solves the problem of projected negative available inventory but puts in clear focus the question of feasibility. Does the company have the capacity to produce five batches during the next 12 weeks, or to immediately deliver a batch that was planned for 2 weeks hence? The capacity issue must be resolved before the new MPS is put into effect. Furthermore, high costs are typically associated with making production changes. The master production schedule should be buffered from overreaction, with changes made only when essential.

Order Promising

For many products, customers don't expect immediate delivery, but place orders for future delivery. The delivery date (promise date) is negotiated through a cycle of order promising,

FIGURE 6.8
Order
Promising
Example:
Week 1

						Week Number							
	1	2	3	4	5	6	7	8	9	10	11	12
Forecast	5	5	5	5	5	5	15	15	15	15	15	15
Orders	5	3	2									
Available	15	10	5	30	25	20	5	20	5	20	5	20
ATP	10			30				30		30		30
MPS				30				30		30		30

On hand = 20

$$ATP = 20 - (5 + 3 + 2) = 10$$

FIGURE 6.9
Order
Promising
Example:
Week 2

						Week Number							
	2	3	4	5	6	7	8	9	10	11	12	13
Forecast	10	10	10	10	10	15	15	15	15	15	15	15
Orders	5	5	2									
Available	30	20	10	30	20	5	20	5	20	5	20	5
ATP	28			30			30		30		30	
MPS	30			30			30		30		30	

On hand = 10

$$ATP = (30 + 10) - (5 + 5 + 2) = 28$$

where the customer either asks when the order can be shipped or specifies a desired shipment date. If the company has a backlog of orders for future shipments, the order promising task is to determine when the shipment can be made. These activities are illustrated in Figures 6.8 and 6.9.

Figure 6.8 builds on the lot-sized MPS depicted in Figure 6.5. The original sales forecast and MPS as of the beginning of week 1 are shown. In addition, we now consider the sales forecast row to be for shipments. That is, we're forecasting when items will be shipped; and we're closing out the forecast with shipments, not with sales. The distinction separates various forms of sales (e.g., receipt of order or billing) from the manufacturing concern with actual physical movement of the goods.

The row labeled "Orders" represents the company's backlog of orders at the start of the first week. Five units were promised for shipment in the first week, three more for week 2, and an additional two units were promised for delivery in week 3. Thus, the cumulative order backlog is 10 units over the three weeks. The **available-to-promise (ATP)** value of 10 units for week 1 is calculated in the bottom portion of Figure 6.8. The on-hand inventory (20 units) has to cover all existing customer orders until the next scheduled MPS (5 + 3 + 2).

As in our previous example, we assume actual shipments in week 1 were 10 units. This means five of the units shipped in week 1 weren't on the books as sold orders at the week's start; that is, 50 percent of the orders shipped during week 1 were received during the week. This percentage varies greatly among companies.

Figure 6.9 shows the status as of the start of week 2. Figure 6.8's sales forecast and MPS have been revised in the same way as the revision from Figure 6.5 to Figure 6.7. Furthermore, additional customer orders were received during the first week for shipping in weeks 2 through 4. At the start of week 1, we had three units due to be shipped during week 2. Two additional units have been booked during week 1 for week 2 shipment, so the total backlog at the beginning of week 2 for shipment during week 2 is five units. An additional three units have been booked for shipment during week 3 and an additional two units for week 4 shipment. We see then that the cumulative order backlog at the beginning of week 2 is 12 units over the 12-week planning horizon. The increase in the cumulative order backlog from 10 to 12 units over a three-week period may well have been one of the key inputs the marketing department used in revising its sales forecasts.

Orders booked for shipment in week 2 in Figure 6.9 are 5 units, while forecast total shipment in this week is 10 units. We expect to receive orders for 5 additional units during week 2 to be shipped during week 2. Carrying this analysis further, we see the cumulative backlog for weeks 2 and 3 to be 10 units, and the cumulative forecast for the same 2 weeks to be 20 units. This implies that, between the start of week 2 and the end of week 3, we expect to receive orders for 10 additional units to be shipped during that two-week period.

A more interesting relationship is seen between the order backlog and the MPS. The order backlog for week 2 in Figure 6.9 is 5 units, and the anticipated production plus beginning inventory is 40 units. This suggests we still have 35 units to use to meet additional customer requests; that is, it looks like we could make total shipments of up to 35 units in addition to what's already promised in week 2.

This isn't true; we can only accept 28 *additional* units for shipment during week 2; that is, we only have 28 units "available to promise." The reason is that the next scheduled production for this item isn't until week 5; therefore, as shown in the bottom portion of Figure 6.9, the beginning inventory of 10 units plus the 30 units in the master schedule for week 2 have to cover all existing orders for weeks 2 through 4. Since we already have orders for 12 units on the books for shipment during that period, we can only accept up to 28 additional units. That is why Figure 6.9 shows a value of 28 units in ATP for week 2. Those 28 units could be shipped any time during weeks 2, 3, or 4, or any other week in the future.

An important convention about the format of the time-phased MPS record in Figures 6.8 and 6.9 concerns the available row. The available row is the expected ending inventory. A frequently encountered convention is to use the greater of forecast or booked orders in any period for projecting the available inventory balance. In our example in Figures 6.8 and 6.9, actual customer orders never exceed forecasts for the periods. The general calculation for the available row is: previous available + MPS − (greater of forecast or orders).

The available-to-promise logic is a bit harder to state neatly. An ATP value is calculated for each period in which there is an MPS quantity. In the first period, it's the on-hand plus any first-period MPS minus the sum of all orders until the next MPS. For later periods, it's the MPS minus all orders in that and subsequent periods until the next MPS. Both of these rules, however, have to be modified to reflect subsequent-period ATP deficiencies. Figure 6.9 now shows 30 units as ATP in weeks 5, 8, 10, and 12. These quantities match the MPS quantities and reflect the lack of customer orders beyond week 4. Suppose an order for 35 units was booked for week 10 in Figure 6.9. The ATP for week 10 would be zero, and the ATP for week 8 would fall to 25. That is, the 35-unit order in week 10 is to be satisfied by 30 units produced in week 10 and 5 from the MPS produced in week 8.

Some companies choose to show the available-to-promise row as cumulative (58 in week 5). However, keeping the additional increments of ATP separate makes order promising easier and also has the advantage of not overstating the availability position; that is, there are not really 58 available to promise in week 5 as well as 28 in week 2. Some software packages provide ATP both as indicated in Figure 6.8 *and* in cumulative format.

In many firms, accurate order promising allows the company to operate with reduced inventory levels; that is, order promising allows the actual shipments to be closer to the MPS. Companies in effect buffer uncertainties in demand by their delivery date promises. Rather than carry safety stocks to absorb uneven customer order patterns, those firms "manage" the delivery dates.

Consuming the Forecast

One authority on master production scheduling, Richard Ling, originated the idea that actual customer orders "consume" the forecast; that is, we start out with an estimate (the forecast), and actual orders come in to consume (either partially, fully, or over) the estimate. We see this in Figure 6.9. Of the 10 units forecast for week 2, 5 have been consumed. For week 3, 5 of 10 have been consumed, as have 2 of the 10 for week 4.

Let's consider Figure 6.9 and see if, during week 2, we can accept the following hypothetical set of customer orders, assuming they were received in the sequence listed:

Order Number	Amount	Desired Week
1	5	2
2	15	3
3	35	6
4	10	5

The answer is yes to all but order number 4. Since the total amount requested is 65, and the cumulative amount available to promise is only 58 for weeks 2 through 6 (28 in week 2 plus 30 in week 5), only 3 units of order number 4 could be shipped in this period. Let's say the customer would not accept a partial delivery, so we negotiated for delivery in week 8. Figure 6.10 shows the time-phased record at the beginning of week 3 if no more orders were received in week 2 and the forecast for week 14 is incorporated.

FIGURE 6.10
Order
Promising
Example:
Week 3

	Week Number												
	3	4	5	6	7	8	9	10	11	12	13	14
Forecast	10	10	10	10	15	15	15	15	15	15	15	15
Orders	20	2		35		10						
Available	10	0	20	−15	−30	−15	−30	−15	−30	−15	−30	−45
ATP	3		0			20		30		30		
MPS			30			30		30		30		
On hand	30											

Obviously, the set of orders received during week 2 represents a major deviation from the forecast. However, it does allow us to see clearly how we can use the record to make decisions as we roll through time. Let's first review the process's arithmetic. To calculate on-hand inventory at the beginning of week 3, we start with week 2's beginning inventory of 10. We add week 2's MPS of 30; then we subtract the orders for 5 units shipped in week 2 (shown in Figure 6.9) and we subtract the order for week 2 just promised (5 units). The result is $10 + 30 - 5 - 5 = 30$.

The available row provides the master production scheduler with a projection of the item availability throughout the planning horizon in a manner analogous to projecting an on-hand inventory balance in an MRP record. The convention of subtracting the "greater of forecast or orders" and adding the MPS quantities to calculate the available row has an effect here. For week 3 in Figure 6.10, for example, the available is the 30 units of inventory minus the 20 units on order, for a total of 10. In week 4, the available quantity is 0, the difference between the week 3 available of 10 and the forecast of 10. The use of the greater of forecasts or orders for calculating the available row is consistent with forecast consumption. If actual orders exceed forecast, there has been an "over" consumption that should be taken into account. As actual orders are less than forecasts, the result will appear in the on-hand balance (a gross-to-net process); this also impacts the available calculations.

The available position at the end of the planning horizon is important information for managing the master production schedule, as is the existence of negative available data during the planning horizon. During the planning horizon there is typically some length of time in which changes are to be made only if absolutely essential, to provide stability for planning and execution. At the end of this period, master production schedulers have maximum flexibility to create additional MPS quantities. If the projected available is positive in the time bucket at the end of this period, then scheduling more production of the item may not be necessary. Note, for example, at the start of week 2 in Figure 6.9 the week 13 available was 5 and no MPS quantity was entered for week 13. At the start of week 3 in Figure 6.10, the available for week 14 is −45, because of consumption of the forecast by orders booked in week 2. This indicates that in week 3 the master production scheduler should consider scheduling production for completion in week 14. The negative available numbers for weeks 6 through 14 indicate desire for more MPS during the planning horizon. Whether this can be achieved is a matter of response time, availability of materials, and competing needs (other items).

The convention of the greater of forecast or orders means large orders will be immediately reflected in the availability position. This signals the master production scheduler to consider responding to the order by increasing future item availability, which can be used for booking future orders. Separately the available-to-promise row controls the actual order promising. A related question for sales is whether a large order "consumes" forecast for only one period.

To calculate the available-to-promise position, we consider only actual orders and the scheduled production, as indicated by the MPS. We calculate only the incremental available to promise. Note that in Figure 6.10 the 30 units on hand must cover actual orders for weeks 3 and 4, since no additional production is scheduled. In week 5, 30 additional units are scheduled, but none of them is available to promise. The 3 units available to promise in week 3 come from the 30 on hand minus the 20 units ordered for week 3 and the 2 units ordered for week 4. Another 5 units of those on hand are needed for the order of 35 in week 6, since the MPS of

30 units in week 5 isn't sufficient. This leaves only 3 units available to promise for weeks 3 through 7. Of the 30 units to be produced in week 8, we see 10 will be used for the order in week 8. This leaves 20 units available to promise in week 8.

Note that the later customer orders are covered by the later MPS quantities. The 10-unit order for week 8 could have been covered by 3 units in week 3 plus 7 units in week 8 instead of all 10 in week 8. This would have left no units for promising from week 3 until week 8, greatly reducing promise flexibility. The convention is to preserve early promise flexibility by reducing the available to promise in as late a period as possible.

The use of both the "Available" row and the "ATP" row is the key to effective master production scheduling. Using the ATP to book orders means that no customer promise will be made that can't be kept. Note this may mean some orders must be booked at the end of a planning horizon concurrently with creating an additional MPS quantity. As actual orders are booked (the "Order" row), or anticipated (the "Forecast" row), or shipped (on-hand inventory), the "Available" row provides a signal for the creation of an MPS quantity. Once created, the MPS quantity provides the items available to promise for future orders.

The final item of interest in Figure 6.10 is to again focus on the negative available quantities from weeks 6 through 14. These negative quantities indicate potential problems—but only *potential* problems. However, costly MPS changes should not be made to solve "potential" problems. But a condition that created a negative ATP represents a "real" problem.

The time-phased records in Figures 6.9 and 6.10 are similar to MRP records. In fact, the same data can be integrated with standard MRP formats. The primary advantage of doing so is to obtain standard record processing. However, it's necessary to keep track of actual customer orders and the timings of MPS quantities to make ATP calculations. The result is the company database will need to be expanded.

Mitel Corporation: Order Promising with ATP

Mitel Corporation, headquartered in Kanata, Ontario, Canada, is an international supplier of telecommunications equipment and services. Its product lines include business telephone systems, semiconductors, public switching systems, network enhancement and gateway products, systems development, and software products. Mitel is active in major growth markets such as computer telephony integration and emerging technology systems. By combining its products, services, and knowledge, the company provides solutions to a variety of telecommunication problems for customers.

One of the company's products is a telephone, the Superset 430. The dark gray version of the phone is part number 9116-502-000-NA. The order promising record for this product is shown as Figure 6.11. At the top of the header information is the part number, and product description. Next, data on stock status and availability are given. The "Whs" is the warehouse where the stock is located. The "OH" is the on-hand balance, which might overstate availability because some product is already allocated ("Alc") for a customer, has been picked ("Opk") and is ready to ship to a customer, or is being inspected for damage ("Dmg"). The net result is the amount of product available ("Avl") for delivery to customers in the future. The record has a 13-month horizon, of which only 9 weeks are shown on the screen. The starting availability refers to the beginning of the first week of the record.

The detailed record itself is used to develop the available-to-promise quantities that are used to make order promises to customers. The record displays nine weeks of information

FIGURE 6.11 Order-Promising Record for Mitel

Product: 9116-502-000-NA Description: SUPERSET 430 DARK GREY

Schedule/Stock-by-Week

```
----Whs------OH-----Alc-----OPk-----Dmg------Avl------BkO-----OnO-----Com-----InT-
DIS   1,039                                   1,039
```

APT Horizon: 13 Starting Avl: 1,039

Week Ending	3/8	3/15	3/22	3/29	4/5	4/12	4/19	4/26	5/3
Unal Ship	2	8	3	188	93				
Sch Rcpt / Mfg Rcpt							84		150
Prj OH	1,037	1,029	1,026	838	745	745	829	829	979
Cum B'log	294	292	284	281	93				
ATP	745	745	745	745	745	745	829	829	979

FIGURE 6.12 Update of ATP after Booking Order

-Product----------Description----------------------------Extended Description----------

9116-502-000-NA SUPERSET 430 DARK GREY

Schedule/Stock-by-Week

```
----Whs------OH-----Alc-----OPk-----Dmg------Avl------BkO-----OnO-----Com-----InT-
DIS   1,039                                   1,039
```

ATP Horizon: 13 Starting Avl: 1,039

Week Ending	3/8	3/15	3/22	3/29	4/5	4/12	4/19	4/26	5/3
Unal Ship	2	8	3	188	93	100			
Sch Rcpt / Mfg Rcpt							84		150
Prj OH	1,037	1,029	1,026	838	745	645	729	729	879
Cum B'log	394	392	384	381	193	100			
ATP	645	645	645	645	645	645	729	729	879

using the week ending date as the indicator of the week. The row labeled "Unal Ship" (unallocated shipments) contains the booked customer orders that have not yet been allocated or picked. The second line shows scheduled receipts ("Sch Rcpt"), for items for which purchasing is an alternative, and manufacturing receipts ("Mfg Rcpt"), which come directly from the master production schedule and are managed using a different record. The projected on-hand balance ("Prj OH") is calculated from the booked orders directly, since there is no forecast information included in the Mitel order-promising record. For instance, the starting availability of 1,039 is reduced by the demand of 2 in the week of 3/8 to leave a balance of 1,037. Similarly, the demand of 8 in 3/15 further reduces the balance to 1,029.

The final row on the record totals the cumulative backlog for each week in the future for all subsequent weeks. For week 3/8 it is the sum of the booked orders for the first five weeks, 294. For week 3/15 it is the sum of the first five weeks minus the first week. Since the last booked order occurs in week 4/12, that is the last week for which there is a backlog. The ATP row shows that there are 745 units available to promise up to week 4/19 where an MPS quantity increases the availability. Another MPS quantity increases the ATP in week 5/3. The ATP amount (745) is just the difference between the starting availability and the cumulative backlog for the first six weeks. The record says that up to 745 units can be promised to customers anytime over the next six weeks and that another 84 will be available in seven weeks.

Figure 6.12 shows the results of booking an order for 100 telephones for the week of 4/12. The order increases the cumulative backlog by 100 units to 394 and reduces the ATP to 645 in the first six weeks. Salespeople use this record to inform customers when orders can be delivered. The actual booking of the orders is done formally, however, so there can be no game playing with the quantities. Once an order has been placed and is booked, the record is immediately updated for all subsequent order promises. The record is also updated when there is a change in the master production schedule.

Bill of Materials Structuring for the MPS

The assemble-to-order firm is typified by an almost limitless number of end-item possibilities made from combinations of basic components and subassemblies. For example, the number of unique General Motors automobiles runs into billions! Moreover, each new product option for consumers tends to double the number of end-item possibilities. This means the MPS unit in the assemble-to-order environment can't feasibly be based on end items. Defining other units for master production scheduling means creating special bills of material. In this section, we present a few key definitions to clarify what a bill of material is and is not. Thereafter, we discuss modular bills of materials and planning bills of materials that aid MPS management. With this background, it's possible to see how master production scheduling takes place in the assemble-to-order environment.

Key Definitions

The **bill of materials** is narrowly considered to be an engineering document that specifies the ingredients or subordinate components required physically to make each part number or assembly. A **single-level bill of materials** comprises only those subordinate components that are immediately required, not the components *of* the components. An **indented bill of**

materials is a list of components, from the end item all the way down to the raw materials; it does show the components of the components.

The **bill of materials files** are those computer records designed to provide desired output formats. The term **bill of materials structure** relates to the architecture or overall design for the arrangement of bill of materials files. The bill of materials structure must be such that all desired output formats or reports can be provided. A **bill of materials processor** is a computer software package that organizes and maintains linkages in the bill of materials files as dictated by the overall architecture (bill of materials structure). Most bill of materials processors use the single-level bill of materials and maintain links or chains between single-level files. It's the bill of materials processor that's used in MRP to pass the planned orders for a parent part to gross requirements for its components.

The single-level bill and the indented bill are two alternative output formats of the bill of materials. Alternative output formats are useful for different purposes. For example, the single-level bill supports order launching by providing the data for component availability checking, allocation, and picking. Industrial engineers often use the fully indented bill to determine how to physically put the product together; accountants use it for cost implosions. A fundamental rule is that a company should have one, and only one, set of bills of materials or **product structure** records. This set should be maintained as an entity and be so designed that all legitimate company uses can be satisfied.

An important element of the bill of materials is the designation of a **low-level code number** for each part, component, subassembly, or finished item in the BOM. These are numbers that indicate where in the product structure a particular part or subassembly is with respect to the end item. By convention the highest level (e.g., the end item) is designated level 0. The components of level 0 are designated as level 1 and so forth until the purchased parts and raw materials are designated. Designating level codes facilitates bill of material processing in that all requirements for items at level 0 can be determined and summarized before processing the requirements for level 2. In structuring bills of material for planning purposes, however, it is not always true that the end item is designated as level zero.

The rest of this section presents concepts providing another way of thinking about the bill of materials. The traditional approach is from an engineer's point of view, that is, the way the product is *built*. The key change required to achieve superior master production scheduling for assemble-to-order products is to include bill of materials structures based on the way the product is *sold*. In this way, the bill of materials can support some critical planning and management activities.

Constructing a bill of materials structure or architecture based on how the product is sold, rather than how it's built, offers important advantages. Achieving them, however, isn't without cost. The primary cost is that the resultant bills of materials may no longer relate to the way the product is built. Activities based on *that* structure (e.g., industrial engineering) will have to be based on some new source of data; that is, if the description of how the parts physically go together isn't found in the bill of materials, an alternative set of records must be maintained. Providing alternative means to satisfy these needs can be costly in terms of both file creation and maintenance.

The Modular Bill of Materials

A key use of bill of materials files is in translating the MPS into subordinate components requirements. One bill of materials structure or architecture calls for maintaining all end-

FIGURE 6.13
The MPS
Hourglass

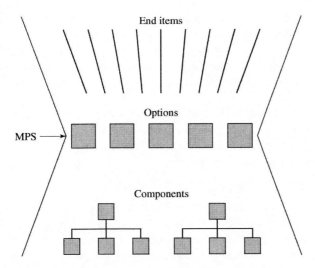

item buildable configurations. This bill of materials structure is appropriate for the make-to-stock firm, where the MPS is stated in end items. For each end item, a single-level bill is maintained, which contains those components that physically go into the item. For General Motors, with its billions of possible end items, this bill of materials structure isn't feasible.

Figure 6.13 shows the dilemma. A solution is to establish the MPS at the option or module level. The intent is to state the MPS in units associated with the "waist" of the hourglass. This necessitates that bill of materials files be structured accordingly; each option or module will be defined fully in the bill of materials files as a single-level bill of materials. Thus, the modular bill of materials structure's architecture links component parts to options, but it doesn't link either options or components to end item configurations. If the options are simply buildable subassemblies, then all that's required for the new architecture is to treat the subassemblies as end items; that is, designate them as level 0, instead of level 1. In most cases, however, the options aren't stated as buildable subassemblies but as options that provide features to the customer.

Consider, for example, the air-conditioning option for a car. The single-level bill of materials would show this option or module as consisting of a particular radiator, fan, hoses, compressor, and interior knobs and levers. These items are not, however, assembled together. They are assembled with still other parts as subassemblies, which eventually are assembled into the automobile.

Using the air-conditioning option as a bill of materials will pass demand from the customer who wants this option down to the necessary parts. It can also be used to forecast demand for air conditioners. However, this bill of materials isn't useful in the physical building process for air conditioners. For example, the air-conditioning knobs are planned by the bill for the air-conditioning option. They aren't planned by the bill of the dashboard assembly where they're installed. Thus, the industrial engineer needs other means to say how the dashboard is to be assembled and from what components. The modular bill of materials focuses on how the car is sold, not how it is made.

Using the modular bill of materials structure for a firm with a situation similar to that in Figure 6.13 permits the MPS to be stated in fewer different units. The MPS is stated in the terms in which the product is *sold,* not in terms in which it's built; that is, air conditioning, two doors, automatic transmission, fancy trim, and so on. The approach is compatible with marketing perceptions of models, options, and trends in options (e.g., more people buying cars with air conditioning), which tends to improve forecasting. Master scheduling may be made easier by using modular bills, but order entry tasks are more complex since each option must be evaluated.

Once the individual customer order (representing a unique collection of options) is entered, it serves the function of a one-time, unique single-level bill of materials; that is, it specifies which options or modules are to be included for the particular customer order. It's controlled by a separate final assembly schedule.

The Planning Bill of Materials

Restructuring the bill of materials to better perform MPS activities has led many people to see that alternative bill of materials approaches have additional applications. An example is the planning bill of materials, which is any use of bill of materials approaches for planning only, as opposed to use for building the products. The modular bill of materials approach just described involves one form of a planning bill, since it's used for developing material plans and modules not all of which are buildable.

The most widely used planning bill of materials is the **super bill.** The super bill describes the related options or modules that make up the *average* end item. For example, an average General Motors J-body car might have 0.6 Chevrolet unique parts, 2.6 doors, 4.3 cylinders, 0.4 air conditioners, and the like. This end item is impossible to build; but using bill of materials logic, it's very useful for planning and master production scheduling. Bill of materials processing dictates that the super bill be established in the product structure files as a legitimate single-level bill of materials. This means that the super bill will show all the possible options as components, with their average decimal usage. The logic of bill of materials processing permits decimal multiples for single-level component usages. The super bill combines the modules, or options, with the decimal usage rates to describe the average car. The bill of materials logic forces arithmetic consistency in the mutually exclusive options; for example, the sum of two possible engine options needs to equal the total number of cars.

The super bill is as much a marketing tool as a manufacturing tool. With it, instead of forecasting and controlling individual modules, the forecast is now stated in terms of total average units, with attention given to percentage breakdowns—to the single-level super bill of materials—and to *managing* module inventories by using available-to-promise logic on a day-to-day basis as actual customer orders are booked.

Let's consider an artificially small example. The Garden Till Company makes rototillers in the following options:

Horsepower: 3 HP, 4 HP, 5 HP.

Drive train: Chain, gear.

Brand name: Taylor, Garden Till, OEM.

The total number of end item buildable units is 18 ($3 \times 2 \times 3$). Management at the end-item level would mean each of these would have to be forecast. Figure 6.14 shows a super bill for 4-horsepower tillers. Using this artificial end item, an average 4-horsepower tiller, only one forecast is needed from marketing. More important, the MPS unit can be the super bill. The entry of 1,000 four-horsepower super bill units into the MPS would plan the

FIGURE 6.14
**The
4-Horsepower
Super Bill**

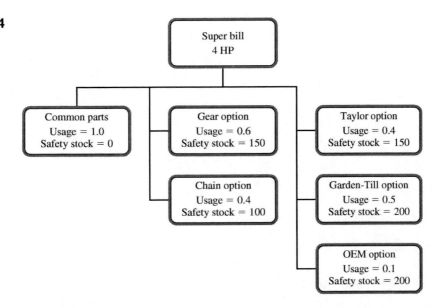

appropriate quantities of each of the options to build 1,000 four-horsepower units in the average option proportions. Actual orders may not reflect the average in the short run, however.

Figure 6.14 shows the use of safety stocks for the options to absorb variations in the mix. No safety stock is shown for the common parts. This means protection is provided for product mix variances but not for variances in the overall MPS quantity of 4-horsepower tillers. A commitment to an MPS quantity for the super bill means exactly that number of common parts will be needed. In Figure 6.14's example, if 1,000 four-horsepower super bills were entered, the bill of materials would call for 1,000 common-parts modules, 600 gear options, 400 chain options, 400 Taylor options, 500 Garden Till options, and 100 OEM options. The safety stocks allow shipments to customers to vary from the usages specified in the bill of materials percentage usage.

Although 600 of the 1,000 four-horsepower tillers are expected to be finished in the gear drive option, as many as 750 can be promised because of the safety stock. Similar flexibility exists for all other options. Safety stocks are maintained with MRP gross to net logic, so appropriate quantities are maintained as actual conditions become reflected in replenishment orders. Moreover, the safety stock will exist in matched sets because of the modular bill of materials structure. Matched sets occur because when one unit of the module is specified for safety stock, *all* parts required for that unit will be planned. Furthermore, costs of all safety stocks are readily visible; marketing can and should have the responsibility to optimize the mix.

Order entry using planning bill of materials concepts tends to be more complex than when the structure is end-item based. To accept a customer order, the available-to-promise logic must be applied to each option in the order, meaning it's necessary to check each of the affected modules. Figure 6.15 shows the flow for a particular customer order, in this case for 25 Taylor 4-horsepower units in the gear option (T4G). The safety stocks are available for promising and will be maintained by the gross to net logic as additional MPS quantities are planned.

FIGURE 6.15
Available-to-Promise Logic with Modular Bill Architecture (order for 25 T4Gs)

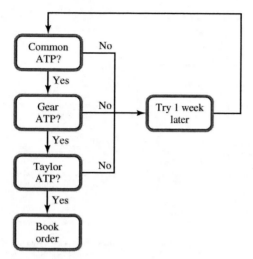

The Final Assembly Schedule

The final assembly schedule (FAS) states the exact set of end products to be built over some time period. It's the schedule that serves to plan and control final assembly and test operations; included are the launching of final assembly orders, picking of component parts, subassembly, painting or other finishing, scheduling the fabrication or purchase of any component items not under MPS control but needed for final assembly, and packing. In short, the FAS controls that portion of the business from fabricated components to completed products ready for shipment. It may be stated in terms of customer orders, end-product items, serial numbers, or special assembly order numbers.

Relation to the MPS

The master production schedule represents an anticipated build schedule. The FAS is the actual build schedule. The MPS disaggregates the production plan into end items, options, or groups of items, whereas the FAS is the last disaggregation—into exact end-item definitions. The distinction is that the MPS generally incorporates forecasts or estimates of actual customer orders in its preparation, with actual orders thereafter imperfectly consuming these forecasts; the FAS represents the last possible adjustment that can be made to the MPS; therefore, it's advisable to make that adjustment as late as possible. Any unsold items on the FAS will become part of the firm's finished-goods inventory.

The FAS is distinct and separate from the MPS. The distinction is most clearly seen in the assemble-to-order environment. There, the MPS is typically stated in super bills and options, whereas the FAS must be stated in terms of the exact end-item configurations. However, even in make-to-stock firms (such as Ethan Allen and Black & Decker), the MPS is stated in consolidated groups of items, such as all models of a table that differ only in finish, or all models of an electric drill that differ only in speed or gearing. In both cases, flexibility is so maintained that the final commitment to end items can be made as late as possible.

It's important to note that in make-to-stock firms a single-level bill of materials is typically maintained for each end item. This means that the conversion from MPS to FAS is simply the substitution of one end-item part number for another. Both are valid, and both explode to components in the same way. For some make-to-stock firms, the MPS is stated in terms of the most common or most complete end item. As actual sales information is received, other end items are substituted. This process continues until a time is reached when all final substitutions are made.

For assemble-to-order and make-to-order firms, end-item bills of materials are not maintained. If the FAS is stated in terms of customer orders, these orders must be translated into the equivalent of a single-level bill of materials; that is, these orders must lead to bill of materials explosion for order release, picking, and so on. This is easily accommodated if the customer order is stated in the same modules as the planning bill. For the tillers, this means that the customer order is stated in brand name, horsepower, and drive train terms.

Avoidance of firming up the FAS until the last possible moment means the time horizon for the FAS is only as long as dictated by the final assembly lead time (including document preparation and material release). Techniques that help to delay the FAS commitment include bill structuring, close coupling of order entry/promising systems, partial assembly, stocking subassemblies, and process/product designs with this objective.

The Hill-Rom FAS

The Hill-Rom Company, a division of Hillenbrand Industries, manufactures hospital furniture and other health-care equipment. One product, an over-bed table, comes in four different models, 10 alternative color high-pressure laminate tops, and four different options of chrome "boots" (to protect the base) and casters. The result is 160 (4 × 10 × 4) end-item possibilities. Let's examine a super bill approach to master production scheduling and final assembly scheduling in this environment.

Figure 6.16 shows a super bill of materials for this group of products. Manufacturing lead time for over-bed tables is 20 weeks, which means that the MPS must extend at least

FIGURE 6.16
Over-Bed Table
Super Bill

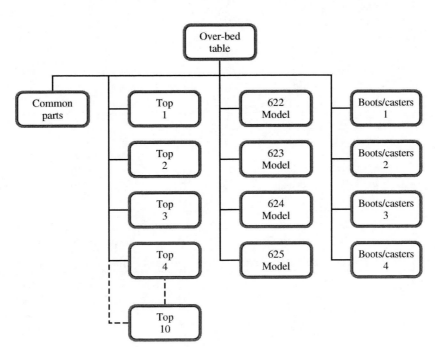

that far into the future. This means that an MPS time-phased record must be maintained over at least this time horizon for each of the 19 common part and option bills of materials shown in Figure 6.16.

The final assembly lead time for this product is four weeks. This involves part availability checking, order launching, component-part release, welding of subassemblies, snag grinding to smooth welded surfaces, degreasing, painting, subassembly, and final assembly.

Hill-Rom is basically an assemble-to-order company, but some finished-goods inventory is held. This means, for each of the 160 end-item over-bed tables, an on-hand balance record must be maintained. This is incorporated in a time-phased FAS record. The overall need is for 19 time-phased MPS records (1 for each option and the common parts) maintained for week 5 through at least week 20, plus 160 time-phased FAS records, maintained for each end item for weeks 1 through 4.

The FAS job is to convert MPS records into FAS records as we roll through time. This is done by the master production scheduler interacting with marketing, since the FAS represents the final culmination of the MPS process.

A related task is order promising, since customer orders may be promised out of the FAS system (on hand or in final assembly) or out of the MPS system (option by option, as done in Figure 6.15). Figures 6.17, 6.18, and 6.19 show this process. Figure 6.17 shows an FAS record for one of the 160 end items; it's maintained only for the length of the FAS lead time, four weeks. The record is for the 622 model, with "gunstock"-colored top, and 01B boots/caster combination; the finished-good item number, which identifies this configuration, is 17123-01B GUN.

FIGURE 6.17
FAS Record for 17123-01B GUN Table

Part No.	Item	FAS Lead Time		On Hand	
7123-01B GUN	Over-bed Table	4		120	

Week	1	2	3	4	
Orders	10			30	Before
Available	160	160	210	230	booking order
Available to promise	160		50	20	F 5264
FAS	50		50	50	

Week	1	2	3	4	
Orders	10		200	30	After
Available	160	160	10	30	booking order
Available to promise	10			20	F 5264
FAS	50		50	50	

MPS Pegging Detail				Actual Order Pegging Detail			
Week	Shop Order	Quantities	Action	Week	Quantity	Customer Order	Code
1	011	50		1	10	F 5117	F
3	027	50		3	200	F 5264	F
4	039	50		4	30	F 5193	F

FIGURE 6.18
MPS Record for Common Parts

Part No.	Item	MPS Lead Time						
1234	Common Parts	20						
Week		5	6	7	8	20	21	Before booking order
Forecast		75	75	75	75	75	75	
Orders		10						
Available		−15	210	235	160	125	50	
Available to promise		50	300	100				
MPS		50	300	100	0			
On hand = 10								

Week		5	6	7	8	20	21	After booking order
Forecast		75	75	75	75	75	75	
Orders		10	200					
Available		−15	85	110	35	0	−75	
Available to promise		50	100	100				
MPS		50	300	100				
On hand = 10								

FIGURE 6.19
Available-to-Promise Logic

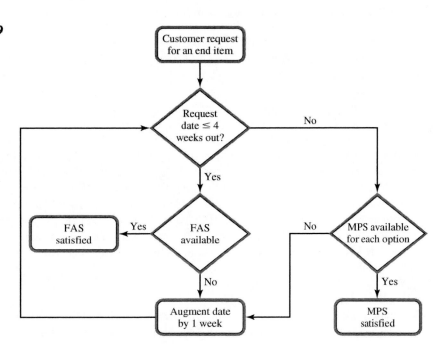

Note the record contains *only* orders (no forecasts), and they're used to compute the "Available" row. This convention recognizes that the FAS is finishing out products in a specific configuration. The 50 units that will be completed this week aren't subject to uncertainty. If no customer order is received for these, they'll go into stock; essentially, the company has written a "sales order."

Figure 6.17 also shows an order for 200 units being booked. The customer has requested shipment of the complete order as soon as possible. The available-to-promise (ATP) logic leads to putting the order into week 3, since only 160 units can be promised prior to week 3. This is shown in the "Before" and "After" sections of Figure 6.17. The bottom section gives supporting pegging data for the orders. Customer orders are pegged with an F code (satisfied from the FAS system).

Next we assume another customer order is received, requesting shipment in week 6. Since this is outside the FAS, it can be satisfied from MPS. Figure 6.18 shows the MPS record for the common-parts option. Note the MPS quantities are for common and option part numbers. Moreover, inventories for these options can exist, even though the physical inventory would be only a collection of parts. (The on-hand balance for common parts is 10.) The MPS option quantities can also be committed for final assembly of specific end items. When final assembly starts, it takes four weeks to finish out the end item. Figure 6.19 shows the ATP logic required to book any customer order in the Hill-Rom system.

The Master Production Scheduler

We turn now to the next topic in master production scheduling: Who's the master production scheduler, what does he or she do, and what's the appropriate job description? First, we briefly examine the use of some MRP concepts for the master scheduler.

The MPS as a Set of Firm Planned Orders

An interesting advantage of using standard MRP records to manage the master production schedule derives from the firm planned order concept. The firm planned order is similar to any planned order in that it explodes through product structures. However, it's *not* changed in either timing or amount as a result of MRP record processing. It's firm, and it can be changed only as the result of an action taken by a responsible person.

It's useful to think of the MPS as a set of firm planned orders. Thereafter, the master production scheduler's job is to convert planned orders to firm planned orders, and to *manage* the timing and amounts of the firm planned orders. The "available" row in the time-phased record provides the primary signal for performing this task. Standard MRP exception codes can provide indications of when and to what extent firm planned orders might not meet the needs.

Managing the timing and amounts of the firm planned orders means that any changes to the MPS have to be carefully evaluated in terms of their impact on material and capacity plans. The key need is to clearly understand trade-offs between customer needs and other MPC system objectives.

The Job

The master production scheduler has the primary responsibility for making any additions or changes to MPS records. He or she also has the primary responsibility for disaggregating the production plan to create the MPS and for ensuring that the sum of the detailed MPS production decisions matches the production plans. This involves analyzing trade-offs and telling top management about situations requiring decisions beyond the scheduler's authority level.

As part of the general feedback process, the master production scheduler should monitor actual performance against the MPS and production plan and distill operating results for higher management. The master production scheduler can also help in the analysis of what-if questions by analyzing the impact on the MPS of changes in plans.

The master production scheduler is often responsible for launching the final assembly schedule. This schedule represents the final commitment, taken as late as possible, to exact end items; that is, the final assembly schedule has to be based on specific finished-good items. Other master production scheduler activities include interface with order entry plus an ongoing relationship with production control to evaluate the feasibility of suggested changes.

Much of this activity involves resolving competing demands for limited capacity. Clearly, if several records for the master production schedule show a negative available at the end of the planning horizon, some trade-offs must be made. Not everything can be scheduled at once. Management of the firm planned orders must be done within capacity constraints. The available position indicates the priority for making those trade-offs. The lower the number of periods of supply or the larger the number of periods of backlog the available position shows, the more urgent the need. If too many are urgent, feedback to marketing may be necessary to change budgets.

Figure 6.20 shows the job description for the master production scheduler at Mitel Corporation. This formal job description makes it clear that the master production scheduler needs to constantly balance conflicting objectives and make trade-offs, especially between customer requirements and the need for stability in manufacturing. Moreover, there is a technical requirement to be able to use Fast-Man, the simulation software that Mitel uses to perform what-if analysis when extraordinary circumstances or opportunities are present. Such computer software can greatly aid the master production scheduler, but judgments will always be required.

Managing the MPS Database

For the master production scheduler to operate effectively, it's also critical that there be one single unified database for the MPS, that it links to the operations plan and to detailed material planning systems, and that clear responsibilities for all transactions be established. This involves not only the usual data integrity issues but also some organizational issues.

In the case of the MPS, many transactions occur in different functional areas. For example, receipts into finished goods may come from completed assemblies (production), shipments from order closing (marketing), or bills of lading (finance). It's critical that exact responsibilities be established for transaction processing, and that data linkages to MPS systems and files be rigorously defined and maintained.

Another critical database requirement for the MPS is proper control over both engineering and nonengineering changes to the bill of materials database. The MPS is often stated in planning bill units that may not be buildable (e.g., an average J-body car). This requires a more complex bill of materials or product structure database. The result is a greater need to procedurally control all changes to the bill of materials and to evaluate the impact of changes both from an engineering point of view and in terms of the effect on nonengineering bills of materials.

FIGURE 6.20 **Mitel's Master Production Scheduler Job Description**

A. Identifying Information

Job Title: *Master Scheduler*

Department/Unit: *Planning & Administration*

Job Location: *Kanata, Ontario*

Date: *February 17*

B. Job Purpose and Mandate

The incumbent of this position is responsible for the day to day management of the Master Production Schedule, as it relates to actioning unplanned forecast demand, forecast shortfalls, production and inventory changes, allowing accurate and up-to-date information which in turn drives material and capacity requirements and customer order dating. An advanced level of material planning and manufacturing process knowledge is required.

C. Organization Structure

The Master Production Scheduler reports to the Manager, Planning who reports to the Director, Planning and Administration.

D. Job Description

1. Specific Activities and Accountabilities:

 - Responsible for the creation and continuous update of the master schedule that satisfies customer demand, maintains stability in terms of material and capacity requirements and minimizes RAW, WIP, and Finished Goods inventory levels by:
   • Managing day to day increases/decreases to the schedule through interface with Materials, Manufacturing, and Order Administration.
   • Working with Materials to ensure smooth E.C.O. transition into factory
   • Continuously monitor the impact of "Performance to Forecast" on inventory levels for the current month, and implement any necessary changes to the schedule; i.e. cut roll-over, increase availability through Fast-Man MRP tool.

 - Act as a focal point between N.A. Order Administration, Manufacturing and Distribution to ensure configured system orders are:
   • Scheduled to meet customer cut-over requirements
   • Scheduled to meet manufacturing cell capacity.
   • Quoted and reviewed with manufacturing, initiating build and test.
   • Free of any discrepancies, with Order Administration notified to correct any problems.

 - Continuously monitor problem inventory, taking advantage of any conversion opportunities, making recommendations for scrapping, or potential "Fire Sales."

 - Assess the impact to capacity, inventory levels, purchase order activity and problem inventory levels that result from any proposed major change to the master schedule, utilizing the Fat-Man MRP tool.

2. Supervisory Responsibilities:　　　　　　　　　Direct ( )　　　　　　　　Indirect ( )

3. Key relationships (internal and external)
   • Internal and external auditors
   • Marketing
   • Order Administration
   • Distribution
   • All levels of management within Mitel

   • Traffic
   • Manufacturing
   • Materials Planning
   • Product Management

E. Job requirements
   • Superior product knowledge
   • 3-4 years progressive experience in materials or production control
   • Knowledge of internal Mitel processes and procedures
   • APICS Certification a definite asset
   • Knowledge gained through APICS Certification
   • Organizational and planning skills
   • Secondary education
   • High degree of initiative and personal motivation
   • Personal computer skills
   • Broad-based knowledge of supply/demand process

To support the master production scheduler, the time-phased MPS-record-oriented software system must produce the time-phased records to maintain the database, provide the linkages to other critical systems, provide MPS monitoring and exception messages, and provide for all MPS transactions. Included are entering of order quantities into the MPS, firm planned order treatment, removing MPS order quantities, changing the latter's timing or amount, converting MPS quantities to final assembly schedule (FAS) quantities, launching final assemblies, monitoring FAS scheduled receipts for timing or quantity changes, closing out FAS receipts into finished-goods inventory, and providing for all customer order entry pegging and promising activities.

Company Examples

We turn now to two actual MPS examples. First we'll show Ethan Allen's approach to master production scheduling. The approach uses a form of time-phased record. We'll see how standard MRP system approaches can be usefully applied and highlight aspects of the master production scheduler's job.

The second example illustrates how Jet Spray uses packaged software with an MPS module. The software incorporates available-to-promise logic and other features.

The Ethan Allen Master Production Schedule

The Ethan Allen Furniture Company produces case goods (wood furniture) in 14 geographically dispersed factories. Its total product line is 980 consolidated item numbers. (Different finishes for the same item make the number of end items about 50 percent larger.) Each consolidated item number is uniquely assigned to a particular assembly line or building station in one of the 14 factories. For each assembly line in each factory, a capacity is established in hours such that, if hours of capacity are fully utilized on all lines, overall company objectives as stated in its production plan will be met.

A forecast of demand is made for each consolidated item number, using statistical forecasting methods. A lot size for each item is also determined, based on economic order quantity concepts. For each assembly lot size, hours required on the assembly line are estimated. For each product, expected weekly priorities are established by dividing the expected beginning inventory by the weekly forecast. In weeks after the first, expected beginning inventory takes account of production and expected sales. The assembly line is loaded to capacity in priority sequence, smallest to largest. Figure 6.21 provides a simplified example for an assembly line with 35 hours of weekly capacity. The simplified example is based on only four products. Actual lines typically manufacture from 15 to 100 different items.

The top section of Figure 6.21 provides the basic data for each of the four products: the beginning inventory, weekly forecast of sales, lot size, and estimated hours to assemble one lot. Note that for product C, there's a beginning back order or oversold condition.

The middle portion of Figure 6.21 is the set of time-phased priority data. For product A in week 1, the beginning inventory of 20 is divided by the weekly forecast of 5, yielding a priority of 4; that is, at the beginning of week 1 there are four weeks of inventory for product A. Similar priority calculations are made for products B, C, and D in week 1.

The rule for assigning products to the assembly line is to first assign that product with the smallest priority—the most urgent need. Thus, product C is scheduled for production first. The assignment of product C to the assembly line in week 1 consumes all of the 35 hours of

196   Chapter 6   *Master Production Scheduling*

FIGURE 6.21
Simplified
Ethan Allen
MPS Example

Basic Data:

Product	Beginning Inventory	Weekly Forecast	Lot Size	Hours Per Lot Size
A	20	5	50	20
B	50	40	250	80
C	−30	35	150	60
D	25	10	100	30

Priorities:

Product	P_1	P_2	P_3	P_4	P_5	P_6	P_7	P_8
A	4	3			0		−2	4.5
B	1.25	.25			3.5		1.5	.5
C	−.86	.64			−.57		.29	.71
D	2.5	1.5			−1.5		6.5	5.5

Schedule:

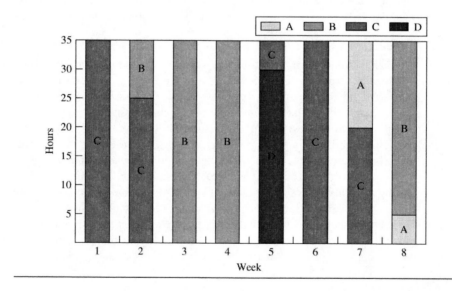

capacity in that week plus 25 hours in week 2. This is so since it takes 60 hours to assemble a batch of 150 of product C.

Moving to week 2, the expected beginning inventory for product A is 15, since forecast sales for week 1 is 5. Divide 15 by the weekly forecast (5) to get the expected priority for week 2 (15 ÷ 5 = 3). Alternatively, if four weeks of sales are in inventory at the beginning of week 1, we'd expect to have three weeks of sales at the beginning of week 2 if no production of product A takes place. This means, for each product not produced, its priority number in the succeeding week is reduced by 1. The expected priority for product C at the start of week 2 can be computed by finding 35/60 of 150, adding this to the beginning inventory of −30, subtracting 35 units of forecast demand for week 1, and dividing the result by the forecast of 35 to give a value of 0.64.

The lowest-priority product for week 2 is B (.25). Since a lot size of the product takes 80 hours, capacity is fully utilized until the end of week 4. This is why no priority data are given for weeks 3 and 4. A similar situation is true for week 6 when product C, started in week 5, uses the full week's capacity. By loading each line to its weekly capacity, no more and no less, the match between the production plan dictated for each assembly line and detailed MPS decision making is maintained. Calculations in subsequent weeks involve adding in any production and reducing inventories by expected sales. For example, product C's priority in week 5 can be calculated as follows:

$$
\begin{aligned}
\text{Beginning inventory} &= -30 \\
\text{Production} &= \underline{150} \\
& \ 120 \\
-4 \text{ weeks' sales at } 35 &= \underline{140} \\
& \ {-20}
\end{aligned}
$$

$$-20/35 = -.57$$

Figure 6.22 shows another way to create the Ethan Allen MPS. Here, the same four products are used. For each, a **time-phased order point (TPOP)** record is developed. The same schedule shown in the bottom portion of Figure 6.21 is achieved when the line is loaded to capacity in the sequence of when planned orders occur in the TPOP records; that is, product C has the first planned order, then B, then D, and so on. Of course, the planned order for D in week 3 isn't placed in week 3 because capacity isn't available until week 5. There's also a tie shown in week 8. Both products B and C have planned orders in that week. The tie-breaking decision could produce a schedule that differs slightly from that shown in Figure 6.21.

The great advantage to using TPOP approaches to developing the MPS is that specialized MPS software development is reduced. TPOP records are produced with standard MRP logic using the forecast quantities as gross requirements. The master production scheduler's job is to convert these planned orders to firm planned orders, so that capacity is properly utilized. At Ethan Allen, conversion of TPOP planned orders to firm planned orders is largely an automatic activity, so it has been computerized. Note, however, the objective is to load the assembly stations to their absolute capacity, in priority sequence. Other firms might use other criteria, such as favoring those jobs with high profitability, favoring certain customers, or allowing flexibility in the definition of capacity. If so, the master production scheduler's detailed decisions would be different.

Master Production Scheduling at Jet Spray

Jet Spray Corporation manufactures and sells dispensers for noncarbonated cold beverages and hot products (coffee and hot chocolate). Jet Spray uses an integrated on-line system encompassing MRP, capacity planning, shop-floor control, master production scheduling, inventory management, and other functions. The software package (Data 3) allows the user to designate part numbers as either being MRP or MPS; that is, MRP part numbers are driven by MPS numbers (but not the opposite). Bills of materials need to be designed accordingly (MPS part numbers are parents to MRP part numbers).

Any MPS part may also be designated as either a make-to-stock or make-to-order item. The distinction is that, when a shop order is created for a make-to-stock MPS item, the order is closed into finished-goods inventory. Subsequent shipment to a customer requires

FIGURE 6.22

Ethan Allen MPS Example Using Time-Phased Order Point

		Week							
		1	2	3	4	5	6	7	8
Gross requirements		5	5	5	5	5	5	5	5
Scheduled receipts									
On hand	20	15	10	5	0	45	40	35	30
Planned orders						50			

A

		Week							
		1	2	3	4	5	6	7	8
Gross requirements		40	40	40	40	40	40	40	40
Scheduled receipts			250						
On hand	50	10	220	180	140	100	60	20	230
Planned orders									250

B

		Week							
		1	2	3	4	5	6	7	8
Gross requirements		35	35	35	35	35	35	35	35
Scheduled receipts									
On hand	−30	85	50	15	130	95	60	25	140
Planned orders		150			150				150

C

		Week							
		1	2	3	4	5	6	7	8
Gross requirements		10	10	10	10	10	10	10	10
Scheduled receipts									
On hand	25	15	5	95	85	75	65	55	45
Planned orders				100					

D

another transaction to remove the items from finished goods into an area awaiting shipment. The inventory in turn is reduced by actual shipment. For a make-to-order item (which includes assemble-to-order), the shop order is driven by an actual customer order and is closed directly into the area awaiting shipment.

One of Jet Spray's best-known products is a two-product cold beverage dispenser, the Twin Jet 3 (TJ3), which is made to stock. Figure 6.23 is a portion of the basic MPS record for the TJ3. It shows the weeks of 11/17 through 1/12, but the system has data to support a one-year planning horizon. Notice that the available-to-promise rows are shown in the

FIGURE 6.23   Jet Spray Corporation Master Planning Schedule

PART NUMBER	DESCRIPTION	QUANTITY ON HAND	SAFETY STOCK	QUANTITY UNAVAIL	LEAD TIME	CUM L/T	FAM GRP	LOT HOR	PLN	TIME FENCE	MASTER SCHEDULE TYPE
S3568	TJ3 DOM. TWIN JET	279	0	21	0	92	TJ	5	001	50	MAKE TO STOCK

BEGIN DATE	11/17/	11/24/	12/01/	12/08/	12/15/	12/22/	12/29/	1/05/	1/12/
DAYS/PERIOD	7	7	7	7	7	7	7	7	7
FORECAST	28	63	147	147	147	146	146	181	181
ACTUAL DEMAND	9	26	8	5	4	4	963	4	1
PROJECTED BAL	240	402	680	830	1,116	1,112	374	493	312
TARGET INV BAL	0	0	0	0	0	0	0	0	0
AVAIL TO PROM	249	171						295	
CUMULATIVE ATP	249	420	420	420	420	420	420	715	715
MPS	0	225	286	155	290	0	225	300	0

format just described as well as in cumulative format. The cumulative date are always the sum of the prior period cumulative plus any ATP in the present period.

The available-to-promise for 11/17 is determined by taking the on-hand quantity (279), subtracting the unavailable (21), and thereafter subtracting the actual demand (9) in the week starting 11/17. The ATP for 11/24 requires looking all the way out to 12/29. In that week, an actual order for 963 completely consumes all MPS quantities for the month of December ($286 + 155 + 290 + 225 = 956$). Thus, 7 units from the MPS for 11/24 must be promised to the order in the week of 12/29. Additionally, the other actual demand quantities for December ($8 + 5 + 4 + 4 = 21$) and 11/24 (26) will have to be covered. Thus, the ATP for 11/24 is the MPS (225) $- 7 - 21 - 26 = 171$. The other ATP figures are relatively straightforward.

The projected balance row (available) for the record is based on a different convention than we've described. The forecast values shown are the *original* forecasts, whereas the software uses the *unconsumed* forecast plus the actual demand in decrementing the projected balance. The unconsumed forecast values are not shown in Figure 6.23. We'd argue for more transparency in the system, but in actual practice, absence of the unconsumed forecast data isn't a great problem. The system is on line, so this number can be obtained whenever it's needed.

The target inventory balance row in Figure 6.23 is worth explaining. The production plan for the TJ3 wasn't shown here. The actual production plan for the TJ3 is constantly monitored against the MPS. There are tolerances for inventory variations, and when projected inventory data exceed limits set by the production plan, this is where those differences are recorded.

This MPS software is an on-line system. Figure 6.23 is only one of several documents available to the master scheduler. Most of the master scheduler's work is supported with a video screen, not paper, and the MPS is reviewed on a daily basis.

Master Production Schedule Stability

A stable master production schedule translates into stable component schedules, which mean improved performance in plant operations. Too many changes in the MPS are costly in terms of reduced productivity. However, too few changes can lead to poor customer service levels and increased inventory. The objective is to strike a balance where stability is monitored and managed. The techniques most used to achieve MPS stability are firm planned order treatment for the MPS quantities, frozen time periods for the MPS, and time fencing to establish clear guidelines for the kinds of changes that can be made in various periods.

Ethan Allen Stability

Construction of the Ethan Allen MPS is based on TPOP records, with assembly lines loaded up to exact capacities, and the sequence of MPS items determined by the date sequence of planned orders. This process might seem to lead to a great deal of repositioning of MPS quantities; that is, as actual sales occur, forecast errors will tend to rearrange the MPS. In fact, this doesn't occur, because planned orders from TPOP records are "frozen," or firm planned, under certain conditions.

FIGURE 6.24
Ethan Allen
Firm Planned
Order
Approach

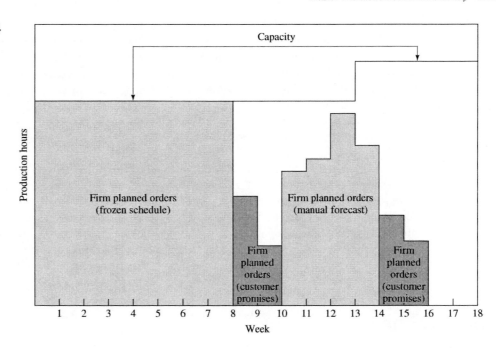

Ethan Allen uses three types of firm planned orders for the MPS, as Figure 6.24 shows. In essence, any firm planned order is frozen in that it won't be automatically repositioned by any computer logic. All MPS quantities for the next eight weeks are considered to be frozen or firm planned at Ethan Allen. In addition, any MPS quantity used to make a customer promise (i.e., a customer order is pegged to that MPS batch) is also a firm planned order. The third type of firm planned order used in Ethan Allen's MPS is for what the company calls the **manual forecast.** Included are contract sales (e.g., items to a motel chain), market specials (i.e., items to go on special promotion), and new items (MPS here being when the product is to be introduced). Finally, all blank space in Figure 6.24 is filled with the TPOP-based scheduling technique discussed earlier. Computerized MPS logic fills in the holes up to the capacity limit without disturbing any firm planned order.

Freezing and Time Fencing

Figure 6.24 shows the first eight weeks in the Ethan Allen MPS as **frozen.** This means *no* changes inside of eight weeks are possible. In reality, "no" may be a bit extreme. If the president dictates a change, it will probably happen, but such occurrences are rare at Ethan Allen.

Many firms don't like to use the term *frozen,* saying that anything is negotiable—but negotiations get tougher as we approach the present time. However, a frozen period provides a stable target for manufacturing to hit. It also removes most alibis for missing the schedule!

Time fencing is an extension of the freeze concept. Many firms set time fences that specify periods in which various types of change can be handled. A common practice, for example, is to have three time fences, say 8, 16, and 24 weeks. The marketing/logistics people could make any changes that they wanted beyond the 24-week fence as long as the sum of all MPS records is synchronized with the production plan. From weeks 16 to 24, substitutions of one end item for another would be permitted, provided required parts would be available and the production plan wasn't violated. From weeks 8 to 16, the MPS is quite rigid; but minor changes within the model series can be made if component parts are available. The period before 8 weeks is basically a freeze period similar to that of Ethan Allen, but occasional changes are made even within this period. In fact, assembly lines have been shut down to make changes—but it's so rare that everyone in the factory remembers when this happens! To achieve the productivity necessary to remain competitive, stability in short-range manufacturing plans is essential.

Two common fences are the **demand fence** and the **planning fence.** The demand fence is the shorter of the two. Inside the demand fence, the forecast is ignored in calculating the available. The theory is that customer orders—not the forecast—matter in the near term. The planning fence indicates the time at which the master production scheduler should be planning more MPS quantities. Within the demand fence it is very difficult to change the MPS. Between the demand fence and the planning fence, management trade-offs must be made to make changes; outside the planning fence, changes can be made by the master production scheduler. Some firms refer to these as the ice, slush, and water zones.

Managing the MPS

We turn now to managing the MPS: How do we measure, monitor, and control detailed day-to-day performance against the MPS? The first prerequisite for control is to have a realistic MPS. Most basic management textbooks say it's critical to hold people accountable only for performance levels that are attainable. This means the MPS can't be a wish list, and it shouldn't have any significant portion that's past due. In fact, we claim that the presence of a significant amount of past due is a major indication of a sick manufacturing planning and control system.

Stability and proper buffering are also important, because the objective is to remove all alibis and excuses for not attaining the performance for which the proper budget has been provided. Successful companies hit the production plan every month, and they do the best job possible to disaggregate the plan to reflect actual product mix in the MPS.

The Overstated MPS

Most authorities have warned that the MPS must not be overstated. To do so destroys the relative priorities developed by MRP and shop-floor control; more important, the overstated MPS erodes belief in the formal system, thereby reinstituting the informal system of hot lists and black books. Walter Goddard, a well-known MPS expert, no longer tells companies not to overstate the MPS, because at some point the temptation is overwhelming; he now tells them to learn from the experience so they won't do it again!

A key to not overstating the MPS is to always force the sum of the MPS to equal the production plan. Then, when someone wants to add something, the question is, "of what do you want less?" The company must give up what's referred to as *the standard manufacturing answer*. The standard manufacturing answer to whether more output of some product is possible is: "We don't know, but we'll try!"

The company *must* know. There should be an overall output budget for manufacturing. Capacity should be in place, and should match (not be more or less than) the budget. Manufacturing and marketing should work diligently to respond to product mix changes, but within the overall budgetary constraint. The correct response to whether more output of some product is possible is, "what else can be reduced?" If nothing, then the answer is either "No" or "The output budget and concomitant resources will have to be changed to increase capacities."

MPS Measures

There's an old Vermont story about the fellow who was asked: "How is your wife?" His answer: "Compared to what?" Likewise, measuring MPS has to be in concrete terms that reflect the firm's fundamental goals. This isn't as easy as it might seem. At one time, Ethan Allen evaluated each factory on the basis of dollar output per week. At one plant, an assembly line produced both plastic-topped tables and all-wood tables. Plastic-topped tables sold for more and could be assembled in roughly half the time, since the top was purchased as a completed subassembly. Obviously, the factory favored plastic-topped tables, even when inventories were high on those items and low on wood tables.

Ethan Allen had to change the measure for evaluating plant performance. Each line in each plant is now scheduled by the techniques we've described, and performance is based upon hitting the schedule.

Another important measure of MPS and other MPC system functions is customer service. In virtually every company, customer service is an area of concern. However, in many firms, a tight definition of precisely how the measure is to be made is lacking. Measurement is a critical step in control, and each firm will need to express how this important aspect of its operation is to be measured.

It's to be expected that whatever measure for customer service is chosen, the firm may have problems similar to those of Ethan Allen when evaluating plants using dollar output. However, the way to find the problems and thereafter eliminate them is, in fact, to start with *some* measure, no matter how crude, and evolve.

Appropriate measures vary a great deal from firm to firm, reflecting the type of market response typical in the industry and the particular company. Ethan Allen measures customer service in terms of hitting the order acknowledgment or promise dates. Jet Spray measures manufacturing performance against the MPS, as well as monthly performance in "equivalent units" of output versus the budget. The goal is a cumulative performance of at least 95 percent. Some assemble-to-order firms evaluate production against the production plan, which is to deliver a specific number of each model to marketing in the agreed upon time frame. They also evaluate customer service in terms of how long customers have to wait until they can get a specific end item. This indicates how well the sales and operations plan is being disaggregated.

Monitoring the MPS at Ethan Allen

Figure 6.24 shows Ethan Allen's planned order approach to its MPS. We also know that each plant is evaluated on hitting the MPS, so it should be useful to see how detailed monitoring takes place and how overall company operations have been affected.

FIGURE 6.25
Ethan Allen Summary MPS Performance

Source: W. L. Berry, T. E. Vollmann, and D. C. Whybark, *Master Production Scheduling: Principles and Practice* (Falls Church, Va.: American Production and Inventory Control Society, 1979), p. 54.

```
                                                          April 5,
To:  Bill Morrissey
From: Marty Stern

                        Production schedule review
                                 4/1

Summary:

     Nine of the 14 factories operation hit their schedules 100 percent.

     Performance against schedule was poor this week at one of the factories:
     Boonville-75 percent

     Packed production was 196 million over total scheduled. 11 of the factories
     reporting met or exceeded their schedule.

     The outside suppliers produced 171 million under their schedule bringing total
     production to 25 million over scheduled goal.

cc:  Marshall Ames
     Barney Kvingedal
     Ray Dinkel
     Walter Blisky
     Andy Boscoe
     Steve Kammerer
     Tom Ericson
     Bob Schneble
     Hank Walker
```

Every Tuesday morning, Ethan Allen's vice president of manufacturing gets a report detailing each factory's performance in the prior week. Figure 6.25 shows this overall performance report. Figure 6.26 is the detail for one factory at Beecher Falls, Vermont.

Figure 6.25 shows one plant, Boonville, as having had poor performance. The last two comments about packed production and outside suppliers show total production achieved in these two categories.

The "STATION" column in Figure 6.26 shows the assembly lines; their capacities are stated in hours. The "PRIORITY" data reflect expected operating conditions 18 weeks in the future. If each priority number were 18, we'd expect the plant to exactly meet customer needs 18 weeks in the future. This particular factory will be seriously behind in terms of meeting anticipated customer demands. This is a question of capacity that's reflected in the comments about each station. For example, for the 06 station, the detail indicates 10 extra weeks of capacity are required to catch up. Note, however, lack of capacity doesn't mean the plant isn't meeting its schedule. All eight lines are reported as "no misses." This means, in the week covered by this report, the plant met its schedule exactly. Jobs in the schedule are being run. The schedule is loaded up to capacity—not in excess of capacity. Lack of adequate capacity means longer delivery times to customers, but not missed schedules.

By evaluating the reports in Figures 6.25 and 6.26, management can tell which plants are performing according to expectations. Life in the factories is much more calm with performance more clearly defined. No longer do salespeople, customers, marketing people, and executives call the factories. The interface between functions is reflected in the master production schedule, and each factory's job is to hit its MPS. In a sense, the entire master

FIGURE 6.26

Ethan Allen Detailed MPS Performance (for one factory)

SUMMARY OF SCHEDULE REVIEW

PLANT: <u>BEECHER FALLS</u>   FROM: MARTY STERN

SCHEDULE DATE <u>3/27/78</u>
THRU WEEK OF   <u>8/28/78</u>

STATION	CAPACITY	PRIORITY	PROD. SCHED. DOLLARS	PRODUCTION GOAL
06-Cases	175.0	1	$240.1	232.0
07-C/Hutch	10.0	11	10.0	9.0
08-Hutch	15.0	14	17.9	19.0
20-Beds	60.0	1	85.7	84.0
21-Misc.	3.0	11	3.7	4.0
22-Bookstack	70.0	3	33.0	31.0
24-Desks	10.0	8	8.8	10.0
26-Mirrors	25.0	12	23.0	19.0
PLANT TOTAL			$422.2	408.0

Station 06 --- Cases: Other than misses caused by reporting date change (Canbury closed Good Friday) no misses. Items such as 10-4017, 4066, 4512P, 4522P, 11-5215, 5223 delayed 1 to 4 weeks. Nine items' service position improved. Some jobs outside frozen schedule should have been made "A" jobs and shifting would not have occurred. Priority down to 1 from 2. To schedule through priority 18 requires 10 weeks capacity, slightly higher than last months' 9 3/4 weeks.

Station 07 --- C/Hutch: No misses. Delayed 3 of 5 items on this line. Priority down to 11 from 14. 7 weeks capacity will schedule thru priority 18, up from 5 weeks.

Station 08 --- Hutch: No misses. Delayed 2 items, pulled 3 ahead. (Plant comments base the shift on purchase parts). Priority up to 14 from 3. To schedule thru priority 18 requires 3 weeks capacity, down from 6 weeks.

Station 20 --- No misses. Delayed the 11-5632-5. Pulled a number of beds ahead. Priority unchanged at 1. Eight weeks capacity, down from 10 3/4 weeks will schedule thru priority 18.

Station 21 --- Misc.: No misses. Some shifting but orders are O.K. Priority up from 10 to 11. Three weeks capacity, same as last month, will schedule thru priority 18.

Station 22 --- Bookstack: No misses. Built 1 assembly ahead. Priority up to 3 from 2. To schedule thru priority 18 requires 4 1/2 weeks capacity down from 6 weeks.

Station 24 --- Desks: No misses. Built 1 assembly ahead. Some shifting no delays. Priority up to 8 from 4. Three and one-half weeks capacity, down from 5 1/2 weeks, will schedule thru priority 18.

Station 26 --- No misses. Some shifting but ahead only. Priority up to 12 from 1. Two and three quarters weeks capacity, down from 8 weeks will schedule thru priority 18.

scheduling effort has enabled Ethan Allen to achieve centralized management of decentralized operations. Factory operations are geographically dispersed over wide areas, but those operations are carefully evaluated in the corporate offices. Execution responsibility and criteria are unambiguously defined for each plant.

One of the master production scheduling system's most important benefits for Ethan Allen is its upward compatibility; that is, the system is transparent and will work with 5 factories or 25 factories, with new ones easily added. Centralized coordination is maintained, and performance is very clear, with the result being an important tool to support orderly growth for the company. The company has roughly tripled in size since the start of the master production scheduling effort.

206 Chapter 6 *Master Production Scheduling*

Concluding Principles

The master production schedule plays a key role in manufacturing planning and control systems. In this chapter, we've addressed what the MPS is, how it's done, and who does it. The following general principles emerge from this discussion:

- The MPS unit should reflect the company's approach to the business environment in which it operates.
- The MPS function should use the common ERP database if such a system is implemented in the firm.
- Common systems, time-phased processing, and MPS techniques facilitate effective scheduling regardless of the firm's environment.
- Customer order promising should be closely linked to the MPS.
- Available-to-promise information should be derived from the MPS and provided to the sales department.
- A final assembly schedule should be used to convert the anticipated build schedule into the final build schedule.
- The master production scheduler must keep the sum of the parts (the MPS) equal to the whole (the operations plan).
- The MPS activity and role of the master production scheduler must be clearly defined organizationally.
- The MPS can be usefully considered as a set of firm planned orders.
- The MPS should be evaluated with a formal performance measurement system.

References

Adenso-Diaz, B., and M. Laguna. "Modelling the Load Leveling Problem in Master Production Scheduling for MRP Systems," *International Journal of Production Research* 34 (1996), p. 483.

Campbell, G. M. "Establishing Safety Stocks for Master Production Schedules," *Production Planning and Control* 6 (1995), p. 404.

Chan, Joseph W. K., and N. D. Burns. "Benchmarking Manufacturing Planning and Control (MPC) Systems," *Benchmarking* 9, no. 3 (2002), pp. 256–277.

Chen, Chien-Yu; Zhenying Zhao; and Michael O Ball. "A Model for Batch Advanced Available-to-Promise," *Production and Operations Management* 11, no. 4 (winter 2002), p. 424.

Chu, S. C. K. "A Mathematical Programming Approach Towards Optimized Master Production Scheduling," *International Journal of Production Economics* 38 (1995), p. 269.

Davis, W. J.; A. Brook; and M. S. Lee. "A New Simulation Methodology for Master Production Scheduling," *1997 IEEE International Conference on Systems, Man, and Cybernetics* (1997), p. 1808.

Ebert, R. J., and T. S. Lee. "Production Loss Functions and Subjective Assessments of Forecast Errors: Untapped Sources for Effective Master Production Scheduling," *International Journal of Production Research* 33 (1995), p. 137.

Guerrero, Hector H., and Gary M. Kern. "How to More Effectively Accept and Refuse Orders," *Production & Inventory Management Journal* 29, no. 4 (1988), pp. 59–64.

Gundogar, E. "A Rule-Based Master Production Scheduling System for an Electro-Mechanical Manufacturing Company," *Production Planning and Control* 10 (1999), p. 486.

Hahn, Chan K.; Edward A Duplaga; and Kee Young Kim. "Production/Sales Interface: MPS at Hyundai Motor," *International Journal of Production Economics* 37, no. 1 (November 1994), p. 5.

Hill, J.; W. L. Berry; G. K. Leong; and D. Schilling. "Master Production Scheduling in Capacitated Sequence Dependent Process Industries," *International Journal of Production Research* 38, no. 18 (December 2000), p. 473.

Johnson, M. Eric, and Gary Scudder. "Supporting Quick Response Through Scheduling of Make-to-Stock Production/Inventory Systems," *Decision Sciences* 30, no. 2 (spring 1999), pp. 441–467.

Kadipasaoglu, Sukran N. "The Effect of Freezing the Master Production Schedule on Cost in Multilevel MRP Systems," *Production and Inventory Management Journal* 36, no. 3 (3rd quarter 1995), pp. 30–36.

Kern, Gary M., and Jerry C. Wei. "Master Production Rescheduling Policy in Capacity-Constrained Just-in-Time Make-to-Stock Environments," *Decision Sciences* 27, no. 2 (spring 1996), p. 365.

Kimms, A. "Stability Measures for Rolling Schedules with Applications to Capacity Expansion Planning, Master Production Scheduling, and Lot Sizing," *Omega* 26 (1998), p. 355.

Krajewski, L. J., and J. Wei. "Modeling MPS Policies for Supply-Chain Flexibility," *Proceedings of the First Asia-Pacific Decision Sciences Institute Conference,* 1996, p. 635.

Kulonda, Dennis J. "MRP in the Third World," *Production and Inventory Management Journal* (3rd quarter 2000).

Lin, N.-P., and L. J. Krajewski. "A Model for Master Production Scheduling in Uncertain Environments." *Decision Sciences* 23, no. 4 (fall 1992), pp. 839–861.

Ling, R. C., and W. E. Goddard. *Orchestrating Success.* New York: John Wiley & Sons, 1988.

Metters, R. D. "A Method for Achieving Better Customer Services, Lower Costs, and Less Instability in Master Production Schedules," *Production and Inventory Management* 34 (4th quarter 1993), pp. 61–65.

Metters, R., and V. Vargas. "A Comparison of Production Scheduling Policies on Costs, Service Level, and Schedule Changes," *Production and Operations Management* 8, no. 1 (spring 1999), pp. 76–91.

Proud, John F. *Master Scheduling: A Practical Guide to Competitive Manufacturing,* 2nd ed. New York: John Wiley & Sons, July 1999.

Spencer, M. S., and J. F. Cox, III. "Master Production Scheduling Development in a Theory of Constraints Environment," *Production and Inventory Management Journal* 36 (1995), p. 8.

Sridharan, V., and W. L. Berry. "Freezing the Master Production Schedule Under Demand Uncertainty," *Decision Sciences* 21, no. 1 (winter 1990), pp. 97–120.

Taylor, Sam G., and Gerhard J. Plenert. "Finite Capacity Promising," *Production and Inventory Management Journal* (3rd quarter 1999).

Vargas, V., and R. A., Metters. "A Master Production Scheduling Procedure for Stochastic Demand," *Proceedings,* Decision Sciences Institute 28th Annual Meeting, 1997, p. 1239.

Verganti, R. "Order Overplanning with Uncertain Lumpy Demand: A Simplified Theory," *International Journal of Production Research* 35 (1997), p. 3220.

Wacker, John G. "Configure-to-Order Planning Bills of Material: Simplifying a Complex Product Structure for Manufacturing Planning and Control," *Production and Inventory Management Journal* 41, no. 2 (2nd quarter 2000), p. 21.

Wallace, T. F., and R. A. Stahl. *Master Scheduling in the 21st Century.* Cincinnati: T. F. Wallace and Co., 2003.

Wright, Nevan. "Master Scheduling," *International Journal of Operations & Production Management* 15, no. 12 (1995), p. 99.

Xiande, Zhao, and Lam Kokin. "Lot-sizing Rules and Freezing the Master Production Schedule in Material Requirements Planning Systems," *International Journal of Production Economics* 53 (1997), p. 281.

Xie, Jinxing; Xiande Zhao; and T. S. Lee. "Freezing the Master Production Schedule Under Single Resource Constraint and Demand Uncertainty," *International Journal of Production Economics* 83, no. 1 (Jan. 25, 2003), pp. 65–84.

Yang, K. K., and F. Robert Jacobs. "Replanning the Master Production Schedule for a Capacity-Constrained Job Shop," *Decision Sciences Journal* 30, no. 3 (summer 1999), pp. 719–748.

Zhao, Xiande; Jinxing Xie; and Qiyuan Jiang. "Lot-sizing Rule and Freezing the Master Production Schedule under Capacity Constraint and Deterministic Demand," *Production and Operations Management* 10, no. 1 (spring 2001), pp. 45–67.

Discussion Questions

1. Why does the text stress that the master production schedule is *not* a forecast?

2. Some companies try to increase output simply by increasing the MPS. Discuss this approach.

3. What do you feel would be the key functions of the MPS in each of the following three environments: make-to-stock, make-to-order, and assemble-to-order?

4. What are the similarities and differences in "rolling through time" for MPS and MRP?

5. Much of the order-promising logic is directed at telling customers when they can honestly expect delivery. Several firms, on the other hand, simply promise their customers delivery within *X* weeks (often an unrealistic claim) and then deliver when they can. Contrast these two approaches.

6. One characterization of the available-to-promise record is that the "Available" row is for the master scheduler and the "Available-to-promise" row is for customers. What's meant by this contention?

7. Explain how determining the "Available" row with the "greater of forecast or orders" logic can overstate required production.

8. Many companies have come to view their master production schedulers as key people in profitably meeting the firm's strategic goals. Would you agree? What qualities would you look for in a master production scheduler?

9. Ethan Allen's approach to master production scheduling puts capacity into a primary position instead of a secondary consideration. What does this statement mean?

10. Discuss the relationship between stability and firm planned orders.

Problems

1. Excelsior Springs, Ltd., schedules production of one end product, Hi-Sulphur, in batches of 80 units whenever the projected ending inventory balance in a quarter falls below 10 units. It takes one quarter to make a batch of 80 units. Excelsior currently has 30 units on hand. The sales forecast for the next four quarters is:

	Quarter			
	1	2	3	4
Forecast	20	70	70	20

a. Prepare a time-phased MPS record showing the sales forecast and MPS for Hi-Sulphur.

b. What are the inventory balances at the end of each quarter?

c. During the first quarter, no units were sold. The revised forecast for the rest of the year is:

	Quarter		
	2	3	4
Forecast	30	50	70

How does the MPS change?

2. Neptune Manufacturing Company's production manager wants a master production schedule covering next year's business. The company produces a complete line of small fishing boats for both saltwater and freshwater use and manufactures most of the component parts used in assembling the products. The firm uses MRP to coordinate production schedules of the component part manufacturing and assembly operations. The production manager has just received the following sales forecast for next year from the marketing division:

	Sales Forecast (Standard Boats for Each Series)			
Product Lines	**1st Quarter**	**2nd Quarter**	**3rd Quarter**	**4th Quarter**
FunRay series	8,000	9,000	6,000	6,000
SunRay series	4,000	5,000	2,000	2,000
StingRay series	9,000	10,000	6,000	7,000
Total	21,000	24,000	14,000	15,000

　　The sales forecast is stated in terms of "standard boats," reflecting total sales volume for each of the firm's three major product lines.

　　Another item of information supplied by the marketing department is the target ending inventory position for each product line. The marketing department would like the production manager to plan on having the following number of standard boats on hand at the end of each quarter of next year:

Product Line	**Quarterly Target Ending Inventory (in Standard Boats)**
FunRay series	3,000 boats
SunRay series	1,000 boats
StingRay series	3,000 boats

The inventory position for each product is:

Product Line	**Current Inventory Level (in Standard Boats)**
FunRay series	15,000 boats
SunRay series	3,000 boats
StingRay series	5,000 boats

　　The master production schedule is to specify the number of boats (in standard units) to be produced for each product line in each quarter of next year on the firm's single assembly line. The assembly line can produce up to 15,000 standard boats per quarter (250 boats per day during the 60 days in a quarter).

　　Two additional factors are taken into account by the production manager in preparing the master production schedule: the assembly line changeover cost and the inventory carrying cost for the finished goods inventory. Each assembly line changeover costs $5,000, reflecting material handling costs of changing the stocking of component parts on the line, adjusting the layout, and so on. After some discussion with the company comptroller, the production manager concluded that the firm's inventory carrying cost is 10 percent of standard boat cost per year. The item value for each of the product line standard units is:

Product Line	Standard Boat Cost
FunRay series	$100
SunRay series	150
StingRay series	200

The master production scheduler has calculated the production lot sizes as 5,000, 3,000, and 4,000 units, respectively.

a. Develop a master production schedule for next year, by quarter, for each of Neptune's fishing boat lines. Identify any problems.

b. Verify the lot size calculations using the EOQ formula.

3. The Zoro Manufacturing Company has a plant in Murphysboro, Georgia. Product A is shipped from the firm's plant warehouse in Murphysboro to satisfy East Coast demand. Currently, the sales forecast for product A at the Murphysboro plant is 30 units per week.

The master production scheduler at Murphysboro considers product A to be a make-to-stock item for master scheduling purposes. Currently, 50 units of product A are on hand in the Murphysboro plant warehouse. Desired safety stock level is 10 units for this product. Product A is produced on a lot-for-lot basis. Currently, an order for 30 units is being produced and is due for delivery to the plant warehouse on Monday, one week from today.

The master production scheduler has heard that an MRP record that uses the forecast for gross requirements and has a lead time of zero can be used for master production scheduling. Complete the following MRP record. How can this be used for master production scheduling?

				Week			
Product A		1	2	3	4	5	6
Gross requirements							
Scheduled receipts							
Projected available balance							
Planned order release							

Q = lot for lot; LT = 0; SS = 10.

4. The MPS planner at Murphy Motors uses MPS time-phased records for planning end-item production. The planner is currently working on a schedule for the P24, one of Murphy's top-selling motors. The planner uses a production lot size of 70 and a safety stock of 5 for the P24 motor.

					Week			
Item: P24		1	2	3	4	5	6	7	8
Forecast		30	30	30	40	40	40	45	45
Orders		13	8	4					
Available									
Available to promise									
MPS									

On hand = 20.

a. Complete the MPS time-phased record for product P24.

b. Can Murphy accept the following orders? Update the MPS time-phased record for accepted orders.

Order	Amount	Desired Week
1	40	4
2	30	6
3	30	2
4	25	3

5. The Spencer Optics Company produces an inexpensive line of sunglasses. The manufacturing process consists of assembling two plastic lenses (produced by the firm's plastic molding department) into a finished frame (purchased from an outside supplier). The company is interested in using material requirements planning to schedule its operations and has asked you to prepare an example to illustrate the technique.

The firm's sales manager has prepared a 10-week sales forecast for one of the more popular sunglasses (the Classic model) for your example. The forecast is 100 orders per week. Spencer has customer orders of 110 units, 80 units, 50 units, and 20 units in weeks 1, 2, 3, and 4, respectively. The sunglasses are assembled in batches of 300. Presently, three such batches are scheduled: one in week 2, one in week 5, and one in week 8.

a. Complete the following time-phased record:

Classic Model MPS Record		Week 1	2	3	4	5	6	7	8	9	10
Forecast											
Orders											
Available											
Available to promise											
MPS											

On hand = 140.

b. Prepare the MRP record for the assembly of the sunglasses using the following record. The final assembly quantity is 300, lead time is 2 weeks, and there's a scheduled receipt in week 2. Note that no inventory is shown for the assembled sunglasses in this record, since it's accounted for in the MPS record.

		Week 1	2	3	4	5	6	7	8	9	10
Gross requirements											
Scheduled receipts			300								
Projected available balance	0										
Planned order release											

Q = 300; LT = 2; SS = 0.

6. Nino Spirelli has constructed the following (partial) time-phased MPS record:

	Week					
	1	2	3	4	5	6
Forecast	20	30	20	30	20	30
Orders	14	8	6			
Available						
Available to promise						
MPS	50		50		50	50

On hand = 5.

a. Complete the record.

b. Are there any problems?

c. What's the earliest Nino can promise an order for 44 units?

d. Assume that an order for 15 is booked for week 4. Assume the order for 44 units in part c is not booked; recompute the record.

7. The Cedar River Manufacturing Company produces a line of furnishings for motels and hotels. Among the items manufactured is an Executive water pitcher with the following product structure:

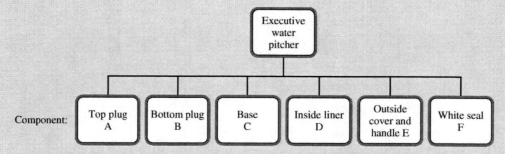

Component items A, B, C, and F are manufactured by the plastic molding shop; components D and E are purchased from a vendor. The Executive water pitcher is completed by the final assembly department.

Currently the following open shop orders for Executive water pitcher components are waiting to be processed at the #101 injection molding press in the plastic molding shop:

Plastic Molding Shop-Floor Control Report

Shop Order Number	Component Item	Order Quantity	Order Due Date	Molding Machine Time (Weeks)
10-XYZ	F	15	ASAP*	2
10-XXX	B	25	ASAP*	2
10-XZV	A	30	ASAP*	1
10-XXY	C	20	ASAP*	2

*As soon as possible.

All the orders shown have their last operation at the #101 injection molding press and are subsequently ready for the final assembly department. (Final assembly time is negligible.)

a. Given the preceding information, complete the MPS and MRP records for all of the Executive water pitcher items.

MPS Record: Executive Water Pitcher

	Week						
	1	2	3	4	5	6	7
Forecast	10	10	10	10	10	10	10
Orders	12	5	2				
Available							
Available to promise							
MPS							

On hand = 15.
MPS lot size = 20.

MRP Records

Component A		Week						
		1	2	3	4	5	6	7
Gross requirements								
Scheduled receipts		30						
Projected available balance	12							
Planned order releases								

Q = 30; LT = 5; SS = 0.

Component B		Week						
		1	2	3	4	5	6	7
Gross requirements								
Scheduled receipts		25						
Projected available balance	22							
Planned order releases								

Q = 25; LT = 5; SS = 0.

Component C		Week						
		1	2	3	4	5	6	7
Gross requirements								
Scheduled receipts		20						
Projected available balance	45							
Planned order releases								

Q = 20; LT = 5; SS = 0.

Component F		Week						
		1	2	3	4	5	6	7
Gross requirements								
Scheduled receipts		15						
Projected available balance	70							
Planned order releases								

Q = 15; LT = 5; SS = 0.

  b. What conclusions can you make regarding the validity of the current order due dates for the open shop orders at the #101 injection molding press?

8. Georgia Clay and Gravel was updating the MPS record for one of its products, Smell Fresh Cat Litter.

  a. Complete the following MPS time-phased record.

Item: Smell Fresh	Week							
	1	2	3	4	5	6	7	8
Forecast	20	20	20	30	30	30	30	30
Orders	5	3	2					
Available	50	30	10	30	50	20	40	10
Available to promise								
MPS	50			50	50		50	

On hand = 20; MPS Lot Size = 50.

The following events occurred during week 1:
- Actual demand during week 1 was 25 units.
- Marketing forecasted that 40 units would be needed for week 9.
- An order for 10 in week 2 was accepted.
- An order for 20 in week 4 was accepted.

- An order for 6 in week 3 was accepted.
- The MPS in week 1 was produced as planned.

b. Update the record below after rolling through time.

	Week							
Item: Smell Fresh	**2**	**3**	**4**	**5**	**6**	**7**	**8**	**9**
Forecast								
Orders								
Available								
Available to promise								
MPS								

On hand =   , MPS Lot Size = 50.

9. The following data have been prepared for master production scheduling purposes at the Pike's Peak Mountain Bike Company:

End Product	Beginning Inventory	Weekly Forecast	Lot Size	Hours Per Lot Size
A	60	10	30	30
B	20	5	20	20
C	30	15	50	50

(Current capacity = 40 hours per week).

a. Prepare the master production schedule for these items during the next four weeks using the Ethan Allen master production scheduling method.

b. Should the Pike's Peak Mountain Bike Company increase or decrease the capacity of the final assembly line? Justify your answer.

c. Suppose that the Pike's Peak master production schedule is frozen for the next three weeks. What specific impact would the policy have on the firm's performance?

10. Figure 6.21, the Ethan Allen example, is based on the following data:

Product	Beginning Inventory	Weekly Forecast	Lot Size	Hours Per Lot Size
A	20	5	50	20
B	50	40	250	80
C	−30	35	150	60
D	25	10	100	30

Priorities are calculated by dividing expected beginning inventory by forecast. In weeks after the first week, expected beginning inventory takes account of production and expected sales.

a. Calculate weekly priorities and determine the master production schedule for weeks 1 through 8 for these data. Check your answers against Figure 6.21.

b. Assume the actual sales in week 1 were as follows:

Product	Sales
A	10
B	30
C	25
D	25

Given these actual sales data, calculate the weekly priorities and determine the MPS for weeks 2 through 9, assuming the forecasts remain unchanged. What impact do these changes have?

c. Given the actual sales data in part b, calculate the priorities for weeks 7, 8, and 9. Determine the MPS for weeks 2 through 9, assuming the forecasts remain unchanged and weeks 2 through 6 are frozen; that is, the schedule in part a can be revised, but only from week 7 on. What impact would the frozen schedule have on the inventory and customer service levels for products A through D?

d. Assume that the time horizon date is extended to 18 weeks resulting in the following scheduling priorities for week 18:

Product	Priority
A	2
B	1.25
C	−1
D	1

Hours	Assembly Load (Week 18)
35	
30	
25	C
20	
15	
10	
5	B
0	

What capacity information can be inferred from this schedule?

11. The master production scheduler at the XYZ Company is concerned with determining the impact of using different MPS freezing intervals on component part shortages and inventory levels in the firm's fabrication shop. Currently, the firm's end products are produced on a make-to-stock basis. A four-period MPS planning horizon is used. Lot sizing is performed at the start of every period covering all four future periods. Assembly orders are issued at the start of each period. The assembly lead time equals zero periods; the beginning finished product inventory is zero.

TABLE A

Period	1	2	3	4
Forecast*	177	261	207	309
Available†	261	0	309	0
MPS	438	0	516	0

Period	2	3	4	5
Forecast	0	207	309	64
Available	0	373	64	0
MPS	0	580	0	0

Period	3	4	5	6
Forecast	207	309	64	182
Available	0	246	182	0
MPS	207	555	0	0

TABLE B

Period	1	2	3	4
Forecast*	177	261	207	309
Available†	261	0	309	0
MPS	438	0	516	0

Period	2	3	4	5
Forecast	0	207	309	64
Available	0	373	64	0
MPS	0	580	0	0

Period	3	4	5	6
Forecast	207	309	64	182
Available	373	64	0	0
MPS	580	0	0	182

*The forecast is net of beginning inventory.
†The available is the closing inventory balance.

Table A shows the forecast, projected inventory, and MPS for three consecutive periods for one of the firm's products, using the current freeze policy of one period and assuming perfect forecasts. Table B provides similar information using a two-period MPS freeze policy. Assuming the component part 1234 is used only on this end product, with a usage rate of one unit per unit of end product, prepare MRP records for this part as of the beginning of each of the three consecutive periods under both MPS freezing policies. Assume that component part 1234 has a planned lead time of two periods, that its lot size is the net requirement for the next two periods whenever a net requirement is observed, that it has zero safety stock and a beginning inventory of 450 units in period 1, and that there are no scheduled receipts.

a. What conclusions can you draw about the two different freezing policies' effectiveness?

b. What other freezing policies should be considered?

c. What are the appropriate time fences?

12. Falcon Sports Inc. makes a line of Jet Skis. There are eight different end items (catalog numbers) in the Jet Ski product line. The skis vary according to horsepower, seating capacity, and

starting mechanism. The company expects to sell one-half of the Jet Skis in the 12-horsepower model and one-half in the 10-horsepower model. The seating capacity breaks down to 60% for dual seating and 40% for single seating. The breakdown for starters is 25% manual and 75% automatic.

Catalog number	2100	2101	1100	1101	2120	2121	1120	1121
Horsepower	10	10	10	10	12	12	12	12
Seating style	Dual	Dual	Single	Single	Dual	Dual	Single	Single
Starter	Manual	Auto	Manual	Auto	Manual	Auto	Manual	Auto
Component parts	602	602	602	602	601	601	601	601
	350	350	360	360	350	350	360	360
	400	400	400	400	400	400	400	400
	235	230	235	230	235	230	235	230
	320	320	315	315	320	320	315	315
	600	600	600	600	600	600	600	600
	250	254	250	254	250	254	250	254
	410	410	410	410	610	610	610	610

    a. Group the component parts. Which are common? Which are associated with horsepower? Seating style? Starter?

    b. Create a super bill for Jet Skis matching the appropriate components with each option (include the usage percentages).

    c. What are the advantages and disadvantages of the super bill approach to planning?

13. The Ace Electronics Company produces printed circuit boards on a make-to-order basis.

    a. Prepare an MPS record for one of its items (catalogue #2400), including the available-to-promise information, using the following data:

        Final assembly production lead time = 2 weeks.
        Weekly forecast = 100 units.
        Current on-hand quantity = 0.
        Booked customer orders (already confirmed):
            95 units in week 1.
            105 units in week 2.
            70 units in week 3.
            10 units in week 5.
        Master production schedule:
            200 units to be completed at the start of week 1.
            200 units to be completed at the start of week 3.
            200 units to be completed at the start of week 5.
            200 units to be completed at the start of week 7.

    b. Suppose the cumulative lead time for the item (catalogue #2400) is eight weeks. What decision must the master scheduler make this week?

14. Brandy Boards produces circuit boards on a make-to-order basis. The company is currently planning production for one of its boards, the Sound Xapper. It has a weekly forecast of 50 boards, current inventory of 70 boards, and uses an MPS quantity of 150. MPS and order information for

the next seven weeks are given below:

Current Booked Orders		Master Production Schedule	
Week	Quantity	Week	Quantity
1	60	2	150
2	70	5	150
3	20		
4	70		
5	40		
6	30		

a. Prepare an MPS record for the Sound Xapper for the next seven weeks, including available-to-promise information.

b. Suppose the planning time fence is six weeks; what decision should the master scheduler make this week?

c. Sales received the following customer requests at the start of week 1. Using the information in the MPS record completed in part a, indicate to Sales which delivery commitments can be made to the customers.

Possible New Orders	
Week	Quantity
1	5
3	10
6	20

15. The Parker Corporation produces and sells a machine for tending golf course greens. The patented device trims the grass, aerates the turf, and injects a metered amount of nitrogen into the soil. Machines are marketed through the Taylor Golf Course Supply Company, under the Parker Company's own original equipment brand, and, recently, through a lawn and garden supply house (Brown Thumb), which serves both commercial and consumer accounts. Addition of the lawn and garden outlet and requests to add a 3-HP version have called into question the production planning and control process for the machines.

Forecasting the products to be produced is difficult. There are now two drive mechanisms (chain and gear), three different body styles (one for each outlet), and two sizes of engine (4- and 5-HP). This gives a total of 12 end items, all of which had some demand. (See Exhibit A.) The 3-HP motor would add six more end items. Forecasting demand for these new items would add to the difficulty of forecasting demand.

Lead times for some of the castings and for 5-HP motors have increased to the extent that it's not possible to wait until firm orders are received for the end items before the castings and motors have to be ordered. In addition, the firm's business is growing; it anticipates selling about 120 units next year. Consequently, the production manager has arranged to purchase enough material for 10 units per month. There's plenty of capacity for the small amount of parts fabrication required, but assembly capacity must be carefully planned. The current plan calls for assembly capacity of 10 units per month.

EXHIBIT A
Last Year's
Sales by
Catalog
Number

Catalog Number			Sales	Key
Body	**Horsepower***	**Drive**	**Total = 100**	
T	4	C	1	
T	4	G	4	Body:
T	5	C	18	T = Taylor Supply
T	5	G	17	O = "OEM" Parker's
O	4	C	13	own
O	4	G	9	B = Brown Thumb
O	5	C	10	
O	5	G	8	
B	4	C	6	Drive
B	4	G	7	C = Chain
B	5	C	2	G = Gear
B	5	G	5	

*Note: The 3-HP machine would be offered in all three body styles and both drives.

With regard to the specific issue of forecasting, the marketing manager summarized the data on the sales of each end item over the past year. (See Exhibit A.) He felt that a 20 percent growth in total volume was about right, and that 3-HP machines will perhaps account for half that growth. Of course, once the forecasts were made, the production manager had to determine which motors and castings (gear or chain) to order. Each machine was made up of many common parts, but the motors, chain or gear drive subassemblies, and bodies were different (though interchangeable).

a. Suggest an improved method of forecasting demand for the firm's products.

b. As the production manager contemplated the difficulty of forecasting demand for the firm's products and determining exactly what to schedule into final assembly, two customers called. The first, from Taylor, wanted to know when the company could deliver a model T3G; the second wanted as early delivery as possible of one of Parker's own machines, an O4C. The Taylor representative said he felt that the three-horsepower models might "really take off."

Before making any commitment at all, it was necessary to check the material availability and get back to the two customers. It was the firm's practice not to promise immediate delivery, since units scheduled for final assembly were usually already promised. The planned assembly schedule called for assembly of three units next week, two units the following week, and alternating three and two thereafter. As a matter of practice, all parts for assembly and delivery in any week would need to be ready at the start of that week.

Exhibit B shows current inventory and on-order positions for the common part "kit," the motors, and the drives. (The production manager didn't concern himself with the body styles since all three styles can be obtained in a week.) Exhibit C lists all booked orders promised for delivery over the next few weeks. Organize this information to respond to the delivery promise requests. (Assume that no safety stocks are held.) What should the delivery promises be?

EXHIBIT B
Inventories and
On-Order

Item	Inventory	On Order in:	Due Date	Lot size
Common "kit"	0	5 each in:	weeks 1,3,5,7,9	5
5-HP motor	10	5 in:	week 5	5
4-HP motor	3	5 in:	weeks 3, 8	5
3-HP motor	0	5 in:	week 1	5
Chain drive	14	—	—	10
Gear drive	6	10 in:	week 3	10

EXHIBIT C
Booked Orders
and Delivery
Dates

		Delivery Week					
		1	**2**	**3**	**4**	**5**	**6**
Models		2T4G*	1B3G	1T5C	1O5G	1T5G	1O4G
		1O5C	1T4C	1B4C			
			1O4G				
	Total	3	3	2	1	1	1

*2 units of T4G.

Chapter

7

Material Requirements Planning

This chapter deals with material requirements planning (MRP), a basic tool for performing the detailed material planning function in the manufacture of component parts and their assembly into finished items. MRP is used by many companies that have invested in batch production processes. MRP's managerial objective is to provide "the right part at the right time" to meet the schedules for completed products. To do this, MRP provides *formal* plans for each part number, whether raw material, component, or finished good. Accomplishing these plans without excess inventory, overtime, labor, or other resources is also important.

Chapter 7 is organized around the following five topics:

- *Material requirements planning in manufacturing planning and control:* Where does MRP fit in the overall MPC system framework and how is it related to other MPC modules?
- *Record processing:* What is the basic MRP record and how is it produced?
- *Technical issues:* What additional technical details and supporting systems should you recognize?
- *Using the MRP system:* Who uses the system, how is it used, and how is the exact match between MRP records and physical reality maintained?
- *System dynamics:* How does MRP reflect changing conditions, and why must transactions be processed properly?

MRP's relationship to other manufacturing planning and control (MPC) concepts is shown in Chapter 1. Many just-in-time (JIT) concepts have emerged as basic approaches for designing MPC systems in some companies. These concepts are discussed in Chapter 8. Advanced MRP techniques are presented in Chapter 14.

Material Requirements Planning in Manufacturing Planning and Control

For companies assembling end items from components produced in batch manufacturing processes, MRP is central to the development of detailed plans for part needs. It is often where companies start in developing their MPC systems. Facility with time-phased planning and the associated time-phased records is basic to understanding many other aspects of the MPC system. Finally, although introduction of JIT and investments in lean manufacturing processes have brought about fundamental changes in detailed material planning for some firms, companies continue to adapt the MRP approach or enhance their existing systems.

For firms using MRP, the general MPC framework depicted in Figure 7.1 shows that detailed requirements planning is characterized by the use of time-phased (period-by-period) requirement records. Several other supporting activities are shown in the front end, engine, and back end of the system as well. The front end of the MPC system produces the master production schedule (MPS). The back end, or execution system, deals with production scheduling and control of the factory and with managing materials coming from vendor plants.

FIGURE 7.1
Manufacturing Planning and Control System

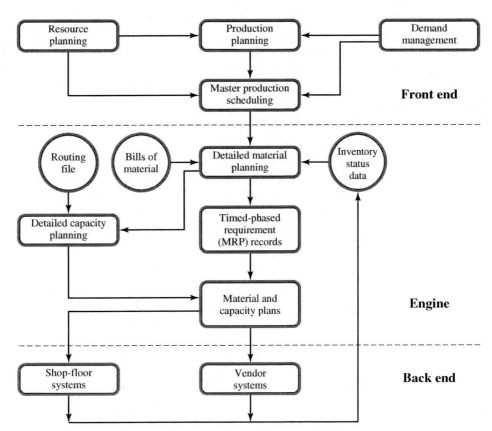

The detailed material planning function represents a central system in the engine portion of Figure 7.1. For firms preparing detailed material plans using MRP, this means taking a time-phased set of master production schedule requirements and producing a resultant time-phased set of component parts and raw material requirements.

In addition to master production schedule inputs, MRP requires two other basic inputs. A bill of material shows, for each part number, what other part numbers are required as direct components. For example, for a car, it could show five wheels required (four plus the spare). For each wheel, the bill of materials could be a hub, tire, valve stem, and so on. The second basic input to MRP is inventory status. To know how many wheels to make for a given number of cars, we must know how many are on hand, how many of those are already allocated to existing needs, and how many have already been ordered.

The MRP data make it possible to construct a time-phased requirement record for any part number. The data can also be used as input to the detailed capacity planning models. Developing material and capacity plans is an iterative process where the planning is carried out level by level. For example, planning for a car would determine requirements for wheels, which in turn determines requirements for tires, and so on. But planning for tires has to be done *after* the planning for wheels; if the company wants to build 10 cars (50 wheels) and has 15 complete wheels on hand, it only needs 35 more— and 35 tires. If 20 wheels have already been ordered, only 15 more must be made to complete the 10 cars.

An MRP system serves a central role in material planning and control. It translates the overall plans for production into the detailed individual steps necessary to accomplish those plans. It provides information for developing capacity plans, and it links to the systems that actually get the production accomplished.

Record Processing

In this section, we present the MRP procedures starting with the basic MRP record, its terminology, timing conventions, and construction. We then turn to an example illustrating coordination of planning component parts and end items. We examine several aspects of this coordination and the relationships that must be accounted for. We then look at linking MRP records to reflect all the required relationships. We intend to show clearly how each MRP record can be managed independently while the *system* keeps them coordinated.

The Basic MRP Record

At the heart of the MPC system is a universal representation of the status and plans for any single item (part number), whether raw material, component part, or finished good: the MRP time-phased record. Figure 7.2 displays the following information:

The anticipated future usage of or demand for the item *during* each period (i.e., **gross requirements**).

Existing replenishment orders for the item due in at the *beginning* of each period (i.e., **scheduled receipts**).

FIGURE 7.2
**The Basic
MRP Record**

		Period				
		1	**2**	**3**	**4**	**5**
Gross requirements			10		40	10
Scheduled receipts		50				
Projected available balance	4	54	44	44	4	44
Planned order releases					50	
Lead time = one period Lot size = 50						

The current and projected inventory status for the item at the *end* of each period (i.e., **projected available balance**).

Planned replenishment orders for the item at the *beginning* of each period (i.e., **planned order releases**).

The top row in Figure 7.2 indicates periods that can vary in length from a day to a quarter or even longer. The period is also called a **time bucket.** A widely used time bucket or period is one week. A timing convention is that the current time is the beginning of the first period. The initial available balance of four units is shown prior to period 1. The number of periods in the record is called the **planning horizon.** In this simplified example, the planning horizon is five periods. The planning horizon indicates the number of future periods for which plans are made.

The second row, "Gross requirements," is the anticipated future usage of (or demand for) the item. The gross requirements are **time phased,** which means they're stated on a unique period-by-period basis, rather than aggregated or averaged; that is, gross requirements are stated as 10 in period 2, 40 in period 4, and 10 in period 5, rather than as a total requirement of 60 or as an average requirement of 12 per period. This method of presentation allows for special orders, seasonality, and periods of no anticipated usage to be explicitly taken into account. A gross requirement in a particular period will be unsatisfied unless the item is **available** during that period. Availability is achieved by having the item in inventory or by receiving either a scheduled receipt or a planned replenishment order in time to satisfy the gross requirement.

Another timing convention comes from the question of availability. The item must be available at the *beginning* of the time bucket in which it's required. This means plans must be so made that any replenishment order will be in inventory at the beginning of the period in which the gross requirement for that order occurs.

The "Scheduled receipts" row describes the status of all open orders (work in process or existing replenishment orders) for the item. This row shows the quantities ordered and when we expect these orders to be completed. Scheduled receipts result from previously made ordering decisions and represent a source of the item to meet gross requirements. For example, the gross requirements of 10 in period 2 cannot be satisfied by the 4 units presently available. The scheduled receipts of 50, due in period 1, will satisfy the gross requirement in period 2 if things go according to plan. Scheduled receipts represent a commitment. For an order in the factory, necessary materials have been committed to the order, and capacity at work centers will be required to complete it. For a purchased item, similar commitments have been made to a vendor. The timing convention used for showing scheduled receipts is also at the *beginning* of the period; that is, the order is shown in the period during which the item will be available to satisfy a gross requirement.

The next row in Figure 7.2 is "Projected available balance." The timing convention in this row is the *end* of the period; that is, the row is the projected balance *after* replenishment orders have been received and gross requirements have been satisfied. For this reason, the "Projected available balance" row has an extra time bucket shown at the beginning. The bucket shows the balance *at the present time;* that is, in Figure 7.2, the beginning available balance is 4 units. The quantity shown in period 1 is the projected balance at the *end* of period 1. The projected available balance shown at the end of a period is available to meet gross requirements in the next (and succeeding) periods. For example, the 54 units shown as the projected available balance at the end of period 1 result from adding the 50 units scheduled to be received to the beginning balance of 4 units. The gross requirement of 10 units in period 2 reduces the projected balance to 44 units at the end of period 2. The term projected *available* balance is used, instead of projected *on-hand* balance, for a very specific reason. Units of the item might be on hand physically but not available to meet gross requirements because they are already promised or allocated for some other purpose.

The "Planned order releases" row is determined directly from the "Projected available balance" row. Whenever the projected available balance shows a quantity insufficient to satisfy gross requirements (a negative quantity), additional material must be planned for. This is done by creating a planned order release in time to keep the projected available balance from becoming negative. For example, in Figure 7.2, the projected available balance at the end of period 4 is 4 units. This is not sufficient to meet the gross requirement of 10 units in period 5. Since the lead time is one week, the MRP system creates a planned order at the beginning of week 4 providing a **lead time offset** of one week. As we have used a lot size of 50 units, the projected available balance at the end of week 5 is 44 units. Another way that this logic is explained is to note that the balance for the end of period 4 (4 units) is the beginning inventory for period 5, during which there's a gross requirement of 10 units. The difference between the available inventory of 4 and the gross requirement of 10 is a **net requirement** of 6 units in period 5. Thus, an order for at least 6 units must be planned for period 4 to avoid a shortage in period 5.

The MRP system produces the planned order release data in response to the gross requirement, scheduled receipt, and projected available data. When a planned order is created for the most immediate or current period, it is in the **action bucket.** A quantity in the action bucket means some action is needed now to avoid a future problem. The action is to release the order, which converts it to a scheduled receipt.

The planned order releases are *not* shown in the scheduled receipt row because they haven't yet been released for production or purchasing. No material has been committed to their manufacture. The planned order is analogous to an entry on a Christmas list, since the list comprises plans. A scheduled receipt is like an order mailed to a catalog firm for a particular Christmas gift, since a commitment has been made. Like Christmas lists versus mailed orders, planned orders are much easier to change than scheduled receipts. Not converting planned orders into scheduled receipts any earlier than necessary has many advantages.

The basic MRP record just described provides the correct information on each part in the system. Linking these single part records together is essential in managing all the parts needed for a complex product or customer order. Key elements for linking the records are the bill of materials, the explosion process (using inventory and scheduled receipt information), and lead time offsetting. We consider each of these before turning to how the records are linked into a system.

An Example Bill of Materials

Figure 7.3 shows a snow shovel, and item part number 1605. The complete snow shovel is assembled (using four rivets and two nails) from the top handle assembly, scoop assembly, scoop-shaft connector, and shaft. The top handle assembly, in turn, is created by combining the welded top handle bracket assembly with the wooden handle using two nails. The welded top handle bracket assembly is created by welding the top handle coupling to the top handle bracket. In a similar way, the scoop assembly combines the aluminum scoop with the steel blade using six rivets.

FIGURE 7.3
The 1605 Snow Shovel Shown with Component Parts and Assemblies

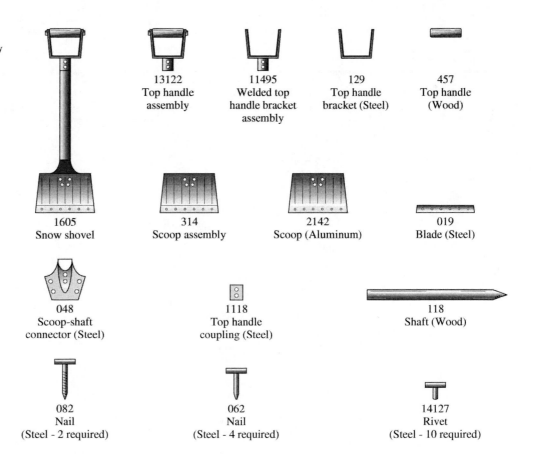

13122 Top handle assembly	11495 Welded top handle bracket assembly	129 Top handle bracket (Steel)	457 Top handle (Wood)
1605 Snow shovel	314 Scoop assembly	2142 Scoop (Aluminum)	019 Blade (Steel)
048 Scoop-shaft connector (Steel)	1118 Top handle coupling (Steel)		118 Shaft (Wood)
082 Nail (Steel - 2 required)	062 Nail (Steel - 4 required)		14127 Rivet (Steel - 10 required)

228   Chapter 7   *Material Requirements Planning*

Explaining even this simple assembly process is a cumbersome task. Moreover, such diagrams as Figure 7.3 get more complicated as the number of subassemblies, components, and parts used increases, or as they are used in increasingly more places (e.g., rivets and nails). Two techniques that get at this problem nicely are the **product structure diagram** and the **indented bill of materials (BOM)** shown in Figure 7.4. Both provide the detailed information of Figure 7.3, but the indented BOM has the added advantage of being easily printed by a computer.

FIGURE 7.4   **Parts for Snow Shovel**

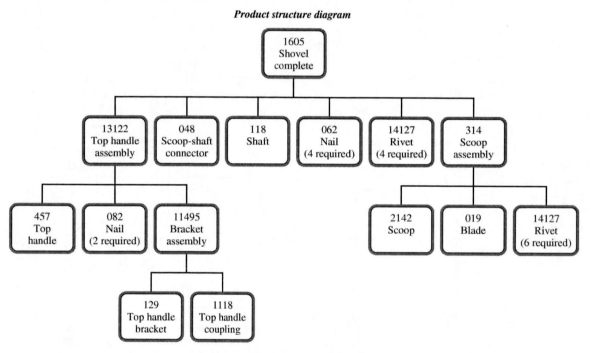

Product structure diagram

Indented bill of materials (BOM)

1605 Snow Shovel

    13122 Top Handle Assembly (1 required)
       457   Top Handle (1 required)
       082   Nail (2 required)
     11495 Bracket Assembly (1 required)
         129   Top Handle Bracket (1 required)
        1118 Top Handle Coupling (1 required)

    048   Scoop-Shaft Connector (1 required)
    118   Shaft (1 required)
    062   Nail (4 required)
    14127 Rivet (4 required)
    314   Scoop Assembly
      2142   Scoop (1 required)
      019   Blade (1 required)
     14127 Rivet (6 required)

Note that both the product structure diagram and the indented BOM show exactly what goes into what instead of being just a parts list. For example, to make one 13122 top handle assembly, we see by the product structure diagram that one 457 top handle, two 082 nails, and one 11495 bracket assembly are needed. The same information is shown in the indented BOM; the three required parts are indented and shown, one level beneath the 13122. Note also that we *don't* need a top handle bracket (129) or a top handle coupling (1118) to produce a top handle assembly (13122). These are only needed to produce a bracket assembly (11495). In essence, the top handle assembly does not care *how* a bracket assembly is made, only that it *is* made. Making the bracket assembly is a separate problem.

Before leaving our brief discussion of bills of material, it is important to stress that the bill of material used to support MRP may differ from other company perceptions of a bill of materials. The BOM to support MRP must be consistent with the way the product is manufactured. For example, if we're making red cars, the part numbers should be for red doors. If green cars are desired, the part numbers must be for green doors. Also, if we change to a different set of subassemblies, indentations on the BOM should change as well. Engineering and accounting may well not care what color the parts are or what the manufacturing sequence is.

Gross to Net Explosion

Explosion is the process of translating product requirements into component part requirements, taking existing inventories and scheduled receipts into account. Thus, explosion may be viewed as the process of determining, for *any* part number, the quantities of *all* components needed to satisfy its requirements, and continuing this process for *every* part number until all purchased and/or raw material requirements are exactly calculated.

As explosion takes place, only the component part requirements net of any inventory or scheduled receipts are considered. In this way, only the *necessary* requirements are linked through the system. Although this may seem like an obvious goal, the product structure can make determination of net requirements more difficult than it seems. To illustrate, let's return to the snow shovel example.

Suppose the company wanted to produce 100 snow shovels, and we were responsible for making the 13122 top handle assembly. We are given current inventory and scheduled receipt information from which the gross requirements and net requirements for each component of the top handle can be calculated, as shown in Figure 7.5.

FIGURE 7.5   **Gross and Net Requirement Calculations for the Snow Shovel**

Part Description	Part Number	Inventory	Scheduled Receipts	Gross Requirements	Net Requirements
Top handle assembly	13122	25	—	100	75
Top handle	457	22	25	75	28
Nail (2 required)	082	4	50	150	96
Bracket assembly	11495	27	—	75	48
Top handle bracket	129	15	—	48	33
Top handle coupling	1118	39	15	48	—

The gross and net requirements in Figure 7.5 may not correspond to what we feel they should be. It might at the outset seem that since one top handle coupling (1118) is used per shovel, the gross requirements should be 100 and the net requirement 46, instead of the 48 and zero shown. To produce 100 shovels means we need (have a demand for) 100 top handle assemblies (part 13122). Twenty-five of these 100 can come from inventory, resulting in a net requirement of 75. As we need to make only 75 top handle assemblies, we need 75 top handles and bracket assemblies. This 75 is the *gross* requirement for parts 457 and 11495 (as indicated by the circled numbers in Figure 7.5). Since 2 nails (part 082) are used per top handle assembly, the gross requirement for 082 is 150. The 25 units of top handle assembly inventory contain some implicit inventories of handles, brackets, and nails, which the gross to net process takes into account. Looking on down, we see that there are 27 units of the bracket assembly in inventory, so the net requirement is for 48. This becomes the gross requirement for the bracket and coupling. Since there are 39 top handle couplings in inventory and 15 scheduled for receipt, there is *no* net requirement for part 1118.

Gross to net explosion is a key element of MRP systems. It not only provides the basis for calculating the appropriate quantities but also serves as the communication link between part numbers. It's the basis for the concept of **dependent demand;** that is, the "demand" (gross requirements) for top handles depends on the net requirements for top handle assemblies. To correctly do the calculations, the bill of material, inventory, and scheduled receipt data are all necessary. With these data, the dependent demand can be exactly calculated. It need not be forecast. On the other hand, some **independent demand** items, such as the snow shovel, are subject to demand from outside the firm. The need for snow shovels will have to be forecast. The concept of dependent demand is often called the fundamental principle of MRP. It provides the way to remove uncertainty from the requirement calculations.

Lead Time Offsetting

Gross to net explosion tells us how many of each subassembly and component part are needed to support a desired finished product quantity. What it does not do, however, is tell us *when* each component and subassembly is needed. Referring back to Figures 7.3 and 7.4, clearly the top handle bracket and top handle coupling need to be welded together before the wooden top handle is attached. These relationships are known as **precedent relationships.** They indicate the order in which things must be done.

In addition to precedent relationships, determining when to schedule each component part also depends on how long it takes to produce the part (that is, the lead time). Perhaps the top handle bracket (129) can be fabricated in one day, while the top handle coupling (1118) takes two weeks. If so, it would be advantageous to start making the coupling before the bracket, since they are both needed at the same time to make a bracket assembly.

Despite the need to take lead time differences into account, many systems for component part manufacturing ignore them. For example, most furniture manufacturers base production on what is called a **cutting.** In the cutting approach, if a lot of 100 chairs were to be assembled, then 100 of each part (with appropriate multiples) are started at the same time. Figure 7.6 is a Gantt chart (time-oriented bar chart) showing how this cutting approach would be applied to the snow shovel example. (Note that processing times are shown on the chart.)

Figure 7.6 shows clearly that the cutting approach, which starts all parts as soon as possible, will lead to unnecessary work-in-process inventories. For example, the top handle bracket (129) doesn't need to be started until the end of day 9, since it must wait for the

FIGURE 7.6
Gantt Chart for Cutting Approach to Snow Shovel Problem (front or earliest start schedule)

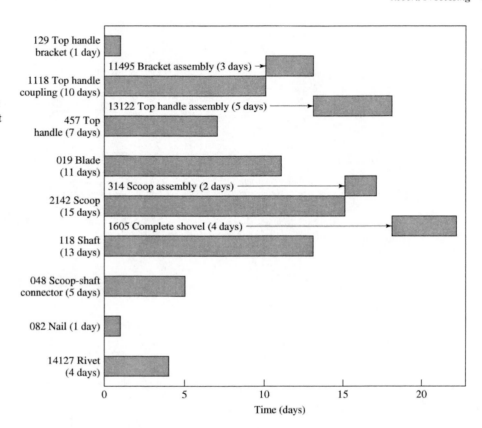

coupling (1118) before it can be put into its assembly (11495), and part 1118 takes 10 days. In the cutting approach, parts are scheduled earlier than need be. This results from using **front schedule** logic (that is, scheduling as early as possible).

What should be done is to **back schedule**—start each item as late as possible. Figure 7.7 provides a back schedule for the snow shovel example. The schedules for parts 1118, 11495, 13122, and 1605 don't change, since they form a critical path. All of the other parts, however, are scheduled later in this approach than in the front scheduling approach. A substantial savings in work-in-process inventory is obtained by this shift of dates.

Back scheduling has several obvious advantages. It will reduce work-in-process, postpone the commitment of raw materials to specific products, and minimize storage time of completed components. Implementing the back schedule approach, however, requires a system. The system must have accurate BOM data and lead time estimates, some way to ensure all component parts are started at the right times, and some means of tracking components and subassemblies to make sure they are all completed according to plans. The cutting approach is much simpler, since all component parts are started at the same time and left in the pipeline until needed.

MRP achieves the benefits of the back scheduling approach *and* performs the gross to net explosion. In fact, the combination of back schedules and gross to net explosion is the heart of MRP.

FIGURE 7.7
Gantt Chart
Based on Back
Schedule
(latest start)

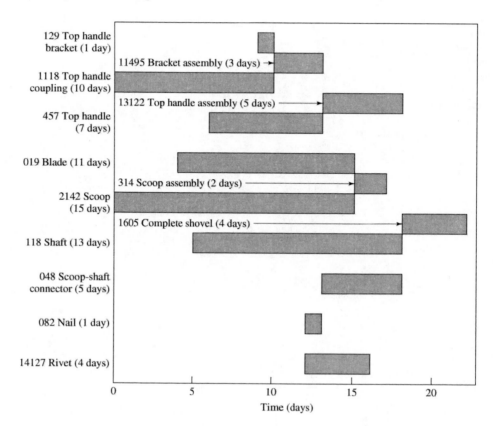

Linking the MRP Records

Figure 7.8 shows the linked set of individual time-phased MRP records for the top handle assembly of the snow shovel. We have already used the first five periods of the 082 nail record shown in Figure 7.8 as the record in Figure 7.2. To see how that record fits into the whole, we start with the snow shovels themselves. We said 100 snow shovels were going to be made, and now we see the timing. That is, the "Gross requirements" row in the MRP record for part number 13122 in Figure 7.8 shows the total need of 100 time phased as 20 in week 2, 10 in week 4, 20 in week 6, 5 in week 7, 35 in week 9, and 10 in week 10. Since each snow shovel takes a top handle assembly, the "Gross requirements" row for the top handle shows when shovel assembly is to begin. Note the total planned orders for the top handle assembly is the net requirement of 75 that we calculated before in the gross to net calculations of Figure 7.5.

The lead time for the top handle assembly is two weeks, calculated as the five days processing time shown in Figure 7.6 plus five days for paperwork. The lead time for each of the other records is similarly calculated; one week (five days) of paperwork time is added to the processing time and the total rounded to the nearest five-day week. The current inventories and scheduled receipts for each part are those shown in Figure 7.5. The scheduled receipts are shown in the appropriate periods. Using the two-week lead time and recognizing a net requirement of five units in week 4 for the top handle assembly, we see the need to plan an order for week 2 of five units.

FIGURE 7.8   **MRP Records for the Snow Shovel Top Handle Assembly**

			Week									
			1	2	3	4	5	6	7	8	9	10
13122 Top handle assembly Lead time = 2	Gross requirements			20		10		20	5		35	10
	Scheduled receipts											
	Projected available balance	25	25	5	5	0	0	0	0	0	0	0
	Planned order releases			(5)		20	5		35	10		
457 Top handle Lead time = 2	Gross requirements			(5)		20	5		35	10		
	Scheduled receipts				25							
	Projected available balance	22	22	17	42	22	17	17	0	0	0	0
	Planned order releases						18	10				
082 Nail (2 required) Lead time = 1 Lot size = 50	Gross requirements			10		40	10		70	20		
	Scheduled receipts		50									
	Projected available balance	4	54	44	44	4	44	44	24	4	4	4
	Planned order releases					50		50				
11495 Bracket assembly Lead time = 2	Gross requirements			5		20	5		35	10		
	Scheduled receipts											
	Projected available balance	27	27	22	22	2	0	0	0	0	0	0
	Planned order releases				3		35	10				
129 Top handle bracket Lead time = 1	Gross requirements				3		35	10				
	Scheduled receipts											
	Projected available balance	15	15	15	12	12	0	0	0	0	0	0
	Planned order releases					23	10					
1118 Top handle coupling Lead time = 3 Safety stock = 20	Gross requirements				3		35	10				
	Scheduled receipts				15							
	Projected available balance	39	39	54	51	51	20	20	20	20	20	20
	Planned order releases				4	10						

This planned order release of five units in week 2 becomes a gross requirement in week 2 for the top handles as shown by the circles in Figure 7.8. Note also the gross requirements for the nails and brackets in period 2 derive from this same planned order release (with two nails per top handle assembly). Thus, the communication between records is the dependent demand that we saw illustrated before in the gross to net calculations of Figure 7.5.

The remaining planned order releases for the top handle assembly exactly meet the net requirements in the remaining periods, offset for the lead time. The ordering policy used for these items is called **lot-for-lot** (i.e., as required) sizing. An exception to the lot-for-lot procedure is the ordering of nails, which is done in lots of 50. In the case of the nails, the total planned orders will not necessarily add up to the net requirements.

Another part for which there is a discrepancy between the planned orders and the net requirements calculated in Figure 7.5 is the top handle coupling. For this part, a safety stock of 20 units is desired. This means the planned order logic will schedule a planned order release to prevent the projected available balance from going below the safety stock level of 20 units. For the top handle couplings, this means a total of 4 units must be planned for period 2 and 10 for period 3 to maintain the 20-unit safety stock.

The one element we have yet to clearly show is the back scheduling effect. We saw in Figure 7.7 that it would be desirable to delay the start of the top handle bracket (part 129) so that this item is completed at the same time as the top handle coupling (part 1118). The MRP records show that the start of the first planned order for part 129 isn't until week 4, two weeks after the first planned order for part 1118. Both of these planned orders are to satisfy a gross requirement of 35 derived from the planned order for the bracket assembly in week 5. We see then that the orders are back scheduled. This relationship can be more complicated than our example, since the planned order release timing depends on the safety stock and inventory levels, as well as the lead times. The MRP system, however, coordinates all of that information and determines the appropriate planned order release dates, based on back scheduling.

At this point, we see fully the linking of the MRP time-phased records. The "Planned order releases" row for the top handle assembly (13122) becomes (with the appropriate multiplier) the "Gross requirements" row for each of its components (parts 457, 082, and 11495), and they are linked together. Once all the gross requirements data are available for a particular record, the individual record processing logic is applied and the planned order releases for the part are passed down as gross requirements to its components, following the product structure (BOM) on a level-by-level basis. In some cases, parts will receive their requirements from more than one source (common parts), as is true for the nails and rivets in the snow shovel. In these cases, gross requirements will reflect needs from more than one planned order release source. Again, the system accounts for this and incorporates it into the gross to net logic.

The MRP records take proper account of gross to netting. They also incorporate back scheduling and allow for explicit timings, desired lot sizing procedures, safety stocks, and part commonality. Even more important, however, is independence of the part number planning. With the MRP approach, the person planning snow shovels need not explicitly coordinate his planning with planning of the component parts. The MRP system accomplishes the coordination. Whatever is done to the MRP record for the snow shovels will result in a set of planned orders that the system will correctly pass down as gross requirements to its components. This means plans for each part number can be developed independently of the product structures, and the plans at each level will be communicated correctly to the other levels.

Technical Issues

In this section, we briefly introduce some technical issues to consider in designing MRP systems.

Processing Frequency

Thus far we've looked only at the static construction of the MRP records and how they're linked together. Since conditions change and new information is received, the MRP records must be brought up to date so plans can be adjusted. This means processing the MRP records anew, incorporating current information. Two issues are involved in the processing decision: how frequently the records should be processed and whether all the records should be processed at the same time.

Processing all of the records in one computer run is called **regeneration.** This signifies that *all* part number records are completely reconstructed each time the records are processed. When a regeneration run is conducted, all current planned orders are removed. Then, starting with the end items, each item is completely rescheduled. This can generate very large processing demands on the system. When initiated on line, the data-intensive run can negatively affect overall system performance and cause inconvenience to other users. To avoid this common problem, it is possible to conduct regeneration runs as background jobs. In addition to operating in the background, these jobs can be scheduled to take place automatically during periods of low system demand, such as late evenings or weekends.

The problem with processing less frequently is that the portrayal of component status and needs expressed in the records becomes increasingly out of date and inaccurate. This decrease in accuracy has both anticipated and unanticipated causes. As the anticipated scheduled receipts are received and requirements satisfied, the inventory balances change. As unanticipated scrap, requirement changes, stock corrections, or other such transactions occur, they cause inaccuracies if not reflected in all the time-phased records influenced by the transactions. Changes in one record are linked to other time-phased records as planned order releases become gross requirements for lower-level components. Thus, some change transactions may cascade throughout the product structure. If these transactions are not reflected in the time-phased records early enough, the result can be poor planning.

More frequent processing of the MRP records increases computer costs but results in fewer unpleasant surprises. When the records reflecting the changes are produced, appropriate actions will be indicated to compensate for the changes.

A logical response to the pressure for more frequent processing is to reduce the required amount of calculation by processing only the records affected by the changes. An alternative to regeneration is the **net change** approach. With net change, only those items that are affected by the new or changed information are reprocessed.

The argument for the net change approach is that it can reduce computer time enough to make daily or even real-time processing possible. Since only some of the records are reviewed at each processing, there's a need for very accurate computer records and transaction processing procedures. Some net change users do an occasional regeneration to clean up all records.

The most challenging aspect of net change is its hypersensitivity, or nervousness. The frequent replanning may result in continual revision of recommended user actions through the revision of planned order releases. Users may be frustrated with these frequent revisions to the plan.

Bucketless Systems

To some extent, the problems of timing are tied to the use of time buckets. When the buckets are small enough, the problems are reduced significantly. However, smaller buckets mean more buckets, which increases review, storage, and computation costs. A bucketless MRP system specifies the exact release and due dates for each requirement, scheduled receipt, and planned order. The managerial reports are printed out on whatever basis is required, including by exact dates.

Bucketless MRP systems are a better way to use the computer. Above and beyond that, the approach allows better maintenance of lead time offsets and provides more precise time-phased information. The approach is consistent with state-of-the-art software, and many firms now use bucketless systems. The major addition is that the planning cycle itself is bucketless. That is, plans are revised as necessary, not on a periodic schedule, and the entire execution cycle is also shortened.

Lot Sizing

In the snow shovel example of Figure 7.8, we use a fixed lot size (50 units for the nails) and the lot-for-lot procedure. The lot size of 50 for the nails could have been someone's estimate of a good lot size or the result of calculation. The time-phased information can be used in combination with other data to develop lot sizes conforming to organizational needs. We might reach the conclusion, for the top handle (1118) in Figure 7.8, that it's undesirable to set up the equipment for 4 parts in week 2, and again for 10 parts in week 3, so we'd combine the two orders. The time-phased record permits us to develop such **discrete lot sizes** that will exactly satisfy the net requirements for one or more periods.

Several formal procedures have been developed for lot sizing the time-phased requirements. The basic trade-off usually involves elimination of one or more setups at the expense of carrying inventory longer. In many cases, discrete lot sizes possible with MRP are more appealing than fixed lot sizes. Compare the residual inventory of nails in week 10, with that of the bracket assemblies in Figure 7.8, for example.

At first glance the lot-for-lot technique seems a bit too simple-minded since it does not consider any of the economic trade-offs or physical factors. However, batching planned orders at one level will increase gross requirements at the next level in the product structure. So larger lot sizing near the end-item level of the bill of materials cascades down through all levels. Thus, it turns out that lot-for-lot is better than we might expect in actual practice, particularly at the intermediate levels in the bill of materials. This is especially the case when a product structure has many levels, and the cascading effect becomes greatly magnified. This cascading effect can be mitigated to some extent for components and raw materials that are very common. When this is the case, again lot sizing may be appropriate. As a consequence, many firms employ lot sizing primarily at the end-item and basic component levels, while intermediate subassemblies are planned on a lot-for-lot basis.

Safety Stock and Safety Lead Time

Carrying out detailed component plans is sometimes facilitated by including **safety stocks** and/or **safety lead times** in the MRP records. Safety stock is a buffer of stock above and beyond that needed to satisfy the gross requirements. Figure 7.8 illustrates this by incorporating safety stock for the top handle coupling. Safety lead time is a procedure whereby shop orders or purchase orders are released and scheduled to arrive one or more periods before necessary to satisfy the gross requirements.

Safety stocks can be incorporated into MRP time-phased records. The result is that the projected available balance doesn't fall below the safety stock level instead of reaching zero. To incorporate safety lead time, orders are issued (planned) earlier and are scheduled (planned) to be received into inventory before the time that the MRP logic would indicate as necessary. Figure 7.9 shows the top handle bracket from Figure 7.8 being planned with a one-week safety lead time. Notice that both the planned release and planned receipt dates are changed. Safety lead time is not just inflated lead time.

Both safety stock and safety lead time are used in practice and can be used simultaneously. However, both are hedges indicating that orders should be released (launched) or that they need to be received when, in fact, this is not strictly true. To use safety stocks and safety lead times effectively, we must understand the techniques' influence on plans. If they are not well understood, wrong orders can be sent to the factory, meaning workers will try to get out part A because of safety lead time or safety stock when, in fact, part B will be required to meet a customer order.

Safety stock tends to be used in MRP systems where uncertainty about quantities is the problem (e.g., where some small amount of scrap, spare part demand, or other unplanned usage is a frequent occurrence). Safety lead time, on the other hand, tends to be used when the major uncertainty is the timing rather than the quantity. For example, if a firm buys from a vendor who often misses delivery dates, safety lead time may provide better results than safety stock.

FIGURE 7.9   **MRP Record with Safety Lead Time**

			1	2	3	4	5	6	7	8	9	10
Part 129	Gross requirements				3		35	10				
Top handle bracket lead time = 1	Scheduled receipts											
Lot-for-lot	Projected available balance	15	15	15	12	35	10	0	0	0	0	0
Safety lead time = 1	Planned order releases				23	10						

Low-Level Coding

If we refer once again to Figure 7.4, we see that the rivet (part 14127) is a common part. The "Planned order" row for completed shovels will be passed down as gross requirements to the rivet. But there are additional requirements for the rivets (14127) from the scoop assembly (314). If we process the time-phased record for this common part before all of its gross requirements have been accumulated, the computations must be redone.

The way this problem is handled is to assign **low-level code numbers** to each part in the product structure or the indented BOM. By convention, the top final assembly level is denoted as level 0. In our example, the snow shovel would have a low-level code of 0. All immediate component part numbers of this part (13122, 048, 118, 062, 14127, and 314 in Figure 7.4) are given the low-level code number 1. The next level down (part numbers 457, 082, 11495, 2142, 019, and 14127) are low-level coded 2. Note the common part (rivet) has just been recoded as level 2, indicating it is used lower in the product structure. The higher the level codes, the lower in the product structure the part is used. Consequently, the last level code assigned to a part indicates the lowest level of usage and is the level code retained for that part. We finish the example when part numbers 129 and 1118 are coded level 3. The level code assigned to any part number is based on the part's usage in all products manufactured by the organization.

Once low-level codes are established, MRP record processing proceeds from one level code to the next, starting at level code 0. This ensures all gross requirements have been passed down to a part before its MRP record is processed. The result is planning of component parts coordinated with the needs of all higher-level part numbers. Within a level, the MRP record processing is typically done in part number sequence.

Pegging

Pegging relates all the gross requirements for a part to all the planned order releases or other sources of demand that created the requirements. The pegging records contain the specific part number or numbers of the sources of all gross requirements. At level 0, for example, pegging records might contain the specific customer orders to be satisfied by the gross requirements in the end-item, time-phased records. For lower-level part numbers, the gross requirements are most often pegged to planned orders of higher-level items, but might also be pegged to customer orders if the part is sold as a service part.

Pegging information can be used to go up through the MRP records from a raw material gross requirement to some future customer order. In this sense, it's the reverse of the explosion process. Pegging is sometimes compared to **where-used data.** Where-used data, however, indicate for each part number, the part numbers of all items on which the part is used. Pegging, on the other hand, is a *selective* where-used file. Pegging shows only the specific part numbers that produce the specific gross requirements in each time period. Thus, pegging information can trace the impact of a material problem all the way up to the order it would affect.

Firm Planned Orders

The logic used to illustrate the construction of an MRP record for an individual part number is automatically applied for every processed part number. The result is a series of planned order releases for each part number. If changes have taken place since the last time the record was processed, planned order releases can be very different from one record-processing cycle to the next. Since planned orders are passed down as gross requirements to the next level, the differences can cascade throughout the product structure.

One device for preventing this cascading down through the product structure is to create a **firm planned order (FPO).** FPO, as the name implies, is a planned order that the MRP system *does not* automatically change when conditions change. To change either the quantity or timing of a firm planned order, managerial action is required. This means the trade-offs in making the change can be evaluated before authorization.

The FPO provides a means for temporarily overriding the system to provide stability or to solve problems. For example, if changes are coming about because of scrap losses on open orders, the possibility of absorbing those variations with safety stock can be evaluated. If more rapid delivery of raw material than usual is requested (say by using air freight) to meet a special need, lead time can be reduced for that one order. An FPO means the system will not use the normal lead time offset from the net requirement for that order.

Service Parts

Service part demand must be included in the MRP record if the material requirements are not to be understated. The service part demand is typically based on a forecast and is added directly into the gross requirements for the part. From the MRP system point of view, the service part demand is simply another source of gross requirements for a part, and the sources of all gross requirements are maintained through pegging records. The low-level code for a part used exclusively for service would be zero. If it's used as a component part as well, the low-level code would be determined the same way as for any other part.

As actual service part needs occur, it's to be expected that demand variations will arise. These can be partially buffered with safety stocks (inventories specifically allocated to service part usage) or by creative use of the MRP system. By careful examination of pegging records, expected shortage conditions for manufacturing part requirements can sometimes be satisfied from available service parts. Conversely, critical service part requirements can perhaps be met with orders destined for higher-level items. Only one safety stock inventory is needed to buffer uncertainties from both sources, however.

Planning Horizon

In Figure 7.8, the first planned order for top handle assemblies occurs in week 2 to meet period 4's gross requirement of 10 units. This planned order of 5 units in week 2 results in a corresponding gross requirement in that week for the bracket assembly (part 11495). This gross requirement is satisfied from the existing inventory of part 11495. But a different circumstance occurs if we trace the gross requirements for 35 top handle assemblies in week 9.

The net requirement for 35 units in week 9 becomes a planned order release in week 7. This, in turn, becomes a gross requirement for 35 bracket assemblies (part 11495) in week 7 and a planned order release in week 5. This passes down to the top handle coupling (part 1118), which creates a planned order release for 4 units in week 2. This means the **cumulative lead time** for the top handle assembly is 7 weeks (from release of the coupling order in week 2 to receipt of the top handle assemblies in week 9).

Scheduled Receipts versus Planned Order Releases

A true understanding of MRP requires knowledge of certain key differences between a scheduled receipt and a planned order. We noted one such difference before: the scheduled receipt represents a commitment, whereas the planned order is only a plan—the former is much more difficult to change than the latter. A scheduled receipt for a purchased item means a purchase order, which is a formal commitment, has been prepared. Similarly, a scheduled receipt for a manufactured item means there's an open shop order. Raw materials and component parts have *already* been specifically committed to that order and are no longer available for other needs. One major result of this distinction, which can be seen in Figure 7.8, is that planned order releases explode to gross requirements for components, but scheduled receipts (the open orders) do not.

A related issue is seen from the following question: Where would a scheduled receipt for the top handle assembly (13122) in Figure 7.8 of, say, 20 units in week 2 be reflected in the records for the component parts (457, 082, and 11495)? The answer is nowhere! Scheduled receipts are not reflected in the current records for component parts. For that scheduled receipt to exist, the component parts would have already been assigned to the shop order representing the scheduled receipt for part 13122 and removed from the available balances of the components. As far as MRP is concerned, the 20 part 457s, 40 part 082s, and 20 part 11495s don't exist! They're on their way to becoming 20 part 13122s. The 13122 record controls this process, not the component records.

Using the MRP System

In this section, we discuss critical aspects of using the MRP system to ensure that MRP system records are exactly synchronized with physical flows of material.

The MRP Planner

The persons most directly involved with the MRP system outputs are planners. They are typically in the production planning, inventory control, and purchasing departments. Planners have the responsibility for making detailed decisions that keep the material moving through the plant. Their range of discretion is carefully limited (e.g., without higher authorization, they cannot change plans for end items destined for customers). Their actions, however, are reflected in the MRP records. Well-trained MRP planners are essential to effective use of the MRP system.

Computerized MRP systems often encompass tens of thousands of part numbers. To handle this volume, planners are generally organized around logical groupings of parts (such as metal parts, wood parts, purchased electronic parts, or West Coast distribution center). Even so, reviewing each record every time the records are processed would not be an effective use of the planners' time. At any time, many records require no action, so the planner only wants to review and interpret those that do require action.

The primary actions taken by an MRP planner are:

1. Release orders (i.e., launch purchase or shop orders when indicated by the system).
2. Reschedule due dates of existing open orders when desirable.

3. Analyze and update system planning factors for the part numbers under her control. This would involve such things as changing lot sizes, lead times, scrap allowances, or safety stocks.

4. Reconcile errors or inconsistencies and try to eliminate root causes of these errors.

5. Find key problem areas requiring action now to prevent future crises.

6. Use the system to solve critical material shortage problems so actions can be captured in the records for the next processing. This means the planner works *within* formal MRP rules, *not* by informal methods.

7. Indicate where further system enhancements (outputs, diagnostics, etc.) would make the planner's job easier.

Order Launching

Order launching is the process of releasing orders to the shop or to vendors (purchase orders). This process is prompted by MRP when a planned order release is in the current time period, the **action bucket.** Order launching converts the planned order into a scheduled receipt reflecting the lead time offset. Order launching is the opening of shop and purchase orders; closing these orders occurs when scheduled receipts are received into stockrooms. At that time, a transaction must be processed—to increase the on-hand inventory and eliminate the scheduled receipt. Procedures for opening and closing shop orders have to be carefully defined so all transactions are properly processed.

The orders indicated by MRP as ready for launching are a function of lot sizing procedures and safety stock as well as timing. We saw this in Figure 7.8 where we worked with lot-for-lot approaches and fixed lot sizes. A key responsibility of the planner is managing with awareness of the implications of these effects. For example, not *all* of a fixed lot may be necessary to cover a requirement, or a planned order that's solely for replenishment of safety stock may be in the action bucket.

When an order is launched, it's sometimes necessary to include a shrinkage allowance for scrap and other process yield situations. The typical approach allows some percentage for yield losses that will increase the shop order quantity above the net amount required. To effect good control over open orders, the *total* amount, including the allowance, should be shown on the shop order, and the scheduled receipt should be reduced as actual yield losses occur during production.

Allocation and Availability Checking

A concept closely related to order launching is **allocation**—a step prior to order launching that involves an availability check for the necessary component or components. From the snow shovel example, if we want to assemble 20 of the top handle assembly (13122) in period 4, the availability check would be whether sufficient components (20 of part 457, 40 of part 082, and 20 of part 11495) are available. If not, the shop order for 20 top handle assemblies (13122) should not be launched, because it cannot be executed without component parts. The planner role is key here, as well. The best course of action might be to release a partial order. The planner should evaluate that possibility.

Most MRP systems first check component availability for any order that a planner desires to launch. If sufficient quantities of each component are available, the shop order can be created. If the order is created, then the system allocates the necessary quantities to the particular shop order. (Shop orders are assigned by the computer, in numerical sequence.) The allocation means this amount of a component part is mortgaged to the particular shop order and is, therefore, not available for any other shop order. Thus, the amounts shown in Figure 7.8 as projected available balances may not be the same as the physical inventory balances. The physical inventory balances could be larger, with the differences representing allocations to specific shop orders that have been released, but whose component parts have not been removed from inventory.

After availability checking and allocation, **picking tickets** are typically created and sent to the stockroom. The picking ticket calls for a specified amount of some part number to be removed from some inventory location, on some shop order, to be delivered to a particular department or location. When the picking ticket has been satisfied (inventory moved), the allocation is removed and the on-hand balance is reduced accordingly.

Availability checking, allocation, and physical stock picking are a type of double-entry bookkeeping. The result is that the quantity physically on hand should match what the records indicate is available plus what is allocated. If they don't match, corrective action must be taken. The resulting accuracy facilitates inventory counting and other procedures for maintaining date integrity.

Exception Codes

Exception codes in MRP systems are used "to separate the vital few from the trivial many." If the manufacturing process is under control and the MRP system is functioning correctly, exception coding typically means only 10 to 20 percent of the part numbers will require planner review at each processing cycle. Exception codes are in two general categories. The first, checking the input data accuracy, includes checks for dates beyond the planning horizon, quantities larger or smaller than check figures, nonvalid part numbers, or any other desired check for incongruity. The second category of exception codes directly supports the MRP planning activity. Included are the following kinds of exception (action) messages or diagnostics:

1. Part numbers for which a planned order is now in the most immediate time period (the action bucket). It's also possible to report any planned orders two to three periods out to check lead times, on-hand balances, and other factors while there's some time to respond, if necessary.

2. Open order diagnostics when the present timing and/or amount for a scheduled receipt is not satisfactory. Such a message might indicate that an open order exists that's not necessary to cover any of the requirements in the planning horizon. This message might suggest order cancellation caused by an engineering change that substituted some new part for the one in question. The most common type of open order diagnostic shows scheduled receipts that are timed to arrive either too late or too early and should, therefore, have their due dates revised to reflect proper factory priorities. An example of this is seen with each of the three scheduled receipts in Figure 7.8. The 457 top handle open order of 25 could be delayed one week. A one-week delay is also indicated for the 082 nail scheduled receipt. For part 1118 (the top handle coupling), scheduled receipt of 15 could be delayed from week 2 until week 5. Another open order exception code is to flag any past-due scheduled receipt (scheduled to have been received in previous periods, but

for which no receipt transaction has been processed). MRP systems assume a past-due scheduled receipt will be received in the immediate time bucket.

3. A third general type of exception message indicates problem areas for management; in essence, situations where level 0 quantities can't be satisfied unless the present planning factors used in MRP are changed. One such exception code indicates a requirement has been offset into the past period and subsequently added to any requirement in the first or most immediate time bucket. This condition means an order should have been placed in the past. Since it wasn't, lead times through the various production item levels must be compressed to meet the end-item schedule. A similar diagnostic indicates the allocations exceed the on-hand inventory—a condition directly analogous to overdrawing a checking account. Unless more inventory is received soon, the firm will not be able to honor all pick tickets issued, and there will be a material shortage in the factory.

Bottom-up Replanning

Bottom-up replanning—using pegging data to solve material shortage problems—is best seen through an example. Let's return again to Figure 7.8, concentrating on the top handle assembly and the nails (parts 13122 and 082). Let's suppose the scheduled receipt of 50 nails arrives on Wednesday of week 1. On Thursday, quality control checks them and finds the vendor sent the wrong size. This means only 4 of the 10 gross requirement in week 2 can be satisfied. By pegging this gross requirement up to its parent planned order (5 units of 13122 in week 2), we see that only 7 of the gross requirement for 10 units in week 4 can be satisfied (the 5 on hand plus 2 made from 4 nails). This, in turn, means only 7 snow shovels can be assembled in week 4.

The pegging analysis shows that 3 of the 10 top handle assemblies can't be available without taking some special actions. If none are taken, the planned assembly dates for the snow shovels should reflect only 7 units in week 4, with the additional 3 scheduled for week 5. This should be done if we cannot overcome the shortfall in nails. The change is necessary because the 10 snow shovels now scheduled for assembly in week 4 also explode to other parts—parts that won't be needed if only 7 snow shovels are to be assembled.

There may, however, be a critical customer requirement for 10 snow shovels to be assembled during week 4. Solving the problem with bottom-up replanning might involve one of the following alternatives (staying *within* the MRP system, as planners must do):

1. Issue an immediate order to the vendor for six nails (the minimum requirement), securing a promised lead time of two days instead of the usual one week. This will create a scheduled receipt for six in week 2.

2. Order more nails for the beginning of week 3, and negotiate a one-week reduction in lead time (from two weeks to one week) for fabricating this one batch of part 13122. The planned order release for five would be placed in week 3 and converted to a firm planned order, so it would not change when the record is processed again. The negotiation for a one-week lead time might involve letting the people concerned start work earlier than week 3 on the two part 13122s, for which material already exists, and a reduction in the one-week paperwork time included in the lead times.

3. Negotiate a one-week lead time reduction for assembling the snow shovels; place a firm planned order for 10 in week 5, which will result in a gross requirement for 10 top handle assemblies in period 5 instead of period 4.

FIGURE 7.10 Example MRP Record

```
DATE-01/21
*******PART NUMBER*********
NONJEK OPTY SSV LAM PP UPHL          MATERIAL STATUS-PRODUCTION SCHEDULE
USTR040                                    DESCRIPTION
        ******USAGE*******          3/16 × 7/8 MR P & C STL STRAP
  YTD   LAST YR   YTD                                        PLNR   BYR
 SCRAP                               POLICY                  CODE   COE
                                      CODE                    01    9
                                       3
******************************ORDER POLICY AND LOT SIZE DATA**************************
         STANDARD   PERIODS        REJECT    SAFETY    SHRINKG   LEAD    FAMILY
         QUANTITY   TO COMB.  U/M   QUANTITY   STOCK    ALLOWNE   TIME    DATA
                      04      LFT              497        1       08
         MINIMUM   PERIODS          MAXIMUM   MULTIPLE   MIN ORD
           QTY     TO COMB.           QTY       QTY      POINT
```

	PAST DUE	563 01/22	564 01/29	565 02/05	566 02/12	567 02/19	568 02/26	569 03/05	570 03/12	571 03/19	572 03/28	573 04/02
REQUIREMENTS	495											
SCHEDULED RECEIPTS												
PLANNED RECEIPTS				483				516				
AVAILABLE ON-HAND	1,500		508	25	25	25	508	491				
PLANNED ORDERS	491			337		334		334			337	

	574 04/09	575 04/16	576 04/23	577 04/30	578 05/07	579 05/14	580 05/21	581 05/28	582 06/04	583 06/11	584 06/18	585 06/25
REQUIREMENTS	337											
SCHEDULED RECEIPTS												
PLANNED RECEIPTS					334							
AVAILABLE ON-HAND				334	334							
PLANNED ORDERS												

	586 07/16	587 07/23	588 07/30	589-592 08/06	593-596 09/03	597-600 10/01	601-604 10/29	605-608 11/26	609-612 12/24
	VACATION								
REQUIREMENTS									
SCHEDULED RECEIPTS									
PLANNED RECEIPTS									
AVAILABLE									
PLANNED ORDERS									

```
*********EXCEPTION MESSAGES*********
PLANNED ORDER OF   491 FOR M-WK   568   OFFSET INTO A PAST PERIOD BY 03 PERIODS
********PEGGING DATA (ALLOC)*********
79016 455 JN2220
*********PEGGING DATA (REQMT)********
790205 483 F 17144    790305 516 F 19938    790409 337 F 17144
790507 334 F 19938
```

Thus, we see the solution to a material shortage problem might be made by compressing lead times throughout the product structure using the system and bottom-up replanning. Planners work within the system using firm planned orders and net requirements to develop workable (but not standard) production schedules. The creativity they use in solving problems will be reflected in the part records at the next MRP processing cycle. All implications of planner actions will be correctly coordinated throughout the product structure.

It's important to note that the resolution of problems cannot *always* involve reduced lead time and/or partial lots. Further, none of these actions are free. In some cases, customer needs will have to be delayed or partial shipments made. Pegging and bottom-up replanning will provide advance warning of these problems so customers can take appropriate actions.

An MRP System Output

Figure 7.10 is an MRP time-phased record for one part number out of a total of 13,000 at the Batesville, Indiana, facility of the Hill-Rom Company. The header information includes the date the report was run, part number and description, planner code number, buyer code number (for purchased parts), unit of measure for this part number (pieces, pounds, etc.), rejected parts that have yet to receive disposition by quality control, safety stocks, shrinkage allowance for anticipated scrap loss, lead time, family data (what other parts are similar to this one), year-to-date scrap, usage last year, year-to-date usage, and order policy/lot size data. The policy code of 3 for this part means the order policy is a **period order quantity (POQ).** In this case, "periods to comb. = 04" means each order should combine four periods of net requirements.

The first time bucket is "past due." After that, weekly time buckets are presented for the first 28 weeks of data; thereafter, 24 weeks of data are lumped into 4-week buckets. In the computer itself, a bucketless system is used with all data kept in exact days, with printouts prepared in summary format for one- and four-week buckets. The company maintains a manufacturing calendar; in this example, the first week is 563 (also shown as 1/22), and the last week is 612.

In this report, safety stock is subtracted from the on-hand balance (except in the past-due bucket). Thus, the exception message indicating that a planned order for 491 should have been issued three periods ago creates no major problem, since the planner noted that this amount is less than the safety stock. This report also shows the use of safety lead time. *Planned* receipts are given a specific row in the report and are scheduled one week ahead of the actual need date. For example, the 337-unit planned order of week 565 is a planned receipt in week 573, although it's not needed until week 574.

The final data in the report is the pegging data section tying specific requirements to the part numbers from which those requirements came. For example, in week 565 (shop order no. 790205), the requirement for 483 derives from part number F17144. MRP records are printed at this company only for those part numbers for which exception messages exist.

System Dynamics

Murphy's law states that if anything can go wrong, it will. Things are constantly going wrong, so it's essential that the MRP system mirror actual shop conditions; that is, both the physical system and the information system have to cope with scrap, incorrect counts,

246   Chapter 7   *Material Requirements Planning*

FIGURE 7.11
MRP Record for Part 1234 as of Week 1

Lead time = 2
Lot size = 50

		1	2	3	4	5
Gross requirements		30	20	20	0	45
Scheduled receipts		50				
Projected available balance	10	30	10	40	40	45
Planned order releases		50		50		

changes in customer needs, incorrect bills of material, engineering design changes, poor vendor performance, and a myriad of other mishaps.

In this section, we look at the need for quick and accurate transaction processing and review the MRP planner's replanning activities in coping with change. We discuss sources of problems occurring as a result of database changes plus actions to ensure the system is telling the truth, even if the truth hurts.

Transactions During a Period

To illustrate transaction processing issues, we use a simple example for one part. Figure 7.11 shows an MRP record (for part 1234) produced over the weekend preceding week 1. The planner for part 1234 would receive this MRP record on Monday of week 1.

The planner's first action would be to try to launch the planned order for 50 units in period 1; that is, the MPC system would first check availability of the raw materials for this part and then issue an order to the shop to make 50, if sufficient raw material is available. Launching would require allocating the necessary raw materials to the shop order, removing the 50 from the "Planned order release" row for part 1234, and creating a scheduled receipt for 50 in week 3, when they're needed. Thereafter, a pick ticket would be sent to the raw material area and work could begin.

Let's assume during week 1 the following changes occurred, and the transactions were processed:

- Actual disbursements from stock for item 1234 during week 1 were only 20 instead of the planned 30.
- The scheduled receipt for 50 due in week 1 was received on Tuesday, but 10 units were rejected, so only 40 were actually received into inventory.
- The inventory was counted on Thursday and 20 additional pieces were found.
- The requirement date for the 45 pieces in week 5 was changed to week 4.
- Marketing requested an additional five pieces for samples in week 2.
- The requirement for week 6 has been set at 25.

The resultant MRP record produced over the weekend preceding week 2 is presented as Figure 7.12.

FIGURE 7.12
MRP Record for Part 1234 as of Week 2

Lead time = 2
Lot size = 50

		2	3	4	5	6
Gross requirements		25	20	45	0	25
Scheduled receipts			50			
Projected available balance	50	25	55	10	10	35
Planned order release				50		

Rescheduling

The MRP record shown in Figure 7.12 illustrates two important activities for MRP planners: (1) indicating the sources of problems that will occur as a result of database changes and (2) suggesting actions to ensure the system is telling the truth. Note the scheduled receipt presently due in week 3 is not needed until week 4. The net result of all the changes to the database means it's now scheduled with the wrong due date, and the due date should be changed to week 4. If this change is not made, this job may be worked on ahead of some other job that is really needed earlier, thereby causing problems. The condition shown in Figure 7.12 would be highlighted by an MRP exception message, such as "reschedule the receipt currently due in week 3 to week 4."

Complex Transaction Processing

So far, we've illustrated system dynamics by using a single MRP record. However, an action required on the part of an MRP planner may have been caused by a very complex set of database transactions involving several levels in the bill of materials. As an example, consider the MRP records shown in Figure 7.13, which include three levels in the product structure. Part C is used as a component in both parts A and B as well as being sold as a service part. Part C, in turn, is made from parts X and Y. The arrows in Figure 7.13 depict the pegging data.

The part C MRP record is correctly stated at the beginning of week 1. That is, no exception messages would be produced at this time. In particular, the two scheduled receipts of 95 and 91, respectively, are scheduled correctly, since delaying either by one week would cause a shortage, and neither has to be expedited to cover any projected shortage.

While the two scheduled receipts for part C are currently scheduled correctly, transactions involving parts A and B can have an impact on the proper due dates for these open orders. For example, suppose an inventory count adjustment for part A resulted in a change in the 30-unit planned order release from week 1 to week 3. In this case, the 95 units of part C would not be needed until week 3, necessitating a reschedule. Similarly, any change in timing for the planned order release of 25 units of part A in week 4 would call for a reschedule of the due date for 91 units of part C. Finally, suppose a transaction requiring 75 additional units of part B in week 5 were processed. This would result in an immediate release of an order for 100 units of part C. This might necessitate rescheduling for parts X and Y. The point here is that actions required on the part of an MRP planner can occur because of

FIGURE 7.13
MRP Record Relationships for Several Parts

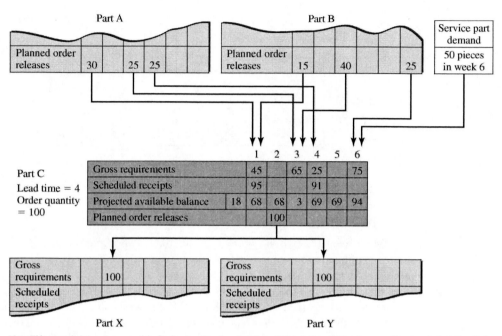

Note: This example is based on one originally developed by Joseph Orlicky. *Orlicky's Material Requirements Planning,* 2nd ed. New York: McGraw-Hill, 1994, chap. 4, pp. 69–99.

a complex set of database transactions involving many different parts. They may not necessarily directly involve the particular part being given attention by the MRP planner.

Procedural Inadequacies

MRP replanning and transaction processing activities are two essential aspects of ensuring the MPC database remains accurate. However, while these activities are necessary, they aren't sufficient to maintain accurate records. Some of the procedures used to process transactions simply may be inadequate to the task.

To illustrate inadequate transaction procedures, let's return to the example in Figure 7.13. Note that, if 4 or more pieces are scrapped on the shop order for 95, there will be a shortage in week 3, necessitating rescheduling of the order for 91 one week earlier.

It's even more interesting to see what would happen if 4 pieces were scrapped on the order for 95, and this scrap transaction weren't processed. If the scrap isn't reported, MRP records would appear as shown in Figure 7.13, indicating no required rescheduling—when, in fact, that's not true. *If* the shortage were discovered by the person in charge of the stockroom when he or she puts away this order, then only one week would be lost before the next MRP report shows the problem. If, however, the stockroom person doesn't count, or if the person who made the scrap puts the defective parts at the bottom of the box where they go undetected by quality control, then the problem will be discovered only when the assembly lines are trying to build As and Bs in week 3. Such a discovery comes under the category of unpleasant surprises. An interesting sidelight to this problem is that the cure will be to rush down to the shop to get at least 1 piece from the batch of 91. The very person who failed to report the earlier scrap may well now be screaming. "Why don't those idiots know what they need!"

Still another aspect of the scrap reporting issue can be seen by noting the 95 and 91 were originally issued as lot sizes of 100. This probably means 5 and 9 pieces of scrap have occurred already, and the appropriate adjustments have been made in the scheduled receipt data. Note that, if these adjustments had *not* been made, the two scheduled receipts would show as 100 each. The resultant 14 (or $5 + 9$) pieces (that don't, in fact, exist) would be reflected in the MRP arithmetic. Thus, the projected available balance at the end of period 5 would be 83 (or $69 + 14$); this is more than enough to cover the gross requirement of 75 in period 6, so the planned order release for 100 in period 2 would not exist and the error would cascade throughout the product structure. Further, even if shop orders are carefully counted as they are put into storage, the five-piece shortage in period 1 is not enough to cause the MRP arithmetic to plan an order. Only after period 4 (the beginning of period 5) will the additional nine pieces of scrap be incorporated in the MRP record showing a projected shortage in period 6. This will result in an immediate order, to be completed in one week instead of four! What may be obvious is that, if accurate counting isn't done, then the shortage is discovered in week 6, when the assembly line goes down. This means procedures for issuing scrap tickets when scrap occurs and procedures for ensuring good parts are accurately counted into inventory must be in place. If not, all the MPC systems will suffer.

The long and the short of all this is that we have to believe the numbers, and an error of as little as *one* piece can cause severe problems. We have to know the truth. We have to tightly control transactions. Moreover, we have to develop iron-clad procedures for processing MPC database transactions.

Concluding Principles	Chapter 7 provides an understanding of the MRP approach to detailed material planning. It describes basic techniques, some technical issues, and how MRP systems are used in practice. MRP, with its time-phased approach to planning, is a basic building-block concept for materials planning and control systems. Moreover, there are many other applications of the time-phased record. We see the most important concepts or principles of this chapter as follows:

- Effective use of an MRP system allows development of a forward-looking (planning) approach to managing material flows.
- The MRP system provides a coordinated set of linked product relationships, thereby permitting decentralized decision making on individual part numbers.
- All decisions made to solve problems must be done within the system, and transactions must be processed to reflect the resultant changes.
- Effective use of exception messages allows focusing attention on the "vital few," not on the "trivial many."
- System records must be accurate and reflect the factory's physical reality if they're to be useful.
- Procedural inadequacies in processing MRP transactions need to be identified and corrected to ensure material plans are accurate.

250   Chapter 7   *Material Requirements Planning*

References   Conway, R. W. "Linking MRPII and FCS." *APICS—The Performance Advantage,* June 1996.

Fisher, D. "MRP at 'Lightspeed' without the MRP." *IE Solutions,* May 1996.

Hiquet, Bradley D. *SAP R/3 Implementation Guide: A Managers Guide to Understanding SAP.* Indianapolis: Macmillan Technical Publishing, 1998.

Miller, J. G., and L. G. Sprague. "Behind the Growth in Materials Requirements Planning." *Harvard Business Review,* September–October 1975.

Plossl, G. *Orlicky's Material Requirements Planning.* 2nd ed. New York: McGraw-Hill, 1994.

Ptak, Carol A. *ERP Tools, Techniques, and Applications for Integrating the Supply Chain.* Boca Raton, Fla.: St. Lucie Press, 2000.

Discussion Questions

1. Why is the MRP activity in the "engine" part of the MPC system shown in Figure 7.1?

2. What additional information would be helpful to you in using or following the basic MRP record?

3. Compare a bill of materials (BOM) and a cookbook recipe.

4. How does the *system* coordinate the individual item records and provide back schedule information?

5. Provide examples of potential differences between the information system and the physical reality for university activities. What are the consequences of some of these mismatches?

6. What are some of the reasons for wanting to process the records in an MRP system frequently? Provide examples and consequences of delaying the processing of the information.

7. The chapter uses a Christmas list and Christmas gift order analogy for planned order releases and scheduled receipts. What are other analogies of these two concepts? Why is it important to keep them separate in the MRP records?

8. What are the implications of *not* allocating material to a shop order after availability checking?

9. Give some examples of transaction processing for individual students at a university. What happens if they are not done well?

Problems

1. Joe's Burgers sells three kinds of hamburgers—Big, Giant, and The Football. The bills of materials are:

Big Burger		**Giant Burger**		**Football Burger**	
$\frac{1}{4}$ lb. patty	1.0	$\frac{1}{2}$ lb. patty	1.0	1 lb. patty	2.0
Regular bun	1.0	Sesame bun	1.0	Sesame bun	1.0
Pickle slice	1.0	Pickle slices	2.0	Pickle slices	4.0
Catsup	0.1 oz.	Catsup	0.2 oz.	Lettuce	0.3 oz.
		Onion	0.2 oz.	Catsup	0.2 oz.
				Cheese	0.5 oz.
				Onion	0.2 oz.

a. If the product mix is 20 percent Big, 45 percent Giant, and 35 percent Footballs, and Joe sells 200 burgers a day, how much hamburger meat is used per day?

b. How many pickle slices are needed per day?

c. Suppose buns are delivered every second day. Joe is ready to order. His on-hand balance of regular buns is 25, and his on-hand balance of sesame buns is 20. How many buns should be ordered?

d. Reconsider question c if Joe has 10 Big hamburgers, 5 Giant, and 15 Footballs all made.

2. The following illustration shows how to assemble your own computer.

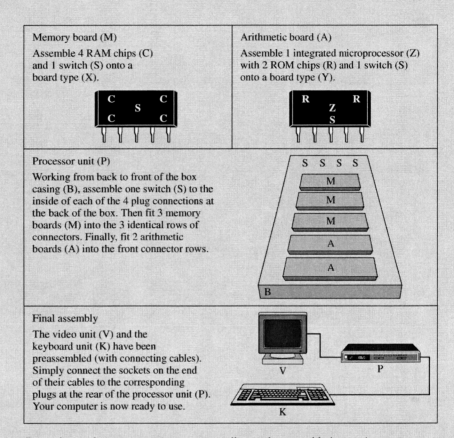

Memory board (M)

Assemble 4 RAM chips (C) and 1 switch (S) onto a board type (X).

Arithmetic board (A)

Assemble 1 integrated microprocessor (Z) with 2 ROM chips (R) and 1 switch (S) onto a board type (Y).

Processor unit (P)

Working from back to front of the box casing (B), assemble one switch (S) to the inside of each of the 4 plug connections at the back of the box. Then fit 3 memory boards (M) into the 3 identical rows of connectors. Finally, fit 2 arithmetic boards (A) into the front connector rows.

Final assembly

The video unit (V) and the keyboard unit (K) have been preassembled (with connecting cables). Simply connect the sockets on the end of their cables to the corresponding plugs at the rear of the processor unit (P). Your computer is now ready to use.

a. Draw the product structure tree corresponding to the assembly instructions.

b. Determine low-level codes for the following items: (1) A—Arithmetic board, (2) B—Box casing, (3) C—RAM chip, (4) K—Keyboard unit, (5) M—Memory board, (6) P—Processor unit, (7) R—ROM chip, (8) S—Switch, (9) V—Video unit, (10) X—Board type X, (11) Y—Board type Y, and (12) Z—Integrated microprocessor.

c. Assume no inventory of any item. How many of each part should be available to assemble one completed unit?

3. Power Tools (PT) has just received an order for 70 PT band saws, to be shipped at the beginning of week 9. Information concerning the saw assembly is given below:

PT Band Saw		
Item	**Lead Time (weeks)**	**Components**
Saw	2	A(2*), B, C(3)
A	1	E(3), D
B	2	D(2), F(3)
C	2	E(2), D(2)
D	1	
E	1	
F	3	

*Number of parts required to make one parent.

   a. Draw the product structure tree.

   b. Construct a Gantt chart for the new order using front schedule logic.

   c. Construct a Gantt chart for the new order using back schedule logic.

4. The recipe for 6 servings of Martha's Triple Chocolate Smoothie calls for 4 dashes of cinnamon, $1\frac{1}{2}$ liters of vanilla ice cream, 2 liters of chocolate ice cream, $\frac{1}{2}$ liter of chocolate milk, and 1 bag of chocolate chips.

   a. Martha is planning an ice cream social for 12 people and wants to make Triple Chocolate Smoothies. How much chocolate ice cream does she need for 12 servings if her chocolate ice cream is totally gone?

   b. How many liters of vanilla ice cream must be bought if Martha already has one liter of vanilla on hand?

   c. Martha is planning her party for November 15. It's now November 11. The local dairy will deliver liters of ice cream and milk if given a one-day notice. Fill in the following MRP record for chocolate milk if Martha has $\frac{1}{2}$ liter on hand and wants the rest delivered. Assume she can make the Smoothies on the day of the social.

		November			
	11	12	13	14	15
Gross requirements					
Scheduled receipts					
Projected available balance					
Planned order release					

5. Develop an MRP spreadsheet record for six periods using the following parameters for the item:

Period	1	2	3	4	5	6
Gross requirements	20	20	40	30	30	30

Lead time	1 period
Lot size	50 units
Safety stock	0 units
Inventory	2 units
Scheduled receipt	50 units in period 1

   a. In what periods are there planned order releases?

   b. What happens to the timing, number of planned order releases, and average inventory (for periods 1 through 6) if 15 units of safety stock are required?

   c. What happens to the timing, number of planned order releases, and average inventory (for periods 1 through 6) if a one-week safety lead time is used instead of the safety stock?

6. Given the following product structure diagram, complete the MRP records for parts A, B, and C.

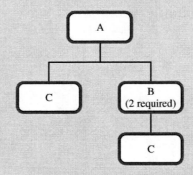

	Week						
Part A		**1**	**2**	**3**	**4**	**5**	**6**
Gross requirements		5	25	18	8	12	22
Scheduled receipts							
Projected available balance	21						
Planned order release							

Q = 20; LT = 1; SS = 0.

	Week						
Part B		**1**	**2**	**3**	**4**	**5**	**6**
Gross requirements							
Scheduled receipts		32					
Projected available balance	20						
Planned order release							

Q = 40; LT = 2; SS = 0.

	Week						
Part C		**1**	**2**	**3**	**4**	**5**	**6**
Gross requirements							
Scheduled receipts							
Projected available balance	70						
Planned order release							

Q = LFL; LT = 1; SS = 10.

7. Given the product structure diagrams at Traci's Tomahawk shown below, complete the MRP records for Parts A, F, and G using the data provided for each.

Product Structures

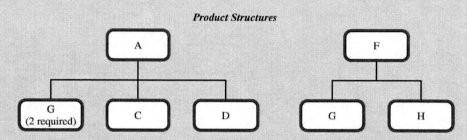

		Week				
Part A		**1**	**2**	**3**	**4**	**5**
Gross requirement		5	3	10	15	15
Scheduled receipt		5				
Projected available balance	10					
Planned order release						

Lead time = 1; Q = L4L; SS = 0.

		Week				
Part F		**1**	**2**	**3**	**4**	**5**
Gross requirement		10	20	25	15	5
Scheduled receipt			15			
Projected available balance	15					
Planned order release						

Lead time = 2; Q = L4L; SS = 0.

		Week				
Part G		**1**	**2**	**3**	**4**	**5**
Gross requirement						
Scheduled receipt		20				
Projected available balance	30					
Planned order releases						

Lead time = 1; Q = multiples of 20; SS = 10.

8. Ajax produces two basic products called A and B. Each week, Paul, the owner, plans to assemble 20 product As and 8 product Bs. Given this information and the following product structure dia-

grams for A and B, fill out the MRP records (inventory status files) for component parts G and Y for the next seven weeks.

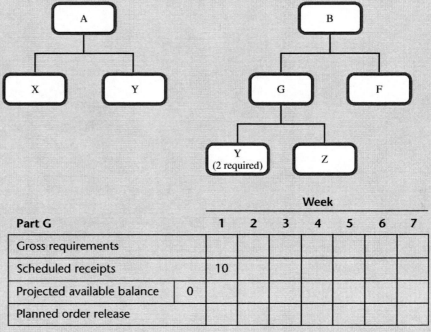

		Week						
Part G		1	2	3	4	5	6	7
Gross requirements								
Scheduled receipts		10						
Projected available balance	0							
Planned order release								

Q = lot for lot; LT = 1; SS = 0.

		Week						
Part Y		1	2	3	4	5	6	7
Gross requirements								
Scheduled receipts		10						
Projected available balance	48							
Planned order release								

Q = lot-for-lot; LT = 2; SS = 0.

Suppose 10 units of safety stock are required for part Y. What changes would result in the records? Would the MRP system produce any exception messages?

9. Consider the following product structure and inventory information:

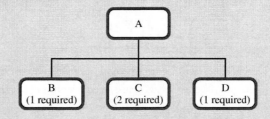

256 Chapter 7 *Material Requirements Planning*

Item	Inventory
A	10
B	40
C	60
D	60

Lead time = 1 week for all items. There are no scheduled receipts for any item. How many units of product A can be delivered to customers at the start of next week (i.e., in one week) under each of the following circumstances? (Treat each independently; that is, only a, only b, or only c.)

a. The bill of materials for B is wrong. It actually takes 2 units of B to make an A.

b. The inventory for D is only 30 units.

c. There was need to scrap 5 units of the inventory for item C.

10. XYZ Manufacturing Company has collected 10 periods of data for two of its products, A and B. Using the two data sets as gross requirements data, construct MRP time-phased records. Using a spreadsheet program, create four time-phased records, two for each data set. For one case, use a lot size of 150 units, and for the other use an order quantity equal to the total net requirements for the next three periods. In all four records, start with a beginning inventory of 150 units, and compute the average inventory level held over the 10 periods. What do the results mean?

	Period									
Demand	1	2	3	4	5	6	7	8	9	10
A	71	46	49	55	52	47	51	48	56	51
B	77	83	90	22	10	10	16	19	27	79

11. Consider the information contained in the planned order row of the following MRP record. The planned order releases in weeks 2 and 4 are firm planned orders and cannot be changed without managerial approval.

		Period			
	1	2	3	4	5
Gross requirements	10	30	20	15	20
Scheduled receipts	40				
Projected available balance	10	40	10	30	15	35
Planned order release (firm)		40		40	

Q = 40; LT = 1; SS = 5.

Use an MRP spreadsheet to answer the following questions:

a. What transactions would cause an action message on the firm planned order in week 2?

b. What transactions would cause an action message on the firm planned order in week 4?

12. Consider the following MRP record:

	Week					
	1	**2**	**3**	**4**	**5**	**6**
Gross requirements		25	30	5	15	5	10
Scheduled receipts			50			15	
Projected available balance	35	10	30	25	10	20	10
Planned order releases							

Q = lot-for-lot; LT = 5; SS = 0.

Suppose 15 units of the scheduled receipt for 40 units due on Monday of week 2 are scrapped during week 1, and no scrap ticket is issued. Furthermore, assume this lot isn't counted before it's put away in the stockroom on Monday of week 2, but is recorded as a receipt of 50 units. What impact will these actions have on factory operations?

13. Complete the following MRP time-phased record:

Item: Toaster	Week							
	1	**2**	**3**	**4**	**5**	**6**	**7**	**8**
Gross requirements	20	20	35	25	35	35	35	35
Scheduled receipts	50							
Projected available balance	10							
Planned order release								

Q = 50; LT = 2; SS = 5.

The following events occurred during week 1:

1. Actual demand during week 1 was only 5 units.
2. A scheduled receipt of 45 was received during week 1.
3. A cycle count of on-hand units showed 17 units at the start of week 1.
4. Marketing forecasted that 40 easy chairs would be required in week 9.

Update the record below after rolling through time.

Item: Easy Chair	Week							
	2	**3**	**4**	**5**	**6**	**7**	**8**	**9**
Gross requirements	20	25	25	35	35	35	35	
Scheduled receipts								
Projected available balance								
Planned order release								

Q = 50; LT = 2; SS = 5.

14. The MPC system at ABC Manufacturing Company is run weekly to update the master production schedule (MPS) and MRP records. At the start of week 1, the MPS for end products X and Y is:

Master Production Schedule						
Week Number	1	2	3	4	5	6
Product X	10	—	25	5	10	—
Product Y	5	30	—	20	—	20

One unit of component C is required to manufacture one unit of either end product X or Y. Purchasing lead time for component C is two weeks, an order quantity of 40 units is used, and no (zero) safety stock is maintained for this item. Inventory balance for component C is 5 units at the start of week 1, and there's an open order (scheduled receipt) for 40 units due to be delivered at the beginning of week 1.

a. Complete the MRP record for component C as it would appear at the beginning of week 1:

		Week					
		1	2	3	4	5	6
Gross requirements							
Scheduled receipts							
Projected available balance							
Planned order releases							

b. During week 1, the following transactions occurred for component C:

1. The open order for 40 units due to be received at the start of week 1 was received on Monday of week 1 with a quantity of 30 (10 units of component C were scrapped on this order).

2. An inventory cycle count during week 1 revealed that five units of component C were missing. Thus, an inventory adjustment of −5 was processed.

3. Ten units of component C were actually disbursed (instead of the 15 units planned for disbursement to produce end products A and B). (The MPS quantity of 5 in week 1 for product B was canceled as a result of a customer order cancellation.)

4. The MPS quantities for week 7 include 15 units for product X and 0 units for product Y.

5. Because of a change in customer order requirements, marketing has requested that the MPS quantity of 25 units for product X scheduled in week 3 be moved to week 2.

6. An order for 40 units was released.

Given this information, complete the MRP record for component C as it would appear at the beginning of week 2:

		Week					
		2	3	4	5	6	7
Gross requirements							
Scheduled receipts							
Projected available balance							
Planned order releases							

What action(s) are required by the inventory planner at the start of week 2 as a result of transactions occurring during week 1?

15. Use a spreadsheet program to develop the MRP records for parts A and B from the following product structure. Use the data from the following table:

Part	A	B
Requirements	50/period	–
Initial inventory balance	63	8
Lead time	1	1
Lot size	lot-for-lot	250
Safety stock	10	–
Scheduled receipt	–	250 in period 1

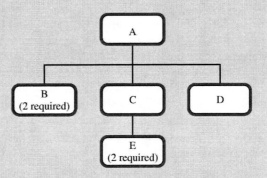

a. What are the planned orders for item B?

b. On an unlucky day (it must have been the 13th), the planner for part A found that the inventory was wrong by 13 units. Instead of 63, there were only 50 on hand. What happens to the planned orders for part B?

c. Use the spreadsheet model to generate a 10-period material plan for parts A and B. Assume that the 63 units of inventory for A were correct. Suppose that in period 1, actual demand for part A was 60 units instead of 50. Regenerate the spreadsheet for periods 2 through 11. What changes occur in the material plans for parts A and B?

Chapter **9**

Just-in-Time

This chapter addresses just-in-time (JIT) approaches for manufacturing planning and control. JIT is a key building block for modern approaches to manufacturing planning and control (MPC), and is both a philosophy and a set of techniques. Moreover, the techniques go beyond traditional manufacturing planning and control systems. JIT changes manufacturing practices, which in turn affect MPC execution. JIT greatly reduces the complexity of detailed material planning, the need for shop-floor tracking, work-in-process inventories, and the transactions associated with shop-floor and purchasing systems. These gains come at the cost of more tightly coordinated manufacturing processes—both inside a company and with supplier firms that produce under JIT. The chapter concentrates on the MPC aspects of JIT but necessarily touches on broader aspects as well. It is organized around the following seven topics:

- *JIT in manufacturing planning and control:* What are JIT's key features and how do they impact MPC systems?
- *A JIT example:* How can the basic principles of JIT be illustrated in one simplified example?
- *JIT applications:* What are some concrete examples of JIT practice?
- *Nonrepetitive JIT:* How can JIT concepts be applied to the nonrepetitive manufacturing environment?
- *Joint-Firm JIT:* How is supplier-customer coordination supported with JIT?
- *JIT software:* What features of computer packages support JIT?
- *Managerial implications:* What changes are required to fully pursue the benefits of JIT?

JIT is one of two classic approaches to detailed material planning and control. Chapter 7 describes the other—material requirements planning (MRP). JIT techniques have the most influence on the "back-end" execution concepts in Chapter 11. Chapter 17 focuses on supply chain management—where the MPC systems need to be interfirm in their orientation. This is quite the case when JIT includes suppliers' firms. In addition, the integration of JIT and MRP, as well as the market requirements that drive MPC choices, are described in Chapter 13. Chapter 15 describes advanced concepts in JIT. More fundamentally, JIT influences will be referred to in many other chapters where the techniques used are essentially different when JIT is in place.

JIT in Manufacturing Planning and Control

Figure 9.1 shows how just-in-time programs relate to our manufacturing planning and control framework. The shaded area indicates the portions of MPC systems that are most affected by implementation of JIT. The primary application area is in back-end execution. However, JIT extends beyond manufacturing planning and control. JIT programs raise fundamental questions about manufacturing strategy and effectiveness. For this reason, we begin with a discussion of the major elements in a JIT program. Thereafter, we turn to the impact on the MPC system and the overhead cost savings from reduced MPC system transaction processing. The section closes by describing four fundamental JIT building blocks.

Major Elements of Just-in-Time

Many definitions have been put forward for just-in-time, and they have evolved over time. One popular definition of JIT is an approach to minimize waste in manufacturing. This focus is too broad: it helps to subdivide waste into time, energy, material, and errors. A useful common denominator running through this and other JIT definitions is a broad philosophy of pursuing zero inventories, zero transactions, and zero "disturbances" (*zero disturbances* means routine execution of schedules day in—day out).

The JIT literature is largely one of cases. The best-known JIT examples are from firms with high-volume repetitive manufacturing methods, such as the classic case of Toyota. The most important features of these applications have been the elimination of discrete manufacturing batches in favor of production rate goals, the reduction of work-in-process inventories, production schedules that level the capacity loads and keep them level, mixed

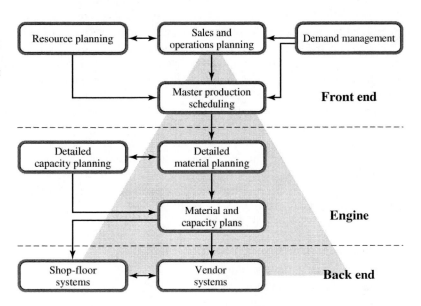

FIGURE 9.1
Manufacturing Planning and Control System and JIT

model master production schedules where all products are made more or less all the time, visual control systems where workers build the products and execute the schedule without paperwork or complex overhead support, and direct ties to vendors who deliver high-quality goods frequently. All of these have MPC implications.

Just-in-time objectives require physical system changes—and programs to make the changes. A prime example is setup time reduction and a drive toward constantly smaller lot sizes. This is necessary to make all of the products constantly. It's also consistent with reducing inventory levels. Setup times are typically reduced by applying common industrial engineering techniques to analyzing the setup process itself, often by workers themselves using a video camera. The results of setup time reduction have been impressive indeed. Changeovers of several hours have been reduced to less than 10 minutes. The goal now being achieved by many firms is expressed by Shigeo Shingo: SMED (single-minute exchange of dies, meaning all changeovers take place in less than 10 minutes).

Another physical program is improved quality through process improvements. Most JIT firms have programs of quality awareness and statistical process control. In a repetitive manufacturing system, any quality problem will result in a stoppage of the entire flow line, unless undesirable buffer inventories are held.

Quality improvement has taken many forms and is largely beyond our present scope. Two critical aspects for JIT are *TPM* and *poka-yoke*. TPM can stand for both total preventative maintenance and total productive maintenance. The goal is to apply the diligence of product quality improvement to equipment and process quality. Poka-yoke means foolproof operations. This is achieved by building checking operations into processes so that quality is evaluated as it's created. This also ensures low cost through finding defects at the time they're created. These quality programs have an impact on MPC system requirements and design.

Most JIT programs include continual improvement as a maxim for day-to-day operations. Every day, each worker should get better in some dimension, such as fewer defects, more output, or fewer stoppages. Continual improvement is achieved by making thousands of small improvements in methods and products in a never-ceasing quest for excellence. JIT best practice includes a strong degree of worker involvement and worker participation. In the words of a union official at the GM/Toyota (NUMMI) plant in Fremont, California, "This is the way work ought to be. [With JIT] this plant employs our hearts and minds, not just our backs."

JIT firms often group their equipment for cellular manufacturing: a group of machines manufactures a particular set of parts. The equipment layout minimizes travel distances and inventories between machines. Cells are typically U-shaped to increase worker interactions and reduce material handling. Cross-trained workers can run several machines. Cellular manufacturing makes "capacity" more flexible, so surges or mix changes are more readily handled. An extension of the cellular concept is the plant within a plant, where a portion of a factory focuses solely on one group of products.

In summary, a JIT orientation includes several action programs:

1. Reduction of setup times and lot sizes
2. A "no defects" goal in manufacturing
3. A focus on continual improvement

4. Worker involvement

5. Cellular manufacturing

Figure 9.2 lists the typical benefits gained in a JIT program.

JIT's Impact on Manufacturing Planning and Control

JIT influences all three areas of our MPC framework (front end, engine, and back end). JIT's primary contribution is in the back end, providing greatly streamlined execution on the shop floor and in purchasing. JIT can eliminate standard shop-floor reporting systems, reduce costs of detailed shop scheduling, significantly reduce work in process and lead times, and support better vendor scheduling.

However, JIT is not without influence on the front end and engine. In the detailed MRP planning of the engine, JIT reduces the number of part numbers planned and the number of levels in the bill of materials. Many part numbers formerly planned by MRP analysts can now be treated as "phantoms" (i.e., as part numbers still in the bill of materials but not transacted into and out of inventories). This means that instead of MPC being based on detailed operation steps to make individual parts, the planning is at the level of assemblies, using cross-trained workers and cellular manufacturing to eliminate the detailed planning. The result is often an order of magnitude reduction in the complexity of detailed material planning, with a concomitant reduction in planning personnel. Moreover, with planning/execution at the assembly level instead of with detailed operations and parts, the overall flow time from parts to finished goods is significantly reduced.

In the front end, JIT also gives rise to important changes. JIT production plans and master production schedules require relatively level capacity loading for smooth shop operations. In many cases, this is a rate-based MPS—that is, producing so many units per hour or day. This drive toward more stable, level, daily-mix schedules dictates many of the required JIT activities, such as setup time reduction. To the extent that lead times are sufficiently reduced, many firms that had to provide inventories in anticipation of customer orders (made-to-stock firms) now find themselves more like make-to-order or assemble-to-order companies, better able to respond to customer orders. This, in turn, can affect demand management.

FIGURE 9.2
JIT Benefits

Manufacturing throughput time reductions
Materials moved shorter distances
Less material movements in/out of storage
Reduced transactions
Simplified MPC systems
Reduced changeover times
Greater responsiveness to market demands
Inventory reductions
Labor cost reductions
More satisfied/cohesive workers
Better team working
Space reductions
Quality cost reductions
Quality improvements

In JIT execution, orders move through the factory so quickly that it's not necessary to track their progress with a complex production activity control system. A similar argument holds for purchased items. If they're converted into finished goods within hours or days of receipt, it's unnecessary to put them into stockrooms, pick them, and go through all the details normally associated with receipts from vendors. Instead, the JIT firm can simply pay the vendor for the purchased components in whatever products are completed each time period; there will be so little work-in-process inventory that it's not worth either party keeping track of it.

The concept of updating component inventory balances when finished items are received into stock is called **backflushing.** Instead of detailed work-in-process accounting systems based on shop-order transactions, some JIT firms just reduce component part inventory balances by exploding the bills of material for whatever has been delivered into finished goods. However, backflushing implies a very high level of data integrity.

JIT execution is focused on simplicity. The intent is to design manufacturing cells, products, and systems so goods flow through routinely. With problems of quality and disturbances largely eliminated, routine execution becomes just that: routine. Simple systems can be employed by shop people without detailed records or the need for extensive overhead staff support.

The Hidden Factory

A manufacturing firm comprises two "factories." One makes products and the other (the hidden factory) processes transactions on papers and computer systems. Over time, the former factory has been decreasing in cost, relative to the latter. A major driver for these costs is transactions. **Logistical transactions** include ordering, execution, and confirmation of materials moving from one location to another. Included are the costs of personnel in receiving, shipping, expediting, data entry, data processing, accounting, and error follow-up. Under JIT, the goal is to eliminate the vast majority of this work and the associated costs. Work orders that accompany each batch of material as it moves through the factory are eliminated. If the flow can be simplified, fast, and guaranteed, there is no need for paperwork.

Balancing transactions are largely associated with the planning that generates logistical transactions. Included are production control, purchasing, master scheduling, forecasting, and customer order processing/maintenance. In most companies, balancing transaction costs are 10 to 20 percent of the total manufacturing overhead costs. JIT again offers a significant opportunity to sharply reduce these costs. MRP planning can be cut by perhaps 75 to 90 percent in complexity. Improvements generated by vendor scheduling can also be extended. Vendor firms no longer need to process *their* sets of transactions.

Quality transactions extend far beyond what one normally thinks of as quality control. Included are identification and communication of specifications, certification that other transactions have taken place, and recording of backup data. Many of the costs of quality identified by Juran and others are largely associated with transactions. JIT, with closer coupling of production and consumption, has faster quality monitoring and response capability.

Still another category is **change transactions.** Included are engineering changes and all those that update MPC systems, such as routings, bills of materials, and specifications.

Engineering change transactions are some of the most expensive in the company. A typical engineering change might require a meeting of people from production control, line management, design engineering, manufacturing engineering, and purchasing. The change has to be approved, scheduled, and monitored for execution.

One way that firms attack the hidden factory is by finding ways to significantly reduce the number of transactions. Stability is another attack, and again JIT is important since it is based on stabilized operations. Still another attack on hidden factory transaction costs is through automation of transactions (as with bar coding), eliminating redundancies in data entry, and better data entry methods. But stability and transaction elimination should be pursued before turning to automation of transactions. JIT is clearly a key.

JIT Building Blocks in MPC

As Figure 9.3 shows, JIT links four fundamental building blocks: product design, process design, human/organizational elements, and manufacturing planning and control. JIT provides the connecting link for these four areas.

Critical activities in product design include quality, designing for manufacture in cells, and reducing the number of "real" levels in the bill of materials to as few as possible. By having no more than three real levels in the bill of materials, products have to go into inventory and out again, with MRP-based planning, only once or twice as they are produced.

Reducing bill of materials levels and process design are closely related. For fewer levels to be practical, the number of product conversion steps must be reduced through process design changes, often through cellular manufacturing. Equipment in cellular manufacturing is positioned (often in a U shape) to achieve rapid flow of production with minimal

FIGURE 9.3
**Building
Blocks for
Just-in-Time**

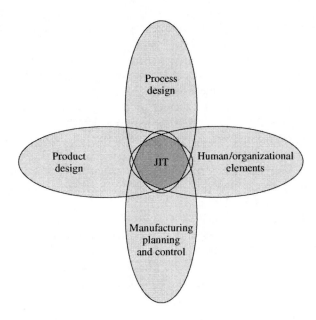

inventories. The object is to concentrate on material velocity. Jobs must flow through in short cycle times, so detailed tracking is unnecessary.

Bandwidth is an important notion in designing manufacturing processes. A wide bandwidth system has enough surge capacity to take on some variation in demand for the products as well as a fairly mixed set of products. The impact on MPC systems is the focus on inventory and throughput time reductions, where inventory is not built to level out capacity requirements. JIT systems are designed to be responsive to as large a set of demands as possible. Superior manufacturing processes support greater bandwidth. The objective is for MPC systems to schedule any product, right behind any other, with minimal disruption.

Human/organizational elements are another building block for JIT. One aspect of this is continual improvement, which implies cross training, process improvements, and whatever else is needed to enhance worker performance. The objective is continual learning and improvement. Human/organizational elements recognize that workers' range of capabilities and level of knowledge are often more important assets to the firm than equipment and facilities. Education is a continuing investment in the human asset base. As the asset base's capabilities grow, need for overhead support is reduced and overhead personnel can be redeployed to address other issues.

Linking human/organizational elements into the other activities has a significant effect on operation of the production process and MPC system. Bandwidth and the avoidance of building inventories to utilize direct labor mean surge capacity must be available. Implementing surge capacity with direct labor personnel means these people will not be fully utilized in direct production activities. In fact, the **whole person** concept is based on the premise of hiring *people,* not just their muscles. As a consequence, direct workers take on many tasks not usually associated with "direct labor." This work can be done in nonpeak production times. This includes equipment maintenance, education, process improvement, data entry, and scheduling. From a JIT standpoint, the human/organizational elements building block puts a greater emphasis on scheduling by workers and less on scheduling by a centralized staff function. The entire process is fostered by the inherent JIT push toward simplification. With no defects, zero inventories, no disturbances, and fast throughput, detailed scheduling is easier; moreover, any problems tend to be local in nature and amenable to solution on a decentralized basis. The whole person concept implies a shift from indirect labor to direct, where jobs are more widely defined.

The final building block in Figure 9.3 is the manufacturing planning and control system and its link to JIT. Applying JIT requires most of the critical MPC functions described in this book. It will always be necessary to do master production scheduling, production planning, capacity planning, and material requirements planning. If the bill of materials is reduced to two or three levels, detailed material planning and associated transaction costs can be cut significantly. If detailed tracking is done by direct laborers under the whole person concept, additional savings can be achieved.

We see then that JIT has the potential for changing the character of manufacturing in a company, since it reduces MPC transactions. JIT can significantly reduce the size of the "hidden factory" that produces papers and computer transactions instead of products. Figure 9.4 provides a more detailed listing of JIT's building blocks and objectives. Many of these will be described in the next section, which presents a detailed JIT example.

FIGURE 9.4
JIT Objectives and Building Blocks

Ultimate objectives:
- Zero inventory
- Zero lead time
- Zero failures
- Flow process
- Flexible manufacture
- Eliminate waste

Building blocks:
- Product design:
  Few bill of materials levels
  Manufacturability in production cells
  Achievable quality
  Appropriate quality
  Standard parts
  Modular design

- Process design:
  Setup/lot size reduction
  Quality improvement
  Manufacturing cells
  Limited work in process
  Production bandwidth
  No stockrooms
  Service enhancements

- Human/organizational elements:
  Cross training/job rotation
  Flexible labor
  Continual improvement
  Whole person
  Limited direct/indirect distinction
  Cost accounting/performance
    measurement
  Information system changes
  Leadership/project management

- Manufacturing planning and control:
  Pull systems
  Rapid flow times
  Small container sizes
  Paperless systems
  Visual systems
  Level loading
  MRP interface
  Close purchasing/vendor relationships
  JIT software
  Reduced production reporting/
    inventory transaction processing
  Hidden factory cost reductions

A JIT Example

In this section we develop a detailed but simple example to show how MPC approaches based on MRP would be modified to implement JIT and describe the necessary building blocks (Figure 9.4) to achieve this. The product is a 1-liter saucepan produced in four models by the Muth Pots and Pans Company. (See Figure 9.5.) The product's brochure sums up its importance: "If you ain't got a Muth, you ain't got a pot." We'll look at elements of a JIT program for the saucepan that range from leveling production to redesigning the product. Some of these elements have direct MPC relevance; others will affect MPC only indirectly.

Leveling the Production

We start the saucepan's JIT program by considering how to "level and stabilize" production. This means planning a level output of 1-liter saucepans with the full mix of models each day (or week or some other short interval). Full-mix production in a short interval provides less inventory buildup in each model. Moreover, the schedule can respond to actual customer order conditions more quickly. Level output implies "freezing" to stabilize production and related activities on the floor. Before seeing how this might be done, let's compare Muth's manufacturing situation with traditional MRP-based approaches.

308   Chapter 9   *Just-in-Time*

FIGURE 9.5
The 151
One-Liter
Saucepan Line

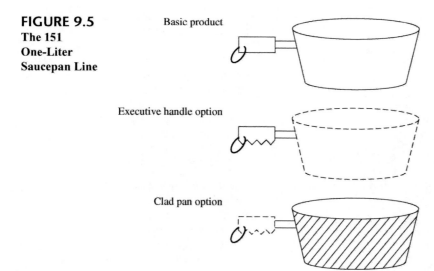

Basic product

Executive handle option

Clad pan option

FIGURE 9.6
Annual
Forecast Data

Completed Pan Model Number	Description of Model		Annual Forecast
	Handle	Metal	
151A	Basic	Sheet	200,000
151B	Basic	Clad	2,500
151C	Executive	Sheet	25,000
151D	Executive	Clad	100,000

Currently, Muth uses production planning to set the overall production rate, necessarily building inventories in anticipation of the Christmas season demand peak. The annual forecast for each of the four models is given in Figure 9.6. A master production schedule, for each of the four models, is exploded to produce a material requirements planning record for each of the 14 component part numbers shown on the part listing in Figure 9.7. Safety stock is carried for all components, and production is in the lot sizes indicated in Figure 9.7. Figure 9.8 gives lead times and routing data; lead times are computed on the basis of two days per operation, rounded up to the next whole week using five-day weeks. A typical MRP record is shown as Figure 9.9.

To plan for level production, the first step is converting the forecasts to the daily requirements for each model. Using a 250-day year, this conversion is shown in Figure 9.10. Note the difference between the current lot sizes and the daily requirements. Daily production will put pressure on process design to reduce setup times. Two other possible mixed-model master production schedules are shown in Figure 9.10, in addition to the one based on daily production batch sizes. The first shows quantities to be produced if hourly batches are to be made. The second shows an MPS with the minimum batch size of one for model 151B.

FIGURE 9.7   **Product Structure and Parts List**

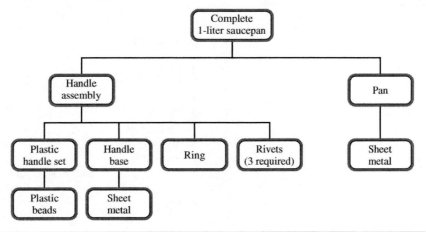

			Finished Item Number			
	Lot Size	Safety Stock	151A	151B	151C	151D
Models (end items)						
Complete pan 151A	8,000	5,000	X			
Complete pan 151B	900	1,000		X		
Complete pan 151C	3,000	3,000			X	
Complete pan 151D	6,000	5,000				X
Component part						
Regular pan 1936	14,000	10,000	X		X	
Clad pan 1937	8,000	6,000		X		X
Basic handle assembly 137	14,000	8,000	X	X		
Exec. handle assembly 138	8,000	5,000			X	X
Basic handle set 244	9,000	8,000	X	X		
Exec. handle set 245	9,000	8,000			X	X
Basic handle base 7731	14,000	8,000	X	X		
Exec. handle base 7735	12,000	5,000			X	X
Ring 353	24,000	15,000	X	X	X	X
Rivets 4164	100,000	50,000	X	X	X	X
Sheet metal 621	1 coil	1 coil	X		X	
Clad sheet 624	1 coil	1 coil		X		X
Handle sheet 685	1 coil	1 coil	X	X	X	X
Plastic beads 211	5 tons	1 ton	X	X	X	X

Pull System Introduction

A "pull" system exists when a work center is authorized to produce only when it has been signaled that there's a need for more parts in a downstream (user) department. This implies no work center is allowed to produce parts just to keep workers or equipment busy. It also means no work center is allowed to "push" material to a downstream work center. All movements and production are authorized by a signal from a downstream work center when it has a need

FIGURE 9.8 **Routing and Lead Time Data**

Department	Item	Routing	Lead Time
Final assembly	Complete pan	1. Spot weld	2 days
		2. Inspect	2 days
		3. Package	2 days
		Total = 6 days = 2 weeks	
Punch press	Pan	1. Blank and form	2 days
		2. Roll lip	2 days
		3. Test for flat	2 days
		4. Straighten	2 days
		5. Inspect	2 days
		Total = 10 days = 2 weeks	
Handle base	Handle base	1. Blank and form	2 days
		2. Inspect	2 days
		Total = 4 days = 1 week	
Handle assembly	Handle assembly	1. Rivet	2 days
		2. Inspect	2 days
		Total = 4 days = 1 week	
Injection molding	Plastic handle set	1. Mold	2 days
		2. Deburr	2 days
		3. Inspect	2 days
		Total = 6 days = 2 weeks	
	Purchased Items		
Purchasing	Sheet metal		Purchased
	Clad sheet metal		lead time
	Plastic beads		one week
	Ring		for all
	Rivets		items

FIGURE 9.9
MRP Record for Basic Handle Assembly (Part 137)

			Week								
		1	2	3	4	5	6	7	8	9	10
Gross requirements			8		8	3	8		8		8
Scheduled receipts											
Projected available balance	10	10	16	16	8	19	11	11	17	17	9
Planned order releases		14			14			14			

Q = 14; LT = 1; SS = 8.
All quantities are in thousands.

for component parts. Frequently, it's believed that the pull system creates the benefits in JIT. In fact, primary payoffs come from the discipline required to make the system work. Included are lot size reductions, limited work in process, fast throughput, and guaranteed quality.

Signals for communicating downstream work center demand vary widely. They include rolling a colored golf ball from a downstream work center to its supplying work center when the downstream center wants parts; yelling "Hey, we need some more"; sending an

FIGURE 9.10
Master Production Schedule Data*

	Model			
	151A	**151B**	**151C**	**151D**
Option configurations:				
Handle	Basic	Basic	Executive	Executive
Pan	Sheet	Clad	Sheet	Clad
Annual forecast (units)	200,000	2,500	25,000	100,000
Possible mixed model master production schedules:				
Daily batch MPS	800	10	100	400
Hourly batch MPS	100	1.25	12.5	50
Minimum batch MPS	80	1	10	40

*Data are based on a 250-day year and an eight-hour work day.

empty container back to be filled; and using cards (kanbans) to indicate more components are needed. A widely used technique is to paint a space on the floor that holds a specific number of parts. When the space is empty, the producing department is authorized to produce material to fill it. The consuming or using department takes material out of the space as it needs it; typically, this occurs only when the space authorizing that department's output is empty. For the Muth example, we'll use an empty container as the signal for more production; that is, whenever a using department empties a container, it sends the container back to the producing department. An empty container represents authorization to fill it up.

Given that Muth has committed to a level schedule where all models are made every day, the firm is almost ready to move into a pull mode of operation. Two additional issues need to be faced. First, there's the question of stability. For most pull systems, it's necessary to keep the schedule firm (frozen) for some reasonable time. This provides stability to the upstream work centers, as well as overall balance to the workflow. For Muth, assume the schedule is frozen for one month, with the daily batch quantities given in Figure 9.10 (1,310 pots per day).

The second issue is determining the container sizes to transport materials between work centers—a fairly complicated issue. It involves material handling considerations, container size commonality, congestion in the shop, proximity of work centers, and, of course, setup costs. For example, consider the container used between handle assembly and final assembly of the pots using the basic handle, part 137 (810 being used per day). The center is currently producing in lots of 14,000. We'll choose a container size that holds 100 pieces representing just under an eighth of a day's requirements. Note this choice puts a great deal of pressure on the handle assembly work center to reduce setup times.

Figure 9.11 shows the flow of work in Muth's new system for handle assembly to the final assembly line. Only two containers are used for part 137; while one is being used at the final assembly line, the other is being filled at handle assembly. This approach is very simple and is facilitated by the two departments being in close proximity. Figure 9.12 shows the factory layout. A worker from the final assembly line or a material handler can return empty containers. Any empty container is a signal to make a new batch of handles (i.e., fill it up). It's interesting to note the difference in average inventory that will be held in this system, compared with the former MRP methods and the lot size of 14,000. The system with a small container approaches "zero inventory," with an average inventory of about 100 units. Compare this to the inventories shown in the MRP record of Figure 9.8 (average inventory = 14,400).

312   Chapter 9   *Just-in-Time*

FIGURE 9.11
Pull System for Muth Pots and Pans

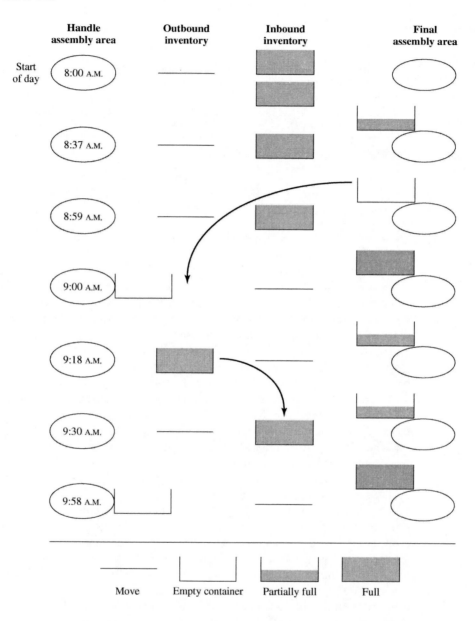

This pull system example has no buffer at either work center. It would be possible to add another container, which would allow greater flexibility in handle assembly, at the cost of extra inventory in the system. As it is, the final assembly area would use up a container in just under one hour. This means the system has to be responsive enough for the empty container to be returned to handle assembly and a batch made in this time frame. An extra container allows more time for responding to a make signal (an empty container) and also allows more flexibility in the supplying department. The extra inventory helps resolve problems—for example, when several production requests for different parts (containers) arrive at the same time.

FIGURE 9.12
Factory Layout

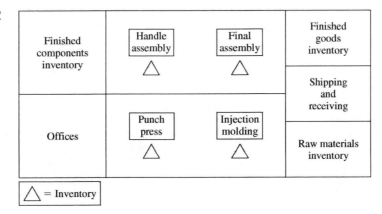

FIGURE 9.13
Redesigned
Handle Base

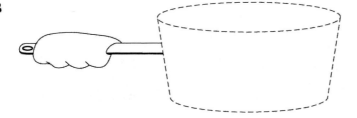

Product Design

To illustrate the implications for product design, consider the basic and executive handles for Muth's 1-liter saucepan shown in Figure 9.5. There are two differences between the handles: the grips and the ring placement. With some redesign of the plastic parts on the executive handle, the handle base becomes a common part and the ring placement is common between the two handle models; the methods for handle assembly could also be standardized. The only difference would be the choice of plastic handle parts. Such a redesigned handle base is shown in Figure 9.13.

In addition to the improvements this design change makes in handle subassembly, there are potential impacts in other areas as well. For example, handle bases would have one combined lot of production instead of two, with attendant reductions in inventory. It might now be possible to run the handle base area on a pull system as well, with containers passing between the handle base area and the handle subassembly area. Another advantage is a simplification in the bill of materials, a reduction in the number of parts that must be planned and controlled with MRP, and a concomitant reduction in the number of transactions that have to be processed.

Process Design

The product redesign, in turn, opens opportunities for process improvement. For example, it may now be possible to use the same equipment to attach both kinds of plastic handles to the handle base. Perhaps a cell can be formed, where handle bases are made and assembled as a unit. Figure 9.14 shows one way this might be accomplished, including an integration

FIGURE 9.14
Cellular
Manufacturing
of Handle
Assembly and
Final Assembly

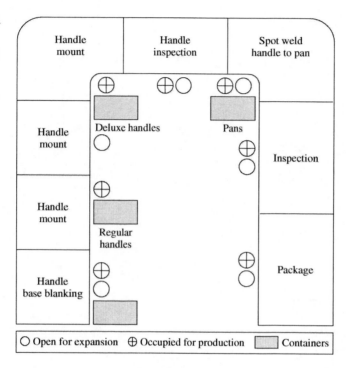

of the handle assembly cell and the final assembly line in a U-shaped layout. Note in this example that no significant inventories are anywhere on the line, and both handle base material and plastic handle parts are replenished with a pull system based on containers.

Figure 9.14 also illustrates the bandwidth concept. Several open stations along the line would permit adding personnel if volume were increased. Moreover, perhaps Muth would like to establish different production rates for certain times. For example, perhaps this pan might be manufactured in higher volumes near the Christmas season. What's needed is the capacity at the cell to move from one level of output to another. This added capacity probably means the dedicated equipment will not be highly utilized.

The cell is designed to permit variations in staffing to better respond to actual customer demands. If an unexpected surge in demand for executive handle pots comes through, the cellular approach will allow Muth to make the necessary changes faster—and to live with this kind of problem with smaller finished goods inventories. Over time, perhaps this cell can be further expanded in terms of bandwidth and flexibility to produce handles for other Muth products.

The value of quality improvement can be seen in Figure 9.14. The inspection station takes up valuable space that could be used for production. It adds cost to the product. If bad products are being culled by inspection, buffer stocks will be required to keep the final assembly line going. All of this is waste to be eliminated.

Bill of Materials Implications

The product redesign results in a streamlined bill of materials. The number of options from the customer's point of view has been maintained, but the number of parts required has

FIGURE 9.15
Simplified
Product
Structure

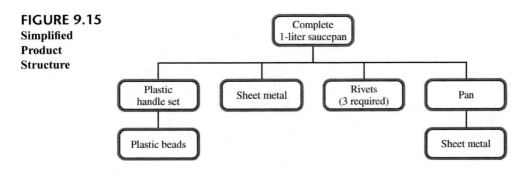

FIGURE 9.16   **MRP Record for Phantom (Part 137)**

	Week									
	1	2	3	4	5	6	7	8	9	10
Gross requirements	4,050	4,050	4,050	4,050	4,050	4,050	4,050	4050	4,050	4,050
Scheduled receipts										
Projected available bal.	15,000	10,950	6,900	2,850						
Planned order releases				1,200	4,050	4,050	4,050	4050	4,050	4,050

Q = lot for lot; LT = 0; SS = 0.

gone down (e.g., components have been reduced from 14 to 10). With the cellular layout shown in Figure 9.14, the handle base and handle assembly no longer exist as inventoriable items. They are "phantoms" that won't require direct planning and control with MRP. The product structure given as Figure 9.7 now will look like Figure 9.15.

Several observations can be made about Figure 9.15. One is that handle assemblies have ceased to exist as part of the product structure. If we wanted to maintain the handle assembly for engineering and other reasons, it could be treated as a phantom. Figure 9.16 shows what the MRP record would look like in this case. In Figure 9.16, there's some existing inventory to use up; phantom treatment allows this to occur, and will always use this inventory before making more.

Another observation is that pans *do* remain as inventoriable items. Elimination of these two part numbers and their associated inventories may well be the next goal for product and process redesign. Still another is to understand the magnitude of the reduction in transactions represented by the JIT approach illustrated in Figure 9.14. All MRP planning for the eliminated part numbers (or phantom treatment) is now gone. This affects MRP planning as well as stockrooms—and all other indirect labor associated with MRP control.

Finally, we need to consider the effect on lead times, the resultant ability to better respond to market conditions, the reductions in work-in-process inventories, and the greater velocity with which material moves through the factory. If the combined lead times are computed for the product structure in Figure 9.7 and lead time data in Figure 9.8, five weeks are required for the flow of raw materials into pots. The JIT approach cuts that to just over two weeks, which could be reduced even further.

316   Chapter 9   *Just-in-Time*

JIT Applications

Toyota is the classic JIT company in that it has gone further than any other discrete manufacturing firm in terms of truly making the production process into a continuous flow. Much of the basic terminology and philosophy of JIT have their origins at Toyota. A key issue in JIT at Toyota is understanding that automobile manufacturing is done in very large factories that are much more complex than our simplified example. Parts will flow from one work center to many others with intermediate storage, and flows into work centers will also come from many work centers with intermediate storage. The JIT systems at Toyota have to reflect this complexity. Before delving into the complexity, however, it's useful to first see how a **single-card kanban system** functions in a manufacturing environment with many work centers and intermediate storage.

Single-Card Kanban

Figure 9.17 depicts a factory with three work centers (A, B, and C) producing component parts, three work centers (X, Y, and Z) making assemblies, and an intermediate storage area for component parts. A single component (part 101) is fabricated in work center C and used by work centers Y and Z. To illustrate how the system works, suppose work center Z wishes to assemble a product requiring component 101. A box of part 101 would be moved from the storage area to work center Z. As the box was removed from storage, the accompanying kanban card would be removed from the box; shortly thereafter, the card would be placed

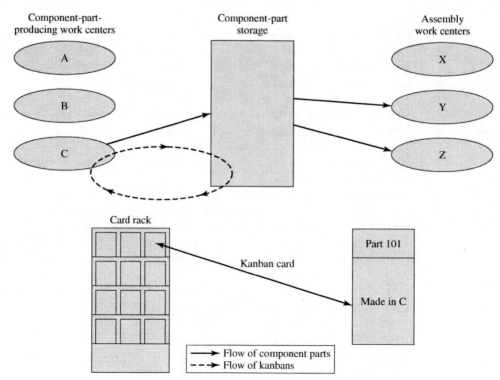

FIGURE 9.17
Single Kanban System

Component-part-producing work centers

Component-part storage

Assembly work centers

A

B

C

X

Y

Z

Card rack

Kanban card

Part 101

Made in C

→ Flow of component parts
--→ Flow of kanbans

in the card rack at work center C. The cards in the rack at any work center represents the authorized production for that work center.

The greater the number of kanban cards in the system, the larger the inventory, but also the greater the autonomy that can be attained between the component-producing work centers and the assembly work centers. Some priority system can be implemented in the component work centers, such as working on a first-come/first-served basis or imposing some time requirements (such as all cards delivered in the morning will be returned with filled containers in the afternoon of the same day and all afternoon cards will be delivered the next morning).

Toyota

The production system at Toyota is in many ways the most advanced JIT system in the world. Its results are seen on the highways of the world. By virtually any yardstick, Toyota is truly a great manufacturing company. For example, Toyota turns its inventories 10 times as fast as U.S. and European car manufacturers and about 50 percent faster than its Japanese competitors. It's also very competitive in price, quality, and delivery performance.

Figure 9.18 shows the Toyota production system and where JIT fits within the overall approach. To some extent, the role given to JIT in Figure 9.18 may appear less encompassing

FIGURE 9.18 **Toyota's Production System**

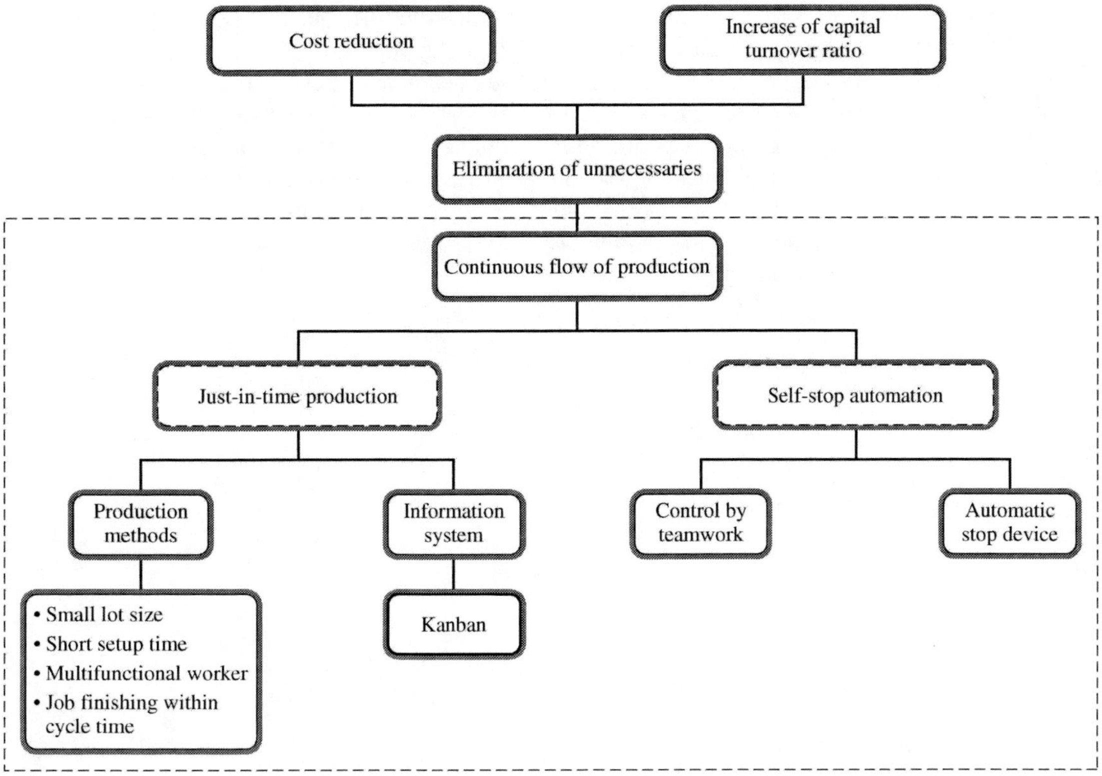

Source: European Working Group for Production Planning and Inventory Control, Lausanne, Switzerland.

than that just described. For example, the "elimination of unnecessaries" is seen as fundamental. All of the objectives and building blocks for JIT listed in Figure 9.4 are in basic agreement with those in Figure 9.18. The box for production methods is basically the same as process design in Figure 9.3. Included under this heading is the multifunctional worker, which matches with several aspects of the human/organizational element building block. Also included is "job finishing within cycle time"; this is consistent with the dominance of material flow velocity and the subservient role of direct labor utilization.

Toyota's Kanban System

The Toyota view of just-in-time production shown in Figure 9.18 includes "Information system" with "Kanban" below it. The information system encompasses the MPC activities necessary to support JIT execution. Kanban is the Toyota technique for controlling material flows. The situation at Toyota is much more complex than that illustrated in the single-card kanban example. Toyota has intermediate storage after production of components and additional intermediate storage in front of assembly work centers. This means the work flows from a producing work center into an inventory, then to another inventory, and then to the next work center. For this reason, Toyota uses a two-card kanban system, but the principles are the same as for the single kanban card system. The chain of dual kanban cards can extend all the way back to the suppliers. Several of Toyota's suppliers receive their authorizations to produce via kanban cards.

Figure 9.19 gives the formula used to calculate the number of kanban cards needed. In this formula, there's a factor for including safety stock, which Toyota says should be less than 10 percent. Using the formula, no safety stock, and a container size of 1, we can see the philosophy of the system. If a work center required eight units per day (one per hour) and it took one hour to make one unit, only one set of two kanban cards would be theoretically necessary; that is, just as a unit was finished, it would be needed at the subsequent operation.

The container sizes are kept small and standard. Toyota feels that no container should have more than 10 percent of a day's requirements. Since everything revolves around these containers and the flow of cards, a great deal of discipline is necessary. The following rules keep the system operating:

- Each container of parts must have a kanban card.
- The parts are always pulled. The using department must come to the providing department and not vice versa.
- No parts may be obtained without a conveyance kanban card.

FIGURE 9.19
Calculating the Number of Kanbans

$$Y = \frac{DL(1+\alpha)}{a} \qquad (9.1)$$

where:

Y = number of kanban card sets
D = demand per unit of time
L = lead time
a = container capacity
α = policy variable (safety stock)

FIGURE 9.20
**Toyota's View
of Inventory**

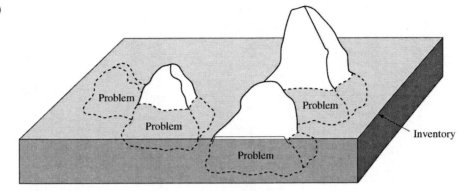

- All containers contain their standard quantities and only the standard container for the part can be used.
- No extra production is permitted. Production can only be started on receipt of a production kanban card.

These rules keep the shop floor under control. The execution effort is directed toward flawlessly following these rules. Execution is also directed toward continual improvement. In kanban terms, this means reducing the number of kanban cards and, thereby, reducing the level of work-in-process inventory. Reducing the number of cards is consistent with an overall view of inventory as undesirable. It's said at Toyota that inventory is like water that covers up problems that are like rocks. Figure 9.20 depicts this viewpoint. If the inventory is systematically reduced, problems are exposed—and attention can be directed to their solution. Problems obscured by inventory still remain.

Hewlett-Packard

Hewlett-Packard (HP) has been one of the more successful users of JIT in the United States. An interesting approach to JIT was implemented at its Medical Electronics Division in Waltham, Massachusetts. JIT was used for assembling two major patient-monitoring products called Pogo and Clover. Figure 9.21 shows the assembly area layout for these products. Clover was the older, more expensive product, with a larger number of customer-specified options. Pogo was designed as a lower-cost alternative with JIT manufacture in mind. The Clover assembly process was made up of four feeder subassemblies (A to D) and a final assembly and test area (E). Pogo was designed to be built in four successive assembly stations in a U shape with a test performed in each. A final test was performed at station V. Both Clover and Pogo went into a heat test area, shown at the top of Figure 9.21. The series of tests performed on Pogo at each station (I to IV) allowed HP to reduce the failure rate in heat testing more quickly than it did for Clover.

Both Clover and Pogo were supported by dedicated component stock areas. Each was also supported with a printed circuit board stock. In Pogo's case, 12 types of circuit boards were maintained, with a single-card kanban approach. They were supplied in lot sizes of four, with coded clothespins acting as the single kanban. On the other hand, the printed circuit boards for Clover were maintained with traditional MRP lot sizes. Both Pogo and Clover used a single-card kanban approach to pull kits of parts from the controlled stock areas.

FIGURE 9.21   **Hewlett-Packard Waltham Division Pogo/Clover Production U Stations**

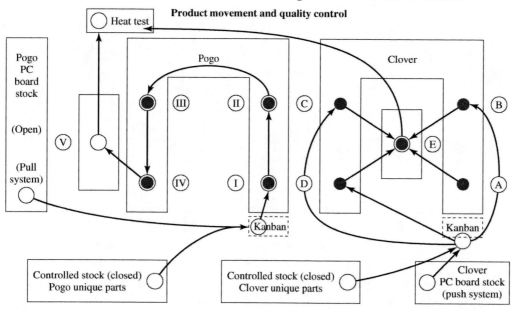

This JIT system was supported by several MRP-based computer systems. These company-wide systems were mainly used for component-part planning. As time went by, however, the semimonthly MRP explosion, weekly allocation quantities, and daily release against these allocation quantities became more cumbersome for JIT manufacturing. JIT operates in a very different time frame.

A more profound issue concerned HP's overall philosophy in adopting JIT. The primary emphasis was on stability. In Pogo, for example, the goal was to make 10 units per day, each and every day. This goal was achieved; then it became possible to get 10 good units between 8 A.M. and 1:30 P.M. on most days. To concentrate on stability, the Pogo assembly area was buffered on both ends. Extra supplies of component materials were held, as were extra finished goods inventories.

Once stability was achieved, relatively flawless output could be achieved with regularity. The continuous improvement attention then shifted to reducing buffers and increasing responsiveness. If the assembly area could produce 15 units on a particular day when necessary, the finished goods could be reduced. With flawless production, lower component inventories could also be attained. The JIT results were impressive. Total plant inventory fell from $56 million to $40 million in 15 months. Work-in-process inventory for the Pogo line was reduced from 50 units to 4, and the assembly floor space required decreased 65 percent. Quality increased substantially by the JIT approach, as well. But there were still new avenues for improvement. Included were further reductions in the printed circuit board inventories and tackling what appeared to be bottlenecks in circuit board production.

Nonrepetitive JIT

Many JIT principles for high-volume repetitive manufacturing apply in low-volume production environments as well. However, most low-volume manufacturers have balked at two basic problems: (1) the requirement of setting up high-volume flow lines dedicated to a few products and (2) level loading. However, merging of the two camps is taking place: even for the high-volume repetitive manufacturer, it's increasingly important to respond to customer pressures for greater flexibility in volume, product mix, and other service features. The lower-volume job shop manufacturers are in turn learning to adapt JIT concepts to their environments.

A Service-Enhanced View of Manufacturing

An examination of service operations provides insights into producing products faster with greater variety. Rapid response is critical, the number of possible product/service combinations continues to grow, end-item forecasting is more difficult, and large buffer inventories are unacceptable. One example was a repair facility for Palm Pilots and other electronics products, placed in the DHL (worldwide parcel shippers) facilities in Singapore. Using DHL's rapid product movements and tracking, a product could be picked up, repaired, and returned in two to three days, instead of supplying a replacement.

All of this argues for a JIT mode of manufacture—one whose objective is to be able to accept any customer order and turn it out right behind any other, with flexibility to handle surges in volume or mix changes, all done on a routine basis. Service industries provide an example. McDonald's can handle two busloads of Boy Scouts or an unexpected shift from Big Macs to fish sandwiches without resorting to some "panic mode" of operation. Fast-food operations provide still another example. Most have seen an evolution toward a broader product line (greater bandwidth). McDonald's no longer just serves hamburgers, for example. The objective is to increase market appeal while maintaining maximum responsiveness, minimal inventories, small lot sizes, and short lead times.

The traditional JIT view of level capacity must be adapted in nonrepetitive situations. Responsiveness to fickle demand requires a large bandwidth in terms of surge capacity. No one wants the fire department to be operated at high capacity utilization; immediate response is essential. Surge capacity must be in place in both equipment and labor. A different view of asset management and labor utilization is required. Fixed assets (both capital and people) will be less intensively utilized to increase material velocity and overall system responsiveness.

Flexible Systems

Leading-edge firms are coming to understand requirements for volume and product flexibility. Some have had experience in repetitive manufacturing applications of JIT and are now moving into nonrepetitive applications. An example is a telecommunications equipment manufacturer, which began JIT in its high-volume telephone handset operations. The firm had a limited number of high-selling models; in two years its inventory turns were tripled, work in process was reduced by 75 percent, failure rates in manufacturing were cut in half, and setup times fell 50 percent. Thereafter, the firm turned to its low-volume telecom systems plant, where more than 150 basic circuit boards were manufactured, and every end item was somewhat of a custom order. The company learned it needed to go back to the basics of JIT—product engineering, process engineering, and the whole person concept—to successfully implement JIT for its nonrepetitive products.

The firm developed cellular designs, began cellular manufacturing with great flexibility, and cross trained people with an emphasis on being able to handle volume surges in the telecom systems plant. MRP was still used for overall planning, but far fewer transactions were processed by the hidden factory of indirect labor. In the first six months, first pass yields improved 27 percent, work in process fell 31 percent, and manufacturing cells under JIT hit 100 percent of schedule. The people then helped out other parts of the company that were behind schedule!

Simplified Systems and Routine Execution

A major issue in any JIT firm, repetitive or nonrepetitive, is flow times. Work must flow through the factory so quickly that detailed tracking is not required. A related idea is responsiveness. In several JIT systems for nonrepetitive environments, the firm installed what might be called a **weekly wash.** In its simplest form, weekly wash means week 1's sales orders become week 2's production schedule.

As an example, Stanley Hardware in New Britain, Connecticut, was a make-to-stock firm for most items, but some were unique to particular customers. It applied JIT with the weekly wash concept to three different production areas. In each case, weekly sales for a particular week were determined on Friday, with resultant quantities manufactured the next week within some change parameters. In one case, the week-to-week variation in production could be plus or minus 20 percent. For a second product group, the swing was plus or minus 35 percent, and for a third group any adjustment could be handled. Because response times were shortened, customer service was enhanced.

The weekly wash approach to JIT for nonrepetitive manufacturing shifts the emphasis from scheduling material to scheduling time blocks. The focus is on what's scheduled in the next time frame, rather than on when we'll make product X. This focus is driven by the actual requirements, rather than a forecast of needs. It's as though we were scheduling a set of trains or buses. We don't hold the train until it's full, and we can always cram a few more people into a car, within reason. By scheduling trains on a relatively frequent basis, attempting to keep capacity as flexible as possible, and assigning "passengers" only to a time frame, responsiveness to actual demand can be increased, and detailed scheduling can be made more simple. A hospital administrator once expressed the idea well: We do not make people sick to fill the beds!

Joint-Firm JIT

JIT has been applied and misapplied by companies with their suppliers. Some firms simply ask the suppliers to buffer poor schedules. On the other hand, when done well, a joint JIT approach can lead to greater bottom-line results for both firms and increased competitiveness in the marketplace. It is critical to understand the need for joint efforts in JIT. For example, we are told by several automotive component suppliers that they are able to provide lower prices to Toyota than other firms, because Toyota is easy to do business with—the company makes a schedule and sticks to it. Others change their requirements often, with serious cost implications.

The Basics

The first prerequisite to joint-firm JIT is a scheduling system producing requirements that are reasonably certain. Without predictability, JIT for vendors is a case of the customers exporting the problems. Although this may work in the short run, in the long run it can't. We've seen a factory where JIT benefits were extolled, only to find a new paving project—for vendors' trucks. Inventory had moved from the warehouse to trailer trucks! Similar war stories abound about warehousing firms in Detroit that are needed to buffer suppliers as auto companies implement JIT.

Joint-firm JIT needs, to whatever extent possible, a stable schedule. This is consistent with level schedules for the repetitive manufacturer. To the extent that a firm makes the same products in the same quantities every day—without defects and without missing the schedule—a supplier firm's schedule is extremely simple. For the nonrepetitive manufacturer, the issue isn't leveling as much as it is avoiding surprises. The level schedule may be violated in nonrepetitive environments, but there is a greater need for coordinated information flows and, perhaps, larger buffer inventories. However, there's a major difference between a *stable* (albeit nonlevel) schedule and one that's simply uncertain. The only cure for the latter case is buffer inventories.

Certainty is a relative commodity. A vendor might be able to live fairly well with a schedule that's unpredictable on a daily basis but very predictable on a weekly basis. A weekly MRP-based total, with some kind of daily call-off of exact quantities, could be reasonably effective. In fact, some firms have developed "electronic kanbans" for this purpose. The notion of weekly wash could also be used; that is, an inventory equal to some maximum expected weekly usage could be maintained and replenished on a weekly basis. For high-value products, it might be worth it to go to some kind of twice-weekly wash, or to obtain better advance information from the customer via an e-based system.

Other "basics" for joint-firm JIT include all the objectives and building blocks discussed earlier in the chapter. A JIT basic uniquely associated with suppliers relates to pruning their number. Many companies have reduced their vendor base by as much as 90 percent to work on a truly cooperative basis with the remaining vendors. Hidden factory issues have to be considered in vendor relations as well. Some people feel the secret in joint-firm JIT is to connect MRP systems in the firms. This isn't a good idea. The focus must be on coordinated execution. A better approach might be to use blanket orders (or *no* orders), MRP for weekly quantities, agreed-upon safety stocks, or amounts by which the sum of daily quantities can exceed weekly totals, and e-based systems to determine the next day in-shipment. All this could be done without intervention of indirect labor personnel.

A telecom equipment manufacturer has such a system: Each day at about 4 P.M., an e-mail is sent to a vendor specifying how many of a particular expensive item to deliver the day after tomorrow. The units delivered never enter a stockroom or inventory record. They're delivered directly to the line without inspection and assembled that day. The vendor is paid on the basis of item deliveries into finished goods inventory. Stability is handled by providing the vendor weekly MRP projections, using time fences that define stability. Daily fluctuations reflect actual market conditions.

Tightly Coupled JIT Supply

Major suppliers to automobile manufacturers utilize JIT extensively. As an example, consider a seat supplier, such as Johnson Controls, and a manufacturer such as Volkswagen. In such a case, the two firms need to develop a form of synchronous manufacturing, operating almost as a single unit. The execution is driven by JIT. JIT execution between these two firms means that the automobile manufacturer will pass the exact build sequence (models, colors of seats, etc.) to the seat supplier, perhaps something like 30 hours in advance. The supplier needs to *build* the seats and deliver them in this time frame. Seats are not built to inventory at the supplier, and no seats are inventoried at the auto manufacturer. The seats are delivered directly to the assembly line, to match the sequence, so the assembly team simply takes the next seat, and installs it in the next car.

This synchronization allows for almost no transactions between the firms, with the supplier paid by backflushing completion of cars off the line. Inventory costs are avoided, as well as damage from multiple handling with minimal use of protective packaging. But achieving the synchronization on a continuous basis requires *flawless execution* in both firms. The auto manufacturing company cannot change the schedule or take a car off of the line for repairs, since this would change the seat installation sequence. The supplier must make each seat perfectly, since there is no stock of seats to replace one that is imperfect. The bottom line here is that this form of joint-firm JIT is highly productive. But it is rigidly connected and requires joint excellence in execution. It works well—for certain kinds of products.

Less Tightly Coupled JIT Supply

In the majority of cases, two firms will not couple their manufacturing activities as closely as those of a seat supplier to its automotive customer. The supplier will have multiple customers, only some of which will be supplied by JIT. Similarly, the customer has multiple suppliers, and not all of these will be expected to deliver directly to the line. An alternative solution is for the customer to pick up goods from vendors on some prearranged schedule. This is increasingly done for several reasons. The most obvious is the savings in transportation costs over having each vendor deliver independently. In some cases JIT has been called "just-in-traffic." A second reason relates to stability and predictability. If the customer picks up materials, some uncertainty inherent in vendor deliveries can be eliminated. Finally, pickup offers more chances to directly attack hidden factory costs. The customer can, for example, provide containers that hold the desired amounts and that will flow as kanbans through the plant. Savings in packaging materials as well as costs of unpacking are helpful to both parties. Items can also be placed on special racks inside the truck to minimize damage. Defective items can be returned easily for replacement without the usual costly return-to-vendor procedures and paperwork. Other paperwork can similarly be simplified when third parties aren't involved and when the loop is closed between problem and action in a short time frame.

Pickup can also be done in geographic areas beyond the factory. A Hewlett-Packard factory in Boise, Idaho, has key suppliers in Silicon Valley, California (about 600 miles away). Pickup from them is done by a trucking firm, with the entire shipment moved to Boise on a daily basis. New United Motor Manufacturing, Inc. (NUMMI) in Freemont, California, did the same thing with its Midwest suppliers: a Chicago-based trucking company collected trailer loads for daily piggyback shipments to California about 2,000 miles away. NUMMI started off holding a three-day safety stock of these parts but reduced it to one day after experience had been gained.

"JIT" Coordination through Hubs

A relatively new innovation that has JIT characteristics is the supply of materials through hubs. A hub is most easily seen as an inventory, placed close to the customer, and filled by the suppliers. The costs of carrying the inventories is born by the suppliers, and they are paid for their goods either as they leave the hub or as they are backflushed into finished goods at the customer. This form of supply is called **vendor-managed inventory (VMI).** VMI is well liked by customers, since it moves inventory carrying costs off their books and onto those of the suppliers. But the "no free lunch" principle applies: If the customer only exports its problems, and does not aid in the solution, the prices will have to be adjusted to make this work. Moreover, the firm with the lowest cost of capital in the chain is ideally suited to absorb inventory-carrying costs.

There is, however, a major potential saving in this relationship. When it is done well, the supplier should eliminate its own finished goods inventory, while the customer in turn also eliminates any inventories of these materials. All inventories are in the hub and are visible to both customer and supplier. The customer needs to take the responsibility for providing highly accurate information on its expected removals from inventory (i.e., its build schedules). This is typically provided via an e-based system. The supplier thus has *knowledge* of exact customer usage: no forecasts (guesses), and no surprise orders. The supplier also has the option of working in what we call the **uphill skier** mode, where it is the supplier's responsibility to supply, but in whatever ways it wishes (just as the uphill skier has the responsibility for not colliding with the downhill skier). Having a few customers who can be supplied with the uphill skier concept allows the supplier to use its capacities and logistics more effectively. For example, if a supplier knows the customer will take 55 units out of inventory 11 days from today, this provides a window for manufacturing and delivery, which is much less constraining than classic JIT coordination.

Lessons

The primary lesson to be learned in joint-firm JIT is to not shift the execution problems from the customer back to its suppliers: joint-firm JIT means *joint.* Many firms have made this mistake, demanding that their suppliers support them in closely coordinated execution—while the suppliers see the customer as "waking up in a new world every morning." Typically, when the consequences become known, the emphasis necessarily shifts to joint problem identification and solution, a focus on joint (chain) measures, the need for stabilized schedules, a true partnership, and help from the customers for the suppliers to implement JIT with *their* suppliers. The results for a manufacturer of office equipment were impressive: overcoming a 40 percent cost disadvantage, reducing its vendor base from 5,000 to 300, and winning several important awards for manufacturing excellence.

JIT Software

The MPC systems required to execute JIT are relatively straightforward. Most ERP systems include software that supports JIT execution. Figure 9.22 shows how this software typically functions.

FIGURE 9.22   **Block Diagram of JIT Software**

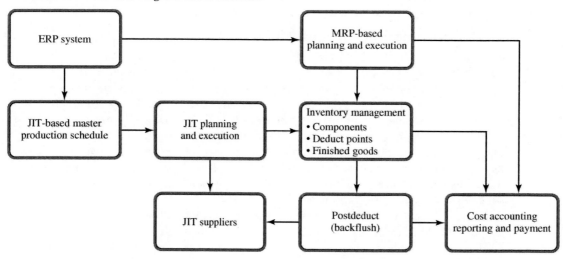

The MRP-JIT Separation

Figure 9.22 depicts the way JIT typically functions as a part of the overall MPC system. An ERP system, such as SAP, provides the overall platform and integration with other company systems. Figure 9.22 shows a split into those items that are to be planned/controlled with JIT and those that will utilize classic MRP-based systems. For the JIT products, it is necessary to first establish a master production schedule, which typically is rate based. This MPS is then passed to a JIT planning and execution subsystem that utilizes simplified bills of materials (phantoms) and cellular manufacturing. The detailed planning is also passed to JIT suppliers, typically with an e-based system providing the exact build sequence.

JIT Planning and Execution

JIT planning and execution is driven by a daily build schedule, supported by the JIT dictates of flawless execution, zero failures, no buffer inventories, cellular manufacturing, pull systems, cross-trained personnel, etc. JIT planning and execution also utilizes an inventory management subsystem for any components that are planned with MRP-based systems. This subsystem also keeps track of finished goods, any hub inventories, and **deduct points.** A deduct point is a stage in the manufacturing process where the inventories for certain parts are backflushed. That is, in some JIT systems, the backflushing is not held off until the goods are finally passed into finished goods inventory. The accounting is done in stages. This is most usually seen in early stages of JIT, when the flow times are longer and the yields less certain. The use of deduct points also helps in migrating from MRP-based planning to JIT-based planning/execution. In fact, a typical improvement is to decide when a deduct point can be eliminated, since a deduct step requires production reporting to indicate that product completion has reached this stage. Figure 9.22 also depicts an accounting/reporting subsystem to collect performance data and support supplier payments.

An Example

Let us illustrate how this software might work by returning to the HP case depicted in Figure 9.21. Concentrating on the Pogo product, let us assume that originally this product was built as five separate subassembly and test steps (I to V), going into inventory after each stage of assembly or test. For each discrete step, the prior assembly would be picked from inventory, along with the unique components associated with the particular subassembly stage. Withdrawals of subassemblies and component parts would be deducted from on-hand inventory balances as they occurred in classic MRP fashion.

Under JIT planning the entire flow might be considered one step from I to V; that is, the deduct point for inventory reductions would be when step V is completed (note that this only becomes feasible when steps I to V occur quickly). Completion of step V would be the only transaction needed through production reporting. When this occurs, a deduct list for all the components used in steps I to V would trigger inventory reporting through backflushing (in this case including the Pogo printed circuit board stocks and controlled stock area for unique Pogo parts). We also noted that HP controlled the PC boards for Pogo with a JIT system. This means that receipt of boards into this area would be a deduct point for PC components. It is worth noting that this approach could lead to serious problems if there is significant scrap in PC board manufacturing (i.e., usage would be under-reported, leading to unreliable inventory values).

Parts and bills of material in JIT systems are the equivalent of the usual product structure files in MRP, but they are defined according to deduct points. That is, the deduct point is like an assembly that is planned as one part and supported by cellular manufacturing to execute the manufacturing accordingly. As products are converted from MRP to JIT, it is necessary to reformat the data according to deduct points. In execution, it is imperative, in fact, to utilize the exact quantities of materials indicated by the deduct lists (flawless execution). As reengineering efforts allow deduct points to be eliminated, the data also need to be reformatted.

JIT Execution with SAP Software

Most ERP systems incorporate some means to accomplish JIT execution within their system structure. SAP, providing the most widely used ERP system, has the following approach to support JIT planning, as reported by Knolmayer et al.:

> The R/3 module supports the Kanban principle. Objects are cards, production supply areas, control cycles, and Kanban boards that provide an overview of the current status (e.g., full, empty, in progress, being transported) of the containers. The board visualizes bottlenecks and problems arising with material supply. The R/3 Kanban system allows external procurement, internal production, and supply from a warehouse. The initiating event for delivery of the material is a status change at the container; when the container status is altered from "full" to "empty," R/3 automatically generates replacement bookings. The status of the containers can be changed directly on the Kanban board, in an input mask, or by scanning a barcode printed on the card. When a receiver sets the status of a container to empty, a replacement element is created and the associated source is requested to supply the material. As soon as the status changes to "full," the arrival of the material is booked automatically with reference to the procurement element. A supplier can view the inventory levels of materials via the Internet and determine what quantities of the materials need to be provided. It can define a delivery due list and inform the customer by setting the status at "in progress."

Managerial Implications

The vision of JIT presented here is much broader than manufacturing planning and control. JIT is best seen as an integrated approach to achieving continued manufacturing excellence. A holistic view of JIT encompasses a set of programs, as well as a process where human resources are continually redeployed in better ways to serve company objectives in the marketplace. In the balance of this chapter, we feel compelled to speculate a bit on what this implies for manufacturing planning and control and related areas.

Information System Implications

Since JIT requires changes in the ways manufacturing is managed and executed, changes are required in the computer-based systems to support JIT manufacturing. The changes run counter to some classic IT systems in manufacturing. JIT calls for continuous improvement, reducing transactions, and eliminating the hidden factory. This implies an ongoing migration of MPC systems to support reengineered manufacturing processes. To the extent that JIT is for nonrepetitive manufacturing, personal computers are often used on the shop floor to support detailed scheduling. For joint-firm JIT planning and execution, the increasing use of e-based systems is taking place. In practice, there tends to be an evolution from simple buying and routine transaction processing to more coordinated work, including new product developments and other less structured activities. Many firms now are implementing extranets to support these objectives, where individual company pairings work on achieving increasingly unique benefits.

Manufacturing Planning and Control

JIT has profound implications for all detailed MPC activities. JIT (including its extensions into less tightly linked supply chains) offers the potential for eliminating or sharply reducing inventories, incoming quality control, receiving, kitting, paper processing associated with deliveries and shipments, detailed scheduling done by central staff, and all the detailed tracking associated with classic production activity control systems. It is important to understand these benefits as the MPC system is enhanced to embody JIT thinking. Many of them are well hidden.

It is never easy to change IT systems. Organizations have grown around them, cost accounting and other areas seem to require data generated by these systems, and many jobs are involved. However, the potential is real, and leading-edge companies are increasing their competitiveness through JIT and related concepts.

Scorekeeping

A firm adopting JIT in its fullest context will need to think carefully about reward systems and managerial scorekeeping. Traditional measurement systems focus attention on producing the products, using cost accounting systems that have changed little since the Industrial Revolution. These systems are from an era when direct labor was the major cost source. Now, in many companies, material costs dominate, with direct labor cost (using traditional definitions) continually decreasing in relative importance. Far too many manufacturing firms are hobbled by antiquated measures such as tons or other overall productivity measures. For example, a large ice cream manufacturer evaluates its factories on "liter-tons" produced. A 1-liter brick of ice cream has less gross margin than a particular ice cream bar—but 1-liter bricks are always put in inventory at year-end to make the numbers look good.

JIT thinking focuses on material velocity, which is consistent with inventory reduction and lead-time compression. Under JIT, we must be wary of how "costs" are measured and the resultant implications for decision making. The values of bandwidth, flexibility, responsiveness, and worker skill enhancement need to be recognized. None of these is incorporated in traditional accounting systems. The entire approach to capacity utilization needs to be rethought in JIT. Utilization of capital assets may not be as important as responsiveness and material velocity. Being able to take any customer order, even when vastly different from forecast, and doing so with short lead times with minimal use of "shock troops" is the goal. Improved responsiveness to marketplace needs will separate successful firms from the also-rans.

What all of this means for cost accounting is that many traditional views will need to be scrapped. For example, some companies have given up the cost category of direct labor. The distinction between direct and indirect isn't useful, and basing product costs on multiples of direct labor cost leads to more erroneous implications than some other scheme. The whole person concept leads to the conclusion that the labor pool is an asset to be enhanced. It also dictates using direct labor for activities not normally associated with direct labor. Trying to apportion labor into various categories is constraining. A final scorekeeping issue is the top-management challenge to create the organizational climate where the JIT/supply chain management journey can best take place. We see this journey is the best means for survival in the years ahead. Leadership will be required to guide manufacturing firms through the necessary changes.

Pros and Cons

There are situations where JIT will work well and ones where it won't. Many authorities believe JIT to be what every Japanese company strives for. In fact, many Japanese firms with complex product structures are now actively working to implement MRP-based systems. However, JIT's realm seems to be expanding. At one time JIT was thought to apply only to repetitive manufacturing with simple product structures and level schedules. Increasingly, companies are applying JIT concepts to nonrepetitive schedules; product complexity is being partially overcome with decentralized computing on the shop floor; make-to-order schedules are being adapted to JIT; and JIT is being applied to interfirm contexts.

Some companies ask if they need to install MRP before adopting JIT, since JIT implementation often means they must dismantle parts of the MRP-based system. Although it's conceptually possible to implement JIT without first implementing MRP, for firms that can benefit significantly from MRP, it's usually not done. Unless we can find some other way to develop the discipline of MRP, JIT operations are at great risk. In the discipline's absence, when JIT takes away the buffers, there will usually be costly disruptions of the manufacturing process, poor customer service, and panic responses to the symptoms rather than to the underlying problems.

Concluding Principles

This chapter is devoted to providing an understanding of JIT and how it fits into MPC systems. Our view of JIT encompasses more than MPC-related activities, but there's a significant overlap between JIT and our approach to MPC systems. In summarizing this chapter, we emphasize the following principles:

- Stabilizing and in some cases leveling the production schedules are prerequisites to effective JIT systems.

- Achieving very short lead times supports better customer service and responsiveness.

- Reducing hidden factory costs can be at least as important as reducing costs more usually attributed to factory operations.

- Implementing the whole person concept reduces distinctions between white- and blue-collar workers and taps all persons' skills for improving performance.

- Cost accounting and performance measurements need to reflect the shift in emphasis away from direct labor as the primary source of value added.

- To achieve JIT's benefits in nonrepetitive applications, some basic features of repetitive-based JIT must be modified.

- JIT is not incompatible with MRP-based systems. Firms can evolve toward JIT from MRP-based systems, adopting JIT as much or as little as they want, with an incremental approach.

References

Brown, J. S.; S. Durchslag; and J. Hagel III. "Loosening Up: How Process Networks Unlock the Power of Specialization," *McKinsey Quarterly,* no. 2 (2002).

Dixon, Lance. *JITII, Revolution in Buying and Selling.* Boston: Cahners, 1994.

Fine, C. H.: *Clockspeed: Winning Industry Control in the Age of Temporary Advantage.* Reading, Mass.: Perseus Books, 1998.

Hall, R. W. *Driving the Productivity Machine.* Falls Church, Va.: American Production and Inventory Control Society, 1981.

————. *Zero Inventories.* Homewood, Ill.: Dow Jones–Irwin, 1983.

Hall, R. W.; H. T. Johnson; and P. B. B. Turney. *Measuring Up: Charting Pathways to Manufacturing Excellence.* Homewood, Ill.: Business One Irwin, 1990.

Hammer, M., and S. Stanton. "How Process Enterprises Really Work," *Harvard Business Review,* November–December 1999, pp.108–118.

Hyer, N., and U. Wemmerlov. *Reorganizing the Factory: Competing through Cellular Manufacturing.* Portland, Ore.: Productivity Press, 2002.

Juran, J. M., and A. B. Godfrey. *Juran's Quality Handbook,* fifth edition. New York: McGraw-Hill, 1999.

Karmarkar, Uday S. "Getting Control of Just-in-Time." *Harvard Business Review,* September–October 1989.

Kern, G. M., and J. C. Wei. "Master Production Rescheduling Policy in Capacity Constrained Just-In-Time Make-To-Stock Environments," *Decision Sciences* 27, no. 2 (spring 1996), pp. 365–387.

Knolmayer, G.; P. Mertens; and A. Zeier. *Supply Chain Management Based on SAP Systems.* Berlin: Springer-Verlag, 2002.

Lummus, R. R. "A Simulation Analysis of Sequencing Alternatives for JIT Lines Using Kanbans," *Journal of Operations Management* 13, no. 3 (1995).

Miller, J. G., and T. E. Vollmann. "The Hidden Factory," *Harvard Business Review,* September–October 1985, pp. 141–150.

Monden, Yasuhiro. *Toyota Production System,* Norcroos, Ga.: Industrial Engineering and Management Press, 1983.

Nakane, J. R., and R. W. Hall. "Management Specs for Stockless Production," *Harvard Business Review,* May–June 1983, pp. 84–91.

Ohno, Taiichi. *Toyota Production System: Beyond Large-Scale Production.* Cambridge, Mass.: Productivity Press, 1988.

Schmenner, R. "Looking Ahead by Looking Back: Swift Even Flow in the History of Manufacturing," *Production and Operations Management* 10, no. 1 (2001), pp. 87–96.

Schonberger, R. *World-Class Manufacturing: The Next Decade,* New York: The Free Press, 1996.

Shingo, Shigeo. *A Revolution in Manufacturing: The SMED System.* Cambridge, Mass.: Productivity Press, 1985.

Wantuck, Kenneth A. *Just-In-Time for America: A Common Sense Production Strategy,* Ken Wantuck Associates, June 1989.

Wemmerlov, U., and D. J. Johnson. "Empirical Findings on Manufacturing Cell Design," *International Journal of Production Research,* no. 3 (2000), pp. 481–507.

Womack, J. P., and D. T. Jones. *Lean Thinking: Banish Waste and Create Wealth in Your Corporation,* New York: Simon & Schuster, 1996.

Voss, C. A., and L. Okazaki-Ward. "The Transfer and Adaptation of JIT-Manufacturing Practices by Japanese Companies in the U.K.," *Operations Management Review* 7, nos. 3 and 4 (1990).

Discussion Questions

1. Some people have argued that just-in-time is simply one more inventory control system. How do you think they could arrive at this conclusion?

2. Take a common system at a university—for example, registration. Describe what kinds of "waste" can be found. How might you reduce this waste?

3. "Surge" capacity is the ability to take on an extra number of customers or product requests. Tell how the following three facilities handle surges: a football stadium, a clothing store, and an accounting firm.

4. List several ways to signal the need for more material in a pull-type system. Distinguish between situations where the feeder departments are in close proximity and those where they're at some distance.

5. Some companies contend that they can never adopt JIT because their suppliers are located all over the country and distances are too great. What might you suggest to these firms?

6. "We just can't get anywhere on our JIT program. It's the suppliers' fault. We tell them every week what we want, but they still can't get it right. I've been over to their shops, and they have mountains of the wrong materials." What do you think is going on here?

7. One manager at a JIT seminar complained that he couldn't see what he would do with his workers if they finished their work before quitting time. How would you respond to this comment?

8. How do you go about creating the organizational climate for successful JIT? Where do you start?

Problems

1. Calculate the number of kanbans needed at the ABC Company for the following two products, produced in a factory that works eight hours per day, five days per week:

	Product 1	Product 2
Usage	300/week	150/day
Lead time	1 week	2 weeks
Container size	20 units	30 units
Safety stock	15 percent	0

2. Calculate the number of kanbans required for the following four components at the ABC Company in problem 1.

	Component			
	W	**X**	**Y**	**Z**
Daily usage	900	250	1,200	350
Lead time	2 hours	5 hours	1 hour	3 hours
Container size	25 units	40 units	50 units	20 units
Safety stock	25 percent	20 percent	15 percent	10 percent

3. The BCD Company has successfully implemented JIT internally, and now wishes to convert one of its main suppliers to JIT as well. As a test of feasibility, the firms have selected one item made by this supplier for BCD. The supplier currently manufactures and delivers this item in batches of 6,000, the price paid is $150/unit, and the average usage rate at BCD is 250 units per day. Under JIT, the kanban container size would be 100 units, 10 percent safety stock, and lead time of 2 weeks (10 days).

   a. What is the current investment in work-in-process inventory for this item at BCD (assume average inventory is Q/2)?

   b. What is the change in investment if the proposed JIT system is implemented?

   c. A consulting study indicates that under JIT and an additional investment of $100,000, the lead time could be reduced from 2 weeks to 1 week. Evaluate the feasibility of this investment.

4. The CDE Company buys 200 different capacitors from 25 suppliers, with most of the capacitors purchased with an individual purchase order. An analysis indicates that the annual number of purchase orders placed for capacitors is roughly 2,000, and a cost analysis estimates the cost to place an order as $30. Additional annual cost estimates for these items include:

Obsolescence	$ 20,000
Maintaining multiple vendors	10,000
Extra shipping costs	5,000
Expediting/shortages	5,000

   One of the suppliers has offered to provide all capacitors, in a racking system, which will be replenished weekly, where each week CDE only pays for what it has used. There will be no orders at all. The supplier offers to provide this service for $25,000 per year, plus the standard cost per item. What are the potential cost savings to CDE in this proposal?

5. The DEF Company produces three products using a mixed-model assembly line, which is operated 16 hours per day (2 shifts of 8 hours each) for 250 days per year. The annual demand forecasts for the products are as follows:

Products	Forecasts
1	20,000
2	10,000
3	5,000

   a. Determine a mixed-model master production schedule for a daily batch, based on the minimum batch size for each product.

b. Prepare a daily schedule indicating the number of each product to be produced each day.

c. Product 1 requires 2 units of component A and one unit of component B. If component A is manufactured internally at DEF, how many kanbans would be required for this component if the lead time is 2 days, the safety factor is 15 percent, and the container size is 25 units?

6. The EFG Company works an 8-hour/day, 250-day/year schedule, producing four models with the following annual demand forecasts:

Model	Forecast
I	500
II	1,500
III	4,500
IV	6,000

a. Determine a mixed-model minimum batch master production schedule for EFG, based on a daily batch and an hourly batch.

b. Construct a detailed mixed-model schedule for an eight-hour day using minimum batch sizes.

7. The FGH Company assembles nine products, working 8 hours/day, 250 days/year. All products are assembled in batches of 120 units, on a line with capacity of 360 units per hour. The forecasted demands for the nine products are as follows:

Product	Forecast
1	180,000
2	150,000
3	120,000
4	120,000
5	90,000
6	30,000
7	15,000
8	7,500
9	7,500

Develop a level-minimum-batch (120 units) scheduling cycle for the assembly line at FGH.

8. The GHI Company produces models W, X, Y, and Z on an assembly line that operates 250 eight-hour days per year. The demand forecasts are:

	Model			
	A	B	C	D
Annual forecast	1,000	3,000	7,000	9,000

a. Determine the mixed-model master production schedule for a daily batch and hourly batch with minimum batch sizes.

b. Determine the schedule of production for an eight-hour day using mixed-model minimum batch production.

9. The GHI Company makes air conditioners, in either the standard model or additionally with a special option it calls the "turbo-charger," using the following indented bill of materials. The air conditioners are assembled at a rate 600 per five-day week, and the turbo-charger is added to every fourth unit. Develop the ten-week MRP record for the turbo-charger, using a one-week lead time, no safety stock, a lot size of 800, and a starting inventory of 200.

   Air Conditioner

   > Part no. 101 (1 required)
   >
   > Part no. 102 (1 required)
   >
   > Part no. 103 (1 required)
   >
   > Turbo-charger assembly ($\frac{1}{4}$ required)
   >
   > Coupling (1 required)
   >
   > Bracket (1 required)
   >
   > Alternator (1 required)

10. Continuing with problem 9, suppose the turbo-charger assembly was phantomed (i.e., the coupling, bracket, and alternator were assembled directly onto the air conditioner).

    a. What would the new bill of materials look like?

    b. Construct the phantom MRP record and compare it to that in problem 9. What are the differences?

    c. Construct the MRP record for the coupling (lot size = 200, safety stock = 20, 250 on hand, lead time = 2 weeks).

11. The air conditioner line is now to be run with JIT. In order to stabilize the planning for components, the GHI Company committed to producing exactly 125 units per each day in the week. Productivity on the air conditioner line started at a somewhat low level, but has been steadily increasing. At the outset, the four-person line could assemble 125 units per day, but it required 10.5 hours per day to do so (2.5 hours of overtime). After six weeks (3,600 units cumulative) the team could assemble 125 units with little or no overtime. Thereafter, the team followed a classic learning curve (90 percent) pattern. At about 7,000 units cumulative, the daily time requirement to assemble 150 units fell to 7.2 hours.

    a. What would be a good estimate of the cumulative average time for the first 3,600 units?

    b. How long will it be before the team can assemble 125 units in 6 to 6.5 hours?

    c. If after 30,000 units the team can assemble 125 units in 5.5 hours, what is the weekly "surge capacity" of the line? In particular, if there was a special promotion, how many units could be built in a week where the team worked 10 hours per day?

12. ZMW Motorwerks buys its car seats from Slippery Seats, Inc. Slippery puts 10 different fabrics on the same seats delivered to one of ZMW's assembly plants. Slippery sells and delivers each seat to ZMW in batches of 500, which ZMW orders when its inventory on a particular seat reaches 100 units—the expected use by ZMW during the two-week lead time (guaranteed as a maximum by Slippery). Every day, the particular 100 seats expected to be used the next day are removed from the inventory at ZMW and transported to the line where the seats are installed (at a rate of 10/hour during a 10-hour day (100/day, 250 days/year). As the cars pass through the seat section, the workers pick the right seat to go with the particular car. In the event that a seat is damaged, another of the same fabric is used (there is a safety stock of 5 seats in each fabric, which is replenished each day as needed). Slippery tries to maintain a finished goods inventory of one batch of each seat-fabric combination. This allows it to almost always be able to ship a batch of seats quickly when ordered by ZMW. The lead time required to make a batch of 500 seats is 3 weeks, and slippery has promised to deliver in 2 weeks at a maximum. The lead time is based on one week to make the frames, one week to order/receive the fabric, which is cut and

sewn in week 2, with the final seats assembled in week 3 (when all the other materials have been ordered and delivered). A new batch is started whenever an order is received, which will replenish the batch removed from inventory to fill the order.

a. What is the expected inventory level (average) of seats at ZMW?

b. What is the expected inventory level (finished goods) at Slippery?

c. What is the expected inventory level (work-in-process) at Slippery?

d. What are the hidden factory costs in both companies?

13. Returning to problem 12, Slippery sees its own operation as a type of kanban system. It has a batch of finished products in inventory, and whenever that is removed, this becomes the trigger to make another batch.

a. What are the fundamental differences between this approach and one based on a mixed-model daily schedule?

b. What is the average batch size for each product that would be run in the latter case?

c. What are the changes that would be required at ZMW?

d. What changes would be required at Slippery?

14. Slippery presently wraps each seat in plastic to protect it from damage and soiling during assembly/delivery. Assume that the plastic material costs $1, the labor to install it costs $2, and at the dealer it costs $3 to remove the plastic and dispose of it. Slippery is now telling ZMW that other auto manufacturers are able to train their assemblers to be more careful, thereby eliminating the plastic wrapping.

a. What would be the annual benefits of this change to Slippery?

b. What would be the annual benefits of this change to ZMW?

c. What would be the annual benefits of this change to the dealers?

d. How might the end customers benefit?

e. How might one resolve any conflicts between Slippery, ZMW, and the dealers over implementing this change?

15. Suppose ZMW provides the daily build schedule to Slippery, and Slippery delivers four times per day (every 2.5 hours), in the exact build sequence, when the inventory at ZMW is down to only 1 hour of stock.

a. What is the reduction in inventory at ZMW?

b. What is the potential reduction in inventory at Slippery if it *builds* to the schedule?

c. What other advantages are gained in the two firms?

d. What kind of information system is needed to support this JIT execution?

e. What else has to be implemented in both firms to make it a reality?

SIX-SIGMA QUALITY

chapter 9

General Electric (GE) has been a major promoter of Six Sigma for more than 10 years. Jack Welch, the legendary and now retired CEO, declared that "the big myth is that Six Sigma is about quality control and statistics. It is that—but it's much more. Ultimately, it drives leadership to be better by providing tools to think through tough issues. At Six Sigma's core is an idea that can turn a company inside out, focusing the organization outward on the customer." GE's commitment to quality centers on Six Sigma. Six Sigma is defined on the GE Web site as follows:

First, What is Six Sigma? First, what it is not. It is not a secret society, a slogan or a cliché. Six Sigma is a highly disciplined process that helps us focus on developing and delivering

After reading this chapter you will:

1. Understand total quality management.
2. Describe how quality is measured and be aware of the different dimensions of quality.
3. Explain the define, measure, analyze, improve, and control (DMAIC) quality improvement process.
4. Understand what ISO certification means.

near-perfect products and services. Why "Sigma"? The word is a statistical term that measures how far a given process deviates from perfection. The central idea behind Six Sigma is that if you can measure how many "defects" you have in a process, you can systematically figure out how to eliminate them and get as close to "zero defects" as possible. To achieve Six Sigma Quality, a process must produce no more than 3.4 defects per million opportunities. An "opportunity" is defined as a chance for nonconformance, or not meeting the required specifications. This means we need to be nearly flawless in executing our key processes.

At its core, Six Sigma revolves around a few key concepts.

Critical to Quality:	Attributes most important to the customer
Defect:	Failing to deliver what the customer wants
Process Capability:	What your process can deliver
Variation:	What the customer sees and feels

286   *section 2*   Manufacturing, Service, and Health Care Processes

Stable Operations:	Ensuring consistent, predictable processes to improve what the customer sees and feels
Design for Six Sigma:	Designing to meet customer needs and process capability

In this chapter, we first review the general subject of total quality management and the quality movement. We then develop the basic features and concepts of the Six-Sigma approach to TQM. We then describe the Shingo system, which takes a unique approach to quality by focusing on preventing mistakes. This is followed by a review of ISO 9000 and 14000 standards for quality certification used by many companies throughout the world. Finally, we provide the major steps of external benchmarking for quality improvement.

TOTAL QUALITY MANAGEMENT

Total quality management

Global

Total quality management may be defined as "managing the entire organization so that it excels on all dimensions of products and services that are important to the customer." It has two fundamental operational goals:

1. Careful design of the product or service.
2. Ensuring that the organization's systems can consistently produce the design.

These two goals can only be achieved if the entire organization is oriented toward them—hence the term *total* quality management. TQM became a national concern in the United States in the 1980s primarily as a response to Japanese quality superiority in manufacturing automobiles and other durable goods such as room air conditioners. A widely cited study of Japanese and U.S. air-conditioning manufacturers showed that the best-quality American products had *higher* average defect rates than those of the poorest Japanese manufacturers.[1]

THE MALCOLM BALDRIGE NATIONAL QUALITY AWARD

The Award is given to organizations that have demonstrated outstanding quality in their products and processes. Three Awards may be given annually in each of these categories: manufacturing, service, small business, education, health care, and nonprofit.

Applicants for the Award must submit an application of 50 pages or less that details the processes and results of their activities under seven major categories: Leadership; Strategic Planning; Customer and Market Focus; Measurement, Analysis and Knowledge Management; Workforce Focus; Process Management; and Results. The applications are scored on total points out of 1,000 by the Baldrige Board of Examiners and Judges. High-scoring applications are selected for site visits and Award recipients are selected from this group. The president of the United States traditionally presents the Awards at a special ceremony in Washington, DC. A major benefit to all applicants is the feedback report prepared by Examiners that is based on their processes and practices. Many states have used the Baldrige criteria as the basis of their quality programs. A report, *Building on Baldrige: American Quality for the*

21st Century, by the private Council on Competitiveness, said, "More than any other program, the Baldrige Quality Award is responsible for making quality a national priority and disseminating best practices across the United States."

So severe was the quality shortfall in the United States that improving it throughout industry became a national priority, with the Department of Commerce establishing the **Malcolm Baldrige National Quality Award** in 1987 to help companies review and structure their quality programs. Also gaining major attention at this time was the requirement that suppliers demonstrate that they are measuring and documenting their quality practices according to specified criteria, called ISO standards, if they wished to compete for international contracts. We will have more to say about this later.

Malcolm Baldrige National Quality Award

The philosophical leaders of the quality movement, notably Philip Crosby, W. Edwards Deming, and Joseph M. Juran—the so-called Quality Gurus—had slightly different definitions of what quality is and how to achieve it (see Exhibit 9.1), but they all had the same general message: To achieve outstanding quality requires quality leadership from senior management, a customer focus, total involvement of the workforce, and continuous improvement based upon rigorous analysis of processes. Later in the chapter, we will discuss how these precepts are applied in the latest approach to TQM—Six Sigma. We will now turn to some fundamental concepts that underlie any quality effort: quality specifications and quality costs.

The Quality Gurus Compared

exhibit 9.1

	CROSBY	DEMING	JURAN
Definition of quality	Conformance to requirements	A predictable degree of uniformity and dependability at low cost and suited to the market	Fitness for use (satisfies customer's needs)
Degree of senior management responsibility	Responsible for quality	Responsible for 94% of quality problems	Less than 20% of quality problems are due to workers
Performance standard/motivation	Zero defects	Quality has many "scales"; use statistics to measure performance in all areas; critical of zero defects	Avoid campaigns to do perfect work
General approach	Prevention, not inspection	Reduce variability by continuous improvement; cease mass inspection	General management approach to quality, especially human elements
Structure	14 steps to quality improvement	14 points for management	10 steps to quality improvement
Statistical process control (SPC)	Rejects statistically acceptable levels of quality (wants 100% perfect quality)	Statistical methods of quality control must be used	Recommends SPC but warns that it can lead to tool-driven approach
Improvement basis	A process, not a program; improvement goals	Continuous to reduce variation; eliminate goals without methods	Project-by-project team approach; set goals
Teamwork	Quality improvement teams; quality councils	Employee participation in decision making; break down barriers between departments	Team and quality circle approach
Costs of quality	Cost of nonconformance; quality is free	No optimum; continuous improvement	Quality is not free; there is not an optimum
Purchasing and goods received	State requirements; supplier is extension of business; most faults due to purchasers themselves	Inspection too late; sampling allows defects to enter system; statistical evidence and control charts required	Problems are complex; carry out formal surveys
Vendor rating	Yes; quality audits useless	No, critical of most systems	Yes, but help supplier improve

QUALITY SPECIFICATION AND QUALITY COSTS

Fundamental to any quality program is the determination of quality specifications and the costs of achieving (or *not* achieving) those specifications.

DEVELOPING QUALITY SPECIFICATIONS

Design quality

The quality specifications of a product or service derive from decisions and actions made relative to the quality of its design and the quality of its conformance to that design. **Design quality** refers to the inherent value of the product in the marketplace and is thus a strategic decision for the firm. The dimensions of quality are listed in Exhibit 9.2. These dimensions refer to features of the product or service that relate directly to design issues. A firm designs a product or service to address the need of a particular market.

A firm designs a product or service with certain performance characteristics and features based on what the intended market expects. Materials and manufacturing process attributes can greatly impact the reliability and durability of a product. Here the company attempts to design a product or service that can be produced or delivered at reasonable cost. The serviceability of the product may have a great impact on the cost of the product or service to the customer after the initial purchase is made. It also may impact the warranty and repair cost to the firm. Aesthetics may greatly impact the desirability of the product or service, in particular consumer products. Especially when a brand name is involved, the design often represents the next generation of an ongoing stream of products or services. Consistency in the relative performance of the product compared to the state of the art, for example, may have a great impact on how the quality of the product is perceived. This may be very important to the long-run success of the product or service.

Conformance quality

Conformance quality refers to the degree to which the product or service design specifications are met. The activities involved in achieving conformance are of a tactical, day-to-day nature. It should be evident that a product or service can have high design quality but low conformance quality, and vice versa.

Quality at the source

Quality at the source is frequently discussed in the context of conformance quality. This means that the person who does the work takes responsibility for making sure that his or her output meets specifications. Where a product is involved, achieving the quality specifications is typically the responsibility of manufacturing management; in a service firm, it is usually the responsibility of the branch operations management. Exhibit 9.3 shows two examples of

Dimensions of quality

the **dimensions of quality**. One is a laser printer that meets the pages-per-minute and print density standards; the second is a checking account transaction in a bank.

Both quality of design and quality of conformance should provide products that meet the customer's objectives for those products. This is often termed the product's *fitness for use,* and it entails identifying the dimensions of the product (or service) that the customer wants (that is, the voice of the customer) and developing a quality control program to ensure that these dimensions are met.

exhibit 9.2   The Dimensions of Design Quality

DIMENSION	MEANING
Performance	Primary product or service characteristics
Features	Added touches, bells and whistles, secondary characteristics
Reliability/durability	Consistency of performance over time, probability of failing, useful life
Serviceability	Ease of repair
Aesthetics	Sensory characteristics (sound, feel, look, and so on)
Perceived quality	Past performance and reputation

	MEASURES	
DIMENSION	PRODUCT EXAMPLE: LASER PRINTER	SERVICE EXAMPLE: CHECKING ACCOUNT AT A BANK
Performance	Pages per minute Print density	Time to process customer requests
Features	Multiple paper trays Color capability	Automatic bill paying
Reliability/durability	Mean time between failures Estimated time to obsolescence Expected life of major components	Variability of time to process requests Keeping pace with industry trends
Serviceability	Availability of authorized repair centers Number of copies per print cartridge Modular design	Online reports Ease of getting updated information
Aesthetics	Control button layout Case style Courtesy of dealer	Appearance of bank lobby Courtesy of teller
Perceived quality	Brand name recognition Rating in *Consumer Reports*	Endorsed by community leaders

Examples of Dimensions of Quality

exhibit 9.3

COST OF QUALITY

Although few can quarrel with the notion of prevention, management often needs hard numbers to determine how much prevention activities will cost. This issue was recognized by Joseph Juran, who wrote about it in 1951 in his *Quality Control Handbook*. Today, **cost of quality (COQ)** analyses are common in industry and constitute one of the primary functions of QC departments.

Cost of quality

There are a number of definitions and interpretations of the term *cost of quality*. From the purist's point of view, it means all of the costs attributable to the production of quality that is not 100 percent perfect. A less stringent definition considers only those costs that are the difference between what can be expected from excellent performance and the current costs that exist.

How significant is the cost of quality? It has been estimated at between 15 and 20 percent of every sales dollar—the cost of reworking, scrapping, repeated service, inspections, tests, warranties, and other quality-related items. Philip Crosby states that the correct cost for a well-run quality management program should be under 2.5 percent.[2]

Three basic assumptions justify an analysis of the costs of quality: (1) failures are caused, (2) prevention is cheaper, and (3) performance can be measured.

The costs of quality are generally classified into four types:

1. **Appraisal costs.** Costs of the inspection, testing, and other tasks to ensure that the product or process is acceptable.
2. **Prevention costs.** The sum of all the costs to prevent defects such as the costs to identify the cause of the defect, to implement corrective action to eliminate the cause, to train personnel, to redesign the product or system, and to purchase new equipment or make modifications.

A GOODYEAR ASSOCIATE INSPECTS A RADIAL TIRE AT THE SAO PAULO, BRAZIL, FACTORY. GOODYEAR PRACTICES BOTH VISUAL AND INTERNAL INSPECTIONS OF TIRES, EVEN PULLING SOME TIRES FROM THE PRODUCTION LINE TO BE X-RAYED.

exhibit 9.4

Quality Cost Report

	CURRENT MONTH'S COST	PERCENTAGE OF TOTAL
Prevention costs		
Quality training	$ 2,000	1.3%
Reliability consulting	10,000	6.5
Pilot production runs	5,000	3.3
Systems development	8,000	5.2
Total prevention	25,000	16.3
Appraisal costs		
Materials inspection	6,000	3.9
Supplies inspection	3,000	2.0
Reliability testing	5,000	3.3
Laboratory testing	25,000	16.3
Total appraisal	39,000	25.5
Internal failure costs		
Scrap	15,000	9.8
Repair	18,000	11.8
Rework	12,000	7.8
Downtime	6,000	3.9
Total internal failure	51,000	33.3
External failure costs		
Warranty costs	14,000	9.2
Out-of-warranty repairs and replacement	6,000	3.9
Customer complaints	3,000	2.0
Product liability	10,000	6.5
Transportation losses	5,000	3.3
Total external failure	38,000	24.9
Total quality costs	$153,000	100.0

3. **Internal failure costs.** Costs for defects incurred within the system: scrap, rework, repair.
4. **External failure costs.** Costs for defects that pass through the system: customer warranty replacements, loss of customers or goodwill, handling complaints, and product repair.

Exhibit 9.4 illustrates the type of report that might be submitted to show the various costs by categories. Prevention is the most important influence. A rule of thumb says that for every dollar you spend in prevention, you can save $10 in failure and appraisal costs.

Often increases in productivity occur as a by-product of efforts to reduce the cost of quality. A bank, for example, set out to improve quality and reduce the cost of quality and found that it had also boosted productivity. The bank developed this productivity measure for the loan processing area: the number of tickets processed divided by the resources required (labor cost, computer time, ticket forms). Before the quality improvement program, the productivity index was 0.2660 [2,080/($11.23 × 640 hours + $0.05 × 2,600 forms + $500 for systems costs)]. After the quality improvement project was completed, labor time fell to 546 hours and the number of forms rose to 2,100, for a change in the index to 0.3088, an increase in productivity of 16 percent.

Service

FUNCTIONS OF THE QC DEPARTMENT

Although the focus of this chapter is on corporatewide quality programs, it is useful to comment on the functions of QC departments.

The typical manufacturing QC department has a variety of functions to perform. These include testing designs for their reliability in the lab and the field; gathering performance data on products in the field and resolving quality problems in the field; planning and budgeting the QC program in the plant; and, finally, designing and overseeing quality control systems and inspection procedures, and actually carrying out inspection activities requiring special

J. D. Power and Associates Initial Quality Study of New Cars

The J. D. Power and Associates Initial Quality Study[SM] serves as the industry benchmark for new-vehicle quality measured at 90 days of ownership. The study is used extensively by manufacturers worldwide to help them design and build higher quality vehicles and by consumers to help them in their purchase decisions. Initial quality has been shown over the years to be a good predictor of long-term durability, which can significantly impact consumer purchase decisions. The study captures problems experienced by owners in two distinct categories: 1) design-related problems and 2) defects and malfunctions.

1 Exterior
 a Design-related problems: front or sliding doors with handles that are difficult to operate.
 b Defects/Malfunctions: front or sliding doors that are difficult to open or close, excessive wind noise, or paint imperfections—including chips or scratches at delivery.

2 The Driving Experience
 a Design-related problem: too much play or looseness in the steering system, excessive brake dust, or foot pedals that are too close together.
 b Defects/Malfunctions: brakes that pull noticeably, are noisy, or emit excessive brake dust.

3 Features/Controls/Displays
 a Design-related problems: problems with the remote keyless entry system, door locks, or cruise control

systems that are difficult to use. Controls that are awkwardly located.
 b Defects/Malfunctions: problems with remote keyless entry systems, door locks, or cruise control systems that are not working properly.

4 Audio/Entertainment/Navigation
 a Design-related problems: audio and entertainment systems with controls that are difficult to use or awkwardly located, or hands-free communication systems that don't recognize commands.
 b Defects/Malfunctions: CD players with loading problems or radios with poor/no reception on AM/FM stations.

5 Seats
 a Design-related problems: forward/backward seat adjustments or memory seat controls that are difficult to understand or use.
 b Defects/Malfunctions: forward/backward seat adjustment or memory seats that are broken or not working properly.

6 Heat, Ventilation and Air Conditioning
 a Design-related problems: a vehicle heater that doesn't get hot fast enough or windows that fog up too often.
 b Defects/Malfunctions: a fan/blower with excessive noise or vents that emit air with a moldy or stale smell.

7 Interior
 a Design-related problems: a glove box or center console that is difficult to use.
 b Defects/Malfunctions: instrument panel or dash lights that are not working or a glove box or center console that is broken or damaged.

8 Engine/Transmission
 a Design-related problems: an engine that loses power when the AC is on or a manual transmission that is hard to operate.
 b Defects/Malfunctions: an engine that runs and then dies/stalls or an automatic transmission that shifts at the wrong time.

SOURCE: DIRECT COMMUNICATION WITH J. D. POWER AND ASSOCIATES.

technical knowledge to accomplish. The tools of the QC department fall under the heading of statistical quality control (SQC) and consist of two main sections: acceptance sampling and process control. These topics are covered in Chapter 9A.

SIX-SIGMA QUALITY

Six Sigma refers to the philosophy and methods companies such as General Electric and Motorola use to eliminate defects in their products and processes. A defect is simply any component that does not fall within the customer's specification limits. Each step or activity in a company represents an opportunity for defects to occur, and Six-Sigma programs seek to   **Six Sigma**

section 2   MANUFACTURING, SERVICE, AND HEALTH CARE PROCESSES

reduce the variation in the processes that lead to these defects. Indeed, Six-Sigma advocates see variation as the enemy of quality, and much of the theory underlying Six Sigma is devoted to dealing with this problem. A process that is in Six-Sigma control will produce no more than two defects out of every billion units. Often, this is stated as four defects per million units, which is true if the process is only running somewhere within one sigma of the target specification.

One of the benefits of Six-Sigma thinking is that it allows managers to readily describe the performance of a process in terms of its variability and to compare different processes using a common metric. This metric is **defects per million opportunities (DPMO)**. This calculation requires three pieces of data:

DPMO

1. **Unit.** The item produced or being serviced.
2. **Defect.** Any item or event that does not meet the customer's requirements.
3. **Opportunity.** A chance for a defect to occur.

A straightforward calculation is made using the following formula:

$$DPMO = \frac{\text{Number of defects}}{\text{Number of opportunities for error per unit} \times \text{Number of units}} \times 1{,}000{,}000$$

Service

Step by Step

EXAMPLE 9.1

The customers of a mortgage bank expect to have their mortgage applications processed within 10 days of filing. This would be called a *critical customer requirement*, or CCR, in Six-Sigma terms. Suppose all defects are counted (loans in a monthly sample taking more than 10 days to process) and it is determined that there are 150 loans in the 1,000 applications processed last month that don't meet this customer requirement. Thus, the DPMO = 150/1,000 × 1,000,000, or 150,000 loans out of every million processed that fail to meet a CCR. Put differently, it means that only 850,000 loans out of a million are approved within time expectations. Statistically, 15 percent of the loans are defective and 85 percent are correct. This is a case where all the loans processed in less than 10 days meet our criteria. Often there are upper and lower customer requirements rather than just a single upper requirement as we have here. ●

There are two aspects to Six-Sigma programs: the methodology side and the people side. We will take these up in order.

SIX-SIGMA METHODOLOGY

While Six Sigma's methods include many of the statistical tools that were employed in other quality movements, here they are employed in a systematic project-oriented fashion through the define, measure, analyze, improve, and control (**DMAIC**) cycle. The DMAIC cycle is a more detailed version of the Deming **PDCA cycle**, which consists of four steps—plan, do, check, and act—that underly **continuous improvement**. (Continuous improvement, also called **kaizen**, seeks continual improvement of machinery, materials, labor utilization, and production methods through applications of suggestions and ideas of company teams.) Like Six Sigma, it also emphasizes the scientific method, particularly hypothesis testing about the relationship between process inputs (X's) and outputs (Y's) using design of experiments (DOE) methods. The availability of modern statistical software has reduced the drudgery of analyzing and displaying data and is now part of the Six-Sigma tool kit. The overarching focus of the methodology, however, is understanding and achieving what the customer wants, since that is seen as the key to profitability of a production process. In fact, to get across this point, some use the DMAIC as an acronym for "Dumb Managers Always Ignore Customers."

DMAIC
PDCA cycle
Continuous improvement
kaizen

The standard approach to Six-Sigma projects is the DMAIC methodology developed by General Electric, described below:[3]

1. Define (D)
   - Identify customers and their priorities.
   - Identify a project suitable for Six-Sigma efforts based on business objectives as well as customer needs and feedback.
   - Identify CTQs (critical-to-quality characteristics) that the customer considers to have the most impact on quality.

2. Measure (M)
   - Determine how to measure the process and how it is performing.
   - Identify the key internal processes that influence CTQs and measure the defects currently generated relative to those processes.
3. Analyze (A)
   - Determine the most likely causes of defects.
   - Understand why defects are generated by identifying the key variables that are most likely to create process variation.
4. Improve (I)
   - Identify means to remove the causes of defects.
   - Confirm the key variables and quantify their effects on the CTQs.
   - Identify the maximum acceptance ranges of the key variables and a system for measuring deviations of the variables.
   - Modify the process to stay within an acceptable range.
5. Control (C)
   - Determine how to maintain the improvements.
   - Put tools in place to ensure that the key variables remain within the maximum acceptance ranges under the modified process.

ANALYTICAL TOOLS FOR SIX SIGMA AND CONTINUOUS IMPROVEMENT

The analytical tools of Six Sigma have been used for many years in traditional quality improvement programs. What makes their application to Six Sigma unique is the integration of these tools in a corporatewide management system. The tools common to all quality efforts, including Six Sigma, are flowcharts, run charts, Pareto charts, histograms, checksheets, cause-and-effect diagrams, and control charts. Examples of these, along with an opportunity flow diagram, are shown in Exhibit 9.5 arranged according to DMAIC categories where they commonly appear.

Flowcharts. There are many types of flow charts. The one shown in Exhibit 9.5 depicts the process steps as part of a SIPOC (supplier, input, process, output, customer) analysis. SIPOC in essence is a formalized input-output model, used in the define stage of a project.

Run charts. They depict trends in data over time, and thereby help to understand the magnitude of a problem at the define stage. Typically, they plot the median of a process.

Pareto charts. These charts help to break down a problem into the relative contributions of its components. They are based on the common empirical finding that a large percentage of problems are due to a small percentage of causes. In the example, 80 percent of customer complaints are due to late deliveries, which are 20 percent of the causes listed.

Checksheets. These are basic forms that help standardize data collection. They are used to create histograms such as shown on the Pareto chart.

Cause-and-effect diagrams. Also called *fishbone diagrams,* they show hypothesized relationships between potential causes and the problem under study. Once the C&E diagram is constructed, the analysis would proceed to find out which of the potential causes were in fact contributing to the problem.

Opportunity flow diagram. This is used to separate value-added from non-value-added steps in a process.

Control charts. These are time-sequenced charts showing plotted values of a statistic, including a centerline average and one or more control limits. It is used here to assure that changes introduced are in statistical control. See Chapter 9A for a discussion of the various types and uses of charts for process control.

Other tools that have seen extensive use in Six-Sigma projects are failure mode and effect analysis (FMEA) and design of experiments (DOE).

Failure mode and effect analysis. This is a structured approach to identify, estimate, prioritize, and evaluate risk of possible failures at each stage of a process. It begins with

exhibit 9.5   Analytical Tools for Six Sigma and Continuous Improvement

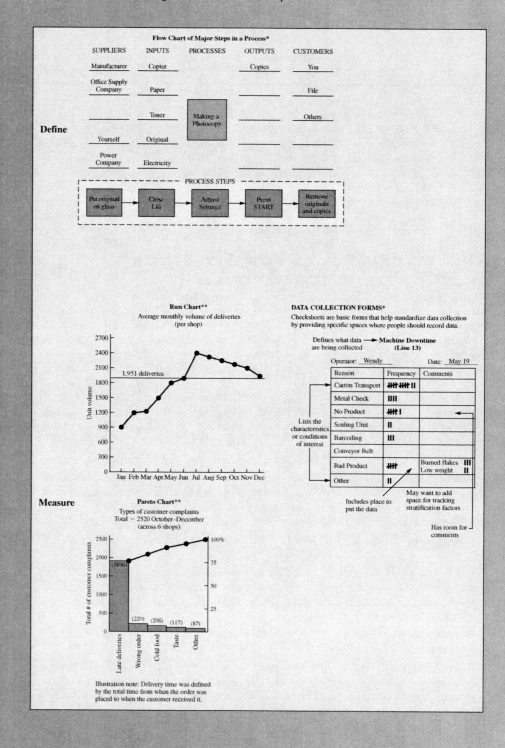

Flow Chart of Major Steps in a Process*

SUPPLIERS	INPUTS	PROCESSES	OUTPUTS	CUSTOMERS
Manufacturer	Copier		Copies	You
Office Supply Company	Paper			File
	Toner	Making a Photocopy		Others
Yourself	Original			
Power Company	Electricity			

Define

PROCESS STEPS

Put original on glass → Close Lid → Adjust Settings → Press START → Remove originals and copies

Run Chart**
Average monthly volume of deliveries
(per shop)

1,951 deliveries

Unit volume — Jan Feb Mar Apr May Jun Jul Aug Sep Oct Nov Dec

DATA COLLECTION FORMS*
Checksheets are basic forms that help standardize data collection by providing specific spaces where people should record data.

Defines what data → **Machine Downtime** are being collected   **(Line 13)**

Operator: __Wendy__   Date: __May 19__

Reason	Frequency	Comments
Carton Transport	IIII IIII II	
Metal Check	IIII	
No Product	IIII I	←
Sealing Unit	II	
Barcoding	III	
Conveyor Belt		
Bad Product	IIII	Burned flakes III, Low weight II
Other	II	

Lists the characteristics or conditions of interest

Includes place to put the data

May want to add space for tracking stratification factors

Has room for comments

Measure

Pareto Chart**
Types of customer complaints
Total = 2520 October–December
(across 6 shops)

Total # of customer complaints — Late deliveries (1890), Wrong order (220), Cold food (206), Taste (117), Other (87)

100%, 75, 50, 25

Illustration note: Delivery time was defined by the total time from when the order was placed to when the customer received it.

*SOURCE: RATH & STRONG, *RATH & STRONG'S SIX SIGMA POCKET GUIDE*, 2001.
**SOURCE: RAYTHEON SIX SIGMA, *THE MEMORY JOGGER* II, 2001.

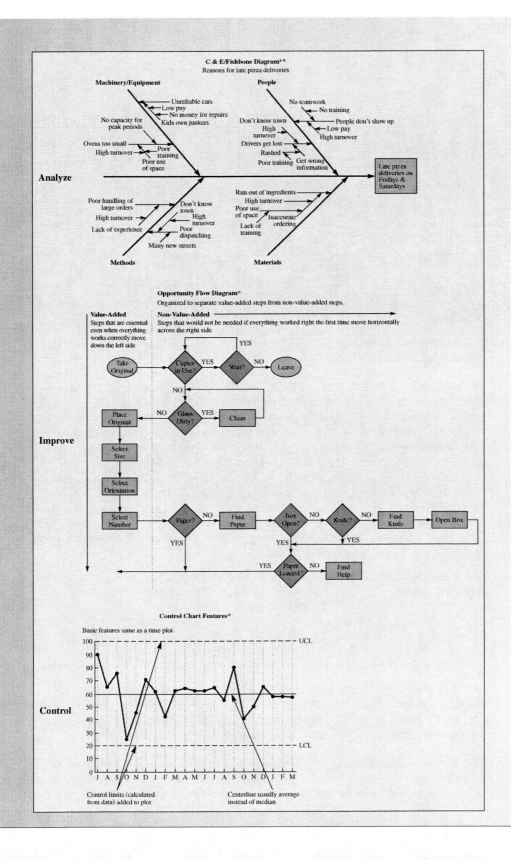

C & E/Fishbone Diagram**
Reasons for late pizza deliveries

Analyze

Machinery/Equipment — Unreliable cars, Low pay, No money for repairs, Kids own junkers, No capacity for peak periods, Ovens too small, High turnover, Poor training, Poor use of space

People — No teamwork, No training, Don't know town, People don't show up, High turnover, Low pay, High turnover, Drivers get lost, Rushed, Poor training, Get wrong information

Late pizza deliveries on Fridays & Saturdays

Methods — Poor handling of large orders, High turnover, Lack of experience, Don't know town, High turnover, Poor dispatching, Many new streets

Materials — Run out of ingredients, High turnover, Poor use of space, Inaccurate ordering, Lack of training

Opportunity Flow Diagram*
Organized to separate value-added steps from non-value-added steps.

Improve

Value-Added — Steps that are essential even when everything works correctly move down the left side

Non-Value-Added — Steps that would not be needed if everything worked right the first time move horizontally across the right side

Take Original → Copier in Use? YES → Wait? YES → Leave, NO → Glass Dirty? YES → Clean, NO → Place Original → Select Size → Select Orientation → Select Number → Paper? NO → Find Paper → Box Open? NO → Knife? NO → Find Knife → Open Box, YES → Paper Loaded? YES / NO → Find Help

Control Chart Features*

Control

Basic features same as a time plot

UCL ... 100 90 80 70 60 50 40 30 20 10 0

LCL

J A S O N D J F M A M J J A S O N D J F M

Control limits (calculated from data) added to plot

Centerline usually average instead of median

section 2   MANUFACTURING, SERVICE, AND HEALTH CARE PROCESSES

---

exhibit 9.6   FMEA Form

FMEA Analysis

Project: _____   Date: _____ (original)

Team: _____   _____ (revised)

Item or Process Step	Potential Failure Mode	Potential Effects of Failure	Severity	Potential Cause(s)	Occurrence	Current Controls	Detection	RPN	Recommended Action	Responsibility and Target Date	"After" → Action Taken	Severity	Occurrence	Detection	RPN

Total Risk Priority Number: _____   "After" Risk Priority Number: _____

SOURCE: RATH & STRONG, *RATH & STRONG'S SIX SIGMA POCKET GUIDE*: 2001, P. 31.

---

identifying each element, assembly, or part of the process and listing the potential failure modes, potential causes, and effects of each failure. A risk priority number (RPN) is calculated for each failure mode. It is an index used to measure the rank importance of the items listed in the FMEA chart. See Exhibit 9.6. These conditions include the probability that the failure takes place (occurrence), the damage resulting from the failure (severity), and the probability of detecting the failure in-house (detection). High RPN items should be targeted for improvement first. The FMEA suggests a recommended action to eliminate the failure condition by assigning a responsible person or department to resolve the failure by redesigning the system, design, or process and recalculating the RPN.

Design of experiments (DOE).   DOE, sometimes referred to as *multivariate testing,* is a statistical methodology used for determining the cause-and-effect relationship between process variables (X's) and the output variable (Y). In contrast to standard statistical tests, which require changing each individual variable to determine the most influential one, DOE permits experimentation with many variables simultaneously through carefully selecting a subset of them.

Lean Six Sigma

Lean Six Sigma combines the implementation and quality control tools of Six Sigma with materials management concepts of *lean manufacturing*. Lean manufacturing (discussed in detail in Chapter 13) achieves high-volume production and minimal waste through the use of just-in-time inventory methods. The term *lean* in this context is a focus on reducing cost by lowering raw material, work-in-process, and finished goods inventory to an absolute minimum. Lowering inventory requires a high level of quality as processes need to be predictable since extra inventory is not available. Reducing variability is a key driver in successful lean Six-Sigma programs.

SIX-SIGMA ROLES AND RESPONSIBILITIES

Successful implementation of Six Sigma is based on using sound personnel practices as well as technical methodologies. The following is a brief summary of the personnel practices that are commonly employed in Six-Sigma implementation.

1. *Executive leaders,* **who are truly committed to Six Sigma and who promote it throughout the organization, and** *champions,* **who take ownership of the processes that are to be improved.**   Champions are drawn from the ranks of the executives, and managers are expected to identify appropriate metrics early in the project and make certain that the improvement efforts focus on business results. (See the Breakthrough box "What Makes a Good Champion?")

BREAKTHROUGH

WHAT MAKES A GOOD CHAMPION?

At a manufacturing company implementing Six Sigma, a designated champion regularly met with his black belts. At one report-out meeting, a black belt informed him that she needed to purchase and install a table for sorting defects off-line. It would cost about $17,000, but it would provide an alternative to shutting down the entire line, which would cost far more. The controller told her to go through the normal requisition process and she'd have her table in about four months. That delay would have killed the project

right then and there: to submit the project to "business as usual" would have shown little real commitment to supporting Six Sigma. So the champion asked for the data that backed up her request, analyzed it, agreed with it, and then got immediate executive sign-off on securing a table the following week.

This is the stuff of a good champion: removing barriers and sending a clear signal that he and upper management are aligned and committed to Six Sigma. The champion does whatever it takes to support the black belts.

SOURCE: GREG BRUE, *SIX SIGMA FOR MANAGERS* (NEW YORK: MCGRAW-HILL, 2002), P. 84.

---

2. **Corporatewide training in Six-Sigma concepts and tools.** GE spent over a billion dollars training its professional workforce in the concepts. Now, virtually every professional in the organization is qualified in Six-Sigma techniques. To convey the need to vigorously attack problems, professionals are given martial arts titles reflecting their skills and roles: **black belts,** who coach or actually lead a Six-Sigma improvement team; **master black belts,** who receive in-depth training on statistical tools and process improvement (they perform many of the same functions as black belts but for a larger number of teams); and **green belts,** who are employees who have received enough Six-Sigma training to participate in a team or, in some companies, to work individually on a small-scale project directly related to their own job. Different companies use these "belts" in different combinations with sponsors and champions to guide teams.

    Black belts
    Master black belts

    Green belts

3. **Setting of stretch objectives for improvement.**
4. **Continuous reinforcement and rewards.** At GE, before any savings from a project are declared, the black belt in charge must provide proof that the problems are fixed permanently.

THE SHINGO SYSTEM: FAIL-SAFE DESIGN

The Shingo system developed in parallel and in many ways in conflict with the statistically based approach to quality control. This system—or, to be more precise, philosophy of production management—is named after the codeveloper of the Toyota just-in-time system, Shigeo Shingo. Two aspects of the Shingo system in particular have received great attention. One is how to accomplish drastic cuts in equipment setup times by *single-minute exchange of die* (SMED) procedures. The other, the focus of this section, is the use of source inspection and the poka-yoke system to achieve zero defects.

Shingo has argued that SQC methods do not prevent defects. Although they provide information to tell us probabilistically when a defect will occur, they are after the fact. The way to prevent defects from coming out at the end of a process is to introduce controls within the process. Central to Shingo's approach is the difference between errors and defects. Defects arise because people make errors. Even though errors are inevitable, defects can be prevented if feedback leading to corrective action takes place immediately after the errors are made. Such feedback and action require inspection, which should be done on 100 percent of the items produced. This inspection can be one of three types: successive check, self-check, and source inspection. *Successive check* inspection is performed by the next person in the process or by an objective evaluator such as a group leader. Information on defects is immediate feedback for the worker who produced the

exhibit 9.7   Poka-Yoke Example (Placing labels on parts coming down a conveyor)

Before Improvement

The operation depended on the worker's vigilance.

After Improvement

Device to ensure attachment of labels

The tape fed out by the labeler turns sharply so that the labels detach and project out from the tape. This is detected by a photoelectric tube and, if the label is not removed and applied to the product within the tact time of 20 seconds, a buzzer sounds and the conveyor stops.

Effect: Label application failures were eliminated.
Cost: ¥ 15,000 ($145)

Labeler

Label

Blank tape

Photoelectric tube

product, who then makes the repair. *Self-check* is done by the individual worker and is appropriate by itself on all but items that require sensory judgment (such as existence or severity of scratches, or correct matching of shades of paint). These require successive checks. *Source inspection* is also performed by the individual worker, except instead of checking for defects, the worker checks for the errors that will cause defects. This prevents the defects from ever occurring and, hence, requiring rework. All three types of inspection rely on controls consisting of **fail-safe procedures** or devices (called **poka-yoke**). Poka-yoke includes such things as checklists or special tooling that (1) prevents the worker from making an error that leads to a defect before starting a process or (2) gives rapid feedback of abnormalities in the process to the worker in time to correct them.

Fail-safe procedures
Poka-yoke

There are a wide variety of poka-yokes, ranging from kitting parts from a bin (to ensure that the right number of parts are used in assembly) to sophisticated detection and electronic signaling devices. An example taken from the writings of Shingo is shown in Exhibit 9.7.

There is a good deal more to say about the work of Shingo. Blasting industry's preoccupation with control charts, Shingo states they are nothing but a mirror reflecting current conditions. When a chemical plant QC manager proudly stated that it had 200 charts in a plant of 150 people, Shingo asked him if "they had a control chart for control charts."[4]

ISO 9000 AND ISO 14000

Global

ISO 9000

ISO 9000 and ISO 14000 are international standards for quality management and assurance. The standards are designed to help companies document that they are maintaining an efficient quality system. The standards were originally published in 1987 by the International Organization for Standardization (ISO), a specialized international agency recognized by affiliates in more than 160 countries. **ISO 9000** has become an international reference for quality management requirements in business-to-business dealing, and ISO 14000 is primarily concerned with environmental management.

The idea behind the standards is that defects can be prevented through the planning and application of *best practices* at every stage of business—from design through manufacturing and then installation and servicing. These standards focus on identifying criteria by which any organization, regardless of whether it is manufacturing or service oriented, can ensure that product leaving its facility meets the requirements of its customers. These standards ask a company first to document and implement its systems for quality management and then to verify, by means of an audit conducted by an independent accredited third party, the compliance of those systems with the requirements of the standards.

The ISO 9000 standards are based on eight quality management principles that are defined in the ISO 9000:2000 document. These principles focus on business processes related to the following areas in the firm: (1) customer focus, (2) leadership, (3) involvement of people, (4) process approach, (5) system approach to management, (6) continual improvement, (7) factual approach to decision making, and (8) mutually beneficial supplier relationships. The ISO documents provide detailed requirements for meeting the standards and describe standard tools that are used for improving quality in the firm. These documents are intended to be generic and applicable to any organization producing products or services.

The ISO 14000 family of standards on environmental management addresses the need to be environmentally responsible. The standards define a three-pronged approach for dealing with environmental challenges. The first is the definition of more than 350 international standards for monitoring the quality of air, water, and soil. For many countries, these standards serve as the technical basis for environmental regulation. The second part of ISO 14000 is a strategic approach defining the requirements of an environmental management system that can be implemented using the monitoring tools. Finally, the environmental standard encourages the inclusion of environment aspects in product design and encourages the development of profitable environment-friendly products and services.

In addition to the generic ISO 9000 and ISO 14000 standards, many other specific standards have been defined. The following are some examples:

- QS-9000 is a quality management system developed by DaimlerChrysler, Ford, and General Motors for suppliers of production parts, materials, and services to the automotive industry.
- ISO/TS 16949, developed by the International Automotive Task Force, aligns existing American, German, French, and Italian automotive quality standards within the global automotive industry.
- ISO 14001 environmental standards are applied by automobile suppliers as a requirement from Ford and General Motors.
- ANSI/ASQ Z1.4-2003 provides methods for collecting, analyzing, and interpreting data for inspection by attributes, while Z1.9-2003 relates to inspection by variables.
- TL 9000 defines the telecommunications quality system requirements for the design, development, production, delivery, installation, and maintenance of products and services in the telecommunications industry.

The ISO standards provide accepted global guidelines for quality. Although certification is not required, many companies have found it is essential to be competitive in the global markets. Consider the situation where you need to purchase parts for your firm and several suppliers offer similar parts at similar prices. Assume that one of these firms has been ISO 9000–certified and the others have not. From whom would you purchase? There is no doubt that the ISO 9000–certified company would have the inside track in your decision making. Why? Because ISO 9000 specifies the way the supplier firm operates as well as its quality standards, delivery times, service levels, and so on.

Supply Chain

There are three forms of certification:

1. First party: A firm audits itself against ISO 9000 standards.
2. Second party: A customer audits its supplier.
3. Third party: A "qualified" national or international standards or certifying agency serves as an auditor.

The best certification of a firm is through a third party. Once passed by the third-party audit, a firm is certified and may be registered and recorded as having achieved ISO 9000 status and it becomes a part of a registry of certified companies. This third-party certification also has legal advantages in the European Community. For example, a manufacturer is liable for injury to a user of the product.

The firm, however, can free itself from any liability by showing that it has used the appropriate standards in its production process and carefully selected its suppliers as part of its purchasing requirements. For this reason, there is strong motivation to choose ISO 9000–certified suppliers.

EXTERNAL BENCHMARKING FOR QUALITY IMPROVEMENT

External benchmarking

Global

The quality improvement approaches described so far are more or less inward looking. They seek to make improvements by analyzing in detail the current practices of the company itself. **External benchmarking**, however, goes outside the organization to examine what industry competitors and excellent performers outside of the industry are doing. Benchmarking typically involves the following steps:

Identify processes needing improvement. Identify a firm that is the world leader in performing the process. For many processes, this may be a company that is not in the same industry. Examples would be Procter & Gamble using L.L Bean as the benchmark in evaluating its order entry system, or ICL (a large British computer maker) benchmarking Marks and Spencer (a large U.K. clothing retailer) to improve its distribution system. A McKinsey study cited a firm that measured pit stops on a motor racing circuit as a benchmark for worker changes on its assembly line.[5] *Contact the managers of that company and make a personal visit to interview managers and workers.* Many companies select a team of workers from that process as part of the team of visitors.

Analyze data. This entails looking at gaps between what your company is doing and what the benchmarking company is doing. There are two aspects of the study: one is comparing the actual processes; the other is comparing the performance of these processes according to a set of measures. The processes are often described using flowcharts and subjective evaluations of how workers relate to the process. In some cases, companies permit videotaping, although there is a tendency now for benchmarked companies to keep things under wraps for fear of giving away process secrets.

SUMMARY

How to achieve TQM is no secret any more. The challenge is to make certain that a quality program really does have a customer focus and is sufficiently agile to be able to make improvements quickly without losing sight of the real-time needs of the business. The quality system must be analyzed for its own quality. There is also a need for sustaining a quality culture over the long haul. Some companies (which will remain nameless) that gained a great reputation for quality in the 1980s and 90s simply ran out of gas in their quality efforts—their managers just couldn't sustain the level of enthusiasm necessary for quality to remain a top priority goal. As Tom Peters said, "Most Quality programs fail for one of two reasons: they have system without passion, or passion without system."[6]

KEY TERMS

Total quality management (TQM) Managing the entire organization so that it excels on all dimensions of products and services that are important to the customer.

Malcolm Baldrige National Quality Award An award established by the U.S. Department of Commerce and given annually to companies that excel in quality.

Design quality The inherent value of the product in the marketplace.

Conformance quality The degree to which the product or service design specifications are met.

Quality at the source The person who does the work is responsible for ensuring that specifications are met.

Dimensions of quality Criteria by which quality is measured.

Cost of quality Expenditures related to achieving product or service quality such as the costs of prevention, appraisal, internal failure, and external failure.

Six Sigma A statistical term to describe the quality goal of no more than four defects out of every million units. Also refers to a quality improvement philosophy and program.

DPMO (defects per million opportunities) A metric used to describe the variability of a process.

DMAIC An acronym for the **D**efine, **M**easure, **A**nalyze, **I**mprove, and **C**ontrol improvement methodology followed by companies engaging in Six-Sigma programs.

PDCA cycle Also called the "Deming cycle or wheel"; refers to the plan–do–check–act cycle of continuous improvement.

Continuous improvement The philosophy of continually seeking improvements in processes through the use of team efforts.

Kaizen Japanese term for continuous improvement.

Lean Six Sigma Combines the implementation and quality control tools of Six Sigma with the materials management concept of lean

manufacturing with a focus on reducing cost by lowering inventory to an absolute minimum.

Black belts, master black belts, green belts Terms used to describe different levels of personal skills and responsibilities in Six-Sigma programs.

Fail-safe or poka-yoke procedures Simple practices that prevent errors or provide feedback in time for the worker to correct errors.

ISO 9000 Formal standards used for quality certification, developed by the International Organization for Standardization.

External benchmarking Looking outside the company to examine what excellent performers inside and outside the company's industry are doing in the way of quality.

REVIEW AND DISCUSSION QUESTIONS

1 Is the goal of Six Sigma realistic for services such as Blockbuster Video stores?
2 "If line employees are required to work on quality improvement activities, their productivity will suffer." Discuss.
3 "You don't inspect quality into a product; you have to build it in." Discuss the implications of this statement.
4 "Before you build quality in, you must think it in." How do the implications of this statement differ from those in question 3?
5 Business writer Tom Peters has suggested that in making process changes, we should "Try it, test it, and get on with it." How does this square with the DMAIC/continuous improvement philosophy?
6 Shingo told a story of a poka-yoke he developed to make sure that the operators avoided the mistake of putting fewer than the required four springs in a push-button device. The existing method involved assemblers taking individual springs from a box containing several hundred and then placing two of them behind an ON button and two more behind an OFF button. What was the poka-yoke Shingo created?
7 A typical word processing package is loaded with poka-yokes. List three. Are there any others you wish the packages had?

PROBLEMS

1 A manager states that his process is really working well. Out of 1,500 parts, 1,477 were produced free of a particular defect and passed inspection. Based upon Six-Sigma theory, how would you rate this performance, other things being equal?
2 Professor Chase is frustrated by his inability to make a good cup of coffee in the morning. Show how you would use a fishbone diagram to analyze the process he uses to make a cup of his evil brew.
3 Use the benchmarking process and as many DMAIC/CI analytical tools as you can to show how you can improve your performance in your weakest course in school.
4 Prepare a SIPOC flowchart (Exhibit 9.5) of the major steps in the process of boarding a commercial flight. Start the process with the passenger arriving curbside at your local airport.
5 Prepare an opportunity flow diagram for the same process of boarding a commercial flight.
6 The following table lists all costs of quality incurred by Sam's Surf Shop last year. What was Sam's appraisal cost for quality last year?

Annual inspection costs	$ 155,000
Annual cost of scrap materials	$ 286,000
Annual rework cost	$ 34,679
Annual cost of quality training	$ 456,000
Annual warranty cost	$1,546,000
Annual testing cost	$ 543,000

7   Below is a table of data collected over a six-month period in a local grocery store. Construct a Pareto analysis of the data and determine the percentage of total complaints represented by the two most common categories.

All Other	71
Checker	59
General	58
Service Level	55
Policy/Procedures	40
Price Marking	45
Product Quality	87
Product Request	105
Checkout Queue	33
Stock Condition	170

8   A common problem that many drivers encounter is a car that will not start. Create a fishbone diagram to assist in the diagnosis of the potential causes of this problem.

INTERNET ENRICHMENT EXERCISES

1   Visit the Baldrige Award Web site and see who won this year. What quality ideas did the winner demonstrate? What did the winner do that was particularly creative?
2   Visit the Six-Sigma Web site to see how companies are applying the concept.

CASE: HANK KOLB, DIRECTOR OF QUALITY ASSURANCE

Hank Kolb was whistling as he walked toward his office, still feeling a bit like a stranger since he had been hired four weeks before as director of quality assurance. All that week he had been away from the plant at a seminar given for quality managers of manufacturing plants by the corporate training department. He was now looking forward to digging into the quality problems at this industrial products plant employing 1,200 people.

Kolb poked his head into Mark Hamler's office, his immediate subordinate as the quality control manager, and asked him how things had gone during the past week. Hamler's muted smile and an "Oh, fine," stopped Kolb in his tracks. He didn't know Hamler very well and was unsure about pursuing this reply any further. Kolb was still uncertain of how to start building a relationship with him since Hamler had been passed over for the promotion to Kolb's job; Hamler's evaluation form had stated "superb technical knowledge; managerial skills lacking." Kolb decided to inquire a little further and asked Hamler what had happened; he replied, "Oh, just another typical quality snafu. We had a little problem on the Greasex line last week [a specialized degreasing solvent packed in a spray can for the high-technology sector]. A little high pressure was found in some cans on the second shift, but a supervisor vented them so that we could ship them out. We met our delivery schedule!" Because Kolb was still relatively unfamiliar with the plant and its products, he asked Hamler to elaborate; painfully, Hamler continued:

We've been having some trouble with the new filling equipment and some of the cans were pressurized beyond the upper specification limit.

The production rate is still 50 percent of standard, about 14 cases per shift, and we caught it halfway into the shift. Mac Evans [the inspector for that line] picked it up, tagged the cases "hold," and went on about his duties.

When he returned at the end of the shift to write up the rejects, Wayne Simmons, first-line supervisor, was by a pallet of finished goods finishing sealing up a carton of the rejected Greasex; the reject "hold" tags had been removed. He told Mac that he had heard about the high pressure from another inspector at coffee break, had come back, taken off the tags, individually turned the cans upside down and vented every one of them in the eight rejected cartons. He told Mac that production planning was really pushing for the stuff and they couldn't delay by having it sent through the rework area. He told Mac that he would get on the operator to run the equipment right next time. Mac didn't write it up but came in about three days ago to tell me about it. Oh, it happens every once in a while and I told him to make sure to check with maintenance to make sure the filling machine was adjusted; and I saw Wayne in the hall and told him that he ought to send the stuff through rework next time.

Kolb was a bit dumbfounded at this and didn't say much—he didn't know if this was a big deal or not. When he got to his office, he thought again what Morganthal, general manager, had said when he had hired him. He warned Kolb about the "lack of quality attitude" in the plant and said that Kolb "should try and do something about this." Morganthal further emphasized the quality problems in the plant: "We have to improve our quality; it's costing us a lot of money, I'm sure of it, but I can't prove it! Hank, you have my full support in this matter; you're in charge of these quality problems. This downward quality–productivity–turnover spiral has to end!"

The incident had happened a week before; the goods were probably out in the customers' hands by now, and everyone had forgotten about it (or wanted to). There seemed to be more pressing problems than this for Kolb to spend his time on, but this continued to nag him. He felt that the quality department was being treated as a joke, and he also felt that this was a personal slap from manufacturing. He didn't want to start a war with the production people, but what could he do? Kolb was troubled enough to cancel his appointments and spend the morning talking to a few people. After a long and very tactful morning, he learned the following information:

1   **From personnel.**   The operator for the filling equipment had just been transferred from shipping two weeks ago. He had no formal training in this job but was being trained by Wayne, on the job, to run the equipment. When Mac had tested the high-pressure cans, the operator was nowhere to be found and had only learned of the rejected material from Wayne after the shift was over.

2   **From plant maintenance.**   This particular piece of automated filling equipment had been purchased two years ago for use on another product. It had been switched to the Greasex line six months ago and maintenance completed 12 work orders during the last month for repairs or adjustments on it. The equipment had been adapted by plant maintenance for handling the lower viscosity of Greasex, which it had not originally been designed for. This included designing a special filling head. There was no scheduled preventive maintenance for this equipment and the parts for the sensitive filling head, replaced three times in the last six months, had to be made at a nearby machine shop. Nonstandard downtime was 15 percent of actual running time.

3   **From purchasing.**   The plastic nozzle heads for the Greasex can, designed by a vendor for this new product on a rush order, were often found to have slight burrs on the inside rim, and this caused some trouble in fitting the top to the can. An increase in application pressure at the filling head by maintenance adjustment had solved the burr application problem or had at least forced the nozzle heads on despite burrs. Purchasing agents said that they were going to talk to the sales representative of the nozzle head supplier about this the next time he came in.

4   **From product design and packaging.**   The can, designed especially for Greasex, had been contoured to allow better gripping by the user. This change, instigated by marketing research, set Greasex apart from the appearance of its competitors and was seen as significant by the designers. There had been no test of the effects of the contoured can on filling speed or filling hydrodynamics from a high-pressured filling head. Kolb had a hunch that the new design was acting as a venturi (carrier creating suction) when being filled, but the packaging designer thought that was unlikely.

5   **From the manufacturing manager.**   He had heard about the problem; in fact, Simmons had made a joke about it, bragging about how he beat his production quota to the other foremen and shift supervisors. The manufacturing manager thought Simmons was one of the "best foremen we have . . . he always got his production out." His promotion papers were actually on the manufacturing manager's desk when Kolb dropped by. Simmons was being strongly considered for promotion to shift supervisor. The manufacturing manager, under pressure from Morganthal for cost improvements and reduced delivery times, sympathized with Kolb but said that the rework area would have vented with their pressure gauges what Wayne had done by hand. "But I'll speak with Wayne about the incident," he said.

6   **From marketing.**   The introduction of Greasex had been rushed to market to beat competitors, and a major promotional advertising campaign was under way to increase consumer awareness. A deluge of orders was swamping the order-taking department and putting Greasex high on the back-order list. Production had to turn the stuff out; even being a little off spec was tolerable because "it would be better to have it on the shelf than not there at all. Who cares if the label is a little crooked or the stuff comes out with a little too much pressure? We need market share now in that high-tech segment."

What bothered Kolb most was the safety issue of the high pressure in the cans. He had no way of knowing how much of a hazard the high pressure was or if Simmons had vented them enough to effectively reduce the hazard. The data from the can manufacturer, which Hamler had showed him, indicated that the high pressure found by the inspector was not in the danger area. But, again, the inspector had used only a sample testing procedure to reject the eight cases. Even if he could morally accept that there was no product safety hazard, could Kolb make sure that this would never happen again?

Skipping lunch, Kolb sat in his office and thought about the morning's events. The past week's seminar had talked about the role of quality, productivity and quality, creating a new attitude, and the quality challenge; but where had they told him what to do when this happened? He had left a very good job to come here because he thought the company was serious about the importance of quality, and he wanted a challenge. Kolb had demanded and received a salary equal to the manufacturing, marketing, and R&D directors, and he was one of the direct reports to the general manager. Yet he still didn't know exactly what he should or shouldn't do, or even what he could or couldn't do under these circumstances.

QUESTIONS

1   What are the causes of the quality problems on the Greasex line? Display your answer on a fishbone diagram.

2   What general steps should Hank follow in setting up a continuous improvement program for the company? What problems will he have to overcome to make it work?

CASE: APPRECIATIVE INQUIRY—A DIFFERENT KIND OF FISHBONE

The standard cause-and-effect, or fishbone, diagram approach focuses on identifying the root cause of a problem. Finding this cause then becomes an input into developing a solution. On the other hand, improvements aren't always about finding out what went wrong; rather, they may be about identifying what was done right. This is what the AI approach is designed to do. The way it works is

exhibit 9.8   Identifying Excellence Drivers (the Hows of Excellence)

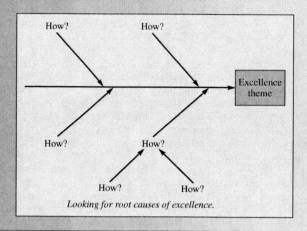

Looking for root causes of excellence.

exhibit 9.9   Root Causes of Excellence

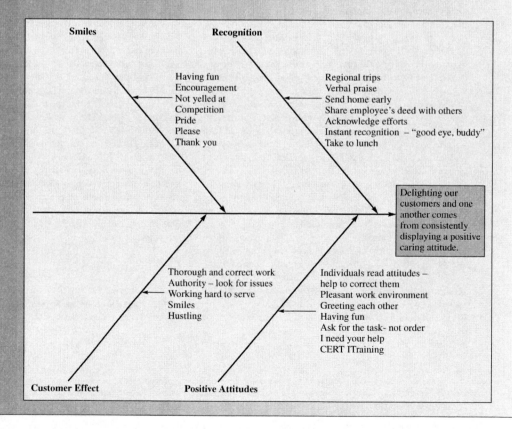

it solicits success stories from employees about how, for example, they delighted their customers. These are then put on the head of the fishbone diagram as the theme for study. (See Exhibit 9.8.) The approach then gathers the causes of success, which are entered on the fishbone as the "hows" of success. One of the particular benefits

of this is that it builds on the unique capabilities of the company rather than copying approaches taken by others.

This approach has been used successfully by Direct Discount Tires executive Steve Fornier Jr., who says, "AI is a simple tool that we can use to find out what and why things are done the way they are done. It gives our employees a chance to think for themselves, find solutions, and execute at higher levels rather than being recipients of a 'do this' 'do that' kind of speech. Because they are figuring out answers for themselves, it drives the entrepreneurial spirit, promotes innovation, and eventually creates new leaders and new best practices from the front line that will continue to keep us 'The Best.' Without this new innovation, we risk becoming stagnated." (The fishbone diagram for Direct Discount Tires is shown in Exhibit 9.9.)

SOURCE: WILLIAM YOUNGDAHL AND CAREN SIEHL, LECTURE NOTES, AMERICAN GRADUATE SCHOOL OF INTERNATIONAL MANAGEMENT, 2006.

QUESTIONS

1 From a worker's perspective, what do you see as the major benefit of appreciative inquiry compared to standard cause-and-effect analysis?

2 As an interesting exercise, think about your favorite instructor. Develop an appreciative inquiry fishbone diagram that identifies why you feel this instructor is so outstanding.

SUPER QUIZ

1 This refers to the inherent value of the product in the marketplace and is a strategic decision for the firm.

2 Relates to how well a product or services meets design specifications.

3 Relates to how the customer views quality dimensions of a product or service.

4 The series of international quality standards.

5 What is the enemy of good quality?

6 A Six-Sigma process that is running at the center of its control limits would expect this defect rate.

7 The standard quality improvement methodology developed by General Electric.

1. Design quality 2. Conformance quality 3. Fitness for use 4. ISO 9000 5. Variation 6. 2 parts per billion units 7. DMAIC cycle

SELECTED BIBLIOGRAPHY

Bemowski, K., and B. Stratton, eds. *101 Good Ideas: How to Improve Just About Any Process.* Washington, DC: American Society for Quality, 1999.

Blakeslee, J. A., Jr. "Implementing the Six Sigma Solution." *Quality Progress,* July 1999, pp. 77–85.

Brue, G. *Six Sigma for Managers.* New York: McGraw-Hill, 2002.

Chowdhury, S. *Design for Six Sigma.* Chicago: Dearborn Trade Publishing, 2002.

Chowdhury, S., and K. Zimmer. *QS-9000 Pioneers—Registered Companies Share Their Strategies for Success.* Burr Ridge, IL: Richard D. Irwin, 1996.

Crosby, P. B. *Quality Is Free.* New York: McGraw-Hill, 1979 (reissue 1992).

———. *Quality Is Still Free.* New York: McGraw-Hill, 1996.

Deming, W. E. *Quality, Productivity and Competitive Position.* Cambridge, MA: MIT Center for Advanced Engineering Study, 1982.

Eckes, G. *Six Sigma Revolution: How General Electric and Others Turned Process into Profits.* New York: John Wiley & Sons, 2001.

Evans, J. R., and W. M. Lindsay. *The Management and Control of Quality.* Cincinnati: South-Western/Thomson Learning, 2002.

Feigenbaum, A. V. *Total Quality Control.* New York: McGraw-Hill, 1991.

Gitlow, H.; A. Oppenheim; and R. Oppenheim. *Quality Management: Tools and Methods for Improvement.* 2nd ed. New York: Irwin/ McGraw-Hill, 1995.

Juran, J. M. *Quality Control Handbook.* 3rd ed. New York: McGraw-Hill, 1979.

Juran, J. M., and F. M. Gryna. *Quality Planning and Analysis.* 2nd ed. New York: McGraw-Hill, 1980.

Pande, P. S.; R. P. Neuman; and R. R. Cavanagh. *The Six Sigma Way.* New York: McGraw-Hill, 2000.

———. *The Six Sigma Way Team Fieldbook.* New York: McGraw-Hill, 2002.

Robinson, A. *Modern Approaches to Manufacturing Improvement: The Shingo System.* Cambridge, MA: Productivity Press, 1990.

Shingo, S. *Zero Quality Control: Source Inspection and the Poka-Yoke System.* Stamford, CT: Productivity Press, 1986.

Taormina, T. *Virtual Leadership and the ISO 9000 Imperative.* Englewood Cliffs, NJ: Prentice Hall, 1996.

Welch, J. *Jack: Straight from the Gut.* New York: Warner Business Books, 2001.

FOOTNOTES

1 D. A. Garvin, *Managing Quality* (New York: Free Press, 1988).

2 P. B. Crosby, *Quality Is Free* (New York: New American Library, 1979), p. 15.

3 S. Walleck, D. O'Halloran, and C. Leader, "Benchmarking World-Class Performance," *McKinsey Quarterly,* no. 1 (1991), p. 7.

4 A. Robinson, *Modern Approaches to Manufacturing Improvement: The Shingo System* (Cambridge, MA: Productivity Press, 1990), p. 234.

5 Walleck, O'Halloran, and Leader, "Benchmarking World-Class Performance," p. 7.

6 T. Peters, *Thriving on Chaos* (New York: Knopf, 1987), p. 74.

Chapter

10

Capacity Planning and Utilization

In this chapter we discuss the role of capacity planning and utilization in MPC systems. We focus primarily on techniques for determining the capacity requirements implied by a production plan, master production schedule, or detailed material plans. One managerial problem is to match the capacity with the plans: either to provide sufficient capacity to execute plans, or to adjust plans to match capacity constraints. A second managerial problem with regard to capacity is to consciously consider the marketplace implications of faster throughput times for making products, at the expense of reduced capacity utilization. For example, JIT production results in very fast throughput times for manufacturing products, but typically some capacities are underutilized. Similarly, by scheduling the highest-priority jobs through all work centers—taking explicit account of available capacity—it is possible to complete these jobs in much shorter times than under more conventional MPC approaches. But this gain in speed for high priority jobs comes at the expense of lower priority job throughput times and some underutilization of capacity.

This chapter is organized around five topics:

- *The role of capacity planning in MPC systems:* How does it fit and how is capacity managed in various manufacturing environments?
- *Capacity planning and control techniques:* How can capacity requirements be estimated and capacity utilization controlled?
- *Scheduling capacity and materials simultaneously:* How can finite scheduling techniques be applied, and what are the costs/benefits of these techniques?
- *Management and capacity planning/utilization:* What are the critical managerial decisions required to plan/utilize capacity most effectively?
- *Example applications:* How are techniques for capacity planning applied and what are some best practices?

Some of the techniques developed in this chapter are closely analogous to approaches for demand management and operations planning as described in Chapters 2 and 3. Finite loading techniques and the theory of constraints are described here as forms of capacity planning to produce detailed schedules; these are described in further detail under production activity control in Chapter 11. Perhaps the major linkage between capacity planning and other MPC modules is with the master production schedule, the subject of Chapter 6.

The Role of Capacity Planning in MPC Systems

MPC is often seen as encompassing two major activities: planning/control of materials and planning/control of capacities. The two need to be coordinated for maximum benefits, on the basis of managerial perceptions of what is required in the marketplace. Capacity planning techniques have as their primary objective the estimation of capacity requirements, sufficiently far enough into the future to be able to meet those requirements. A second objective is execution: the capacity plans need to be executed flawlessly, with unpleasant surprises avoided. Insufficient capacity quickly leads to deteriorating delivery performance, escalating work-in-process inventories, and frustrated manufacturing personnel. On the other hand, excess capacity might be a needless expense that can be reduced. Even firms with advanced MPC systems have found times when their inability to provide adequate work center capacities has been a significant problem. On the other hand, there are firms that continually manage to increase output from what seems to be a fixed set of capacities. The bottom line difference can be substantial.

Hierarchy of Capacity Planning Decisions

Figure 10.1 relates capacity planning decisions to other MPC system modules. It depicts a scope of capacity planning starting from an overall plan of resource needs, and then moves to planning procedures to estimate the capacity implications of a particular master production

FIGURE 10.1
Capacity Planning in the MPC System

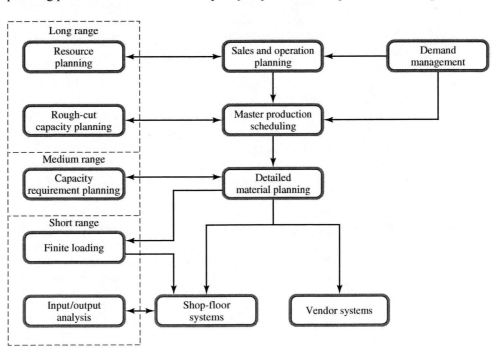

schedule. Thereafter the hierarchy depicts middle-range capacity planning, which evaluates the capacity implications of the detailed material plans, then to the short-range actual scheduling/capacity trade-offs, and finally to the evaluation of particular capacity plans.

These five levels of capacity planning range from large aggregate plans for long time periods to the detailed scheduling decisions as to which job to run next on a particular machine. In this chapter the focus is first on the several rough-cut capacity planning procedures. With this background, one can see how capacity requirements planning (CRP) systems are a logical extension, with a more detailed view of capacity needs. Understanding these systems allows one to appreciate the different approaches, with each providing a more exact estimate of capacity needs, but with a corresponding need for more information and system complexity. Thereafter, we can see how advanced production scheduling (APS) based on finite loading provide still another approach to the planning/management of capacity. Finally, Figure 10.1 shows input/output analysis as the last of the five levels of capacity planning. Here, the focus is on capacity management, in which capacity plans are continually compared with actual results.

Many authorities distinguish between long-, medium-, and short-range capacity planning horizons as indicated in Figure 10.1. This is a useful distinction, but the time dimension varies substantially from company to company. Moreover, in the last several years, the focus has shifted more to the short term, as firms operate with lower inventory levels and faster response times to customer needs. In this chapter, we will examine capacity planning/utilization decisions ranging from one day to a year or more in the future.

Links to Other MPC System Modules

System linkages for the capacity planning modules follow the basic hierarchy shown in Figure 10.1. **Resource planning** is directly linked to the sales and operations planning module. It's the most highly aggregated and longest-range capacity planning decision. Resource planning typically involves converting monthly, quarterly, or even annual data from the sales and operations plan into aggregate resources such as gross labor-hours, floor space, and machine-hours. This level of planning involves new capital expansion, bricks and mortar, machine tools, warehouse space, and so on, and requires a time horizon of months or years.

The master production schedule is the primary information source for **rough-cut capacity planning.** A particular master schedule's rough-cut capacity requirements can be estimated by several techniques: *capacity planning using overall planning factors (CPOF), capacity bills,* or *resource profiles.* These techniques provide information for modifying the resource levels or material plan to ensure execution of the master production schedule.

For firms using material requirements planning to prepare detailed material plans, a much more detailed capacity plan is possible with the **capacity requirements planning (CRP)** technique. To provide this detail, time-phased material plans produced by the MRP system form the basis for calculating time-phased capacity requirements. Data files used by the CRP technique include work in process, routing, scheduled receipts, and planned orders. Information provided by the CRP technique can be used to determine capacity needs for both key machine centers and labor skills, typically covering a planning horizon of several weeks to a year.

Resource planning, rough-cut capacity planning, and capacity requirements planning link with the sales and operations plan, master production schedule, and MRP systems, respectively. Linkages are shown as double-headed arrows for a specific reason. There must be a correspondence between capacity required to execute a given material plan and capacity made available to execute the plan. Without this correspondence, the plan will be either impossible to execute or inefficiently executed. We don't claim capacity must always be changed to meet material plans. In fact, whether this is worthwhile or whether plans should be changed to meet capacity is a managerial judgment. Capacity planning systems provide basic information to make that a *reasoned* judgment.

Finite loading in some ways is better seen as a shop scheduling process, and therefore part of production activity control (PAC), but it is also a capacity planning procedure. There are an increasing number of software systems provided by vendors, usually called **advanced production scheduling (APS)** techniques to do finite loading. The fundamental difference between the other capacity planning approaches and finite loading is that the former set does not consider any adjustment to plans because of planned capacity utilization. The latter starts with a specified capacity and schedules work through work centers only to the extent that capacity is available to do so. Moreover, by scheduling within exact capacity constraints, the APS systems allow work to flow through the necessary set of work centers more quickly. The jobs are scheduled with exact timing on all work centers—not merely in some general way, such as during a particular week.

Input/output analysis provides a method for monitoring the actual consumption of capacity during the execution of detailed material planning. It is necessarily linked to the shop floor execution systems, and supported by the database for production activity control (PAC). Input/output analysis can indicate the need to update capacity plans as actual shop performance deviates from plans, as well as the need to modify the planning factors used in the capacity planning systems.

This overview of capacity planning's scope sets the stage for the techniques the chapter discusses. The primary interaction among these techniques is hierarchical: long-range planning sets constraints on medium-range capacity planning, which in turn constrains detailed scheduling and execution on the shop floor.

Capacity Planning and Control Techniques

Here we describe four procedures for capacity planning. The first technique is *capacity planning using overall factors (CPOF)*. The simplest of the four techniques, CPOF is based only on accounting data. The second, *capacity bills,* requires more detailed product information. The third, *resource profiles,* adds a further dimension—specific timing of capacity requirements. The first three procedures are rough-cut approaches and are applicable to firms with or without MRP systems. The fourth, *capacity requirements planning,* is used in conjunction with time-phased MRP records and shop-floor system records to calculate capacity required to produce both open shop orders (scheduled receipts) and planned orders. To describe the four planning techniques, we use a simple example. The example allows us to clearly see differences in approach, complexity, level of aggregation, data requirements, timing, and accuracy among the techniques.

Capacity Planning Using Overall Factors (CPOF)

Capacity planning using overall factors (CPOF), a relatively simple approach to rough-cut capacity planning, is typically done on a manual basis. Data inputs come from the master

FIGURE 10.2
Example
Problem Data

Master production schedule (in units):

End Product							Period							
	1	2	3	4	5	6	7	8	9	10	11	12	13	Total
A	33	33	33	40	40	40	30	30	30	37	37	37	37	457
B	17	17	17	13	13	13	25	25	25	27	27	27	27	273

Direct labor time per end product unit:

End Product	Total Direct Labor in Standard Hours/Unit
A	0.95 hours
B	1.85

FIGURE 10.3   **Estimated Capacity Requirements Using Overall Factors (in standard direct labor-hours)**

Work Center	Historical Percentage	Period													Total Hours
		1	2	3	4	5	6	7	8	9	10	11	12	13	
100	60.3	37.87	37.87	37.87	37.41	37.41	37.41	45.07	45.07	45.07	51.32	51.32	51.32	51.32	566.33
200	30.4	19.09	19.09	19.09	18.86	18.86	18.86	22.72	22.72	22.72	25.87	25.87	25.87	25.87	285.49
300	9.3	5.84	5.84	5.84	5.78	5.78	5.78	6.96	6.96	6.96	7.91	7.91	7.91	7.91	87.38
Total required capacity		62.80*	62.80	62.80	62.05	62.05	62.05	74.75	74.75	74.75	85.10	85.10	85.10	85.10	939.20

*$62.80 = (0.95 \times 33) + (1.85 \times 17)$ for the standards in Figure 10.2.

production schedule (MPS), rather than from detailed material plans. This procedure is usually based on planning factors derived from standards or historical data for end products. When these planning factors are applied to the MPS data, overall labor or machine-hour capacity requirements can be estimated. This overall estimate is thereafter allocated to individual work centers on the basis of historical data on shop workloads. CPOF plans are usually stated in terms of weekly or monthly time periods and are revised as the firm changes the MPS.

The top portion of Figure 10.2 shows the MPS that will serve as the basis for our example that was developed by Berry, Schmitt, and Vollmann. This schedule specifies the quantities of two end products to be assembled during each time period. The first step of the CPOF procedure involves calculating capacity requirements of this schedule for the overall plant. The lower portion of Figure 10.2 shows direct labor standards, indicating the total direct labor-hours required for each end product. Assuming labor productivity of 100 percent of standard, the total direct labor-hour requirement for the first period is 62.80 hours, as shown in Figure 10.3.

The procedure's second step involves using historical ratios to allocate the total capacity required each period to individual work centers. Historical percentages of the total direct labor-hours worked in each of the three work centers the prior year were used to determine allocation ratios. These data could be derived from the company's accounting records. In the example, 60.3 percent, 30.4 percent, and 9.3 percent of the total direct labor-hours were worked in work centers 100, 200, and 300, respectively. These percentages are used to estimate anticipated direct labor requirements for each work center. The resulting work center capacity requirements are shown in Figure 10.3 for each period in the MPS.

The CPOF procedure, or variants of it, is found in a number of manufacturing firms. Data requirements are minimal (primarily accounting system data) and calculations are straightforward. As a result, CPOF approximations of capacity requirements at individual work centers are valid only to the extent that product mixes or historical divisions of work between work centers remain constant. This procedure's main advantages are ease of calculation and minimal data requirements. In many firms, data are readily available and computations can be done manually.

The CPOF procedure will work reasonably well for many manufacturing environments. For example, in a just-in-time (JIT) manufacturing company, the CPOF approach would allow the firm to make fairly good estimates of capacity needs under different planning scenarios. The inherent inaccuracies of CPOF will present fewer problems in a JIT environment where execution is fast, with virtually no work-in-process inventories to confound the analysis. This might be particularly useful for estimating the capacity needs for firms that supply a JIT manufacturing company.

Capacity Bills

The **capacity bill procedure** is a rough-cut method providing more-direct linkage between individual end products in the MPS and the capacity required for individual work centers. It takes into account any shifts in product mix. Consequently, it requires more data than the CPOF procedure. A bill of materials and routing data are required, and direct labor-hour or machine-hour data must be available for each operation.

To develop a bill of capacity for the example problem, we use the product structure data for A and B shown in Figure 10.4. We also need the routing and operation time standard data in the top portion of Figure 10.5 for assembling products A and B, as well as for manufacturing component items C, D, E, and F. The bill of capacity indicates total standard time required to produce one end product in each work center required in its manufacture. Calculations involve multiplying total-time-per-unit values by the usages indicated in the bill of materials. Summarizing the usage-adjusted unit time data by work center produces the bill of capacity for each of the two products in the lower portion of Figure 10.5. The bill of capacity can be constructed from engineering data, as we've done here; similar data might be available in a standard cost system. Some firms' alternative approach is to prepare the bill of capacity only for those work centers regarded as critical.

Once the bill of capacity for each end product is prepared, we can use the master production schedule to estimate capacity requirements at individual work centers. Figure 10.6 shows the determination of capacity requirements for our example. The resultant work center estimates differ substantially from the CPOF estimates in Figure 10.3. The differences reflect the period-to-period changes in product mix between the projected MPS and historical average figures. Estimates obtained from CPOF are based on an overall historical ratio of work between machine centers, whereas capacity bill estimates reflect the actual product mix planned for each period.

It's important to note that the total hours shown for the MPS (939.20) are the same in Figure 10.3 and Figure 10.6; the differences are in work center estimates for each time

342   Chapter 10   *Capacity Planning and Utilization*

FIGURE 10.4
Product
Structure Data

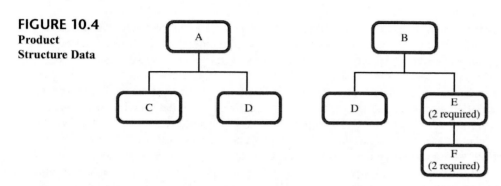

FIGURE 10.5   Routing and Standard Time Data

	Lot Sizes	Operation	Work Center	Standard Setup Hours	Standard Setup Hours per Unit	Standard Run Time Hours per Unit	Total Hours per Unit
End Products							
A	40	1 of 1	100	1.0	0.025*	0.025	0.05†
B	20	1 of 1	100	1.0	0.050	1.250	1.30
Components							
C	40	1 of 2	200	1.0	0.025	0.575	0.60
		2 of 2	300	1.0	0.025	0.175	0.20
D	60	1 of 1	200	2.0	0.033	0.067	0.10
E	100	1 of 1	200	2.0	0.020	0.080	0.10
F	100	1 of 1	200	2.0	0.020	0.0425	0.0625

	Bill of Capacity: End Product	
	A	**B**
Work Center	**Total Time/Unit**	**Total Time/Unit**
100	0.05	1.30
200	0.70‡	0.55§
300	0.20	0.00
Total time/unit	0.95	1.85

*0.025 = Setup time ÷ Lot size = 1.0/40.
†0.05 = Standard setup time per unit + Standard run time per unit = 0.025 + 0.025.
‡0.70 = 0.60 + 0.10 for one C and one D from Figure 10.4.
§0.55 = 0.10 + 2(0.10) + 4(0.0625) for one D, two E's, and four F's.

FIGURE 10.6   Capacity Requirements Using Capacity Bills

Work Center	Period													Total Hours	Projected Work Center Percentage
	1	2	3	4	5	6	7	8	9	10	11	12	13		
100	23.75*	23.75	23.75	18.90	18.90	18.90	34.00	34.00	34.00	36.95	36.95	36.95	36.95	377.75	40%
200	32.45	32.45	32.45	35.15	35.15	35.15	34.75	34.75	34.75	40.75	40.75	40.75	40.75	470.05	50%
300	6.60	6.60	6.60	8.00	8.00	8.00	6.00	6.00	6.00	7.40	7.40	7.40	7.40	91.40	10%
Total	62.80	62.80	62.80	62.05	62.05	62.05	74.75	74.75	74.75	85.10	85.10	85.10	85.10	939.20	100%

*23.75 = (33 × 0.05) + (17 × 1.30) from Figures 10.2 and 10.5.

period. These differences are far more important in firms that experience significant period-to-period mix variations than in those that have a relatively constant pattern of work.

Resource Profiles

Neither the CPOF nor the capacity bill procedure takes into account the specific timing of the projected workloads at individual work centers. In developing **resource profiles,** production lead time data are taken into account to provide time-phased projections of the capacity requirements for individual production facilities. Thus, resource profiles provide a somewhat more sophisticated approach to rough-cut capacity planning.

In any capacity planning technique, time periods for the capacity plan can be varied (e.g., weeks, months, quarters). However, when time periods are long relative to lead times, much of the time-phased information's value may be lost in aggregating the data. In many firms, this means time periods longer than one week will mask important changes in capacity requirements.

To apply the resource profile procedure to our example, we use the bills of material, routing, and time standard information in Figures 10.4 and 10.5. We must also add the production lead time for each end product and component part to our database. In this simplified example, we use a one-period lead time for assembling each end product and one period for each operation required to produce component parts. Since only one operation is required for producing components D, E, and F, lead time for producing these components is one time period each. For component C, however, lead time is two time periods: one for the operation in work center 200 and another for work center 300.

To use the resource profile procedure, we prepare a time-phased profile of the capacity requirements for each end item. Figure 10.7's operations setback charts show this time phasing for end products A and B. The chart for end product A indicates that the final assembly operation is to be completed during period 5. Production of components C and D must be completed in period 4 prior to the start of the final assembly. Since component C requires two time periods (one for each operation), it must be started one time period before component D (i.e., at the start of period 3). Other conventions are used to define time phasing, but in this example we assume the master production schedule specifies the number of units of each end product that must be completed by *the end* of the time period indicated. This implies *all* components must be completed by the end of the preceding period.

For convenience, we've shown the standard hours required for each operation for each product in Figure 10.7. This information is summarized by work center and time period in Figure 10.8, which also shows the capacity requirements the MPS quantities generated in time period 5 from Figure 10.2 (40 of end product A and 13 of end product B). The capacity requirements in Figure 10.8 are only for MPS quantities in period 5. MPS quantities for other periods can increase the capacity needed in each period. For example, Figure 10.8 shows that 7.9 hours of capacity are needed in period 4 at work center 200 to support the MPS for period 5. The MPS for period 6 requires another 27.25 hours from work center 200. This results in the total of 35.15 hours shown in Figure 10.9, which provides the overall capacity plan for the current MPS using the resource profile procedure.

Comparing the capacity plans produced by the capacity bills and the resource profile procedures (Figures 10.6 and 10.9), we see the impact of the time-phased capacity information. Total workload created by the master production schedule (939.2 hours) remains the same, as do the work center percentage allocations. But the period requirements for

344 Chapter 10 *Capacity Planning and Utilization*

FIGURE 10.7
Operation Setback Charts for End Products A and B

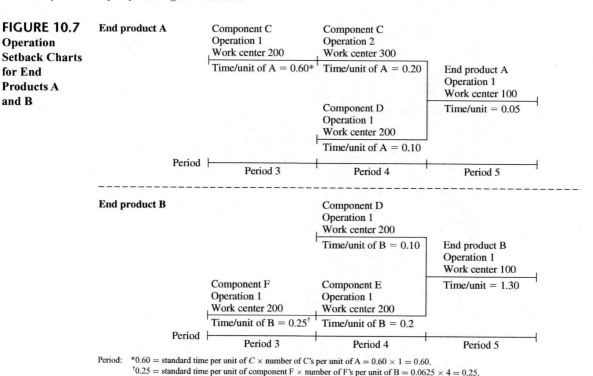

Period: *0.60 = standard time per unit of C × number of C's per unit of A = 0.60 × 1 = 0.60.
†0.25 = standard time per unit of component F × number of F's per unit of B = 0.0625 × 4 = 0.25.

work centers 200 and 300 projected by the two techniques vary somewhat. A capacity requirement of 8 hours was projected for work center 300 in time period 6 using capacity bills versus 6 hours using resource profiles, a difference of more than 30 percent. This change reflects the difference in the timing of resources required to produce the component parts, which is taken into account by the resource bill procedure.

Capacity Requirements Planning (CRP)

Capacity requirements planning (CRP) differs from the rough-cut planning procedures in four respects. First, CRP utilizes the time-phased material plan information produced by an MRP system. This includes consideration of all actual lot sizes, as well as lead times for both open shop orders (scheduled receipts) and orders planned for future release (planned orders). Second, the MRP system's gross-to-net feature takes into account production capacity already stored in the form of inventories of both components and assembled products. Third, the shop-floor control system accounts for the current status of all work-in-process in the shop, so only the capacity needed to *complete the remaining work* on open shop orders is considered in calculating required work center capacities. Fourth, CRP takes into account demand for service parts, other demands that may not be accounted for in the MPS, and any additional capacity that might be required by MRP planners reacting to scrap, item record errors, and so on. To accomplish this, the CRP procedure requires the same input information as the resource profile procedure (bills of material, routing, time standards, lead times) plus information on MRP-planned orders and the current status of open shop orders (MRP-scheduled receipts) at individual work centers.

FIGURE 10.8
Resource Profiles by Work Center

Time required during preceding periods for one end product assembled in period 5:

	Time Period		
	3	**4**	**5**
End product A			
Work center 100	0	0	0.05
Work center 200	0.60	0.10	0
Work center 300	0	0.20	0
End product B			
Work center 100	0	0	1.30
Work center 200	0.25	0.30	0

Time-phased capacity requirements generated from MPS for 40 As and 13 Bs in time period 5:

	Time Period		
	3	**4**	**5**
40 As			
Work center 100	0	0	2
Work center 200	24	4	0
Work center 300	0	8	0
13 Bs			
Work center 100	0	0	16.9
Work center 200	3.25	3.9	0
Work center 300	0	0	0
Total from period 5 MPS			
Work center 100	0	0	18.9
Work center 200	27.25	7.9	0
Work center 300	0	8.0	0

FIGURE 10.9   **Capacity Requirements Using Resource Profiles**

Work Center	Past Due*	Period													Work Total Hours	Center Percentage
		1	2	3	4	5	6	7	8	9	10	11	12	13		
100	0.00	23.75*	23.75	23.75	18.90	18.90	18.90	34.00	34.00	34.00	36.95	36.95	36.95	36.95	377.75	40%
200	56.50	32.45	35.65	35.15	35.15	32.15	34.75	34.75	39.45	40.75	40.75	40.75	11.80		470.05	50%
300	6.60	6.60	6.60	8.00	8.00	8.00	6.00	6.00	6.00	7.40	7.40	7.40	7.40		91.40	10%
Total	63.10	62.80	66.00	66.90	62.05	59.05	59.65	74.75	79.45	82.15	85.10	85.10	56.15	36.95	939.20	100%

*This work should be completed already for products to meet the master production schedule in periods 1 and 2. (If not, it's past due and will add to the capacity required in the upcoming periods)

As a medium-range capacity planning procedure, CRP exploits MRP information so as to calculate only the capacity required to complete the MPS. By calculating capacity requirements for actual open shop orders and planned orders in the MRP database, CRP accounts for the capacity already stored in the form of finished and work-in-process inventories. Since MRP data include timing of both these open and planned orders, the potential for improved accuracy in timing capacity requirements is realized. This accuracy is most important in the most immediate time periods. Rough-cut techniques can overstate required capacity by the amount of capacity represented in inventories. In Figure 10.9, for example, the past due or already completed portion of the capacity requirements is 63.1 hours—about a full time period's capacity. This work should already have been completed if we expect to meet the MPS in periods 1 and 2. CRP's potential benefits aren't without cost. A larger database is required, as well as a much larger computational effort.

The process of preparing a CRP projection is similar to that used for resource profiles. The major difference is that detailed MRP data establish exact order quantities and timing for calculating capacity required. The resultant capacity needs are summarized by time period and work center in a format similar to Figure 10.9. The CRP results would differ from those of the other techniques, primarily in the early periods, but would be a more accurate projection of work center capacity needs. Since calculations are based on all component parts and end products from the present time period through all periods included in the MRP records (the planning horizon), we can see the enormity of the CRP calculation requirements. Some firms have mitigated this cost by collecting data as the MRP explosion process is performed.

Figure 10.10 presents one of the MRP records that drive the CRP procedure for our example. To simplify the presentation, we show the MPS only for end product A and the MRP record for one of its components, component C. We've used these data to calculate capacity requirements for work center 300. These capacity requirements incorporate the influence of lot sizes, inventories, and scheduled receipts for component C. Since item C is processed at work center 300 during the second period of the two-period lead time, the planned order for 40 units due to be released in period 1 requires capacity in period 2 at work center 300.

FIGURE 10.10
CRP Example:
Detailed
Calculations

		Period											
	1	**2**	**3**	**4**	**5**	**6**	**7**	**8**	**9**	**10**	**11**	**12**	**13**
Product A *MPS*	33	33	33	40	40	40	30	30	30	37	37	37	37

Component C

Lot size = 40		Period											
Lead time = 2	**1**	**2**	**3**	**4**	**5**	**6**	**7**	**8**	**9**	**10**	**11**	**12**	**13**

		1	**2**	**3**	**4**	**5**	**6**	**7**	**8**	**9**	**10**	**11**	**12**	**13**
Gross requirements		33	33	33	40	40	40	30	30	30	37	37	37	37
Scheduled receipts			40											
Projected available balance	37	4	11	18	18	18	18	28	38	8	11	14	17	20
Planned order releases		40	40	40	40	40	40		40	40	40	40		

Work center 300 Capacity Requirements Using CRP

		Period											
	1	**2**	**3**	**4**	**5**	**6**	**7**	**8**	**9**	**10**	**11**	**12**	**13**
Hours of capacity* Total = 88	8	8	8	8	8	8	8	0	8	8	8	8	

*The eight hours of capacity required is derived from the scheduled receipt and planned order quantities of 40 units multiplied by the time to fabricate a unit of component C in machine center 300, 0.20 hours (see Figure 10.7).

Required capacity is calculated using the setup and run time data from Figure 10.5 for component C.

For a lot size of 40 units, total setup and run time in work center 300 is eight hours [1.0 + (40 × .175)]. Each planned order for component C in Figure 10.10 requires eight hours of capacity at work center 300, one period later. Similarly, the scheduled receipt of 40 units due in period 2 requires eight hours of capacity in week 1. Note the eight hours of capacity required for the scheduled receipt may not, in fact, be required if this job has already been processed at work center 300 before the beginning of period 1. The shop order's actual status is required to make the analysis.

In comparing CRP to the other capacity planning procedures, we shouldn't expect total capacity requirements for the 13 periods or the period-by-period requirements to be the same. Comparing capacity requirements for work center 300 developed by the resource profile procedure (Figure 10.9) and CRP (Figure 10.10) indicates estimated total capacity requirements for the 13 periods are less using CRP than resource profiles (88 versus 91.4 hours) and vary considerably on a period-by-period basis. Differences are explained by the initial inventory and use of lot sizing. Any partially completed work-in-process would reduce the capacity requirements further.

Scheduling Capacity and Materials Simultaneously

Thus far in the chapter we have taken what has been the traditional view of capacity in MPC systems: one first plans the materials, and thereafter examines the capacity implications of those plans. The underlying assumption in all of this is that if one knows of capacity requirements in sufficient time, adjustments to capacity can be effected. The capacity planning techniques we have examined thus far all make this assumption: their major difference is only in sophistication of the plans produced.

Moreover, the material plans produced by classic MRP systems are based on batches of materials traveling between work centers for subsequent operations, then flowing through inventories in order to be subsequently processed/integrated into higher-level part numbers. The overall lead times associated with producing end products on this basis tend to be quite long as a multiple of actual manufacturing times, particularly when the products have many levels in the bill of materials. For many firms today this just will not do: they must respond to actual customer demands faster, without holding large inventories. This implies "smarter" scheduling, which must simultaneously reflect actual capacity conditions. Furthermore, those "capacity conditions" are tighter and tighter: in order to be profitable one must utilize capacities more effectively, and satisfy end customer demands faster with lower inventories. The bottom line is a need to simultaneously schedule both capacity and materials.

Finite Capacity Scheduling

Finite scheduling systems can first be seen as an extension of the approach used by capacity requirements planning (CRP) systems, with one major difference: CRP calculates only capacity needs—it makes no adjustments for infeasibility. If, for example, we take the capacity requirements data for work center 300 coming from Product A, as shown in Figure 10.10, these would be depicted in either a CRP or finite workload capacity profile as the top part of Figure 10.11. If similar capacity requirements were collected from *all* the MRP

FIGURE 10.11
Infinite versus Finite Loading (CRP Profile for Work Center 300)

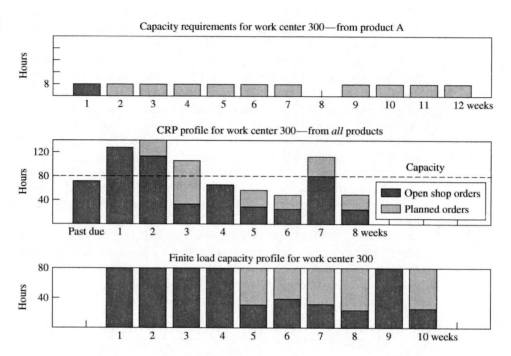

records, for all the jobs passing through work center 300, the CRP record might look like the middle portion of Figure 10.11 (here we have expanded the example to realistically include more products).

The bottom portion of Figure 10.11 shows the difference in the approach using finite scheduling. Here the capacity is scheduled only up to the 80-hour capacity limit. Thus the 75 hours of work shown as past due in the middle of Figure 10.11 would be scheduled in week 1 in the finite scheduling approach. Finite scheduling does not solve the undercapacity problem shown here. If capacity is not increased, only 80 hours of work can be completed in any week, regardless of the scheduling procedure. Finite scheduling will determine *which* jobs will be completed, according to how the jobs are scheduled—and there are various methods used to prioritize these decisions.

Finite scheduling systems simulate actual job order starting and stopping to produce a detailed schedule for each shop order and each machine center; that is, finite scheduling *loads* all jobs in all necessary work centers for the length of the planning horizon. For this reason, the terms *finite scheduling* and *finite loading* tend to be used interchangeably. The result of finite loading is a set of start and finish dates for each operation at each work center. Finite scheduling explicitly establishes a detailed schedule for each job through each work center based on work center capacities and the other scheduled jobs. Figure 10.1 depicts finite loading as a short-term capacity planning technique. Since it produces a detailed schedule of each work center, it tends to be most correct in the short term. That is, predictions of exact job schedules will be less valid in the longer term.

One output of finite scheduling is a simulation of how each machine center is to operate on a minute-by-minute basis for whatever time horizon is planned. For example, suppose we begin with work center 300 on Monday morning of week 1. A job is already in process and 150 pieces remain with a standard time of one minute per piece. This order consumes the first 150 minutes of capacity; if work starts at 8 A.M., the machine is loaded until 10:30 A.M. The finite scheduling system would pick the next job to schedule on this machine, and load it, taking account of setup time and run times. The process is repeated to simulate the entire day, then the next day, and so on.

Selection of the next job to schedule is not based just on those jobs physically waiting at the work center. Most finite scheduling systems look at jobs coming to the work center, when they will be completed at the prior work centers, and these jobs' priorities to decide whether to leave the work center idle and immediately available for the arrival of a particular job. Also, some systems allow for overlap operations, where a job can start at a downstream work center before all of it is complete at the upstream work center.

The approach we have just described, where a work center is scheduled, job by job, is called **vertical loading.** Its orientation is on planning/utilizing the capacity of a work center—independently. This is consistent with how most job shop scheduling research is conducted where the focus is on establishing relative job order priorities for deciding which job to schedule next in a work center. A different approach used in finite scheduling is **horizontal loading.** In this case the orientation is on entire shop orders. Here, the highest-priority shop order or job is scheduled in *all* of its work centers, then the job with the next highest priority, and so on. The horizontal loading approach is often in conflict with using the work centers to their highest capacity, since it will have more "holes" in the schedule than the vertical loading approach.

There is a temptation to see vertical loading as better than horizontal because of the capacity utilization. This is not the case. Horizontal loading will complete whole jobs faster than vertical loading. And it is whole jobs that are sold to the customers, not partial jobs, and it is harder to sell jobs that take long times to complete. It is far better to have 50 percent of the jobs completed than 90 percent that are not quite completed!

In addition to the horizontal-vertical distinction, there is also the issue of **front scheduling** versus **back scheduling.** The back scheduling approach starts with scheduling jobs backward from their due dates, whereas front scheduling starts with the current date scheduling into the future, where each job is completed as early as possible. If a back scheduling approach produces a past due start date for a shop order, this indicates infeasibility; similarly, if a front schedule does not produce jobs by the dates needed, it is also infeasible

Since any plan produced by any finite scheduling model is indeed a simulation, it is to be expected that errors will result. That is, the times used for the schedule are only estimates, and randomness will occur. This means that many times a job is expected to be at a work center and it is not complete at the prior center, raising the question as to whether to wait or choose another job. Furthermore, the further out the simulation model is extended, the greater the uncertainty in the expected results. If the finite schedule is prepared on Sunday night, schedules for Monday might be fairly good, while those for Tuesday will have to deal with the actual results achieved on Monday. The validity of the schedule will decay as the time horizon for scheduling is extended. One way to improve the scheduling is to reschedule more often. Even though today's computers are fast, redoing an entire finite schedule every time a job is completed is still too expensive for most firms.

Finite Scheduling with Product Structures: Using APS Systems

The complexity of scheduling increases if one wishes to schedule not only *component parts* but also *products* with part structures. Thus if we return to Figure 10.4, the real problem is in scheduling products A and B, not just in scheduling the components C, D, E, and F. Again if all the components are 90 percent completed, we cannot ship anything! The approach used by classic MRP systems is to take a long time to complete these jobs or else to have plenty of capacity available. With present imperatives on deliveries, inventories, and capacity investments, many firms are turning to finite loading systems that schedule the entire product as an entity. These systems are called **advanced production scheduling (APS)** systems, and several leading edge software companies provide them.

Essentially, APS systems use horizontal loading, and either front or back scheduling depending on whether the product is desired as soon as possible (front scheduling). But now the entire product structure is scheduled. Thus, for product A (see Figure 10.4), it is necessary to schedule A, C, and D. Let us illustrate the methodology, with back scheduling, for the 30-unit master schedule quantity shown for week 8 in Figure 10.2, the lot sizes for C and D (40 and 60) shown in Figure 10.5, and the assumptions that the MRP records are run without safety stock and that there would be no projected available balances to offset the calculations by the time week 8 is planned.

Figure 10.12 shows how the master production schedule and component MRP records would be depicted for this example. Note that the records show *only* the requirements for this particular MPS quantity (e.g., not including any requirements for component D to support end product B). Figure 10.13 shows the capacity requirements for the MPS (work center 100) as well as for work centers 300 and 200 that would be produced by the resultant APS back schedule. This figure is based on the two-shift capacity (80 hours per week) assumption

FIGURE 10.12
**Data for APS
Approach to
End Product A**

Master production schedule

MRP records for components C and D

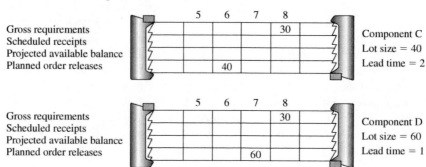

FIGURE 10.13
Back Schedules
for the MPS
and Work
Centers 300
and 400

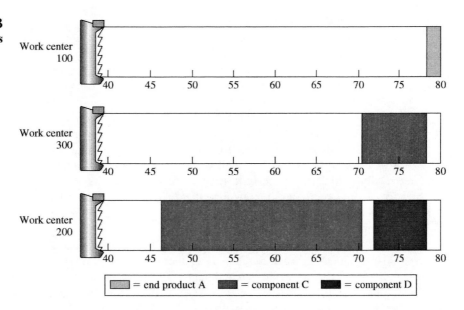

= end product A   = component C   = component D

used in the other calculations for this example. For work center 100, the capacity requirement is 1.5 hours, based on the data in Figure 10.7 (0.05 hours per unit × 30). Component C requires 24 hours of capacity in work center 200 (0.6 hours per unit × 40), followed by 8 hours of capacity in work center 300 (0.2 hours per unit × 40). Also shown in Figure 10.13 is a capacity requirement of 6 hours for work center 200 (0.1 hours per unit × 60) in order to fabricate the batch of component D needed to support the MPS for end product A.

Figure 10.13 allows us to discuss some of the key issues raised by using APS systems. First, let us be clear on the major benefit: The entire schedule for the MPS quantity has been fulfilled in less than $\frac{1}{2}$ week (total elapsed time = 33.5 hours/80 = .41 weeks). This can be contrasted with an expected time of 3 weeks for standard MRP based approaches (86 percent lead time reduction). This implies a corresponding reduction in work-in-process inventories as well as a faster response to market conditions.

Executing the schedule planned in Figure 10.13 may make some people nervous. But it has been shown that this problem will absolutely not be made better by overstating the times used for the APS scheduling. Doing so puts in a *consistent* bias that degrades the planning process. The better approach is to focus on improving time estimates as much as possible (unbiased) and thereafter focus on flawless execution and recovery from any problems (work to the plan). More frequent rescheduling by the APS system allows errors to be reflected and compensated for in updated plans.

Figure 10.13 is simplified to show only the capacity requirements for one MPS quantity and its supporting components. In reality, the APS will schedule all MPS quantities, producing an overall capacity profile and detailed schedules for each work center. The *next* MPS quantity that is scheduled has to deal with the realities established by the prior schedules. That is, for example, if end product B is scheduled next in week 8, it will be back-scheduled to complete at hour 78.5 in work center 100, and its needs for capacity in work center 200 can end only at hour 46.5. One might therefore ask if the scheduling of end product B should precede that of end product A. This is a complex issue. Sequential processing of MPS quantities in APS means that one needs to determine the priorities for scheduling these end products. We will come back to this issue.

Figure 10.13 shows a "hole" in the schedule for work center 200 between hours 70.5 and 72.5. An APS system would allow this capacity to be used for another job or work order, but only if the work order had a capacity requirement equal or less than 2 hours. That is, the criterion here is to respect the schedules for the *end products,* not to optimize work center utilizations. The hole also illustrates another choice: The capacity requirement for Component D has been back-scheduled from the time when it is needed to produce end product A. This will result in the lowest inventory levels. But it could start at time 70.5 (front-schedule it), but then it would be completed 2 hours before needed. Doing so provides more surety that the MPS can proceed as planned, since now only the schedule for component C might upset it, rather than the schedules for either component part.

Front-scheduling component D will increase the work-in-process inventory, since it is started in production earlier. But there is another issue here, similar to when you arrive with enough time to take an earlier plane though not having a ticket for that flight. For the airline, if there is a seat available on the earlier flight, it is in their interest to put you on the earlier flight—regardless of what the payment/ticket conditions are—since the seat is empty, and the one you will occupy on the subsequent flight might be sold to someone else. The same issue comes up in Figure 10.13. The front schedule allows the "hole" to be shifted later, when it has a much better chance to be used, since there is not presently any work scheduled beyond hour 80 in work center 200. Front scheduling of component D allows work on another shop order to begin at hour 78.5 instead of hour 80.

What all of this illustrates is that there are "many ways to skin the cat." APS systems typically provide the ability to look at the schedules visibly—to allow manual intervention—and thereafter to see the resultant effects throughout the company (work centers, shop orders, MPS, customer orders). The outputs from APS are often displayed as schedule boards (bar charts showing each shop order being processed over time in each work center). APS systems are also usually linked to spread sheet models to allow users to examine the implications of various choices/schedule changes.

Management and Capacity Planning/Utilization

Capacity planning is one side of the coin; capacity management is the other. Plans need to be executed, and this needs to be done effectively; moreover, well-developed demand management can provide conditions that are much more favorable to routine execution. For example, Toyota and several other Japanese auto manufacturers develop production plans with a stable rate of output (cars per day). Product mix variations are substantially less than those for other auto companies because they carefully manage the number and timing of option combinations. The result is execution systems that are simple, effective, and easy to operate with minimal inventories and fast throughput times. Capacity planning is straightforward and execution is more easily achieved, not only for the company itself but for its suppliers as well. That is, well-managed front-end planning can rationalize the entire supply chain.

Capacity Monitoring with Input/Output Control

One key capacity management issue concerns the match between planning and execution. This implies monitoring on a timely basis to see whether a workable capacity plan has been created and whether some form of corrective action is needed. The best-known approach to this issue is **input/output control,** where the work flowing through a work center is monitored: the planned work input and planned output are compared to the work actual input and output.

Input/Output Control

The capacity planning technique used delineates the planned input. Planned output results from managerial decision making to specify the capacity level; that is, planned output is based on staffing levels, hours of work, and so forth. In capacity-constrained work centers, planned output is based on the rate of capacity established by management. In non-capacity-constrained work centers, planned output is equal to planned input (allowing for some lead-time offset).

Capacity data in input/output control are usually expressed in hours. Input data are based on jobs' expected arrivals at a work center. For example, a CRP procedure would examine the status of all open shop orders (scheduled receipts), estimate how long they'll take (setup, run, wait, and move) at particular work centers, and thereby derive when they'll arrive at subsequent work centers. A finite loading system would do the same, albeit with better results. The approach would be repeated for all planned orders from the MRP database. The resultant set of expected arrivals of exact quantities would be multiplied by run time per unit from the routing file. This product would be added to setup time, also from the routing file. The sum is a planned input expressed in standard hours.

Actual input would use the same routing data, but for the *actual* arrivals of jobs in each time period as reported by the shop-floor control system. Actual output would again use the shop-floor control data for exact quantities completed in each time period, converted to standard hours with routing time data.

The only time data not based on the routing file are those for planned output. In this case, management has to plan the labor-hours to be expended in the work center. For example, if two people work 9 hours per day for five days, the result is 90 labor-hours per week. This value has to be reduced or inflated by an estimate of the relation of actual hours to standard hours. In our example, if people in this work center typically worked at 80 percent efficiency, then planned output is 72 hours.

A work center's actual output will deviate from planned output. Often deviations can be attributed to conditions at the work center itself, such as lower-than-expected productivity, breakdowns, absences, random variations, or poor product quality. But less-than-expected output can occur for reasons outside the work center's control, such as insufficient output from a preceding work center or improper releasing of planned orders. Either problem can lead to insufficient input or a "starved" work center. Another reason for a variation between actual input and planned input was shown by our capacity planning model comparisons—some models don't produce realistic plans!

Input/output analysis also monitors backlog. Backlog represents the cushion between input and output. Backlog decouples input from output, allowing work center operations to be less affected by variations in requirements. Arithmetically, it equals prior backlog plus or minus the difference between input and output. The planned backlog calculation is based

FIGURE 10.14
Sample
Input/Output
for Work
Center 500*
(as of the end
of period 5)

		Week				
		1	**2**	**3**	**4**	**5**
Planned input		15	15	0	10	10
Actual input		14	13	5	9	17
Cumulative deviation		−1	−3	+2	+1	+8
Planned output		11	11	11	11	11
Actual output		8	10	9	11	9
Cumulative deviation		−3	−4	−6	−6	−8
Actual backlog	20	26	29	25	23	31

Desired backlog: 10 hours

*In standard labor-hours.

on planned input and planned output. Actual backlog uses actual input and output. The difference between planned backlog and actual backlog represents one measure of the total, or net, input/output deviations. Monitoring input, output, and backlog typically involves keeping track of cumulative deviations and comparing them with preset limits.

The input/output report in Figure 10.14 is for work center 500 shown in weekly time buckets with input and output measured in standard labor-hours. The report was prepared at the end of period 5, so the actual values are current week-by-week variations in planned input. These could result from actual planned orders and scheduled receipts; that is, for example, if the input were planned by CRP, planned inputs would be based on timings for planned orders, the status of scheduled receipts, and routing data. The *actual* input that arrives at work center 500 can vary for any of the causes just discussed.

Work center 500's planned output has been smoothed; that is, management decided to staff this work center to achieve a constant output of 11 hours per week. The results should be to absorb input variations with changes in the backlog level. Cumulative planned output for the five weeks (55 hours) is 5 hours more than cumulative planned input. This reflects a management decision to reduce backlog from the original level of 20 hours. The process of increasing capacity to reduce backlog recognizes explicitly that flows must be controlled to change backlog; backlog can't be changed in or of itself.

Figure 10.14 summarized the results after five weeks of actual operation. At the end of week 5, the situation requires managerial attention. The cumulative input deviation (+8 hours), cumulative output deviation (−8 hours), current backlog (31 hours), or all three could have exceeded the desired limits of control. In this example, the increased backlog is a combination of more-than-expected input and less-than-expected output.

One other aspect of monitoring backlog is important. In general, there's little point in releasing orders to a work center that already has an excessive backlog, except when the order to be released is of higher priority than any in the backlog. The idea is to not release work that can't be done, but to wait and release what's really needed. Oliver Wight summed this up as one of the principles of input/output control: "Never put into a manufacturing facility or to a vendor's facility more than you believe can be produced. Hold backlogs in production and inventory control." With today's APS system, a similar dictate results: concentrate on executing the most immediate schedule—exactly. The APS system will take care of the future schedules.

FIGURE 10.15
The Capacity
Bathtub

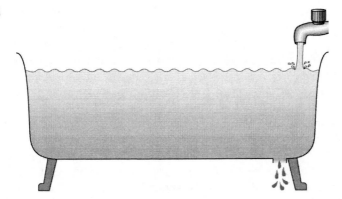

Figure 10.15 depicts a work center "bathtub" showing capacity in hydraulic terms. The input pipe's diameter represents the maximum flow (of work) into the tub. The valve represents MPC systems like MPS, MRP, and JIT, which determine **planned input** (flow of work) into the tub. Actual input could vary because of problems (like a corroded valve or problem at the water department) and can be monitored with input/output analysis. We can determine **required capacity** to accomplish the planned input to the work center with any of the capacity planning techniques. The output drain pipe takes completed work from the work center. Its diameter represents the work center's planned or **rated capacity,** which limits planned output. As with actual input, actual output may vary from the plan as well. It too can be monitored with input/output analysis. Sometimes planned output can't be achieved over time even when it's less than maximum capacity and there's a backlog to work on. When that occurs, realized output is called **demonstrated capacity.** The "water" in the tub is the **backlog** or **load,** which can also be monitored with input/output analysis.

Managing *Bottleneck* Capacity

Eliyahu Goldratt developed a key capacity management idea that he popularized more than 20 years ago in *The Goal.* Fundamentally, one needs to find the bottlenecks in any factory, and thereafter manage their capacities most effectively. Goldratt's maxim is that an hour of capacity lost in a bottleneck work center is an hour of capacity lost to the entire company—worth a fortune. But an hour of capacity gained in a nonbottleneck work center will only increase work-in-process inventory and confusion. Eli Goldratt has gone on to other things, but this fundamental concept remains at the base of his work. Today, he and his colleagues have generalized the ideas into what they refer to as "theory of constraints" (TOC). For the purposes of capacity planning and management, TOC teaches that the capacities of bottleneck work centers need to be planned and managed much more carefully than those of nonbottlenecks. In fact, Goldratt points out that for nonbottlenecks it may not be important to even have decent data. If sufficient capacity exists, execution of capacity plans is easy. Spend the time and energy on execution of what at first seems impossible.

Goldratt has many suggestions for how to execute the impossible. For example, why shouldn't bottleneck work centers run through lunch hours and coffee breaks—others can run these work centers while the primary personnel eat lunch and drink coffee. Alternative routing is another solution, and this is a good idea even when it "costs" much more. Usually the costs are calculated with unrealistic assumptions. Extra work done in an underutilized work center has no real cost, and if the bottleneck workload is thereby reduced, it is an excellent idea to do it.

The TOC approach to capacity planning is essentially to first determine the bottleneck work centers. This can be done with a rough-cut capacity planning model or with CRP. Where are the bottlenecks? Next, TOC would try to find the quick solutions for eliminating bottlenecks. Finally, scheduling will concentrate on best managing bottleneck capacity. Essentially, TOC will separate those jobs that pass through the bottlenecks from those that do not. Only the jobs or work orders requiring capacity in the bottleneck resource are finite scheduled, using horizontal loading and back scheduling for the most critical jobs.

If we return to the hole in the schedule of Figure 10.13, the TOC approach would definitely front-schedule component D for the reason described there: it is the schedule for component C that constrains the start of end product A. Do not let component D become a constraint to this overall product schedule. TOC treats this early schedule (front-loaded) as a buffer in order to reduce the possibility of missing the overall goal: Ship the end product!

TOC uses APS systems, but concentrates their attention on what is truly critical. For nonbottleneck work centers it is more than unimportant to utilize their capacity—it is fundamentally *wrong*. Increasing utilization of nonbottlenecks will result in more work being in the factory than necessary, yielding higher inventories and confusion. Nonbottleneck work will be done easily since there is basically no constraint to it. Restricting the use of APS systems to focus on the bottlenecks allows smart users to examine the best ways to "skin the cat."

The most critical capacity requirements need to be identified and thereafter utilized to maximum effectiveness. Capacity planning techniques can help with the former, but effective management is needed for the latter. Moreover, managerial policies can also create environments that are easier to execute—environments where capacities are utilized in a predictable and stable fashion.

Capacity Planning in the MPC System

To illustrate the importance of the interrelationships in designing and using the capacity planning system, let's consider the impact of production planning and resource planning decisions on shorter-term capacity planning decisions. To the extent that production planning and resource planning are done well, problems faced in capacity planning can be reduced, since appropriate resources have been provided. If, for example, the production plan specifies a very stable rate of output, then changes in the master production schedule (MPS) requiring capacity changes are minimal. If the material planning module functions effectively, the MPS will be converted into detailed component production plans with relatively few unexpected execution problems.

A quite different but equally important linkage that can affect capacity planning system design is the linkage with shop-floor execution systems. A key relationship exists in scheduling effective use of capacity. With sufficient capacity and efficient use of that capacity ensured by good shop-floor systems, we'll see few unpleasant surprises requiring capacity analysis and change. Effective shop-floor procedures utilize available capacity to process orders according to MRP system priorities, provide insight into potential capacity problems in the short range (a few hours to days), and respond to changes in material plans. Thus, effective systems reduce the necessary degree of detail and intensity of use of the capacity planning system. The result is a better match between actual input/output and planned input/output. Again, we see attention to the material planning side of the MPC system, in this case the shop-floor module, having an effect on the capacity planning side.

Choosing the Measure of Capacity

The choice of capacity measures is an important management issue. Alternatives run from machine-hours or labor-hours to physical or monetary units. The choice depends on the constraining resource and the firm's needs. In any manufacturing company, the "bundle of goods and services" provided to customers increasingly includes software, other knowledge work, after-sales service, and other customer services. In every case, providing these goods and services requires resources—"capacities" that must be planned, managed, and developed. Appropriate measures of capacity must be established and changed as evolution in the bundle of goods and services occurs.

Several current trends in manufacturing have a significant bearing on the choice of capacity measures. Each can have a major impact on what's important to measure in capacity. One important trend is considerable change in the concept of direct labor. Direct labor has been shrinking as a portion of overall manufacturing employment. Distinctions between direct and indirect labor are becoming less important. The ability to change labor capacity by hiring and firing (or even using overtime) has been reduced; notions of "lifetime employment" have further constrained this form of capacity adjustment.

Since one objective in JIT systems is continual improvement, the basis for labor capacity is constantly changing. This mandates control procedures for identifying and changing the planning factors as improvements take place.

Another important trend is decreased internal fabrication and increased emphasis on outside purchasing, i.e., outsourcing. This trend can alter the conception of what capacity requirements are important. Procurement analysis, incoming inspection, and engineering liaison may become the critical capacities to be managed, as well as planning and scheduling the capacities in vendor firms. In fact, one of the major benefits ascribed to major outsourcing companies such as Solectron and Flextronics is their ability to more flexibly respond to changing capacity needs.

For many firms engaged in fabrication, machine technology is changing rapidly. Flexible automation has greatly increased the range of parts that can be processed in a machine center. Future product mixes are likely to be much more variable than in the past, with a marked effect on the equipment capacity required. Moreover, as equipment becomes more expensive, it may be necessary to plan and control the capacity of key pieces of equipment at a detailed level.

To the extent that cellular technologies are adopted as part of JIT manufacturing, the unit of capacity may need to change. Usually the entire cell is coupled and has only as much capacity as its limiting resource. Often, the cell is labor limited, so the unit of capacity is labor-hours (continually adjusted for learning). Sometimes, however, the capacity measure needs to be solely associated with a single aspect of the cell. Also, when dissimilar items are added to the cell for manufacture, it's necessary to estimate each new item's capacity requirements in terms of individual processing steps.

The first task in choosing a capacity measure is to creatively identify resources that are critical and in short supply. Capacity control is too complicated to apply to all resources. The next step is to define the unit of measure. If the key resource is people, then labor-hours may be appropriate. In other instances, such measures as tons, gallons, number of molds, number of ovens, hours of machine time, square yards, linear feet, lines of code, customer calls, and cell hours have been used. In some cases, these are converted to some "equivalent" measure to accommodate a wider variety of products or resources.

After the resources and unit of measure have been determined, the next concern is to estimate available capacity. The primary issue here is theory versus practice. The engineer can provide theoretical capacity from the design specifications for a machine or from time studies of people. A subissue is whether to use "full" capacity or some fraction thereof (often 75 to 85 percent). A further issue is "plasticity" in capacity. For almost *any* resource, if it's *really* important, more output can be achieved. We've seen many performances that fall short of or exceed capacity calculations.

Choice of capacity measure follows directly from the objective of providing capacity to meet production plans. The appropriate measure of capacity most directly affects meeting these plans. The measure, therefore, should be appropriate to the critical limited resources and be based on what's achievable, with allowances for maintenance and other necessary activities. It must be possible to convert the bundle of products and services into capacity measurement terms. The results must be understood by those responsible, and they should be monitored.

Choice of a Specific Technique

In this chapter's discussion, the capacity planning techniques for converting a material plan into capacity requirements include three different methods for rough-cut capacity planning (CPOF, capacity bills, and resource profiles). We also examined capacity requirements planning, CRP, which is particularly useful for medium range planning. For the detailed day-to-day capacity planning APS systems can be valuable under some circumstances. The choice of method depends heavily on characteristics of the manufacturing environment.

The three rough-cut methods are most general, being applicable even in companies using just-in-time methods for shop-floor control. Rough-cut approaches can be useful in JIT operations to estimate the impact of changes in requirements called for by revisions to the master production schedule. For example, under level scheduling conditions, a change from a production rate of 480 units per day (one unit per minute) to 528 units per day (1.1 units per minute) might be needed. A rough-cut procedure could be used to examine the impact on each work center or manufacturing cell through which this volume would pass (including those of suppliers). Any indicated problems or bottleneck conditions could be addressed *before* the crisis hits. Similarly, a planned reduction in MPS could be evaluated to determine resources that might be freed to work on other tasks.

Rough-cut approaches do vary in accuracy, aggregation level, and ease of preparation. There's a general relationship between the amount of data and computational time required, and the quality and detail of the capacity requirements estimated. The issue is whether additional costs of supporting more complex procedures are justified by improved decision making and subsequent plant operations.

The capacity bills procedure has an advantage over capacity planning using overall factors (CPOF) because it explicitly recognizes product mix changes. This can be important in JIT operations, particularly where the level schedule is based on assumptions of product mix and where different products have different capacity requirements. On the other hand, if changes in mix are easily accommodated, and there are minimal differences in capacity requirements for different products, then CPOF's simplicity can be exploited. Under JIT operations, however, there's often little need to incorporate the added sophistication of the resource profile procedure. There simply won't be any added advantage to making lead time offsets in the planning process. Work is completed at virtually the same time as it's started.

Capacity requirements planning is only applicable in companies using time-phased MRP records for detailed material planning and shop-order-based shop scheduling systems. CRP is unnecessary under JIT operations anyway since minimal work-in-process levels mean there's no need to estimate the impact in capacity requirements of partially processed work. All orders start from "raw material" with virtually no amount of "capacity" stored in component inventories. Also, under JIT, there's no formal PAC procedure. There are no work orders. Thus, there are no status data on work orders.

Input/output control isn't usually an issue under JIT operations because attention has been shifted from planning to execution. As a result, actual input should equal actual output. Actual input becomes actual output with an insignificant delay. The backlog is effectively a constant zero. However, planned input can indeed vary from actual input and so can planned output vary from actual output. These variations should be achievable without violating the equality between actual input and actual output—with backlog remaining at zero. To the extent that plan-to-actual variations are possible, the result reflects the flexibility, or bandwidth, of the JIT unit.

Using the Capacity Plan

All the techniques we've described provide data on which a manager can base a decision. The broad choices are clear—if there's a mismatch between available capacity and required capacity, either the capacity or the material plan should be changed. If capacity is to be changed, the choices include overtime/undertime authorization, hiring/layoff, and increasing/ decreasing the number of machine tools or times in use. Capacity requirements can be changed by alternate routing, make-or-buy decisions, subcontracting, raw material substitutions, inventory changes, or revised customer promise dates.

Choice of capacity planning units can lead to more effective use of the system. Capacity units need not be work centers as defined for manufacturing, engineering, or routing purposes. They can be groupings of the key resources (human or capital) important in defining the factory's output levels. Many firms plan capacity solely for key machines (work centers) and gateway operations. These key areas can be managed in detail, while other areas fall under resource planning and the shop-floor control system.

Capacity planning choices dictate the diameter of the manufacturing pipeline. Only as much material can be produced as there's capacity for its production, *regardless of the material plan*. Not understanding the critical nature of managing capacity can lead a firm into production chaos and serious customer service problems. In the same vein, the relationship between flexibility and capacity must be discussed. You can't have perfectly balanced material and capacity plans *and* be able to easily produce emergency orders! We know one general manager who depicts his capacity as a pie. He has one slice for recurring business, one for spare parts production, one for downtime and maintenance, and a final specific slice for opportunity business. He manages to pay for this excess capacity by winning lucrative contracts that require rapid responses. He *does not add* that opportunity business to a capacity plan fully committed to the other aspects of his business.

Example Applications

We finish this chapter with three example applications of capacity planning/utilization. The first example, Montell USA, Inc., is a straightforward application of rough-cut capacity planning used to compare capacity plans with actual customer demands on an ongoing basis. The second example, Applicon, is tailored to the company's JIT manufacturing environment, allowing it to make systematic adjustments to the labor force. Finally, we see how the Manugistics APS software can be applied.

Capacity Planning at Montell USA, Inc.

Montell USA, Inc., manufactures plastic pellets used in injection molding machines. The pellets are made up of combinations of plastic material, coloring agents, and other chemicals. The company's primary customers use injection molding machines to make plastic components for the automotive industry. Montell currently utilizes a combination of two software packages in its manufacturing planning and control system. Front-end activities, like master production scheduling and demand management, are done with a system termed Picaso. MRP and back-end activities, like shop-floor control and vendor scheduling, are accomplished with an enterprise resource planning system provided by SAP. The Picaso system is used to produce the capacity planning reports for the company.

Montell prepares a rough-cut capacity plan from the master production schedule. It is a rolling plan, revised each month for the coming six months. It is prepared for each of the company's production lines, using a capacity measure of thousands of pounds of output. An example of part of a plan is given in Figure 10.16. For each of the next six months, two figures are shown for each production line: FINL and PLAN. The first of these, FINL, shows the booked customer orders for the month.

The second column for each month is the PLAN column. This gives the master production schedule quantity for each of the production lines. There are a few instances where booked orders exceed the planned capacity (e.g., months 12 and 01 for line B1). In some of these cases, management action (like overtime or a partial extra shift) may be needed to meet the requirements; in others, no action is needed because of the specific products being produced. To help determine where action should be taken, the rough-cut capacity plan is also detailed by specific product. An example showing part of the capacity plan detailed by product is provided in Figure 10.17. In this report the planners can see, for instance, the breakdown of specific products that sum up the quantities of 616 FINL and 561 PLAN for line G2 in month 12. The planners at Montell use this data to determine if changes need to be made in the MPS and/or in the commitments to customers.

Capacity Planning at Applicon

Applicon, a division of Schlumberger, designs and manufactures computer-aided engineering (CAE), computer-aided design (CAD), and computer-aided manufacturing (CAM) systems. Applicon implemented numerous JIT concepts and replaced some of its MRP system modules. Its dramatic results included a reduction in lead time (20 weeks to 4 days), an inventory reduction of over 75 percent, virtual elimination of obsolescence costs, little or no inspection, and a decline in MPC personnel (86 to 14).

FIGURE 10.16   **Part of Montell's Capacity Plan by Production Line**

Line	FINL 12*	PLAN 12	FINL 01	PLAN 01	FINL 02	PLAN 02	FINL 03	PLAN 03	FINL 04	PLAN 04	FINL 05	PLAN 05
B 1	2,327	1,685	2,610	2,598	2,758	2,530	2,818	2,862	2,763	2,621	508	2,842
BW-8	887	649	792	892	713	752	686	810	615	837	76	997
C 1	264	330	426	247	672	225	262	254	42	313	42	311
CK	180	162	190	159	180	116	52	201	132	134	0	159
CT-1	0	88	0	0	0	0	0	0	0	0	0	0
E 1	0	0	0	0	0	0	0	0	0	0	0	0
E 2	0	0	0	0	0	0	0	0	0	0	0	0
E 4	0	0	0	0	0	0	0	0	0	0	0	0
E 7	0	0	0	0	0	0	0	0	0	0	0	0
G 1	910	532	1,076	1,180	887	1,230	752	1,255	440	1,265	160	1,297
G 2	616	561	645	719	637	634	509	639	600	661	16	665
G 3	582	431	716	438	600	411	458	414	219	514	62	416
G 4	1,347	791	1,494	1,391	1,182	1,222	1,074	1,292	1,102	1,471	82	1,409
G 5	1,802	1,698	2,430	1,571	2,211	1,631	2,127	1,708	1,669	1,424	320	1,449

*Month 12.

FIGURE 10.17   **Part of Montell's Capacity Plan by Product and Line**

Line	Name	FINL 12	PLAN 12	FINL 01	PLAN 01	FINL 02	PLAN 02	FINL 03	PLAN 03	FINL 04	PLAN 04	FINL 05	PLAN 05
G 2	722-44-06 BB73F KZE	30	10	25	35	33	45	35	35	35	35	0	35
	722-44-07 BB73F DC4A	60	95	70	80	99	90	100	90	90	80	0	90
	722-44-08 BB73F YCD	90	100	10	110	10	110	10	110	0	110	0	110
	722-44-09 BB73F MDD	0	0	90	0	90	0	90	0	100	0	0	0
	722-46-01 BB73F DCC	15	20	10	50	15	20	15	25	15	50	0	25
	722-46-04 BB73F YCC	10	20	15	25	10	20	10	25	10	20	0	25
	840-43-05 EXP149628	0	0	0	0	0	0	0	0	0	0	0	0
	840-43-06 EXP149629	0	0	0	0	0	0	0	0	0	0	0	0
		616	561	645	719	637	634	509	639	600	661	16	665
G 3	102-64-08 RTA3184 6P	0	0	0	0	0	0	0	0	0	0	0	0
	102-64-13 RTA3184 JA	0	0	0	0	0	0	0	0	0	0	0	0
	105-02-01 RTA3363E B	0	0	0	0	0	0	0	0	0	0	0	0
	109-03-05 CL37BC BLA	0	0	0	0	0	0	0	0	0	0	0	0
	120-05-17 CA45GC PA7	0	0	0	0	0	0	0	0	0	0	0	0
	120-05-52 CA45GC SPN	17	36	25	0	25	0	25	0	25	0	0	0

Figure 10.18 shows an Applicon "Capacity Status Report." Applicon divided the factory into 17 capacity groupings (work centers) for planning purposes. It used actual customer orders as a monthly MPS to drive capacity planning. Capacity bills were used to convert the MPS into the present "load" over the next month (20 working days) in standard hours (the second column in Figure 10.18). The capacities in column 3 are based on a total workforce of 48 people (e.g., ALF-A had three workers who worked 8 hours per day for 20 days in the month = 480 standard hours). Work center OLD-P's zero capacity indicates no worker is presently assigned to this activity.

The fourth column reduces the capacity amounts by 30 percent (the desired rate of direct production activity for Applicon workers). The remaining time was used for "whole person" activities. That is, the company operated with the direct workers taking on many

362   Chapter 10   *Capacity Planning and Utilization*

FIGURE 10.18
Applicon
Capacity
Status Report

Work Center	Load (Std. Hours)	Capacity (Standard)	Capacity (Adj. Std.)	Capacity (Maximum)
ALF-A	70	480	336	528
ALF-T	5	80	56	88
HLT-A	438	800	560	880
HLT-T	85	160	112	176
MIS-A	270	800	560	880
MIS-T	14	80	56	88
MVX-A	399	1,120	784	1,232
MVX-T	79	80	56	88
OLD-P	81	0	0	0
PCB-A	52	160	112	176
PCB-H	44	160	112	176
PCB-I	124	320	224	352
PCB-M	441	480	336	520
PCB-P	408	960	672	1,056
PCB-T	918	1,680	1,176	1,848
PCB-V	123	160	112	176
PCB-W	56	160	112	176
Totals	3,634	7,680	5,376	8,440

20 total workdays included.

other tasks, such as design of work methods, new drawings, and database maintenance. On the average, Applicon expected that 30 percent of the time would be spent on this indirect work. This was *instead* of having a larger number of indirect workers. The last column provides a "maximum" capacity value based on 10 percent overtime. Applicon felt that it had the flexibility to operate easily between these two capacity levels. Where the volume was much higher or lower, they needed to make adjustments.

This report was run on June 12 for the next 20 days. Differences between "load" and the three capacities represented Applicon's ability to take on additional work in the next month. Large orders could be included into a trial run of the MPS to examine the orders' impact in terms of existing capacity availabilities. Total load (3,634 hours) represented 47 percent of standard capacity, 68 percent of adjusted capacity, and 43 percent of maximum capacity. Management reviewed these numbers carefully—particularly if possible large orders were under negotiation. It was relatively easy to make trial runs with those orders included to examine the impact of accepting the orders.

Of all the work centers in Figure 10.18, MVX-T appeared to be in the most trouble. However, this could easily be fixed. MVX-T only had one-half person allocated to it (80 hours/month). Reducing MVX-A (or some other work center) by one-half person and increasing MVX-T's capacity to one person for the month solved the problem. OLD-P similarly needed to have a person allocated to it.

This rough-cut capacity planning system serves Applicon well. Problems can be anticipated. JIT operations mean results are very current, with little or no bias because of work-in-process inventories. Results of the capacity planning are given to shop personnel, who make their own adjustments as they see fit, making allowances for absenteeism, particular workers' relative strengths, and other local conditions.

Capacity Planning with APS at a Consumer Products Company

A large European based consumer products company uses APS extensively in one of its factories. The APS software package is provided by Manugistics, and is called NetWORKS Scheduling. It is essentially a horizontal loading, back-scheduling system operating like the one illustrated in this chapter. It produces schedules for each work center that are similar to that of Figure 10.14. Figure 10.19 is a portion of a sample output report as generated by the APS software. Here we see a work center (packing line 250 ml. sauce), and the 10 pasta sauces that are scheduled for production over the next seven days. Each of the items shown is a 250-milliliter bottle of a particular end product. For each item there are two values shown: the planned production in each day, and the expected inventory in days of supply. By using days of supply, the system makes comparisons of inventory positions more transparent. To accomplish this, there is a linkage to a demand management system that allows the calculations for days of supply to reflect forecasts, actual orders, and provisions for special promotions.

Figure 10.19 seems to reflect ample capacity to meet demands at this company. There do not appear to be any shortages predicted in this plan, except perhaps for the third item (103), which might run out on 15/9. The match of production with capacity seems fairly close, with most production quantities scheduled to occur just when the days of supply approach zero. Thus, items 102, 105, and 107 are all scheduled the day after the days of supply is one day. It is only items 108 and 109 that seem to be scheduled earlier than necessary.

FIGURE 10.19
Sample APS Output—Pasta Sauce Line

Res: 250 ml. Sauce

Item	Description	10/9	11/9	12/9	13/9	14/9	15/9	16/9
101	250 ml.			6,600				
				5D	4D	3D	2D	1D
102	250 ml.						5,400	
		5D	4D	3D	2D	1D	8D	7D
103	250 ml.							5,100
		5D	4D	3D	2D	1D		3D
104	250 ml.	2,700						
		9D	8D	7D	6D	5D	4D	3D
105	250 ml.			7,200				
		2D	1D	12D	11D	10D	9D	8D
106	250 ml.	10,800						7,200
		6D	5D	4D	3D	2D	1D	3D
107	250 ml.						3,100	
		5D	4D	3D	2D	1D	4D	3D
108	250 ml.						1,800	
		12D	11D	10D	9D	8D	14D	13D
109	250 ml.						3,600	3,900
		6D	5D	4D	3D	2D	5D	9D
110	250 ml.				5,000			

One might look at Figure 10.19 and ask why item 103 is not scheduled a day earlier with item 108 moved one day later, in order to better balance the inventory days of supply across all items. The answer is that there are many reasons for scheduling decisions, and balanced inventory is only one of them. The Manugistics APS software package allows for many scheduling options. For example, the four items now scheduled for 15/9 might be scheduled as a group because they share a common setup. Another possibility is that they are all made from a common raw material. Perhaps this is the day that the company schedules all the pasta sauce made with mushrooms or some other common material.

The Manugistics APS software allows the schedulers at this consumer products company to evaluate output schedules like Figure 10.19 with graphical review. A user can view a schedule (it can be tailored with 14 different colors), changing schedule assignments by pointing/clicking. The schedules produced can be analyzed with a user-specified set of tools called "Troubleshooter," which alerts the user to any conditions he/she would like to flag. Particular assignments (schedules) can be frozen, which allows one to override whatever basic logic is used for making scheduling decisions. Thereafter, the APS model can be rerun to determine the shifts that result from these user imposed decisions. Changes in schedules also automatically generate the changes in setup/changeover costs if these are particularly relevant.

The APS software has been found to be quite versatile, allowing the company to use it in somewhat different kinds of manufacturing environments. For example, some packing lines necessarily need to complete all the jobs before the ends of days, while in other cases equipment can simply be turned off at night and back on in the morning, with work taking up where it has left off. The software also has helped coordinate scheduling of the packaging lines with scheduling of bulk products to be packed in multiple packages.

Concluding Principles

Clear principles for design and use of the capacity planning system emerge from this chapter:

- Capacity plans must be developed concurrently with material plans if the material plans are to be realized.
- The particular capacity planning technique(s) chosen must match the level of detail and actual company circumstances to permit making effective management decisions.
- Capacity planning can be simplified in a JIT environment.
- The better the resource and production planning process, the less difficult the capacity planning process.
- The better the shop-floor system, the less short-term capacity planning is required.
- The more detail in the capacity planning system, the more data and database maintenance are required.
- It's not always capacity that should change when capacity availability doesn't equal need.
- Capacity not only must be planned, but use of that capacity must also be monitored and controlled.
- Capacity planning techniques can be applied to selected key resources (which need not correspond to production work centers).
- The capacity measure should reflect realizable output from the key resources.

References

Berry, W. L.; T. Schmitt; and T. E. Vollmann. "Capacity Planning Techniques for Manufacturing Control Systems: Informational Requirements and Operational Features," *Journal of Operations Management* 3, no. 1 (November 1982).

_____. "An Analysis of Capacity Planning Procedures for a Material Requirements Planning System," *Decision Sciences* 15, no. 4 (fall 1984).

Blackstone, J. H. Jr. *Capacity Management.* Cincinnati: Southwestern, 1989.

Chakravarty, A., and H. K. Jain. "Distributed Computer Systems Capacity Planning and Capacity Loading," *Decision Sciences Journal* 21, no. 2 (spring 1990), pp. 253–262.

Fine, C. H. *Clockspeed Winning Industry Control in the Age of Temporary Advantage.* Reading: Perseus Books, 1998.

Goldratt, E. *Critical Chain.* Great Barrington, Mass.: North River Press, 1997.

Goldratt, E. M., and J. Cox. *The Goal: Process of Ongoing Improvement,* 2nd revised edition. Crofon-on-Hudson, NY: North River Press, 1992.

Hoover, W. E. Jr.; E. Eloranta; J. Holmstrom; and K. Huttunen. *Managing the Demand-Supply Chain.* New York: Wiley 2002, pp. 127–152.

Hyer, N., and U. Wemmerlov. *Reorganizing the Factory.* Portland: Productivity Press, 2002, pp. 311–368.

Karmarker, U. S. "Capacity Loading and Release Planning with Work-in-Progress (WIP) and Lead-times," *Journal of Manufacturing and Operations Management* 2, no. 2 (1989), pp. 105–123.

Knolmayer, G.; P. Mertens; and A. Zeier. *Supply Chain Management Based on SAP Systems.* Berlin: Springer, 2002, pp. 116–147.

Material and Capacity Planning Reprints. Falls Church, Va: APICS, 1993.

Metters, R., and V. A. Vargas. "A Comparison of Production Scheduling Policies on Costs, Service Levels, and Schedule Changes," *Production and Operations Management* 17, no. 3 (1999), pp. 76–91.

Matsuura, H; H. Taubone; and K. Katoka. "Comparisons between Simple Infinite Loading and Loading Considering a Workload Status under Uncertainty in Job Shop Operation Times," *International Journal of Production Economics* 40, no. I (1995).

Miller, T. *Hierarchical Operations and Supply Chain Planning.* London: Springer, 2001.

Vakharia, A. J.; D. A. Parmenter; and S. M. Sanchez, "The Operating Impact of Parts Commonality," *Journal of Operations Management* 14, no. 1 (1996).

Waller, D. L., *Operations Management.* London: Thompson, 2002, pp. 417–457.

Discussion Questions

1. Figure 10.1 shows a hierarchy of capacity planning and material planning processes. How does a better job of long-range planning affect the medium-range planning? Is the issue similar between production planning and master production scheduling?

2. Why does JIT execution require a less-intensive capacity planning approach?

3. What are the advantages and disadvantages of using CRP over rough-cut capacity planning?

4. What are the relative advantages of horizontal versus vertical loading?

5. How does input-output analysis provide a reality check on material and capacity planning processes?

6. Why is an hour of capacity lost in a bottleneck work center so valuable?

7. How might the Montell capacity plan (Figure 10.16) allow the company to determine if its revenue projections are on target?

8. What is the thinking behind Applicon's three different capacity values for its work centers?

9. In the Manugistics APS system, what would it mean if the days of supply were negative whenever a new batch of the products was scheduled? What would it mean if each time a new batch was scheduled, the days of supply was at 5D?

10. What are some examples of capacity planning in a University? What are good and poor practices?

Problems

1. A firm makes car seats for an automaker in two varieties: leather and fabric. The standard labor hours for these are 1.2 and 1.0 hours, respectively. The seats are made in two work centers, sewing and assembly, where the average percentage of work has been 55 percent for sewing and 45 percent for assembly. Given the following schedule for the next six weeks, calculate the labor hours needed in each of the two work centers:

Week	1	2	3	4	5	6
Leather	15	20	18	21	15	13
Fabric	65	60	62	59	65	67

(All quantities are in hundreds of units)

2. Returning to problem 1, what are the average labor hours needed over the six-week period, and how might the company handle deviations for the average? How might they staff their departments?

3. Returning again to problem 1, the leather requires incoming inspection for each car seat in order to be sure the colors match. The time required for this is five minutes per set of car seats. What are the expected capacity requirements for the inspection department over the next six weeks? Is there any way that this problem can usefully be combined with problem 1?

4. Returning to problem 3, what if inspection is done by the seat manufacturer in combination with assembly? How does this influence analysis of problem 1?

5. A metal fabricating company has the following master production schedule for one of its items (a frame), as well as the accompanying product structure.

	Week 1	Week 2	Week 3	Week 4
MPS	20	30	35	20

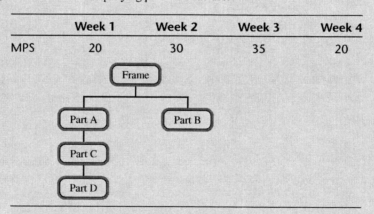

The resource profile for the frame is as follows:

Item	Work Center	Setup Hours	Run Hours/Unit	Lead Time
Frame	200	4	1.5	0 weeks
Part A	300	3	1.0	1 week
Part B	300	3	.8	1 week
Part C	400	2	1.2	2 weeks
Part D	500	2	1.0	1 weeks

Determine the capacity requirements for all work centers, assuming all usages are one, and that a new setup is required in each week at each work center.

6. A furniture manufacturer makes a bookcase from two end panels, four shelves, fasteners, and hangers. The end panels and shelves have the following data:

		End Panel	
Operation	Machine	Run Time	Setup Time
1	Saw	5 minutes	.6 hours
2	Planer	3 minutes	.3 hours
3	Router	4 minutes	.8 hours

		Shelf	
Operation	Machine	Run Time	Setup Time
1	Saw	4 minutes	.5 hours
2	Molder	5 minutes	1.3 hours
3	Router	5 minutes	.7 hours
4	Sander	1 minute	.1 hours

The master schedule for the next three weeks is 35, 50, and 40 bookcases, respectively. Each MPS quantity requires a setup.

a. What is the total number of hours required on each of the five machine centers for each week?

b. If each of the two parts is started into production one week (five days) before needed in assembly, and it takes one day per operation, generate the week-by-week load on the routing machine.

c. If in b the two parts arrive at the router on the same day, which would you process first? Why?

7. An office supply company makes notebooks with the following product structure:

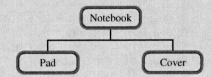

The company uses an MRP system, and has the following records for these three items.

		Week					
Notebook		**1**	**2**	**3**	**4**	**5**	**6**
Gross requirements		25	25	25	25	25	25
Scheduled receipts							
Projected available balance	30	5	0	0	0	0	0
Planned order releases		20	25	25	25	25	0

Q = L4L, LT = 1, SS = 0.

Pad		**1**	**2**	**3**	**4**	**5**	**6**
Gross requirements		20	25	25	25	25	0
Scheduled receipts		15					
Projected available balance	10	5	10	15	20	25	25
Planned order releases		30	30	30	30	0	0

Q = 30, LT = 1, SS = 0.

Cover		1	2	3	4	5	6
Gross requirements		20	25	25	25	25	0
Scheduled receipts		50					
Projected available balance	10	40	15	40	15	40	40
Planned order releases		50	0	50	0	0	0

$Q = 50, LT = 2, SS = 0.$

The notebooks are fabricated in the following work centers, listed with accompanying time requirements.

Operation	Work Center	Setup Time	Run Time
Notebook assembly	100	2 hours	10 minutes
Pad production	200	3 hours	5 minutes
Cover production	300	2 hours	9 minutes

Determine the weekly capacity requirements in each of the work centers. For the two scheduled receipts, assume that the setup is complete, and that in each case they are half complete.

8. Returning to Figures 10.12 and 10.13 and the supporting data, construct the APS back schedule that would be based on product B being horizontally loaded, not product A.

9. Continuing with problem 8, construct the APS back schedule for *both* products A and B, first with B given priority, then with A given priority.

10. Suppose the best customer asked for one unit of product B. How quickly could it be delivered if only enough component parts for one unit were made and assembled, and all existing work in the affected work centers was halted as necessary to make this unit?

11. Suppose that product B had a gross margin of $100/unit, while that of product A was $30. Which product should be the APS system schedule first? Why?

12. The following input-output data were gathered at the end of week 8 for a work center:

	Week							
	1	2	3	4	5	6	7	8
Planned input	60	60	60	60	60	60	60	60
Actual input	68	70	75	70	68	60	55	55
Planned output	65	65	65	65	65	65	65	65
Actual output	60	62	63	63	64	65	63	60

Beginning backlog = 50 hours.

a. Complete the input output document

b. What was the planned objective?

c. Was it met?

d. What recommendations would you make

13. A company with three product lines has estimated its weekly capacity requirements for four work centers as follows.

	Product Line		
Work Center	**A**	**B**	**C**
100	35 hours	28 hours	12 hours
200	25 hours	37 hours	56 hours
300	46 hours	35 hours	33 hours

    a. How many workers (and duplicate machines) are needed in each work center if they are to work 40 hours per week?

    b. What is the difference if the firm decides to work two shifts (80 hours per week)?

14. Suppose in the Montell example (Figure 10.16) a customer wanted to place the maximum order possible for the B1 line. What is the total quantity that could be provided in the next months (12, 01, and 02) with the current capacity? What might be done to improve the response?

15. Applicon has the following capacity bills for its popular items A and B.

A		B	
Work Center	**Hours/Unit**	**Work Center**	**Hours/Unit**
ALF-A	1.0	ALF-T	0.4
HLT-A	0.5	HLT-T	0.7
MIS-A	0.7	MIS-T	0.5
MVX-A	0.7	MVX-T	1.0
PCB-A	0.4	PCB-P	0.8
PCB-P	1.2	PCN-B	1.6

It is now June 15, and an important customer wishes to have 100 units of both A and B during the next month (20 working days). Analyze the effect of accepting this order. Assume there are adequate materials, and work center MVX-T has had its capacity increased to one full person (capacity now = 160). This was accomplished by reducing MVX-A to 6.5 persons, and no other orders have been booked since June 12. Use the capacity data and conditions of Figure 10.18 as the basis for your analysis.

Chapter **11**

Production Activity Control

This chapter concerns the execution of detailed material plans. It describes the planning and release of individual orders to both factory and outside vendors. Production activity control (PAC) also concerns, when necessary, detailed scheduling and control of individual jobs at work centers on the shop floor, as well as vendor scheduling. An effective production activity control system can ensure meeting the company's customer service goals. A PAC system can reduce work-in-process inventories and lead times as well as improve vendor performance. A key element of an effective PAC system is feedback on shop and suppliers' performance against plans. This loop-closing aspect provides signals for revising plans if necessary.

This chapter is organized around three topics:

- *A framework for production activity control:* How does PAC relate to other aspects of material planning and control, and how do just-in-time production of individual firm decisions affect PAC system design?
- *Production activity control techniques:* What basic concepts and models are used for shop-floor and vendor scheduling and control?
- *Production activity control examples:* How have PAC systems been designed and implemented in several different kinds of companies?

Chapter 11 is linked closely to Chapter 7 in that many PAC techniques are designed to execute the detailed material plans produced by material requirements planning (MRP) systems. Much of the detail order tracking of PAC is not required in a just-in-time (JIT) environment, so many of the appropriate JIT shop-floor systems are described in Chapter 9. Chapter 16 deals with advanced scheduling techniques. Chapter 17 treats supply chain linkages where vendor schedules are coordinated with customer schedules.

A Framework for Production Activity Control

Production activity control (PAC) concerns execution of material plans. It encompasses activities within the shaded areas of Figure 11.1. The box entitled "Shop-floor scheduling and control," which we refer to as shop-floor control, falls completely within PAC. Vendor

FIGURE 11.1
Production Activity Control in the MPC System

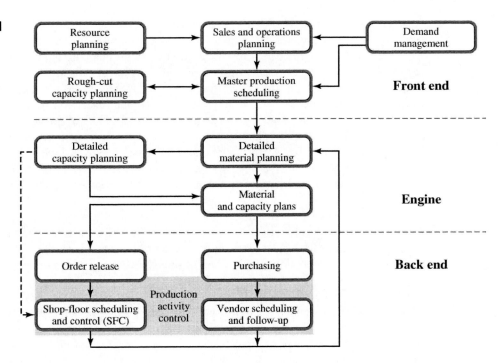

scheduling and follow-up is depicted as largely being part of production activity control, but not completely. Many firms, particularly those with JIT material control approaches, assign most vendor scheduling to PAC. Order release (which authorizes release of individual orders to the factory and provides accompanying documentation) is similarly becoming more a part of PAC. In purchasing, **procurement** is seen as a professional activity where information networks, relationships, terms, and conditions are established with vendor companies outside of PAC, while release of individual orders and follow-up activities are a part of PAC.

The extension of the definition of *production activity control* is accentuated by the growing use of computers on the shop floor as well as **electronic data interchange (EDI)** and Internet-based system linkages with vendors. As more and more traditional staff work is integrated into the basic manufacturing infrastructure, it will expand PAC as well.

MPC System Linkages

The primary connection between PAC and the rest of the MPC systems shown in Figure 11.1 comes from the box marked "Material and capacity plans." The capacity plan is especially critical to managing the detailed shop-floor flow of materials. In essence, the capacity provided represents resource availabilities for meeting material plans.

Capacity's importance for shop-floor control (SFC) is illustrated by considering two extremes. If insufficient capacity is provided, no SFC system will be able to decrease backlogs, improve delivery performance, or improve output. On the other hand, if more than enough capacity exists to meet peak loads, almost *any* SFC system will achieve material flow objectives. It's in cases with bottleneck areas and where effective utilization of capacity is important that we see the utility of good SFC systems.

A related issue is the extent to which good capacity planning is done. If the detailed capacity planning activity in Figure 11.1 provides sufficient capacity, with relatively level loading, shop-floor control is straightforward. On the other hand, if peaks and valleys in capacity requirements are passed down to the back end, execution becomes more complex and difficult. The same general issues apply to vendor follow-up systems: vendor capacity must be carefully planned to ensure effective execution. If one does not help vendors utilize capacity effectively, total system costs increase, which in the end must be borne by the end customers. Thus, several automobile suppliers report that Toyota is the easiest customer to work for since it maintains a much more level schedule, with fewer changes/surprises.

The material plan provides information to the SFC and vendor follow-up systems and sets performance objectives. The essential objective of both execution systems is to achieve the material plan—to provide the right part at the right time. This will result in being able to hit the master production schedule and to satisfy customer service objectives.

The Linkages between MRP and PAC

The shop-floor and vendor scheduling activities begin when an order is released. A critical information service provided by MRP is apprising the SFC systems of all changes in material plans. This means revising due dates and quantities for scheduled receipts so correct priorities can be maintained. The job thereafter might be likened to that of a duck hunter following a moving target. Control and follow-up systems must keep each order lined up with its due date—one that's moving—so overall MPC is supported.

Linkages between PAC and the engine aren't all one-way. There's important feedback from the shop-floor control and vendor follow-up systems to material and capacity planning. Feedback is of two types: status information and warning signals. Status information includes where things are, notification of operational completions, count verifications, order closeout and disposition, and accounting data. The warning signals help flag inadequacies in material and capacity plans: that is, will we be able to do what was planned?

Just-in-Time Effect on PAC

Shop-order-based systems are founded on the premises of job shop (now more frequently called *batch*) manufacturing, where parts are routed to different parts of the factory for processing steps, with relatively long lead times, high work-in-process inventories, and high utilization of work center capacities. JIT has none of these. Manufacturing takes place in facilities, often in cells, where jobs are easily kept track of; work is completed quickly; work-in-process inventory levels are insignificant; and work centers have surge capacity or else are level loaded. In either case, capacity utilization is not a key issue.

Formal systems for shop-floor control are largely unnecessary under JIT. Release of orders is still part of PAC, but the typical "shop order" with associated paperwork isn't maintained. Therefore, the PAC functions in Figure 11.1 are greatly simplified. Order release can be accomplished with kanbans or other pull system methodologies, and work-in-process inventories in the factory are severely limited. Detailed scheduling is also unnecessary since orders flow through cells in predictable ways so that workers know the sequence of conversion operations. Work is completed fast enough that "order scheduling" isn't required. Detailed scheduling of workers and equipment is similarly not an issue, since design of the JIT system itself determines schedules. There's no need for data collection or monitoring since JIT basically assumes only two kinds of inventories: raw materials and finished goods. Receipt of finished goods is used to "backflush" required raw materials from inventory. The JIT-based systems dramatically reduce the number of transactions to be processed, as well as the associated inventories and lead times.

Vendor scheduling under JIT can be a bit more complex than shop-floor control, but if the relationship with the vendors is good, differences are very small. Many firms use some form of electronic kanban to authorize work at the vendor factories, and excellent vendors don't build inventories in anticipation of orders from their customers. Well-run auto companies, for example, transmit an exact build schedule to their seat vendors several times a day, as actual cars are started. By the time these cars are ready for seats to be installed, seats will be delivered by the vendor in the exact sequence required. The seats are not pulled from inventory. They are built to order and delivered in the exact sequence to match the build schedule at the assembly plant. There is no need for transactions such as shipping or receiving documents. The seat manufacturer is paid on the basis of the build schedule; one just assumes that each car has the requisite seats!

The Company Environment

The primary PAC objective is managing the materials flow to meet MPC plans. In some firms, other objectives relate to efficient use of capacity, labor, machine tools, time, or materials. Under JIT and time-based competition, the objective is material velocity. A firm's particular set of objectives is critical to PAC design.

The choice of objectives for PAC reflects the firm's position vis-à-vis its competitors, customers, and vendors. It also reflects the company's fundamental goals and the constraints under which it operates. In many countries firms find changing capacity to be more difficult than in the United States. This viewpoint colors the view of PAC. Similarly, some firms have more complex products and/or process technologies than others. The result can be a difficult shop-floor management problem and a resultant difference in the appropriate PAC system. As a result PAC system design must be tailored to the particular firm's needs.

Production Activity Control Techniques

This section begins by describing basic concepts for production activity control under batch manufacturing with an MRP system. It covers basic shop floor concepts, including the elements of lead time, operation setback charts, and lead-time management. It then examines three approaches to shop-floor control. The first, **Gantt charts,** provides graphic understanding of the shop-floor control problem; moreover, Gantt chart models can be used in manual shop-floor control systems. The second approach is based on **priority sequencing rules** for jobs at a work center under MRP. The third approach to shop-floor control, **theory of constraints scheduling,** involves the preparation of an exact schedule of jobs for bottleneck work centers, and sequencing the nonbottleneck work centers by a priority sequencing rule. We next look at vendor scheduling where the concepts are applied to supplier operations.

Basic Shop-Floor Control Concepts

Figure 11.2, an example product structure for end item A, demonstrates basic concepts underlying shop-floor control techniques. One essential input to the SFC system is the routing and lead-time data for each product item. Figure 11.3 presents this for parts D and E of the example. The routing specifies each operation to be performed to make the part and which work center will perform the operation.

FIGURE 11.2
Example Product Structure Diagram

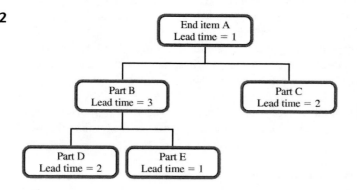

FIGURE 11.3
Routing Data and Operation Setback Chart

Operation	Work Center	Run Time	Setup Time	Move Time	Queue Time	Total Time	Rounded Time
Part D routing							
1	101	1.4	0.4	0.3	2.0	4.1	4.0
2	109	1.5	0.5	0.3	2.5	4.8	5.0
3	103	0.1	0.1	0.2	0.5	0.9	1.0

Total lead time (days) 10.0

Operation	Work Center	Run Time	Setup Time	Move Time	Queue Time	Total Time	Rounded Time
Part E routing							
1	101	0.3	0.1	0.2	0.5	1.1	1.0
2	107	0.2	0.1	0.3	0.5	1.1	1.0
3	103	0.3	0.2	0.1	1.5	2.1	2.0
4	109	0.1	0.1	0.1	0.5	0.9	1.0

Total lead time (days) 5.0

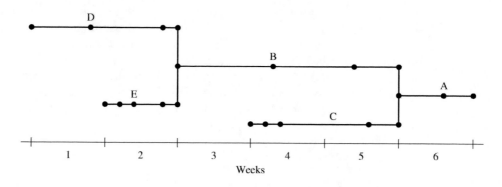

Production of part D, for example, requires three operations of 4, 5, and 1 days, respectively, for a total of 10 days, or two weeks. Part E requires four operations of 1, 1, 2, and 1 days, respectively, for a total of 5 days, or one week. The remaining lead times in Figure 11.2 are all derived the same way. Lead times used for MRP should match those in the routing file. If the MRP time for part E was set at two weeks instead of one week, orders would constantly be released one week early.

Lead times are typically made up of four elements:

Run time (operation or machine run time per piece × lot size).

Setup time (time to prepare the work center, independent of lot size).

Move time (delay waiting to be moved plus time spent moving from one work center to the next).

Queue time (time spent waiting to be processed at a work center, which depends on workload *and* schedule).

Queue time (the critical element) frequently accounts for 80 percent or more of total lead time; it's the element most capable of being managed. Reducing queue time means shorter lead time and, therefore, reduced work-in-process inventory. This reduction requires better scheduling.

The bottom of Figure 11.3 shows an **operation setback chart** based on each part's lead times. Here we clearly see the implications of incorrect MRP lead time. If the MRP lead time for part E isn't the one week calculated from the routing data, the part will be released either early or late to the shop. Neither of these is a desirable outcome. Note that Figure 11.3 shows that both parts D and E go through work center 101 for their first operation. The top of Figure 11.4 shows the partial schedule for work center 101, with parts D and E scheduled according to the timing in Figure 11.3.

The bottom of Figure 11.4 shows two alternative detailed schedules for part D in week 1 at work center 101. The shaded portion represents the 1.8 days of lead time required for

FIGURE 11.4
Work Center
101 Schedules

Parts D and E with MRP lead times

	Week 1					Week 2					Week 3			
M	T	W	T	F	M	T	W	T	F	M	T	W	T	F

Part D

E

Alternative detailed schedules for Part D
(The shaded area represents setup and run time only)

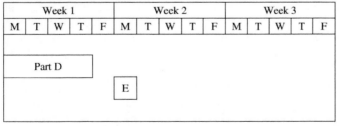

Monday	Tuesday	Wednesday	Thursday
Part D			

Early schedule

		Part D	

Late schedule

setup and run time. The early schedule has part D loaded as soon as possible in the four days. The late schedule loads part D into the latest possible time at work center 101. The key differences between the top and bottom of Figure 11.4 are the timing of the setup and run times. The blank area in both schedules includes queue time. Queue time represents slack that permits the choice of alternative schedules—a form of flexibility. This slack can be removed by good SFC practice; that is, this schedule allows 4 full days to complete part D, when actual time on the machine is only 1.8 days. For the remaining 2.2 days, the part waits in a queue or is moving between work centers.

The shaded portion of the schedules shown at the bottom of Figure 11.4 contains no queue time. These schedules represent loading a particular job onto a particular work center for a particular time period. The two alternatives in the bottom of Figure 11.4 are different loadings; one typically chooses between alternative loadings to utilize the machine center effectively.

Lead-Time Management

Many people think of **lead time** as a constant, such as π. In fact, it's not a value to be measured as much as a parameter to be managed. Of the four elements of lead time (run, setup, move, and queue), the last two can be compressed with good PAC design and practice.

Lead time and work in process (WIP) are directly related. Moreover, some critical feedback linkages operate. The longer the lead time is perceived to be, the longer the time between the order launching date and due date. The longer this time, the more orders in the shop. The more orders in the shop, the longer the queue time (and WIP); we have a self-fulfilling prophecy.

Some WIP is needed at work centers where high utilization is important. However, a basic principle of MPC systems is to *substitute information for inventory*. The firm doesn't need to have jobs physically in front of machines. Orders can be held in a computer and converted to physical units only as needed. For many plants, setup and run time constitute only 10 to 20 percent of total lead time. The rest is slack that can be substantially cut.

One interesting question is how to manage lead time. This means changing database elements for both SFC and MRP. One alternative is to go through the database and systematically change all lead times. Reducing them could result in a transient condition of dry work centers at early gateway operations. This might be a reasonable price to pay for the resulting WIP reduction.

Changing lead-time data elements naturally leads to the question of how they're established in the first place. For most firms, lead-time data are usually an input from some functional area, such as production control. An alternative is to *calculate* lead time. When we think about changing lead times as part of a management process, and when we remember that SFC lead time must be in tune with MRP lead-time offset data, this approach has increasing appeal. One firm calculated lead times as follows:

1. Nonqueue time for each operation was set equal to setup plus run (time per piece × lot size) plus move times.

2. Nonqueue time was converted to days by dividing total hours by number of shifts per day, assuming seven productive hours per day.

3. Queue time was set equal to two days if the next work center routing was in another department, one day if it was in the department but a different work center, and zero days if it was on the same machine.

4. Lead time for the total order was the sum of the queue and nonqueue times. This time was calculated with an average order quantity, rounded to a weekly lead time, and used for MRP lead-time offsetting.

Selecting queue time is the critical element in this formula. Values were chosen by taking a sample of 50 parts and using different queue time estimates to yield lead times consistent with production control personnel opinions. The initial estimates were padded, but the company was not very concerned. Once the system was in operation, estimates for queue times were systematically reduced a bit at a time. The result was a managed approach to shorter lead times and reduced work in process.

Before leaving this discussion, let's look at one firm's results. David A. Waliszowski says a $25 million division of Hewlett-Packard reduced lead time 70 percent and increased customer service levels 80 percent. This amounted to a $1.7 million reduction in work-in-process inventory that was achieved in three months.

Gantt Charts

Gantt or **bar charts,** like those in Figure 11.4, show a schedule. The operation setback chart in Figure 11.3 is very similar. It too is a schedule for when to make each of the five parts based on lead times that include move and queue times.

One form of shop-floor control is to prepare operation setback charts similar to Figure 11.3 for each job, and use them with the kind of data in Figure 11.3 to prepare Gantt charts, such as those in Figure 11.4. The objective is to prepare a schedule for each machine center. This schedule can be based on the assumptions in either the top or bottom of Figure 11.4; that is, the schedule may or may not use lead times that include queue and move times.

The more usual practice is to prepare the detailed work center schedule *without* move and queue times. Many firms' systems do this. The typical approach is a **schedule board** with racks to hold pieces of paper. Each paper is a job and its length represents the setup plus run time required.

The primary problem with this kind of system is updating. Actual data must be captured and integrated into an ongoing replanning cycle. Moreover, a means to communicate with the shop floor is usually required since schedule boards typically reside in planning offices. However, with personal computers on the shop floor, some firms have in essence created a fairly dynamic version of the schedule board.

Priority Sequencing Rules

Priority sequencing rules determine which job to run next at a work center. To some extent, these rules can be seen as producing a loading of jobs onto individual machines, but usually only one job is committed at a time; that is, the job to run *next* is determined only near the time when the prior job has been completed. The priority (sequencing) rule is just what the name suggests: a *rule* for what job to process next.

Many different priority rules have been established. A fairly common one is to base priorities on the type of data in Figure 11.3. The lower half of that figure contains scheduled due dates for parts and operations. These due dates can be used as priorities. For example, a priority rule could be: the job to process next is the job with the earliest operation due date. An alternative is to next process the job with the earliest *part* due date. Four other commonly used sequencing rules are:

- *Order slack:* Sum the setup times and run times for all remaining operations, subtract this from the time remaining (now until the part due date), and call the remainder slack. The rule is to work on that job with the least slack. This rule addresses the problem of work remaining.

- *Slack per operation:* A variant of order slack is to divide the slack by the number of remaining operations, again taking next the job with the smallest value. The reasoning behind slack per operation is that it will be more difficult to complete jobs with more operations because they will have to be scheduled through more work centers.

- *Critical ratio:* A rule based on the following ratio:

$$\frac{\text{Time remaining}}{\text{Work remaining}}$$

For calculation, the rule is expressed as

$$\frac{\text{Due date} - \text{Present time}}{\text{Lead time remaining (including setup, run, move, and queue)}}$$

If the ratio is 1.0, the job is on time. A ratio below 1.0 indicates a behind-schedule job, while a ratio above 1.0 indicates an ahead-of-schedule condition. The rule is to always process that job with the smallest critical ratio next.

- *Shortest operation next:* This rule ignores all due date information as well as all information about work remaining. It simply says, take as the next job the one that can be completed in the shortest time at the work center. This rule maximizes the number of shop orders that go through a work center and minimizes the number waiting in queue.

In an MRP system, each shop order would be a scheduled receipt for the part. As such, the scheduled receipt has a due date. From this due date, operational due dates could be established by backing off expected operation times, if these data are needed to establish priority sequence. The great advantage of this computer-based system is that, whenever the due date for a scheduled receipt changes, operation due dates can be changed accordingly. These changes, in turn, lead to priority changes for shop-floor control, resulting in an execution system that works on the most-needed shop orders first. The objective is for high-priority jobs to move through the shop very quickly, while low-priority jobs are set aside. In this way, the shop-floor control system can indeed execute the dictates of the detailed material plan. In recent times, many companies have developed a preference for sequencing rules that are easy to understand. One straightforward approach is to develop operation start and operation due dates, and use them for determining priority sequence decisions. In a computer-based shop-floor control system, due dates wouldn't be printed on any shop paper that travels with the work-in-process inventory. The shop paper would show the routing or sequence of operations (static data), but no due dates. The changing (dynamic) due date information would be printed daily or be displayed on line in the form of a work center schedule or dispatch list. It's the dispatch list, not the traveling paper, that shows the priority sequence. The dispatch list can be updated as rapidly as transactions are processed to the MRP database.

Theory of Constraints (TOC) Systems

An increasing number of firms have been implementing a plant scheduling system that uses theory of constraints (TOC) concepts. Initially, TOC scheduling systems were viewed as a replacement of an integrated MPC system. In fact, TOC scheduling systems encompass the functions performed in the engine and back end of Figure 11.1, but combine these functions so that material and capacity are planned simultaneously. TOC systems accomplish many functions in the MPC framework, but not all.

Basic Concepts of TOC Systems

Most manufacturing firms have a very limited number of constraints. Any resource whose capacity is equal to or less than the required demand is referred to as a *bottleneck*. As a consequence the fundamental principle of TOC systems is that only those work centers (or other types of resources) that are bottlenecks are of critical concern in scheduling. This is because the bottleneck work centers limit the overall production output of a plant. Further output beyond the constraint of the bottleneck can be achieved only by improved utilization of the bottleneck facilities, using approaches such as reduced downtime, improved productivity, and reduced changeover times. The objective of TOC scheduling is to maximize throughput. Since throughput is limited by the bottleneck resources, all efforts are devoted to maximizing capacity utilization in these work centers. Therefore, TOC scheduling systems focus on the identification of bottleneck work centers, and the scheduling of these work centers.

The concept of a bottleneck has been generalized into "constraints," which include marketplace constraints. In fact, it is argued that the goal is to have company output constrained by the marketplace, not by constraints over which the firm has more control. Further, TOC adds some operational concepts for dealing with constraining situations. Constraints are explicitly identified, and they're buffered with inventory. Also, the constraint's importance is made clear to the entire factory. For example, bottleneck work centers are operated over coffee breaks and lunch, and are worked a maximum of overtime hours. Moreover, jobs are closely examined to find any that can be alternatively routed, even if the result is "excess cost" for the work so routed. The goal is always to break a constraint, or bottleneck condition, and thereafter identify the next constraint. Continuous improvement is an integral part of the theory of constraints philosophy. Moreover, the path for the improvement is directed by the theory, always following the constraints.

TOC Scheduling

The scheduling approach used in TOC systems is called **drum-buffer-rope.** The bottleneck work centers (constraints) are the drums, and are, therefore, used to control the workflow in a plant. Any resource whose capacity is more than the demand is called a *non drum*. The rope refers to "pull" scheduling at the nonbottleneck work centers. The purpose of the rope is to tie the production at each resource to the drum. Buffers exist at all of the bottleneck work centers, and the shipping dock, but not at nonbottleneck work centers. These buffers are used to protect the throughput of the bottleneck work centers from the inevitable minor fluctuations through the use of time buffers (WIP inventory) at a relatively few critical points in the plant. The basic concept is to move material as quickly as possible through nonbottleneck work centers until it reaches the bottleneck. The work at the bottleneck resources is scheduled for maximum efficiency. Thereafter, work again moves at maximum speed to the shipping dock (finished goods).

The diagram shown in Figure 11.5 outlines the basic TOC scheduling steps. TOC begins its process by combining data in the bill of materials file with data in the routing file. The result is a network, or extended tree diagram, where each part in the product structure also has its operational data attached directly. These data are then combined with the MPS to form the "product network." Figure 11.6 provides an example of a TOC product

FIGURE 11.5
TOC
Scheduling

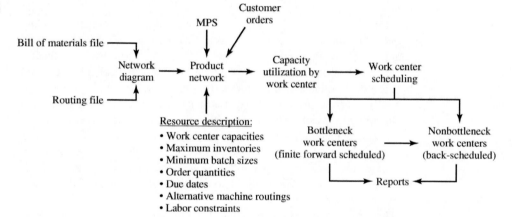

FIGURE 11.6
Sample
Product
Network

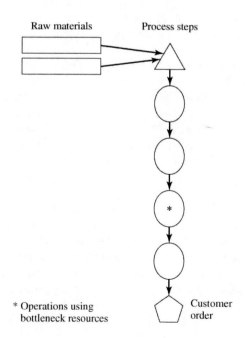

network. Here customer orders are linked to the final operation (such as the final assembly process), which, in turn, is linked to previous operations (such as the detailed fabrication steps for components), and then to raw materials. Additional data typically included in the TOC files are: capacities, maximum inventories, minimum batch quantities, order quantities, due dates, alternative machine routing, labor constraints, and other data typically used in finite scheduling models. In Figure 11.5, these data would be part of the "Resource description."

Next, the product network and resource descriptions are fed into a set of routines that identify the bottleneck resources. This routine combines the product network and resource information to form a TOC network of the bottleneck resources. To determine the bottleneck resources an initial analysis is prepared that provides reports indicating bottleneck resources. This involves using a rough-cut capacity planning routine that provides much of the information of other capacity planning procedures. Since the TOC product network includes both the parts and their routings, a pass through this network can result in an estimate of the capacity required at each work center. Lot sizes at this rough-cut stage are based on lot-for-lot rules. The resultant capacity needs, when divided by the number of weeks in the planning horizon, are the average capacity requirements for each resource. When divided by the resource capacities, the result is the average expected load.

As illustrated in Figure 11.7, the average loads on machine centers are sorted, and the most heavily loaded are studied by analysts. Typical questions include: Are the data correct? Are the time standards accurate? Can we easily increase capacity? Can we use alternative routings for some items? Any changes based on these questions result in another run to see if the bottleneck resources change. Those work centers in Figure 11.7 having a utilization exceeding 80 percent would be considered bottleneck work centers.

At this point the TOC product network is split into two portions, as shown in Figure 11.5. The left-hand portion incorporates all bottleneck resources and all succeeding operations, including market demand for end products with parts that have processing on the bottleneck resources. *This portion of the network is forward finite loaded.*

The right-hand portion includes all of the nonbottleneck resources. *This portion of the network is not forward finite loaded.* Operation start dates/times are, however, established by using the setup times, run times, and queue times for the nonbottleneck resource operations. An initial scheduling pass is made through the product network, and the raw material release dates are offset from customer order due dates by taking into account the processing and queue times for all part operations. In a second pass, however, due dates for any part operations that feed bottlenecks are based on those established by the TOC scheduling of bottlenecks. Schedules for these part operations are set so that material will be available in time for the first operation in the TOC network. This scheduling logic provides a dispatch list for the nonbottleneck resources.

One advantage of the TOC network split is that we can readily see where attention should be focused. Not only is bottleneck capacity utilized more intensively by finite scheduling of this small subset of work centers, but identifying bottlenecks allows us to target efforts in quality and production improvements on these resources.

Buffers

One issue with TOC is the assumption of certainty of the processing times. TOC buffers the schedules for critical operations at bottleneck operations by using both safety stock and

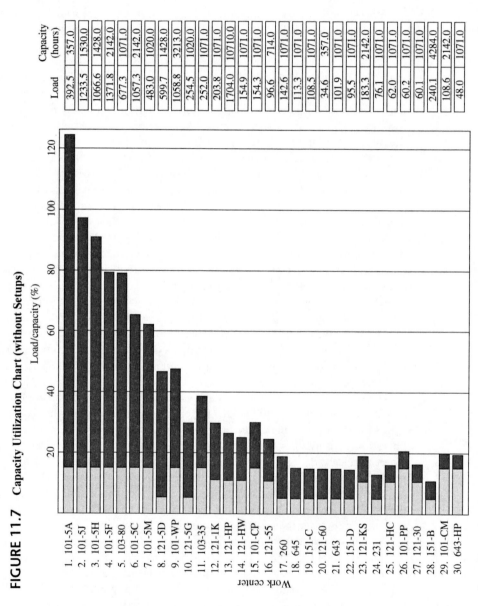

FIGURE 11.7   Capacity Utilization Chart (without Setups)

Work center	Load	Capacity (hours)
1. 101-5A	392.5	357.0
2. 101-5J	1233.5	1530.0
3. 101-5H	1066.6	1428.0
4. 101-5F	1371.8	2142.0
5. 103-80	677.3	1071.0
6. 101-5C	1057.3	2142.0
7. 101-5M	483.0	1020.0
8. 121-5D	599.7	1428.0
9. 101-WP	1058.8	3213.0
10. 121-5G	254.5	1020.0
11. 103-35	252.0	1071.0
12. 121-1K	203.8	1071.0
13. 121-HP	1704.0	10710.0
14. 121-HW	154.9	1071.0
15. 101-CP	154.3	1071.0
16. 121-55	96.6	714.0
17. 260	142.6	1071.0
18. 645	113.3	1071.0
19. 151-C	108.5	1071.0
20. 121-60	34.6	357.0
21. 643	101.9	1071.0
22. 151-D	95.5	1071.0
23. 121-KS	183.3	2142.0
24. 231	76.1	1071.0
25. 121-HC	62.0	1071.0
26. 101-PP	60.2	1071.0
27. 121-30	60.1	1071.0
28. 151-B	240.1	4284.0
29. 101-CM	108.6	2142.0
30. 643-HP	48.0	1071.0

Source: Company Records

safety lead time. In scheduling a sequence of jobs on the same machine, safety lead time can be introduced between subsequent orders. This provides a cushion against variations adversely affecting the flow of jobs through this machine.

To protect against having these variations affect subsequent bottleneck operations on the same job, safety lead time is employed. In this case, the start of the next bottleneck operation on the same job isn't scheduled immediately after the current operation is completed. A delay is introduced to perform the buffering here. (*Note:* there can be another job in process during the delay; its completion will affect the actual start date for the arriving job.) Each of these allowances means actual conditions will vary from the TOC schedule. While the schedule for bottleneck resources is clear, an important question for the supervisors at some point could easily be *which* job to run next at nonbottleneck resources. Such decisions can be made by using a priority sequencing rule.

To ensure there's always work at the bottleneck operation (to provide maximum output), there is safety lead time in front of these work centers. Thus, whenever one job is completed, another is ready to go on the bottleneck machine. Further, in order to protect the final assembly schedule against shortages that could severely cut output, a safety stock of nonbottleneck operation completed parts is held before final assembly. The idea is to not disrupt the flow of material from a bottleneck operation. Parts shortages that can be made up by going through nonbottleneck operations won't cut capacity.

Other management considerations also enter the TOC scheduling system to reduce the effect of uncertainty. These include making realistic schedules that meet material and capacity limitations. Considerations involving the appropriate level of work-in-process inventory, the capacity utilization attainable, degree of schedule protection, and batch size controls can all be applied to the TOC procedure. These help take into account the company culture as the TOC procedure is implemented.

TOC and Lot Sizing

TOC calculates different batch sizes throughout the plant, depending on whether a work center is a bottleneck. This has several MPC implications. In typical finite scheduling procedures, the batch size is fixed. Such isn't the case with TOC. It also follows that a batch size for one operation on a part could be different than for other operations on the same part. This implies special treatment will be required for any paperwork that travels with shop orders. In fact, TOC is designed to do order splitting at nonbottleneck resources. In usual practice, order splitting is done on backlogged (bottleneck) machines; in this situation TOC would do the opposite in order to reduce setup time and maximize output at the bottleneck resources.

The key to lot sizing in TOC is distinguishing between a *transfer* batch (that quantity that moves from operation to operation) and a *process* batch (the total lot size released to the shop). Any differences are held as work-in-process inventories in the shop. In essence, no operation can start until at least a transfer batch is built up behind it.

The transfer batches are predetermined integral fractions of the original order quantity (process batch). They provide a work center with the flexibility to start producing an order before it is completed at the previous work center. Such flexibility, frequently referred to as *lot splitting* and *overlap* or *line scheduling*, reduces order flow times and smooths work flow in the shop to yield better use of capacity. This flexibility also means the number of

384   Chapter 11   *Production Activity Control*

FIGURE 11.8   **TOC Example**

Product	Customer Order Number	Order Quantity	Raw Material Specification Number	First Machining, Operation 1	Heat Treating, Operation 2	Testing, Operation 3	Final Machining, Operation 4	Requested Customer Shipping Date	Hour
				Processing Time (in Hours)					
A	1XXX	100	124	3	6	1	4	Day 5	32
B	2XXX	10	101	2	4	1	2	Day 6	40
C	3XXX	50	88	4	6	1	4	Day 6	40

Notes: 1.   Shop operates 8 hours each day.
   2.   All orders require 2 hours in shipping department.
   3.   All raw material is stocked and available.
   4.   An 8-hour buffer is maintained at the final machining work center.

units produced during a given work center setup, the *operation batch size,* can vary between a transfer batch and the original order quantity.

This lot-sizing concept can be applied by using any standard priority scheduling method (e.g., shortest processing time, critical ratio). When an order is completed under traditional priority scheduling rules, the highest-priority order in the queue is selected for processing next. Under this lot-sizing concept, a work center may contain transfer batches coming from many released orders. In this case, the queue is searched for transfer batches of the same part order that has just been completed at the work center in order to save setup time at a bottleneck resource. If such an item is available, it is processed next, regardless of priority; otherwise, the highest-priority transfer batch in the queue is selected and a new setup is made at the work center. If the queue is empty, the next batch to arrive at the work center is processed.

Managing the TOC Schedule

Managing the TOC schedule on a daily basis involves five basic steps that are illustrated by the example products shown in Figure 11.8. In this example, each product requires processing on four work centers: first machining, heat treating, testing, and final machining. The processing time (setup and run time) for each operation is shown in Figure 11.8. The first three operations are performed in a fabrication cell. Capacity is sufficient in this cell, so these are nonbottleneck operations. The fourth operation, final machining, is a bottleneck operation. Other data such as the customer order number, order quantity, and requested customer delivery date are included in Figure 11.8.

Scheduling the Drum

The first step is scheduling new orders on the bottleneck operations, referred to as the *drums.* This is accomplished by using the following logic:

- Calculate the earliest start time on the first constraint by adding the processing time before the constraint to the raw material lead time and the first constraint buffer time.
- Place the order after and as close as possible to the earliest start time on the constraint.
- Calculate the earliest start time on the next constraint (or the shipping date) by adding the processing time after the first constraint and the next buffer time to the completion time on the current constraint.

Product A in Figure 11.8 illustrates this logic. Note that in Figure 11.8 the processing time for the three operations before the first constraint (final machining) is 10 hours, the raw material lead time is zero (since this material is stocked), and the buffer time for the first constraint (final machining) is 8 hours. As a result, the earliest start time on the first constraint is in 18 hours, or at the end of hour 2 in day 3 (assuming the plant works one eight hour shift each day). Figure 11.9 shows a workload profile of the drum (the final machining work center), indicating that the last 4 hours of day 3 have not yet been scheduled. Therefore, the order for Product A is scheduled to start at the end of hour 4 and complete at the end of hour 8 on day 3.

Figure 11.10 shows a flow diagram of the process and indicates the key dates that are set by using the TOC scheduling logic. These include: the date/time that the order is scheduled to enter the final machining buffer, the date that the final machining operation starts, the date that the order is to enter the shipping buffer, and the customer delivery date. Figure 11.11 shows these dates/times for Product A. The raw material release for Product A is planned for the end of hour 2 on day 1, and this product is scheduled to enter the final machining buffer at the end of hour 12 (day 2, hour 4). This job is therefore expected to wait

FIGURE 11.9
Final Machining Work Load Profile

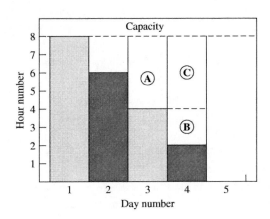

FIGURE 11.10
TOC Example: Plant Scheduling— Bottleneck Work Centers

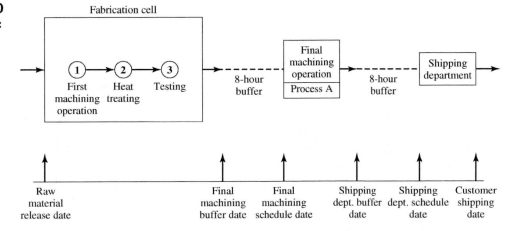

386   Chapter 11   *Production Activity Control*

FIGURE 11.11   TOC Example—Plant Schedule

Product	Customer Order Number	Order Quantity	Raw Material Release	First Machining	Heat Treat	Test	Final Machining Buffer	Final Machining	Shipping Buffer	Shipping Department	Promised Scheduled Shipping Date Hour	Promised Scheduled Shipping Date Day
A	1XXX	100	2	2	5	11	12	20	24	32	34	Day 5 Hour 2
B	2XXX	10	11	11	13	17	18	26	28	36	38	Day 5 Hour 6
C	3XXX	50	9	9	13	19	20	28	32	40	42	Day 6 Hour 2

Notes: 1. All times represent scheduled start times as of the end of the hour indicated.
   2. First machining, heat treat, and test are nonbottleneck work centers and are not finite capacity scheduled.
   3. Final machining and shipping are bottleneck work centers and are, therefore, finite capacity scheduled.

8 hours before processing at the bottleneck machining process. This ensures that errors in processing time estimates do not affect the 100 percent utilization of the bottleneck. Likewise, this order is scheduled to enter the shipping buffer at the end of hour 24 (day 3, hour 8) with shipment scheduled for the end of hour 34 (day 5, hour 2).

Orders are scheduled by using finite backward scheduling. This logic proceeds as follows:

- Subtract the shipping buffer and the processing time after the final constraint from the scheduled ship date. This provides the latest completion time.
- Place the order on the final constraint (drum) before and as close as possible to the latest completion time.
- Determine the start time on the final constraint by subtracting the processing time on the constraint from the completion time.
- Subtract the final constraint buffer time and the processing time back to the latest completion time of the previous constraint (or the raw material release time) from the final constraint start time.
- Once the material release is determined, the delivery schedule for the raw material can be determined.

Product C in Figure 11.8 illustrates this scheduling logic. The customer-requested shipping date for this order is the end of hour 8 on day 5 (or hour 40 in the example). Since no processing occurs on this order after the drum (final machining), the latest completion time can be determined by subtracting the shipping department time of 2 hours plus the shipping buffer of 8 hours from the scheduled shipping date of hour 40. This means that the latest completion time for the final machining operation is the end of hour 30, and that the order should enter the shipping buffer at that time. Since the drum is currently scheduled for the first four hours on day 4, product C can be scheduled from the end of hour 4 through 8 on day 4 (hours 28 through 32). The latest raw material release date can be determined for product C by subtracting both the processing time prior to the drum and the drum buffer time from the drum start time. In this case 11 hours of processing time and a drum buffer time of 8 hours is subtracted from the drum start time of the end of hour 28 to yield a raw material release time of the end of hour 9. The schedule for product C is also shown in Figure 11.11.

Exploiting the Drums

In scheduling the drums, product demand may exceed the available capacity at the drums. In this case it may be necessary to take steps to augment the capacity of the drum. This may involve offloading some of the orders scheduled on the drum to other machines that are nondrums, or outsourcing this work to suppliers. Other options would include working the drums through lunches and breaks, adding overtime, and increasing the batch sizes at the drum to minimize setup time. Batch sizes should, however, not be increased if this would result in delaying the scheduled shipment dates for customer orders. This is a good example of how lot splitting might be usefully employed. By dividing the batch into that which services customers and that which goes into inventory, the overall constraint utilization (selling the throughput) is maximized.

Material Release—Rope

In managing plant operations, raw material should not be released earlier than the scheduled TOC raw material release date. Releasing the raw material on these dates will minimize the WIP inventory and reduce the choice of orders to be run on the nonbottleneck operations.

Proactive Management of Buffers

Buffers are put in place for unforseen variations in production at the nonconstraint work centers. While the entire buffer time is scheduled for every order, it is not expected that every order will arrive at the drum on time. Therefore, the key to a successful implementation of TOC is the proactive management of the buffers. In many plants the management of the buffers is the responsibility of a shop-floor scheduling person designated as the *buffer coordinator.*

One way of accomplishing this is to divide the buffers in thirds. The first third is the **red zone.** The red zone includes the orders that are scheduled next on the constraint. The middle third is the **yellow zone,** and the final third is the **green zone,** which includes the orders that are the furthest out in the drum schedule.

The red zone should rarely have missing orders. Orders that are missing from the red zone represent an immediate danger to the drum schedule. If an order is missing from the red zone, the buffer coordinator should be working nonstop on getting this order to the machine. Management should be aware of the situation and actively working to assist the buffer coordiator to resolve the problem. If the red zone is always full, consideration should be given to reducing the buffer size. The larger the buffer size, the more money invested in WIP inventory. Therefore, buffers should be only large enough to ensure delivery performance to the drums.

The yellow zone will occasionally have missing orders. The buffer coordinator should be actively working to get these orders to the buffer as quickly as possible. Likewise, the green zone will regularly have orders missing. The buffer coordinator should know where these orders are, and verify that they should arrive at the buffer shortly.

Elevating the Drum

This is really a planning step. Once the shop floor is running smoothly, consideration should be given in the planning process to increasing the capacity at the drum. If the capacity is increased at the constraint, it is possible for the organization to grow the business.

TOC and the MPC Framework

Returning to Figure 11.1, we see that TOC can't uniquely be put in the front end, the engine, or the back end. It works in all three areas and does some things quite differently than when scheduling is done by other approaches. However, TOC uses most of the same data as other MPC applications. We still need a front end, engine, and back end (both shop-floor and vendor systems). For the firm with an operating MPC system, the basic database and closed-loop understanding exist. Implementing TOC as an enhancement seems to be a logical extension. TOC is another example of separating the vital few from the trivial many, and thereafter providing a mechanism to exploit this knowledge for better manufacturing planning/control. It allows a firm to simultaneously plan materials and capacities and to integrate important concepts from finite scheduling into the MPC system.

It's been argued TOC doesn't have the same needs for data accuracy that MRP scheduling has. This is partially correct, if you feel less accuracy is required for nonbottleneck parts and work centers. But going into the process of using TOC, you may not realize very well what these bottleneck operations are. Both TOC and MRP require detailed knowledge of product structures and processes. Databases, accurate transaction processing, and the right managerial commitment are required for both as well.

TOC Contributions

Now we can identify clearly one of TOC's primary contributions. When finite scheduling through bottleneck resources is complete, the result is a doable master production schedule. For this reason, TOC is sometimes considered to be a "front-end" system (i.e., a master production scheduling technique). We see it less as an MPS technique than an enhancement to the MPS. TOC conceivably can take any MPS as input and determine the extent to which it is doable.

This means TOC makes an explicit computer-based analysis of the feedback from engine (and back end) to the front end—an important enhancement to MRP systems. It means a valid MPS is generated—one the firm has a strong chance of achieving—that is based on the capacity parameters used in the scheduling.

A secondary contribution at this stage comes from the way TOC schedules the nonbottleneck resources. The easiest way to see this is to assume (as is often the case in practice) there are no bottlenecks. In that case, TOC schedules are based on MRP logic. The difference is that TOC in this case will change batch sizes (reducing them) to the point where some resources almost become bottlenecks. The result is less WIP, reduced lead time, greater material velocity, and a move toward "zero inventory" manufacturing. TOC does much of this by overlapping schedules, using unequal batch sizes for transferring and processing.

TOC's third important contribution is to virtually eliminate the fundamental issue of conflicting priorities between MRP and finite scheduling. With finite scheduling of only a small fraction of the work centers priority conflict issues should largely disappear. Moreover, computational time required to do finite scheduling should be dramatically cut by dealing only with a subset of orders and work centers/resources.

In operation as a shop-floor control technique, TOC has a few other differences from usual practice. A fundamental tenet in TOC is that an hour lost in a bottleneck resource is an hour lost to the entire factory's output, while an hour lost in a nonbottleneck resource has no real cost. This means capacity utilization of bottleneck resources is important. TOC increases utilization by using WIP buffers in front of bottlenecks, and where output from a bottleneck joins with some other parts. TOC also runs large batch sizes at bottleneck operations, thereby reducing relative time spent in setup downtime.

In practice, the variable lot size issue has two major implications. First, lead times should be shorter: smaller batches will move faster through nonbottleneck work centers. Second (and less felicitous), procedures have to be developed to split/join batches as they go through production.

Implementation Issues

A major paradigm shift is required in order to obtain the benefits of TOC scheduling. Management needs to recognize that the plant culture needs to change from one of keeping people busy and equipment fully loaded to one of maximizing throughput at the critical resources—the bottleneck. This means that under TOC, as with JIT, it's quite all right to not work if there's no work to do at nonbottleneck resources. In fact, working (by the usual definition) in this situation will cause problems. If people at the nonbottleneck work on orders that are not needed to maximize flow through the bottleneck work centers, the net result of their work will be to simply increase WIP and cause confusion for scheduling at other work centers. Understanding the basic concepts is critical in obtaining the benefits of TOC scheduling.

TOC presents further difficulties in implementation. Companies also need sound basic systems, education, top-management support, and a willingness to unlearn some ingrained habits. One firm we know of has been working for several years to implement finite scheduling, without great success, because it has strong pressures to fully utilize all direct labor-hours. In this case, the fundamental principles of TOC have not been accepted.

Vendor Scheduling and Follow-up

The **vendor-scheduling** and **follow-up** aspects of PAC are the direct analog of the shop-floor scheduling and control systems. There are some important differences, however. From the vendor's perspective, each customer is usually only one of a number of demand sources. Customer demands are managed in the vendor's plant with its MPC system. The MPC relationship is largely through information exchanged between vendor and customer, often from the back-end activities of the customer directly to the vendor's MPC system.

From the customer's standpoint, the objectives of vendor scheduling are the same as those for internal work center scheduling: keep the orders lined up with the correct due dates from the material plan. This means the vendor must have a continually updated set of relative priority data. A typical approach to providing this information is a weekly updated report reflecting the current set of circumstances in the customer's plant and, sometimes, the final customer requirements that dictate them. Increasingly, computer-to-computer communication is used to transmit this information.

Since the vendor follow-up system is often concerned with changes to the schedule and keeping priorities correct, there must be limits to the amount of change the vendor will be asked to accommodate. Contractual agreements with the vendor typically define the types and degree of changes that can be made, time frames for making changes, additional elements of flexibility required, and so on. In addition, the agreement specifies procedures for transmitting needs to the vendor plus the units in which the vendor's capacity is planned and controlled. This sets the stage for vendor PAC including order release, scheduling, and follow-up.

The Internet and Vendor Scheduling

The Internet provides several ways in which manufacturing companies and their vendors can share information for the purpose of improving the timing and reliability of supplier deliveries. For manufacturing companies the use of information technology can provide improvements such as quicker delivery response to customers, improved delivery reliability, and reductions in operating costs involving both purchasing staff costs and inventory. These improvements have also had an important effect on the national economy. Rapid response times are a result of technological advances. Increased use of real-time information, such as computerized order tracking, enables business to know when demand is shifting and to instantly change output schedules, workshifts, inventory levels, and capital spending plans. Like increased productivity and greater labor flexibility, quick reflexes became a key characteristic of the U.S. economy.

Websites and E-Mail

Increasingly, companies are creating websites to provide a routine way of communicating with vendors. These websites include forward planning information such as listings of open purchase orders (scheduled receipts from MRP), planned future purchase orders from MRP records, and vendor requirements stated in terms of capacity, as well as information on accounts payable status for completed vendor shipments and vendor report cards indicating on-time delivery, shipment quantity shortfalls, and quality performance. Websites are also important sources of historical information on item usage that is helpful to vendors in improving their sales forecasting methods. Furthermore, companies are increasingly sharing engineering information with their vendors through their websites. Websites now contain product management data that includes product specifications and part drawings. Sharing such information electronically enables vendors to access up-to-date information that contains the latest engineering designs and change notices. Sharing this type of information reduces costs on the part of both manufacturers and their vendors, since both are working with the same latest information on product designs.

Another important area of electronic information sharing between manufacturers and their vendors involves the routine use of e-mail to communicate schedule changes, new orders, and order revisions/cancellations. The use of e-mail eliminates much of the more expensive communication with vendors, involving phone calls, letters, and fax documents. E-mail reduces the time and effort of buyers and planner-schedulers in purchasing and customer service coordinators at vendors, thereby improving productivity in both companies. Further, e-mail updates on schedule changes in open orders enables both parties to know the current status and availability of specific items. Accurate order status information enables manufacturers to better plan their operations, and leads to improved delivery reliability on customer orders.

Implementation Issues

While the use of e-mail is gaining widespread usage in improving customer/vendor communications, the use of websites appears to be more limited under certain operating conditions. First, companies that are able to make real progress with vendors in developing JIT supply programs have little need to communicate open orders to vendors on websites. The JIT delivery of goods eliminates the need to develop future plans and schedules for vendor items using MRP. The JIT delivery of vendor items is less expensive, involves shorter lead times, and provides less exposure to a purchasing commitment on the part of the manufacturer. However, other website items such as historical data on item usage and vendor report cards may still have value.

A second reason that limits the use of websites to communicate future plans and orders to vendors involves the stability of the manufacturer's MPS. Companies that face major changes in the MPS on a routine basis can pass a high degree of schedule uncertainty to the vendors through the communication of open orders and future planned orders on their websites. This can create considerable confusion at the vendors. Further, companies with poor inventory accuracy can also pass highly uncertain schedules to their suppliers. Therefore, vendors need to assess the quality and the value of the information provided by the customer websites in planning and scheduling their operations. Simply making effective use of the historical data provided on a customer's website to improve the supplier's sales forecasting methods may yield better plans.

Finally, in some cases issues of confidentially and information security can be reasons for not sharing planning and scheduling information with suppliers on websites. Clearly, some of these concerns can be reduced through careful attention to system security, and avoiding the sharing of sensitive information about costs and prices. In many companies production order quantities and production volumes are considered less sensitive information.

Some of the limitations of using websites to communicate open and planned order information to vendors have to do with economic conditions. During times of economic downturn and recession, companies typically do not have full order books and often take orders in less than normal lead time in order to maintain operations. Under these conditions the MPS can be very unstable, producing less valuable planning information for the vendors. However, when economic conditions improve, and economic expansion is underway, company order backlogs increase and lead times often lengthen. In these conditions, when the production and supplier lead times are long, and the MPS is stable, open and future planned order information on the websites can often provide more stable information to suppliers.

Production Activity Control Examples

This section applies production activity control techniques in three quite different examples. The first example covers Tosoh SMD, Inc. This company has implemented a TOC finite loading system for shop-floor control. Special alloy products for the computer industry are processed in manufacturing cells that include machining, heat treating, and testing operations. The company produces products on a make-to-order basis for companies that often face highly cyclical demand. As a result, resulting capacity requirements vary widely at individual work centers. The firm employs a technically based, highly paid workforce that is not easily expanded or contracted.

The second example is vendor scheduling at Liebert. Here MRP-based planning is extended into vendor follow-up with excellent results. Finally, PAC procurement practice using electronic data interchange (EDI) is examined at the Caterpillar Tractor Company.

TOC Scheduling at TOSOH

TOSOH is a manufacturer of special alloy materials for computer manufacturing firms. The products are custom designed to meet the specifications of the customer's production process and product design. The product unit selling price ranges from $500 to $6,000. The annual sales are $100 million, with 80 percent of the sales volume going to 10 customers.

Products are manufactured on a make-to-order basis with approximately 500 open shop orders at any given time. Each product passes through 10 to 20 operations, and there are four focused factory operations within the main plant, each of which has about 10 work centers. Each product is manufactured from a special metal alloy, and the master database contains approximately 1,500 end-product items. The bill of material has two levels: product items and raw materials.

Before installing the TOC system, the plant used a manual scheduling system that was based on very rough estimates of process setup and run times. While bills of material and product routings existed, these were poorly maintained. There was no clear measure of plant capacity nor an ability to forecast the upcoming capacity constraints.

The company chose to implement TOC to achieve several business objectives. The foremost objective was to deliver product faster and more reliably in a market characterized by life cycles approximating 6 to 12 months a relatively short time. The company also wanted to maximize the throughput of the factory and to achieve a better utilization of the expensive machine tools and heat-treatment facilities. The company felt that the TOC system would enable manufacturing to minimize batch sizes, reducing cycle time and WIP inventory while improving responsiveness to customers. Finally, because of the short product life cycle, and the costs of product obsolescence, the company wanted to reduce the investment in finished goods inventory.

The TOC project began with a one-year manual pilot implementation of the TOC system. Subsequently, the TOC software was purchased, the manufacturing database was developed, and the software was tested. An example of the TOC schedules at TOSOH, using product item 3596C-13-108-501 is illustrated. This item is being manufactured for shop order RWO502, which has a due date of 10/16/XX. The process routing for this item is shown in Figure 11.12. Note that *only* operation 500 on this order is performed on a drum work center.

Portions of the schedule at all of the work centers in the example are shown in Figure 11.13a. Figure 11.13a shows the schedule for shop order RW0502 for the five work centers preceding the drum (work center 101-5M). The material release date of 9/19/XX in Figure 11.13a is back-scheduled from the drum schedule, and all of the operations in between (operations 100 through 400) are run on a first-in, first-out basis, using process and delay time data. A portion of the drum schedule for work center 101-5M is shown in Figure 11.13b. Shop order RWO502 is scheduled to start at 10:20 A.M. on 10/11/XX and to be completed 2 hours and 15 minutes later. (The setup time of 45 minutes and the run time of

FIGURE 11.12
Process Routing, Product Item 3596C-13-108-501

Operation Number	Work Center	Work Center Status
100	101-KS	Nonconstraint
200	101-WP	Nonconstraint
300	101-5C	Nonconstraint
400	101-80	Nonconstraint
500	101-5M	Constraint
600	101-CM	Nonconstraint
700	255-XRF	Nonconstraint
800	260	Nonconstraint
900	231	Nonconstraint
1000	Stores	Nonconstraint

1 hour and 30 minutes is shown in the upper portion of Figure 11.13b.) Likewise, all of the nonconstraint operations following the drum (600 through 1000) are expected to be complete by the order due date (10/16/XX), using first-in, first-out scheduling priorities. The TOC schedule for this product allows a buffer of 56 hours for the drum (operation 500), and a buffer of 72 hours for the shipping dock buffer. These are shown in the "buffer plan" columns of Figures 11.13a and b.

The company learned several lessons during implementation. First, the culture needed to change in order to achieve the benefits of TOC scheduling. The importance of educating all of the manufacturing personnel on the basic concepts of TOC scheduling became clear. Other changes included the elimination of traditional cost accounting performance measures relating to productivity, efficiency, product cost, etc. Manufacturing people needed to understand that it is all right for the nondrum work centers to be idle. Further, this training needed to be performed on a company wide basis for the system to be totally effective.

Second, in using TOC the company needed to emphasize the elimination of obstacles to the flow of materials through the plant. In addition to the physical constraints, these obstacles included such items as paperwork, procedural roadblocks, and work rules. This effort involved ensuring raw material availability, instilling a sense of urgency in people regarding the TOC schedule, achieving a high level of process reliability, and reducing waste in time and materials. Both TOC scheduling and the focus on process improvement at TOSOH have produced important achievements in operating performance. This includes a sales revenue increase of 14 percent, a 38 percent improvement in delivery reliability, a 14 percent reduction in customer lead times, a doubling of the overall inventory turns, and a 50 percent reduction in the reserve for obsolete inventory. These results were achieved over a four-year period.

Vendor Scheduling at Liebert

Liebert is the world's leading supplier of computer support systems and the largest supplier of precision air-conditioning and power-protection systems worldwide. At Liebert the procurement group is responsible for strategic sourcing efforts, while the materials control

FIGURE 11.13a Plant Schedule

Analyst ID: JB

Release on: 9/19/XX

Part ID	Work Order ID	Qty	Work Center ID	Order ID	Line No.	Order Due Date Target	Order Due Date Projected	Product ID	Customer ID	Buffer Planned	Buffer Remaining
3596C-13-108-501	RWO502	1.00	101-KS	C10402	18	10/16/XX	10/16/XX	3596C-13-108-501	7138568-4	56	103
4028H-13-108-501	RWO500	10.00	101-KS	01090062	2	10/8/XX	10/8/XX	4028H-13-108-501	7011585-1	56	114

Part ID	Job Step	Qty	Work Order ID	Setup Time	Run Time	Start Date	Buffer Plan	Buffer Remain	Order ID	Target Date	Proj. Date	Product ID
Priority list for work center 101-KS—KASTO SAWS (2)												
Calendar: Default												
3596C-13-108-501	100.00	1.00	RWO502	00:15	00:01	09/19/XX	56	103	C10402	10/16/XX	10/16/XX	3596C-13-108-501
Priority list for work center 101-WP—WISCONSIN COLD												
Calendar: Default												
3596C-13-108-501	200.00	1.00	RWO502	00:30	12:00	09/19/XX	56	103	C10402	10/16/XX	10/16/XX	3596C-13-108-501
Priority list for work center 101-SC—MAZAK II & III PLANAR												
Calendar: 10 hour												
3596C-13-108-501	300.00	1.00	RWO502	00:30	00:45	09/19/XX	56	108	C10402	10/16/XX	10/16/XX	3596C-13-108-501
Priority list for work center 101-80—OUTSIDE WELD												
Calendar: Default												
3596C-13-108-501	400.00	1.00	RWO502	01:00	168:0	09/19/XX	56	116	C10402	10/16/XX	10/16/XX	3596C-13-108-501
3596C-13-108-501	400.00	1.00	RWO508	01:00	168:0	10/03/XX	56	221	C10402	10/30/XX	10/30/XX	3596C-13-108-501
3596C-13-108-501	400.00	1.00	RWO519	01:00	168:0	10/17/XX	56	431	C10402	11/13/XX	11/13/XX	3596C-13-108-501
3596C-13-108-501	400.00	1.00	RWO527	01:00	168:0	10/31/XX	56	536	C10402	11/27/XX	11/27/XX	3596C-13-108-501

FIGURE 11.13b Drum Schedule: Grouped By Unit

Work Center: 101-5M : AMAT CELL   Unit: 1   Calendar: 14 Hour

Part ID	Job Step	Qty	Qty Finished	Work Order	Setup	Duration	Start Time	Actual Start	Order ID	Target Data	Proj. Data	Product ID	Customer ID
Start date: 10/11/XX													
3596C-13-108-501	500.00	1.00	0.00	RW0502	00:45	01:30	10:20		C10402	10/16/XX	10/16/XX	3596C-13-108-501	7138568-4
Start date: 10/18/XX													
3596C-13-108-501	500.00	1.00	0.00	RW0508	00:45	01:30	10:20		C10402	10/30/XX	10/30/XX	3596C-13-108-501	7138568-4
Start date: 11/08/XX													
3596C-13-108-501	500.00	1.00	0.00	RW0519	00:45	01:30	10:20		C10402	11/13/XX	11/13/XX	3596C-13-108-501	7138568-4
Start date: 11/15/XX													
3596C-13-108-501	500.00	1.00	0.00	RW0527	00:45	01:30	10:20		C10402	11/27/XX	11/27/XX	3596C-13-108-501	7138568-4

Part ID	Job Step	Qty	Work Order ID	Setup Time	Run Time	Start Date	Buffer Plan	Order ID	Buffer Remain	Target Date	Proj. Date	Product ID
Priority list for work center 101-CM—CMM (2)												
Calendar: Default												
3596C-13-108-501	600.00	1.00	RW0502	00:00	00:00	10/11/XX	72	C10402	357	10/16/XX	10/16/XX	3596C-13-108-501
3596C-13-108-501	600.00	1.00	RW01139	00:00	00:00	10/18/XX	72	C10402	462	10/30/XX	10/30/XX	3596C-13-108-501
3596C-13-108-501	600.00	1.00	RW01375	00:00	00:00	11/08/XX	72	C10402	672	11/13/XX	11/13/XX	3596C-13-108-501
Priority list for work center 255—XRF												
Calendar: Default												
3596C-13-108-501	700.00	1.00	RW0502	00:00	00:00	10/11/XX	72	C10402	357	10/16/XX	10/16/XX	3596C-13-108-501
3596C-13-108-501	700.00	1.00	RW01139	00:00	00:00	10/18/XX	72	C10402	462	10/30/XX	10/30/XX	3596C-13-108-501
3596C-13-108-501	700.00	1.00	RW01375	00:00	00:00	11/08/XX	72	C10402	672	11/13/XX	11/13/XX	3596C-13-108-501
Priority list for work center 260—CLEAN/PACK/SHIP C/P												
Calendar: Default												
3596C-13-108-501	800.00	1.00	RW0502	00:00	00:00	10/11/XX	72	C10402	357	10/16/XX	10/16/XX	3596C-13-108-501
3596C-13-108-501	800.00	1.00	RW01139	00:00	00:00	10/18/XX	72	C10402	462	10/30/XX	10/30/XX	3596C-13-108-501
3596C-13-108-501	800.00	1.00	RW01375	00:00	00:00	11/08/XX	72	C10402	672	11/13/XX	11/13/XX	3596C-13-108-501
Priority list for work center 231—INSP MEDIA/PM												
Calendar: Default												
3596C-13-108-501	900.00	1.00	RW0502	00:10	00:03	10/11/XX	72	C10402	357	10/16/XX	10/16/XX	3596C-13-108-501
3596C-13-108-501	900.00	1.00	RW01139	00:10	00:03	10/18/XX	72	C10402	462	10/30/XX	10/30/XX	3596C-13-108-501
3596C-13-108-501	900.00	1.00	RW01375	00:10	00:03	11/08/XX	72	C10402	672	11/13/XX	11/13/XX	3596C-13-108-501
Priority list for work center STORES—KITTED												
Calendar: Default												
3596C-13-108-501	1,000.00	1.00	RW0502	00:00	00:00	10/11/XX	72	C10402	357	10/16/XX	10/16/XX	3596C-13-108-501
37000-13-950-100	300.00	1.00	130313	00:00	00:00	10/17/XX	56	C10402	418	11/13/XX	11/13/XX	3596C-13-108-501
3596C-13-108-501	1,000.00	1.00	RW01139	00:00	00:00	10/18/XX	72	C10402	462	10/30/XX	10/30/XX	3596C-13-108-501
37000-13-950-100	200.00	1.00	RW01411	00:00	00:00	10/31/XX	56	C10402	523	11/27/XX	11/27/XX	3596C-13-108-501
3596C-13-108-501	1,000.00	1.00	RW01375	00:00	00:00	11/08/XX	72	C10402	672	11/13/XX	11/13/XX	3596C-13-108-501

group manages the operational functions that include order release and vendor scheduling functions for suppliers. Although Liebert uses MRP II to plan and schedule end product, component, and purchased items, it continues to currently introduce JIT into both its manufacturing and vendor operations.

Liebert utilizes an e-procurement system that issues purchase orders to suppliers and provides each supplier with access to computer files that contain a listing of all open purchase orders, forecast information, and usage history data on the items supplied by the individual vendor. Figure 11.14 shows a sample open purchase order report that can be accessed on the Internet by a supplier. Each vendor can obtain a listing of all of the open purchase orders that have been placed with that company by Liebert. This information includes the due date, the ship-to location, and status update notes that can be routinely accessed by both Liebert and supplier personnel.

As shown in Figure 11.15, suppliers can also download to a spreadsheet forecast information for each of the items that are supplied by the company to Liebert. This information contains actual released orders (scheduled receipts) over the item's vendor lead time, and forecast (planned orders) information up to one year beyond the vendor's lead time. In addition, a supplier can also download historical usage information on the items supplied to Liebert by the vendor. This is shown in Figure 11.16. The "Netable" column in this figure indicates the on-hand inventory for the individual items at Liebert, and the "Wgt Mth Use" column indicates the average historical usage for each item. Further, Liebert's suppliers can download a supplier performance report indicating their performance over the past year. An example of this report is shown in Figure 11.17. It includes quality, cost, and delivery metrics.

Currently, about 50 percent of Liebert's suppliers are linked to the e-procurement system. Because of the important overhead savings involved in Liebert's procurement and material control groups, the company is planning to extend this system to all of its vendors. In addition, Liebert has incorporated accounts payable status information into this system to provide easy access to the payment status of supplier invoices.

Liebert is also expanding its efforts with suppliers to implement JIT deliveries of low-value items such as hardware. Since a kanban signal will be used to initiate the replenishment of a JIT vendor item, issuing and tracking of individual purchase orders in the e-procurement system (Figure 11.14) will no longer be required. On delivery, a manual transaction will initiate an invoice payment request. However, the forecast and historical sales information shown in Figures 11.15 and 11.16 will continue to be available to suppliers on the e-procurement system.

Vendor Scheduling at Caterpillar

As the number of purchased components increases, many firms routinely use electronic data interchange (EDI) to communicate with their suppliers on a routine basis. Caterpillar Tractor Company illustrates use of EDI in PAC. Nearly 400 of the firm's domestic and off-shore supplier locations are connected by EDI using standards developed by the Automotive Industry Action Group (AIAG). Each supplier is assigned an electronic mailbox on the network. Suppliers retrieve information from their mailboxes and can forward information though the mailboxes to Caterpillar. By adopting AIAG, the "mail" is read in a language common to computers of Caterpillar and its vendors.

FIGURE 11.14   Review and Reschedule Purchase Orders

Liebert® KEEPING BUSINESS IN BUSINESS*

eProcurement Home | Phone Book | Liebert Facilities | Procurement News | View/Download Documents | Part Look-up
Choose Supplier # | Open Purchase Orders | Historical Usage | Forecasted Usage | Your Preferences | Feedback | Log Off

SUPPLIER SELECTED:

| submit | preview changes |

☐ check this box to include yourself on the 'SUBMIT' audit e-mailing (for your records)

Row	Pls Cnfrm	PO Number	Line/Sch	Liebert Part #/ Supplier Part #	Ord Qty	Bal Due	Ship To:	Request Date			Due on Liebert Dock Date	Evaluation Date	Status note	Contact e-mail Phone
1	☐	P00694893 view	001/Y1		1	1	Q	10	16	Y1	10/16/Y1	10/16/Y1		E-mail
2	☐	P23606412 view	003/Y1		1	1	K	10	20	Y1	10/20/Y1	10/20/Y1		E-mail
3	☐	P23606519 view	001/Y1		1	1	K	10	29	Y1	10/29/Y1	10/29/Y1		E-mail
4	☐	P23606587 view	001/Y1		1	1	K	10	29	Y1	10/29/Y1	10/29/Y1		E-mail
5	☐	P00694886 view	001/Y1		1	1	Q	11	05	Y1	11/05/Y1	11/05/Y1		E-mail
6	☐	P23606622 view	001/Y1		2	2	K	11	05	Y1	11/05/Y1	11/05/Y1		E-mail
7	☐	P00694895 view	001/Y1		2	2	Q	11	06	Y1	11/06/Y1	11/06/Y1		E-mail
8	☐	P00694899 view	001/Y1		1	1	Q	11	26	Y1	11/26/Y1	11/26/Y1		E-mail
9	☐	P23606416 view	001/Y1		2	2	K	01	07	Y2	01/07/Y2	01/07/Y2		E-mail

FIGURE 11.15   Forecasted Inventory Usage as of 10/28/Y1

⊕Liebert® KEEPING BUSINESS IN BUSINESS*

eProcurement Home I Phone Book I Liebert Facilities I Procurement News I View/Download Documents I Part Look-up

Choose Supplier # I Open Purchase Orders I Historical Usage I Forecasted Usage I Your Preferences I Feedback I Log Off

SUPPLIER SELECTED:

Download Forecast Data

Plant	Liebert Part. / Vendor Part.	Net-able	Non-Net-able	Type	Past Due	10/28	11/04	11/11	11/18	11/25	12/02	12/09	12/16	12/23	12/30	01/06	01/13	01/20 02/16	02/17 03/16	03/17 04/13	04/14 05/11	05/12 06/08	06/09 07/06	07/07 08/03	08/04 08/31	09/01 09/28	09/29 10/26
001		2304	0	Fcast	0	0	0	200	200	70	200	200	210	0	0	0	0	0	720	1152	864	720	864	864	720	864	0
				Orders	0	0	0	0	0	0	0	0	0	0	0	0	0	432	0	0	0	0	0	0	0	0	0
001		563	0	Fcast	0	0	0	0	0	144	288	0	288	0	0	144	0	432	288	720	288	432	432	432	288	432	0
				Orders	0	0	0	0	0	0	0	0	0	0	0	0	0	432	0	0	0	0	0	0	0	0	0
001		225	330	Fcast	0	40	0	0	0	0	0	0	0	0	0	0	0	342	156	226	156	160	160	156	156	148	0
				Orders	0	0	35	0	0	0	27	35	70	0	70	0	35	141	140	210	140	140	140	140	140	140	0
001		57	64	Fcast	47	0	0	0	0	25	0	0	0	0	0	0	0	0	0	0	0	0	0	0	0	0	0
				Orders	0	0	115	240	0	0	60	500	70	0	0	0	0	407	420	660	352	0	656	0	352	320	0
001		60	3	Fcast	0	0	0	0	0	0	0	0	0	0	0	0	0	0	0	0	0	0	0	0	0	0	0
				Orders	0	0	0	0	0	0	0	0	0	0	0	0	0	0	0	0	0	20	65	72	0	90	0
001		585	0	Fcast	0	0	0	0	0	0	0	0	0	0	0	0	0	0	0	0	0	0	0	0	0	0	0
				Orders	0	0	0	0	300	300	0	0	400	0	0	300	0	700	700	800	900	500	800	500	500	700	600
012		328	4	Fcast	0	0	0	0	0	0	0	0	0	100	0	200	100	200	200	200	300	200	300	200	200	300	200
				Orders	0	0	0	0	100	0	100	0	0	0	0	0	0	0	0	0	0	0	0	0	0	0	0
012		156	0	Fcast	0	0	0	200	0	0	0	0	0	0	12	0	12	56	102	114	180	144	114	120	144	0	0
				Orders	0	0	0	0	110	0	0	0	0	0	0	0	0	0	0	0	0	0	0	0	0	0	0
001		159	0	Fcast	0	0	0	0	0	0	0	0	0	0	0	0	0	0	0	0	0	0	0	0	0	0	0
				Orders	0	0	0	0	266	380	0	0	93	290	190	190	0	222	614	700	700	700	0	0	0	0	0
001		0	0	Fcast	0	0	0	157	266	266	0	0	206	128	0	142	450	457	244	258	442	256	256	32	256	232	0
				Orders	0	0	0	31	0	0	0	0	0	0	0	0	0	0	0	0	0	0	0	0	0	0	0
001		547	39	Fcast	131	62	82	62	128	0	64	64	0	0	0	0	0	190	244	258	442	256	256	32	256	232	0
				Orders	0	0	0	0	0	0	0	0	0	0	0	0	0	0	0	0	0	0	0	0	0	0	0
001		0	1	Fcast	0	0	0	0	0	0	0	0	0	0	0	0	0	0	0	0	0	0	0	0	0	0	0
				Orders	0	0	0	271	357	0	0	280	344	266	284	322	282	1241	1282	1716	1264	1001	678	779	761	795	0
001		79	8	Fcast	0	0	0	0	0	0	0	0	0	0	0	80	0	240	349	368	330	202	256	0	202	252	202
				Orders	0	0	0	0	0	0	0	0	0	0	0	0	0	0	0	0	0	0	0	0	0	0	0
012		2300	1	Fcast	0	0	0	480	0	0	480	480	0	0	480	0	0	480	960	960	480	960	480	960	480	480	0
				Orders	0	0	0	0	0	0	0	0	0	0	0	0	0	0	0	0	0	0	0	0	0	0	0

FIGURE 11.16 Historical Usage

Liebert® KEEPING BUSINESS IN BUSINESS*

eProcurement Home | Phone Book | Liebert Facilities | Procurement News | View/Download Documents | Part Look-up
Choose Supplier # | Open Purchase Orders | Historical Usage | Forecasted Usage | Your Preferences | Feedback | Log Off

SUPPLIER SELECTED:

Download Historical Data

Usage is from all supplier sources

Plant	Liebert Part	Vendor Part	Net-able	Wgt Mth Use	Hgh Mth Use	11/Y1	10/Y1	09/Y1	08/Y1	07/Y1	06/Y1	05/Y1	04/Y1	03/Y1	02/Y1	01/Y1	12/Y0	11/Y0
001			2304	457.7	1322	269	145	645	646	593	1005	699	864	991	797	709	672	1322
001			563	332	1214	242	465	343	218	480	409	333	1214	366	811	975	997	759
001			225	99.1	144	88	68	89	144	58	116	96	132	62	91	57	1	3
001			57	112.2	179	117	85	179	71	74	85	109	92	103	40	157	32	14
001			60	423.5	882	365	82	882	326	394	308	253	413	509	0	0	0	0
001			585	49.9	70	46	43	70	38	28	31	25	14	13	8	1	11	0
012			328	632.2	941	547	576	702	647	646	740	525	517	622	941	789	804	750
012			156	151.6	296	154	140	163	151	179	168	153	200	203	296	233	222	285
001			159	536.1	2505	261	86	582	1032	2505	700	0	0	0	0	0	0	0
001			0	44	440	440	0	0	0	0	0	0	0	0	0	0	0	0
001			547	532.2	589	288	510	579	589	456	530	199	0	0	0	0	0	0
001			0	14.6	143	143	1	0	0	0	0	0	0	0	0	0	0	0
001			79	258.1	331	196	266	331	198	90	0	0	0	0	2	0	0	0
001			2300	97	872	49	128	76	103	90	90	75	155	208	633	823	527	872
012			69	3.6	20	0	10	0	2	0	0	10	20	0	0	0	0	0
001			921	967	3000	889	898	1053	976	1075	1902	1522	2617	3000	2776	2388	2486	2545
012			658	240.5	544	179	192	231	319	269	279	533	509	544	190	4	38	19
001			456	621.3	2830	624	558	643	662	880	1062	1121	2696	1966	2230	2830	2216	2296

400   Chapter 11   *Production Activity Control*

FIGURE 11.17   Supplier Performance

Liebert

SUPPLIER PERFORMANCE REPORT   SUPPLIER: ORG   CODE

SUPPLIER NAME

MONTH	DELIVERY	%	#	QTY FAILED	QTY RECVD.	PPM	COST RED	AVG LT	LT PCT	SHORT AGES	AVG DAYS OUT	SPEND
Jul/Y0	LATE	37.5%	15	57	4,417	12,905	$0	22	0.00	0	0	$70,016.00
	EARLY	17.5%	7									
	ONTIME	45.0%	18									
Aug/Y0	LATE	20.6%	7	0	4,026	0	$0	22	0.00	0	0	$39,057.00
	EARLY	5.9%	2									
	ONTIME	73.5%	25									
Sep/Y0	LATE	16.1%	5	18	3,670	4,905	$0	22	0.00	0	0	$89,512.00
	EARLY	6.5%	2									
	ONTIME	77.4%	24									
Oct/Y0	LATE	29.2%	14	18	5,444	3,306	$0	22	0.00	1	2	$46,310.00
	EARLY	16.7%	8									
	ONTIME	54.2%	26									
Nov/Y0	LATE	31.6%	6	37	2,292	16,143	$0	22	0.00	0	0	$53,311.00
	EARLY	31.6%	6									
	ONTIME	36.8%	7									
Dec/Y0	LATE	33.3%	6	34	2,793	12,173	$0	22	0.00	0	0	$74,238.00
	EARLY	0.0%	0									
	ONTIME	66.7%	12									
Jan/Y1	LATE	12.5%	1	2	2,103	951	$0	21	0.00	0	0	$56,402.00
	EARLY	0.0%	0									
	ONTIME	87.5%	7									
Feb/Y1	LATE	5.0%	1	3	1,016	2,953	$0	22	0.00	0	0	$14,253.00
	EARLY	0.0%	0									
	ONTIME	95.0%	19									
Mar/Y1	LATE	3.0%	1	19	2,966	6,406	$0	22	0.00	0	0	$29,261.00
	EARLY	9.1%	3									
	ONTIME	87.9%	29									
Apr/Y1	LATE	9.7%	3	0	5,248	0	$55,031	22	33.00	0	0	$14,550.00
	EARLY	0.0%	0									
	ONTIME	90.3%	28									
May/Y1	LATE	0.0%	0	15	2,429	6,175	$0	23	0.00	0	0	$18,142.00
	EARLY	0.0%	0									
	ONTIME	100.0%	16									
Jun/Y1	LATE	13.0%	3	101	2,621	38,535	$76,741	26	0.00	0	0	$56,990.00
	EARLY	0.0%	0									
	ONTIME	87.0%	20									

Tuesday, July 17, Y1

MONTH: 06/Y1   Page 1

Caterpillar's EDI network for suppliers and purchasers electronically exchanging data is called "Speed." Although Caterpillar has been building the Speed network for several years, it began as an outgrowth of the company's existing MPC systems. The company recognized the need to add effective electronic communications with the outside suppliers to facilitate JIT. The company viewed the Speed network's advantages to be applicable to both Caterpillar and its vendors. Direct benefits include:

- Reducing transaction time to a few hours, compared with processing through the mail.
- Quicker response to changes for revised material requirements.
- Reduced paper-handling expenses.
- Fewer errors involving transmitting information.

Concluding Principles

We see the following principles emerging from this chapter:

- Production activity control system design must be in concert with the firm's needs.
- Vendor capacities should be planned and scheduled with as much diligence as are internal capacities.
- Lead times are to be managed.
- Feedback from PAC should provide early warning and status information to other MPC modules.
- E-based systems can dramatically improve customer/vendor communication, reducing lead time and overhead cost.
- TOC scheduling provides improved performance by focusing on the constraining resources.
- TOC implementation requires a change in plant culture in order to obtain the full benefits of this approach.
- Adapting standards for communication is a prerequisite to global EDI.
- Traditional priority rules can play a role in nonbottleneck scheduling.
- Stability in the manufacturing loads and capacity planned facilitates shop-floor execution.

References

Arnold, J. R. T., and S. N. Chapman. *Introduction to Materials Management*, 4th ed. Columbus, Ohio: Prentice Hall, 2001, pp. 141–175 and pp. 396–427.

Atwater, J. B., and S. S. Chakravorty. "A Study of the Utilization of Capacity Constrained Resources in Drum-Buffer-Rope Systems," *Production and Operations Management* 11, no. 2 (summer 2002), pp. 259–273.

"APS/Finite Scheduling Software Comparison," *APICS—The Performance Advantage*, September 2001, pp. 48–53.

Bihun, T. A. "Electronic Data Interchange: The Future," *American Production and Inventory Control Society 1990 Annual Conference Proceedings,* pp. 605–609.

Carter, J. R., and L. D. Fredendall. "The Dollars and Sense of Electronic Data Interchange," *Production and Inventory Management Journal* 31, no. 2 (2nd quarter 1990), pp. 22–26.

Chakravorty, S. S. "Improving a V-Plant Operation: A Window Manufacturing Case Study," *Production and Inventory Management Journal* 43, no. 3 (3rd quarter 2000), pp. 37–42.

Christy, D. P., and J. J. Kanet. "Open Order Rescheduling in Job Shops with Demand Uncertainty: A Simulation Study," *Decision Sciences* 19, no. 4 (fall 1988), pp. 801–818.

Davis, D. J., and Vincent A. Mabert. "Order Dispatching and Labor Assignment in Cellular Manufacturing Systems," *Decision Sciences Journal* 31, no. 4 (fall 2000), pp. 745–771.

Fogarty, D. W.; J. H. Blackstone, Jr.; and T. R. Hoffmann. *Production & Inventory Management,* 2nd ed. Cincinnati: Southwestern, 1991.

Frazier, G. V., and P. M. Reyes. "Applying Synchronous Manufacturing Concepts to Improve Production Performance in High Tech Manufacturing," *Production and Inventory Management Journal* 43, no. 3 (3rd quarter 2000), pp. 60–65.

Goldratt, E. M., and J. Cox. *The Goal,* New York: North River Press, 1984.

Greenstein, Irwin. "Caterpillar Erects Paperless Network," *Management Information Systems Week,* January 20, 1986.

Hyer, N. L., and Karen A. Brown. "The Discipline of Real Cells," *Journal of Operations Management* 17, no. 5 (August 1999), pp. 557–574.

Jensen, E. B.; P. R. Philipoom; and M. K. Malhotra. "Evaluation of Scheduling Rules with Commensurate Customer Priorities in Job Shops," *Journal of Operations Management* 13, no. 3 (1995).

McCollum, Benjamin D. "How Changing Purchasing Can Change Your Business," *Production and Inventory Management Journal* 44, no. 2 (2nd quarter 2001).

Melnyk, S. A.; P. L. Carter; D. M. Dilts; and D. M. Lyth. *Shop Floor Control.* Homewood, Ill.: Dow Jones–Irwin, 1985.

———. *Production Activity Control.* Homewood, Ill.: Dow Jones–Irwin, 1987.

Melnyk, S. A.; S. Ghosh; and G. L. Ragatz. "Tooling Constraints and Shop Floor Scheduling: A Simulation Study," *Journal of Operations Management* 8, no. 2 (April 1989), pp. 69–89.

Philipoom, P.; R. E. Markland; and T. D. Fry. "Sequencing Rules, Progress Milestones and Product Structure in a Multistage Job Shop," *Journal of Operations Management* 8, no. 3 (August 1989), pp. 209–29.

Plenert, G., and B. Kirchmier. *Finite Capacity Scheduling.* New York: Oliver Wight Publications, John Wiley & Sons, 2000.

Production Activity Control Reprints. Falls Church, Va.: American Production and Inventory Control Society, 1993.

Production Flows at Timken Steel, I2 Technologies, Web: www.i2.com, 1999.

Sabuncuoglu, I., and H. Y. Karapinar. "A Load-Based and Due-Date-Oriented Approach to Order Review/Release in Job Shops," *Decision Sciences Journal* 31, no. 2 (spring 2000), pp. 413–447.

Scherer, E., ed. *Shop Floor Control—A Systems Perspective.* Berlin: Springer Verlag, October 15, 1998.

Schorr, J. E. *Purchasing in the 21st Century: A Guide to State-of-the-Art Techniques and Strategies.* New York: John Wiley & Sons, 1995.

Schragenheim, E., and B. Ronen. "Drum-buffer-rope Shop Floor Control," *Production and Inventory Management Journal* 31, no. 3 (1990), pp. 18–22.

Simons, Jacob B., and Wendell P. Simpson III. "An Exposition of Multiple Constraint Scheduling as Implemented in the Goal System (Formerly Disaster ™), *Production and Operations Management* 6, no. 1 (spring 1997).

Smunt, T. L., and Charles A. Watts. "Improving Operations Planning with Learning Curves: Overcoming the Pitfalls of 'Messy' Shop Floor Data," *Journal of Operations Management* 21, no. 1 (January 2003), pp. 93–107.

Spearman, M. L. "On the Theory of Constraints and The Goal System," *Production and Operations Management* 6, no. 1 (1997), pp. 28–33.

Taylor, S. G., and S. F. Bolander. *Process Flow Scheduling*, APICS, 1994.

Umble, M., and M. L. Srikanth. *Synchronous Manufacturing*, Spectrum Publishing, 1995.

Umble, M., E. Umble, and L. Von Deylen. "Integrating Enterprise Resources Planning and Theory of Constraints: A Case Study," *Production and Inventory Management Journal* 42, no. 2 (2nd quarter 2001), pp. 43–48.

Waliszowski, David A. "Lead Time Reduction in Multi Flow Job Shops," *APICS Annual Conference Proceedings,* 1975.

Wassweiler, W. L. "Fundamentals of Shop Floor Control," *APICS Conference Proceedings,* 1980, pp. 352–354.

Discussion Questions

1. Suppose an average of 20 students per year were in your major and the number of graduates varied between 15 and 30 each year. One required course, open to both juniors and seniors, is offered once a year and has a capacity of 20 students. What system would you use to assign students to that course? Would it make any difference if the course capacity was 40 students or 10 students per year?

2. What kind of warning signals would you like fed back from PAC to the MRP system?

3. Lead times have sometimes been called "rubbery." What accounts for this concept of elasticity in lead times?

4. In the list of priority rules, there is no first-come/first-served (FCFS) rule, yet most banks, cafeterias, and theater ticket booths use this rule in waiting on patrons. Why isn't it a suggested rule for the shop floor?

5. What are the differences in how bottleneck and nonbottleneck work centers are scheduled under TOC? Why are these differences desirable?

6. Why should buffers be located in front of bottleneck work centers under TOC scheduling? How should the size of these buffers be determined?

7. How would you determine how much discretion to give the foreman in combining and reprioritizing jobs?

8. What benefits might be gained by having clerks in a retail store use a wand to read tags on items?

9. Discuss the merits of separating the daily transaction people (schedulers) from the buyers in the purchasing organization.

Problems

1. Tom's Sailboard manufactures custom wind surfers in Seattle. The incoming orders follow different routes through the shop, but all orders must stop at each of the three work centers (WCs) in the plant. The following table contains information regarding the four jobs that arrive over five days and need to be scheduled at the company. It is currently November 10 and Tom works a seven-day week.

Order	Arrival Date	Job/WC Routing	Processing Time (Days)		
			WC 1	WC 2	WC 3
(B)iff	Nov. 10	1-3-2	1	3	1
(G)riff	Nov. 10	2-3-1	2	2	2
(H)erbie	Nov. 12	3-2-1	3	1	2
(K)erri	Nov. 14	2-1-3	1	3	1

Assume that the material for all orders is ready for processing as soon as the orders arrive and that a first-come/first-served sequencing rule is used at all work centers. All three work centers are idle as work begins on orders B and G on November 10.

   a. Construct a Gantt chart depicting the processing and idle times for the three work centers for these four jobs.

   b. How many days does each job wait in queue for processing at work center 2?

2. The production manager at the Knox Machine Company is preparing a production schedule for one of the fabrication shop's machines, the P&W grinder. He has collected the following information on jobs currently waiting to be processed at this machine. (There are no other jobs and the machine is empty.)

Job	Machine Processing Time, Days*	Date Job Arrived at this Machine	Job Due Date
A	4	6-23	8-15
B	1	6-24	9-10
C	5	7-01	8-01
D	2	6-19	8-17

*Note: This is the final operation for each of these jobs.

   a. The production manager has heard about three dispatching rules: the shortest operation next rule, the first-come/first-served rule, and the earliest due date rule. In what sequence would these jobs be processed at the P&W grinder if each rule were applied?

   b. If it's now the morning of July 10 and the shortest operation next rule is used, when would each of the four jobs start and be completed on the P&W grinder? (Express your schedule in terms of the calendar dates involved, assuming that there are seven working days each week.)

3. Jobs A, B, and C are waiting to be started on machine center X and then be completed on machine center Y. The following information pertains to the jobs and work centers.

Job	Hours Allowed for Machine Center X	Hours Allowed for Machine Center Y	Day When Due
A	36	20	10
B	96	24	17
C	60	28	25

Machine center X and machine center Y have 40 hours of capacity per weekday. Two days are allowed to move jobs between machine centers.

   a. If these jobs are rescheduled by earliest due date, can they be completed on time?

   b. Can they be completed on time using the critical ratio technique?

   c. Can the jobs be completed on time (using the earliest due date or critical ratio technique) if 20 hours of overtime are run in work center X each week?

   d. Can the jobs be completed on time (using the earliest due date or critical ratio technique) if only one day is required between operations?

4. The customer for job B in problem 3 has agreed to take half the order on day 17 and the rest on day 28. Use earliest due date rule to schedule the four jobs (A, Bl, B2, C). Can they be completed on time, assuming no extra setup time is required for splitting job B?

5. Ms. Mona Hull is in charge of a project to build a 50-foot yacht for a wealthy industrialist from Jasper, Indiana. The yacht is scheduled to compete in the famous Lake Lemon Cup Race. Eight weeks remain for constructing the yacht. Assume that each week consists of 5 workdays, for a total lead time of 40 days. The work required to complete the yacht comprises 10 operations, 4 days for each.

   a. On Tuesday morning of week 3, 3 of the 10 operations had been completed and the yacht was waiting for the fourth operation. What's the critical ratio priority?

   b. What's the critical ratio priority if only 2 of the 10 operations are completed by Tuesday morning of week 3?

6. Big Dan's Machine Shop is considering the use of a priority scheduling rule in the fabrication shop and must decide whether to use: (1) critical ratio (CR), (2) earliest due date (EDD), (3) shortest operation next (SON), or (4) order slack. The current shop status of the company is given below:

Order Number	Total Remaining Manufacturing Time	Time Remaining until Due Date	Current Operation Processing Time
1	15	12	8
2	12	15	5
3	10	14	4
4	15	18	3
5	20	19	6

   a. Using the four sequencing rules, compute the scheduling priority for each order given in the table above.

   b. What order should be run first under each of these scheduling rules?

7. Marucheck's makeshift manufacturing facility had three departments: shaping, pickling, and packing. Marucheck's orders averaged 100 pieces each. Each of the three shaping machines required one hour setup, but could run a piece in one minute. The pickling department lowered baskets of pieces into brine tanks and subjected them to low-voltage current, a heating and cooling, and a rinse. The whole process took four hours for any number of baskets or pieces. The only brine tank could hold four baskets, each of which could contain 50 pieces. (Baskets were loaded while another load was in the tank.) Each piece was inspected and wrapped in bubble pack in the packing department. Each of the four people in the department could do this at the rate of 25 pieces per hour. Marucheck had heard of optimized production technology (OPT) and wanted to identify the bottleneck department. Which is it?

8. The Ace Machine Company is considering using a priority scheduling rule in its fabrication shop and must decide whether to use: (1) the critical ratio rule, (2) the order slack rule, (3) the shortest operation next rule, or (4) the slack per operation rule. Exhibit A shows the company's current inventory and shop status.

   a. State the formula for calculating the priority index for each of sequencing rules given previously.

   b. Compute the scheduling priority for each order in Exhibit A, four sequencing rules.

EXHIBIT A

Order Number	Manufacturing Lead Time Remaining	Time Remaining Until Due Date	Current Operation Processing Time	Number of Operations Remaining	Total Processing Time Remaining
1	15	7	2	3	8
2	15	11	3	4	8
3	20	−2	5	2	8
4	15	−5	4	3	8
5	15	3	1	12	8

Note: Time is measured in days. Manufacturing lead-time remaining includes both the machine processing time and the length of time orders spend moving and waiting to be processed in a machine queue. Current operation processing time (as well as total processing time remaining) includes no move or queue times.

	Big Mess	No Problem
Customer order 1	Part A: setup 5, run 10 Part B: setup 2, run 5	Part C: setup 1, run 2
Customer order 2	Part A: setup 5, run 3	Part D: setup 2, run 2
Customer order 3	Part B: setup 2, run 5	Part C: setup 1, run 3

9. The Optima Shop has two work centers: Big Mess and No Problem. The Monday list of orders to be filled this week shows the total setup and total run time requirements (in hours) at the two centers.

   Joe Biggs, the scheduler of Optima, said his first criterion is to minimize setups, and the second is to prioritize customer orders in numerical order.

   a. How should he schedule part production in the two centers? (Please illustrate using a Gantt chart.)

   b. Can customer delivery promises be met without overtime if capacity is 40 hours in each work center?

   c. How does the answer to part b change if only one person is assigned to do the setup in *both* work centers?

   d. Is the schedule consistent with the OPT philosophy?

10. The XYZ Company uses MRP to plan and schedule plant operations. The plant operates five days per week with no overtime, and all orders are due at 8 A.M. Monday of the week required. It's now 8 A.M. Monday of week 1, all machines are currently idle, and the production manager has been given the information in Exhibit B.

    a. Assuming that the shortest operation next rule is used to schedule orders in the shop, how should the open orders (scheduled receipts) for items A, B, and C be sequenced at their current operations? What are the implications of this schedule?

    b. Assuming that the critical ratio rule is used to schedule orders in the shop, how should the open orders for items A, B, and C be sequenced at their current operations? What are the implications of this schedule?

    c. Suppose that 32 additional units of item B have just been found in the stockroom as a result of a cycle count. What actions are required on the part of the MRP planner?

11. The Ace Tool Company is considering implementing the transfer batches in scheduling the firm's fabrication shop. The production manager selected an example order to use in evaluating benefits and potential costs of this scheduling approach. A transfer batch size of 100 units was suggested for this item. The example order is for a quantity of 1,000 units and has the

EXHIBIT B
System Data

MRP System Data

Item A		Week							
		1	2	3	4	5	6	7	8
Gross requirements		3	16	8	11	5	18	4	2
Scheduled receipts			30						
Projected available balance	10	7	21	13	2	27	9	5	3
Planned order release			30						

$Q = 30; LT = 2; SS = 0.$

Item B		Week							
		1	2	3	4	5	6	7	8
Gross requirements		2	5	12	4	18	2	7	10
Scheduled receipts				30					
Projected available balance	12	10	5	23	19	1	29	22	12
Planned order release			30						

$Q = 30; LT = 4; SS = 0.$

Item C		Week							
		1	2	3	4	5	6	7	8
Gross requirements		14	4	12	7	8	3	17	2
Scheduled receipts			20						
Projected available balance	17	3	19	7	0	12	9	12	10
Planned order release		20		20					

$Q = 20; LT = 4; SS = 0.$

Shop-Floor Control System Data

Item	Routing					Current Operation Number
A	Operation number	1	2	3	4	3 (machine 2)
	Machine number	4	6	2	3	
	Processing time*	1	1	1	1	
B	Operation number	1	2	3	4	2 (machine 2)
	Machine number	4	2	6	1	
	Processing time*	4	2	5	3	
C	Operation number	1	2	3	4	4 (machine 2)
	Machine number	6	3	1	2	
	Processing time*	3	4	6	1.5	

*In days. For computing lead times, assume that there are 1.5 days of move and queue time associated with each operation, including time to complete paperwork after the last operation.

following routing data:

Operation	Work Center	Setup Time	Run Time/Unit
2	1	40 minutes	2.4 minutes/unit
2	2	20 minutes	1.44 minutes/unit

a. Assuming a single-shift, 8-hour day, 5-day week for work centers 1 and 2, prepare a Gantt chart showing the earliest start- and finish-time schedule for this order under a conventional scheduling approach where all items in the order are processed at one time. Do the same when transfer batches are used. What are the earliest start and finish times for each transfer batch at work center 2, assuming none of the transfer batches are processed together to save setup time?

b. What's the difference in the order-completion times under the two scheduling approaches in part a above?

c. What are the benefits and potential costs of this scheduling approach?

12. This morning, Pete Jones, integrated circuit buyer at Flatbush Products, Inc., received the following purchased part MRP record:

Circuit 101		Week											
		1	2	3	4	5	6	7	8	9	10	11	12
Gross requirements		50									50	50	50
Scheduled receipts													
Projected available balance	65												
Planned order releases													

$Q = 50$; $LT = 3$; $SS = 2$.

a. Complete the circuit 101 MRP record.

b. Pete noted that the vendor for circuit 101 recently indicated its plant has limited production capacity available. At most, this supplier can provide 50 units per four-week period. Pete wondered what action, if any, needs to be taken on this item as a result of this capacity limitation.

13. To remain competitive, Ed's Sheet Metal must reduce manufacturing lead time for a product that typically sells in lots of 800 units. The product goes through two operations in different departments. The company wants to evaluate the value of using a transfer batch between operations. Its idea is to split the order at the first operation and transfer an amount to the second operation to get it started while the rest of the order is finished at the first operation. The setup of operation 2 can start as soon as parts arrive, but not sooner. Other data are:

Order size	800 units
Operation 1 processing time	6 minutes/unit
Operation 2 processing time	8 minutes/unit
Transfer time from operation 1 to 2	20 minutes
Setup time for operation 1	1.0 hours
Setup time for operation 2	1.5 hours

a. What is the *minimum* transfer batch that assures that operation 2 has no idle time?

b. How much would manufacturing lead time be reduced by using the transfer batch instead of the full order of 800 units?

14. On a busy day in June, the Framkrantz Factory had five jobs lined up for processing at machine center 1. Each job went to machine center 2 after finishing at machine center 1. After that they had different routings through the factory. It's now shop day 83 and due dates have been established for each job. Machine time includes setup time, but it takes one day to move between centers and two days of queue time at each center (including Finish).

Shop Day = 83	Machine Center Sequence for the Jobs and Days of Machine Time Required						
Job	1	2	3	4	5	Finish	Due Date
A	1	4				X	102
B	3	2	8			X	123
C	3	8		2		X	104
D	6	2	1		2	X	98
E	4	1		8	3	X	110

a. Use a spreadsheet program to calculate the priorities for each job using the critical ratio rule.

b. All jobs were at machine 2 by the morning of shop day 96. (Job A took 2 days instead of 1 and Job D took 1 day instead of 6 on machine 1.) Unfortunately, there was a long job on machine 2 and none of the five jobs had started yet. What would their priorities be for machine 2?

c. What would priorities be if Job N's due date were 96?

15. Shown below is the MRP record for part no. 483. The current shop day is 100 (with five-day weeks); it's now Monday of week 1. Open orders (scheduled receipts) are due Mondays (shop days 100, 105, 1, 10, etc.) of the week for which they're scheduled. The shop floor has just reported that the batch of 40 on shop order number 32 has just finished at machine center A43 and is waiting to be moved to C06. It takes one day to move between machine centers (or to I02, the inventory location) and one day of queue time at the machine centers. (The inventory location doesn't require the queue time, but one day of "machine time" is shown for clearing the paper work.) Part number 483's routing and status are also given below.

Part No. 483		Week					
		1	2	3	4	5	6
Gross requirements		14	4	10	20	3	10
Scheduled receipts			40*				
Projected available balance	20	6	42	32	12	9	39
Planned order releases					40		

Q = 40; LT = 2; SS = 5.
*Shop order no. 32.

Part No. 483

Routing (machine center):	A12	B17	A43	C06	I02
Machine time (days)	4	1	1	1	1
Status shop order 32:	Done	Done	Done		

410 Chapter 11 *Production Activity Control*

    a. Use a spreadsheet to replicate the MRP record and calculate the critical ratio for part no. 483. Should the planner take any action?

    b. What would the priorities be if the inventory were 23 instead of 20? What action should be taken now?

    c. What if inventory were 17 instead of 20?

16. Consider the following data for three jobs processed in the boring machine center for Conway Manufacturing.

Job	Setup Time (Minutes)	Run Time/Unit (Minutes)	Batch Size
A	15	0.05	200
B	10	0.15	100
C	20	0.10	200

Queue data for the boring machine center:

Job	Arrival Time	Job	Arrival Time	Job	Arrival Time
A	8:24	B	8:40	B	9:12
B	8:28	C	8:42	C	9:14
C	8:31	C	8:44	A	9:18
A	8:34	A	8:57	B	9:21
B	8:39	A	9:03	B	9:31

    a. If the boring machine center used a first-come/first-served rule to schedule jobs, how long would it take to process the queue? (Assume no other jobs arrive, all jobs in queue are for one batch each, and job B has just been completed.)

    b. How long would it take to process all jobs in the queue, using the transfer batch logic?

17. Howie's Handicraft needs your advice on the production schedule for its Hallowe'en product line. Analyze the information for the three-station four-product line, given below:

Product	Estimated Weekly Sales, (Units)	Selling Price, ($)	Material Cost, ($)	Process Time Work Station* 1	2	3
Witches	60	35	15	10	10	40
Goblins	50	40	15	10	15	40
Ghosts	40	45	20	10	10	20
Ghouls	30	50	20	15	20	20

*The times for workstations 1, 2, and 3 are in minutes per unit. Capacity at each workstation is 2,400 minutes/week and operating expenses are $2,000/week.

    a. What is the bottleneck workstation? What schedule of products at this work station maximized the profit to Howie?

    b. What is the total profit from the schedule in question a above?

18. The Marlborough Manufacturing Company in New Zealand was considering embarking on a program of rationalizing its vendor base. It had heard of the benefits of doing so, but was unsure where to start. To begin the process, it recorded the total New Zealand dollar (NZD) purchases in the last year and the number of orders that it placed with each firm in a sample of 20 suppliers. The data are shown below.

Company	NZD	Orders/Year
Axel	321,760	7
Backer	55,122	2
Booker	186,242	3
Century	16,088	4
Farmic	80,440	22
First	48,262	3
Gentry	1,850,120	10
Grist	40,220	1
Hooker	64,532	2
Hume	63,253	6
Jacobs	965,283	8
Kelvin	8,124	2
Kolst	1,367,484	5
Kume	57,305	4
Locket	563,087	1
Neive	7,944	1
Whist	2,171,886	3
Wolf	31,523	3
Young	17,053	6
Zydec	121,555	2

a. Develop a Pareto diagram of the purchases in this sample. For which suppliers should Marlborough focus its efforts in building relationships?

b. For which might it consider making some deletions?

c. What other questions does the sample information raise about the purchasing policies of the company?